ISBN 978-1-330-51014-8
PIBN 10071633

1 MONTH OF
FREE
READING

at

www.ForgottenBooks.com

By purchasing this book you are eligible for one month membership to ForgottenBooks.com, giving you unlimited access to our entire collection of over 1,000,000 titles via our web site and mobile apps.

To claim your free month visit:

www.forgottenbooks.com/free71633

English
Français
Deutsche
Italiano
Español
Português

www.forgottenbooks.com

Mythology Photography **Fiction**
Fishing Christianity **Art** Cooking
Essays Buddhism Freemasonry
Medicine **Biology** Music **Ancient**
Egypt Evolution Carpentry Physics
Dance Geology **Mathematics** Fitness
Shakespeare **Folklore** Yoga Marketing
Confidence Immortality Biographies
Poetry **Psychology** Witchcraft
Electronics Chemistry History **Law**
Accounting **Philosophy** Anthropology
Alchemy Drama Quantum Mechanics
Atheism Sexual Health **Ancient History**
Entrepreneurship Languages Sport
Paleontology Needlework Islam
Metaphysics Investment Archaeology
Parenting Statistics Criminology
Motivational

CONTRIBUTIONS

TO THE

ECCLESIASTICAL HISTORY

OF

CONNECTICUT;

PREPARED

Under the Direction of the General Association,

TO

COMMEMORATE THE COMPLETION OF

ONE HUNDRED AND FIFTY YEARS

SINCE ITS FIRST ANNUAL ASSEMBLY.

NEW HAVEN:

PUBLISHED BY WILLIAM L. KINGSLEY.

J. H. BENHAM, PRINTER.

1861.

74
74
13

PREFACE.

11135785

A BRIEF statement seems necessary by way of introduction to the somewhat miscellaneous compilation in the volume now offered to the public.

At the annual meeting of the Association of New Haven West, in December, 1857, it was suggested by Rev. E. W. Robinson, then pastor of the church in Bethany, that the hundred-and-fiftieth anniversary of the General Association of Connecticut ought not to pass without some special commemoration. The suggestion was favorably received ; and the assembling of the General Association in 1859, (the first General Association having been convened in 1709,) was fixed upon as the best time for the purpose. A circular to the several Associations was issued, proposing certain arrangements, which, if acceptable, might be ratified by the General Association next to be convened.

The General Association for 1858 was to be held at Norwich ; and by the rule then in force, the meeting for the next year would have fallen to the Windham Association. But no place in the County of Windham seemed large enough for the accommodation of so great a concourse as might be expected to attend upon the proposed commemoration. The good people of Norwich, it was found, were ready to accept an arrangement by which the General Association for 1859 should have the benefit of their large and generous hospitality; and, by general consent, the meeting for 1858 was regularly transferred to Danielsonville, in West Killingly.

Accordingly, the proposal for a commemoration came, in due form, before the General Association convened at Danielsonville on the third Tuesday in June, 1858. Overtures on the subject from New Haven West, Litchfield South and other

Associations, were referred to the Rev. R. C. Learned, W. R. Long, Jason Atwater, L. H. Barber and Orson Cowles. On the report of that Committee, it was resolved—

1. That the hundred-and-fiftieth anniversary of this Association be celebrated at its next annual meeting to be held in the city of Norwich in June, 1859.

2. That the whole of Thursday, if possible, be devoted to this subject; the forenoon being occupied with a historical discourse by the Rev. Dr. Bacon, or, in case of his failure, by the Rev. David L. Parmelee, and the afternoon with addresses by those who have been previously secured for this purpose.

4. That Rev. J. P. Gulliver, Rev. Dr. Bond, Rev. H. P. Arms, Rev. R. P. Stanton, N. A. Fisher, M. D., George Coit, Esq., Lewis Hyde, Esq., and Benjamin Durfee, Esq., be a Central Committee to procure speakers and make all necessary arrangements for said celebration.

4. That Rev. E. W. Robinson, Rev. W. H. Moore, and Rev. M. N. Morris be authorized to collect such facts and statistics as they deem desirable for the purposes of this celebration, and prepare them for presentation at that time, and for subsequent publication, if deemed expedient by the General Association.

5. That the Rev. Messrs. S. H. Allen, Noah Porter, D. D., A. C. Washburn, L. B. Rockwood, S. W. S. Dutton, D. D., A. C. Pierce, A. McEwen, D. D., S. J. M. Merwin, R. C. Learned, J. Eldridge, D. D., D. L. Parmelee, Isaac Parsons and Merrick Knight, be appointed to assist the last named Committee in the collections proposed within the limits of their several Associations.

In conformity with the foregoing arrangements, the hundred-and-fiftieth annual assembly of the General Association was held at the Broadway Church, in the city of Norwich, on the third Tuesday (21) in June, 1859. The first two days of the session were occupied with the routine of business. On Wednesday, "Rev. E. W. Robinson presented the report of the Committee, appointed at the last meeting, on facts and statistics with reference to the celebration of the hundred-and-fiftieth anniversary of the Association,—which was read and referred to a committee consisting of Rev. Messrs. Jonathan Brace, D. D., and D. S. Brainerd." In the afternoon of the same day, "the following report, presented by Rev. Dr. Brace, was accepted and adopted :—

"The committee to whom were referred the collections of the Committee on Facts and Statistics, to report what disposition should be made of the same, and of the historical discourse for the celebration; also to nominate a committee of publication, and present plans and estimates for accomplishing the work; report—

That they recommend the putting of these collections and the historical discourse into a pamphlet, or a bound volume to those who prefer it, and nominate as a committee of publication and to complete the collections, Rev. Messrs. Leonard Bacon, D. D., S. W. S. Dutton, D. D., and E. W. Robinson;—and, since the cost of publishing the same cannot now be correctly estimated, that this matter be left with the publishing committee, in the hope that they will be able to devise some method of publication by which the sales of the work may defray the expense."

On Thursday, after a few items of business, the entire day was devoted to the appointed celebration. The proceedings are recorded on the Minutes of the General Association, as follows :

"The ordinary business of the annual meeting having now been finished, the exercises connected with the celebration of the one hundred and fiftieth anniversary of the General Association were opened, under the direction of the committee of arrangements, by the reading of extracts from historical papers prepared for the occasion.

Rev. E. W. Robinson read a list of the half-century ministers of Connecticut from the beginning.

Rev. W. H. Moore read a paper, prepared by Rev. Henry Jones, on the Relation of the rise and growth of other denominations in this State to Congregationalism.

At 10 o'clock, after singing, and prayer by Rev. David Smith, D. D., a historical discourse was delivered by Rev. Leonard Bacon, D. D.

After prayer by Rev. Dr. Hawes, a recess was taken till half-past 2 o'clock, P. M.

Thursday afternoon, half past 2 o'clock.—The session was opened with singing. Prayer was offered by Rev. Dr. Calhoun.

Voted, That each speaker this afternoon and evening be limited to twenty minutes; and that the Moderator be requested to give notice, when necessary, of the expiration of the allotted time.

Rev. Abel McEwen, D. D., read a paper on Congregationalists in their relations to religious sects characterized by error, fanaticism, or disorder; or the *Isms of Connecticut.*

Prof. E. A. Lawrence, D. D., made an address on the Principles of our Fathers historically considered; Rev. T. D. Woolsey, D. D., on the Catholicity of true Congregationalism; and Rev. Joel Hawes, D. D., on the First Church formed in the State.

A few stanzas of a hymn were sung.

Rev. T. M. Post, D. D., of St. Louis, Mo., then spoke on the Mission of Congregationalism in the West; and Rev. E. P. Barrows, D. D., of Andover, Mass., on Congregationalism as in harmony with the Scriptural idea of Christian Union.

Rev. John Waddington, of Southwark, London, being present, and specially invited by the Moderator, addressed the audience briefly, and very acceptably, with reference to the interests of Congregationalism in the Old and the New World.

He was followed by Rev. A. L. Chapin, D. D., President of Beloit College, whose subject was, Connecticut Puritans in the West.

After the doxology and the benediction, a recess was taken till half-past seven in the evening.

Thursday evening, half-past 7 o'clock.—The session was opened with singing. Prayer was offered by Rev. George Bushnell.

Rev. E. W. Robinson read a paper relative to the First Meeting of the A. B. C. F. Missions at the house of Noah Porter, D. D., in Farmington,—prepared by Dr. Porter. Rev. S. W. S. Dutton, D. D., addressed the audience upon the safety and wisdom of entire religious liberty, as illustrated by our history; Rev. Joseph Eldridge, D. D., upon Consociated Congregationalism; Rev. Samuel Wolcott, of Providence, R. I., upon the Lessons of our day as suggested by the leading aim of our fathers; Rev. Joseph P. Thompson, D. D., of New York City, upon the Congregational Polity as adapted to the highest development of the individual Christian, in harmony with the practical union of all Christians in the faith and the work of Christ; and Rev. William I. Budington, D. D., of Brooklyn, N. Y., upon the Mission of our Churches as defined by our history.

The promiscuous audience convened to listen to the public addresses was dismissed after the singing of a hymn, by the benediction. It was then *Resolved,* That, in view of that inheritance which we have received from our fathers,—the principles of which have been so fully set before us on this occasion,—this Association at this closing hour feel called upon not only unitedly to express our deepest gratitude to God for the same, but also to do all in our power to transmit it to the latest time.

Voted, That the thanks of the General Association be presented to Rev. Leonard Bacon, D. D., for the clear and most important history contained in the able discourse pronounced by him to-day, and that a copy be requested for publication.

Voted, That the thanks of the Association be presented to those gentlemen who have given extempore addresses, and that they be requested to revise them from the printed reports for publication in the forthcoming volume.

Voted, That the thanks of the Association be presented to those who have prepared essays for publication in connection with this occasion.

Voted, likewise, That the thanks of this body be presented to the committee on facts and statistics, and especially to the chairman, Rev. E. W. Robinson, for his diligent, persevering and successful labors.

Resolved, That the thanks of the Association be presented to the families of this city and vicinity for their liberal and courteous hospitality; to the two Congregational societies, for the use of their houses of worship; to the committee of arrangements for their delicate and unwearied attention to our minutest wants; to the choirs of the respective churches, for their attendance and assistance in our public praises; and to the members of the press who have so largely contributed to awaken and keep alive the interest felt on this important occasion.

In the discharge of the duty imposed upon the subscribers by the General Association of 1859, this volume of contributions to the Ecclesiastical History of Connecticut is now offered to the public. Much labor has been bestowed upon the preparation of it since the materials, in an unfinished state, were put into our hands. It will be observed, as one result of the necessary delay in the publication, that the statistical and historical information collected from the District Associations, and from the churches, is brought down to the present year.

In so large a volume, containing contributions of so many different kinds, and from so many different sources, the reader will naturally expect to find some diversity in matters of opinion, and will neither be surprised nor offended at unimportant discrepances of statement in matters of fact. On the question, for example, whether the First Church in Hartford or the the First Church in Windsor is to be regarded as the oldest in the State, the reader may judge for himself, or hold his judgment in suspense. It was not our duty as a publishing committee to decide any such questions. While we have done what we could to perfect the historical and statistical papers which constitute so large a portion of this volume, we trust that neither the Committee nor the General Association will be held responsible for the statements or the arguments of individual contributors. We are sorry to be obliged to add that no inconsiderable number of errors has been discovered in these pages, particularly in the matter of names and dates. It is hoped that most of these will be found to be of no great importance. A full list of ERRATA is given at the end of the volume. It would be well if each person would make the proper corrections in his own copy at the outset.

Important service has been rendered by the members of the committee appointed by the General Association to assist in making collections within their several Associations ; and acknowledgments are due to them and to the Rev. Messrs. W. C. Fowler, H. G. Jesup, J. A. Gallup, W. H. Moore, Abram Marsh, J. H. Newton and A. Putnam ; particularly in the preparation of the Sketches of the District Associations and the Lists of Licentiates.

Our thanks, and the thanks of the General Association and of the churches, are also due to Mr. William L. Kingsley, whose diligence and skill have greatly aided our editorial labors, and whose generous zeal has undertaken the publication of these Contributions to the Ecclesiastical History of his native State, with no prospect of gain, and with no security against pecuniary loss. Only a small edition has been printed. We hope it will not be permitted to remain upon his hands.

LEONARD BACON,
S. W. S. DUTTON, } *Committee*
E. W. ROBINSON, } *of Publication.*

NEW HAVEN, Dec. 1860.

Few readers, save those who have had some experience of such work, can understand how great the labor has been of collecting, condensing, completing and editing the Historical Sketches of the District Associations and the Churches ; and how much of correspondence, and of patient waiting, and of renewed and repeated inquiry, that labor has involved. The two first named members of the Committee may be allowed to say that this great labor could not have been performed but for the zeal and unwearied diligence of their colleague, Rev. E. W. Robinson. From the first suggestion of the commemoration to the completion of the indexes which will make this volume valuable as a book of reference, his industry has never been weary. He has been, as many of the contributors have had occasion to know, the working member of the committee.

LEONARD BACON,
S. W. S. DUTTON.

CONTENTS.

HISTORICAL PAPERS.

HISTORICAL SKETCHES OF THE DISTRICT ASSOCIATIONS, WITH LISTS OF THEIR LICENTIATES.

HISTORICAL SKETCHES OF THE CONGREGATIONAL CHURCHES OF CONNECTICUT,

APPENDIX.

TOPICAL INDEX.

INDEX OF NAMES.

BIBLIOGRAPHY.

_____

SUMMARY.

The following statistical items—some of them scattered through the volume, and a few of them not elsewhere to be found—are here grouped together for convenience of reference.

Associations in the State, ... 15
Churches now existing and reported, . . . 284
Whole Number of Church Members, (Minutes Gen. Assoc.) 47,109
Extinct Churches reported, ... 21
" Separate " Churches, extinct, merged or changed, . . 30
Towns in the State, ... 161
Town having no Congregational Church, (Waterford,) . 1
Pastors who went on Missionary tours before 1798, . . 45
Missionaries sent to New Settlements and the West, . . 279
Amount expended for these Missions, and paid to Am. Home
    Miss. Society, (June, 1859,) . . . $654,304.40
Number of Churches formed by these Missionaries, about, . 500
Churches and Congregations aided in Conn., by the Connec-
    ticut Missionary Society, . 93
    Of these there are now self-supporting, . . . 53
    Still receiving aid, ... 35
    Have become extinct or changed, ... 5
Expended for Home Missions in the State, (June, 1859,) $117,422.29
Foreign Missionaries from Connecticut, . . . 103
Female Foreign Missionaries reported, . . . 72
Foreign Missionaries, Graduates of Yale College, . . 54
Students of Yale Theological Seminary, (1859,) about, . 700
Students of East Windsor Theological Institute, (1859,) . 238
Half-Century Ministers, on both Lists, ... 250
    Those who have ministered in the State, . . . 175
    Natives and Licentiates who have ministered out of the State, 70
    Who have left the Congregational ministry, . . . 5
Licentiates reported, ... 1320
Of these there were licensed before 1760, by six Associations, 125

xiv CONTENTS.

HISTORICAL DISCOURSE,

DELIVERED AT NORWICH, JUNE 23, 1859,

BEFORE THE

General Association of Connecticut,

AT THE CELEBRATION OF ITS

ONE HUNDRED AND FIFTIETH ANNIVERSARY.

———

BY LEONARD BACON, D. D.

HISTORICAL DISCOURSE.

In attempting to fulfill the appointment which I received from the last General Association, I throw myself frankly on that Christian liberality and fraternal kindness, of which the appointment itself was an expression. I am not the pastor of a consociated church. I have been sometimes, and in some quarters, reputed to be unfriendly to that form of confederation which our fathers and predecessors established among the churches in this Puritan commonwealth. Others are in many respects more competent than I am, to the duty of setting forth in a historical discourse the origin and design, the working, and the results of that ecclesiastical constitution. Assured that the appointment was not made inconsiderately, nor without the understood consent of the pastors and other ministers represented in the General Association, I accept the task in the same spirit in which it was assigned to me. Addressing myself on this occasion, not to the General Association as a representative body, but to its constituency assembled as in a mass meeting, I speak in all freedom; for I am sure that what is expected of me is not a set defense of any particular arrangement for maintaining that great principle of "the Congregational way," the communion of churches, but only an honest attempt to set forth those facts of our ecclesiastical history, which are most pertinent to this commemoration.

One hundred and fifty-one years ago, that is in the year 1708, on the 9th, or according to our present calendar, the 20th day of September, a meeting of pastors and lay messengers, hardly more numerous than an ordaining council of these times, was convened in the little town of Saybrook. The

2

time of meeting was the time of commencement in the "Collegiate School," which has since become Yale College, and in which the seventh commencement was then to be celebrated. The place may be presumed, and is reported by the local tradition to have been at the house which Mr. Nathaniel Lynde of Saybrook had generously given for the use of the college, so long as it should be continued in that town. Commencement in those days brought no great concourse to the town ; for as yet the degrees were conferred with no public demonstration, only a few friends of the candidates, in addition to the trustees, being admitted to the ceremony. Nor did the presence of the synod, if we may so call it, add much to the attendance in Saybrook at that commencement; for of the twelve ministers whose names appear upon the roll of that synod, nine were at the time trustees of the Collegiate School. The synod then, (for by that name it will be convenient to speak of it,) was hardly more than a meeting of the trustees in another capacity.

Let us name then, one by one, the men who formed the Saybrook constitution. What else is there to be known concerning them ? What sort of men were they in their generation ?

Small as that synod was numerically, it had two moderators, not so much for use as for dignity ; not so much because the assembly was expected to be turbulent, as because such had been the way in the preceding synods of New England. The senior moderator was JAMES NOYES, of Stonington, at that time a venerated father among the clergy of Connecticut, being in the sixty-ninth year of his age. His father, of the same name, the first teacher of the church in Newbury, Massachusetts, was one of those eminent men among the first ministers of New England, whose lives are recorded in Mather's Magnalia, and was greatly distinguished in his day, like his colleague and kinsman Thomas Parker, by his dissent from the Congregational way, and by the approximation of his views to the Presbyterian system. Our James Noyes was an alumnus of Harvard College, a graduate of 1659. He had been for forty-four years the minister of Stonington, and for thirty-four years the pastor there; the first church in Stonington not having been instituted till ten years after the commencement of his labors in the town.

The adsessor of James Noyes in moderating the synod, was THOMAS BUCKINGHAM, pastor of the church in Saybrook. He was a son of Thomas Buckingham, one of the "seven pillars" who were chosen to begin the church in Milford. As he does not appear among the alumni of Harvard College, it may be presumed that he received his education in the New Haven "colony school." He appears to have commenced his ministry at Saybrook, not far from the year 1667, when the candlestick had been removed out of its place, by the migration of the church with its pastor to Norwich. Before 1669 another church had been gathered in Saybrook, and soon afterwards Thomas Buckingham had become its pastor. At the date of the synod he was sixty-two years of age, and had been in the pastoral office not far from forty years. All the indications of his character and position that appear upon the documents that have come down to us from that age, show that he was one of the most conspicuous among the clergy of the colony. To us assembled here, it is an interesting fact that the honored and beloved chief magistrate of this ancient commonwealth, at the present time, is his descendant.

Where there were two moderators, it is not strange that there were two scribes. These were STEPHEN MIX, of Wethersfield, and JOHN WOODWARD, of Norwich. The former was at that time about thirty-six years old. He was a native of New Haven, the youngest son of one who was a young man among the earliest inhabitants of the town. Educated at Harvard College, a graduate of 1690, he became pastor of the Wethersfield church in 1694, when he was only twenty-two years of age ; and in that place the traditionary remembrance of his ministry, and especially of the authority with which he ruled the people, was long maintained, and I dare say is not yet extinguished. The other scribe, John Woodward, was a still younger man. He had been less than nine years a pastor, though he had been fifteen years a graduate of Harvard.

Another aged pastor, deputed by the council of New London county, was present in the synod, namely, Moses Noyes, of Lyme. He had been minister in that place from the beginning of the settlement there, forty-two years ; but he had sustained the pastoral office only fifteen years, for, from 1666 till 1693, though public worship was maintained in Lyme, and a minister supported, without aid from any Home Missionary Society, no church was instituted in that settlement. It seems difficult to reconcile such a fact with another equally attested fact, namely, that the man who labored as minister of the gospel twenty-seven years in a single parish, without gathering a church, and therefore without any administration of sacramental ordinances, was nevertheless a man of mark among the clergy of the colony, a Calvinist without reproach in his doctrinal scheme, and esteemed by the best judges that knew him, a man of great and extensive learning, an excellent Christian, and judicious divine. He was three years younger than his brother the moderator, but the two were classmates at Harvard College in the class of 1659.

Two other members of the synod, the next after Buckingham in the order of age, were also classmates at Harvard, in the class of 1675. Samuel Andrew, of Milford was at that time in the fifty-second year of his age, and was just completing the twenty-third year of his pastorate. He was the acting rector or president of the Collegiate School, which office he continued to hold without resigning his pastoral charge, till after the removal of the school to New Haven, and the completion of its first college building there in 1718, when his son-in-law, the pastor of Stratford, was appointed rector. His ministry at Milford, prolonged through more than half a century, seems to have been steadily prosperous, and the effects of it upon the habits of the people are visible at this day. His classmate TIMOTHY WOODBRIDGE, of Hartford, was a son of that John Woodbridge who came to New England in 1634, at the age of twenty-one, and was pastor for a little while at Andover, but resigned his charge and returned to England while Puritanism was in the ascendant there, and then, after many years, came back, and was settled in Newbury as colleague with his aged uncle, Thomas Parker, and successor to his kinsman, the father of the Noyeses. Timothy Woodbridge was ordained pastor of the First Church in Hartford, on the same day on which his college classmate was ordained at Milford. He came into the pastoral office in that church, only nineteen years after the decease of Samuel Stone, the surviving colleague of Thomas Hooker. How well he bore himself in that office, and to what degree of honor and public confidence he attained among his contemporaries, is amply testified by the eulogium which Timothy Edwards pronounced upon him, when preaching the election sermon before the authorities of the colony, the week after his death, [1732.] Both the Hartford ministers had died within the year, and both were commemorated by the preacher, standing in the pulpit where both had been for many years accustomed to sit on the occasion of that great solemnity. Having spoken first of the pastor of the South Church who had died six months before, he proceeded to speak more at large of "that aged and eminent servant of Christ, who died in this town this last week, who was one of the principal men of his order in the land. Him, we that were his contemporaries in the sacred work of the evangelical ministry in the towns about him, generally considered as one much our senior and superior; and in cases of weight and difficulty advised with and hearkened to him as our head and guide, yea very much as to a father, who was indeed one of the chief of the fathers of that tribe in Israel which he, by office as a minister of Christ, stood especially related to." All this might seem to be no more than the common-place eulogium that naturally follows the hearse of an aged and respected minister. But when we remember that the preacher who said all this, was himself well advanced in life, these strong expressions of veneration for a departed leader and father, become more significant. Nor was all this enough for his own feeling, or for the expectation of his hearers. He went on to speak of the departed more particularly: "the goodness of his natural temper; the gravity, greatness and superiority that appeared in his countenance; his bodily presence being so far from being mean and contemptible, that it was great, much above what is ordinary, his proper stature, (he being taller than the common size,) with his comely and majestic aspect, being such as commanded reverence;"—"how wise and judicious he was; with his great prudence, his entertaining freedom, obliging courtesy and affability; his superior learning, reading and knowledge; his liberal, bountiful, generous and public spirit;" —"his great ability for, and readiness in giving counsel in difficult and important cases, and how much the care of the churches and of the College lay upon him;"—"and how happy a hand he had in managing of controversies and differences; and what influence, sway, and authority he had with ministers and people;"—"and how from place to place he carried the blessing of peace with him; and how ready and willing he was with love to serve men and do good to all." The hearers were furthermore reminded of "his orthodoxy and soundness in the Christian faith, and how much he savored of a gracious spirit—particularly in his great love to our Lord Jesus Christ, his blessed master; his holy zeal for God and against sin; his humble submission and resignation to divine sovereignty;

[and] his great mortification to the world." It seemed not necessary to tell them, but only to remind them, " for how many years and how well he filled the pulpit, and (in our councils and associations,) the moderator's chair ; and with how amiable a conversation he adorned his profession ;"—" and how becoming a Christian and a minister he carried himself, both living and dying." When such men die," exclaimed the preacher, "we may well weep over them, as the king of Israel wept over the holy prophet, ' *O my father, my father ! the chariots of Israel, and the horsemen thereof !'* "

I may add that he who was the subject of all this eulogy, left in print one specimen of his ability in the ministry,—an election sermon preached in 1727, when he was already far advanced in age. An attentive examination of that sermon, especially in the light of the testimony given so soon afterwards over his recent grave, shows that he was a strong and deep thinker, and that he must have been to an intelligent congregation an eminently impressive preacher.

Another class of graduates from Harvard, that of 1681, gave three members to our little synod, namely, JAMES PIERPONT, of New Haven, NOADIAH RUSSELL, of Middletown, and SAMUEL RUSSELL, of Branford. The first of these is traditionally reported to have made the original draught of the articles adopted by the synod. At the house where some of his descendants live on his old homestead in New Haven, his countenance—slightly shaded with a look of sadness yet expressive of whatever quality can win affection, gentle and scholarly yet full of manly beauty, with the high, thoughtful forehead, the delicately chiseled features, and the dark, keen eye—still looks upon us from the canvas. And well do the rich masses of hair falling upon his shoulders, the neat white bands, and the scholar's gown with its loose folds, set off the serious beauty of that countenance. One printed sermon remains to tell us with what force and fervor, as well as doctrinal sound-

ness, he performed his work in preaching the word. The time
at which he came to the pastoral office in the New Haven
Church, required in the pastor peculiar gifts of influence and
of wisdom, and especially a manifest eminence in the wisdom
that cometh from above. The generation that came out of
England had just passed away. Eaton and Goodyear, Greg-
son and the Newmans, and others like them who had first encountered the temptations of the wilderness, and had laid the
foundations of what they hoped would be a glorious temple,
had left behind them none that could be called their equals.
The first pastor Davenport, seventeen years before, had forsaken
the church in his old age, not only because he felt himself called
to do battle in a broader field for what he esteemed an essential principle of the Congregational way, but also because, in
the midst of thickening disappointments, he was depressed and
discouraged. His colleague, Street, had labored on alone six
years, and his death had left the church for the first time without a minister. Ten years of trouble, of discouragement, of
division, and of steady declension followed, and then, by the
kind providence of God, the young man came to them, in
whom, after a few months of probation, their hearts were
united. His wisdom, his gentleness, his faithfulness, carried
that church through a perilous crisis in its history. His public
spirit, as well as his eminent gifts, made him conspicuous in
the colony. It was out of his consultations with his two next
neighbors in the ministry, Andrew, of Milford, and Russell, of
Branford, that the movement came which resulted in the
founding of a college under the humble name of a collegiate
school. In the words of Cotton Mather, "New Haven valued
him—all Connecticut honored him." When he came to the
commencement at Saybrook, in 1708, making his slow journey through the woods that had as yet receded from the shore
only at distant intervals, and discussing the affairs of the colony, the college, and the churches, with his friend and class-

mate Samuel Russell, as they rode side by side from Branford to the river, he was less than fifty years old, but he had been more than twenty-three years in the pastoral office. He died six years afterwards, at the age of fifty-five, when the college of which he was a principal founder had not yet found its permanent abode, and when the system of church government which he helped to frame had not yet begun to show what it could do. But his usefulness has survived him in his descendants to this day. His beautiful and gifted daughter, Sarah, a great grand daughter of Thomas Hooker, was like a ministering angel to her husband,* that wonderful preacher and theologian, whose name is to this day the most illustrious in the church history of New England, but who could never have fulfilled his destiny without her. A grandson of his† enriched our New England theology with his unanswerable exposition and defense of the divine fact of the atonement for the sins of men. A great grandson of his‡ presided over the college for more than twenty years with eminent success and wide renown, and left to all the evangelical churches that read or worship in our English language, the only System of Theology that ever has become in two hemispheres a popular religious classic. Nor is this all. The humble collegiate school, which in 1708 was sending out a class of three graduates, and which, when James Pierpont died had not yet dared to call itself a college, has grown into a university with five distinct faculties of instruction, with almost six hundred students, and with more than three thousand living alumni; and its beloved and honored president, with those various gifts of genius, of learning and of grace, which so adorn the office made illustrious by his predecessors, is a great great grandson of the same James Pierpont.

Of Pierpont's two classmates, the Russells, we know less;

---

* President Edwards. † The younger President Edwards. ‡ President Dwight.

2

but what we know is of the same sort with what we know of him. The church of Middletown was in its stage of early weakness when Noadiah Russell became the pastor there. His only predecessor in office had died after a ministry of only sixteen years, and an interregnum of four years had followed. That was, as I have intimated, a time of greater depression, and greater peril in church and state than any other time in the history of New England. Just then it was that Noadiah Russell, whose childhood and early youth had been passed under the ministry of Davenport and Street, in New Haven, began his ministry in Middletown. How well he performed his work, how effectually he molded the character, and formed the habits of the people, and how much he had of their grateful affection, may be inferred from the fact that when he died, in the fifty-fifth year of his age, and the twenty-ninth of his pastorate, his son became in a few months his successor, and labored there for almost fifty years—the entire period from the ordination of the father to the funeral of the son being more than three-quarters of a century. In like manner Samuel Russell, son of the first minister of Hadley, came to the pastoral office in Branford at the re-organization of the church there, twenty-two years after the removal of Abraham Pierson' with his flock to New Jersey. He became the second father of the town. His ministry, peaceful and prosperous, was prolonged forty-four years, till his death in 1731, at the age of seventy. It was at his house that the ceremony of founding the college, by the ten ministers who had been designated for that purpose, took place in the year 1700.

Of the twelve clergymen in our little synod, I have already mentioned ten. The two that remain to be commemorated, were contemporaries in college, though not classmates,—CHARLES CHAUNCEY, who graduated in 1686, and JOHN DAVENPORT, who graduated one year later—the one being a grandson of that Charles Chauncey who, in the first generation of our New

England history, was President of Harvard College, and the other being the only grandson of the first pastor of New Haven. The first was forty years old in 1708; the second, one year younger, they being the youngest members of the synod with the exception of the scribes. Chauncey was pastor of the Stratfield church, now the First church in Bridgeport. He was born in Stratford, where his father, the youngest son of President Chauncey, was pastor. He was twenty-seven years old, and had been nine years a graduate, when a new parish was instituted, which received the name of Stratfield as signifying that part of it was in *Strat*ford, and part in Fair*field*. At the organization of the church in that new parish, he was ordained to the pastoral office over a people among whom he had been known from his childhood. In that office he continued till his death in 1714. John Davenport, pastor of the church in Stamford, was not inferior in ability to any other member of the synod. In his own church and town, and among the ministers and churches of that county, he had a commanding influence. In the election sermon for 1731, his death, which had taken place three months before, was spoken of by the preacher (Samuel Whittelsey, of Wallingford) as " the removal of one eminent for learning, and who was a bulwark and a barrier upon our frontiers." Nor was this an unmeaning eulogy. As to his learning, it was testified at his funeral, by one of his neighbors in the ministry, (Samuel Cooke, the successor of Chauncey at Stratfield,) that " he had the advantage of an accurate knowledge of those languages wherein the scriptures were given by Divine inspiration, probably far beyond the compass of any of his survivors within many scores of miles every way ; and so could drink immediately out of the sacred fountain, those languages being almost as familiar to him as his mother tongue." And that he was not a scholar merely, but a man of action and of influence, was largely testified. His relations to the civil interests of the colony, to the college, (of which he had been for fourteen years a trustee,) and to the ecclesiastical commonwealth at large, as well as to his own parish, having been referred to, and his ability and bold fidelity as a minister of God's word, having been commemorated, the speaker went on to say, he "was both our crown and our bulwark";—"it was many years since looked upon by the serious and judicious as a special favor of Divine Providence that a person of such distinction was seated so near the western limits of New England as a bulwark against any irruptions of corrupt doctrines or manners."

Of the four lay messengers who were delegated to that synod from the several constituent councils, little can be reported. "The council of Hartford county sent JOHN HAYNES, Esq., of the First church in Hartford, who was a son of the second pastor of that church, and a grandson of the first governor of that colony. He had been liberally educated at Harvard College, and was eminent in civil life, being a Judge and an "assistant." "From the council of Fairfield county" came Deacon SAMUEL HOYT, an officer of the church in Stamford. "From the council of New London county" there were two, of whom one was ROBERT CHAPMAN, of Saybrook, a man who often represented that town in the colonial legislature, and whose memorial among his descendants is that "he walked with God;" and the other was Deacon WILLIAM PARKER, of whom I have been able to find no traces elsewhere.

The synod, consisting of these sixteen members, was convened by an order from the civil government of the colony. Such a call was in accordance not only with the ideas then prevalent, but with all the precedents in the history of New England. It was universally understood in those days—and rarely was there an election sermon in which it was not explicitly or implicitly repeated—that Moses and Aaron were to embrace each other in the mount; that Christian magistrates were to care for the peace and purity of the churches; and that those who were entrusted with the government of the commonwealth were to be regarded, and were to regard themselves, in their relation to the churches, as *episcopi quoad externa.* Accordingly, in May, 1708, the legislature entered upon the record of its doings an order which not only convened the synod, but prescribed its duties, and which should therefore be read in full on such an occasion as the present.

"This Assembly, from their own observation, and the complaint of many others, being made sensible of the defects of discipline in the churches of this government, arising from the want of more explicit asserting of the rules given for that end in the Holy Scriptures, from which would arise a permanent establishment among ourselves, a good and regular issue in cases subject to ecclesiastical discipline, glory to Christ our head, and edification to his members, hath seen fit to ordain and require, and it is by the authority of the same ordained and required, that the ministers of the several counties in this government shall meet together, at their respective county towns, with such messengers as the churches to which they belong shall see cause to send with them, on the last Monday in June next, there to consider and agree upon those methods and rules for the management of ecclesiastical discipline, which by them shall be judged agreeable and conformable to the word of God, and shall, at the same meeting, appoint two or more of their number to be their delegates, who shall all meet together at Saybrook, at the next commencement to be held there, where they shall compare the results of the ministers of the several counties, and out of and from them to draw a form of ecclesiastical discipline, which, by two or more persons delegated by them, shall be offered to this court, at their session at New Haven in October next, to be considered of and affirmed by them ; and the expense of the above mentioned meetings shall be defrayed out of the public treasury of this colony."

The alleged occasion of this ordinance, and the ends which it was expected to answer, require some attention on our part if we would fully understand this important chapter in the church history of Connecticut. "Defects of the discipline of the churches" are referred to as obvious and notorious, but are not described or specified. What were those defects, so noto- rious that there was no need of naming them? It is affirmed that those defects, whatever they may have been, "arise from the want of a more explicit asserting of the rules given for that end in the Holy Scriptures." What rules for the discipline of the churches are those which, as the framers of this ordinance thought, are given in the scriptures, but which were not suffi- ciently asserted in the then existing platform of the Connecti- cut churches? It was expected that from the more explicit as- sertion of those rules, there would arise "a permanent estab- lishment" in Connecticut. What was the meaning of that phrase " permanent establishment?" Establishment—of what? And how was that expected establishment to differ from the establishment then existing? It was furthermore expected that from this more explicit asserting of scriptural rules, there would arise " a good and regular issue in cases subject to ecclesiasti- cal discipline," as well as " glory to Christ and edification to his members." What did this language mean as used by the framers of the ordinance? If we can fairly answer these ques- tions I think we shall understand the views and aims of the men who projected the Saybrook synod.

We may get some help in our exegesis by remembering what former synods had been held in New England, and with what results. The first—that of 1637—was held that the churches, and their ministers, might come, by discussion and fraternal consultation to some united judgment concerning an enthusias- tic antinomianism, which had become a perilous and disorgan- izing heresy in the Boston church, and was mixing itself dis- astrously with all the interests of the colonies. The second— that which met in 1647, and again by adjournment in 1648— was called to digest and set forth a system of principles for the guidance of the churches in matters of discipline, and its result was the Cambridge Platform. In this as well as at the first synod, the churches, not of Massachusetts only, but of the other colonies, were represented. The platform elaborated by the synod had not indeed the authority of a constitution or of a code of laws ; it was law to the churches, only in the sense in which Kent's Commentaries or Story on the Constitution is law to courts of justice. It was nothing else than an " explicit asserting" of rules given in the scriptures. As such it was accepted in Connecticut not less than in Massachusetts, and was held to be full and sufficient for the guidance of churches in their self-government, and in their relations to each other. Even now, after a lapse of more than two hundred years, that platform, (notwithstanding its errors here and there in the application of proof texts, and its one great error in regard to the power of the civil magistrate in matters of religion,) is the most authentic exposition of the Congregational church order as given in the scriptures. At first, it was the more effectually commended to general acceptance because it was understood as having satisfactorily adjusted whatever differences on the subject of church discipline had been developed in New England. But not many years had passed, when difficulties arose in the churches on the Connecticut, and especially in the Hartford church, from which the admired and venerated Thomas Hooker had recently been removed by death. That passage in our church history is an obscure one, the documents by which it might be illustrated having mostly perished. But we may be sure the conflict was not by any means a merely personal collision between the Teaching Elder Stone and the Ruling Elder Goodwin, or between any other, individuals who were involved in it. Whatever may have been the beginning of it, the controversy itself was a conflict between opposite principles of ecclesiastical order. It is often said that there was a Presbyterian element or tendency among the original Puritans of New England ; and so there was, but what was it ? None but the shallowest and most ignorant readers of our history will undertake to find that Presbyterian element in the fact that every church was to have its eldership, including one at least beside the teaching elders; nor in the fact that the Cambridge Platform insists on the duties of churches toward each other. Neither of these facts has any relation to the difference between the Presbyterianism of that age, and "the Congregational way." Some of the first ministers of New England were avowed Presbyterians. Such were Thomas Parker of Newbury, and his kinsman and colleague James Noyes, the father of the two Noyeses in our Saybrook synod. Such was also John Woodbridge, first of Andover, and afterwards of Newbury, another kinsman of Thomas Parker, and the father of that Timothy Woodbridge who was also a member of our synod. Others were semi-presbyterians, or infected with a presbyterian tendency. Such was Samuel Stone, the famous colleague of the more famous Hooker. He appears to have held firmly enough the principle that all church power inheres in every organized local church; but his Presbyterian tendency is intimated by the tradition which imputes to him the saying that "a church is a speaking aristocracy in the face of a silent democracy." The elders only were to speak in the transaction of church affairs; the brethren were to give their consent in silence. While Thomas Hooker lived, the presby- terianizing tendency in his colleague teacher was effectually counteracted, or perhaps was not developed. But soon after the first pastor's death, the conflict of opinions in that most important church began. And soon, as all the traces of the story show, the conflict involved not only the rights and functions of the brotherhood in the government of the church, but also the qualifications for baptism, and the conditions and nature of church-membership. Soon, thoughtful men, in various parts of New England, were able to discern how far the influence of the principles that had been newly broached at Hartford might extend, and how perilous a defection from the Congregational way was impending. The demand for a promiscuous administration of baptism after the way of national churches, and for the recognized church-membership of all baptized persons not convicted of some overt and positive offence, had been peeped and muttered elsewhere, but had been suppressed without much trouble. It has been often alleged, that this demand originated in the unwise exclusion of all but church members from participation in political power, and that a reasonable extension of the right of suffrage would have silenced the demand. But on such a theory how is it to be explained that the troubles which the theory accounts for, began in just that colony in which no such exclusion had ever been established or attempted? No; the controversy which agitated the churches on the river, however it may have been embittered by political interests, as well as by personal feelings, was essentially nothing else than the fermentation of that leaven of Presbyterianism which came over not with the Pilgrims in the Mayflower, but with the later Puritan emigration, and which the Cambridge Platform, with all its explicitness in asserting the rules given in the Scriptures, had not effectually purged out.

That local controversy at Hartford and Wethersfield, gave origin to the third New England Synod. Once and again the General Court of the colony had interposed in vain. Council after council had given advice in vain. At last, at the request of the government in Connecticut, the government of Massachusetts gave out the invitation for a synod, which was convened in 1657. Twenty-one questions "about church affairs," and especially about the relation of baptized persons as such to the church, had been sent from Connecticut to Massachusetts, and were the subject matter on which the synod was to give light. In one respect this differed from the two former synods. Instead of being a general convention of "elders and other messengers" from the churches, it was rather a select assembly of divines, commissioned by the several governments. Twelve eminent elders were appointed by the General Court of Massachusetts. Four, viz: the aged Warham, of Windsor, Stone, of Hartford, Blinman, of New London, and Russell of Wethersfield, (the father of that Samuel Russell who was a member of our Saybrook synod,) were commissioned from Connecticut. But the General Court of the New Haven jurisdiction having, "seriously considered" the matter, "with the help of such elders as were present," declined the invitation in a courteous but significant letter, which they carefully put upon their own records. They had "heard of some petitions and questions at first unwarrantably procured and presented at Connecticut, but since, under the name of liberty, offensively if not mutinously prosecuted." They "approved the readiness" of Massachusetts "to afford help when the case requires it, yet themselves conceive that the elders of Connecticut colony, with due assistance from their court, had been fully sufficient to clear and maintain the truth, and to suppress the boldness of such petitioners, without calling a synod or any such meeting, which in such times may prove dangerous to the purity and peace of these churches and colonies." They say, "We hear the petitioners, or others closing with them, are very confident they shall obtain great alterations both in civil government and in church discipline, and that some of them have procured and hired one as their agent, to maintain in writing (as is conceived,) that parishes in England, consenting to and continuing their meetings to worship God, are true churches, and such persons coming over hither, (without holding forth any work of faith, &c.,) have right to all church privileges. And probably they expect their deputy should employ himself and improve his interests, to spread and press such paradoxes in the Massachusetts, yea at the synod or meeting." Intimating the probability that "some in all the colonies, affecting such liberty, may too readily hearken and comply," they at the same time expressed their hope that the "general courts who have framed their civil polity and laws according to the rules of God's most holy word, and the elders and churches who have gathered and received their discipline out of the same holy Scriptures, will unanimously improve their power, and endeavor to preserve the same inviolably." They refer to the condition of their churches, weakened within a few years by the removal or death of several elders, whose places had not been supplied, and to " Mr. Davenport's personal unfitness for so long a journey in the heat of summer," as showing that " it would be very inconvenient for them to send or spare any of their remaining teaching officers to a service like to require much time." At the same time the elders of that jurisdiction have perused the twenty-one questions that are to be considered by the synod; and their answer, " drawn up by Mr. Davenport," and " fully approved " by the court, is sent with the letter, and so the whole matter is by them devoutly commended to God, " without whose special blessing, (according to the present state and frame of things in Connecticut colony, which may soon spread farther,) such a meeting if it hold, may produce sad effects."* How much effect this indirect but strong remonstrance had upon the meeting in its discussions and conclusions, does not distinctly appear. The result of the meeting was to some extent, (perhaps not entirely,) what the New Haven authorities, civil and ecclesiastical, had feared; for that meeting of divines first gave authority and credit to the notion of what afterwards became so celebrated in our church history, under the name of the " half way covenant."

At first the churches seem not to have accepted at all the new principle which had been commended to them. But the proposal struck the previously existing system just at its weak-

---

* New Haven Colonial Records, (C. J. Hoadly,) vol. ii, pp. 195, 198.

est point. Some modification of what had been, till then, the actual working of the Congregational church order, was inevitable. Two serious inconveniences (to use the softest phrase) had been developed in attempting to carry into effect that cardinal principle, that "saints by calling" are the only fit material of a church. First, there was felt to be a necessity for some arrangement that should recognize the obvious rights of those who, while they were required to aid in the support of the ministry, had no voice or power in the election of the ministers—the class whose rights are now amply guarded in the constitution and powers of our parishes or ecclesiastical societies ; and, secondly, there must needs be some arrangement that should recognize the Christian standing of those otherwise Christian people, who misled by inadequate or erroneous views of religious experience, or trying their own experience by traditional and technical methods, or for any other reason, dared not profess that they had been effectually called by the work of the Holy Spirit—a class of worshipers whom we now endeavor to instruct and guide by setting before them the primary act of repentance towards God and of trust in Christ, not merely as an experience to be waited for, but rather as an immediate and urgent duty, and by illustrating in every way the simplicity, and (so far as consciousness reaches) the naturalness of a truly Christian experience. The expedient of recognizing a qualified church-membership in all baptized persons, not only during their childhood, but after coming to maturity, and of inviting them to assume and renew the engagements that were made for them in their baptism, and to bind themselves by a public religious vow to live a Christian life, without any profession of a Christian experience,—aggravated, instead of exposing to refutation, the religious and theological error from which it sprung. Thus the synod of 1656 prepared the way for another which was assembled only six years afterwards.

Under the continued and growing pressure of the difficulties

which I have just mentioned, the General Court of Massachusetts issued an order for a general synod of elders and messengers from all the churches of that colony. That fourth synod
met at Boston in 1662. Two questions only were referred to
it for discussion and decision :—*first,* " Who are the subjects
of baptism ?"—and *secondly,* " Whether according to the word
of God there ought to be a consociation of churches, and
what should be the manner of it ?" After much deliberation
and debate, the synod gave its answer, not unanimously, but
by a vote of more than seven to one, as reported by Cotton Mather. Yet in that small minority there were " several reverend
and judicious persons," whose dissent greatly impaired the force
of the result. Most of the seven " propositions " in which the
judgment of the majority concerning the subjects of baptism was
summed up, are substantially accordant with what I suppose
to be the ordinary practice in our churches at the present
time. But the fifth of those propositions reaffirmed and commended to the churches the crude expedient of the half-way
covenant.* It did not merely provide that baptized persons
growing up in the bosom of the church with blameless character, and without any overt denial of the faith in which they
were nurtured, might offer their children for baptism without
being required to demand and obtain at the same time the
privilege of full communion. But it also provided that such
persons, as a condition preliminary to the baptism of their
children, should make a certain public profession of Christian
faith and Christian obedience, including a formal covenant with
God and with the church, which at the same time was to be
understood as implying no profession of any Christian experi-

---

* " Church members who were admitted in minority, understanding the doctrine of
faith, and publicly professing their assent thereto ; not scandalous in life ; and
solemnly owning the covenant before the church, wherein they give up themselves
and children to the Lord, and subject themselves to the government of Christ in the
church,—their children are to be baptized."

ence. The former, by itself, might have been a comparatively harmless innovation. The latter was a grave theological error, hardening and establishing itself in the form of an ecclesiastical system.

Neither of the two western colonies was represented in that synod. Connecticut was occupied just then with the excitement of receiving its charter from the king, and with the effort to extinguish the independent jurisdiction of the New Haven colony, in which there was a strong and united opposition to the principles that seemed likely to prevail. But as soon as it had become certain that New Haven was under a necessity of giving up its independence, and that a new and greater danger, impending over all the colonies, would compel those towns to take refuge under the charter, the General Court of Connecticut availed itself of the opportunity to give a very explicit sanction to the new principle of church-membership, commending it to all the ministers and churches, for adoption, as a rule of practice. It even " desired that the several officers of the respective churches would be pleased to consider whether it be not the duty of the court to order the churches to practice according to the premises, if they do not practice without such order."* Here is evidence not only that the old way of the churches was to be subverted, but also that the churches were slow in yielding to the outside pressure. Had they stood upon their congregational independency alone, they would not have submitted.

Less than two years after that intermeddling of the legislature with a purely ecclesiastical question, the difficulties that had so long existed in the church at Hartford, were coming to a crisis. John Whiting, a son of one of the wealthiest and most honored among the first planters of Hartford, and Joseph Haynes, a son of the first governor of that colony, had be-

* Colonial Records of Conn., (J. H. Trumbull,) vol. i, 438.

come the successors of Hooker and Stone. Both were young; Whiting thirty-one years old, and Haynes only twenty-five. A letter from John Davenport to Gov. Winthrop, dated June 14, [24] 1666, gives us some insight into the state and progress of the controversy. " I feel at my heart," said the stiff old Congregationalist, "no small sorrow for the public divisions and distractions at Hartford. Were Mr. Hooker now *in v'vis*, it would be as a sword in his bones that the church which he had planted there should be thus disturbed by innovations brought in and urged so vehemently by his young successor in office, not in spirit ; who was so far from these lax ways that he opposed the baptizing of grandchildren by their grandfathers' right." " But he is at rest ; and the people there grow wofully divided, and the better sort are exceedingly grieved, while the looser and worser party insult, hoping that it will be as they would have it, viz : that the plantations shall be brought into a parish way, against which Mr. Hooker hath openly borne a strong testimony in print. The most of the churches in this jurisdiction are professedly against this new way, both in judgment and practice, upon gospel grounds, namely: New Haven, Milford, Stratford, Branford, Guilford, Norwalk, Stamford, and those nearer to Hartford, namely Farmington, and the sounder portion of Windsor, together with their reverend pastor Mr. Warham, and I think Mr. Fitch and his church also." Probably the writer suspected, if he did not positively know, that his friend the governor was prudently favoring the innovation. If so, we can easily understand the reason of his writing just in this vein. After having intimated that he and others who were of the same opinion, could not be expected to continue silent when " the faith and order of the churches of Christ " were to be contended for ; and having made allusion to the work which he had published against the propositions of " the Bay-Synod," and to another book of his on the same theme, which remained unpublished, he proceeds to let the governor know how the facts then recent at Hartford, seemed, when reported at a distance. "I shall briefly suggest unto you what I have heard, viz : that before the last lecture-day, when it was young Mr. Haynes' turn to preach, he sent three of his party to tell Mr. Whiting, that the next lecture-day he would preach about his way of baptizing, and would begin the practising of it on that day. Accordingly he preached, and water was prepared for baptism, (which I suppose was never administered in a week-day in that church before,) but Mr. Whiting, as his place and duty required, testified against it, and refused to consent to it. Much was spoken to little purpose by some of Mr. Haynes' party. [The "silent democracy" had found their tongues.] But when Mr. Warham began to speak, one of the church rudely hindered him, saying to this purpose, 'What hath Mr. Warham to do to speak in our church matters?' This check stopped Mr. Warham's proceeding at that time." The writer then interrupts his narrative to show that inasmuch as the matter in hand concerned not that church only, but was " of common concernment to all the churches in these parts," Mr. Warham ought to have been heard ; " but," he adds, with something of an old man's querulousness, " we live in times and places when the faces of the elders are not duly honored." Resuming his narrative, he says, " Yourself prudently concluded that that day was not a fit season to begin their purposed practice, seeing it was not consented to but opposed. And so it ceased for that time." He then proceeds to expostulate against an arrangement which, as he was informed, had been made for a public dispute between the two ministers on the next lecture day, and to propose in place of it, a written discussion of the question. Of the former plan he says, " No good issue can rationally be expected of a verbal dispute, at that time, and in that place, where so many are likely to disturb the business with interruptions and clamors, and to prepare a sufficient number to overvote the better party, for the establishment of the worser way. So truth shall be dethroned, and error set up in the throne." Of his own plan he says, "This is the most suitable way for a peaceable issuing of the dispute, with solid judgment, and with due moderation and satisfaction ; and let all practice of Mr. Haynes' opinion be forborne till the truth be cleared. But if Mr. Haynes refuseth this way, I shall suspect that he more confides in the clamors of his party than in the goodness of his cause, or in the strength of his arguments, or in his ability for disputation."* What the result was of young Mr. Haynes' challenge of his colleague to a public dispute, or of old Mr. Davenport's gratuitously offered advice, we have no means of knowing, except in general that Mr. Haynes and " his way of baptizing," were in the majority ; and that three years afterwards Mr. Whiting and his adherents, under the advice of a council of elders, and with a full permission from the General Court, withdrew from the original church in Hartford, for the sake of *"practicing the Congregational way."* In the preamble to the covenant which they adopted on the day of their being formally constituted a distinct church, (Feb. 12, [22] 1670,) the seceding party made ·a distinct profession of the Congregationalism, from which the First church had departed. " Public opposition and disturbance," such was the language of their preamble, " hath of late years been given, both by preaching and practice, to the Congregational way of church order, by all manner of orderly establishments settled, and for a long time unanimously approved and peaceably practiced in this place." " We," therefore, " declare that according to the light we have hitherto received, the forementioned Congregational way (for the substance of it,) as formerly settled, professed and practiced, under the guidance of the first leaders of this church of

* History and Genealogy of the Davenport Family, pp. 360–364.

Hartford, is the way of Christ." Their statement of the "main heads or principles" which constitute and define the Congregational way, though very brief, is an exact summary of the Congregationalism which we find asserted in the Cambridge Platform.*

Notwithstanding the strenuousness of the opposition, and the divisions among ministers and churches,—of which the proceedings at Hartford are a specimen,—the new principles and practice gradually prevailed. There was no longer any pretense that the new way was really and simply the Congregational way. In 1676, the ecclesiastical and religious character of Connecticut was officially represented to the Lords of trade and plantations, in these words: "Our people, in this colony, are some of them strict Congregational men, others more large Congregational men, and some moderate Presbyterians. The Congregational men of both sorts are the greatest part of the people of the colony. There are four or five Seventh-day men, and about so many more Quakers." A very intelligible classification in the light of what we know about the ecclesiastical movement then in progress! The new system was "LARGE Congregationalism," with some not yet assimilated mixture of "moderate Presbyterianism;" and the "strictness" of the old Congregational way was gradually failing and dying out. As the aged ministers and other old men, honored and influential, who had resisted the conclusions of the Massachusetts synod, passed away, the half-way covenant came in with the new generation of pastors and church members.

From the first, the predominating influence in the government seems to have favored the new system. I have already mentioned one instance of direct legislative intermeddling, which occured even before the absorption of the New Haven colony by Connecticut had been quite consummated. Another instance took place in 1666, while Mr. Whiting and Mr. Haynes,

---

* Trumbull's History, vol. i, pp. 461–463.

in the church at Hartford, were at the hight of their dispute. At that time the General Court undertook to force the new system into operation by means of a clerical convention, including all the teaching elders in the colony, together with those ministers who, like the two Noyeses, were settled in towns where no churches had been gathered, to whom were to be added four from Massachusetts, selected and invited by the same authority. At first it was thought that such a convention might be made to pass for a synod, and it was so denominated in the order. But the jealousy of the churches having had time to manifest itself, the name was changed, and by a new order the meeting was required to take the humbler title of "an assembly of the ministers of this colony." The whole movement, however, notwithstanding this timely concession, seems not to have proceeded according to the intention of its authors, and after one session, [May, 1667] in which it became manifest that the ministers were not very manageable, the assembly was quietly and adroitly got rid of before the time arrived to which it had adjourned itself.

The next year a different movement was made. Four ministers, one from each county,* were commissioned to meet at Saybrook, "to consider of some expedient for our peace, by searching out the rule, and thereby clearing up how far the churches and people may walk together within themselves, and one with another, in the fellowship and order of the Gospel, notwithstanding some various apprehensions among them in matters of discipline respecting membership and baptism, &c." Those commissioners made their report in May, 1669, but what it was does not appear. No trace of it can be found, save one enactment which stands upon the record of that session, and which appears to have been intended as a compromise. The preamble of that act refers to the great divisions

---

* The ministers appointed were James Fitch, of Norwich, Gershom Bulkley, of Wethersfield, Joseph Eliot, of Guilford, and Samuel Wakeman, of Fairfield.

in the colony "about matters of church government." Moved
by a regard "for the honor of God," for the "welfare of the
churches," and for "the public peace so greatly endangered,"
the court undertakes to pronounce upon the matter. First,
"This Court do declare, that whereas the Congregational
churches in these parts, for the general of their profession and
practice, have hitherto been approved, we can do no less than
still approve and countenance the same to be without disturbance until better light in an orderly way doth appear." Is
there not something particularly significant in this? "The
Congregational Churches in these parts," whose way was marked out and defended by Hooker and Davenport, as well as by
Cotton and the authors of the Cambridge Platform, have hitherto been approved "for the *general* of their profession and
practice," and therefore their liberty to continue in their course
is to be undisturbed "*until better light* in an orderly way doth
appear." But this intimation of another ecclesiastical system
looming in the future is not all. In the second place, "Forasmuch as sundry persons of worth for prudence and piety
amongst us are otherwise persuaded, (whose welfare and peaceable satisfaction we desire to accommodate,) this Court doth
declare that all such persons, being also approved according to
law as orthodox and sound in the fundamentals of Christian
religion, may have allowance of their persuasion and profession in church ways or assemblies without disturbance." All
this was right undoubtedly. But it shows, plainly enough,
that the deplored divisions about church government were
caused by the strong preference which "sundry persons of worth
for prudence and piety" had manifested for a new ecclesiastical
system which was not Congregationalism. That system was
old in the old world, but new in New England. It was the
system of all national churches, and therefore of the Presbyterian party in the Long Parliament and the Westminster Assembly. It was what Davenport called the "parish way"—a sys-

tem under which the local church, as a covenanted brother-hood of souls renewed by the experience of God's grace, was to be merged in the parish ; and all persons of good moral character living within the parochial bounds, were to have, as in England and Scotland, the privilege of baptism for their households, and of access to the Lord's table.*

From that time, the Legislature seems not to have meddled again directly with the question, being satisfied, perhaps, that time would bring the change so much desired. And time did bring the change. It is difficult to say where the resistance to the half-way covenant ceased. Gradually, the churches, weary of contention, fell into the new way for the sake of peace. Perhaps the great movement for a moral and religious reformation, inaugurated in Massachusetts by the reforming synod (as it is called) of 1679–80, with those solemn covenantings which ensued, contributed something to the change. The church at New Haven, I suspect, yielded at or soon after the ordination of Mr. Pierpont in 1684. Near the close of the century when Haynes and Whiting had been succeeded by Woodbridge in the First church, and Buckingham in the Second, we find both pastors and both churches united in the half-way covenant method of churchdiscipline. The principles of the synod of 1662 were for the time victorious throughout New England ;

---

* "At a Court of Election held at Hartford, May 13th, 1669"

   *   *   *   *   *   *   *

"The return of the Reverend Mr. James Fitch, Mr. Buckley, Mr. Wakeman and Mr. Eliot was read in this Court, and left upon the file"

   *   *   *   *   *   *   *

" This Court having seriously considered the great divisions that arise amongst us about matters of Church government, for the honor of God, welfare of the churches, and preservation of the public peace so greatly hazarded, do declare that whereas the Congregational churches in these parts, for the general of their profession and prac-tice have hitherto been approved, we can do no less than still approve and counte-nance the same to be without disturbance until better light in an orderly way doth ap-pear ; but yet forasmuch as sundry persons of worth for prudence and piety amongst us are otherwise persuaded, (whose welfare and peaceable satisfaction we desire to accommodate,) this Court doth declare that all such persons, being also approved according to law as orthodox and sound in the fundamentals of Christian religion, may have allowance of their persuasion and profession in church ways or assemblies without disturbance." *J. H. Trumbull's Colonial Records of Connecticut* and the new system was bringing forth fruit after its kind, in the wide growth of a reliance on forms and outward moralities as the only attainable substitute for an unattainable experience of spiritual conversion, and in the development of a portentous though unrecognized tendency toward the hierarchical and sacramentarian type of Christianity. In 1708, when the General Court of Connecticut issued its rescript to convene our Saybrook synod, the venerable Stoddard, of Northampton, a soundly Calvinistic divine, a faithful pastor, an earnest and evangelical preacher, had already published his argument to prove that men confessedly without any spiritual experience are fit subjects of full communion in the church, and ought not to be excluded from that most important means of spiritual quickening, the Lord's Supper, if only they will honestly engage to conform their outward conduct to the accepted rules of Christian morality. Nor was the principle for which he argued, and which afterwards bore his name, a novelty at that time in New England. Silently, widely, and for at least a quarter of a century, the practice had preceded the public vindication of it.

What then remained to carry out and finish the great change which had already been achieved? It will be remembered that two questions had been referred to the Massachusetts synod of 1662. In the great controversy and agitation that arose upon the answer given to the first of those questions, the whole subject matter of the second seems to have been for the time forgotten. But there was an answer to the second question and in proportion as the principles asserted by the synod in relation to church membership prevail, and are carried out to their results, it becomes necessary to provide a government not only in the churches, but over them. To the question, " whether, according to the word of God, there ought to be a consociation of churches, and what should be the manner of it ?"—the synod of 1662 had given a clear and unequivocally Congregational answer. It declared the entire and complete ecclesiastical power of every local or particular church. It re-affirmed, with much accuracy of statement, the principles which the Cambridge Platform had affirmed concerning " the communion of churches one with another." It defined " the consociation of churches " as " their mutual and solemn agreement to exercise communion in such acts as aforesaid among themselves, with special reference to those churches which by Providence are planted in a convenient vicinity, though with liberty· reserved, without offense, to make use of others, as the nature of the case, or the advantage of opportunity may be had thereunto." It commended such consociation to " the churches of Christ in this country having so good opportunity for it," as a duty urged upon them by various considerations of expediency, and warranted by principles laid down in texts of Holy writ. It proposed, as the manner in which this consociation, or explicit covenant of communion between churches, should be effected; that each church should enter into the confederation by giving its open consent to these principles and rules of intercourse. In Massachusetts, the ancient charter of self-government had been abrogated, and the colony had been brought into a stricter dependence on the king, before the theory of the half-way covenant had obtained its full ascendency in the churches ; and there it could not but be felt that any attempt to set up a new and more formal church-establishment, might possibly result in subjecting all their churches to English laws and the English Episcopacy. But in this colony there was a different condition of affairs, and a different feeling. Here the ample charter of political power, obtained by the admirable diplomacy of Winthrop from the easy good-nature of Charles II, and the ignorance or thoughtlessness of his ministers, had been strangely continued in force ; and a more explicit ecclesiastical establishment might seem to be as practicable as it was desirable.

Do we not find, in all this, some illustration to aid in the interpretation of that legislative order by which the synod of 1708 was convened at Saybrook ? What were the "defects in the discipline of the churches of this government ?" What need was there of "a more explicit asserting of the rules given in the Holy Scrictures ?" The notorious defects, and the want of a more explicit asserting of scriptural rules, might all be summed up in two facts. *First*, the old Congregational way had been gradually given up, and what they called a "large" Congregationalism—a loose half-way covenant Congregationalism, "moderately Presbyterian " in its sympathies and tendencies, and more than moderately Presbyterian in its needs, had been gradually accepted ;—and *secondly*, those loosely Congregational churches, with all their Presbyterian need of government over them, were independent of external rule. The General Court, with its constant intermeddling in church quarrels, could only aggravate the evils which it could not control ; and there was no ecclesiastical authority that could decide judicially and conclusively. Here then was the need of a new platform in order to a more formal and explicit church establishment. "Strict Congregationalism," whatever may be its advantages in other respects, is, for such purposes, a very inconvenient and intractable form of organic Christianity.

The original bill for that act of the General Court—the veritable autograph, as it passed through the forms of legislation one hundred and fifty-one years ago, has been preserved in the archives of the State. A few days ago, I had the opportunity of seeing it. The endorsements on that little slip of paper tell us that the bill passed first in the upper House (no date being given)—then, that on the 22d of May, a committee of conference was appointed in the lower House—then, that on the 24th the bill passed. Evidently there was something in it which encountered opposition among the plain honest men of democratic tendencies and sympathies, such as have always constituted the House of Representatives in the General Assembly of Connecticut. Some of them were evidently afraid that some danger to liberty, or to the true order of the gospel, might be concealed in the proposal. It would be interesting to know what was said in the House, and what was done in the committee of conference. Did mere explanation satisfy? Or was some amendment necessary, before the deputies from the towns would consent to the proposal which had come from Governor Saltonstall and the Assistants? Turning from the endorsements to the face of the bill, we find one significant intimation. In its original draft, the order required the *ministers* of the colony to meet at their respective county towns to consult and agree on plans for the government of the churches. The words, "*with such messengers as the churches to which they belong shall see cause to send with them,*" are an interlineation. Whoever may have been the author of this project, the first intention was, that a representative body of ministers, convened by the authority of the civil government, without any opportunity given for the churches to express either approbation or dissent, should prepare a system or "form of ecclesiastical discipline," which might be commended to the churches, perhaps imposed upon them, by the legislative power of the colony. By way of afterthought and concession, an opportunity was given to the churches to participate in the proceeding by sending messengers, or to express their disapprobation by refusing to send.

It is noticeable that the records of the meeting at Saybrook show a very great disparity of numbers between the ministers who were present and the messengers of the churches; the ratio of the ministers to the messengers being that of three to one. How many of the churches had "seen cause" to give their sanction to the constituent county meetings by sending their delegates, does not appear. Was it merely accidental that from New Haven county not one individual appeared as representing any church? Had the old antipathy which the churches in the New Haven jurisdiction cherished against any possibility of subjecting the churches to the civil power, survived so long?

The first act of the synod was one in which we may be sure they were unanimous. As yet there had been in New England, since the synod of 1637, no controversy or discussion properly theological. No indication of any serious difference of judgment among the churches, or among their pastors and teachers, on any doctrinal question, appears till a much later date, so far as I can remember. Doubtless, then, it was with one consent, and without any demurrer or delay, or any suspicion of each other's soundness, that the synod (for so it was in some sense, though it did not formally represent the churches) accepted the Confession of Faith which stands connected with the Saybrook Platform. "We agree that the Confession of Faith owned and assented unto by the elders and messengers assembled at Boston, in New England, May 12, 1780, being the second session of that synod, *be recommended to the Honorable General Assembly of this Colony, at the next session, for their public testimony thereunto as the faith of the churches of this Colony.*" There was no need for them to declare, by any authority of their own, what was, and ever had been the doctrinal belief of the churches of Connecticut. But what they proposed was that the civil government of the Colony should give a " public testimony " to that well known confession— originally drawn up by the Westminster Assembly under a commission from the Long Parliament ; then revised and modified by a meeting of Congregational pastors and delegates convened at the Savoy in London by the permission of the Lord Protector Cromwell ; then modified again by the Reforming Synod of Massachusetts in 1680, and by them brought into a nearer conformity with the original Westminster Confession. By a " public testimony from the civil government," that confession was to be invested with a new authority in Connecticut, and was to become the doctrinal basis of a new ecclesiastical "establishment."   11135785

The next act of the synod, in the order of their report, is given in these words: " We agree also, that the Heads of Agree ment assented to by the United Ministers, formerly called Presbyterian and Congregational, be observed by the churches throughout this Colony." Here we find the synod acting, or seeming to act, as if it were invested with full and final power to impose a Platform on the churches. "We agree" that a certain code of rules and principles " be observed by the churches throughout this Colony." Doubtless it was a very reasonable and proper thing for them to agree in accepting and approving the Heads of Agreement. And if they had commended those Heads of Agreement to the churches for their acceptance and adoption, that also would have been a very reasonable and proper thing. Or if they had commended the Heads of Agreement to the government of the Colony that it might be by them incorporated with the basis of the proposed religious establishment, that would have been in full conformity with the commission under which they were sitting as a synod. But that imperious phrase, " We agree that the Heads of Agreement *be observed* by the churches throughout this Colony " might seem to have been an oversight.

Those " Heads of Agreement, assented to by the United Ministers formerly called Presbyterian and Congregational," were an English platform. In old England, Puritanism had been broken down, and had suffered a total defeat, in consequence of the pertinacious disagreement between the Presbyterians with their passion for a national church and a state establishment of religion, and the Independents or Congregationalists, with their unyielding demand for a more radical reformation, and a larger measure of ecclesiastical liberty. After the restoration of the Stuarts to the throne, and of the old ecclesiastical system, the mutual repulsion between those two bodies

of Nonconformists was gradually weakened under the pressure
of an impartial persecution ; while the restraints and disabil-
ities which hedged them in, made it impossible for them to
organize anything. When a more tolerant policy had begun
to prevail under the reign of William and Mary, the differences
between Presbyterians on the one hand, who could only gather
isolated congregations, and who had lost all hope of ever becoming the national church of England, and Independents on
the other, who repudiated the idea of a national church ; and
who desired no classical . or synodical organizations—was
theoretical rather than practical. At last, in the year 1691, a
formal union of the Pedo-baptist dissenting ministers in and
about London, was effected on a platform of rules and Scriptural principles, which, for the most part, ignored, or covered
up in comprehensive statements, the heads of difference between the Presbyterian and Congregational theories. That
platform, for so it might have been denominated by those who
framed it, was modestly entitled " Heads of Agreement." It
was not a compact among churches, nor was it formed by any
representative convention. It was only the statement of a
method in which certain ministers of the gospel, differing in
the theory of ecclesiastical order, had agreed to recognize each
other, and to bring about, if they could, a more intimate communion among their churches. Framed for such a purpose, it
could not but imply as its basis the right of each congregation
or worshiping society to manage its affairs in its own way ; and
so it was in fact, though not in name, a Congregational platform. While the differences between that and the Cambridge
Platform are not very striking, and are by no means offensive
in expression, even to a rigid Congregationalist, the setting up
of the Heads of Agreement by the Saybrook synod, as a substitute for the old platform, was not without significance. It implied that the new form of ecclesiastical government in Connec-

ticut was to be, in some sort, and to some extent, a compromise with Presbyterian principles.

A single glance at the English platform thus introduced and commended, is sufficient to discover that it is designed to produce some uniformity of discipline in churches mutually independent. But in respect to any method of making an appeal from the erroneous judgment of a particular church, or bringing the influence of neighbor churches to bear on a delinquent church, it is far less explicit than the Cambridge Platform. There remained, therefore, for the synod, another, and more difficult duty. That " permanent establishment among ourselves " which the political leaders of the Colony so much desired, and that "good and regular issue in cases subject to ecclesiastical discipline," without which, the hope of an establishment would be chimerical, had not yet been provided for.

Fifteen "Articles of Discipline "—the synod's own work— were therefore introduced into the report, as having been agreed upon " for the better regulation of the administration of church discipline in relation to all cases ecclesiastical, both in particular churches and councils, to the full determining and executing the rules in all such cases." What the meaning of those articles is, or rather what their meaning was when they were new, remains to this day a doubtful question ; and I believe that I may say that, even now, one of our heads of agreement, here in Connecticut, is that on that question we agree to differ. The synod's fifteen Articles seem to be, in effect, a compromise between that simple and purely Congregational method of consociation which was proposed by the Massachusetts synod of 1662, and something else that was intended to be a great deal more stringent.

Thus the work of the synod was completed. Whether they understood their own work or not, they unanimously voted for it ; 'and the three documents which constitute the Saybrook Platform, were, one month afterward, presented to the legislature, in its October session at New Haven, for approval and establishment. The legislative act which ensued, is, every word of it, worth repeating here.

"The Reverend ministers, delegates from the elders and messengers of this government, met at Saybrook September 9th, 1708, having presented to this Assembly a Confession of Faith, Heads of Agreement, and regulations in the administration of church discipline, as unanimously agreed and consented to by the elders and churches in this government; this Assembly doth declare their great approbation of such an happy agreement, and do ordain that all the churches within this government that are, or shall be, thus united in doctrine, worship, and discipline, be, and for the future shall be owned and acknowledged established by law;—provided that nothing herein shall be intended or construed to hinder or prevent any society or church, that is or shall be allowed by the laws of this government, who soberly differ or dissent from the united churches hereby established, from exercising worship and discipline, in their own way, according to their consciences."

Several particulars in this act seem remarkably significant. First, it is very coolly—and, with due reverence to the memory of Governor Saltonstall and his associates in the government, we might even say, audaciously—affirmed that the Saybrook Platform had been presented to that General Court as a thing *" unanimously agreed and consented to by the elders and churches."* In other words it was pretended that those sixteen men at Saybrook, twelve of them ministers convened only as ministers by the simple mandate of the government without any reference whatever to the consent of the churches, and the other four of them deputies of the deputies whom some of the churches had sent to the several county meetings—*were* " the elders and churches of this government ;" and that what they, in that little conclave, had "agreed and consented to," needed no approbation or acceptance from any of the forty churches then existing in Connecticut. It may be doubted whether a more signal instance of merely arbitrary imputation can be found any where save in some men's science of theology. Yet this is only an instance of the style in which the legislature of Connecticut, from the first, was wont to meddle in ecclesiastical affairs.

In the next place, the new Platform is deliberately and distinctly imposed upon the churches by excluding from the benefits of the previously existing establishment every church that should refuse conformity. Heretofore, all churches, formed with the consent of the government and the approbation of neighbor churches, had been equal in privileges. Their teaching elders, and none others, were the authorized ministry in the several towns and parishes, their administrations the only authorized administrations. But this act expresses the intention of the government to repudiate and disown all churches that should insist on the ancient system of church order, or what was called the Congregational way. Forty years before, it had been ordained that as the Congregational churches had been approved, they should still be countenanced and protected till better light should appear ; though, inasmuch as there were sundry persons of prudence and piety presbyterially inclined, it was provided that such persons, being approved according to law as orthodox in the fundamentals of the Christian religion, should be allowed their own persuasion and profession of church ways without disturbance. But now the long expected light had come, and henceforth the churches of the new Platform were to be the only ecclesiastical establishment in Connecticut.

In the third place, was the proviso at the close of the act fairly understood on all sides ? The fair construction of it seems to be that if the church in New Haven, for example, or the church in Norwich, should refuse submission to the Saybrook Platform, and insist upon proceeding in the Congrega-

tional way, it might indeed maintain its separate worship
without disturbance, but it should no longer be in a legal connection with the town ; it should no longer have a right to the
place of worship established by the town, and its ministers
should no longer have a right to public encouragement and
support. But there is reason to doubt whether the proviso was
so understood by those who enacted it—or at least whether it
was so understood by all of them.

In conformity with this new law, a convention, or council
of ministers and churches was soon held in each of the four
counties into which our territory was then divided. In Hartford County, (which included Waterbury in one direction, and
Windham, Colchester and Plainfield in another,) the thirteen
churches then existing were confederated under the new religious constitution of the Colony in two consociations, and their
elders were accordingly united in two associations. Each of
the other counties became one ecclesiastical district. So that
when the first General Association of the Colony of Connecticut
was convened at Hartford in May, 1709—a meeting of which
no record is extant, but which is incidentally noted in the Colonial Records*—the body included five particular associations.

But how was the new religious constitution received by the
churches? And how did they understand it when they submitted to it? Our venerable historian, Dr. Trumbull, says that
the· Platform "met with a general reception, though some of
the churches were extremely opposed to it." He also tells us
that "somewhat different constructions were put upon the constitution. Those who were for a high consociational govern-

* May, 1709. "It is ordered and enacted by the Governor, Council, and Represen-
tatives in General Court assembled, and by authority of the same, That the Reverend
Elders, the General Delegates of the several Associations of Elders within this Colo-
ny, now assembled in Hartford. do revise and prepare for the press the Confession of
Faith, Articles of Agreement between the united brethren in England, formerly called
Presbyterian and Congregational, together with the Discipline agreed upon by the
General Council of the Reverend Elders and churches of this Colony assembled at
Saybrook " * * * "and being revised, that the same shall be forthwith printed."

ment, construed it rigidly according to the Articles of Discipline ;" and others by the Heads of Agreement ; or at least they
were for softening down the more rigid articles by construing
them agreeably to those heads of union." There remain,
within our reach at this day, some facts and documents to illustrate the testimony of this careful and honest historian.

For example : The convention for New Haven county was
held at Branford on the 13th of April, 1709. Five elders were
present ; and their five churches were represented by eight
messengers. Three churches and their elders made no appearance in the council,—namely, Guilford, where Thomas Ruggles was pastor,—Wallingford, where Samuel Street had been
pastor more than thirty years,—and East Haven, where Jacob
Hemingway had been quite recently ordained to the pastoral
office. The story is that the churches which were represented
in the council had particularly charged their messengers to
"take care to secure their Congregational privileges." Of
course the Articles of Discipline were seriously called in question by some members of the council; and we are told that
"the Rev. Mr. Andrew and Mr. Pierpont interpreted these articles to their satisfaction." Not content with oral explana-
tions, they insisted that the sense of the ambiguous articles
should be written and fixed to prevent a different interpretation in time to come ; and that written interpretation, which
they placed upon their minutes, makes the Platform a purely
and thoroughly Congregational confederation of Congregational
churches. Even "the sentence of non-communion" against
an erring and obstinate church, as provided for in the sixth
article, was not to be declared till the constituent churches
should have been informed of the council's judgment, and
should have expressed their approval of it.*

*Narrative of the Proceedings of the First Society and Church in Wallingford, &c.
By Jonathan Todd, 1759, pp. 33-37. Also, Congregational Order, pp. 284-286.

On the other hand, the convention of elders and messengers for Fairfield County had held its meeting, at Stratfield, just four weeks earlier, [Mar. 16.] Every elder in the county was there, six in all. Of the eight churches, Greenwich only (which seems to have been in a disorganized condition) was not represented ; and Norwalk alone was contented with a single messenger. The record of that meeting is preserved at length upon the record-book of the Stratfield church. It was not till the second day of the session that any vote was taken. Then, after a vote to institute one consociation for the county, an extended ultra-Presbyterian interpretation and construction of the Articles of Discipline was put upon the record. It was distinctly resolved that the *pastors*, met in one consociation, have *power*, with the *consent* of the messengers of our churches chosen and attending, *authoritatively and decisively to determine* ecclesiastical affairs brought to their cognizance, according to the word of God ; and that our pastors, with the concurrence and consent of the messengers to be chosen and that shall attend, upon all future occasions, have like *authoritative, juridical* and *decisive* power of determination of affairs ecclesiastical ; and that in further and fuller meetings of two consociations together * * * there is the like authoritative, juridical, and decisive power," &c. It was also resolved "that, in the sixth paragraph of said conclusions, we do not hold ourselves obliged in our practice to use the phrase of 'the sentence of '*non-communion*' but instead thereof to use the phrase of *the sentence of excommunication*, which, in our judgment, may be formally applied in the case expressed in said paragraph ;" and furthermore, "that the judgment of the consociation or council be executed by any pastor appointed thereto by the council, when the pastor that hath already dealt in the case, hath not a freedom of conscience to execute the same." And as if to show more completely the genius of the system under that construction of it, there was a formal resolution "that all persons that are known to be baptized, shall, in the places where they dwell, be subject to the censures of admonition and excommunication, in case of scandal committed and obstinately persisted in."

How far this new ecclesiastical constitution, as expounded and applied in Fairfield county, differed from the Congregational way as marked out by the fathers of New England—by how many "degrees toward the antarctique" (in the phrase of the first John Davenport,) it had "varied from the first ways of reformation here begun" is evident enough to any who will consult such an authority as our venerable Hooker. He says distinctly. The church "is so far subject to the consociation of churches, that she is bound, in case of doubt and difficulty, to crave their counsel, and if it be according to God, to follow it; and if she shall err from the rule, and continue obstinate therein, *they have authority to renounce the right hand of fellowship with her.*"* He says expressly, in treating of the power of synods or councils, "They have not power *infligendi censuras, utpote excommunicationis.*" "They have no power to *impose* their canons or conclusions on the churches."† And throughout the whole of the fourth part of his Survey of the sum of church discipline, he reasons continually against that same juridical and decisive power of councils or synods, and especially that power of excommunicating individuals or churches, which the Fairfield consociation in 1709 dared to challenge for itself.

John Woodward, pastor of the Norwich church, has already been named as one of the scribes in the Saybrook synod. The incident has been commemorated, doubtless with some degree of correctness, that when the act of the legislature, adopting the new Platform as the ecclesiastical constitution of the colony, had been passed, he read that act to his congregation but without the proviso. Thereupon, as the story is given by

---

* T. Hooker, Survey, part 2, chap. 3, p. 80. † *Ibid.* p. 4, c. 3.

Isaac Backus the Baptist historian, "Richard Bushnell and Joseph Backus, Esquires, who [as representatives of the town] had opposed that scheme in the Assembly, informed the church of the liberty they had to dissent from it; but the minister carried a major vote against them. Therefore these representatives and other fathers of the town withdrew * * and held worship by themselves for three months. For this the minister and his party censured them." "But not long after the Norwich minister had censured their representatives, he consented to refer the matter to a council; and they followed it with council after council for about six years." "At last, by advice of a council that met August 31, 1716, said minister was dismissed, and the church in Norwich determined to abide upon its ancient foundation." The successor of Mr. Woodward, Dr. Lord, was required at the time of his settlement to accept the Cambridge Platform as the assertion of the rules of discipline given in the Scriptures.*

Many incidents may be gleaned from public and private records to show what kind of a government in and over the churches was intended by the anti-congregational party in those times. The first pastor in Durham was Nathaniel Chauncey, a very near relative of that Charles Chauncey who was a member of the Saybrook synod. His ordination took place in February 1711, after nearly five years of service as a candidate. The question of his settlement had been long pending, because a portion of the people were not satisfied with his "judgment as to matters of discipline." Here was an instance of the conflict of opinions which at that period was producing so many divisions in Connecticut. What the particular questions were between Mr. Chauncey and the dissentients from his judgment, does not distinctly appear. But just as the difficulty was coming to a crisis, "I heard" says Chauncey, "of

---

* Hovey, Life and Times of Isaac Backus, pp. 23, 24. Backus, (l. c.) adds, "The church in East Windsor, under the care of Mr. Timothy Edwards, father of Mr. Jonathan, also refused to receive the Saybrook Platform."

the general meeting of the elders to be held at Saybrook. I
told some of them [the malcontents] I thought it was wisdom
to tarry until that was over. * * As soon as I could, I got a
copy [of the new Platform] and let them have it to read among
themselves. And having read and considered it, those that
were members in full communion came to me, and told me
that their business was to tell me they were all suited." Thereupon he was invited to "take the pastoral charge." " At this
meeting," he says, " something was said about the understanding of the Articles, to which I replied, if difficulty should be
there, we must refer ourselves to the same power which drew
them up, which was not objected against." The trouble, however, was not yet disposed of. A mutual council was proposed,
and was agreed to, but was afterwards merged in the ordaining
council. The questions between the candidate and the minority were laid before that council; and according to his statement, " The result was this. I was called for and asked whether, in difficult and weighty cases, I was willing the mind of the
church should be known by some sign. I replied, I designed
never to be any other than tender in such cases, and should like
to have the concurrence of the church. But it may be that
might be insisted on by some in trivial matters ; whereto, reply
was made ' in things that I might judge or account best.' This
I duly assented to. This is the whole of what I was obliga-
ted to at that time ; namely, that the mind of the church be
known by some sign in things that I myself should judge to
be weighty and difficult."* Such was Nathaniel Chauncey's
construction of the first article in the Saybrook Platform,
which is that " the elder or elders of a particular church, with
the consent of the brethren of the same, have power, and
ought to exercise church discipline according to the rule of
God's word in relation to all scandals that fall out within the

---

* Chauncey Memorials, pp 102-103.

same.'' Surely the notion of "a silent democracy" had been fully developed when a pastor was settled with no other concession of privilege to the brotherhood in matters of church government, than that he would permit the mind of the church to be known by some sign in difficult and weighty cases, he himself being the sole judge as to what cases were weighty and difficult.

The history of the churches in Connecticut, under the constitution formed at Saybrook, divides itself naturally into three half-century periods. For nearly fifty years, the working of the constitution was chiefly in the hands of the men who, toward the close of that period, became distinguishable as the "old light" party, They were Calvinists in theory ; they seem to have accepted and held the established Confession of Faith without any difficulty or equivocation ; but they had been molded in their intellectual and religious habits, and in all their ideas of the church and its ordinances, by the influences which brought in the half-way covenant. They were very naturally, not to say inevitably, formalists, if we may use that word without implying that they rejected the idea of spiritual religion. It is not for any of us to say that they were not truly good men, and in their way earnest and faithful ; or that they were not doing a good work in their day, unlike as their ideas and modes of working were to ours. In those fifty years, the ecclesiastical constitution, notwithstanding any imperfections of its own, and notwithstanding any errors or excesses in the administration of it, was gradually bringing the churches, and especially the ministers into a closer union with each other ; and was preparing them for perils and conflicts, and for achievements of which they had little anticipation. During that period, new towns were settled and incorporated, and every new town had its church, its meeting-house, and its minister ; two new counties were organized, and each new county had its consociation of churches, and its association of pastors, according to the

Platform. The collegiate school soon migrated from its temporary abode at Saybrook ; and in the home which, after a perilous conflict, had been gained for it at New Haven, it grew into a flourishing institution in a most intimate connection with the clergy, who, at the close of this period, had been educated there, almost without an exception. Great and persistent efforts were made for the reformation of morals, for the thorough indoctrination of the people by the domestic and parochial catechising of children, and for the general education of the young in such parochial schools as the poverty of that period could provide. The dreadful tendency to barbarism— a tendency incident to the growing up of a colony in such a wilderness, and aggravated by the effects of wars, Indian, French and Spanish, was heroically and not unsuccessfully resisted. By the laborious fidelity of those pastors in their ways of working, the people of their parishes were prepared, in some sort, for the great and memorable religious awakening which marks so signally the latter part of that half-century. And that the enthusiastic excesses, and the acrimonious controversies and recriminations which followed the awakening, did not produce by their repulsive force a far wider defection through cold Aminianism and Socinianism into mere Deism and Infidelity, may perhaps be ascribed in part, to those intimate relations among the churches, and especially among their pastors, which had been effected by the ecclesiastical constitution of the colony.

But we must not forget what were the ends which the projectors and contrivers of this constitution had in view. " A permanent establishment " was indeed obtained, for church and state were more securely bound together than before ; but how was it in regard to that " good and regular issue in cases subject to ecclesiastical discipline," which was hoped for? The venerable Dr. Trumbull, ardent in everything, was an ardent friend to the ecclesiastical constitution ; but the second volume of his history shows what he thought about the way in which it was administered while the " old light" men had the working of it. That it had any efficacy at all in preventing, or in adjusting those local controversies which are inevitably incident to the government of all self-governed churches, does not appear in all the history of that half-century.

For example : In 1728, a difficulty arose in Guilford about the ordination of a pastor. A large minority of the church and parish protested in vain. Finding their protest disregarded by the ordaining council, as well as by the majority of the church and parish, they refused to sit under the ministry that had been thus imposed upon them, and withdrew. Nearly fifty of them were members of the church. They were numerous enough to be a church by themselves ; and they judged themselves able to support the expenses of public worship. They distinctly renounced the Saybrook Platform, and falling back upon rights which they considered older and more sacred than the work of any synod, they set up worship as an independent Christian congregation, having employed a regularly approbated candidate to preach to them. In all these proceedings, we find no interference of the consociation. On the contrary when this seceding minority applied to the legislature, in 1729, for leave to become a distinct ecclesiastical society, their petition was rejected, and a commission of three ministers was appointed by the General Court to visit Guilford and attempt a reconciliation between the parties. That committee, having heard and considered the objections urged by the seceding party against the minister, pronounced the objections insufficient, and simply advised the secession to return and fill up the vacant sittings in the great new meeting house, and to let the past be forgiven and forgotten on both sides. Of course such advice, offered in such a way, was not accepted ; and if the Reverend Commissioners had understood the nature of a Guilford parish controversy as well as we do in these later times, they might have saved the paper on which their advice was written. Those seceders had made up their minds that Mr. Ruggles, the young minister imposed upon them by the majority, was not the minister for them. They had therefore made up their minds to disown the Saybrook Platform, with which, as the ecclesiastical establishment of the Colony, the cause of Mr. Ruggles and the majority seemed to be, in some way identified. On both points they were conscientious as well as willful—perhaps the more conscientious for being willful—certainly the more willful for being conscientious. The result of their petition to the General Court had wakened them to grave doubts concerning the right of the legislature to interpose with unsolicited advice in a dispute about the fitness of a given preacher for a given parish. Guided either by their own ingenuity or by that of some adviser, they came to the conclusion that as British subjects, they had a right to secede from the establishment. An act of Parliament, passed in the reign of William and Mary, and referred to in a statute of the Colony, for similar purposes, provided relief for sober dissenters from the established order, and prescribed the steps by which a dissenting preacher and his congregation might obtain a legal protection. Claiming the benefit of that twofold legislation, the seceding party presented themselves before the county court in New Haven, that by taking the necessary oaths, and subscribing the required declaration, they might be qualified in law to worship by themselves. After a five months' opportunity for deliberation and for consultation, the court yielded to their demand. But this, of course, did not exempt them from the necessity of paying the taxes imposed upon them by the parish from which they had seceded. They, therefore, from the vantage ground which they had gained, renewed their petition to the legislature for relief, and for a full incorporation as an ecclesiastical society. A partial relief was granted; but the legislature adhering to its old habit of playing the bishop

8

over the churches, must needs persist in the preposterous attempt to bring the seceders back, and make them settle down under the ministry of Mr. Ruggles. An ecclesiastical council of ten ministers and churches, selected from three counties by the legislature, was ordered to meet in Guilford, and bring the controversy to a close. In compliance with the advice of that council, the church, acting judicially, suspended from communion those who had seceded from it, already more numerous than those they had left behind. It was yet to be discovered that church-censures in such cases have no efficacy for good. Thus the controversy proceeded. The General Association, at the proposal of the legislature, and with the consent of the separating party, met at Guilford, heard the parties, and adjourned. Then the legislature sent a committee of its own, who heard the parties and reported recommending the appointment of another council. Such a council was appointed, with a commission from the legislature to hear and " finally determine" the case; but it accomplished nothing. Then another committee from the legislature went, heard the parties and reported; then a third legislative committee went, who at last reported that to grant the prayer of the persevering petitioners, whose continual coming had so long wearied that honorable body, would be " for the peace of the town and the interests of religion." Five years that conflict raged, and thus it ended.*

All this while the church in Guilford, so persistently patronized by the General Court, had never accepted the Saybrook Constitution, and therefore was not really one of the established churches according to the act of 1708. In that case, the church was not considered as dis-established by adhering to the original platform of the New England churches. But when a somewhat similar case of difficulty arose in Canterbury, a few years later, a very dissimilar course was taken. The majority of the church refused to accept, as their pastor, the minister whom

---

* Trumbull, Hist. of Conn. vol. ii, chap. 7.

the majority of the parish had chosen. Yet the consociation of Windham county convened ; and by counting in sundry de-linquent members who were under censure, they increased the minority into what they thought might pass for a majority, and then proceeded to ordination. The church withdrew from the consociation, and from the parish, placed itself upon the ancient Congregational platform, and found that its separate meeting for worship was pronounced not only schismatic but illegal.* In Milford, not far from the same time, a minority protesting against the settlement of a pastor, and afterwards seceding, were compelled to take a course like that which had been taken by the minority at Guilford, and were even con-strained to make themselves, for the time being, Presbyterians under the presbytery of New Brunswick, in order to gain a toleration which they could not have as Congregationalists. After twelve years of legalized annoyance, they obtained from the legislature an incorporation as the Second Ecclesiastical Society in Milford, and their Presbyterianism vanished away.†

At an early stage in the progress—or perhaps I might more properly say, in the sequel—of the great awakening, as soon as the irregularities and extravagances incidental to such a move-ment in such times, began to appear, the great body of the ministers throughout the colony were not unreasonably alarm-ed ; and it is not to be wondered at that, in their inexperience as to the way of dealing with such perils, and under the guid-ance of principles which they had always assumed as axioms, they were led into a too conservative policy. In New Haven county especially, the severest measures were employed by the association and the consociation against those pastors who could be charged with any irregularity. The pastor of Derby was excluded from the association because he had preached to a Baptist congregation within some other minister's parochial

* Trumbull, vol. ii, pp. 178–184. Hovey, Life and Times of Isaac Backus, p. 18.
† Trumbull, vol. ii, chap. 13.

bounds. The pastor of West Haven, for some imprudent expressions, was dismissed from his charge, notwithstanding his frankly expressed regret, and thereupon the " old light " men expressed their exultation by saying that they had put out one new light, and would put them all out. Three of the members of the New Haven association assisted in the ordination of a pastor over the church in Salisbury, which had been formed on the Cambridge Platform, and for that reason they were suspended from all associational communion.* The minister of Branford was a new light. On one occasion he preached to a little Baptist church in Wallingford. His so doing was, by the consociation, pronounced disorderly, and he was therefore deprived of his seat in that body. Not long afterwards, he was arraigned for various extravagant expressions in his sermons— some of them obviously perverted and distorted, and for the general course of his policy in regard to the excitements of those times, and at last he was, in form, deposed from the ministry. He went on with his work in his own church and parish, his people, with few exceptions, adhered to him, not forgetting to pay his salary, and even increasing it. The legislature, on the petition of a few disaffected parishioners of his, endeavored to interfere, but did not succeed ; and that was the end of it. About seven years afterwards, he was quietly invited to sit with the consociation ; and no more was said on the subject.†

The extant records of the General Association begin with the year 1738. That year there was a full meeting of ten members, every association being represented by two delegates. In 1741, eight were present, of whom the youngest was Joseph Bellamy. On that occasion, with warm expressions of thankfulness to God " for an extraordinary revival of religion in this land," the most judicious and Christian suggestions were made to the particular associations as to what ministers should do at

---

* Trumbull, vol. ii, pp. 195, 196. † Trumbull, vol. ii, pp. 196–233.

such a time, not only to promote the great awakening, but to maintain mutual confidence and earnest co-operation among themselves. The next year, with renewed expressions of thankfulness, warnings and cautions against errors of doctrine and irregularities in practice, and against the impending danger of divisions in the churches, were given out to the ministers and to the churches. The next year, (1743,) the utterances from the General Association are in a tone of still greater alarm ; yet there is no syllable which we, as their successors, after the lapse of one hundred and sixteen years, have any occasion to regret. But two years afterwards, (1745,) eight members being present, " the following resolve was come into."

" Whereas there has of late years been many errors in doctrine, and disorders in practice, prevailing in the churches of this land, which seem to have a threatening aspect upon these churches—and whereas Mr. George Whitefield has been the promoter, or at least the faulty occasion of many of these errors and disorders, this association think it needful for them to declare that if the said Mr. Whitefield should make his progress through this government, it would by no means be advisable for any of our ministers to admit him into their pulpits, or for any of our people to attend upon his preaching and administrations."

This seems like a harsh judgment. We honor the name of Whitefield. Doubtless,

" the tear
That fell upon his Bible was sincere."

But let us remember that the Whitefield of history, is not exactly the Whitefield of popular traditions. The famous evangelist, whose first visit to New England was coincident in time with the religious revival of 1740, had been received by the pastors and churches of Connecticut with an almost unanimous welcome, as if he were an angel of God. He deserved such a welcome ; for he was a true evangelist, earnest, faithful, fervent, self-sacrificing, eloquent as if gifted with a tongue of fire. But after all, he was only a man with more zeal than judgment, better fitted to rouse and agitate, than to guide and instruct; and in the few years between his first visit and his second, a thick growth of mischievous enthusiasms and disorganizing extravagances had sprung up in his track, and were unquestionably the result, in part, of his unbalanced and unguarded teaching. Against those enthusiastic and destructive practices, and against the erroneous opinions and beliefs with which they were identified, Edwards, and all the New England pastors who were known as sharing in the great revival, had freely and boldly testified. But Whitefield had never offered one word that could be construed as retracting any of the mischievous words or actions which had proceeded from his ill informed and inconsiderate zeal; nor one word of caution against the principles or the proceedings of those frantic admirers of his who were spreading around them confusion and every evil work, and were bringing not the great revival only but religion itself into contempt. Every word alleged against him by that General Association of 1745 was literally true. Yet it must be confessed that in thus denouncing one who, with all his rashness, and with all the shallowness of his views, and with all the incidental mischiefs that attended his ministry, was nevertheless most manifestly a chosen instrument of God for a blessed service, both in Britain and in America, they committed an error as grave perhaps, and as likely to be mischievous, as any error of his.

It is quite in keeping with the spirit then predominating in church and state, that the fulmination against Whitefield, on the record of 1745, is immediately followed by votes about the revival and keeping up of ecclesiastical discipline. The next year we find questions about ecclesiastical discipline again. In 1747, one question about discipline is answered; and, the scarcity of copies of the Saybrook Platform being noticed, a member is appointed to procure and distribute a number of copies which are understood to be in the custody of the secretary of the colony. The next year, Joseph Bellamy being again a member, the importance of catechising is the first theme, and Watts's catechisms are commended, though not as a substitute for the Assembly's shorter catechism; another attempt is made to obtain from the secretary those reported copies of the Saybrook Platform; and, in view of "the great prevalence of vice and profaneness," and of "a lamentable indifference in spiritual concerns among the people," ministers are earnestly entreated to deal with the people of their charge by personal private addresses. For the two years next following, no business was transacted; the records seem as if the General Association was dying if not already dead. But from 1751 onward, there are new signs of life. Soon afterwards a great alarm at the progress of doctrinal errors, Socinian, Arian, Arminian and Pelagian, begins to show itself. The minutes for 1758 are wanting. But in 1759, the record is alive with references to the Wallingford case. It is the beginning of the second half-century.

That Wallingford case—the ordination of James Dana, from Harvard College, (afterwards Dr. Dana,) by an old light council, against the protest of a respectable minority, and against a positive prohibition from the consociation of New Haven county, which had been convened to forbid the ordination of a candidate suspected of doctrinal unsoundness—marks the complete and final overthrow of the "old lights" as a dominant party. Their great fortress, "our ecclesiastical constitution," had been seized, and all its guns were turned upon them. A new generation of ministers, trained under the influences of the great awakening, and indoctrinated to some extent by the writings of Edwards and Bellamy, had come. The era of the New England theology was opening. While the new lights were in the minority, their respect for the ecclesiastical constitution had not been very profound, and on the whole, they can hardly be said to have had much reason to think well of it. But now they found it an exceedingly useful arrangement;—

though some of the churches which they had formed, irregularly, still stood out against it.* Those ministers in New Haven county, who had so exaggerated and perverted the powers of association and of consocation, found those powers no longer under their control. They, in their turn, were censured and excluded for disorderly proceedings, with singular poetic justice; and in their turn they found that as long as their churches and parishes stood by them, such censure and exclusion was not very hard to bear.

The second half century of our ecclesiastical confederation, from 1758 to 1808, has its memorable features. During that half century our missionary work began, under the guidance of the General Association. In 1774 the first notice of missions to the new settlements appears upon our records; and a system of operations was begun which, though often modified according to the lessons of experience and the changes in the work, has never been relinquished. In the year 1800, the first attempt was made by our churches, through the same organization, to send a missionary far hence to the heathen of the wilderness.† But of this topic a special statement has already been given in another form.

---

* One of these was the White Haven Church in New Haven, now commonly known as the North Church. See Dr. Dutton's Historical Discourses.

† The author of this discourse may be allowed to say that his father, the Reverend David Bacon, was the missionary. Nor will it be impertinent to copy here a few sentences concerning him, from a Historical Discourse pronounced at Tallmadge, Ohio, June 24, 1857.

In early life—I know not at what age—he had been the subject of a deep and thorough religious experience; and through his spiritual conflicts and deliverances he had been brought into a special sympathy with the self-sacrificing spirit of Brainerd, that saintly New England missionary who wore his young life out among the Indians of New Jersey and Pennsylvania long ago, and whose biography, written by Jonathan Edwards, has wakened in later ages, and in other lands, such minds as Henry Martyn, to a holy emulation. Thus, at a period when missions to the heathen were little thought of, he cherished in his solitary bosom the fire that is now glowing, less intensely indeed, but with a vital warmth, in millions of Christian hearts. He longed for that self-denying service; but there were none to send him forth. Disappointments in his worldly business inflamed, instead of discouraging, his desire of a service so self-denying, and to worldly minds so uninviting. With limited opportunities and means, he devoted himself to study in preparation for that work. At last the

That date, 1774, which marks the beginning of our missions, is suggestive of another topic. In 1769, the General Association was assembled in this town of Norwich; and then, for the first time, "the dark and threatening aspect of Divine Providence upon our nation and land, in regard to their civil liberties and public interest," is noticed on the record. In 1774, a spirited and patriotic "letter of condolence" is prepared and sent "to the ministers of Boston, under the present melancholy circumstances of that town," "suffering the severe resentment of the British Parliament." In 1775, the General Association, "taking into serious consideration the distressing and melancholy state of public affairs in the British American colonies, and the dangers they are now threatened with from the oppressive measures of the British Court," summon themselves and their brethren, and the churches, to the religious duties of so great a crisis, and especially to devout humiliation and earnest prayer. In 1776, the "General Association of the pas-

---

the Trustees of the Connecticut Missionary Society, two years after the institution of that Board, were persuaded to attempt, on a very small scale, a mission to the Indians; and he was commissioned, for six months, to perform a journey of exploration and experiment among the Indian tribes in that unknown wilderness beyond Lake Erie. On the eighth of August, 1800, he set forth from Hartford; and the scale of liberality on which that mission was to be supported may be estimated from the fact that the missionary went his way, not only alone, but on foot, and with his luggage on his back, to rejoice in whatever opportunities he might find of being helped along by any charitable traveler with a spare seat in his wagon. Having acquired such information as seemed sufficient to determine the location of the mission, he immediately returned, and on the first of January, 1801, having been in the meantime solemnly consecrated to his work by ordination, he set his face towards the wilderness again, with his young wife, and her younger brother, a boy of fourteen years, [Beaumont Parks, Esq., now of Springfield, Illinois,] to encounter the hardships, not of the long journey only, but of that new home to which their journey would conduct them. Of their perils and privations there—of their disappointments and discouragements—I might speak, if the time and the occasion would permit. I will only say that as soon as the inevitable expenses of a mission so far remote from all civilized communities, and involving the necessity of an outlay for schools and for industrial operations, began to confound the limited expectations with which the work had been attempted, the Trustees, frightened by unexpected drafts on their treasury, abandoned the enterprise; and the missionary was ordered to New Connecticut. In the month of August, he left the isle of Mackinaw, with his wife and their two children, the youngest less than six weeks old; and after a weary and dangerous voyage, some part of which was performed in an open canoe, they arrived safe on the soil of the Western Reserve.—*Tallmadge Semi-centennial Commemoration, pp.* 47 48.

9

tors of the consociated churches of the *Colony* of Connecticut" sends out, for the first time, a printed document. That publication contains, among other matters, a formal address to the pastors and the churches, portraying the necessity of repentance and general reformation, and of seeking God's favor and help at such a crisis. In 1777, the quiet change of a single word in the customary heading of the minutes, intimates that a great event in the world's history, had taken place: "At a meeting of the General Association of the STATE of Connecticut." The *Colony* of Connecticut had ceased to be.

Another significant fact records itself upon the minutes for 1788. "On motion made by the Association of the western district of New Haven county, the Association voted that the slave-trade is UNJUST, and that every justifiable measure ought to be taken to suppress it. Voted also that Drs. Goodrich, Edwards and Wales be a committee to draw up an address and petition to the General Assembly, that some effectual laws may be made for the abolition of the slave-trade." A reference to the records of the State will show that at the next session of the legislature the slave-trade was prohibited, and heavy penalties denounced against it. This action, however, in the General Association of 1788, was by no means the beginning of agitation by the pastors of Connecticut against the slave-trade, or against slavery. Long before that date, the pulpit had given an unequivocal testimony against the injustice of converting human beings into merchandize. For example, I have before me here a printed copy of "a sermon preached to the Corporation of Freemen in Farmington, at their meeting on Tuesday, September 20, 1774, and published at their desire." The occasion of the meeting was the semi-annual election of representatives to the legislature. The preacher was Levi Hart a native of Farmington, but then, and for a long time afterwards the honored "pastor of a church in Preston."* Lib-

---

* Dr. Hart's parish in Preston is now the town of Griswold.

erty is the subject of the sermon ; and on the title-page is that
holy motto, " The Spirit of the Lord God is upon me, because
he hath annointed me—to proclaim *liberty* to the captives."
Treating of liberty, the preacher could not but treat of slavery.
In the preface to his pamphlet, he offers it as his reason for
consenting to publish his discourse, " that the subject and occasion gave him opportunity to cast in his mite for the oppressed and injured Africans whose cause he thought himself bound
to plead, and to bear his testimony against the cruel and bar-
barous slave-trade." He " pretends not to pronounce on the
impropriety of the slave-trade in a political view—this would
be out of his province ; but he would submit to the gentlemen
of the law, whether the admission of slavery in a government
so democratical as that of the colony of Connecticut, doth not
tend to the subversion of its happy constitution." He adds,
" Be this as it may, if the slave-trade is contrary to the law of
nature, *which is the law of God*, it is more than time it was effectually prohibited." He professes himself " fully convinced
that there is no more reason or justice in our enslaving the Africans than there would be in their enslaving us." In the sermon itself, he says, " Of all the enjoyments of the present life,
that of liberty is the most precious and valuable, and a state of
slavery the most gloomy to a generous mind ; to enslave men,
therefore, who have not forfeited their liberty, is a most atro-
cious violation of one of the first laws of nature." He pro-
nounces " the horrible slave-trade, carried on by numbers, and
tolerated by authority in this country," " a flagrant violation
of the law of nature, of the natural rights of mankind." Such
preaching was orthodox before the Declaration of Independen-
dence, and however it may be elsewhere, such preaching has
never ceased to be orthodox in Connecticut. In that very year,
1774, the doctrine of that sermon began to take effect upon
the legislation of the Colony that had not yet become a state.
The bringing of another slave into Connecticut was thence-

forward prohibited; and heavy penalties were laid upon the importer and the purchaser. The continued agitation of the great wrong, continued to have its effect upon our legislation. Slavery and the slave-trade, being persistently denounced as wrong, were persistently discouraged by the state. Four years before the date of that memorial from the General Association, slavery itself had been prospectively abolished by an act providing for the freedom of all persons born thereafter. The memorial then, from the General Association in 1788, was not a memorial against the importation of slaves into Connecticut; for that sort of slave-trade was already effectually prohibited. The law which that memorial asked for, and which was enacted accordingly, was a law making it penal for any citizen of Connecticut to have any concern in the African slave-trade anywhere, "as master, factor, supercargo, owner or hirer, in whole, or in part, of any vessel." It ought not to be forgotten, on such an occasion as this, that the abolition of slavery in this State, and in every state in which it has been abolished as yet, is due in no small measure to the testimony which the ministers of God's word have given against the moral wrong of slavery.

It was not found in those days, nor was it pretended, that a fearless holding forth of God's word against the wickedness of oppressing the poor, and of buying and selling men for gain, was inconsistent with the prosperity of spiritual religion. The transition is easy, then, to another feature in the history of our second half-century. It deserves our thankful commemoration that while this period began in the depth of the religious declension which followed the revival of 1740,—and while the first five and twenty years of the half-century [1758–1783] are dark with signs of growing demoralization, and with the progressive decay of godliness under the influence of war, of political agitation and revolution, of universal insolvency, and of every temptation which comes with the fluctuations of a paper currency and with a general failure to fulfill commercial engagements—the close of the eighteenth century and the beginning of the nineteenth, mark the blessed era of the renewed and continued influence of God's Holy Spirit in the reviving of religion. From that time forward the blessing has never been entirely withdrawn from our churches. The steady prosperity and progress of religion in the form of a manifested work of God's grace within the soul,—our increased familiarity with the phenomena of conversion as developed in the consciousness and in the life,—and our habit of distinguishing and teaching our people to distinguish, more carefully and exactly, after the manner of Edwards, between what are and what are not the tests of religious experience—have reacted, perhaps, on our theology in some particulars ; and on the other hand, our theology, coming out of its scholastic formulas, and laying aside, to some extent, in our public ministrations, the costume of technical phrases, brings forth the ancient and immutable truth with more simplicity, and with less danger of its being perverted to enthusiastic or fanatical extravagance, if not with greater power of impression on the conscience and the emotions. May we not say with humility that we have learned, better than our fathers knew—nay that we have learned by their experience and by our own—how to deal with the irregularities and extravagances that frightened them ? By the favor of God, the religious awakenings of the present century, in the field of our immediate care and labor, have been followed with less and less of such reaction and depression as followed the great awakening of 1740, and caused it to stand the glorious but lonely landmark of that age.

There are many here to whom the most memorable changes of the last half-century, beginning in 1808, are matters of personal remembrance. Who of us, for example, needs to be reminded that the missionary aspiration and effort which made its little mark upon our records in 1774, and which, from that time forward, began to mingle itself with all the sympathies and yearnings of devotion in our churches, was only the intimation, or the faintly dawning light of a new era of evangelism, which in 1808 had not yet begun ? At that date, the only organization which our churches had, through which to act for the propagation of the gospel at home or abroad, was the old Connecticut Missionary Society with its annual contribution in the month of May, taken in all the congregations by virtue of a " brief " from the Governor, and in conformity with a legislative order. The entire system of those arrangements by which we are now acting on all the extent of our country, from ocean to ocean, and from the head springs of the Mississippi to the Southern Gulf—the entire system by which we are sending out the knowledge of God in Christ, not only to the waste places and wildernesses of our own broad Union, but to the ends of the earth,—was yet to be developed, and has been the growth of our last half-century.

That annual rescript from the Governor, authorizing a contribution in the churches of our order for missions to the new settlements, reminds us of another and most conspicuous fact in the history of the last fifty years. The legal establishment of the Saybrook Platform—always an equivocal thing, and more of a burthen than a dignity or immunity to the churches that did not distinctly dissent from the system—was silently but finally repealed in 1784, in a revision of the statute book. The churches and parishes were by that repeal left to adopt whatever scheme of doctrine or of discipline they might severally choose, and to change the same at their discretion. But still ours was, in some vague sense, " the standing order. " The adherents of every other religious or ecclesiastical system had been freed from every burthen or shadow of a burthen ; but public worship in some form was still presumed, by law, to be the duty of every citizen, and those who did not prefer to be enrolled elsewhere were members of our parishes. Forty-two years ago, this last vestige of the ancient union of our churches with the civil order of the commonwealth was swept away, and we were placed fairly and unequivocally on that basis of absolute religious liberty which Roger Williams invented as a "permanent establishment" for Rhode Island. That slight change was, in fact, the completed emancipation of our churches.

At the same time, though not wholly by the same process, our churches have recovered their original Congregationalism; and perhaps I may say without offense, they value it so much the more for their having had some experience of what it is to be without it. Our ancient Congregationalism began to be recovered in the great awakening of 1740, and in those sharp and strong discussions by which first the Stoddardean Sacramentalism, and then the half-way covenant were demolished. When that leaven of a national church, and of what John Davenport called a "parish way," had been purged out by sounder doctrine and by the wide revival of religion as a personal experience, there began to be of course a yearning and a half-conscious endeavor after the old Congregational way. A natural reaction against the enthusiastic errors of the Separates, made the name of Congregationalism, to some extent obnoxious to ministers and even to churches, of the "standing order;" and the struggle against the already incipient rationalism of the following age, increased in the clergy at least, a sense of the value of some controlling power over the churches. About sixty years ago, several of the most honored pastors in Connecticut, gave a public certificate to the effect that the system of church order here was Presbyterianism. I myself remember when the name "Congregational" was not ordinarily known as the proper and distinctive designation of our churches; and when the honored successor of Thomas Hooker and immediate predecessor of Dr. Hawes, wrote himself, and printed himself "Pastor of the North* *Presbyterian* Church in Hartford." An alliance with the Americanized Presbyterians of the Middle and Southern States was begun in the common resistance to the proposed establishment of an American Episcopate by the British government before the revolution, and was renewed after the war of independence, in the expectation, doubtless, that both parties would be gradually assimilated to each other, and would ultimately become one great and powerful body. The events of the last thirty years have taught us most effectually, that the idea once so widely cherished, is purely chimerical. We have learned that nothing on earth is more impracticable than the scheme of an organic Presbyterian unity, extending its jurisdiction over the whole territory of our common country, and binding together the Christian sympathies and co-operative efforts of all who hold our evangelical faith, and who reject, on the one hand, the prelatical theory of church government, yet accept, on the other hand, that view of the church and of God's covenant with his people, which regards the children of the church as subjects of baptism. Our exclusive alliance with the Scoto-American Presbyterianism in distinction from the Dutch, the German Reformed, the Lutheran, and all other organizations of like principles and spirit, may have been wise and useful in its day; but it has answered its purpose, and has passed away, leaving no trace of its former importance, save the ceremonious but pleasant interchange of single delegates with one fraction of the now broken organization with which our fathers concerted their "plan of union." Our churches and our ministers, delivered from what had become an "entangling alliance," are content, and more than content with the simple and Scriptural policy which rejects all ecumenical, national, provincial, and classical judicatures ruling the churches of Christ, and recogni-

* At that time what is now "the North Church" in Hartford was not instituted; and the First Church and Society was commonly known as the "North."

zes no church on earth save the local or parochial assembly and fellowship of believers, and the Church Universal which includes all that are Christ's. We have learned, and I trust we shall never forget, that the only visible union attainable or really desirable, is to be found not in the Presbyterian idea of government over churches, but in the Congregational idea of the communion of churches.

Meanwhile in proportion as that old and true idea of the communion of churches, in distinction from the idea of national, provincial and classical jurisdiction, has been more clearly developed,—and in proportion as our ecclesiastical forms and practices have been progressively disentangled from their unnatural connection with principles which our New England polity originally rejected, there has been a steady progress in the feeling of forbearance and kindness toward all evangelical dissenters from our order, and in the free sense of catholic unity with all the churches of Christ around us, whatever their distinctive names or forms. Our relations to other bodies of professed Christians holding the vital truths of the common salvation, are gradually putting off the unseemly form of ecclesiastical separation and non-intercourse, and are becoming more and more transformed by the spirit of Christian brotherhood, of mutual recognition, and of cooperation in the common cause. We have learned that such acts of church fellowship with churches outside of our own connection, as we find to be practicable, are our privilege and our duty. We are learning to avoid all needless conflict with their prejudices against our forms of order and discipline, and of doctrinal statement, and to count it among our advantages that we can recognize them as churches of Christ, even where it happens that by their subjection to some "law of commandments contained in ordinances" they are unable to acknowledge us. I trust we are learning not to annoy with obtrusive offers of cooperation those whose forms forbid them to cooperate with us, nor to demand

a sacramental communion as the first condition of Christian
fraternity with those whose misfortune is that they find themselves forbidden not so much by their feelings as by their logic or their traditions, to commune with us in the recognition
of our sacraments. In this respect the true genius of our Congregational system is better developed with us, than it was with
our fathers; and is it not in this direction that the prospect
opens of the coming age, when differences of judgment in the less
momentous things shall no longer produce alienation of feeling,
or any incapacity of cooperation for Christ and his kingdom,
among those who unite in accepting the faithful saying, that
" Christ Jesus came into the world to save sinners, " and in
maintaining the Apostolic principle that " with the heart man
believeth unto righteousness, and with the mouth confession is
made unto salvation." Let us be willing to learn more thoroughly—as God in his providence and by his grace has already
constrained us to learn in part—the wisdom that can bear the
infirmities of the weak, and that can be tolerant and patient
toward the ignorance and the errors, the defects and the excesses, and even toward the narrowness and schismatic exclusiveness, which are not wholly inconsistent with the reality of
a professed faith in the Saviour of sinners. As we have learned
to cooperate with other churches in all good works in which
they can cooperate with us, let us be willing to learn the added
lesson of a larger and more catholic charity toward those who
separate themselves and work apart. So shall we, cheerfully
following others when they go before us, and gently winning
and leading onward those who can be moved by our example,
leave still further behind us the days and the spirit of sectarian
strife. He who leads the blind by a way which they know
not, has led us in this way; and as we find ourselves brought
out by no wisdom of our own, from the chilling enclosure of
high and strong division walls, into the warm sunshine of a
new and brighter day,—

"The breath of heaven, fresh blowing, pure and sweet,
With day-spring born,"—

let us say to that guiding spirit of catholic freedom and fraternity which we have learned already to enjoy—nay, rather let
us say to that Holy Spirit of God who seals and sanctifies his
elect not under our forms of ministration only, but under many
forms,

"A little onward lend thy guiding hand
To these dark steps,—a little further on."

Our churches then, in recovering their original Congregationalism from an unfortunate complication with ideas and principles derived from other systems, have become, and are still
becoming, not more sectarian, but less so.   They are gaining,
year by year, if I mistake not, a larger and more catholic habit
of thought and practice in relation to other Christian bodies, than
our fathers knew ; and in this way the true genius of our system, with its two cardinal principles of the completeness and
self-government of each local church under Christ, and of the
free communion of the churches with each other,—is finding
its natural and full development.

I feel that the historical survey which we have taken is inadequate to the theme, and may be found to need correction in
many of the particulars, if not in the general outline ; but I
may say that I have endeavored to perform, in a truthful and
impartial spirit, the duty which was assigned to me.   We have
traced imperfectly indeed, and indistinctly, but not without
conscientious care, the circumstances in which the peculiar
confederation of our churches had its beginning, the original
intent and purpose of the arrangement, the method in which
it was established, the measure of success which attended its
early administration as a scheme of ecclesiastical power, and
the modifications which three half-centuries, so full of moral
and political changes, and of religious awakening and progress,
have wrought in the manner and spirit of its working.   What
then has been the use of that "ecclesiastical constitution"

which was set up in the little wilderness colony of Connecticut, one hundred and fifty years ago? What is there which makes the first meeting of our General Association an event worthy of the commemoration which it receives from us to-day? The answer to such a question is incorporated with all the history of American Congregationalism from that day to the present hour. Nowhere in the United States does any intelligent man think of Congregationalism as a method of ecclesiastical organization and communion without including in the thought two elements which are, partly at least, the contribution of Connecticut to the completeness and stability of the system.

Everywhere throughout the United States, we find as an inevitable incident of Congregationalism, the voluntary but formal and recognized association of pastors and other ministers. These clerical " Associations " are not for any jurisdiction or government over the churches; they abjure all pretense of corporate authority, and the churches everywhere have, long ago, ceased to regard them with suspicion. They are simply associations of Congregational ministers for fellowship and mutual improvement, for mutual advice and help in the exigencies of their work, for examining and certifying to the churches the qualifications of candidates for the ministry, for consultation on whatever relates to the interests of Christ's kingdom, and for giving united counsel or testimony on whatever question of ecclesiastical order, of Christian duty, or, if need be, of religious doctrine, may fairly come before them. It has been proved by experience that without the recognized and formal association of pastors for such purposes, the churches will become, in the strife of sects and the fluctuations of opinion, a prey to the spoiler. It was in Connecticut, and as a result of our Saybrook constitution, that such association of pastors, never dreamed of by the framers of the Cambridge Platform, became an established arrangement in the system of Congregationalism. Some rudimental attempts at such association seem to have been made before, especially in the neighborhood of Boston; but the idea now universally accepted, of a system of clerical associations spreading over the whole country, including all Congregational ministers who recognize each other's regular standing in the clerical profession, maintaining a widely extended intercourse by delegation and correspondence, and giving unity and completeness to our ecclesiastical system without infringing at any point on the self-government of the churches, seems not to have been entertained elsewhere till the usefulness of associations had been proved by experience in Connecticut.

The other element of our Saybrook constitution, namely, the special consociation of churches in districts, has found less favor beyond the limits of Connecticut; but the example of our confederation has had its influence everywhere. The stated annual meeting of churches by their delegates in what are called "Conferences of churches," for consultation on the state of religion within their own bounds, and on the ways and means of doing good, is only another form of consociation, which differs from ours by leaving to each church an unlimited liberty to select its own councils in all cases of difficulty in the administration of its own affairs. And everywhere—unless the partiality incident to my position as a Connecticut Congregationalist misleads my judgment—the sentiment of the communion of churches, the consciousness of the duty which churches owe to each other, and the habit of mutual watchfulness and helpfulness among churches of the same vicinity, have been sustained and invigorated by the example of constant fidelity to each other among our churches. Notwithstanding the well defined propositions of the Cambridge Platform concerning "the communion of churches one with another," and notwithstanding the many recorded yearnings of the New England fathers for some stipulated and constant intercourse that should not impair the independence of the churches, our American Congregationalism might have lost, in process of time, that great principle of communion and mutual responsibility which is no less essential to the system than the coordinate principle of independence ; each being the complement of the other. If the churches of Massachusetts, by their chronic jealousy of consociation, have guarded and kept intact, for us and our successors, the independence of the parochial or local church, the churches of Connecticut, on the other hand, by their strict confederation, have guarded and maintained, and have effectually commended to Congregationalists everywhere, that equally important and equally distinctive principle of our polity, the communion of churches.

But it is here chiefly, in our own goodly heritage, that we are to look for the good that has resulted from what our old-time predecessors loved to call " the ecclesiastical constitution of the colony." Our own Connecticut—to our filial hearts the glory of all lands—how much is it indebted for the present aspect of its Christian civilization, to that organized association of its clergy, and that strict confederation of its churches, which were effected when as yet there was within our boundaries neither church nor pastor of any other ecclesiastical order ! The unconsociated churches, yielding to the genius of the system while rejecting its forms, have shared in the blessing. The churches that have been formed by dissent and secession from us—Episcopalian, Baptist, and Methodist—have had in all their growth, the benefit of being planted in our Puritan soil, and of being stimulated and invigorated by the strong religious influence that has not yet ceased to mold the character of our native population. Is there no meaning in the fact that not one of our churches, and only one of our parishes fell in the Unitarian defection? To my thought there is a similar meaning in the fact that while Congregationalism still remains stronger in Connecticut than in any other State, the Episcopalians of Connecticut are, in proportion to our aggregate population, one of the strongest dioceses in the Union, and the Baptist and Methodist churches among us, are also almost as strong in numbers, and quite as strong in the elements of religious character and influence, if I mistake not, as the average of those two most numerous and powerful bodies of Christian churches in all the states and territories of the Union. To my thought there is a meaning of the same sort in the fact that of all the religious organizations commonly regarded as anti-evangelical or anti-orthodox, not one has ever flourished among the native population of our State. Whatever fault we may find in our ecclesiastical system—whatever errors may have been made from time to time in the working of it,—whatever reason we may have to inquire whether the system needs revision and reconstruction, or to blame ourselves as ministers and churches of Christ, that we have not adapted our arrangements with adequate skill and zeal to the changes which have taken place in the habits and condition of our people—our own Connecticut, to-day, with all its imperfections, is the convincing testimony to the value of those two principles—the association of pastors for professional fellowship and mutual cooperation, and the friendly confederation of churches—which were first inaugurated and made effective by our fathers, one hundred and fifty years ago. Where does the sunlight gild a landscape more adorned with the evidences of Christian civilization ? Where can we find so large a body of churches in so small a territory, maintaining more effectually, on the whole, "the unity of the Spirit in the bond of peace," and cherishing at the same time a more catholic charity toward dissenters and seceders from their order ? Where, notwithstanding the perpetually renewed investigation of all truth, and the sometimes personal sharpness of our theological debates, do we find, in so large a body of pastors and ministers, so little of factious partizanship, and so much of fraternal intimacy, as among our clergy ? Where shall we find a happier solution of the difficult problem how to reconcile a complete ecclesiastical liberty with a well guarded ecclesiastical fellowship, evangelical orthodoxy with evangelical liberality and charity ; the conservative reverence that stands upon the ancient paths, with the progressive spirit that prays for new light from the fountain of light, and ever striving to keep pace with the progress of the ages, honors God by expecting a brighter future ?

Such is our inheritance. Such the trust which we have received from those who have lived and labored here before us. It is for us, in our turn, not merely to preserve the inheritance unimpaired, but to amplify it with new riches, and to adorn it with a fairer beauty. May God give us grace so to live and labor through the remnant of our time, that those who are to come after us shall bless him for our memory, as we bless him for the memory of our fathers !

ADDRESSES.

THE THREE PRINCIPLES OF CONGREGA-
TIONALISM.

BY PROF. E. A. LAWRENCE, D. D., EAST WINDSOR HILL.

MR. MODERATOR:

There are epochs in history, or, as Bossuet calls them, stand-still points, at which institutions and principles disclose their character by their results. The present occasion is such a point in the history of the Congregationalism of Connecticut and New England. It is wise, sir, to stop awhile here and question the past respecting those principles which we and our fathers have regarded as fundamental. We do well to come up to this post of retrospection, and ask our history to give us the elements of prophecy and of future guidance.

A little more than two hundred and twenty years ago, a company of men, women and children "with the cattle," started from Dorchester, in the "Bay" Colony for the Connecticut valley. It comprised the larger part of the church in that town, with, as some say, Mr. Wareham, the pastor, at its head. They made their way slowly through the wilderness, up ravines and over mountain-passes, beginning and ending each day's journey with prayer and songs of praise. Their settlement was at Matianuck, now Windsor; and in its spirit of Christian enterprise, was a genuine "church extension movement." They were soon followed by Hooker and his company from Cambridge, who went on to Hartford. After these came Davenport and his companions, just from England, whom, because they were a "very desirable folk," the Massachusetts people wished to have settle in "the Bay." But because, as Davenport said "they were Londoners and not so well fitted for an agricultural as a commercial settlement," they went on "in advance of all others" to Quinnipiac, now New Haven. Their arrival was on Saturday evening, and the next day, Mr. Dav-

12

enport preached on the " Temptation in the wilderness. " At the beat of the drum, they assembled in the forest aisles of that vast temple whose arch is the blue expanse, and where, from forest harps, the winds made rich choral music for the devout worshippers, and sweetly mingled it with their vocal praises.

The animus of these extension-movements in New England, dates back historically to the Puritan struggles for the rights of conscience in Old England, and indicates the three great principles of Congregationalism—Christ the *sole Legislatr* in the church, his Word the *Law*, and his Spirit, the *Life* of the church.

It was upon the first of these principles that the Non-Conformists separated from the Church of England under Elizabeth in 1566. The Kingly office of Christ, so patent in the New Testament, and in early Church History, though remaining in the creeds of the Romish Church, had been practically displaced by the assumption of Pontifical power. The English Reformation only transferred the sovereignty of the Church in England from the Pope to the King, and the evil remained. In connection with this infelicity in the constitution of the church, "as by law established," she who was reigning sovereign when the Puritan struggle began, and who, by the apostolic constitution, was required to " keep silence in the churches, " or if she would learn anything, "ask her husband at home," not only had no husband and would not be silent, but, with her advisers claimed that her word was absolute. This brought on the issue.

It was not a question of doctrine, for the parties were in essential agreement on the Thirty-nine Articles. Nor was it one of apparel, for the Puritans allowed this to be, in itself, non-essential. But it was, of the binding force in the church of this woman's word, as above the kingly authority of Christ. She forbade them to preach, except what she authorized, and as she authorized it. The Puritans protested, and, trusting themselves to the adjudication of the Great Lawgiver, preached on.

In the time of Charles I. and Laud, the restrictions and prohibitions became still more oppressive. The royal will was supreme in matters spiritual as well as temporal. Passive submission was the regnant dogma, and personal freedom was lost in the power of the prince. The rights of conscience were nothing ; the Bible was nothing ; the Kingship of Christ, even in his own spiritual domain, was nothing. Honest and Christian men in vain pleaded it in their defence as free preachers of a free Gospel. This pressure of arbitrary power on *such* men, in *such* a cause, produced the Hegira of Congregationalism, first to free Holland, and afterwards into this wide and freer wilderness.

Here the framers of our polity made loving loyalty to Christ as the sole Lord and Legislator, the chief corner-stone of their ecclesiastical and doctrinal system. " This was and is our cause in coming here, " said honest John Higginson, of Salem, "that Christ alone might be acknowledged by us as the only Head, Lord, and Lawgiver. " This principle gradually, but legitimately worked out the separation of the Church and the State, and gave to them both, liberty, harmony and vitality. It secured religious toleration to all, by the doctrine of a strict accountability of each, in matters of conscience, to one common Head. And so salutary were its results in the mother country, that the sceptical Hume admits that the English nation is indebted to the Puritans for all the liberty of its Constitution. And the Westminster Review, with all its antipathy to the doctrines of Calvin, is forced to yield the eulogium which the historic conscience demands, that his polity was a vigorous effort to supply a positive *education* of the individual soul—to substitute free obedience for passive submission—not a police, but an education, self-government mutually enforced by equals upon each other—that Sparta against Persia, was not such odds as Geneva against Spain with the Jesuits and the Inquisition— that *Calvinism saved Europe.*

The second of these great principles follows logically from the first—Christ's Word the only *law* in the church. This Word, with the Fathers of Congregationalism, was not simply a higher law, but the *highest*. In their constructive work, they applied faithfully the Protestant principle—" The Bible, the whole Bible, and nothing but the Bible. " Cotton Mather says of them " The Bible was their perpetual and only guide. " " The parts of our government," says the Cambridge Platform,

" are all of them exactly described in the Word of God. " And the counsels of the Saybrook fathers, whose wisdom we here commend to-day, by commemorating it, are explicit and in point—" That you be immovably and unchangably agreed in the only sufficient and invariable rule of religion, which is the Holy Scriptures. You ought to account nothing *ancient* that will not stand by this rule, and nothing modern that will. That you be determined by this rule in the *whole* of religion. That your faith be right and divine, the Word of God must be the foundation of it, and the authority of the Word the reason of it."

This Word of God was not indeed, their only book, though it was their Alpha and Omega. They studied it most, and in such a manner, according to the rule of Melancthon, as to judge of the advice and decrees of men, by comparing them with this as a touchstone. They had all of the argument from antiquity which is worth anything, by making this Divine Law, which is the most ancient, the sum or the source of all their authoritative regulations. Their faith and polity were, in the best sense, traditional, because they started from those infallible Scriptures which were " given by inspiration of God." The old writers with whom this principle of Congregationalism brings its adherents into most constant and living communion, are the writers of our old Bible. Whosoever of the reputed fathers stands opposed to these, is not of the fathers, but the children, and those too described by Isaiah, who " behave themselves proudly against the ancients, the base against the honorable. "

The polity which was thus drawn out of the Scriptures, and arranged in the Platform, is not Brownism, as it has sometimes been called,—an absolute independency; for the independency is modified by the community and fellowship of the churches and the moral power of councils. It differs also from Presbyterianism, the community of churches being prevented from becoming an organic external unity by the individualizing influence of the independency. It is simply Congregational, placing the governing power, not in the elders exclusive of the church, but in the church inclusive of the elders. It embraces the Consociation of churches, and the Association of ministers, and makes use of both stated and occasional councils. It holds to the church and the churches, the visible and invisible, the militant and triumphant ; and harmonizes and employs to the practical ends of life and love the elements of freedom and fellowship, dependence and responsibility, law and liberty. The Law stands sentinel to guard the churches from anarchy, and the Liberty in like manner, to preserve the church from despotism.

It is one of the crowning excellencies of these principles, that they allow us to erect no human fences around our most sacred enclosure ; but on the other hand, require us to frater- nize with all Christ-loving evangelists, in seeking what is bet- ter than any mere forms or polity, as our " Plans of Union " and " Heads of Agreement " abundantly testify. With an unsparing hand, under their influence, we have sown our purest seed-wheat upon the virgin soil of the boundless West, and with little unhallowed jealousy, seen the golden harvest gath- ered by Presbyterian reapers into the Presbyterian barns. The flax, even in our own New England fields, has been freely pulled by Presbyterian hands, and the wool clipped, with our consent, from the flocks on our New England hills, by Presby- terian shearers, and spun and woven into Presbyterian fabrics. In a similar spirit, Presbyterianism has in turn placed itself in helpful relations to Congregationalism. Both have joined their forces without stint, as sowers and reapers in the same fields, according to the law of Christ, which makes his church one, and that love of Christ, in the exercise of which, each was more desirous that men should become *Christians* than Congregationalists or Presbyterians.

With the same reverent regard to the authority of Christ's Word as law, the confessions of our faith were framed. When the Saybrook fathers came to their work in 1708, they found a time-honored symbol drawn from the Word of God by the Westminster divines, in 1643. Five years later, after careful examination and comparison with the Bible, it was adopted by the framers of the Cambridge Platform at Boston.—Still again in 1680, a synod in Boston placed this Confession on more thorough trial, according to the Law and the Testimony, and with slight, verbal alterations, made by the Independents at the

Savoy, London, in 1658, it was again adopted as the teaching of scripture, and the faith of the churches.

After all these trial-processes, by the best minds and hearts, the most learned and self-denying of the age, the fathers at Saybrook once more bring it, sentence by sentence, to the Divine standard, and, upon this " diligent inquiry, solicitous search, and faithful prayer," commended it to the churches of Connecticut, as "well and fully grounded upon Holy Scripture."

In its general type of doctrine, it was termed Calvinian, not that Calvin invented it, or gave it authority or efficacy. For it had been germinating in the church long before John Calvin's day, and by God's grace, made him what he was, one of the most lucid expounders and illustrious exemplifiers of its truth, by his life of laborious self-denial and love. It was also, in its main features, Lutheran and Augustinian, yet older than either of these distinguished men, whom it drew, the one from the dead body of forms and will-worship, and the other from the pride of the philosophies, evincing by these and similar sublime moral victories, that it is the power of God and the wisdom of God unto salvation to them that believe. In the present century, it has fought with Unitarianism in New England, and conquered :—with the vaunting hosts of German Rationalism and conquered; and on the same field, with the subtlest forms of spiritualistic Pantheism and conquered. And now it is abroad, in the name and by the power of the Lord, making conquests from Brahmanism, Buddhism and Mohamedanism, causing the wilderness of heathendom to bud and blossom as the rose.

The impugners of this Puritan theology have pronounced upon it as contracted, contradictory and adverse to the culture and advancement of the age. But these pronouncings are contradicted by every fair rendering of the facts of history. These show that the profoundest masters of wisdom and of reason—the most pains-taking and successful students in history, philosophy and the Divine Word, have been the products of its power, and the producers of all the worthiest advancement and culture. In the judgment of Bancroft, our most philosophic historian, the Calvinian theology, instead of being narrow, illiberal, or irrational, "combines and perfects the symbolic wisdom of the Orient, and the reflective genius of Greece ; conforming to reason, yet enkindling enthusiasm, * * * guaranteeing absolute freedom, yet invoking the inexorable restraints of duty ; awakening the inner man to a consciousness of his destiny, and yet adapted with exact harmony to the outer world." Of President Edwards, the most profound, yet practical New England representative of this theology, the same historian has more recently said, " All his teachings bear the marks of universality, and he looked to the establishment of his views as reasonable. The practical character of his system, in its adaptation to Christian life and action, is worthy of particular observation. On the one hand it has ever asserted against the pride and pomp of human oppressors, the doctrines of divine sovereignty and election, thus giving individual freedom to society, under the restraints of self-imposed divine law. On the other, looking to the mediation of Christ, as the manifested fulness of the Godhead, in union with the equally complete, the recovered and fully developed manhood for the world's highest weal, it places 'love as the central point of its view of creation, and the duty of the created.' " This is the judgment of historical criticism upon the doctrinal system of our churches, rendered by the most dispassionate and impartial examiners. It bears the marks of universality because of its derivation from the Word of the Universal Lord and Father of all; because it has from the beginning, been in the bosom of the living, universal church, and has ever fully met the deepest spiritual needs of the universal fallen humanity.

The third grand principle of Congregationalism, completes its basis—Christ's spirit the *life* of the Church.

The former two find their complement in this, not in the Pantheistic theory of an *identity* of substance and life in God and man, but of a fallen, dependent creature, dead in sin, yet created anew in Christ Jesus unto all holy obedience. The commencement of this new life in man is regeneration, and makes him like Christ ; and the fellowship of the regenerate constitutes, in its vital principle, the church. Without this, it fails, whatever may be its doctrines, polity or activities. And whatever of these in the church, does not minister to this Christ-like life in its members is useless, and does not belong to it. And whatsoever obstructs its free and full onward, conquering movement in the individual soul, or the church, is anti-Christ ; and however time-honored, corporate or organic, must be thrown off. In this view our Puritan fathers were most solidly grounded. As everything in the vegetable and animal kingdom holds a subservient relation to the *vital* principle, so they believed it was divinely arranged to be in the church. This spirit of Christ, which is the life of the church, is *central*, and works as in its Head, from the interior outward. The law and order which Christ has established, are its normal forms, and the conditions of its freest and most salutary activities. Little by little it works the soul free from its prejudices, errors and sins, and brings it into the completed likeness of Christ. It incorporates into the church whatsoever of human susceptibilities, sentiments or culture is homogeneous, and beats back and destroys whatsoever in humanity is antagonistic, which it does not transform into an ally.

Hence from this central and vital principle of our polity, Congregationalism is charitable and catholic as well as discriminating. It believes in "the Holy Catholic Church," and embraces in it all who, by faith and obedience, embrace Christ as the head. It opens its communion to all who are in communion with Him, while it makes compromises with none in their errors, or in the evil of their life. Hence, too, the Congregational idea of unity lies deeper, and is more vital than that of uniformity. The true apostolic succession is in the doctrine, life and labors of the apostles, with apostolic results. It is a " unity of the spirit, " with "diversities of gifts," like the law of the vegetable world, which holds all the divers plants and trees, buds and blossoms, fragrance, fruits and beauty— all by the central, organific unity of life, as living subjects of the same vast kingdom.

" All that believe," said Cromwell to the Long Parliament, "have the real unity, which is the most glorious because inward and spiritual, *in* the Body, and *to* the Head."

Our fathers loved their church-order, because it was so simple, so scriptural, and tended to what is superior to any mere polity—to the truth of doctrine, purity of morals and the life of Christian love. And the history of New England from the time the Mayflower moored at Plymouth, amply justifies their preference. Where are churches marked by a more patient and prayerful study of the Scriptures, or a more profound, yet rational reverence for their sovereign wisdom and authority, as a rule of faith and life? Where those distinguished by a purer and more salutary doctrine, or the application of more deep, practical, heaven-guided thought to the great problems of man's being, duties and destiny? Where, since the age of the apostles, has faith wrought out more amply and legitimately the works of godlike charity to the poor at home, and the heathen abroad, than has this faith of Eliot and Mayhew, of Edwards and Brainard, of our Harriet Newells and Mrs. Judson's? Where has been nurtured a purer social ethics, that has made the family more a seminary of all that is pure and lovely and of good report, and raised around the marriage covenant, the sacred center of the family, its heaven-high walls of defense? Where are found such systems of instruction for all classes, such philanthropic and charitable institutions for the poor, the deaf, the dumb, and the blind ;—such Christ-like exertions for mitigating the miseries of this life, and inspiring hope for the life to come, as have sprung up here in New England, where the doctrines and polity of our fathers, for nearly two centuries and a half, have had their existence and action? In what place or period, in, or out of New England, has the *reverse* of this been most realized in history,—or the picture been most marred or darkened by the vices of men and their demoralizing doctrines? Just where this Bible faith and ethics have been most resisted and impugned.

Thus, by an appeal to that trial-word of Christ the Lord, " By their fruits ye shall know them," the faith of our fathers stands historically verified as genuine, and their doctrine as substantial truth. They are verified by the constant endeavors after moral perfection, by the transparent sincerity and self-denial which they have produced, and by a free obedience to every word of the Supreme from the life-forces of truth and love which they have occasioned.

THE CATHOLICITY OF CONGREGATIONALISM.

BY REV. THEODORE WOOLSEY, D. D., PRESIDENT OF YALE COLLEGE.

The subject of President Woolsey's address was the Catholicity of the Congregational Body. Having attempted after many months to revive his recollections of his address, the speaker was able by the aid of very brief notes to give the following outline:

Holding in his hand an ancient copy of the Saybrook Platform, which had come down from President Stiles, as an heirloom of the Presidents of Yale College, he read from the heads of agreement, assented to at the time when the Saybrook Platform was arranged, that the ministers of Connecticut, as others had done before them, received the doctrinal Articles of the Church of England, the Confession or Catechisms, shorter or larger, of the Westminster Assembly, and the Savoy Confession to be agreeable to the word of God. This readiness to receive various expositions of their faith as equivalents, and the habit of accepting them for substance of doctrine, shows the independence of Congregationalists upon any human standards. Connected with this independence is their catholicity.

But what is catholicity? The speaker, while confessing that perhaps his conception of it was not quite as definite as it ought to be, defined it:

1. To be a preponderance of belief, and of interest in the Church Universal, while the particular church or form or polity takes the background in the mind.

2. It consists in an overlooking of things wherein Christians differ, and a disposition to unite in common fundamental doctrines.

3. It is manifested by a readiness to cooperate with other Christians in movements of religion and benevolence. Those who lack the catholic spirit separate themselves from general efforts, and feel that their field lies in promoting the interests

of a particular church or denomination; they suspect true Christian union ; they suspect the theories of other Christian bodies as being heretical or unchristian ; in short the reasons for separate action accumulate before their minds, while those for joint action become faint and few, until they can scarcely contemplate religion in its brightness, but only as it is colored by the goggles of their own sect.

It was then asked whether Congregationalism has a catholic tendency. That it has such a tendency was argued from several facts. *First*, we see willingness to cooperate, without thinking of sectarian advantage. Instances of this were drawn from the old agreement, or plan of union between the General Association of Connecticut and the General Assembly, and from the cooperation in the American Home Missionary Society, in which, to say the least, the churches of New England never asked, and never would have asked, but for movements begun by others, whether they were not doing more than their share.

Another proof was derived from great liberality in doctrine. The Congregationalists have always put faith before forms, and have thought lightly of forms : they might, notwithstanding, have been narrow in doctrine, had not the free spirit of the individual and of the single independent church promoted freedom of thought among them, and given rise to smaller differences of opinion amid agreement in fundamentals. The active spirit of theological inquiry, which has been prevalent in New England, shows that the churches exercise no repressing influence on religious speculation; and the alarms which are continually given out, that they are breaking away from the moorings of the gospel, show that churches nearly akin to them in theology, but unlike them in constitution, cannot understand or receive such freedom.

Still *another* illustration of the catholic spirit was drawn from the ease and freedom with which Congregationalists pass over into another denomination. The Church Universal is the highest idea at home, and when they find the essential elements of that idea realized elsewhere in their emigrations, their chief religious want in regard to a church is satisfied.

But how, it was asked, does Congregationalism promote the

catholic spirit? Two ways were mentioned. First by the simplicity of its worship and organization. It may be liable to the reproach of being naked and disjointed, of being bare bones without flesh, and of being a collection of atoms forming no whole. Whether this reproach be just or not, this is certain: that no great organized body comes between the particular church and the holy Church Universal, to catch and detain the affections as they rise up toward the lofty idea of a Christian community, or to produce party spirit, and sectarian zeal, and mingle a certain selfish interest in efforts for the noblest of causes.

Again, the power of the laity in the Congregational churches favors a catholic spirit. Whether the just balance of power is attained in their system or not may be questioned; but this seems to be sure, that where the clergy have the chief or sole power, a large catholic feeling becomes nearly impossible; that an order of ecclesiastics, placed above, depresses a laity placed below, and by this depression, if it would support its power by argument, must make the church narrow and exclusive. The laity, enjoying power, will not be apt to use that power further than for the purpose of promoting their own freedom, for they are not officers; but the officers, having acquired power, will use it to control the private members of the church, and must maintain themselves by a theory opposed to the doctrine of parity in the body of the faithful.

THE FIRST CHURCH IN CONNECTICUT.

BY REV. JOEL HAWES, D. D. OF HARTFORD.

Mr. Moderator:

I am sure that my brethren in the ministry know well how perplexing it is to a speaker to have several subjects before his mind at the same time, and not know which one to select as the theme of his address. I find myself in just such perplexity at this time. When requested a few weeks since to say something on the present occasion, my thoughts fixed upon a subject which seemed appropriate, and which, having much occupied my mind of late, I intended to make the topic of present remark. "*It is the means of improving and extending our Congregationalism.*" But since I came here I have doubted whether I could do any thing like justice to the subject in the few minutes allowed me. And besides, being, as you know, naturally of a rather timid make, I feared that if I should give full utterance to my sentiments on the subject in question, I might disturb the feelings of some of my too independent brethren, and so I thought it best to pass it by. I then proposed to be silent. But as I could not willingly be excused, I shall confine myself to a few remarks on the first church established in Connecticut. I feel a delicacy in speaking on that subject in this presence, as it comes too nearly in contact with myself. But I wish to forget, and to have my hearers forget, for the time, that I have any connection with the church of which I am to speak, and to say what I have to say simply as a matter of history.

The first church established in this State removed from Newtown, now Cambridge, Mass., to its present locality in Hartford, in the early part of June, 1636,—just two hundred and twenty-three years ago this month.* Its founders were,

---

* As it was claimed by one of the speakers at the late meeting at Norwich that, not

as Cotton Mather calls them, a "choice collection of men" from Braintree and its vicinity in Essex county, England. A portion of them came to this country in 1632, and settled at Newtown. There, on the 11th of October the next year, having been joined by several others who came over the preceding month with Messrs. Hooker and Stone, whose ministry they had enjoyed in England, they were organized into a church, and the two distinguished men just named were ordained its pastor and teacher. It was the eighth church established in New England, and the first in Connecticut. It came through the wilderness with its pastor and teacher, and about one hundred souls ; and after a wearisome journey of fourteen days over hills and valleys, and rivers and swamps, the company of pilgrims arrived on the banks of the " beautiful Connecticut," and set up the standard of the cross on the spot where the church now has its home, and where it has, from the first, maintained uninterruptedly the worship of God and the ordi-

---

the church in Hartford, but the church in Windsor was the first established in Connecticut, it seems proper briefly to state the facts in the case.

The church in Windsor was organized in Plymouth, England, January, 1630, and Messrs. Warham and Maverick were constituted its pastors. It removed to this country the summer following and commenced a settlement in Dorchester. The church in Wethersfield was organized in February, the same year, at Watertown, and Rev. Mr. Phillips became its pastor.

The church in Hartford was organized Oct. 1633, at Newtown—now Cambridge, and Messrs. Hooker and Stone were ordained its pastor and teacher.

The question in regard to removing to Connecticut began to be agitated in each of these churches about the same time. Some of the members visited Connecticut as early as 1632 or 1633. A small company established themselves at Wethersfield in 1634, and made, it is believed, the first settlement on the river.

During the summer of 1635 several of the people of Dorchester congregation removed to a point on the river near the Plymouth trading house, and prepared to lay the foundations of the town of Windsor. In the autumn of this year a company of sixty persons, among whom were many women and children, set out on their tedious march for this new country. Most of these settled in Hartford. As yet no church existed in the State. There were individual Christians but no organized church.

In June, 1636, as stated in the text, the church at Newtown removed with its pastor and teacher, and settled in Hartford. This then was the first church established in the State. There were settlers at Windsor as there were also at Wethersfield, but no church, no minister, no preaching, nor ordinances. Rev. Mr. Phillips never removed with his people to Wethersfield. Rev. Mr Maverick, pastor of the Windsor church, died in 1636, and Rev. Mr. Warham his colleague, did not remove to Windsor till the September following.

The question whether the church in Hartford or the church in Windsor was the first established in the State, is in itself of very little importance. But one does not like to be put in the wrong when he knows he is in the right.

nances of the gospel. It has had ten pastors—I am the tenth, and nine of them lie buried with the people to whom they preached. It has never dismissed a minister—a fact which speaks well for the church and also for the ministers who have served them in the Lord; and I account it a far higher honor to be found in this succession of faithful servants of God, than I should, to be numbered in what is proudly claimed, in certain quarters, as the Apostolical succession. The church, established at the first on sound, evangelical doctrine, has maintained essentially the same doctrine through every successive generation of its membership. Slight deviations there may have been, but never such as to shake or mar the fundamentals of faith, *its first faith.* Always Calvinistic, always holding the great essentials of New England orthodoxy, it has never swung from the foundation on which it was built by Hooker and Stone, nor been carried about or disturbed by any of the many winds of doctrine that have swept over the land; and it deserves to be mentioned as an interesting historic fact, that just the periods when evangelical doctrine was held in highest esteem in the church, and preached most plainly from the pulpit, have been *the* periods of the church's greatest spiritual prosperity and growth. Hooker and Stone were marked men in their day, especially the former. He has been called "the light of the New England churches, and the oracle of the Colony of Connecticut;" and his influence, there can be no doubt, did more than that of any other man to give form and order to the churches of this State. He was the father of the system of consociation. It was a favorite and oft repeated remark of his—"We must have the consociation of the churches, or we are ruined;" and the good working of the system for a hundred and fifty years shows that he did not attach too much importance to it. It has exerted a most happy and efficient influence in preserving the faith and order of our churches, and it has secured to them a measure of peace and prosperity, unsurpassed by any other equal number of churches in the land. The first church in Hartford is a *consociated church,* and such, I trust, it will ever remain, as sure I am that it will, so long as it conducts orderly and well, but should it shake off this character and become unsettled in faith, or impatient of rule and order, it will be quite likely to break off from consociation and unite with others to pull down the system as a useless and hurtful incumbrance to the churches. And this, I am sorry to believe, is one of the unhappy tendencies of our times. There is, I fear, a growing disposition among many to break down the order of the churches established by our fathers and fall back into loose independency. That the effect of this will be to weaken our churches and gradually to open the way for the coming in of error and misrule, I have the deepest conviction; and with this conviction, I cannot forbear to repeat, for the admonition of all whom it may concern, the language of two of the venerable fathers of New England, uttered by them just before they ascended to their reward in heaven. "We do earnestly testify that if any who are given to change, do rise up to unhinge the well established churches in this land, it will be the duty and the interest of the churches to examine whether the men of this trespass are more prayerful, more watchful, more zealous, more heavenly, more universally conscientious, and more willing to be informed and advised, than those great and good men who left unto the churches what they now enjoy; if they be not so, it will be wisdom for the children to forbear pulling down with their own hands the houses of God which were built by their wiser fathers, till they have better satisfaction." You see how the subject on which I first intended to speak *will intrude* itself into my mind. I wished to show that it is no time to weaken or to cut asunder the few bands that bind the several parts of our Congregationalism together. They need rather to be strengthened and drawn closer together so that there may be more compactness and organic unity in our denomination both in this State and throughout the land. *We* want, our *whole* denomination wants, a common platform of faith and order, a *declaration, or manifestation* of doctrine and polity, which shall operate as a band of union to our entire body, and serve both to bind us together in unity of faith and action, and to declare to all who may wish to know, distinctly, and fully, who and what we are ; what we believe ; and what we do in the order and government of our churches ; a fact which cannot now be learnt from any general document of acknowledged authority.

But this is off my track. I shall be pardoned, however, I trust; for I was pressed by an internal force which would not be resisted. I return to my subject. The church of which I am giving a brief historic sketch, as the first established in the State, has been distinguished for its stability, peace and harmony. So far as I can learn it has never been agitated or disturbed, but in a single instance, since its formation, by any serious controversy or dispute either about doctrine or discipline. The case of difficulty referred to occurred in the early history of the church, and was occasioned by a dispute upon some ecclesiastical topic between Mr. Stone and the ruling elder, relating, it is thought, to the qualifications for baptism, church-membership and the rights of the brotherhood. It was of long continuance, and of wide spread and disastrous influence. Cotton Mather, in his quaint style, remarks " that from the fire of the altar there issued thunderings and lightnings and earthquakes through the colony." He says also, that the true original of the misunderstanding was about as obscure as the rise of Connecticut river. It is known, however, that Mr. Stone's ideas of Congregationalism bordered more on Presbyterianism than those of most of the first ministers in New England. His sententious definition of Congregationalism was, " A speaking aristocracy in the face of a silent democracy." From this it would seem not unnatural to infer that the schism referred to had in it a spice of Presbyterianism, and this perhaps was one reason why it was so long continued and so hard to be cured. However this may be, it is good to know that this is the first and only difficulty of any importance that has existed in the church to disturb its peace for more than two hundred years. And I am happy to be able to say that, during the almost forty-two years I have been with the people as their minister, they have never by any associated act or movement of theirs, given me an half hour's uneasiness. Were I to assign the cause of this long continued union and harmony enjoyed by the people, I should say that, under God, it has been owing to a spirit of mutual concession; to the fact that none have assumed to dictate or to rule without the consent of others, and that when the majority have decided a question, the minority have been accustomed peaceably to acquiesce. The church has ever be-

13

lieved in revivals of religion, and owes all its prosperity to these oft repeated visitations of heaven's mercy. The ministry of Mr. Hooker, while in his native land, "was crowned with wonderful success by the Holy Spirit." Multitudes under his preaching became the subjects of renewing grace, many of whom removed to this country and were the founders and first members of the church of which he and Mr. Stone were constituted pastors. After its removal from Cambridge and establishment in its present location, signal were the displays of grace in the midst of it. An early writer referring to this period, exclaims: —" O, that converting glory, which did then appear! Multitudes were converted to thee, O Zion!—Multitudes, multitudes were converted to thee, O Hartford! to thee, O New Haven! to thee, O Windsor!" Passing over the intervening period during which there is evidence that the church was frequently blessed with revivals, we come to the ministry of my immediate predecessor, Dr. Strong. He was ordained in 1774. The first twenty years of his ministry were comparatively unfruitful, owing in part to the disturbed state of the country, occasioned by the revolutionary war, and in part to his own deficiency in fidelity and devotedness to his work. But the last twenty-two or three years of his life, witnessed a great change in *him* and in the *fruits* of *his* labors. A converted man, it is believed, before this, he now experienced what seemed a second conversion, and his ministry was in demonstration of the Spirit and with power. He lived to witness four revivals among the people of his charge. Large numbers were added to the church, among whom were many leading men in the community; and the general tone of religion was greatly elevated and advanced in spirituality and power.

In 1818, I was called to take charge of the church, since which it has been my privilege to witness nine special seasons of revival among the people, the most remarkable of which was in 1821 when nearly two hundred were added to the church during the year. As the result of these revivals the church has been largely increased in numbers, and I trust also in spirituality and fruitfulness unto God. Three colonies have gone forth from it, since I became its pastor, to form other churches in the city. It has sent eighteen* young men into the ministry, once of its membership, and nurtured and trained in its bosom. It has borne a comparatively generous part in sustaining and promoting the cause of home and foreign missions, and the various other benevolent operations of the day. Its contributions (including the congregation,) in aid of these objects have amounted for the last twenty years, to from six to eight thousand dollars annually.

Such is a brief historical sketch of the First Church established in Connecticut. In many respects it may be put down as a model church. And yet it is far, very far removed from the scriptural standard. It has faults, many and great faults, which, if I thought it would do any good either to *it* or to other sister churches, I would be just as frank to name as I have been to speak of its virtues. The millennium has not yet dawned upon it. Indeed it is far from having come to that spirituality and fruitfulness in its membership and communion which I trust it will attain at some future day. Being the oldest church in the State, it is somewhat too staid and *unbendable* in its habits. It is perhaps too much afraid of Young America, and is not sufficiently aware that the best way to guide that fast youngster is not to stand off at a forbidding distance, but to come near, lay a soft hand upon him, and go along by his side speaking kind words and gently holding him in with a flexible rein. The church has always seemed willing to let me do very much as I had a mind to do ; but I have not found them just as ready as I could wish to come forward and help me, especially in occasional religious meetings, and other active labors. I have often complained of this to them, *as they do very well know*—and I have hoped that there has been some improvement of late in a free outflow of feeling and speech, and active co-operation, one with another and with the pastor. Still there is great room for progress in the matters here referred to as well as in many others that might be named. But I must say of the old first church in Connecticut, as Cowper said of his native Old England : " With all thy faults, I love thee still." And I account it

---

* Besides those, seventeen others, though less directly trained in the church, have passed from its membership into the ministry.

the greatest joy and blessing of my life, that I have been permitted to serve the church as its pastor so many laborious, but very happy years. And now as I look to the end of my course—not distant I know, and see the river before me on the shore of which I have parted with so many of my dear people, the loved members of my church, as I clasped them by the hand and bade them farewell on their way to heaven, it gives me new joy to think that I shall ere long cross the same stream, and through grace, as I humbly hope, shall go to join them in the celestial city, and with them rejoice forever in the presence of God and the Lamb.

THE MISSION OF CONGREGATIONALISM AT THE WEST.

BY REV. T. M. POST, D. D., ST. LOUIS, MO.

MR. MODERATOR:

I have interpreted my call to this historic commemoration as a recognition of the fact that Western Congregationalism is a part of your history; a colonial offshoot and exponent. As in the triumphs of ancient Rome, representatives from the frontiers and outposts—from Thrace and Germania, the Euphrates and the Nile—swelled the pageant of the ovation, as exponential of the expansive genius and aspirations of the empire; so your sons from beyond the Mississippi are invited here to-day as representatives not of imperial, but of evangelical aspirations, stretching to the Pacific. I have supposed it the expectation of that call that I should speak of the relations of Congregationalism to that new world where my manly life has been spent. In so doing, I design to speak, not by way of arraignment of those differing from myself—among such are my true brothers, both in blood and in the Gospel of Christ—but, fraternally conceding to them the same right of judgment I claim for myself, I design to look simply to the logic of our position as Congregationalists. All that I would say is the evolution of a few great principles which I can do little but barely state on this occasion.

And, first, I may certainly assume in this presence that Congregationalism is a distinctive, substantive entity, not a mere accident, prejudice, caprice, or custom, commutable into something else at pleasure; but an individual essence, translatable by no synonym, and having characteristic principles, peculiar either in kind or in degree and extent of working, founded on Scripture and the nature of man.

I do not believe that those distinctive principles of church polity for which our fathers in the seventeenth century separated from other Non-conformists, in that conflict which shook down the English monarchy, and those which they so much prized as the great gift of God to them in the wilderness of the

New World—I do not believe these distinctive principles are mere unsubstantial illusions or prejudices.

I will premise, morever, that as these principles lie not within the domain of feeling, but of logic, and are not the creations of feeling, nor to be assumed or laid down at its behests ; so a plea to charity as against their entertainment or assertion is entirely alien and irrelevant. Charity has her own beautiful sphere ; but she cannot make or unmake facts or principles, cannot mend or mar an argument, is no solvent or solderer of logic. Charity worthy the name can live only with clear self-consciousness and ingenuous self-utterance, and, till the millennium, certainly, with variant opinion.

We glory in the large-heartedness of Congregationalism. Long may she wear the honor of catholicity so ably vindicated for her here this day. But certainly this claim to catholicity and charity is not to be vindicated by the abnegation of her own distinctive essence or self-assertion. Our system surely is not so catholic that it is nothing. That which produces such beautiful charity, certainly has no right to carry charity to the extent of suicide—to the destruction of the distinctive individual life-principle that bears a fruit so fair. Charity must not quench the fountain of charity. We may not reason in this wise : " Congregationalism glories in producing a spirit which seeketh not its own but another's good. Therefore let us give it up." We may sacrifice interest and feeling, but never truth and principle. We may die for a brother, but we may not for him suppress a truth or enact or utter a falsehood. If, therefore, the logic of our position and principles demands of Congregationalism a policy of self-diffusion, let not her attempt at duty, due to herself and her Lord, be paralized by that song of the Lotus-eaters to which she has so long listened ;—charming her energies to sleep, by an abuse of the beautiful and blessed name of charity to a mere good feeling, which melts into itself all logic and all distinctive principle and all conscious individuality.

Let not these arguments for the extension of Congregationalism be met by mere deprecation of denominationalism, or by mere pleasant words of the beauty and blessedness of brotherly love. If in the alembic of charity all distinctive organic principles exhale, and nothing is left but a catechism and a kindly feeling, ready to melt into any order that may be presented, the quicker our individual existence is abandoned the better ; we have no right to be. If this adhesion to our church-order cannot abide in the strongest Christian love, then its existence at all is an offense. Our cherished principles are merely prejudice— nothing more ; when we feel right they disappear.

But if our church order stands with us on the only ground on which it is entitled to stand at all—as embracing peculiar principles and forces adapted in their working to glorify Christ and save men, then the stronger our love for Christ and our brethren, the stronger our attachment to it will be.

Self-diffusion, Congregationalism owes to her own principles and to her own life. To limit a principle to geographic boundaries is to destroy it. This denies its universality—its foundation in the nature of things and the Word of God ; and to deny this is abnegation of its own existence. Self-diffusion is the prerogative and duty of Truth. To deny it expansion is to slay it. As well hope to maintain the life of a tree while cutting off its lateral branches and roots. To assume that Congregationalism may not live beyond New England, is fatal to its abiding in New England ; and would necessitate ultimately, as a logical and natural consequence, a contest for the right of your Association to exist in the state of Connecticut.

Again, such diffusion is due to the West. Whether we consider vastness and resources of territory and prospective population, or energy of civilization, never since Christianity strove for the possession of the Roman empire, or the barbaric world in which that empire sunk, or since the Reformation wrestled for the supremacy of Christendon in the sixteenth century—never has so mighty a game been presented, or one staking on its issue such vast results for the kingdom of God, as that now waged by divisive and antagonistic, social and religious forces, for the rising world of the West—never one with necessity more urgent, because of the rapidity of the step of Destiny. While every form of belief and misbelief, from Mormonism to the Papacy, is looking to that world as its quarry, shall the religious order of the founders of our nation alone be excluded ? The cry that this order is unfitted to the West is, in regard to large portions, at least, of the West, sheer, indolent, and hostile cant ; unsupported alike by facts, philosophy or history. All these indicate a peculiar adaptedness of it to that field.

It is due, again, to the history of Congregationalism in the past, that her children should carry her institutions Westward ; that that church-order, which has been the chief social architect of your commonwealths—than which the sun shines on no fairer in all its course—should be introduced amid the plastic and organic forces in the genesis of the new states in the West. Her past protests against her exclusion from the future.

But if self-diffusion be ·a duty, how shall this be effected ? There are two methods. One extensively adopted in the past, is the interpenetration of other denominations with her own ideas, by surrendering her own distinctive organization, and merging herself in them. But whatever we may think of the expediency or the ingenuousness of this procedure in the past, its time is gone. The reactionary spasm is on all the great ecclesiastical systems. The tendency everywhere is to a more stringent ecclesiasticism. Compromises are repelled and resented.

Another mode, that of distinctive assertion and organization, alone is left us. We must advance under our own symbol. And it is better thus. The West loves boldness and frankness. Other denominations appear with generous and explicit self-assertion. Why not the sons of the Pilgrims?

But what means shall we employ to this effect ? Shall we organize a system of crusade and aggression ? Shall we have but one idea? Shall we advocate an impracticable, factious course in our emigrant members ? Do we exalt the church above Christ? Order above life? No, by no means ! The great means is that duty which every system owes to itself, self-indoctrination ; the interpenetration of our own body with a more distinctive, appreciative, grateful self-consciousness. We need to understand better the principles of our own system ; to be taught in our homes and sanctuaries, our theological schools, and by our religious press, its characteristic excellencies ; its beneficent relations, social and religious, to truth, brotherhood, freedom, life, and power. Our great policy is self-instruction. Our weapons are ideas. Our mode of self-diffusion is self-consciousness. We have no great ecclesiastic arm by which to reach into vacant realms and map them into ecclesiastical jurisdictions, and frame outlines into which coming people may shape themselves. Our reliance is on ideas implanted in the minds of our sons and daughters. If there are enduring principles in our system, and we expect posterity to abide by them, our children must be taught what they are ; not to estimate them as the Gospel, or as paramount to Christian life or love ; but to hold them in their true rank, and their proper relations to these interests, and cleave to them for the sake of these interests, and these only. I urge this point, because this duty seems to have been falsely estimated and studiously neglected. In order to cooperation with other ecclesiastical systems, and to facilitate transition to them, we seem purposely to have ignored the principles of our own, till we have well-nigh forgotten it has any, and it stands with us as a mere matter of conveniency, custom or prejudice.

Now, not as against charity, but for the sake of charity, of peace, and of sobriety of thought and feeling, all this should be changed. These can abide permanently only with a clear and comprehensive appreciation of principles, a distinct discernment of their proper limit and consequence, and their due relation and proportion. A system dimly self-conscious, or held merely in prejudice, passion, or custom, is of necessity exposed to the alternative of fanaticism and ultraism on the one hand, or of formalism and indifferentism on the other—an indifferentism extending ultimately to other things than forms of church order. Its adherents must defend it ignorantly, or abandon it with many hazards to character, ever arising from abandonment of what is clearly inwrought in the past with our moral and religious sentiment and practice.

Again, the want of indoctrination, and the sending of your children westward with their church institutions—if borne with them at all—labelled " Things indifferent," breeds a strife of tongues and much uncharitableness. If they cleave to these institutions as matters of principle, they incur suspicion and report as factious and impracticable agitators, troubling the church for mere forms and punctilios. Their attempt at practical assertion of their principles, is resented as stolid or schismatic ob-

14

stinacy ; and often by none more than by those from your own body who, under our past policy of ignoring our distinctive principles, have easily fused with other ecclesiastical systems, and consequently cannot appreciate the difficulties others may find in pursuing the same course. Hence the most bitter opposers of our polity are found among those nurtured in its bosom, educated by its charities, and deriving much of the energy and excellence of character they possess from the influence of its institutions. I do not at all question their conscientiousness. For their position and opinion are the natural consequences of our past policy. But obviously it is for the interests of peace that this policy of self-ignorance should not continue. A distinct self-consciousness will teach us when, how, and to what extent we can cooperate with other denominations, and thus save from the irritation of false expectations and misunderstandings and attempts at impracticabilities. There are primary differences of organic principles between us and other denominations, which, leaving us the power to do something in common, make other things impracticable. If two neighbors have distinct principles of architecture, while they may beneficently unite in many things,—in constructing roads, bridges, and various improvements of a country,—yet clearly if they attempt house-building in common, they incur the hazard of a quarrel. If, for instance, one wishes a circular and the other a rectangular edifice, they cannot compromise by attempting to build a square circle or circular square ; nor will it relieve the difficulty to invent some comprehensive misnomer that may embrace both styles under one term. Nor will it make for peace if one thinks to enter into his neighbor's house and knock off the angles till the rectangular becomes circular, or crowd the curve into angles till the circle becomes a square. Such attempts at unity breed sharper discord in the end. On many things they can beneficially and pleasantly unite ; but in house-building only for temporary shelter, and with the understanding that each, when strong enough, may without impeachment build his own edifice and in accordance with his own taste. So in regard to different churches at work in the West ; similar distinctness of self-consciousness and self-assertion should for the interests of peace mark their relations to each other.

Again, it is due to the maintenance of Puritan manhood among your children going westward, that they be taught rightly to appreciate the Religious Order of their fathers as the bequest of heroic and martyr ages ; and when practicable, to bear them to the wilderness as the most precious part of their birthright. But contrarywise, to inculcate that the emigrant son of New England should initiate life in the West, by casting away the church order connected with what is most sacred and most cherished of his previous years, must tend to set him on a course hazardous often to virtue and principle.

The abandonment of institutions is liable to draw after it that of associated sentiment and principle, and a dangerous relaxation of the entire moral sentiment. No people can abandon what they have in early life been accustomed to regard as sacred, without peril to character. Unless done at the behests of a higher reason and conscience, it enfeebles and demoralizes. Facility of such transition has brought reproach on the New England character ; nor has the fact that this has arisen in many cases from conscientious motives, and often—from want of education in our own church system—with consciousness of little change save in names, prevented that injury to character accruing to the mass, from the general habitude thus induced. This habitude operating on the weak, the ambitious, and the worldly, is wont to betray into a career of moral degeneracy, ending often in apostacy. The whole man ultimately becomes venal ; yielding to the opinions and usages of all majorities. With his inbred love and faculty of gain, and his peculiar energy and adroitness of character, he devotes himself, mind and soul, to the "main chance." The result is a type of character which becomes a reproach to the land of his birth, and a by-word in the land of his adoption ; a type of sad notoriety in the history of the West. For while we are grateful to recognize among the sons of New England specimens of the noblest manhood, in all ecclesiastical connections, or in none ; the most effective and honored agents in various interests, social, commercial, educational, and political; still we are constrained to acknowledge among them types of degeneracy proverbial for opposite qualities and influence ; that—as the highest may sink lowest, as the sweetest things corrupt to the most acrid of acids, as the most beautiful by degeneracy become foulest, as the holiest become in their fall the most deformed, as the types of bestial life approaching nearest the man, disgust us the more from their carricature of humanity—so amid all types of character wandering up and down amid the melange of Western life, the most offensive and deformed is the *faded Yankee.* His moral manhood is perfectly blanched out of him. He is ready for any color to strike through him. He slips out of his early life as the serpent from his slough. He has overcome his prejudices, and his principles are all prejudices. His nativity is renounced. He has no longer a manly individuality. His personality is gone. He is vacant for the occupancy of all majorities. He reminds one of the process by which the masters of the mesmeric art sometimes break the will and subdue the personality of their subject. In this process a glittering coin is held up before him, and he is commanded to follow it with his eye. It is waved above, around, below ; but he must keep it constantly in sight. He pursues it with fascinated eye in all its motions, now with upraised gaze, now with manifold contortions of body, chasing the shining charm around him ; now crawling on hands and knees, now peering after it under chairs and tables. By this preparation his independence of will and his personality seem subdued ; and he is now ready for his master's uses. He now feels, sees, touches, tastes, believes as he is bidden. He sees black or white ; shudders with cold or heat ; tastes sweet or bitter ; sings, dances, prays, blasphemes as the operator chooses; catching up chips for gold, having glorious fishing with his cane, or smelling the attar of rose from the tobacco box. He is no longer anybody in particular, but anybody you please. He doffs and dons, at command, all personages from General Taylor to the last executed murderer.

With similar process and result, often the New Englander placed amid the tumult and scramble of Western life, and chasing through all the charm of the glittering dollar— all principle ignored and forgotten in the fascinated gaze—seems at last divested of his own personality, and subdued to the acceptance of all opinions and characters the popular voice may command. He now is ready to ride each popular wave. He becomes the most fierce in championship of servile usage, or opinion, and the most bitter in denunciation of his former sentiments. He caters to vulgar prejudice in slang abuse of the land of his birth. From the demagogue of Kansas frauds and atrocities to the hardest of overseers, he is the prince of social charlatans and mountebanks; emulating the individuality of the chameleon or the sponge—a mere absorbent or reflector.

Such is the "Yankee" fully "faded." His case may be regarded as an extreme one. But a feeling which initiates the New Englander into Western life with a renunciation of the ecclesiastical institutions of his fathers, transferring itself to his modes of thinking and acting in other interests, tends legitimately toward such results. Self-respect which shall protect his individuality and innerve his moral manhood, demands he should not—unlike every other race and sect—be required on passing certain lines of longitude to abandon his principles of church-order.

I will add, in conclusion: One of the happiest means of arousing a beneficent self-consciousness in our system, and of protecting against tendencies to degeneracy, is oftimes to do what you are doing here this day, viz., revitalizing with solemn celebration, with graphic and philosophic narrative, and with grateful and genial reminiscences, the old metropolitan heart. For such a heart, fathers and brethren, we of the West still recognize as beating from your climes along the sea. Let it ever beat strong and healthful. Infuse into it the life of elder times—the life of a love of Truth and Liberty that shall grow only the more intense as well as more holy, in the love of Christ and the Brotherhood. We shall feel its pulses, thus invigorated, beating beyond the Alleghanies and the Mississippi, up the streams of the Missouri, and through the passes of the mountains to the Pacific seas.

And now, brethren, though in my argument I have challenged for the principles which we in common hold, that practical respect due to their truth and value, which all true men ever owe to their own convictions, I believe I am as far removed as any man, in both feeling and practice, from invoking in their behalf sectarian passion and strife. Our principles are alien to such agencies; nor can our system be served of such. I simply urge that we should act truthfully from our own position ; should fulfill the mission and occupy the sphere assigned us by the principles we hold, and by the Providence of God. To that mission and sphere, as our allotment in Christ's work, let us be faithful ; holding fast faith, hope, and charity ; and working patiently on, whether with the multitude favoring, or under overshadowing adverse majorities, as the Master may appoint. And when another century, rolling this occasion and its actors far into the past, shall bring up a recurrence of this day, let our fidelity to God's work assigned us in our time, present for us a record worthy to rank beside our fathers, of whom we have heard from a legitimate son this day—a record fitting us to share with them, and the faithful of every name or school on earth, in that song of victory which from a redeemed world shall at last climb the hights around the Throne.

CONGREGATIONALISM AS IN HARMONY WITH THE SCRIPTURAL IDEA OF CHRISTIAN UNION.

BY REV. PROF. E. P. BARROWS, ANDOVER, MASS.

MR. MODERATOR:

If the Congregational polity is in harmony with the scriptural idea of Christian union, then it is the right polity, and will work well, and be successful in accomplishing the ends for which the Christian Church was established; if not, it is a wrong polity, and will not work well. I propose to show how this system is permeated throughout with the true spirit of Christian union, as it is delineated in the New Testament.

If we go back to the old Jewish theocracy, there we find a religious state; not a mongrel union of church and state, as two distinct organizations, after the modern European fashion; but simply a state invested by God's appointment with all the functions of religion; and as such, entrusted by God with the sword which every state must bear, and punishing with the sword idolatry and witchcraft, as it did murder and adultery. But our Lord Jesus took out of the state the church elements which had hitherto lain embosomed in it, and constituted them into a separate organization, which is the Christian church. In doing this he left behind the sword, and all outward force of which the sword is the representative. He did not give the state one sword and the church another, that the two might be used against each other; he did not take the sword from the state and commit it to the church, that she might have dominion over the state; he did not make the state the menial of the church (after the Romish notion) to use the sword at her direction and for her aggrandizement; nor did he make the church the menial of the state, to be used in subservience to her secular ends. But he simply constituted churches independent of the state in all their proper functions as churches, while yet the individual members remain in all civil matters subject to the state. And these churches he left without any sword.

For the principle of outward force he substituted that of inward affinity of character. His plan was, by the glorious gospel which he revealed, and the glorious power of the Spirit accompanying it, to transform men into a likeness to himself, and thus into a likeness to each other. He first draws men, one by one, into union with himself, and in this way into an inward union with each other. To all his followers he is the great central point of unity. By making them one with himself and the Father he makes them one with each other.

Upon this simple principle the Apostles proceeded in organizing churches. They went every where preaching the gospel, having full faith in its divine power to accomplish the end for which it was given. And wherever a body of men and women had been brought by it into inward union with Christ and each other, they formed them into a church under the few and simple rules and ordinances which Christ had given, and thus gave them also a visible and outward unity. Thus arose the church in Jerusalem, the church in Antioch, the church in Ephesus, the church in Rome. From the necessity of the case, as well as from Christ's authority, these churches had the officers necessary for the administration of their proper functions as churches, as also the power of admission to their fellowship and exclusion from it. This is the length, breadth, and thickness of the New Testament doctrine of church polity. A common faith united these churches in a holy fellowship with each other. They recognized each other as co-ordinate branches of Christ's body; as such they honored each other, they took counsel with each other, they helped each other in difficulties. But we do not find in the New Testament any trace of a plan on the part of our Saviour and his Apostles to gather these churches or sections of them, outwardly and organically, into one compact body; thus subjecting each individual church to the proper authority and judicial power of the whole, and making it no longer *a* church of Christ in the full sense of the words, but only a part and parcel of *the* Church.

Now let us look for a moment at the Congregational polity. Here, to guard against misapprehension, I premise that in what I have to say about ecclesiastical organizations, I have no refer-

ence to any minor differences that exist among Congregationalists. Coming, as I do, from another commonwealth, this
would not be becoming in me on the present occasion. My remarks will apply only to those organizations that have proper
judicial power and binding authority over the separate churches,
as just now explained. I would simply say then, sir, that we
are content to take up the system of church polity as Christ
and his Apostles left it. If any think that this is not adequate
to the proper office of Christian churches, and that they must,
therefore, go on to compact the individual churches into extended organizations, we have no quarrel with them. In this
matter liberty of judgment belongs to them, as well as to us.
We only say that for their warrant they must go to the same
volume to which Rome goes—the volume of human tradition
and human wisdom. We are satisfied with the system as
Christ and his Apostles left it.

It may be objected that it is not strong enough. For what
ends is it not strong enough? If the office of Christ's churches
be to control, in a direct way, the counsels of kings and cabi-
nets, and pull the wires of party organizations, doubtless the
Congregational polity is not strong enough for this end. If
their business be to legislate Christ's body into uniformity in
outward details—to prescribe, for example, what dress the
preacher shall wear in the pulpit, and whether the congregations shall use written or unwritten prayers—doubtless for this
purpose also it is not strong enough. But if, as we believe,
the great office of Christ's churches is to make men like Christ;
to build up their members in piety and fruitfulness, and to
spread every where the knowledge of the gospel, we think
that for this high and glorious end, our polity is strong enough.
Its freedom and elasticity give us full scope for every Christian enterprise. Take, for example, that of missions, foreign
and domestic. Under the simple system of Congregationalism
we have been able to work up to advantage every particle of
the missionary spirit that existed in our churches. Here we
have been, it is true, far, very far from doing what we ought to
have done. Shame and confusion of face belong to us. But
the fault has lain not in our organization, but in the fact that
we have had so little of the spirit of Christ. Had there been

15

in our churches a hundred fold more of this spirit, and couse-
quently a hundred fold more of missionary zeal, and a hundred fold more of men and of money at our disposal, we should
not have been straitened one jot in our ecclesiastical system.
We could have worked up all these increased means to advantage. And we are willing, sir, that our churches should look
directly in the face the great truth that the missionary spirit
can never be maintained separately from the solid every day
piety of the churches; and, further, that this piety is to be fed
and nourished not by great and strong ecclesiastical systems,
but by the spiritual instrumentalities that Christ has appointed.

For the maintenance of sound doctrine, also, we think that
our polity has sufficient strength. If a minister of the gospel
departs from the faith, we can withdraw from him our approbation for the exercise of the functions of the ministry (in technical language, we can depose or silence him,) and this is precisely the kind and degree of power that Christ has entrusted
to us. If he still goes on to preach, he does it on his own
foundation, and the Master releases us from all further respon-.
sibility in the matter. Once more, if a church, or a portion of
its members, departs from the faith, we can labor with it ; can
give it our counsel and judgment ; can provide for the relief of
a minority in it that adheres to the truth as it is in Jesus ; and,
as a last step, can withdraw our fellowship from it. This,
again, is precisely that moral power which our Master has given
to us. Any further power he does not wish us to exercise. If
the church refuses to listen, and persists in its errors, Christ
will attend to that in his own way. It is true that in our
order one lamentable apostacy from the faith has taken place.
But to ascribe this to the proper operation of our polity would
be a palpable *non sequitur.* We have heard this morning
abundantly of other causes that operated to bring about that
defection. If we unroll the scroll of history, we find that it
is precisely that church which has the strongest organization
that is the most corrupt ; and, further, that it is this very
strength of hierarchical power that makes it irreclaimable in its
corruptions. If it be said that a strong organization with a
sound creed is the bulwark of orthodoxy, then we point to the
church of England in the days when Whitfield and the Wes-

leys arose; which, with both these defenses, had sunk into a deplorable state of worldliness and corruption in both doctrines and morals; and was rescued, so far as it was rescued, not by these, but by God's ancient method of raising up an evangelical ministry, and pouring out his spirit upon the churches. We point also to the Reformed and Lutheran churches of Europe, which, with the same two defenses, have lamentably departed from the truth as it is in Jesus, and are now in the process of regeneration by the same spiritual instrumentalities. Sir, I am not going to say a word in disparagement of creeds. I reverence them, and hold firmly to their necessity. But let us not ascribe to either creeds or ecclesiastical organizations a power which Christ has not given them. Vain is the idea that one generation, by any outward system however elaborate, can do up the work of orthodoxy for all coming ages. No sir. Each generation must fight the battle against error for itself, with the scriptural weapons which God has put into its hands. We consider it an excellency of our system that it does not in any way conceal or cover up the fact that, under God, the hope of sound doctrine is in holy and zealous churches under the instruction of holy and zealous teachers, rather than in any elaborate ecclesiastical machinery.

In the matter of bearing testimony against great national sins, we think that the freeness and elasticity of our system gives us some pre-eminent advantages. Take, for example, the system of American slavery, which overhangs our nation like a dark and portentous cloud big with awful thunders. Nobly, sir, have our churches borne their testimony against this great evil. And it has been with less friction and collision than can be the case under strong and extended ecclesiastical organizations. In truth, we find that just in proportion as an ecclesiastical body spreads itself out over wide regions, as one compact, organic whole, the difficulties thicken in the way of its finding resolutions on the subject of slavery that suit all sides. Every resolution that can be framed then becomes subject to the evil which a venerable clergyman of my state, somewhat distinguished for his wit, has ascribed to definitions in metaphysics. He compares a definition in metaphysics to the cover of a tin pail that is a little grain too small.

You carefully adjust it on one side, and up it hops on the other. Then you go to work too on that side, but just as you have fixed it to your mind up hops the first side. In the same manner one may see a denomination under one of these compact and extended organizations working at its resolutions on slavery—resolutions, counter-resolutions and amendments, without either end or satisfying result—till at last God, who loves his churches and desires their peace, sends them deliverance by a secession, a process which needs only to be repeated a sufficient number of times to produce something resembling our Congregational way of disposing of the matter, namely, that of leaving each body to satisfy itself.

That strong ecclesiastical organizations have their advantages it is not necessary for us to deny. But we think that these advantages may be purchased at too dear a price. To us it seems that nothing is more conspicuous on the page of history than the tendency of such organizations to excess of legislation. When a body of good men thus constituted has become thoroughly penetrated with the high idea that God has committed to it the care of the orthodoxy and the order of all the churches, it feels conscience-bound to be always supervising them. It has taken upon itself a responsibility which the great Head of the church never committed to it, and the almost certain result will be excessive legislation. A hundred things of minor importance will be brought under the trammels of fixed law, that might be much better left to the good sense of the individual churches; and thus the cause of spiritual Christianity will be burdened instead of aided.

Mr. Moderator : allow me to say, in conclusion, that I have the honor to be a native of this State, and the high honor to have been ordained to the work of the ministry by one of its associations—the Hartford North. I see before me the reverend and honored father in the Lord, who preached my ordination sermon on that occasion—"*clarum et venerabile nomen.*"* I remained within the limits of the State three years. Then I was two years connected with a purely Presbyterian body. After that I was fifteen years in a Presbytery of

---

* Rev. Joel Hawes, D. D.

Ohio, formed upon the plan of Union. Far be it from me, sir, to lisp one word to the disparagement of the beloved and honored men in another denomination with whom I have been in former years so pleasantly associated. Many of them it is my privilege to reckon among my dearest friends in the ministry. They have always treated me with Christian kindness. I simply feel it my privilege to say, on the present occasion, that as years roll on, I am becoming, as the result of observation (and I may add experience also) more strongly attached to the Congregational polity. Of that polity in your State I say : *Esto perpetua!* May it live and flourish to the end of time, and bring forth, as hitherto, the fruits of righteousness in this ancient commonwealth !

THE PILGRIM FATHERS.

BY REV. JOHN WADDINGTON, LONDON, ENGLAND.

Rev. John Waddington, of the Southwark Church, London, England, then addressed the Association; but unfortunately only the most meagre outline of his speech has been preserved. He began by congratulating the Association on the harmonious and fraternal spirit which had reigned over their meetings. He then took a review of the Pilgrim principles which, he said, it greatly pleased him to see fostered by this Association. He hoped that all the papers that had been read would be published. Mr Waddington concluded with the prayer that the two nations—America and England, in holy fellowship, might yet together work a great work, the glory of which would be heard in all lands.

PURITAN PIONEERING IN NEW ENGLAND, COMPAR-
ED WITH PURITAN PIONEERING AT THE WEST

BY REV. A. L. CHAPIN, D. D., PRESIDENT OF BELOIT COLLEGE, WIS.

MR. MODERATOR:

I seem, to-day, to be living in two eras. The historic memorials which this occasion has gathered and spread before us,
set me down in the past. Sixteen years of life and labor in the
West have induced the habit of living much in the future.
The vividness with which past scenes have been here presented as fact, gives intense glow to the bright visions sketched by
fancy of things to come. You have all, no doubt, seen that
beautiful print, just published, entitled " The Past and the Future." The rapid alternations of thought and emotion here
seem to realize with me, at once, all that is expressed in the
two significant faces of the picture—the earnest reflection of a
soul chastened by experience, and the eager, expectant outlook
of one full of youthful hope and aspiration.

The speaker who preceded me, led us back to the fountain
of Pilgrim principles and movements in that little, persecuted,
Puritan church of London. The field of my labors pre-
sents a full, clear view of the breadth and depth which the
life-giving stream of blessed influences that proceeded from
that fountain, has attained, in its onward flow. Like the river
of classic fable, those principles crossed the ocean and burst
forth, unmixed and pure, at Plymouth Rock. Thence, they
have traversed the continent. The great central valley of the
Mississippi has been enriched by their presence, and precious
are the fruits already developed there. Over the Rocky Mountains they have found a passage ; and into the heterogeneous
composition of society on the Pacific coast, these Puritan principles are infusing themselves as saving elements. We find
them incorporated into the civil as well as the religious institutions of the land: And, viewed simply as principles of religious
faith and ecclesiastical polity, their presence and influence may

be traced, not only in the churches of pure Congregationalism, but also, through the whole structure and action of other kindred evangelical denominations. Wherever we find them, simple, or in combination, they appear full of life and power, the active elements of true progress for the spiritual growth of individual souls and the Christian civilization of human society. It is in their very nature to live and flourish. Drawn directly from the divine word, they are already identified with the advancement of Christ's kingdom ; and all the precious promises of the ultimate triumph of that kingdom are to us sure pledges of what shall yet, by the blessing of God, be accomplished through the spread and ascendancy of these principles. It is good to stand thus, on this mount of vision and look both ways—back to the apparently feeble beginnings, out upon the wide-spread results already realized, and on to the greater and better things to be hereafter developed. We see much to be thankful for—much to confirm our faith in God and his word —much to kindle higher aspirations and to prompt firmer purposes and nobler undertakings and more fervent prayers.

The historical discourse, to which it was our privilege to listen this morning, brought before us in graphic sketch that scene of one hundred and fifty years ago, which gives chief interest to this occasion. Let me now, for the few minutes allotted me, bring to your notice some points of contrast and resemblance suggested by a comparison of the actors and the acts of that date, with things pertaining to the more recent but similar work of organizing Christian institutions in the West.

Look again upon that little synod at Saybrook, in the olden time. Sixteen men of God, mostly advanced in years and of great dignity, are gathered in conclave. Two, of ripest age and wisdom preside over the council as moderators, while the two youngest are set as scribes to record the doings. Their personal appearance and all their proceedings are characterized by the calm deliberation and stately courtesy which marked that former age. With earnest look and solemn speech they take up the matter before them. They see not all the future growth which is to come of their planting, but their expectations are large enough to convince them that the business they are undertaking is of serious moment, as it concerns the vital interests of the Redeemer's kingdom and the welfare of coming generations. So they deal with it and lay foundations fit to bear up, for centuries, this edifice of organized Christian union, most simple in its structure, yet full of enduring beauty and strength.

Now look on another scene. Its date about a dozen years ago, and its place in the mining region of Wisconsin. There, in one of the ravines which break the country and make it as wild and rough as this hilly Connecticut, is assembled a band of nearly forty Christian men, charged as they believe with the duty of setting up and maintaining in that new state, the institutions of the gospel on the Pilgrim plan. They are mostly young men, with scarcely a gray head to give dignity or sobriety to their council. Where two men of gravest learning would hardly be able to moderate the impetuous zeal of young life on that broad arena, there is set as the single official moderator, one, not yet turned of thirty, who has had less than five years of service in the ministry, to give him wisdom by experience. But these are not *"faded Yankees."* In the New England homes of their nativity, (some in that old first church of Hartford,) they were baptized into the spirit of those venerable Saybrook fathers, and educated in their principles of Christian faith and polity, too thoroughly to lose them by mere change of place. The precious fruits of those principles, which passing years have developed so richly, inspire them with full confidence in their soundness, and efficiency. The swift progress of our country, since its independence, prompts sanguine, almost unlimited hope for the future contemplated in their work. So, with no less of devotion to the master's service, and solemn, prayerful regard for the consequences of their action, but with a quicker pulse, and bolder faith and a freer swing than the Connecticut fathers, they move in a style which would have seemed in the former age, frightful presumption and recklessness. Yet shall their foundations also stand ; for in the true spirit of the fathers, they are laying down the solid granite blocks, the same enduring principles of gospel truth and order.

Observe the contrast yet further, with respect to some circumstances of each scene. The area of the State of Connecticut is less than five thousand square miles. Wisconsin embraces more than fifty thousand. At the date we have in mind, the population here has grown slowly, through three quarters of a century, to fifteen thousand souls. There, ten years have spread over the Indian hunting grounds more than three hundred thousand. Here, the population is select and homogeneous in respect of origin, domestic and social customs and religious faith and practice. There, it is mixed and diverse, drawn by immigration from all civilized nations, with different languages and habits and representing all shades of Christian faith and unchristian skepticism. Here, the pressure of tyranny, felt by the earlier fathers and remembered by their sons, binds all together for the maintenance of highest public freedom. There, freedom enjoyed, without being appreciated, tends to disintegrate society under the prevalent maxim, " Every man for himself in greatest individual liberty." Here, a sterile soil and the struggles and hardships incident to those times which tried men's souls, have developed habits of careful thrift and a spirit of self-sacrifice, There, the idolatry of mammon prevails, and genders wild speculation rather than patient industry ; and the abundant fruits of a fertile soil, gathered in peace, without care or fear, encourage profusion for present self indulgence. Here, all the institutions of civilized society make progress under a process of slow development, in which the depths are sounded and the bearings all taken, and with narrow sails, the whole movement is safe and strong and grand. There, every thing goes with a rush, and careless confidence at the helm hardly deigns to glance at the charts and tables prepared by past labor, and reckless presumption in the engine-room crowds on steam to the utmost, and the excitement of the race makes the eager voyagers almost heedless of the awful collapse or tremendous explosion by which, ever and anon, nature protests against the violation of her laws and warns them to "make haste slowly."

Now, for a moment, suppose those venerable Saybrook fathers suddenly called forth from their graves and sent out West to settle foundations there, in just the present condition of things ; or conversely, suppose those young western pioneers, such as they are, carried back a hundred and fifty years and

entrusted with that ancient work of the giants. Surely, it is
no disparagement to them of the former age and no affectation
of modesty in us of the present, to say that, in either case,
nothing could have been fitly or succesfully done. See, then,
the wisdom with which divine providence ordered the times
and circumstances and relations of things. Wisely did God
choose the time, and the place, and the men, and guide the
process for the slow and sure unfolding of these precious Puritan principles, and the form of organization, through which
their value was to be tested by first experiments. And, not in
false assumption, but in simple faith, we may add, wisely has
God chosen the time and the place and the men for carrying
out the process on a grand scale by giving wide, rapid and
varied application of these principles to all kinds of people for
the ultimate transformation of the world. We have made out
many points of strong contrast; yet the work is really one,
only viewed at different stages, widely separated. The labor
of discovery and invention must precede that of application.
The care and wisdom with which the fathers defined and illustrated their principles is the conservative element in the enthusiastic
swift action of their descendants, the inheritors of those principles ; and the very difficulties which attend and embarass the
present stage of the work in those newer portions of the country present that as the proper field for the ultimate triumph of
those principles, and promise to unfold in due time, even in
these striplings, the true strength and mettle of the noble stock
from which they sprang. So we see realized another feature
of the picture before referred to. She, whose face glows with
the inspiration of hope as her eye dwells on bright visions of
the future, sits leaning back upon her sister, whose soul wrapped
in meditation on the past reads its lessons of wisdom, and the
lessons of wisdom read by the one are the true source of inspiration to the other.

Yes, the work is one. The contrast respects only external
circumstances. The Puritan pioneers of the West, in organizing Christian institutions there, have to study the same problem
which exercised the minds of the Connecticut fathers. That
problem may be propounded in a threefold form thus :

1. How shall beliefs be harmonized and defined in fixed

symbols of evangelical faith, without restricting private judgment, or abating the sense of personal accountability for
opinions?

2. How shall mutual co-operation and efficient combination
be secured, without infringing individual liberty or relieving
personal responsibility?

3. How shall the great agencies for the work of education
and the thorough evangelization of the country be established
and maintained, without centralizing power, stimulating selfish
ambition and chilling the glow of piety?

This is no place to enter upon the discussion of this problem. Yet it must and will surely be discussed. Earnest
minds are now actively engaged in its discussion. Nowhere
does the dispute run higher than in the region of country from
which I come. Just now, the work which most needs to be
done there seems to be hindered by the heat of this discussion
Yet we may believe that God will overrule even this, in the
final issue, for the more rapid extension of the Redeemer's kingdom. A *final* solution of the problem has not yet been found,
and will not be, very likely, till the millenium.

By the very statement of the question, in either form, we
make a balanced sentence. Two opposite tendencies of the
human mind are to be reconciled. A great and good end is to
be attained and a danger to be guarded against. Diverse an-
swers will be given, according as he who attempts the solution
leans, through the bias of natural temperament, education or
existing relations, to the one side or the other. So we have
two solutions proposed. *Ecclesiastical control* is the watchword,
on the one hand, and *untrammeled independency* on the other.
Each answer bears upon the problem, but the trouble is that
either taken by itself provides for only one side of the case.
Therefore, either pushed to its extreme is false and mischievous. The one, seeking efficiency by centralization tends towards the despotism of the Papacy. The other, guarding
liberty by standing aloof from necessary bonds and alliances,
tends towards latitudinarianism in matters of faith and separate, discordant and therefore inefficient action. We approxi-
mate a true solution only as we expand our views to embrace the
whole end to be attained. In other words we must free our-

selves from intolerance and exclusiveness and with genuine
catholicity of spirit, contemplate with single eye the wide-
sweeping interests of the Redeemer's kingdom. We need not
believe that all wisdom died with the fathers of Connecticut.
Yet who can fail, considering what they did in their day and
their circumstances, to wonder and rejoice that they were enabled with such large comprehension and clear foresight, to
provide so well for the interests involved in both parts of the
great question. I will not say that they reached a perfect
result, or that the form of organization adopted by them is to
be exactly imitated in all circumstances. But I do believe that
the happiest result will be reached in all cases, in proportion
as the question is met in the large, free spirit which animated
them. In this respect they present a worthy example.

As a last remark, I offer a thought suggested by some of the
historical facts presented this morning. It appeared that the
times of greatest agitation and hottest dispute were times of
great spiritual declension in the churches. The two things
are reciprocally cause and effect. Our grand safeguard therefore in all this work of building up the temple of God, which
is the church of Christ, is in *the pervading presence of the
Holy Ghost*, keeping each soul true in supreme devotion to
the Head, and therefore humble, and because humble and obe-
dient, *wise* to carry out his blessed plan. " Not by might nor
by power, but by my Spirit, saith the Lord." Let us all take
the lesson. May the Spirit of God ever dwell in these old
churches of Connecticut to make them live and flourish, for
centuries to come, on the foundations so wisely laid, centuries
ago! May the same Spirit animate and guide the sons of Connecticut and those associated with them in the present work of
laying foundations for the building of God in the newer states!
May the one Spirit thus make the work one and advance all
parts in harmony towards a blessed consummation for the good
of men and the glory of God!

THE SAFETY AND WISDOM OF COMPLETE RELIGIOUS LIBERTY, AS ILLUSTRATED IN CONNECTICUT DURING THE LAST ONE HUNDRED AND FIFTY YEARS.

BY REV S. W. S. DUTTON, D. D., NEW HAVEN, (THE MODERATOR.)

MR. SCRIBE:

I propose to speak briefly of the illustration, which we have in the history of the past one hundred and fifty years in Connecticut, of the safety and wisdom of complete religious liberty, and of the peril and folly of restricting it: or the safety and wisdom of leaving the reception and support of religion wholly to the voluntary principle, without any legal or civil compulsion.

This seems very plain to us. But it was not so to our fathers. From the beginning of the colonies down to 1818, in Connecticut, and to a later period in Massachusetts, religious liberty was more or less restricted. It was not till then complete. It advanced to completeness by slow steps, and *resisted* steps as it regards Congregationalists—steps directly against the protests, the prayers and the efforts of our fathers. In this we see that God in his providence is wiser than the wisest of men.

Let us look at some of these steps or stages in the progress of religious liberty here.

At the beginning, in these Puritan colonies, all were compelled to support the Congregational order, which was the order of religion established by the civil government. And not only that, none had any liberty to worship publicly in any other way. Moreover, in those colonies, Connecticut excepted, men could not vote or hold any civil office, unless they were members of some Congregational church. So close at first was the union of Church and State. The rigor of this rule began to be abated in 1708, when the General Assembly of the State passed the *Act of Toleration*, as it was called, by which all persons, who soberly dissented from the worship and ministry by law established, (i. e. the Congregational,) were permitted to enjoy the same liberty of conscience with the Dissenters in England, under the act of William and Mary; i. e. they were exempt from *punishment* for not conforming to the established religion, but not exempt from *taxation* for its support. By appearing before the County Court, and there in legal forms declaring their "sober dissent," they could obtain permission to have public worship in their own way, but were still obliged to pay for the support of the Congregational churches in the places of their residence. There was a further relaxation, as it regards Episcopalians, in 1727, and as it regards Quakers and Baptists in 1729. They were then exempted from taxation by the established churches, provided they attended on the worship of God in a tolerated society of their own denomination. But Congregationalists and Presbyterians had no such exemption. If, for any reason, any of them wished to secede from churches or societies, and worship by themselves, they were still obliged to pay their taxes for the support of the churches from which they had seceded. And even this small degree of liberty for seceding Congregationalists and Presbyterians, was restricted by special acts of the Legislature, in the time of the "Great Awakening" of 1740, through the influence of the "Old Lights," or opposers of that Awakening. The Legislature, to suppress enthusiasm, as was alleged, repealed, in 1743, the Act of Toleration, so that thereafter none could secede from the established ecclesiastical societies, (Congregational,) and worship by themselves, without punishment, unless they should ask and obtain *special permission from the Legislature;* which special permission, it was plainly intimated, *Congregationalists and Presbyterians* should not have. And in the previous year, 1742, for the same purpose of suppressing enthusiasm, i. e. suppressing the "New Lights," a law was passed to this effect, that if any *ordained* or *licensed* preacher should preach, or exhort, within the limits of any parish, without the consent of the pastor and majority of that parish, if he was from without the colony, he should be arrested and carried out of the colony as a vagrant. If he was from within the colony, he should be deprived of his salary, and that without any trial, simply upon information, whether true or false, lodged by any person, with the clerk of his parish. Also, if any person *not licensed* to preach, should *exhort*, within the limits of any parish, without the consent of the pastor and majority of that parish, he should for every such offense be bound to keep the peace, by any assistant or Justice of the Peace, in the penal sum of one hundred pounds.

The operation of these severe restrictions on religious liberty is so well illustrated in the history of the church of which I am pastor, the North Church in New Haven, that I will make a few references to that history.

That church was organized in 1742, by a Council consisting of five ministers, one of whom was Dr. Bellamy, and was composed of members who favored the revival of religion which was then in progress, and seceded from the First Church in New Haven on account of the opposition of the pastor of that church, Rev. Mr. Noyes, and of the majority of the church to that revival, and to its chief promoter, the celebrated Whitfield. Yet they could gain no permission to form an ecclesiastical society, nor to hold public worship. They did have public worship however, but under much oppression. For eighteen years they were taxed for the support of the church which they had left, besides bearing a heavy voluntary burden for the support of their own church. Then, for a large part of that eighteen years they could have no regular minister, at least not without having him molested, fined and punished by the officers of the law. For attempting to preach to that church, Rev. Samuel Finley—afterward President of Princeton College, whose name is familiar to all who have read Dr. John Mason's eloquent Contrast between the Death of David Hume and that of Samuel Finley—was arrested and carried out of the colony as a vagrant. He had previously been treated in the same way for preaching to a church which seceded, or "separated," as the term was, for the same purpose, in Milford. The tradition is, that Finley having been arrested on Saturday, in anticipation of his preaching, was kept in custody by the officer of justice on the Sabbath, and by him was taken to Rev. Mr. Noyes's church, and made to sit in the aisle—probably to expose him as an offender against the laws, and to give him the privilege of hearing preaching and praying specially designed for his benefit.

Great was the hostility against the "Separates" of that day, who, according to our present views of religious liberty, should have been freely allowed to secede and form distinct churches; and whose motive was, to say the least, honorable to their Christian zeal and devotion. And their oppression was often severe, as is seen by the laws enacted and enforced against them. One or two illustrations of this hostile feeling occur to me. The father of one of the deacons of the new (the Separate) church in New Haven was deacon of the First Church. The child of the son died. The father, in a written note, declined to attend the funeral, because the son belonged to the "New Light" church! After the frame of the "New Light" meeting house was prepared to be raised, all the long pieces of timber were cut in two in the night. The "New Lights" replaced them by others, over which they kept guard. The late Chief Justice Daggett used to illustrate this state of feeling by an anecdote, which I will relate. He said that his father, who resided in the town of Attleboro, Mass., attended the Congregational church; but being a Baptist in sentiment, he had some sympathy with the "Separates," many of whom were, or became, Baptists. Rev. Mr. Thacher, a minister of the vicinity, preaching on a certain Sabbath in Attleboro, in giving a summary catalogue of those who would be excluded from the kingdom of heaven, ended off with the expression, "*and all Separates.*" Mr. Daggett, meeting him during the week, said to him: "Mr. Thacher, I did not like that passage in your sermon, last Sabbath, in which you classed the Separates with thieves and liars, and others who would be excluded from the kingdom of heaven." "Oh," said he, "Brother Daggett, I meant those who are separate *from all righteousness!*" "Ah! Was that your meaning? Then, I think that when you preach here again, you had better explain it: for you was understood to have a very different meaning." Mr. Thacher's reply may as well be added: for, though it does not further illustrate the point in hand, it does illustrate something else. "Brother Daggett, I am well aware that I am very liable to err. But, Brother Daggett, I have *no knack at confessing!*" There are many who have "no knack at confessing," especially men of strong will.

17

The Saybrook Platform, or the consociational system, was at that time made an instrument of restricting religious liberty. The Presbyterian or strict construction of its articles prevailed at that period, which made the consociation a *judicial and authoritative* tribunal. And this power was used to prevent the formation of "New Light" churches; the ruling party insisting that no new churches should be formed, unless they would agree to be bound by the Saybrook Platform, i. e. be consociated, and so far forth give up their Congregational liberty.

In the year 1784, another of the steps toward complete religious liberty, which I am noticing, was taken. The legal establishment of the Saybrook Platform was abrogated, leaving all free to worship with whatever denomination they preferred. All, however, were still taxed for the support of some church, the church of their choice. In the year 1818, when the new constitution was formed, this last restriction was removed; and religion was left entirely to voluntary support. A plan which the experience of forty years has proved to be by far the best. And yet our fathers feared it, and protested, prayed and strove against it. They dared not trust complete religious liberty. They feared to leave religion to the free reception and support of the people. They thought that it would not do not to compel men to support that which they disbelieve. I have lately read over again a sermon, preached by Dr. Lyman Beecher, during the period when the question of the new constitution was pending, in which with all his eloquence he sets forth the plan of leaving religion to voluntary support, as one which would open the floodgates of ruin on the state.

I need spend only a few moments, in conclusion, in adverting to the evils of these restrictions on religious liberty, as they have appeared in our history.

1. The strict union of church and state which existed at the first was very disastrous. As only members of the established churches were allowed to vote or hold office, unrenewed men were tempted to become members of the church; membership was construed, also, to include all baptized persons; and then, in order that children of parents not members in full standing, not participants of the Lord's supper, might be baptized, and so be

called members so far forth as to vote and hold civil office, the pernicious "*Half-way-covenant*" was invented and practised. Under such influences, the vital church was merged to a lamentable extent in a mass of unconverted members. Unconverted men, to some extent, were in the ministry. The distinction between those renewed by the grace of God and the unrenewed, between the real church and the world, was in a great measure obliterated; and the standard, both of religion and morals, became very low,—so low that it seemed that nothing but the extraordinary grace of God in the great Awakening of 1740 could have saved the churches from apostasy.

2. These restrictions, or some of them, tended to decrease Congregationalism and to increase other sects. At one period, as I have shown, if Congregationalists, dissatisfied with the administration of the church to which they belonged, seceded and formed another *Congregational* church, they were doubly taxed—*i. e.* for the new church and the old one also—by law for the old one, and voluntarily for the new one; whereas, if they formed a church of another denomination, they were released from taxation to the church which they had left. This, especially in the time of the great Awakening, resulted in the formation of many Baptist churches. The larger part of the Separate churches became Baptist, not because they preferred distinctive Baptist principles, but because the Baptists were Congregational in government, and for the most part in doctrine, and they, by calling themselves Baptist, could escape the oppression of double taxation. Indeed, the formation of those Separate churches, and the earlier growth of the Baptist denomination in this state, was little more than a practical protest against the prevalent violation of religious liberty.

3. That state of the laws which obliged all to pay for the support of some church, but allowed them to choose which, was found to favor the laxer kinds of religion. Infidels and Nothingarians, compelled to support some kind of religion and allowed to choose which, of course chose the *least strict*, both as to orthodoxy and practice. They practised on the principle of an infidel, who attended Matthew Hale Smith's church, when he was a Universalist minister in Hartford. Said he to Mr. Smith: "I go to hear you preach. But I don't believe your

doctrine. I go to hear you, *because your doctrine is nearest to nothing of any that I know of!*" This result, which I have described, was what might have been expected from such a state of the laws. And accordingly it has been found in Massachusetts especially, that the repeal of the law for the compulsory support of religion has been a very severe blow to Unitarianism, so prevalent there, and to all the laxer forms of Christianity.

On the other hand, it has been found since religion has been put upon the voluntary principle and the free choice of men for support, that men generally have more interest in it, and are more active to extend it. And voluntary enterprise and generosity in the work of Home Missions have done far more to build up waste places, and to prevent places from becoming waste, than was ever done, or could be done, by force of law.

But my time is up, and I must conclude. Let us lay to heart the great lesson of this subject, and *have entire faith, under God, in full religious freedom.*

CONSOCIATED CONGREGATIONALISM.

BY REV. JOSEPH ELDRIDGE, D. D., NORFOLK.

MR. MODERATOR:

Congregationalism, Consociated Congregationalism is my theme.

I love Congregationalism of every description, but acknowledge a preference for Consociated Congregationalism; that of Connecticut, as distinguished from that of Massachusetts. My preference is not a hereditary feeling; for I was born and received my early training in the Old Bay State. It is the result of my observation of its working in Litchfield County during a period of more than a quarter of a century. The Congregational churches of that county have been consociated from the beginning. During nearly the entire period of their history, they have settled and dismissed their pastors, and transacted all that ecclesiastical business, that is elsewhere performed by Councils, through the agency of the Consociation. In proof of the salutary operation of the system, I appeal with confidence to the general character of their pastors, past and present,—and to the condition of the churches.

Consociation has supplied those churches with a succession of ministers, competent and orthodox, faithful and devoted. Among the fathers, were Halleck, Griffin, Hooker, Bellamy, Backus, and others. There were giants in those days. Speaking of my immediate predecessors and cotemporaries, I can testify to their soundness in character and doctrine, to their fidelity and usefulness.

The churches in that connection have been a sort of seed plot for the West; and subjected to a constant drain from emigration. Yet they have lived and flourished. They have been the lights in their own region, and have done their part in originating and sustaining the Christian and benevolent enterprises of modern times, both domestic and foreign. The best evidence that a machine is adapted to any end—is to be found in the fact that it successfully accomplishes the end in question.

Consociated Congregationalism, thus judged by its fruits, challenges our approval ; but Mr. Moderator, I think the *rationale* of its successful working may be explained.

Consociation is a mixed body—in which the clerical and lay elements exist in equal proportions. It is a permanent body on the same ground. Its discretion is limited—its powers being defined, and its duties specified. Its mixed character, being composed equally of laymen and clergymen, is at once a check and protection to both parties. Neither can easily infringe upon the rights and privileges of the other. Then the speculative wisdom of the clergy and the practical experience of the laymen both come into useful play in all matters of interest that come before the Consociation.

The permanence of the Consociation on the same ground where its action takes effect is a very important circumstance. An independent Council may be packed in reference to the object for which it is called ; a Consociation cannot be. A Council has no permanent existence, and consequently no character to maintain. Its decision having been given, its members disperse in every direction never to meet more. It is soon out of sight, and out of hearing of any trouble that its proceedings may create.

Consociation, on the contrary, has a permanent existence ; it has a character to sustain for intelligence, impartiality and consistency. The members of it are to remain in the vicinity of the place where the action takes effect ; they are to see and hear the results of that action, and to be held in a degree responsible for them. Still further, the pastors and representatives of the churches know that their decision in each case is to be put on record—that it will be a rod in pickle, a precedent to be applied in their own case, should occasion arise. Who that knows anything of human nature can doubt that these circumstances will tend to produce caution, deliberation, and fairness ? Then Consociation is not left to unlimited discretion ; not merely to the common law of usage and undefined customs. Its powers are defined, its duties are specified, and it acts under a constitution that has been framed and accepted by the churches themselves. The moral authority of their decisions is thereby greatly enhanced.

I have found Consociation also eminently conducive to mutual acquaintance and sympathy among the pastors and churches embraced in its limits. They are often summoned together—they become acquainted with each others state, condition, interests, duties, and the best means to be employed to promote the great cause of the Lord. These matters are discussed, good feeling is elicited, and judicious plans are struck out and adopted—and executed. We recall the good men that have preceded us, we anticipate those who are to come after us, we are stimulated by our recollections of the past, we are animated with hope for the future. (Here the Moderator of the Association said—Your time is up!) Well, then, in my judgment, Consociation is a precious legacy of our ancestors, and I pray God, it may be transmitted to the latest generation of our posterity.

THE LESSONS OF OUR DAY AS SUGGESTED BY THE LEADING AIM OF OUR FATHERS.

BY REV. SAMUEL WOLCOTT, PROVIDENCE, R. I.

MR. MODERATOR:

I am present at this festival as *a son of Connecticut*—a relationship which has always seemed to me so near akin to the family connection, that the two have been scarcely separate in my heart. As such, I feel an interest in her churches and in the history of Congregationalism within her borders, not merely as embraced in the graphic delineation which a master's hand has sketched to-day—the rise and the decline of that Consociationism, which is such a favorite with the respected speaker, who has just preceded me; but also as embodied in the forms of that earlier and broader Congregationalism, which came to Connecticut with her first churches, and will be found, I trust, abiding with her last. Thus comprehensively viewed, what collection of churches in our land comprises, in its records, a more complete exhibition of the elements which, through a protracted and eventful period, have entered into the very constitution of a civil society, and made the history of a community memorable, than this? What were the history of Connecticut, without *this* history, and God's hand therein? The heroic days of this Commonwealth, the days when her direct influence in the national confederacy, of which she was one of the smallest members, was almost unsurpassed; when her Trumbulls, and Griswolds, and Ellsworths, and Shermans were her representative statesmen, and Washington leaned upon her counsels in the cabinet, and her armies in the field—those days, with all their fruitful achievements, had their root and growth and fair development in the faith and polity of her churches, here represented. Through the combined instrumentality of the school, the college, and the sanctuary, were molded by these churches the characters that adorn her historic eras.

The lesson of the hour is obvious to us all, and the simple narrative which has been rehearsed in our ears is its best enforcement. It will be conceded by all who are familiar with our annals, that for the agencies which have advanced and elevated us as a people, and for the results accomplished which constitute our distinctive crown and glory, we are mainly indebted, under God, to the views and aims which brought our forefathers to this land—to the tendencies impressed upon our early life and forming character, upon all our sentiments and habits, by their cherished principles. And this admission involves another, viz : that in a faithful adherence to the course on which the favor of heaven has so manifestly rested, and which has been fraught with such signal benefits in the past, we shall find our continued safety and permanent prosperity.

This gathering, then, is designed to remind us of the leading object which governed the men who sought their homes in this land and planted these churches and gave tone to our history, and to bring us into fresh sympathy with the spirit which animated them. Nor can we be too often reminded of the truth, familiar as it may be, that the ships which brought over the Pilgrim Fathers did not convey to the savage coast of New England companies of trading adventurers, or individual emigrants, seeking each a separate and selfish end. They brought the household, with all its dependent members, the aged and the young, and with all its dear and sacred ties. They brought the civil government in an organic form, with its written constitution and its appointed officers. They brought the Christian church, with its simple, scriptural polity, its covenant, its sacraments, and its pastor and teacher. The vessels which bore to their several destinations the early colonists of New England, came freighted—with what ? With social, civil, and religious institutions.

In the quiet and venerable churchyard of the ancient town of Windsor, rest the mortal remains of that company of Pilgrims, already described, who traversed the unbroken forests of Massachusetts, and accomplished, with untold hardships, in a weary fortnight, a journey which may now be made with ease in four or five hours. Some of them had left in the Old World homes of comfort and affluence, but they cheerfully

18

shared the toils, privations, and perils of the way; and on reaching the banks of the River, they gratefully welcomed the common termination of their earthly journeyings.

> " They thought on England's fields of green,
> Nor wept that Ocean rolled between,
> But praised the Lord their guide, whose hand
> Had brought them to their promised land."

Along those smiling meadows they reared their humble dwellings; on that swelling upland they built their sanctuary; in that lone cemetery they made their graves. Beneath a monument, the tablet of which has been piously renewed, sleeps the dust of the learned and sainted *Warham*, their beloved and venerated Pastor. On another monument which has happily escaped the ravages of time, is inscribed the name of a worthy fellow-pilgrim,* one of the first Magistrates of the Colony. Around these are scattered the rude memorials of others of the company, men and women, who left the shores of England together in the spring of 1630. Here, undisturbed by the noise of the loaded trains which thunder daily along the iron track by their side, startling with strange echoes that sweet and sacred solitude, they rest, pastor and flock, where two centuries ago they laid them down together, in the joyful hope of an associated rising on the morning of the resurrection. But the bond of this tender relation, as has been stated here to-day, was formed before they left their native land. After their passage had been engaged, they were granted the privilege of assembling in an apartment of the new hospital at Plymouth, and forming a church organization. They came as such, with their confession of faith and covenant, and enjoyed church ordinances and pastoral ministrations on shipboard. It was not a company of individual passengers—it was a church of Christ that crossed the ocean in the good ship which brought them over. And other companies, that were not distinct organizations, were actuated by the same principles and purposes; they all came to plant permanent institutions in these wild solitudes which had been reserved for the purpose—the only spot in the world where *such* institutions could have a fair trial and room for full expansion.

---

* Henry Wolcott.

If our privileges and blessings are to be perpetuated, it is most evident that a work is to be done in this generation, similar to that which our honored ancestors did in theirs, and that this service is to be repeated in coming generations, until our territory is subdued and our population evangelized. The principles and the institutions which were worth transporting across the ocean at such cost and peril, are worth preserving at every cost, and worth transplanting in the newly settled portions of our land at every personal sacrifice. The spirit of emigration to our Western States,—now Western, but soon to be Central, and the seat of empire and of destiny to our Republic—is not to be stimulated as a spirit of commercial speculation and private gain; but as a spirit of patriotic, philanthropic, and Christian enterprise, it deserves our fostering care and warmest encouragement. There, as here, must be laid the deep and broad foundations of those institutions which cluster around a living faith, and with which are identified the stability, purity, and safety of the community. That faith, which is consecrated to us by hallowed memories, and which has been the source and basis of our highest prosperity, we are to preserve and propagate, guarding it alike against the "rampant ecclesiasticism" which would corrupt its simplicity, and the more hateful despotism which would crush its moral life. We are to disseminate it in its integrity, and through it secure, if possible, to the new settlements of the West the same auspicious beginnings with the early settlements of the East.

I cannot but think that it is in this field that Connecticut has done her greatest work, reproducing herself in the young and growing West. Within a few years, as I was passing through the thriving towns and villages of northern Ohio, I was constantly and pleasantly reminded of my native State. More than once have I thought of her with pride and gratitude, as I have stood on the gentle ascent which overlooks the most charming scene in Illinois, the site of a college which a band of her youthful students consecrated to sound learning and to Christ, and which does not dishonor its parentage as a daughter of Yale. And she has her memorial in the New England churches, and Plymouth churches, and nameless Christian churches, springing up over all the boundless West, and whose filial greetings have reached us here to-day. I deem it worthy of special mention, that she has furnished settlers, good men and true, for that dark "Border Line," along which the stern resolve of Christian freemen, under God, now holds to the angry surges of the menacing curse of our Republic the relation of that decree of the Almighty which binds the ocean tides— "Hitherto shalt thou come, *but no further.*"

We have every encouragement to prosecute this good work of Christian emigration and colonization. While colonists and emigrants who have gone forth in the spirit of worldly adventure, or in quest of gain, have met with various, and often, adverse fortunes, never, to my knowledge, have they borne with them a principle which was vital, in behalf of which they were ready to dare and to suffer, and failed, sooner or later, to effect its permanent establishment. The history of New England, from the day that the Mayflower moored in Plymouth harbor, is the glorious witness to this truth. Our own shores are its special monuments; for our pleasant homes and sanctuaries, our dearest possessions and privileges, are the fair product of that tender germ of freedom, which distressed men brought across these waters, and planted in this solitude, and which has here expanded and blossomed and ripened into forms of social beauty and the fruits of a religious liberty, which is now the boast of our land, and the immortal treasure of our age and of the ages. And what is this banded emigration of New England Freemen, but the exodus of another Pilgrim Brotherhood, bearing with them the principles of our fathers, and transplanting to the fertile bosom of the far West the perfected institutions of civil and religious freedom? May we not believe, that the guardian Power, that brought out of oppression the choice vine that was planted on these coasts, and which has here sent out her boughs unto the sea, and her branches unto the river. will watch over and protect it there, and prepare room before it, and cause it to take deep root and fill the land, until the hills of Kansas and Nebraska shall be covered with the shadow of it, and the boughs thereof shall wave on the summits of Oregon like the goodly cedars of Lebanon?

I cannot refrain from a grateful recognition of the Providence which has assembled us for such a celebration on this spot, combining with the unrivaled charms of the natural landscape and the pleasant social life that dwells beneath its shades, the associations of a town distinctively Puritan in its origin and history, in which the principles that are dear to us have had an ascendency from the beginning—represented to-day in her sons, appreciated and honored throughout the State, and represented in her model schools and pleasant sanctuaries; and blessed, early and late, with the special influences of the Holy Spirit. Have we not been brought here to-day, that we may have before us a happy illustration of the legitimate fruits of our system, and an example of the kind of community which it must be our aim to establish across the breadth of our Continent, from shore to shore?

THE CONGREGATIONAL POLITY ADAPTED BOTH TO INDIVIDUAL AND TO UNITED ACTION IN THE CAUSE OF CHRIST.

BY REV. JOSEPH P. THOMPSON, D. D., NEW YORK CITY.

MR. MODERATOR:

No careful reader of the New Testament can fail to be impressed with these two facts, as comprising the method and adaptation of Christianity as a working system, viz. : The *intense personality* of the Gospel in its instructions, addresses, appeals, commands and promises ; and the *spiritual unity* and *moral co-operation* of all who accept it. The feature of *individualism* is always prominent. All that the Gospel is, in its blessings, its hopes, its promises—all that the Gospel requires, in its obligations and commands, pertains to the individual soul. Each man renewed in Christ is made a king and priest unto God, and each disciple is commissioned to preach the Gospel to every creature.

Out of this individual, personal union with and resemblance to Christ, arises the moral affinity of all true believers, which draws them together in associations for his service and glory, and combines them for more efficient action.

It is the beauty of Congregationalism, that it combines in their just proportions these two features or elements of the embodied Christianity of the New Testament. This polity recognizes to the full the individualism of which I have spoken. It looks for the elements of a church to individual souls renewed and sanctified ; then it unites these under natural laws of association, with Christ as their common head ; but in the association called a church, it guards every right, reserves every privilege, of the individual. Moreover, by the very nature of the association—one of equality in power, privilege and responsibility—it developes, in the highest degree, individual character. Now, wherever organic unity is placed first in order, the source of vital power in the organization itself is wanting ; for the vital power resides not in the organization, but in individual souls composing that organization, and making it vital through their personal union with Christ, by his Spirit. Ecclesiasticism, under whatever form, cripples, if it does not destroy this power. The moment the church as an organization, is preferred before the individual as a Christian, the church stands in the way of its own life, and hinders the power of the Gospel. This may be true of the simplest as well as the most elaborate system; for as there may be just as much of formalism in the manner in which the Quaker takes his seat in meeting, as in the bows and genu-flexions with which the stoled priest performs the mass—just as much pride in the Quakeress when selecting the most subdued mouse-color for her shawl or bonnet, as in Eugenie when ordaining a new fashion for the world ;—so there may be just as much of Ecclesiasticism in the administration of our simple polity, as in the most imperious Churchism. Indeed our very liberty of association may become a bondage. The tendency to association and to organic action has been pushed in our times as far as it will bear. No man can go beyond me in valuing that principle for all its legitimate ends ; but how natural it is for us when we desire to accomplish a particular object, to form an Association for that purpose, and imagine that the thing is done. But this is just like the many patent inventions for perpetual motion, which are perfect in every respect but one—they will not move. How much rhetoric, of which I confess my full share, was wasted over the telegraphic cable ; but just at the moment when we were chaining the sea, and girdling the world, and flashing intelligence in advance of time, the magnetism oozed out, and the batteries refused to speak. We frame our complicated organizations, nicely adjusted, wheel within wheel, but they stand a gazing stock, or a monument of folly and extravagance ; but when the living spirit enters within the wheels, they move, not with the noise and clatter of human machinery, but are lifted up from the earth, and their noise is as the voice of the Almighty, the voice of speech, as the noise of a host.

Whenever any organization, however wisely planned, however piously designed, comes to regard itself as *indispensable* to the cause of Christ, this is a sign that the time has come when it should be *dispensed with*. The laudation of associations or societies, the making these paramount or essential to individual churches, and to the efficiency of individual Christians, the attempt to submerge individualism in mere organization, argues that the time has come for modifying the principle of associated effort, or for making associations conform to the laws and principles of the New Testament. And here lies the power of our Congregational system. The remedy for an abuse of the principle of voluntary association, does not lie in Ecclesiasticism. *That* were even a greater evil, for how tremendous the pressure, and how corrupting the influence of Ecclesiasticism on the individual Christian life, all history testifies. .But this system, keeping the individual alive, making him conscious of his rights, and privileges, and duties under the Gospel, supplies the safe corrective for all such evils.

Professor Barrows, in his admirable portraiture of the New Testament polity, said of it, that it had no power as against kings and temporal power. But is this so? Is not the individual soul, living for truth, greater than the organized power against it? Is not the simple association of believing, praying men, for the worship of God and the defence of his truth, mightier than church-and-state organization against them? When Algernon Sydney was condemned by the brutal Jeffries for having written, in an unpublished manuscript, that kings have no right to govern except for the good of the people, and laid his hoary head upon the block, he made his appeal to God and to posterity. Ten years after, the English Revolution answered that appeal. A new dynasty came in at the call of the people. The parliament effaced from his name the attainder of treason. The liberties of England to-day bear witness that the martyr Sydney was mightier than the House of Stuart. Barrowe, Penry, Greenwood, the noble pioneers of religious freedom and of our Congregational polity, seemed weaker in their time than the judges and prelates who shut them up in prison and condemned them to the scaffold. But which lives to-day as a power in the world, that persecuting ecclesiasticism of Elizabeth, or that free polity of those heroic souls? Our brother said also, that this system is weak for wire-pulling. And so it is;—but it is not weak *against the wire pullers*. For when they have held their caucuses and laid their plans to triumph over individual rights, and to manage everything in their own way, men trained in that simple regard for truth and duty, which our system inculcates, bolt up before them some great principle of God's word, some fact of Christian obligation, and in the attempt to pull this down, the wires snap and the wire-pullers fall to the ground discomfitted.

De Tocqueville, who was a most sagacious and philosophical observer of our institutions, remarked that the individualism fostered by democracy tends to Atheism. This may be true of a purely natural individualism. So it may be that physical science and speculative philosophy, apart from religion, with their freedom of investigation and their pride of discovery, tend to Atheism, though I deny that this is the *legitimate* tendency of any science, and where there is Atheism in science, it is found rather in Pantheistic tendencies, which neutralize or absorb the individual. But we speak of a *sanctified* individualism, which proceeds from God and lives in God, so that the man is nothing in himself, but everything in Christ and because Christ dwells in him. There is no danger of Atheism here, for the whole strength of the individual Christian lies in his humility, and his dependence. And for the same reason, this secures the highest conservatism; for he who has the weightiest interests committed to his trust, a soul to save, a kingdom on earth to win for his Master, a kingdom in heaven to enjoy as his reward, will not knowingly thrust aside or destroy anything that God approves or values or has appointed for the good of man. This sanctified individualism also favors the moral co-operation of Christians under the best forms, leaving them free to choose the time and mode of their organic action. Who has not felt to-day that the men who framed that Platform whose history has been reviewed, were greater than the Platform which they made; and that the instrument made for the exigency of their times derives for us much of its value from their characters. Let us go down then, from this glad fellowship one with another, from this high and sacred fellowship with the illustrious dead, with a renewed determination to be as individuals, faithful to our times, as they were to theirs; and to vitalize our churches, under God, by summoning them anew to the highest individual consecration and the most zealous and efficient, because the simplest and the purest united effort for the advancement and the glory of His kingdom.

19

THE MISSION OF OUR CHURCHES AS DEFINED BY OUR HISTORY.

BY REV. WM. I. BUDINGTON, D. D., OF BROOKLYN, N. Y.

MR. MODERATOR :

The design of history is to teach every man and every body of men their true mission. We who are assembled here, in this scene of commemoration, ourselves a part of history, in the midst of its solemn processes, do not come to celebrate a consummation already completed, but to feel for and find the threads of influence which are passing through our hands into the immeasurable future before us ;—we look behind, that we may look forward and go forward. We do not claim, we scarce need to say it, that we are *the* church ; we have no disposition to fence off other claimants from the common heritage. We have no wish even to determine which of all the various churches, bearing the name of Christ, has the most honorable position, and renders the most distinguished service in the work of Christ's kingdom. Our purpose is simply by a study of the past, to ascertain, who and what we are ; the principles we have inherited, the work we have done, and the contributions which we, as a distinct communion, are to make to the church of the future ; and how to do our work wisely and well.

The great truth, that confronts us all, is that we have received and are to transmit to others, the common faith of Christ's church, in connection with the simplest and freest polity which any denomination of Christians has inherited. We have to combine the largest liberty with the strictest and broadest fellowship. This describes our danger and our glory. We find our being, and are to exercise our mission, in freedom as between man and man, and fidelity as toward God. In common with all orthodox Christians we are to contend earnestly for the faith as delivered to the saints ; while more than others we are to contend for the rights of private judgment, and the independence of local churches. Fidelity to our distinctive mission, therefore, if we intelligently apprehend it, will not only make us catholic, but make catholicity our necessary manifestation. Polity with us is so subordinate to doctrine, that in many places and for long periods Congregationalism has been synonymous with orthodoxy, and we have scarcely been conscious what our polity is, and when conscious, oftimes indifferent to it; and where its distinctive features have been zealously espoused, it has been because of their supposed indispensableness to the reorganization of the church upon a catholic basis.

If this be true, it will not be disputed that catholicity itself requires us to move on in the line of our history. We believe that we are carrying through the centuries a most precious and indispensable contribution to the church of the future. Other churches have something we have not, we deny not to other and fellow laborers, the honor and blessedness of bringing each their contribution to this great building of God; we shall not contend with them about the relative values of our several tributes, we will not say that God hath provided " some better thing for us," we are content to believe, " that they without us should not be made perfect." God has set men in families and families in states, and attachment to the family does not conflict with fidelity to the state. Just so is it in the household of faith, our fidelity to the Christian family, in which the Providence and grace of God has inserted us, will but make us the more serviceable to that church which has the world for its field and the ages for its history. We are to contribute to the solution of a problem, which touches the central life of the coming age; it is to determine whether an untrammelled freedom of the individual conscience and of the local church can be made to consist with conservation of the truth, and the strictest Christian fellowship. How much more important will be our office-work and function among the tribes of Israel, if we shall be able to show that the gospel of Christ unrestrained by governmental rule has been preserved in its greatest purity, and has freed itself most easily from error, when it has been connected with the largest liberties of the individual and the church. We have entered

upon an age of critical investigation, and of rapid advancement in knowledge ; tastes the most differing and activities the
most diverse, are mingled and opposed ; every polity will
be subjected to severe strains ; but the most rigorous, the most
minutely prescriptive, that which offers an inelastic mold, to
which the church's thought and action must shape themselves,
will infallibly be broken in pieces. Let us therefore be true to
the traditions of our churches, and show our catholicity by
doing well the work which Providence assigns us.

Let us cherish our history. It is a great and distinctive advantage, that we have behind us the beginning and growth
of an orderly history ; that our civil and ecclesiastical histories
are similar, that they spring from the same fountains. We
ought not to forget that our fathers came here, to practise "the
positive part of church reformation." They laid down principles, which we are bringing more and more to the test ; they
began to apply them, and we are to carry on the application in
the new method our new circumstances require. Let us honor
our fathers' memory, by preserving their memorials ; and let
us unite, under the auspices of the " Library Association," in
gathering together our treasures, and making their rooms in
Boston our historic galleries. Let us also follow our brethren
westward, with our sympathies, and our co-operation ; and encourage them to build upon their own foundations, by making
the " Union" at New York the almoner of our charity, and the
bond of our fellowship. Let us at the same time encourage,
around these earlier homes and more ancient seats, the full and
free expression of every grace that God vouchsafes our members, and every endowment of mind and taste by which He
has enriched us. Our maxim should be, not repression, but
development and comprehension. Freedom is the summer
sunshine. Power is a winter's sun ; and the most it can effect
is but the growth of a hot-house.

But suffer me to add one more suggestion, now that these
commemorative services are about to end. We leave behind
us the century and a half of our history, and begin amid hopes
and fears, the experience of another half century. We who have
taken part in these services, and have been gathering up the
influences of this occasion, shall drop by the way, we shall not

live to carry on the history we now begin to its issues; but
with us or without us, it will go on, and the centennial or semi-
centennial will come round again, and amid those future com-
memorations, what shall be the aspect of our churches, and of
the Redeemer's kingdom? It may be that our posterity will
re-assemble here, to review their past, which is in part our future; and shall it be amid joy or sorrow? We know that
some things will be here to welcome them, as they have us.
This leafy month of June will return with its beauty and its
fragrance. These broad and shady streets, these hospitable
homes, this picturesque environment of hills will remain to
attract and charm them, as they do us. The monument of
Uncas will be here, and it shall be re-visited by young men
and maidens of that coming day. But what shall be the spirit
that is to actuate them, and amid what scenes of millennial
glory in the earth shall they come? Will other Lathrops and
Huntingtons, and Winslows and Aitchisons, and Tracys be
treading these streets, and gathering in these consecrated
places? Will the treasured dust of Norwich in other generations be left to hallow other and distant lands, and her cemetery claim a share in almost every acre throughout the missionary field? The answer to this question is left in part to
us; and upon the spirit with which we return to our respective charges and spheres of labor, will depend, in some measure, the spirit with which our children re-assemble here the
next century!

HISTORICAL PAPERS.

MEETINGS OF THE GENERAL ASSOCIATION.

BY REV. MYRON N. MORRIS, REGISTER, WEST HARTFORD.

The records of the General Association of Connecticut, now in the hands of the Register, commence with the year 1738. From a note in the CONGREGATIONAL ORDER, page 67, it appears that "Hartford was designated as the place where the first meeting should be held for the purpose of organization. The delegates met there accordingly on the 18th of May, 1709. Where the meeting was held in 1710 is not certainly known; the presumption is it was held in New Haven. It was in New London in 1711, in Fairfield 1712, Wethersfield 1713, Milford 1714, Norwich 1715, and Stratford 1717. Where it was in 1716, 1718, 1719, 1720 and 1721, we are unable to state." "When it met twice a year, as it did from 1721 until 1735, unless 1732 be an exception, it met at Hartford and New Haven." The place of meeting in 1735 is not known. In 1736 it was in Killingworth, and in 1737 in Middletown.

No record appears to have been made of the Associational sermon previous to 1770. It had been the custom, however, to have an annual sermon, or "public lecture," so called, as appears from the following action taken in 1768. "The Association, finding some inconveniences attending the present practice of this body in delaying the public lecture upon these occasions to the second day of the session, ordered that it be declared as our advice that, for the future, the lecture be attended on the first day of the session." Formerly, and for many years it was the practice to have two or three sermons, besides that to the Association, preached by clergymen who, as delegates from other bodies, or otherwise, were providentially present.

The following table gives, so far as has been ascertained, the place of meeting, and the names of the Moderator, Scribes and Preacher for each year from 1738 to the present time:

YR.	PLACE.	MODERATOR.	SCRIBE.	PREACHER..
1738	Stratford,	William Burnham,	Thomas Clapp.	
1739	{ Appointed at Wallingford, no record,			
1740	Hartford,	Timothy Edwards,	Ashbel Woodbridge.	
1741	Lebanon,	Eleazer Williams,	Ephraim Little.	
1742	New London,	Eliphalet Adams,	Benjamin Colton.	
1743	Fairfield,	Jacob Hemmingway,	William Russel.	
1744	Durham,	Nathaniel Chauncey,	William Russel.	
1745	Newington,	Benjamin Colton,	Elnathan Whitman.	
1746	Lebanon, (Goshen,)	Stephen Steele,	Ephraim Little.	
1747	{ Saybrook, W'st Parish, now Westbrook,	Jared Eliot,	Jonathan Merrick.	
1748	Reading,	Benjamin Colton,	Sam'l Whittelsey Jr.	
1749	New Haven,		William Russel.	No business done, so few present.
1750	West Hartford,	William Russel,	John Trumbull.	
1751	Windham,	William Gaylord,	Noah Welles.	
1752	Killingworth,	Jared Eliot,	Thomas Ruggles,	
1753	{ Fairfield, West Parish, now Green's Farms,	Noah Hobart,	Samuel Whittelsey.	
1754	{ New Cheshire, in Wallingford, now Cheshire,	Samuel Hall,	Timothy Pitkin.	
1755	{ Middletown, North Society, now Cromwell,	Jared Eliot,	Noah Welles.	
1756	Windham,	Solomon Williams,	Elnathan Whitman.	
1757	{ Stonington, East Society,	Jacob Eliot,	{ Joseph Fish. EbenezerDevotion.	
1758	{ No Record, appointed at Woodbury,			
1759	Danbury,	Moses Dickinson,	Elnathan Whitman.	
1760	North Branford,	Samuel Hall,	Elnathan Whitman.	
1761	Hartford,	Jared Eliot,	Elnathan Whitman.	
1762	Mansfield,	George Beckwith,	Noah Welles.	
1763	Lyme, 3d Parish	Ephraim Little,	Ebenezer Devotion.	
1764	Woodbury,	Jedediah Mills,	Robert Ross.	
1765	Norwalk,	Edward Eells,	Izrahiah Wetmore.	
1766	Guilford,	Thomas Ruggles,	Edward Eells.	
1767	Middletown,	Thomas Ruggles,	William Russel.	
1768	Coventry,	Solomon Williams,	Noah Welles.	
1769	Norwich,	Solomon Williams,	Ebenezer Devotion.	

YR.	PLACE.	MODERATOR.	SCRIBE.	PREACHER.
1770	New Milford,	Daniel Humphrey,	Robert Ross,	Jonathan Lee.
1771	Reading,	Joseph Bellamy, D.D.	Simon Waterman,	
1772	Westbury, now Watertown,	Elnathan Whitman,	Samuel Lockwood,	Benj. Woodbridge.
1773	New Cambridge, now Bristol,	George Beckwith,	Benj'n Boardman,	Hezekiah Bissel.
1774	Mansfield,	Benjamin Throop,	Ebenezer Baldwin,	James Cogswell.
1775	Norwich, New Concord Soc'y, now Bozrah,	Elnathan Whitman,	Elizur Goodrich,	Eliph't Huntington
1776	Cornwall,	John Trumbull,	Ebenezer Baldwin,	
1777	Fairfield,	Nathaniel Bartlett,	Samuel Wales,	Enoch Huntington.
1778	Northford,	Joseph Bellamy, D.D.	Andrew Eliot,	Nicholas Street.
1779	Haddam,	Benj. Pomeroy, D.D.	David Ely,	Benj. Pomeroy, D.D.
1780	Tolland,	Samuel Lockwood,	Joseph Huntington,	Theodore Hinsdale
1781	Lebanon (Goshen,)	Ephraim Little,	Thomas Wells Bray,	Jeremiah Day.
1782	Ripton, now Huntington,	Samuel Newell,	Cyprian Strong,	Elisha Rexford.
1783	Lyme,	James Cogswell,	Elizur Goodrich,	Josiah Whitney.
1784	Torringford,	Timothy Pitkin,	Justus Mitchell,	Jeremiah Day.
1785	Franklin,	James Cogswell,	Josiah Whitney,	
1786	Durham,	Joseph Bellamy, D.D.	Enoch Huntington,	Jo'n Edwards, D.D.
1787	Berlin, Britain Society, now New Britain,	John Smalley,	Benjn Trumbull,	Benj. Trumbull.
1788	West Hartford,	Nathaniel Taylor,	Cyprian Strong,	John Willard.
1789	Lebanon, 2d Parish, now Columbia,	Samuel Lockwood,	William Lockwood,	Timothy Stone.
1790	Greenfield,	Nathaniel Taylor,	Benj. Trumbull,	William Seward.
1791	Washington,	Nathaniel Bartlett,	Jon'n Edwards, D.D.	Cotton M. Smith.
1792	Waterbury,	Mark Leavenworth,	Cyprian Strong,	Isaac Lewis.
1793	Cheshire,	Elizur Goodrich, D.D.	Jon'n Edwards, D.D / Nathan Perkins,	Noah Benedict.
1794	Berlin, Kensington Soci'y,	Nathan Williams,	Jon'n Edwards, D.D / Nathan Perkins,	Jona. Edwards, D.D.
1795	Killingworth,	Elizur Goodrich, D.D.	Jon'n Edwards, D.D / N^{a}t'an Fenn,	Eli'r Goodrich, D.D.
1796	Norwich,	Nathan Williams D.D.	Jon'n Edwards, D.D / Henry A. Rowland	Cyprian Strong.
1797	Windham,	John Smalley,	Jon'n Edwards, D.D / Daniel Smith,	Achilles Mansfield.
1798	Hebron,	Benj. Trumbull, D.D.	Nathan Perkins, / John Marsh,	Samuel Nott.
1799	Hartford,	Levi Hart,	Samuel Blatchford, / John Elliot,	Moses C. Welch.
1800	Norfolk,	Levi Hart,	Samuel Blatchford, / William Lyman,	Charles Backus.

YR.	PLACE.	MODERATOR.	SCRIBES.	PREACHER.
1801	Litchfield,	Jeremiah Day,	Asahel Hooker, Nathan Perkins,	Nathan Perkins.
1802	Norwalk,	Noah Benedict,	Henry Channing, David Ely,	Asahel Hooker.
1803	Stratford,	Noah Benedict,	William Lyman, Lemuel Tyler,	Noah Benedict.
1804	North Haven,	Cyprian Strong, D. D.	Lemuel Tyler, Andrew Yates,	Hez. Ripley, D. D.
1805	Guilford,	John Foote,	Calvin Chapin, Samuel Goodrich,	David Ely.
1806	Wethersfield,	Cyprian Strong, D. D.	John Elliot, Azel Backus,	Ben. Trumbull, D.D.
1807	Saybrook, 2d Society, now Saybrook,	Nathan Perkins, D.D.	David Ely, Bezaleel Pinneo,	Thomas W. Bray.
1808	New London,	Azel Backus,	Chauncey Lee, Abel Flint,	Calvin Chapin.
1809	Lebanon.	Nehemiah Prudden,	Chauncey Lee, Elijah Waterman,	David Selden.
1810	Ellington,	Moses C. Welch,	Samuel Merwin, Heman Humphrey,	Walter King.
1811	Farmington,	Nathan Perkins, D.D.	Wm. Lyman, D. D. David Smith,	Zebulon Ely.
1812	Sharon,	Elijah Parsons,	Andrew Yates, Daniel Dow,	William L. Strong.
1813	Watertown,	David Ely, D. D.,	Elijah Waterman, Bezaleel Pinneo,	Nathaniel Gaylord.
1814	Fairfield,	Samuel Goodrich,	Henry A. Rowland, Dan Huntington,	Peter Starr.
1815	Danbury,	Daniel Smith,	Sam'l Whittlesey, Horatio Waldo,	Uriel Gridley.
1816	New Haven,	Nathan Perkins, D.D.	Lyman Beecher, Sam'l P. Williams,	Heman Humphrey.
1817	East Guilford, now Madison,	William Lyman, D.D.	Ira Hart, David D. Field,	William Andrews.
1818	Middletown,	Abel Flint,	Aaron Hovey, Caleb J. Tenney,	Samuel Merwin.
1819	Lyme, now Old Lyme,	Moses C. Welch, D.D.	Thomas Robbins, Samuel Merwin,	John Elliot.
1820	Colchester,	Samuel Nott,	Nath'l W. Taylor, Joseph Harvey,	Royal Robbins.
1821	Thompson,	Samuel Nott,	Samuel Merwin, William Andrews,	Fred. W. Hotchkiss
1822	Tolland,	Aaron Dutton,	Joab Brace, Hart Talcott,	Abel McEwen.
1823	Windsor,	William L. Strong,	Abel McEwen, Nathaniel Hewit,	Erastus Learned.
1824	Goshen,	Samuel Goodrich,	Noah Porter, Timothy P. Gillet,	Hubbel Loomis.
1825	Litchfield,	Calvin Chapin, D. D.,	Thomas Robbins, Joshua L. Williams,	Thomas Robbins.
1826	Stamford,	Samuel Goodrich,	Thomas Prudden, Epaphras Goodman	James Beach.
1827	Stratford,	Daniel Dow,	Samuel Merwin, Caleb J. Tenney,	Noah Smith.
1828	New Haven,	Henry A. Rowland,	John Marsh, Edw'd W. Hooker,	Edw. W. Hooker.
1829	Wallingford,	Jeremiah Day, D.D.,	Abel McEwen, Isaac Parsons,	Thom. Punderson.
1830	Wethersfield,	N. W. Taylor, D. D.	Edward Bull, Leon'd E. Lathrop,	Nat. W. Taylor, D.D.
1831	Saybrook, now Old Saybrook,	Luther Hart,	Ansel Nash, Samuel Merwin,	Daniel Smith, D. D.
1832	Norwich,	Caleb J. Tenney, D.D.	Timothy P. Gillet, Joseph Harvey,	C. J. Tenney, D.D.
1833	Brooklyn,	Aaron Dutton,	Cyrus Yale, George A. Calhoun,	Chester Colton.
1834	Vernon,	Calvin Chapin, D.D.,	L. P. Hickok, Joel Mann,	C. B. Everest.
1835	Enfield,	Jeremiah Day, D. D.,	Thomas F. Davies, Tho's L. Shipman,	Anson Atwood.

20

YR.	PLACE.	MODERATOR.	SCRIBES.	PREACHER.
1836	Norfolk,	George A. Calhoun,	Anson Rood, Sam'l H. Riddel,	George A. Calhoun.
1837	New Milford,	Noah Porter, D. D.,	Anson Rood, Eleazer T. Fitch,	Bennett Tyler, D. D.
1838	Norwalk,	Nath. W. Taylor, D.D.	Horace Bushnell, Alvan Bond,	Jairus Burt.
1839	Danbury,	Jeremiah Day, D. D.,	Oliver E. Daggett, Theophilus Smith,	Gurdon Hayes.
1840	New Haven,	David D. Field, D.D.	Theophilus Smith, Henry N. Day,	Nath'l Hewitt, D.D.
1841	New Haven,	Nath. W. Taylor, D.D.	Zebulon Crocker, L. H. Atwater,	Abner Brundage.
1842	Wethersfield,	James Beach,	Sam. N. Shepard, Geo. J. Tillotson,	Leonard Bacon.
1843	Westbrook,	Nath'l Hewit, D. D.,	Leverett Griggs, Spofford D. Jewett,	C. A. Goodrich D.D.
1844	New London,	Joab Brace,	S. W. S. Dutton, Joseph Eldridge,	Zebulon Crocker.
1845	Plainfield,	Leonard Bacon, D. D.,	Edwin Hall, A. L. Whitman,	Isaac Parsons.
1846	Somers,	Abel McEwen,	E. L. Cleaveland, Ephraim Lyman,	Alvan Bond.
1847	Suffield,	Jeremiah Day, D. D.,	Tryon Edwards, J. F. Norton.	Geo. J. Tillotson.
1848	Hartford,	Samuel Merwin,	Theophilus Smith, D. M. Seward,	Albert Smith.
1849	Salisbury,	C. A. Goodrich, D.D.,	Rollin S. Stone, Davis S. Brainerd,	W. Thompson, D.D.
1850	Litchfield,	Nath'l Hewit, D. D.,	Hiram P. Arms, Edward Strong,	Noah Porter, D. D.
1851	Bridgeport,	Hiram P. Arms,	S. W. S. Dutton, S. J. M. Merwin,	Cyrus Yale.
1852	Danbury,	Nath'l Hewit, D. D.,	Jonathan Brace, Chauncey Goodrich	John Churchill.
1853	Waterbury,	George J. Tillotson,	Chauncey Goodrich W. H. Moore,	S. B. S. Bissell.
1854	New Haven,	Joel H. Linsley, D. D.	William T. Eustis, L. B. Rockwood,	William B. Weed.
1855	Meriden,	Theo. D. Woolsey, D.D.	M. N. Morris, Burdett Hart,	T. D. Woolsey D.D.
1856	Middletown,	David L. Parmelee,	Lavalette Perrin, E. C. Jones,	Jonathan Brace.
1857	Lyme,	Jared R. Avery,	Tho'sH.Fessenden, W. H. Moore,	George I. Wood.
1858	West Killingly,	Elisha C. Jones,	Robert C. Learned, Robert G. Williams,	J. L. Dudley.

REGISTERS OF THE GENERAL ASSOCIATION.

No Register was appointed until 1774. Previous to this time, the Scribe, each year, recorded the minutes, and passed the book to his successor.

Benjamin Trumbull, appointed in 1774, resigned 1795.
Cyprian Strong, " 1795, " 1807.
Calvin Chapin, 1807, died 1851.
Theophilus Smith, 1851, " 1853.
Myron N. Morris, " 1854.

TREASURERS.

Abel Flint,	appointed in	1799,	served till	1824.
Joel H. Linsley,	"	1824,	"	1832.
Samuel Spring,		1832,	"	1836.
Horace Bushnell,		1836,	"	1837.
Samuel H. Riddel,		1837,	"	1841.
Edward R. Tyler,		1841,	"	1846.
Edward Strong,		1846,	"	1847.
Edward R. Tyler,		1847,	"	1848.
Austin Putnam,		1849.		

STATISTICAL SECRETARY AND TREASURER.

Austin Putnam,	"	1857,	"	1859.
William H. Moore,		1859.		

MOOR'S INDIAN CHARITY SCHOOL.

After the Great Awakening, Rev. Eleazar Wheelock, pastor of the church in Lebanon, Second Society, now Columbia, commenced his labors as a teacher of youth. In December, 1743, he was induced to receive among the boys in his school, *Samson Occum*, a Mohegan Indian, aged about nineteen, whom he kept in his family for four or five years and educated. This Indian, as it is well known, became a preacher of distinction. Mr. Wheelock soon formed the plan of an Indian Missionary School. He conceived that educated Indians would be more successful than white men, as missionaries among the red men, though he proposed also to educate a few English youth as missionaries. The project was new, for the labors of Sargent and the Brainerds, as well as those of Eliot and the Mayhews, were the labors of missionaries among the Indians, and not labors designed to form a band of Indian missionaries. Two Indian boys of the Delaware tribe entered the school in Dec., 1754, and others soon joined them. In 1762 he had more then twenty youths under his care, chiefly Indians. For their maintenance, funds were obtained by subscription, from benevolent individuals, from the Legislatures of Connecticut and Massachusetts, and from the Commissioners, in Boston, of the Scotch Society for Propagating Christian Knowledge. Joshua Moor, a farmer in Mansfield, having, about the year 1754, made a donation of a house and two acres of land in Lebanon contiguous to Mr. Wheelock's house, the institution received the name of "Moor's Indian Charity School." In this school several gentlemen were associated with Mr. Wheelock as teachers; but in 1764, the Scotch Society appointed a Board of Correspondents in Connecticut, who, in 1765, sent out white missionaries and Indian school masters to the Indians on the Mohawk, in New York.

In 1766, Mr. Wheelock sent Mr. Occum, and Rev. Nathaniel Whitaker to Great Britain, to solicit benefactions to the school, that its operations might be enlarged. The success of this mission was great, and was owing chiefly to the labors of Mr. Occum. He was the first Indian preacher from America, who ever visited Great Britain, and he preached several hundred sermons, with great acceptance, to numerous assemblies in England and Scotland. The King subscribed £200, and Lord Dartmouth 50 guineas. The amount of monies collected in England was about £7000 sterling, and between £2000 and £3000 in Scotland, held by a board of trustees, of which Lord Dartmouth was president, and by the Scotch Society. To them Mr. Wheelock presented his accounts, on the allowance of which he drew for the monies voted. The expenditures were chiefly for the support of the scholars in the school, (of whom, in some years there were thirty or forty,) of their teacher, and of missionaries and school masters among the Indians.

After conducting Moor's School in Lebanon about fifteen years, Dr. Wheelock, in order to increase its usefulness, determined to remove it to some new country, and to obtain for it an incorporation as an academy, in which a regular and thorough education might be given to the youth, Indian and English, who should be assembled in it. At this time there were only three colleges in New England: Harvard, Yale, and Brown University, in its infancy, at Warren, R. I. When the design was made known to the public, he received various offers from the owners of new lands, and from different towns. At length, in 1770, he removed to Hanover, New Hampshire, and obtained the charter of Dartmouth College, which was partly endowed by Gov. Wentworth. But the school was not merged in the college, though the President of the college was the President of the school. Of Moor's school the Earl of Dartmouth was a benefactor, but not of Dartmouth College, —to the establishment of which he and the other trustees were opposed, as being a departure from the original design.

Dr. Wheelock lived but nine years in his new location, but was succeeded by his son, John Wheelock, as President of the school and college. Soon after Dr. Wheelock began to send out missionaries into the wilderness, the controversy with Great Britain commenced, which blighted his fair and encouraging prospects; and during the last few years of his life, there was actual war, in which many of the Indians acted with the enemy.

The whole number of missionaries, educated at this school, we are unable to state ; but, at the period of the first college commencement, in 1771, the number of scholars destined to be missionaries was twenty-four, of whom eighteen were white and only six were Indians.   The change which Wheelock made from his original plan was the result of experience,   He had found that of forty Indian youths who had been under his care, twenty had returned to the vices of savage life.   The celebrated Brant was one of his pupils.   Among the missionaries whom he employed were Occum, C. J. Smith, T. Chamberlain, S. Kirkland, L. Frisbie, and D. McClure.   The missionary Kirkland, was the father of President Kirkland of Harvard College, and the missionary Frisbie was the father of Professor Frisbie of the same college.   The missionary McClure was the Rev. D. McClure of East Windsor, Connecticut.   Dr. Wheelock died in 1771.   See notice of his life in Sprague's Annals, Vol. 1., 397, and Dr. Allens' Biog. Dict. ; of Samson Occum, Sprague's Annals. Vol. 3, 192.

FIRST MEETING OF THE AMERICAN BOARD OF COMMISSIONERS FOR FOREIGN MISSIONS.

BY REV. NOAH PORTER, D. D., FARMINGTON.

The American Board of Commissioners for Foreign Missions was first organized at Farmington, in this State, Sept. 5, 1810. At the annual meeting of the General Association of Massachusetts, held in Bradford, in June of that year, four young men, Adoniram Judson, Jr., Samuel Nott, Jr., Samuel J. Mills and Samuel Newell, members of the Theological Seminary in Andover, had offered themselves to be Missionaries of Christ to the heathen, and committed themselves to the Association for advice and direction as to the course they should take in entering on the work to which they were devoted; and the Association had proceeded, with solemn deliberation and prayer, to institute a Board for that purpose, and for the general object to which these young men had consecrated themselves, under the name of " *The American Board of Commissioners for Foreign Missions*," consisting of nine members, all of them, in the first instance, chosen by that Association, and afterwards to be chosen annually, five of them by that body, and four of them by the General Association of Connecticut; and had chosen the following gentlemen to constitute the Board: His Excellency John Treadwell, Esq., Rev. Dr. Timothy Dwight, Gen. Jedediah Huntington, and Rev. Calvin Chapin, of Connecticut; Rev. Dr. Joseph Lyman, Rev. Dr. Samuel Spring, William Bartlett, Esq., Rev. Samuel Worcester and Deacon Samuel H. Walley, of Massachusetts. In complaisance to Governor Treadwell, chairman of the Commissioners, their first meeting was held in Farmington; and, circumstances making it inconvenient to accommodate them at *his* house, the meeting was held at the house of Rev. Noah Porter, the pastor of the church there, who was invited to take part in their deliberations. A majority only were present, viz., Governor Treadwell, Doctors Lyman and Spring, and Messrs. Worcester and Chapin. The first day and part of the second were employed in anxious consultations relative to the Constitution of the Board, the direction to be given to its missionaries, and the raising of the necessary funds.   The Constitution being formed, the Board was organized by the choice of the following gentlemen as its officers :*

His Excellency, JOHN TREADWELL, ESQ., *President.*
        REV. DR. SPRING, *Vice President.*
        WILLIAM BARTLETT, ESQ.,
        REV. DR. SPRING,   } *Prudential Committee.*
        REV. SAMUEL WORCESTER,
        REV. CALVIN CHAPIN, *Recording Secretary.*
        REV. SAMUEL WORCESTER, *Corresponding Secretary.*
        Deacon SAMUEL H. WALLEY, *Treasurer.*
        Mr. JOSHUA GOODALE, *Auditor.*

The sensation excited by this movement, among the pastors and churches of New England, was profound.   No doubt was entertained that the young men, in whose minds it began, were moved by the Spirit of Christ.   They were now publicly devoted to the service of Christ among the heathen, for life. Their example furnished an appeal to the churches for their co-operation that could not be unheeded; and the Commissioners selected to receive and apply their charities, and to direct and superintend their missions, were among the choicest of New England's sons.   Of Governor Treadwell, a few years after his death, it was said that he was "the last of the Puritan Governors of Connecticut."   Perhaps this could not now be said with due consideration of the piety of some who have succeeded him ; but it was said of him, with reference not to his piety alone, but also to his theological knowledge, his simplicity of manners, his firmness of purpose, and the interest which he took in the order of the churches, the propagation of the Gospel, and the cause of evangelical religion.   When he was made the first President of the Board of Commissioners for Foreign Missions, he had long been prized by the ministers of New England as one of the ablest theological writers in this country; and had for many years been the Chairman of the Trus-

* A more ample account of the above may be found in the Panoplist, Vol. 3, pp. 88—90, and 181.

tees of the Missionary Society of Connecticut, to which office he had been chosen at the first organization of that Board. Dr. Spring, of Newburyport, also was eminently a public man, and was honorably connected with some of the most important philanthropic, educational and evangelical enterprises of his day. Dr. Lyman, of Hatfield, was one of the earliest friends and patrons of the Hampshire Missionary Society, and in 1812 was chosen its President. On the death of Dr. Spring in 1819, he was chosen Vice President of the American Board of Commissioners, and in 1823 its President. Dr. Worcester, of Salem, also stood eminent among the ablest ministers of New England, as a preacher and an author, an expounder of the Christian faith, and its defender ; and as the Corresponding Secretary of the American Board from its institution till his death in 1821, he contributed, probably, more than any other man to the high and honorable character which it has sustained. Dr. Chapin, of Rocky Hill, was too well known to need any extended notice. He was distinguished for exactness, enterprise and humor, and a constant interest in all Christian and benevolent enterprises. He continued the Recording Secretary of the Board from its organization till near the close of his useful life.

MISSIONARIES TO FOREIGN LANDS FROM CONNECTICUT.*

NAME.	PLACE OF BIRTH OR EARLY RESIDENCE.	FIELD OF MISSIONARY LABOR.
Rev. William Aitchison,	Norwich,	China.
Mrs. Samuel Allis, (Emeline Palmer.)		Pawnees.
Rev. Lorin Andrews,		Sandwich Islands.
Mrs. S. L. Andrews, (Parnelly Pierce.)	Woodbury,	Sandwich Islands.
Rev. William T. Arms,	Norwich Town,	Armenians.
Mr. Daniel H. Austin,	Winchester,	Osages.
Mrs. D. H. Austin, (Lydia Hovey.)	Mansfield,	Osages.
Mrs. P. Auten, (Lydia Chapman.)	Fairfield,	Choctaws.
Rev. David Avery,	Franklin,	N. Y. Indians.
Rev. David Bacon,	Woodstock,	Mackinaw.
Mrs. David Bacon, (Alice Parks.)	Bethlem,	Mackinaw.
Rev. D. Baldwin, M. D.,	Durham,	Sandwich Islands.
Mrs. D. Baldwin, (Charlotte Fowler.)	Northford,	Sandwich Islands.
Mrs. Dyer Ball, (Lucy H. Mills.)	New Haven,	Singapore.
Mrs. Elias R. Beadle, (Hannah Jones.)	Hartford,	Syria.
Rev. William A. Benton,	Tolland,	Syria.
Rev. Isaac Bird,	Salisbury,	Syria.
Rev. William Bird,	Hartford,	Syria.
Rev. Lemuel Bissell,	East Windsor,	Ahmednuggur.
Abraham Blatcheley, M. D.	Madison,	Sandwich Islands.
Mrs. A. Blatcheley, (Jemima Marvin.)	Lyme,	Sandwich Islands.

* The list of missionaries here given, includes the names of several who went to different Indian tribes before the formation of the American Board of Commissioners for Foreign Missions ; also the names of a few who, though not born in Connecticut, spent their youth in the state, made here a profession of their faith, and were members of our churches at the time of their leaving for their fields of labor. The names of missionaries who were born in other states and who came to Connecticut only for the purpose of education, or who resided here only while they were pursuing their college studies, are not given.

Mrs. A. C. Blunt, (Harriet Ellsworth.)	Chatham,	Cherokees.
Rev. H. Bradley,	East Haven,	N. Y. Indians.
Mrs. H. Bradley, (Catharine Wheeler.)	Fairfield,	N. Y. Indians.
Rev. D. Brainerd,	Haddam,	N. Y. Indians.
Rev. J. Brainerd,	Haddam,	N. Y. Indians.
Rev. David Breed,	New Haven,	Choctaws.
Mrs. David Breed, (Sarah A. Griswold,)	Colchester,	Choctaws.
Mrs. Ebenezer Burgess, (Mary Grant.)	Colebrook,	Satara.
Rev. E. Butler, M. D.,	Norfolk,	Cherokees.
Mrs. E. Butler, (Esther Post.)	Canaan,	Cherokees.
Rev. Cyrus Byington,	Bristol,	Choctaws.
Mrs. W. Chamberlin, (Flora Hoyt.)	Danbury,	Cherokees.
Rev. G. Champion,	Westchester,	Zulus.
Rev. J. E. Chandler,	N. Woodstock,	Madura.
Mrs. Henry Cherry, (Charlotte H. Lathrop.)	Norwich,	Madura.
Mrs. H. Cherry, (Jane E. Lathrop.)	Bozrah,	Madura.
Rev. Epaph's Chapman,	East Haddam.	
Rev. Edward Chester,	New Haven,	Madura.
Rev. Titus Coan,	Killingworth,	Sandwich Islands.
Mr. Amos S. Cooke,	Danbury,	Sandwich Islands.
Miss Delia Cooke,	New Hartford,	Ojibwas.
Mrs. C. C. Copeland, (Cornelia Ladd.)	Franklin,	Choctaws.
Henry DeForest, M. D.	Seymour,	Syria
Rev. J. T. Dickinson,	Norwich,	Singapore.
Mr. Henry Dimond,	Fairfield,	Sandwich Islands.
Miss Lucinda Downer,	Norwich,	Choctaws.
Mrs. Sylvester Ellis, (Sarah Hoyt.)	Danbury,	Cherokees.
Mr. J. C. Ellsworth,	Chatham,	Cherokees.
Rev. James Ely,	Lyme,	Sandwich Islands.
Mrs. James Ely, (Louisa Everest.)	Cornwall,	Sandwich Islands.
Rev. Levi Frisbie,	Branford,	Delaware Indians.
Rev Stephen Fuller,	East Haddam.	
Rev. Charles Gager,	Bozrah.	

Rev. Anson Gleason,	Hartford,	Choctaws.
Mrs. A. Gleason, (Bethiah W. Tracy.)	Lebanon,	Choctaws.
Rev. J. Goodrich,	Wethersfield,	Sandwich Islands.
Rev. Jona'n S. Green,	Lebanon,	Sandwich Islands.
Mrs. J. S. Green, (Theodocia Arnold.)	Millington,	Sandwich Islands.
Rev. Elnathan Gridley,	Farmington,	Turkey.
Mrs Peter J. Gulick, (Fanny H. Thomas.)	Lebanon,	Sandwich Islands.
Mrs. C. Hall, (Matilda Hotchkiss.)	Cheshire,	Stockbridge Ind's.
Mrs. Wm. Hall, (Emeline Gaylord.)	Norfolk,	Senecas.
Mrs. Charles Harding, (Julia M. Terry.)	Plymouth,	Bombay.
Mrs. Sarah Haskell, (Sarah Brewster.)	Norwich,	Assyria.
Mrs. Allen Hazen, (Martha R. Chapin.)	Somers,	Ahmednugger.
Mrs. Story Hebard, (Rebecca W. Williams.)	Lebanon,	Syria.
Rev. Abel H. Hinsdale,	Torrington,	Assyria.
Rev. H. R. Hitchcock,	Manchester,	Sandwich Islands.
Mrs. J. Hitchcock, (Nancy Brown.)	Eastbury,	Cherokees.
Mrs. Thomas Holman, (Lucia Ruggles.)	Brookfield,	Sandwich Islands.
Miss Elizabeth J. Hough,	New Britain,	Choctaws.
Rev. A. Hoyt,	Danbury,	Cherokees.
Mrs. A. Hoyt, (Esther Booth.)	Southbury,	Cherokees.
Mrs. S. Hutchings, (Elizabeth C. Lathrop.)	New London,	Ceylon.
Mrs. William Hutchison, (Forresta G. Shepherd.)	New Haven,	Turkey.
Rev. Mark Ives,	Goshen,	Sandwich Islands.
Mrs. M. Ives, (Mary A. Brainerd.)	Haddam,	Sandwich Islands.
Rev. Stephen Johnson,	Griswold,	China.
Rev. Samuel Kirkland,	Lisbon,	N. Y. Indians.
Mr. H. O. Knapp,	Greenwich,	Sandwich Islands.
Mrs. H. O. Knapp, (Charlotte Close.)	Greenwich,	Sandwich Islands.
Mrs. E. Lathrop, (Cornelia F. Dolbear.)	Montville,	Choctaws.
Mrs. J. Y. Leonard, (Amelia A. Gilbert.)	New Haven,	Armenians.

Rev. Charles Little,	Columbia,	Madura.
Rev. H. Lobdell, M. D.,	Danbury,	Assyria.
Mrs. H. Lobdell,	Ridgefield,	Assyria.
(Lucy C. Williams.)		
Rev. J. Lockwood,	New Haven,	Choctaws.
Rev. Nathan L. Lord,	Norwich,	Ceylon.
Rev. D. B. Lyman,	New Hartford,	Sandwich Islands.
Rev. David McClure,		Delaware Indians.
Mrs. Dwight W. March,	New Haven,	Assyria.
(Julia W. Peck.)		
Mrs. Samuel D. Marsh,	Fairfield,	Zulus.
(Mary Skinner.]		
Rev. Samuel J. Mills,	Torringford,	Africa.
Rev. C. C. Mitchell,	Groton,	Nestorians.
Mrs. C. C. Mitchell,	Meriden,	Nestorians.
(Eliza A. Richards.)		
Rev. Samuel Moseley,	Mansfield,	Choctaws.
Mr. W. H. Manwaring,	Norwich,	Cherokees.
Rev. Benjamin C. Meigs,	Bethlem,	Ceylon.
Mrs. B. C. Meigs,	Bethlem,	Ceylon.
(Sarah M. Peet.)		
Rev. J. Miner,	Guilford,	Stockbridge Ind's.
Mr. Eastman S. Minor,	New Haven,	Ceylon.
Mr. Samuel Moulton,	Bolton,	Choctaws.
Mrs. S. Moulton,	Killingworth,	Choctaws.
(Lucinda Field.)		
Mrs. Murgee,	Lyme,	India.
(Mary ——.)		
Rev. Samuel Nott,	Franklin,	Mahrattas.
Rev. Samuel Occum,	Columbia.	
Mr. J. Olmsted,	Ridgefield,	Choctaws.
Mrs. Benjamin Parker,	Branford,	Sandwich Islands.
(Mary E. Baker.)		
Mr. Henry Parker,	Litchfield,	Cherokees.
Mrs. H. Parker,	Simsbury,	Cherokees.
(Philena Griffin.)		
Rev. M. Palmer, M. D.	Stanwich,	Cherokees.
Mrs. M. Palmer,	Colchester,	Cherokees.
(Clarissa Johnson.)		
Mrs. M. Palmer,	Colchester,	Cherokees.
(Jerusha Johnson.)		
Mrs. J. W. Parsons,	Derby,	Armenians.
(Catharine Jennings.)		
Rev. John M. S. Perry,	Sharon,	Ceylon.

Mrs. J. M. S. Perry, (Harriet J. Lathrop.)	Norwich,	Ceylon.
Rev. Benj. Parsons,	Fairfield,	Armenians.
Rev. Gideon H. Pond,	Washington,	Sioux.
Rev. S. W. Pond,	Washington,	Dakotas.
Mrs. S. W. Pond, (Rebecca Smith.)	Washington,	Dakotas.
Rev. Rollin Porter,	Somers,	Gaboon.
Mrs. Rollin Porter, (Nancy A. ——.)	Somers,	Gaboon.
Rev. William Potter,	Lisbon,	Cherokees.
Mrs. W. Potter. (Laura Weld.)	Hampton,	Cherokees.
Rev. A. T. Pratt, M. D.	Berlin,	Armenians.
Mrs. A. T. Pratt, (Sarah F. Goodyear.)	New Haven,	Armenians.
Mrs. Wm. C. Requa, (Susan Comstock.)	Wilton,	Osages.
Rev. Elijah Robbins,	Thompson,	Zulus.
Mrs. E. Robbins, (Adaline Bissell.)	Rockwell,	Zulus.
Mrs. Samuel P. Robbins, (Martha R. Pierce.)	Enfield,	Siam.
Miss Emily Root,	Farmington,	N. Y. Indians.
Mr. Samuel Ruggles,	Brookfield,	Sandwich Islands.
Mrs. Samuel Ruggles, (Nancy Wells.)	East Windsor,	Sandwich Islands.
Rev. J. L. Seymour,	Plymouth,	Ojibwas.
Charles S. Shelton, M. D.	Huntington,	Madura.
Mrs. C. S. Sherman, (Martha E. Williams.)	Stonington,	Syria.
Rev. Wm. C. Shipman,	Wethersfield,	Sandwich Islands.
Miss Pamela Skinner,	Glastenbury,	Choctaws.
Miss Juliette Slate,	Manchester,	Choctaws.
Rev. Eli Smith, D. D.	Northford,	Syria.
Mrs. E. Smith, (Sarah L. Huntington.)	Norwich,	Syria.
Mrs. Henry H. Spaulding, (Eliza Hart.)	Berlin,	Oregon.
Rev. S. M. Spencer,	West Hartford.	
Miss Eunice Starr,	Norwich,	Choctaws.
Rev. Edwin Stevens,	New Canaan,	China.
Rev. W. R. Stocking,	Middletown,	Nestorians.
Mrs. W. R. Stocking, (Jerusha E. Gilbert.)	Weston,	Nestorians.

Rev. Seth B. Stone,	Madison,	Zulus.
Rev. John C. Strong,	Granby,	Choctaws.
Mrs. Charles L. Stewart, (Harriet Tiffany.)	Stamford,	Sandwich Islands.
Rev. H. S. Taylor,	West Hartford,	Madura.
Mrs. D. Temple, (Eliza Hart.)	Hartford,	Turkey.
Mr. W. A. Thayer,	Roxbury,	N. Y. Indians.
Mrs. W. A. Thayer, (Susan Whiting.)	Colebrook,	N. Y. Indians.
Rev. J. L. Thompson,	Montville,	Cyprus.
Miss Cynthia Thrall,	Windsor,	Cherokees.
Rev. R. Tinker,	Hartford,	Sandwich Islands.
Mrs. E. S. Town, (Hannah E. Cone.)	Manchester,	Choctaws.
Miss Susan Tracy,	Norwich,	Choctaws.
Rev. William Tracy,	Norwich,	Madura.
Rev. William F. Vaill,	Hadlyme,	Osages.
Mrs. W. F. Vaill, (Asenath Selden.)	Hadlyme,	Osages.
Mrs. H. J. Van Lennep, (Mary E. Hawes.)	Hartford,	Turkey.
Mrs. H. J. Van Lennep, (Emily F. Bird.)	Hartford,	Turkey.
C. H. Wetmore, M. D.,	Lebanon,	Sandwich Islands.
Rev. Samuel Whitney,	Branford,	Sandwich Islands.
Rev. E. Whittlesey,	Salisbury,	Sandwich Islands.
Rev. S. G. Whittlesey,	New Preston,	Ceylon.
Mrs. Miron Winslow, (Harriet W. Lathrop.)	Norwich,	Madras.
Mr. Abner Wilcox,	Harwinton,	Sandwich Islands.
Mrs. A. Wilcox, (Lucy E. Hart.)	Norfolk,	Sandwich Islands.
Mrs. L. S. Williams, (Matilda Loomis.)	Winchester,	Choctaws.
Rev. Samuel Wolcott,	East Windsor,	Syria.
Rev. A. Wright,	Columbia,	Choctaws.

CORNWALL MISSION SCHOOL.

At the meeting of the Board for Foreign Missions in 1816, it was resolved that a school for the education of foreign youths should be established in this country, and a committee of seven were appointed to carry out the design of the Board in this respect. The committee met October 29th, 1816, in New Haven, at the house of Dr. Dwight, and adopted a constitution, in which the object of the school, and the means for securing the object were specified. The object of the school was stated to be " to educate heathen youth in such a manner, that with future professional studies they might be qualified for missionaries, schoolmasters, interpreters and physicians among heathen nations; and to communicate such information in agriculture and the arts as should tend to promote Christianity and civilization." To carry out this design, a farm and suitable buildings were to be provided for the practice of agricultural pursuits; the useful branches of education were to be taught, and also the leading truths of the Christian religion. Accordingly a farm was purchased at Cornwall, suitable buildings erected, and a school commenced about the first of May, 1817, with twelve pupils.

Rev. Herman Daggett, of New Canaan, for several years a pastor on Long Island, and also a teacher of academies in different places, was soon thought of as a suitable person to be placed at the head of it; but as he was detained by his engagement in the academy at New Canaan, Mr. Edwin W. Dwight, of Stockbridge, Massachusetts, took his place for one year. Mr. Daggett, at his inauguration, in May, 1818, delivered an address. Gov. Treadwell also made an address; and Rev. Joseph Harvey, of Goshen, preached a sermon. All of these were published in connection with the memoirs of Obookiah. Considering the great variety of taste, disposition, age, language and character of the pupils, a more difficult task can hardly be conceived than the management of such a school; and Mr. Daggett, by his great kindness and wisdom succeeded in giving to the school a very harmonious character, and in rendering it for a season, the instrument of no inconsiderable usefulness. His pupils were greatly attached to him, and not a few of them thought to have been radically and permanently benefitted by his influence. But Mr. Daggett's health gave way, and his connection with the school ceased in a little less than six years. Being thus obliged to retire from all public service, he still resided in Cornwall about eight years longer, and died in March, 1832. Rev. Amos Bassett, D. D., who had just left the pastorate at Hebron, (subsequently settled at Monroe,) succeeded Mr. Daggett in 1824, and continued in charge of the school, till it was disbanded. Dr. Bassett died in 1828, having been a member of the corporation of Yale College from 1810. He was an excellent scholar, a sensible and solemn preacher, and especially distinguished for the gravity of his deportment, and for godly simplicity and sincerity. Rev. Herman L. Vaill, now of Litchfield, was for a time an assistant in the school.

The Prudential Committee reported in 1817, that the condition of the school was highly satisfactory; five of the scholars were from the Sandwich Islands; four of whom were hopefully pious and exemplary in their conduct; Henry Obookiah was of the number. For several following years the school seems to have grown in numbers, and in the confidence and regard of the Christian public. The reports of the Prudential Committee for the successive years indicate a satisfactory progress in the various branches of education, and an encouraging degree of interest in spiritual things.

The committee in their report for the year 1821 say, " The expectations of the community are surpassed—the history of its progress is such as to encourage the education of heathen youth, and it is hoped that the number of scholars may be greatly increased through the agency of our commerce, which extends to all parts of the world." The conduct of the scholars was declared good, and their progress in study commendable.

In 1822 the whole number of scholars was thirty-four, of whom twenty-nine were heathen, representing more than half as many different nations and tribes. There were natives of Sumatra, China, Bengal, Hindostan, Mexico, New Zealand; of the

22

Society, Sandwich and Marquesas Islands, the Isles of Greece and the Azores; and from among the North American Indians, there were Cherokees, Choctaws, Osages, Oneidas, Tuscaroras, Senecas, and of the St. Regis tribe, in Canada. In age they ranged from mere childhood to adult years. The languages which they spoke rivalled in number, those which were heard at Jerusalem on the day of Pentecost. Though the ends of the school were secured, and its general interests were remarkably sustained amid all the difficulties attending it; yet it became, after a few years, obnoxious to public censure,—perhaps to an undue measure of prejudice,—on account of the intermarriage of two or three Indians with respectable young ladies in the neighborhood. In 1825 the Prudential Committee raised the question whether the school should be continued. It had answered the expectations of its friends, but the relations of the Board with foreign lands had changed, so that the reasons which led to the establishment of the school had lost their force. It was thought best, however, to continue it for the present, but without special effort to increase its numbers.

The committee appointed in 1827 for investigating the whole subject, reported that the school be discontinued. Their reason was not that the school in itself was a failure, but that the objects which it was designed to secure could now be secured better in some other way. Schools had now become established at the various Missions. Natives could be educated at these schools cheaper, and with a better prospect of being directly engaged in the service of the Missions. Besides, there were difficulties in educating them here, arising from the curiosity of the public from visiting, and consequently too much diversion from their studies and pursuits.

In view of these and various other reasons the Board thought best to discontinue the school, though not regretting the establishment and continuance of it thus far.

For full accounts of the origin, progress and results of the School, see Missionary Herald, and Reports of the Board, 1816–1827; and for notices of Mr. Daggett and Dr. Bassett, see Dr. Sprague's Annals, vol. 2, page 291, and Dr. Allen's Biographical Dictionary.

CONGREGATIONAL HOME MISSIONS IN CONNECTICUT.

BY REV. HORACE HOOKER, HARTFORD.

Connecticut, from the character of its founders and their aim in its settlement, ought to be, and in fact to a good degree has been a misssionary State.

First in order, we may reckon the attempts at different times to Christianize the native tribes within the limits of the colony. For our present purpose, it is enough to say that these attempts were both more numerous and successful than is generally supposed.

The next exhibition of the home missionary spirit, as it would now be regarded, was by " divers ministers in the eastern part of the colony, who, early in the last century, were at the pains and charge of going and preaching in the town of Providence, R. I., by turns." In 1722, " the Association of New London County petitioned Gov. Saltonstall to grant a brief for contributions in so many towns and congregations as his wisdom should see meet," for the support of preaching in that place. In 1724, the General Court, upon application, allowed a brief to " be emitted " to " encourage the building and finishing of a meeting house in Providence"—the beginning of that care of Connecticut for her " little sister," which has been exercised so beneficially in later days.

In 1774, the General Association recommended subscriptions among the people for supporting missionaries " to the scattered back settlements in the wilderness to the northwestward," in what is now Vermont and the northern part of New York These settlements, to a large extent, were composed of emigrants from Connecticut. Rev. Messrs. Williams of Northford, Goodrich of Durham, and Trumbull of North Haven, were chosen a committee to receive funds and supply the place of missionaries, when those appointed by the General Association failed. Rev. Messrs. Taylor of New Milford, Waterman of Wallingford, and Bliss of Ellington, were selected as missionaries, to spend five or six months on a missionary tour, "if the committee are able to provide for their support so long." The war of the revolution interrupted the scheme and the growth of the settlements.

In 1788, the subject came again before the General Association, in consequence of an address by New Haven West Association ; and Rev. Messrs. Jonathan· Edwards, Timothy Dwight, Joseph Huntington and Cotton M. Smith, were chosen a committee to consider and report what was proper to be done in the matter. It was again before the General Association in 1791. In 1792, Middlesex County Association having reported to the General Association that they had appointed Rev. Mr. Vaill as missionary to the new settlements, the General Association voted its approval of the measure, and a committee was chosen to ask liberty from the General Assembly to take up collections in the churches for the support of missionaries in this service. In 1793, it was voted that the missionaries spend four months on their tours. Pastors were allowed $5.00 per week for their services and $4.00 per week for supplying their pulpits in their absence. For several succeeding years, a Committee of Missions was appointed by the General Association—annual contributions were taken up in our churches—and numbers of missionaries entered the field—chiefly pastors, who left their flocks, temporarily, to minister to the destitute in the wilderness.

What, at that time, were the location and condition of the ever shifting *West*, may be gathered from the directions given by the Committee of Missions to one of the missionaries, [Rev. Aaron Kinne,] "to go north and south of the Mohawk river, in Otsego and Herkimer counties, as far westward as there are settlements proper to be visited." In 1793, a misssionary from Connecticut held the "first regular meeting ever attended," at Manlius, in the center of New York, and the next day, another at Pompey, ten miles further south, also "the first ever attended" there. Finding the settlements, to use his own language, "more numerous than had been suspected," he ventured to deviate from the course prescribed in his instructions, that he might be able to give to the committee, composed of such men as the younger President Edwards and Dr. Trumbull, information "which might be useful to them in regulating future missions," and save others from the embarrassments he had experienced from his "ignorance of the country," and from not meeting a person who could give him "any extensive description of it." The labor of the missionary seems more strange than it was needless, in preparing for the use of such a committee a rude map of this region, now filled with populous towns, and even cities, which were then of too recent origin to have a fixed name. A year later, Utica was composed of "a log tavern and two or three other buildings." On this map it is called "Fort Schuyler;" and on a later one by the same missionary, has still the alias, "Old Fort Schuyler;" while Rome is called "*Fort Stanwix.*"

The fields entered by the missionaries from Connecticut, during this period, were chiefly in Vermont and New York. The western part of New Hampshire was also visited.

LIST OF MISSIONARIES APPOINTED BY THE GENERAL ASSOCIATION,

FROM 1774 TO 1798.*

1774—Rev. Messrs. Taylor, Waterman, Bliss.

1788—*Rev. Jeremiah Day.

1793—Rev. Messrs. David Huntington, Ammi. R. Robbins, *Samuel J. Mills, *Cotton M. Smith, Jos. Vaill, Samuel Eells, Theodore Hinsdale, *John Shepherd.

1794—Rev. Messrs. Theodore Hinsdale, Aaron Kinne, *Moses C. Welch, *Jeremiah Day, *Asahel Hooker, Azel Backus, Cyprian Strong, William Lyman, *David Higgins, and Mr. Benjamin Wooster.

1795—Rev. Messrs. *Kinne, Robbins, Knapp, *Hart and Justus Mitchell.

1796—Rev. Messrs. *Joel Benedict, Nott, *Rexford, Vaill, *Mitchell, *McClure, W. Lyman, *Prudden, and John D. Perkins.

1797—Rev. Messrs. Solomon Morgan, *David Huntington, P. V. Booge, Alexander Gillet, Simon Waterman, *Jesse Townsend.

1798—Andrew Judson, Ammi Lewis, Seth Williston, Walter King, Zebulon Ely, Amos Bassett.

---

*Those marked thus * are known to have gone on missionary tours; others, doubtless, did the same, but the scanty documents do not show the fact.

1795—Rev. P. V. Booge, Rev. *Lemuel Tyler, (Huntington,)
    *Rev. J. D. Perkins, (Plainfield)
1796—Rev. John Gurley, (Lebanon,) Rev. Mr. King.

At the meeting of the General Association, in 1797, Rev. Messrs. Levi Hart, Joseph Strong, and Samuel Miller—the last a delegate from the General Assembly of the Presbyterian Church in the United States—"were appointed to draft an address to the several associations on the subject of a Missionary Society" for the state. " Drs. Dwight, Dana and Trumbull were appointed a committee of correspondence" on the same subject. At the meeting of the General Association, at Hebron, in 1798, Rev. Messrs. Hart, Edwards, Nathan Strong and Nathaniel Irwin—the last a delegate from the Presbyterian General Assembly—were appointed to draft a constitution of a Missionary Society, which, "after due consideration," was adopted. The General Association is the " *Missionary Society of Connecticut,*" the objects of which are "to Christianize the heathen in North America, and to support and promote Christian knowledge in the new settlements of the United States,"—" both to be pursued as circumstances shall point out, and as the trustees, under the superintendence of the General Association, shall direct." The trustees, twelve in number, six clergymen and six lay brethren of our churches, were to be appointed by ballot. In 1802, the trustees were incorporated by the General Assembly, with power to hold property not exceeding $100,000. Collections, authorized for some time by the state, were made annually in our denomination, on the first Sabbath in May, from 1798 to 1830, except in the years 1809, 1810, 1811. The whole amount contributed is $77,223.29.

A Narrative of Missions was published annually by the trustees. The Connecticut Evangelical Magazine devoted no small share of its pages, and all its profits, amounting to $11,520.07, to promote the interests of the society. This society is among the oldest of the kind in the country, in respect to organization; and in effect it is the oldest, the General Association having begun to act by a committee in 1792. For many years, its operations were more extensive than those of any kindred institution in the land. Its resources were, perhaps, as well proportioned to the wants of that period, as the larger resources of national societies are to the existing wants.

" To Christianize the Heathen in North America," is the first object mentioned in the constitution to be accomplished by the society, and several of its early donations were for that specific purpose. In 1800, Mr. David Bacon was sent to explore the condition of the Indian tribes south and west of Lake Erie. On his return, he was ordained at the close of the same year—and taking his station at Mackinaw, established a mission among the Chippeways. Here, he continued laboring faithfully in hardships and sufferings, till 1805;—when the enterprise proving more expensive than the limited means of the Society could bear, consistently with the increasing demands of the white settlements, the mission was discontinued. He returned to New Connecticut, where he is still held in grateful remembrance.

With the exception of a small grant ($100) to the Wyandott Indians in 1809, and the more recent aid to the Mohegans in supporting a minister eleven years, in Connecticut—no further attempts have been made for the conversion of the natives, through the medium of this society. The *whole amount* it has expended on account of Indian missions, is $3,665.61.

At the beginning of the present century, missionaries sent out by the Board, were found among the granite mountains of New Hampshire—on the beautiful hills of Vermont, then covered with woods, or sparsely dotted with log huts or lowly cottages—among the scattered settlements of middle or northern New York, and a little later, along the delightful borders of the Seneca Lake, and in the rich valley of the Genesee. They searched for "the lost sheep of the house of Israel" on the pine-clad acclivities of northern Pennsylvania, and wended their solitary way through the dense and lofty forests of New Connecticut. This region the society began to cultivate when its whole population was less than twelve hundred.

In 1812–13, the trustees, in connection with the Missionary Society of Massachusetts, sent out Rev. Samuel J. Mills, with an associate, to explore the valley of the Mississippi, which was then almost a terra incognita, in regard to its religious condition. Their report was widely circulated, and had more influence, probably, than any measure of the period, in awaking public attention to the bearing of that valley on the future destinies of our country. The trustees soon after established Kentucky, the Missouri Territory, and Louisiana as missionary fields.

In 1816, the venerated Giddings, a missionary of this society, organized a Presbyterian church in St. Louis, the first, it is believed, in Missouri. In 1817, Rev. Elias Cornelius, also commissioned by the trustees, laid the foundation of a church in New Orleans, of which the lamented Larned soon after became pastor.

The Missionary Society of Connecticut, has, it is reckoned, organized not far from 500 churches—some of them now among the most flourishing in the land. Its receipts from 1798 to 1859, have been $252,512.83.

In 1799, the trustees began to procure books for the new settlements—and in 1803, a committee, among whom were his Honor John Treadwell, Chief Justice Ellsworth, and Rev. Drs. Strong and Perkins, was appointed to prepare a " *Summary of Christian Doctrine*," for distribution among the destitute—of which 6000 copies were published in 1804, as a first edition. · Before societies were organized specially for this part of the work, the trustees had expended, in 1820, more than $6000 for books—beside distributing large numbers presented by authors and benevolent individuals.

At first, the missionaries of the society were, of necessity, itinerant—as there were no churches, and the population was scattered. Afterwards, the trustees availed themselves of the services of local pastors, for what time these could spare from their own congregations. For many years, their grants have been chiefly confined to aiding in the support of pastors over one or two churches. Not a few of the missionaries were settled in churches which they had organized. The whole number of missionaries employed by this society is 277.

To prepare the way for a change in the mode of conducting our home missionary operations, the Missionary Society of Connecticut, in 1830, ceased to solicit annual contributions from the churches—though still acting independently in expending the income of its Permanent Fund, and such legacies as now and then come into its treasury.

MISSIONARIES EMPLOYED BY THE MISSIONARY SOCIETY OF CONNECTICUT FROM 1798.*

Rev. Walter King,	New York and Vermont.
Rev. Amos Bassett,	New Hampshire.
Rev. Publius V. Booge,	New York.
John Spencer,	New York.
Alexander Gillet,	
Andrew Judson,	New York.
George Colton,	New York and Pennsylvania.
Seth Williston,	New York.
Thomas Punderson,	New York.
Henry Chapman,	Yew York.
Salmon King,	Vermont.
Sylvester Dana,	Pennsylvania, (probably.)
Aaron Kinne,	New York and Vermont.
Royal Phelps,	New York.
Jedediah Bushnell,	Vermont.
Holland Weeks,	Vermont and New York.
Marshfield Steele,	Vermont and New York.
Silas Hubbard,	New York.
Amasa Jerome,	New York.
William Storrs,	Vermont.
David Bacon,	Indians.
Robert Porter,	New York.
David Huntington,	Vermont.
Josiah B. Andrews,	Pennsylvania and New York.
Joseph Badger,	Western Reserve.
Jeremiah Hallock,	Western Reserve and Vermont.
Abraham Scott,	Western Reserve.
Job Swift,	Vermont.

* It was intended that the names of the missionaries in this list should be arranged in the order of their appointment. Only an approximation to chronological order however has been attained, and it must be acknowledged that the list in this respect is very defective. It is a matter of regret also that the specific dates of the commissions given to the missionaries cannot be added; but to do this would require a review of the Records of the Board, and of the Committee of Missions, the annual narratives of missions, the books of accounts, and to a great extent, the reports of missionaries, from the beginning. This would be *"renovare dolorem,"* for which time is wanting.

Simon Waterman,	New York.
Thomas Barr,	Western Reserve.
Hezekiah May,	New York and Pennsylvania.
Ezekiel J. Chapman,	Western Reserve.
James W. Woodward,	New York.
Daniel Higgins,	New York.
Solomon Morgan,	Vermont.
William Wick,	Western Reserve.
John Willard,	Vermont.
William F. Miller,	New York.
Samuel Leonard,	Vermont.
Samuel P. Robbins,	Ohio.
Thomas Robbins,	Western Reserve.
Thomas Williams,	New York.
Ira Hart,	New York.
Calvin Ingalls,	Vermont, New York and Penn.
Timothy Harris,	Ohio.
Oliver Wetmore,	Vermont.
Ebenezer Kingsbury,	New York and Pennsylvania.
Eli Hyde,	New York.
William Graves,	New York.
Israel Day,	Vermont.
Calvin Chapin,	Western Reserve.
Joseph Vaill,	New York.
Asa Carpenter,	Vermont and New York.
Ebenezer J. Leavenworth,	New York.
John Hough,	Vermont.
Israel Brainerd,	New York and Pensylvania.
Archibald Bassett,	New York.
Aaron Cleveland,	New York and Vermont.
Jonathan Leslie,	Western Reserve.
John Denison,	Vermont.
David Harrower,	New York and Pennsylvania.
Mark Mead,	New York.
Nathan B. Darrow,	Western Reserve and Ind.
Joel Byington	Vermont.
Silas L. Bingham,	Vermont.
Enoch Burt,	Western Reserve.
Erastus Ripley,	Vt. and N. Y., Penn. and Ohio.
Chauncey Lee,	Vermont and New York.
Daniel Waldo,	New York and Pennsylvania.
Joshua Beer,	Western Reserve.
Samuel Sweezey.	New York.
Samuel Baldridge,	Illinois.

Oliver Ayer,	New York and Pennsylvania.
Reuben Porter,	Pennsylvania.
Abner Benedict, Jr.	New York.
Lemuel Haynes,	Vermont and New York.
Eleazer Fairbanks,	New York.
Joseph Avery,	Vermont, New York and Penn.
John Bascom,	Pennsylvania.
James Boyd,	Western Reserve.
Salmon King,	Vermont and New York.
Hubbel Loomis,	New York.
Elihu Mason,	New York.
Israel Shailer,	Western Reserve.
Giles H. Cowles,	Western Reserve.
Cyrus Nichols,	Missouri.
William Lockwood,	New York and Pennsylvania.
Alvan Coe,	Western Reserve.
John F. Bliss,	New York and Pennsylvania.
Daniel G. Sprague,	West of Alleghanies.
Joseph M. Sadd,	Missouri.
Asahel Gaylord,	Vermont and New York.
Ammi Nichols,	Vermont.
James Parker,	Vermont and New York.
Asa Johnson,	Missouri.
Benj. F. Hoxey,	Missouri.
Jonathan A. Woodruff,	Illinois.
Caleb Pitkin,	Western Reserve.
Henry Frost,	New York.
Worthington Wright,	Pennsylvania.
Ebenezer Fitch,	New York.
John Matthews,	Missouri.
Simeon Parmelee,	Vermont and New York.
John Lawton,	Vermont.
Samuel Royce,	Louisiana.
Alfred H. Betts,	Western Reserve.
Joel F. Benedict,	New York and Pennsylvania.
Caleb Alexander,	New York.
Daniel Miller,	Western Reserve.
John Field.	Western Reserve.
Nathan Waldo,	New Hampshire and Vermont,
David H. Williston,	Vermont.
Lucas Hart,	Pennsylvania.
Moses Elliot,	Vermont.
Jonathan Hovey,	Vermont.
Ephraim T. Woodruff,	Western Reserve.

Nathaniel Cobb,	Western Reserve.
John Seward,	Western Reserve.
Flavel S. Gaylord,	Western Reserve.
M. M. York,	Pennsylvania and New York.
Samuel J. Mills,	Mississippi Valley.
Orange Lyman,	New York.
Orin Fowler,	Indiana.
William Shedd,	New Orleans.
John F. Schermerhorn,	Mississippi Valley.
David D. Field,	New York.
Joel Davis,	Vermont.
George C. Wood,	Missouri.
Elias Cornelius,	Louisiana.
Harvey Coe,	Western Reserve.
Oliver Hill,	Pennsylvania and New York.
Asaph Morgan,	Vermont and New Hampshire.
Abiel Jones,	Western Reserve.
Joel Goodell,	Missouri.
Simeon Woodruff,	Western Reserve.
Simeon Snow,	New York.
Eli Hyde,	New York.
Charles B. Storrs,	Western Reserve.
Harvey Coe,	Western Reserve.
Isaac Reed,	Kentucky and Indiana.
Joseph Treat,	Western Reserve.
Comfort Williams,	New York.
Orin Catlin,	Illinois.
Josiah Hopkins,	Vermont.
David M. Smith,	New York.
William Hanford,	Western Reserve.
Ard Hoyt,	Pennsylvania.
Hezekiah Hull,	Louisiana.
John F. Crow,	Indiana.
William Williams,	New York.
Eliphalet Austin, Jr.	Western Reserve.
William Wisner,	Pennsylvania.
Ahab Jincks,	Indiana.
Chester Colton,	New York.
Amos Chase,	Pennsylvania.
William R. Gould,	Ohio.
Warren Swift,	Western Reserve.
Luther Humphrey,	Western Reserve.
Justin Parsons,	Vermont.

Timothy Flint,	Ohio and Missouri.
Daniel W. Lathrop,	Western Reserve.
Daniel C. Banks,	Ohio and Kentucky.
Salmon Giddings,	Missouri.
Matthew Taylor,	Ohio.
Amasa Loomis,	Ohio.
Cyrus Kingsbury,	Tennessee.
John Sanford,	Virginia and Tennessee.
Dexter Witter,	Western Reserve.
Stephen Mason,	Kentucky.
Stephen W. Burritt,	New York.
Hervey Lyon,	Western Reserve.
Jason Olds,	Western Reserve.
Herman Halsey,	Kentucky.
Henry Cowles,	Illinois.
Dewey Whitney,	Kentucky.
Luther G. Bingham,	Ohio.
Prince Hawes,	New York.
William Fisher,	New York.
Joseph H. Breck,	Western Reserve.
Horace Smith,	Missouri and Illinois.
Lot B. Sullivan,	Western Reserve.
David Smith,	New York.
Eli Smith,	Kentucky, Indiana and Illinois.
Edward Hollister,	Illinois and Missouri.
Elbridge G. Howe,	Illinois.
Daniel Gould,	Illinois and Missouri.
Edson Hart,	Western Reserve.
Jesse Townsend,	Illinois.
Isaac W. Warner,	Western Reserve.
William Boies,	Ohio.
Luke Wood,	New York and Pennsylvania.
William W. Niles,	Tennessee.
Myron Tracy,	Western Reserve.
Randolph Stone,	Western Reserve.
Lyman Whitney,	Kentucky.
Ludovicus Robbins,	Western Reserve.
David C. Proctor,	Illinois.
Noah Smith,	New York.
Caleb Burbank,	Western Reserve.
Alfred Wright,	Missouri.
Asa Johnson,	Missouri.
Nathaniel Cobb,	Western Reserve.

Benjamin Fenn,	Western Reserve.
Thomas H. Rood,	Wisconsin.
William Johnson,	Western Reserve.
O. Parker,	Michigan.
Gideon C. Clark,	Illinois.
Jonathan Sampson,	Western Reserve.
E. I. Montague,	Wisconsin.
L. H. Parker,	Illinois.
Benj. Walker,	Western Reserve.
James Langhead,	Western Reserve.
John L. Seymour,	Western Reserve.
John Wilcox,	Western Reserve.
J. B. Parlin,	Western Reserve.
Franklin Maginnis,	Western Reserve.
Joel Talcott,	Western Reserve.
Ansel R. Clark,	Western Reserve.
Calvin Porter,	Western Reserve.
Z. K. Hawley,	Illinois.
Eldad Barber,	Western Reserve.
Nelson Slater,	Western Reserve.
George Schlosser,	Western Reserve.
Warren C. Fiske,	Wisconsin.
Edward C. Betts,	Western Reserve.
A. G. Hibbard,	Illinois.
Anson Gleason,	Mohegans.
Octavius Fitch,	Pennsylvania.
Erastus Cole,	Western Reserve.
D. R. Miller,	Illinois.
William Whittlesey,	Illinois.
James Nall,	Michigan.
Luther Shaw,	Western Reserve.
Ithamar Pillsbury,	Illinois.
S. S. Brown,	Michigan.
Sherman B. Canfield,	Western Reserve.
Christian Sans,	Wisconsin.
John W. Beecher,	Western Reserve.
Mark Gould,	Western Reserve.
Elery Curtis,	Western Reserve.
Louis F. Lane,	Western Reserve.
Josephus Morton,	Western Reserve.
M. P. Kinney,	Wisconsin.
Jonathan W. Goodell,	Western Reserve.
H. H. Morgan,	Minnesota.

Solomon Stevens,	Western Reserve.
Philip Everleth,	Western Reserve.
Enos H. Rice,	Michigan.
Hiram Smith,	Western Reserve.
A. L. Leonard,	Iowa.
E. N. Bartlett,	Michigan and Iowa.
Charles Morgan,	Wisconsin.
Urban Palmer,	Western Reserve.
Benson C. Baldwin,	Western Reserve.
Frederic H. Brown,	Western Reserve.
William Carter,	Illinois.
William Kirby,	Illinois.
Thomas Riggs,	Western Reserve.
William F. Vaill,	Illinois.
Samuel Lee,	Western Reserve.
Xenophon Betts,	Western Reserve.
F. E. Lord,	Michigan.
W. T. Bartle,	Illinois.
Aaron K. Wright,	Western Reserve.
Stephen C. Hickok,	Western Reserve.
George D. Young,	Western Reserve.
J. H. Dill,	New York.
Warren Taylor,	Western Reserve.
William Wolcott,	Michigan.
O. Hosford,	Michigan.
M. W. Fairfield,	Illinois and Michigan.
J. H. Payne,	Wisconsin.
W. B. Atkinson,	Iowa.
Joseph C. Cooper,	Iowa.
J. O. Knapp,	New York.
J. A. R. Rogers,	Illinois.
Burdett Hart.	Minnesota.

DOMESTIC MISSIONARY SOCIETY OF CONNECTICUT.

For a long period after the settlement of the colony of Connecticut, there was within its borders no call for that form of home missions which consists in aiding existing churches. The civil government, which was virtually a home missionary society, provided against such a contingency, by refusing to incorporate a town, unless there were inhabitants enough to support a minister—by taxing for the support of religious as well as other institutions—by allowing *winter* privileges to those too far from the place of worship to attend meeting conveniently at that season of the year—by fixing the limits of new parishes when a division became necessary, and suffering no church to be formed " without consent of the general court, and approbation of neighboring elders."

At length, however, from a variety of causes which this is not the place to detail, the churches became weakened, and it required some outward impulse to secure their existence. In 1783, the " Eastern Association of New London County " proposed to the General Association, sitting in Lyme, the question —" What shall be done respecting our destitute churches and congregations whose re-settlement in the enjoyment of Gospel ordinances is improbable ?" The General Association resolved in substance, at its next meeting, that a church guilty of "a faulty neglect to settle a minister"—if on conference and admonition it continued its neglect—should be cut off from the consociation ;—a measure which would rather aggravate than cure the disease. The evil continued to grow in magnitude, until it was said, in 1814, in a sermon which had no small share in hastening the application of a remedy—" There are, in this state, districts as far from heaven—and without help, as hopeless of heaven—as the pagans of Hindoostan and China.*"

At the meeting of the General Association in 1815, Rev. Messrs. Bassett, Nelson, and James Buchanan, the last named, a delegate from the General Assembly of the Presbyterian church in the United States—were chosen a committee to report on the request of the New London County Association, for the formation of a Domestic Missionary Society.† The result was

---

* *Beecher's Sermon on Waste Places in Connecticut.* Among the means suggested in this sermon, for building up these wastes is the formation of a "general society for the special purpose."

† " When I was ordained here, (New London,) in 1806, I was the only pastor of a Congregational church, on a territory in Connecticut, of fifty miles in length by twelve in width. Eleven large contiguous parishes, stretching from Sterling to the sea-board on the line of Rhode Island—thence to the western boundrey of East Lyme; thence northward to the southern line of Colchester, were, except New London, destitute of Congregational ministers. In 1808, the Rev. Ira Hart took charge of the church in Stonington, and in 1811, the Rev. Timothy Tuttle became the pastor of the church in Groton—an event better than our hope. In all the residue of the wide waste, nothing indicated resuscitation or improvement. Wealth enough there was ; people enough there were : a meeting house stood in every parish ; but men of energy, influence, and device, to step forth and regain the minis-

the choice of a committee to consider the subject and report at the next meeting of the body. On their report, at its next meeting in New Haven, it was resolved, unanimously, to form "a Domestic Missionary Society, for Connecticut and its vicinity."

At their first meeting, the directors voted that 17 churches of our denomination in this state needed aid. Six more were soon added to the list, while others seem not to have had energy enough to attempt recovery. Annual contributions were taken up, in September and October. By circulars and other measures, the directors endeavored to awaken interest in the object —but the receipts of the Society seldom exceeded $1500, and sometimes were less than $1000, annually,—a sum entirely inadequate to the wants of the feeble churches. The whole amount of contributions, from 1816 to 1830, was $20,386.69.

During the 14 years of its independent action, 50 churches sought its aid. Two or three of these are extinct, and but for its aid, others now self-sustaining might have shared the same fate.

In 1831, this Society became auxiliary to the American Home Missionary Society. The terms of union secure to the Auxiliary the control of the raising and application of funds, the selection and appointment of missionaries within this state—and the right to nominate for appointment by the Executive Committee of the American Home Missionary Society, missionaries out of the state, to the amount of its surplus funds ; such missionaries to be commissioned by the American Home Missionary Society, and to report to the Auxiliary whenever required by its directors.

The result of this union has been eminently happy. The treasury of the Auxiliary has never wanted means to minister

---

try, were not to be found. The few pastors, who were at length established on the outposts of this waste, were impatient of this rapid and constant degeneracy toward a state of heathenism, in a land of Christianity. At the old parsonage of this parish, one evening in 1815, the Rev. Ira Hart and myself conversed on the subject, and formed a project for a county missionary society, to restore the dilapidated churches and societies. The project, after a few weeks, was referred to the association ; who, after consultation resolved to forward a petition to the General Association of the State, soon to meet at Farmington, that a Home Missionary Society might be instituted for repairing the waste places of Connecticut and its vicinity."—*McEwen's Half-Century Sermon.*

to the necesities of our own churches, and for liberal supplies
to the destitute in other portions of the field. Very little has
been expended for foreign agencies—the services of local pastors and churches having proved sufficient to place Connecticut
among the foremost, in proportion to its population, resources
and number of churches, in the amount devoted to home
missions.

The receipts by the treasury of the Auxiliary to June 1,
1859, are $176,785.91. The treasury of the A. H. M. S. has
received directly from Connecticut, $342,427.95—making in
the whole, as the contribution of our churches and congregations to Home Missions, since the union of the Domestic Missionary Society of Connecticut, with the American Home
Missionary Society, $519,213.86, of which $401,791.57
were for missions out of the state.

The Auxiliary has aided about 80 churches in this state, of
which 42 became self-supporting under its patronage. Three or
four of the number have found it necessary to re-apply for aid,
which will be only temporarily needed, it is hoped, except in
a single case. It has aided several other congregations where
no church has been organized.

CHURCHES AND SOCIETIES AIDED BY THE DOMESTIC AND AUXILIARY
MISSIONARY SOCIETIES OF CONNECTICUT.

	Begun.	Ended.		Begun.	Ended.
North Stonington,	1816	1818	West Stafford,	1816	
East Lyme,	1816		Milton,	1816	
Chesterfield,	1816	1833	Bridgewater,	1817	1852
Voluntown and			East Franklin,	1817	1818
Sterling,	1816		Westfield,	1817	1833
Poquonnoc,	1816		Newtown,	1817	
Middlefield,	1816		Chaplin,	1817	1818
Ridgebury,	1816	1836	Seymour,	1817	
Bethel,	1816	1842	Salem,	1817	
New Stratford,			Naugatuck,	1833	1834
(Monroe,)	1816	1846	Eastford,	1817	
Northfield in Weston,	1816	1824	Eastbury,	1822	1858
Greenwich,	1816	1817	Darien,	1824	1836
Oxford,	1816	1837	New Fairfield,	1825	1845
Union,	1816		Willimantic,	1827	1839
Stafford, (East,)	1816	1836	West Suffield,	1827	1854

Bozrahville,	1827	1846	Windham,	1836	
Hamden, (E. Plains)	1827	1846	South Glastenbury,	1837	
Westford,	1828	1856	West Hartland,	1839	
Exeter,	1827	1853	Col'd Church, New		
East Hampton,	1828	1845	Haven,	1840	
North Stamford,	1828	1829	Groton,	1841	1848
Turkey Hills,	1829	1857	South Canaan,	1842	1843
Jewett City,	1829	1855	Hitchcockville,	1842	
Andover,	1829	1836	Abington,	1844	1845
Killingworth,	1829	1830	Sherman,	1844	1845
North Madison,	1831		Rainbow,	1844	1850
Grassy Hill,	1831		Windsor Locks,	1845	1852
North Mansfield,	1824		Middle Haddam,	1845	
Burlington,	1831		Kensington,	1845	1846
Mohegan Indians.	1832	1834	East Hartland,	1847	
Wolcottville,	1832	1835	North Lyme,	1847	
Wapping,	1832	1860	Putnam,	1847	1857
Millington,	1832	1833	Ashford,	1850	
Greenville,	1832	1839	Barkhamsted,	1849	
New Fairfield,	1832	1845	Daysville,	1849	1850
South Killingly,	1832	1856	German Mission in		
Hadlyme,	1832		Connecticut,	1848	
Tariffville,	1832	1843	Stafford Springs,	1850	1858
Unionville,	1833	1852	Ansonia,	1850	1851
West Avon,	1834	1848	Broad Brook,	1850	
Col'd Cong. Church,			Staffordville,	1852	
Hartford,	1834		Danbury, 2d Church,	1852	1854
West Haven,	1834	1843	Essex,	1852	1853
Long Soc., Preston,	1833	1850	Wauregan,	1855	
Bolton,	1834		West Woodstock,	1854	
Westville,	1835	1855	Northfield,	1855	1856
Franklin,	1835	1840	Falls Village,	1859	
North Goshen,	1835	1845			

With regard to some churches on the list, it is impossible to present all the facts in the case in a brief table. For example, some to whom aid was extended in 1816 are still on the list, though they have not been aided every year since. In some cases there may have been half a dozen breaks in the chain of aid. For perfect accuracy in individual churches, it will be necessary to consult the original records.

GRADUATES OF YALE COLLEGE WHO HAVE SERVED AS FOREIGN MISSIONARIES.

GRAD.

1809,	Benjamin C. Meigs,	Ceylon.
1816,	Isaac Bird,	Western Asia.
	Asa Thurston,	Sandwich Islands.
1819,	Elnathan Gridley,	Western Asia.
1821,	Dwight Baldwin, M. D.	Sandwich Islands.
	Josiah Brewer,	Western Asia.
	Joseph Goodrich,	Sandwich Islands.
	Eli Smith,	Western Asia.
1826,	James T. Dickinson,	Singapore.
1827,	John M. S. Perry,	Ceylon.
1828,	Edwin Stevens,	China.
1829,	George H. Apthorp,	Ceylon.
	John F. Lanneau,	Western Asia.
1831,	George Champion,	South Africa.
	Peter Parker, M. D.,	China.
1832,	Henry A. DeForest, M. D.,	Western Asia.
1833,	Samuel Wólcott,	Western Asia.
1834,	Henry S. G. French,	Siam.
	Samuel G. Whittlesey,	Ceylon.
1835,	Charles S. Sherman,	Western Asia.
1837,	Azariah Smith, M. D.,	Western Asia.
1838,	David T. Stoddard,	Western Asia.
1840,	Timothy Dwight Hunt,	Sandwich Islands.
	Charles S. Shelton, M. D.,	India.
1842,	Lewis Grout,	South Africa.
	Seth B. Stone,	South Africa.
1843,	William A. Benton,	Western Asia.
1844,	John W. Dulles,	India.
	Henry Kinney,	Sandwich Islands.
	Charles Little,	India.
	William A. Macy,	China.
	Samuel D. Marsh,	South Africa.
1845,	Oliver Crane,	Western Asia.
1846,	William B. Capron,	India.

1847, Andrew T. Pratt, M. D.,   Western Asia.
1848, William Aitchison,   China.
      Henry Blodget,   China.
1849, Augustus Walker,   Western Asia.
1850, Benjamin Parsons,   Western Asia.
1851, Henry H. Jessup,   Western Asia.
      Julius Y. Leonard,   Western Asia.
1853, William Frederick Arms,   Western Asia.
      Hiram Bingham, Jr.,   Micronesia.
      Charles Harding,   India.
1854, William Hutchison,   Turkey.
1855, Henry N. Cobb,   Kurdistan.

MISSIONARIES OF THE PROTESTANT EPISCOPAL CHURCH.

1825, Thomas S. Savage, M. D.,   West Africa.
1831, Wm. I. Kip, Mis'y Bishop,   California.
1850, Robert Smith,   Western Africa.

MISSIONARIES AMONG THE NORTH AMERICAN INDIANS.

1720, Jonathan Edwards,   Stockbridge Indians.
1729, John Sergeant,   Stockbridge Indians.
1746, John Brainerd,   New York Indians.
1806, William F. Vaill.   Osages.

MISSIONARY OF THE DUTCH REFORMED BOARD.

1853, Samuel R. Brown,   Japan.

We have no knowledge of a time in the history of Yale College when there were not resident graduates preparing for the ministry. From the year 1755, this class of pupils were in the habit of pursuing their studies under the guidance of the Professor of Divinity. By Dr. Dwight and by his predecessors Doctors Daggett and Wales, several hundred of the Alumni of the college were educated for the pastoral office. Among the persons who studied theology under the direction of Dr. Dwight, may be named, for example, Rev. Moses Stuart, who was converted in the revival of 1801, united with the College Church in 1803, and was the first Professor of Sacred Literature at Andover. As the need of a more extensive course of theological study came to be felt, Dr. Dwight began to cherish the purpose of increasing the means of instruction thus furnished. When the project of a seminary at Andover was under discussion in Massachusetts, his advice was sought by Dr. Morse of Charlestown, and Dr. Spring of Newburyport, who visited New Haven for the purpose of consulting him. He expressed to them his warm approval of the proposed undertaking, at the same time assuring them that he had long been desirous of providing a more complete and systematic course of theological instruction in Yale College ; and that he should embrace the earliest opportunity of carrying out, in this particular, what he deemed to be the design of its founders. After the interview with these gentlemen, he stated confidentially to his young friend and amanuensis, Mr Taylor, (the late Rev. Dr. Taylor,) that his eldest son, Mr. Timothy Dwight, a merchant of New Haven, had invested a sum of money in a business enterprise, which, with the profits arising from it, was to be ultimately given for the object above mentioned. In 1822, fifteen young men, graduates of the college, laid before the faculty a petition that they might be received as a theological class for the ensuing year. This petition was made at the suggestion of Rev. Professor Fitch, and to him belongs in no small measure the credit of its success. He addressed to the corporation an able argument on the subject.

The question was thus distinctly presented whether Yale College should cease to be a school for theological education. The faculty considering the original design of the pious founders of the institution, and the importance of maintaining its dignity and religious usefulness, determined to recommend to the corporation to establish a theological department upon an improved and permanent basis. At this time Mr. Dwight came forward with a subscription of $5,000 towards an endowment for a Professor of Didactic Theology. Had he not been prevented by misfortunes in trade, he would have fulfilled his intention of greatly increasing his first donation. The sum of $20,000 was collected for the professorship. This was accepted by the corporation, who proceeded to establish the Theological Department, grounding their action on the fact that "one of the principal objects of the pious founders of this college, was the education of pious young men for the work of the ministry." The corporation likewise voted "that in commemoration of the high sense which this board entertains of the distinguished merits of the Rev. Timothy Dwight, D. D., late President of this college, and of his eminent services and usefulness while in office, the professorship this day established, shall take his name, and be styled the Dwight Professorship of Didactic Theology." The Rev. Nathaniel W. Taylor, then Pastor of the First Church in New Haven, who had been a beloved pupil of Dr. Dwight, was elected to fill the office. Instruction in Hebrew was first given by Professor Kingsley, the Professor of Languages in College, and in the Greek of the New Testament by Dr. Fitch, Professor of Divinity. Subsequently, in 1824, Mr. Josiah W. Gibbs was invited to act as Professor of Sacred Literature. The Professorship in that department was instituted in 1826, and Mr. Gibbs was then elected Professor. The Rev. Dr. Goodrich was afterwards made Professor of the Pastoral charge, and Dr. Fitch retained his connection with the Seminary, as instructor in Homiletics. The death of Dr. Taylor occurred in 1858, and that of Dr. Goodrich in 1860. Mr. Timothy Dwight, grandson of President Dwight, was made an Assistant Professor of Sacred Literature, in the same year.

The number of students who have received instruction in the theological school since its re-organization is about 700.

FACULTY.

*Presidents.**

ELECTED.		RETIRED.
1822.	Rev. Jeremiah Day, D.D., LL.D.	1846.
1840.	Rev. Theo. D. Woolsey, D.D., LL.D.,	

Livingston Professors of Divinity.

1755.	Naphtali Daggett, D.D.	1780.
1782.	Samuel Wales ,D. D.	1794.
1805.	Timothy Dwight, D. D.	1817.
1817.	Eleazar T. Fitch, D. D.	1852.
1854.	George P. Fisher.	

Professor of Ecclesiastical History.

1777.	Ezra Stiles, D. D.	1795.

Dwight Professor of Didactic Theology.

1822.	† Nathaniel W. Taylor, D. D.	1858.

Professor of Sacred Literature.

1824.	Josiah W. Gibbs, LL.D.

Professor of the Pastoral Care.

1839.	Chauncey A. Goodrich, D. D.	1860.

Assistant Professor of Sacred Literature.

1858.	Timothy Dwight.

---

* According to the present organization, the President of the College is the President of the Theological Faculty.

† Since the death of Dr. Taylor, the duties of this professorship have been discharged by Rev. Noah Porter, D. D., Clark Professor of Moral Philosophy and Metaphysics in the Academical Department.

THEOLOGICAL INSTITUTE OF CONNECTICUT.

BY REV. CHARLES HYDE, ELLINGTON.

The establishment of the Theological Seminary at East Windsor Hill now forms part of the history of Congregationalism in Connecticut. Whatever difference of opinion there may be as to its expediency, the facts connected with its establishment cannot be altered; and simply as matters of history they are here presented.

This Seminary originated, as its friends have no wish to disguise, principally, in the solicitude felt at the time by many, especially of the Congregational ministers of this state, in reference to certain doctrines taught, and the mode of instruction and principles of interpretation adopted, at New Haven. It seemed to them that the sound doctrines of New England Calvinism, as taught by Edwards, Bellamy, Smalley, and Dwight, were in danger of being undermined and swept away. And they felt constrained to devise, if possible, some judicious and practicable method to preserve and perpetuate them.

As early as January 1833, at the suggestion and earnest request of the venerable Dr. Perkins, of West Hartford, a conference of ministers on the state of the churches was held at Hartford. Invitations had been sent to all the associations of the state, requesting them to send each two pastors. A few, also, in the nearest portions of Massachusetts were invited. About twenty only were present.

On invitation of a committee appointed at this meeting, another was held at East Windsor on September 10th, 1833, for consultation, and such action as should seem to be desirable. About forty ministers were present. Two days were spent in prayerful deliberation, resulting in the determination to establish a new Theological Seminary, provided a subscription of twenty thousand dollars could be obtained. These brethren formed themselves into a Pastoral Union, adopted a constitution and creed as the basis of their organization, and appointed a board of trustees. They then opened a subscription upon the spot, and the twenty thousand dollars were secured in the January following.

The wish and design of these ministers was not only to check the prevailing tendencies to error, but, as far as human means could avail, to guard against future lapses. Hence they not only adopted what they considered a sound creed, to which the professors in the new institution should be required to give their assent, renewing it yearly, but sought to establish a seminary that should be in closer connection with the churches than any then existing in New England. The trustees are elected by the "Pastoral Union," and amenable, directly, and through them the professors, to that body.

"The growing demand for ministers of the gospel, and the rapid increase of theological students, the liability of such institutions to become corrupt in doctrine, and the necessity of increasing their number that they might operate as a check upon each other, and that no one shall become overgrown," were also assigned as reasons for establishing the new seminary.

In the Constitution of the Pastoral Union, its object is stated to be, the promotion of ministerial intercourse, fellowship and pastoral usefulness; the promotion of revivals of religion, the defense of evangelical truth against prevailing errors in doctrine or in practice, and the raising up of sound and faithful ministers for the supply of the churches. The "Articles of Agreement" adopted by our brethren convened at Hartford, January 9, 1833, as amended, shall be the doctrinal basis of this union. The number of articles is twenty, and they are too long to be here inserted. The Constitution also provides that pastors and ordained ministers may become members of the Union by nomination and vote, and signing the Articles of Agreement; the Union may establish seminaries and periodical publications; the Constitution, but not the Articles of Agreement, may be altered; and ministers out of the state may become members.

This constitutional basis being adopted, the Pastoral Union immediately adopted a plan for the regulation of the contemplated Seminary, the distinguishing features of which are that its title should be the Theological Institute of Connecticut, that its general management and oversight should be vested in a Board of Trustees, consisting of at least twelve ministers, and eight laymen, to be appointed annually by the Pastoral Union, and that " every trustee and officer in the Institute shall, on entering upon his duties, subscribe the Creed of the Pastoral Union of Connecticut." He shall also declare his full assent to it every year during his continuance in office.

In virtue of their appointment, and in accordance with the constitution of the Institute, the Trustees proceeded to locate the Institute, to elect a Faculty, to provide the requisite buildings and library, and to do whatever was necessary to put the Seminary into operation.

The Institute was located at East Windsor Hill. The Rev. Bennet Tyler, D. D., of Portland, Maine, was chosen President and professor of Theology, and Rev. Jonathan Cogswell, D. D., of New Britain, professor of Ecclesiastical History.

On the 13th May, 1834, the corner stone of the seminary edifice was laid by Rev. Dr. Perkins, and on the same day the two elected professors were inducted into office. In October following, Rev. William Thompson of North Bridgewater, Mass., was chosen professor of Biblical Literature, and the seminary went into full operation with a respectable number of students.

The course of instruction in this institution has ever been peculiarly Biblical. The professors have aimed to inculcate God's truth. The great question has been what has God said, and not what does human philosophy teach. The doctrines taught are such as for the most part have been held by the great lights of New England already named, but with no slavish regard to human authority. Associations and Ecclesiastical Councils have borne pleasing testimony to the thoroughness of instruction, as well as soundness in the faith of the graduates of the Institute.

The friends of the Institute, though struggling against many opposing influences, feel that they have not labored in vain. They think that something has been done to maintain and perpetuate what they believe to be the true gospel, to check the tendencies to error, and greatly to modify the theological views of those who had strongly sympathized with the speculations and doctrines which led to their enterprise.

Within a few years past several friends of the two institutions of the state have cherished the hope that they might be united.   The heat of the controversy had subsided, both institutions were depressed, each having but few students, and great advantages it was thought would result from their union. Seeming obstacles it was thought could be removed.   At all events it was worth while to make the attempt.   The matter was laid before the trustees, committees were appointed to confer with the New Haven gentlemen and see on what terms the union could be consummated.   But it was soon found that difficulties insuperable were in the way, and the design was relinquished.

It should be gratefully recorded, that the leaders in the controversy which so long continued, while they earnestly contended for their respective views, never ceased to cherish and to manifest to each other feelings of Christian kindness and charity.   The senior professors of the two institutions have now gone to their account, and we doubt not their gracious reward.   They doubtless now see eye to eye.   New professors have been chosen in their places.

Its whole number of students have been, to September 1859, 238; its graduates, 148.

The Institute has revived from its late depression, and with what may be esteemed for its age, a liberal endowment, and provision to a considerable extent for the aid of necessitous students.   Under the smiles of a gracious Providence it is hoped it may be a fountain, yearly sending forth streams to make glad the city of God.

FACULTY.

President and Professor of Christian Theology.

ELECTED.   RESIGNED.
1833.   Rev. Bennet Tyler, D. D.   1857.

Professor of Ecclesiastical History.

1834.   Rev. Jonathan Cogswell, D. D. 1844.

Nettleton Professor of Biblical Literature.

1834.   Rev. William Thompson, D. D.

Professor of Sacred Rhetoric.

1844.   Rev. Edward W. Hooker, D. D. 1848.

Waldo Professor of Ecclesiastical History and Pastoral Duty.

1851.   Rev. Nahum Gale, D. D.   1853.
1854.   Rev. Edward A. Lawrence, D. D.

Riley Professor of Christian Theology.

1858.   Rev. Robert G. Vermilye, D. D.

Dr. Nettleton, also, gave occasional familiar lectures to the students on *Revivals of Religion* and kindred topics, from 1834 to 1844.

SABBATH SCHOOLS.

BY REV. JOEL HAWES, D. D., HARTFORD.

As Sabbath schools have come to be regarded as a permanent agency in promoting the cause of Christ, it has been thought proper to present on this occasion, a brief notice of their origin, progress, and present condition, especially in connection with our denomination.

It is not easy to mark the precise time of the commencement of Sabbath schools. It is the common belief that they originated with Robert Raikes in the city of Gloucester, England, in 1781. And this is probably true, if reference be had only to the *present system* of Sabbath school instruction. But something equivalent to this mode of instruction, and often approaching very near to it in form, can be traced through every period of the history of the church. Not to refer to earlier examples, as far back as the beginning of the 16th century, Carlo Borromeo, Archbishop of Milan, though a Catholic, feeling a deep interest in the instruction of the young, founded within his diocese 740 schools, with 3,040 teachers and 40,098 scholars. At the Cathedral in Milan he gathered children by thousands on the Sabbath, classified under catechetical teachers, and superintended by himself. The Waldenses pursued a very similar course in the religious instruction of their children and youth. Schools though in a somewhat different form from the present system, have been coeval with the settlement of New England. Our pilgrim fathers showed the greatest care in the religious instruction of the young. They were accustomed to spend a portion of each Sabbath in gathering around them the younger members of their households, and teaching them from the word of God. The pastors, too, had their appointed seasons for catechising the children and youth of their charge on the Sabbath, and at other times ; and in this good work they were wont to be urged by the officers and other members of the church.

In Roxbury, Masachusetts, a Sabbath school was established in the Congregational church there in 1764, in which the male youth remained every Sabbath, after morning service, to be instructed by their elders, and the female youth by their elders, in the catechism and the Scriptures. Dr. Bellamy, pastor of the church in Bethlehem in this state, from 1740 till the time of his death, was accustomed to meet the youth of his congregation on the Sabbath, not merely for a catechetical exercise, but for a recitation from the Bible, accompanied with familiar instruction, suited to the capacities of the young. In this exercise, too, he was often assisted by members of his church. And it was said by the Rev. Mr. Langdon, who was settled for some time in the same parish, that he had reason to believe they had never been without a Sabbath school from the earliest settlement of the town.

In Washington, in this state, about the year 1781, the same year in which Robert Raikes commenced the first Sabbath school in Gloucester, some of the fathers of the church gathered their children around them under the trees which shaded the Green, and there, during the Sabbath intermissions in the summer, instructed them in the word of God and the Assembly's Catechism. Examples similar to the two last named might be multiplied to almost any extent. Indeed it has been characteristic of our Congregational churches, from their earliest history, to care for the religious training of the rising generation, and this duty has always been faithfully performed just in proportion as religion has revived and flourished among the people. The modern system of Sabbath school instruction has changed somewhat the form, but did not originate the fact of the social teaching of the young in our congregations on the Sabbath in the knowledge of God and salvation.

The first Sabbath school, or among the first, after *the modern system*, in this country, was established, it is said, in Philadelphia in 1791, ten years after its origin in England. In 1803 the late Mr. Bethune, with his wife and her mother, Mrs. Isabella Graham, of blessed memory, opened a school at her own expense in the city of New York, and superintended two or three others, established through their instrumentality. From 1812 to 1824, Sabbath schools were established to a wide extent in New

England and the middle states. The system was introduced into this state about this period. I find it stated that a Sabbath school was opened by six young men in the city of Norwich in 1816. In 1818, about a month after my ordination, the four churches in Hartford united and formed a Sabbath school society, and adopted measures for an efficient organization of a Sunday school in each of the congregations. Something had been done in the way of collecting and teaching the young on the Sabbath some time before. But the system as such was inaugurated on the 8th of April, 1818. Soor the same system spread into other parts of the state, and ere long a Sabbath school came to be regarded as an essential appendage to every healthy and growing church. The system was at first very imperfect. But experience worked improvement, and gradually it has grown to what it is, not yet perfect, but far in advance of what it was in the beginning ; and it is now justly regarded as one of the most efficient agencies we have for instructing the young, and building up our churches in truth and faithfulness unto God. It reaches not the young alone, but all ages and classes of society. There is not a church of our denomination in the state, nor of any other, having a well conducted Sabbath school, that is not the better in all its interests, for sustaining such an institution. Take a few facts. It is estimated that there are now 66,000 scholars of all ages in the various Sabbath schools in this state, some 15,000 of whom are over 18 years of age. There are 9,500 teachers in these schools, engaged from Sabbath to Sabbath in planting the seed of the Word in these 66,000 tender, receptive minds. Instruction is given, sympathy is expressed, prayer is offered, and God sends down His Spirit to bless both the teachers and the taught. During the year 1858, memorable for the great revival, 8,000 were reported as having been hopefully converted and brought to Christ in all the Sabbath schools of the state. What number of these were of our denomination I have not the means of stating. For many years past it appears from the best evidence that a very large proportion, at least seventy-five per cent., probably more, of all that unite with our churches on a profession of religion, are gathered

from those who have been or were at the time, members of
the Sabbath school.

And very gratifying it is to mark the steady progress of the
Sabbath school system, not only in the character and extent of
its influence, but in the methods and subjects of its instruction.
At first the chief aim was to gather the poor and the neglected
into the schools and teach them the common rudiments of
learning, and to commit texts of Scripture with the catechism
to memory. Soon the better classes of society, observing the
happy influence of this mode of instruction, sought to place
their children in Sabbath schools, and now the youthful members of our first families are found, in large proportion, in these
nurseries of Bible knowledge and early piety. At first those
who taught were hired to do their work, as was the fact in the
schools established by Mr. Raikes in Gloucester, and for a time
this practice seems to have been common. To John Wesley,
in 1785, is attributed the credit of introducing the present system of unpaid teaching, and of exclusive religious instruction.
Now the whole work is by a voluntary agency, and teachers,
prompted by benevolence, rejoice to engage in this method of
doing good. At first only small children were thought to be
proper subjects of Sabbath school instruction, and almost any
one, who could be obtained, was deemed qualified to instruct
them. Now thousands of our youth, over eighteen years of
age, with large numbers of adult persons, are found in the
Sabbath school, and a full share of the best talent in our
churches is engaged in the business of instruction. At first,
and indeed for a long time, there were very few helps in the
work of Sabbath school instruction; the Bible, *always* in
place, and the catechism being almost the only books in use.
There were no appropriate Sunday school books, or teachers,
or libraries, and few commentaries that were suited to aid in
the work to be done. But in process of time, a Sabbath school
literature of a high character has grown up; hundreds, not to
say thousands of Sunday school books, excellently adapted to
interest, and instruct the young, have been published and assorted into libraries; and these, with the numerous helps now
afforded the teacher, to assist him to understand the Bible and
the best mode of communicating its precious truth to the young

26

mind, leave scarcely anything to be desired in the way of external appliances to make our Sabbath school apparatus complete. At first, the object of Sabbath schools scarcely rose higher than to keep children out of mischief, or teach them to recite from memory passages of Scripture, in the hope that perchance some good influence might emanate from the exercise. But this low aim has long since passed away, and one much more elevated and spiritual has taken its place. The object now in every well conducted Sabbath school is to teach the young the way of salvation, to lodge in their minds the saving truths of the gospel, and bring them all into the fold of the good shepherd. This is as it should be, and corresponding have been the tokens of God's approbation.

Such are some of the marks of progress in the system of Sabbath school instruction. And they are certainly very encouraging. But the system, though greatly in advance of what it was only a few years since, is still far from being perfect. There are, no doubt, defects, both in organization, mode of teaching, and books, which more experience will discover and correct ; and happy will he be, who shall be enabled to do anything to add to the completeness and efficiency of a system which has been and is productive of wide spread and most beneficent results.

The phrase " well conducted Sabbath school " occurs in what is said above. Were I to describe such a school it would be in this wise ;—the superintendent, who is in fact the motive power at the center of the whole machine, should be a man well qualified for his place, intelligent, kind, genial, warm-hearted, with aptness and skill to discern character, and adapt himself to different temperaments, and earnestly devoted to his work, *from the love of it.* He should be surrounded with a band of intelligent, faithful, cooperative teachers of different ages and of both sexes, who shall be prompt and punctual in their places, thoroughly prepared in their lessons, and ready to meet their classes with hearts of love and words of kindness, earnestly desiring to win them to Christ. The scholars should be taught, both at home and in the school, to be always in season, ready to meet their teacher and listen to his instruction the moment the exercises commence ; and it should be understood both by teachers and pupils, that the hour they spend together is not to be spent, as it sometimes is, in small talk, or in telling stories to entertain and amuse, but in the serious, earnest study of the Bible, in order to communicate and learn its truths, and so become wise unto salvation. Measures should be adopted by visitation, or otherwise, to draw all the children and youth of the congregation into the school, with as many others of adult age as can be persuaded to attend ; and then all should be organized in well assorted classes, and each class furnished with a well qualified teacher, suited to their different ages and characters. The pastor should feel a deep and lively interest in the school ; he should look upon it as the right arm of his ministry ; as the pleasantest and most hopeful part of the garden he is called to cultivate ; and encouraging all who labor in it by his counsels and presence, he should tenderly nurture the plants gathered there, that they may grow and bring forth fruit unto eternal life. With the pastor, the parents of the scholars, and all the members of the church should join their influence ; the one instructing and preparing the children at home in the lessons which are appointed in school, and all remembering both scholars and teachers in their prayers, and all coming together at the monthly Sabbath school concert, which should by all means be kept up, to unite in mutual counsel, sympathy and supplication, for the blessing of God to rest upon the good work and crown it with success in the salvation of those for whom this labor of love is performed. Added to all, the missionary element should enter prominently into the management of the school, and all the members of it should be taught from their earliest age to feel an interest in the poor and perishing, wherever they are, and to contribute their mites, from time to time, to aid in sending to them the blessings of the gospel.

Something like this is the idea in my mind of a well conducted Sabbath school. I would, of course, have it well furnished with a teacher's library, and a library of judiciously selected books for the scholars ; and then I would concentrate upon it the united, intelligent, Christian influence of superintendent, teachers, pastor, parents, members of the church, and all, in the one great object, of making the school a school for training up immortal beings to serve God and their generation on earth, and to inherit everlasting happiness in Heaven.

What proportion of the Sabbath schools in the state, or in connection with our denomination, realize in any good measure this idea of what they should be, I have no means of knowing. But I cannot avoid thinking, that a Sunday school conducted after the model here presented, or coming near to it, would send a constant flow of increase both of piety and of members into the churches, first training its pupils for the communion of the church on earth, and then transferring them to the communion of saints above. And the time will come, I am sure, when this will be the process of nurturing the rising generation ; it will commence in early and faithful parental instruction in the family ; then pass into the Sabbath school to be. advanced there ; and next into the church, to be carried still further on ; and finally be perfected in Heaven, in the happy reunion of parents, children, teachers, pastors and all who have heartily aided in the good work, with the great family of the redeemed in Heaven. Such a day is yet to rise and bless the church and the world ; and happy they who contribute anything by their prayers and efforts to hasten so glorious a consummation !

REVIVALS OF RELIGION.

The history of special revivals of religion in Connecticut need not be written here. Contemporaneous memoirs of two important periods are preserved in Prince's Christian History, (2 vols. Boston 1743, 1744,) and in the Connecticut Evangelical Magazine, (Hartford, 1800—1814.) Tracy's "Great Awakening" sums up with much ability the memoirs of the former period, and the late Dr. Tyler re-edited the materials which had been collected in the successive volumes of the Evangelical Magazine, but had ceased to be generally accessible. Both these works are published by the Congregational Board of Publication. In this article nothing more is proposed than briefly to indicate the distinct periods of spiritual reviving in our churches, the extent of those revivals, the means which have been used, and some of the results.

Probably all our churches have been visited, at one time or another, with special revivals of religion. Some of them have been blessed in this way very frequently. The first general awakening which makes its mark distinctly in our religious history was about the year 1740, commencing in some churches four or five years earlier, and continuing for several years. That movement began at Northampton, Mass., in 1735, under the ministry of Jonathan Edwards, and extended into various parts of New England. The formalism of the preceding age, the general use of the half way covenant, and at last the Stoddardean principle that the Lord's Supper is to be used as a means of regeneration, had brought into full communion in the churches a body of confessedly unregenerate men. Edwards and others saw that in faithfulness to that class of hearers, it was necessary to preach to them such truth, and with such personal application, as they had not been wont to hear. His sermons on justification by faith, and his sermons proving that "every mouth shall be stopped," had a powerful effect, and several persons were wrought upon in a remarkable manner, —some to all appearance savingly converted. According to Tracy's account, the report of this state of things at North-

ampton spread into other towns; great numbers went to Northampton to see for themselves, and not a few of them from
various places were awakened and apparently brought to repentance. The revival began to be general in Suffield and in
Windsor about the same time as at Northampton. Edwards
himself preached in some places in Connecticut, as at Enfield
in July 1740, what was noted as his Enfield sermon, "Sinners
in the hands of an angry God." The work had spread before
this into almost all the region. It was "remarkable" at East
Windsor, and "wonderful" at Coventry. Similar scenes were
also witnessed at Lebanon, Durham, Stratford, Huntington,
New Haven, Guilford, Mansfield, Tolland, Hebron, Bolton,
Preston, Groton and Woodbury. Prince's "Christian History,"
contains accounts of the revival in fourteen churches, written
or subscribed by their pastors ; thirty churches in Connecticut
are mentioned as having shared in the blessing.

Among a portion of the ministers, and of the churches, there
was great opposition to this revival, or rather to some of its ac-
companiments. The measures adopted by some excited their
fears, and the extravagances practiced led them to use all the
caution and influence in their power, in opposition. Resulting
from these and other causes, there was a great decay of revivals for many years after. At the close of the great revival of
1740, James Davenport, and others misled by him, fell into
grievous fanatical excesses, rent asunder churches, and occasioned much confusion in the estimate of many who did not
sufficiently discriminate, thus bringing all revivals into suspicion and discredit. After that, the rise of the Separate churches,
growing partly out of opposition to the revival, and occasioning much controversy not favorable to high religious feeling ;
the civil troubles of the times, in the old French war from 1756
to 1763, the revolutionary war from 1775 to 1783 ; the gradual
restoration of domestic tranquility on the conclusion of peace ;
the agitation of questions concerning the establishment of a
general government ;—all constituting so many exciting and
important public matters, crowded upon the attention of the
people, and thereby the things of true religion were kept in
the back-ground and there were scarcely any revivals in the
land. These causes partly account for the infrequency of

special effusions of the Spirit, without ascribing it wholly to the judgment of Heaven for opposition, from differences of views and spirit, to the great awakening. Considering all the exciting topics of the times, and the state of the people in their civil and ecclesiastical affairs, it had been strange if revivals had been as numerous from 1750 to 1790, as before and since.

But even in those troublous times, the churches were not wholly forsaken. There were here and there revivals, which made considerable additions to their membership, 10, 20, 30, and in one instance in 1774, 85. There were some revivals in 1783, several in 1768–9, and others from 1780 to 1785.

But the era of modern revivals dates from the year 1792. During all the closing years of the last century and as many of the present, revivals were very general, not only in this state, but throughout New England. Dr. Griffin says, " from that date I saw a continued succession of heavenly sprinklings, until I could stand at my door in New Hartford, and number fifty or sixty congregations laid down in one field of divine wonders." The Evangelical Magazine contains accounts of these works of grace during that period, in every part of the state. There were also revivals in many more places, concerning which no accounts were published.

Since that revival period at the beginning of the century, these seasons of refreshing have been frequent. Particularly the years 1816, '21, '26, '31, '38, '49; '53 and '58, and in many cases, years preceding or succeeding these, have been the most favored.

The great Awakening originated under the preaching of Edwards as already stated. Among the chief instruments of furthering the work were pastors Parsons of Lyme, Wheelock of Columbia, Pomroy of Hebron, Bellamy of Bethlem, Griswold of East Lyme, Croswell of Ledyard, and others. These and others labored more or less beyond the bounds of their own parishes, as they were invited to aid other pastors. Whitfield made one rapid tour across the state from Springfield by Hartford and New Haven to New York. The fervor of Parsons, who learned quickly by experience the dangers of the times, the zeal of Wheelock and Pomroy, and the activity and wisdom and doctrinal depth of Bellamy, gave a powerful impulse to the work. They found kindred spirits in both clergy and laity to cooperate with them.

In 1755 and for several years after, circular fasts were adopted as means for awakening and promoting attention to true religion, in some parts of the State. Several churches by their ministers, delegates and members voluntarily attending, went from church to church to hold seasons of fasting and religious services for the reviving of true religion ; and these means proved instrumental of much good.

In the revivals of 1792 to 1808, the means used were little else than the official preaching of the doctrines of the cross, with such illustrations and applications as resulted from the thoroughly Calvinistic views advanced by Bellamy and Smalley, and taught by them and by Backus, Hooker and others of a kindred spirit, to their pupils in theology. Dr. Bellamy died just before these last revival days, Dr. Backus in the midst of them, and Smalley and Hooker lived several years after. But their teachings and the kind of preaching which characterized the ministry of Griffin, Hallock, Mills, Gillett and many others might well result in a general revival. Other states also shared in the divine effusions of these days.

Next came in 1813, and till after the revival of 1831, the labors of Dr. Nettleton. His judicious and well-directed efforts in aid of pastors and the almost unexceptionable measures and influence he used, are well known, though in the view of some his itinerating has furnished an example and occasion for other evangelists, destitute of his wisdom and respect for the settled ministry, to run into excesses and extremes in their measures, productive of infinite mischief for the time being, rendering the ordinary means of grace inefficient in following their excitements, causing many men to lose all respect for revivals and thus doing incalculable and lasting evil, though not without some partial good.

In 1821, there seemed to be no immediate cause of the remarkable awakening, in the special efforts of ministers and Christians, but while they were mourning over the low state of Zion, suddenly the Lord appeared to build up Zion in his glory.

In 1826–7, conferences of churches were held—pastors and

particularly laymen of several churches visited particular churches in turn, and attended public meetings for conference and prayer.

In 1831, and for a few years following, continuous or protracted meetings for some days were held, and when wisely and cautiously conducted, were productive of much good. The extravagances and extreme measures practiced in some other states never accorded with the staid habits and religious principle of our churches and people, and were but seldom adopted. From that time,—after these meetings had passed away, occasional itinerant evangelists have labored in here and there a church, assisting its pastor during a time of religious interest, but more frequently pastors have aided one another, as the most judicious and unexceptional method.

The revival of 1858 seemed to be chiefly originated and carried on by means different from any preceding, by prayer and conference meetings, with comparatively a small number of extra meetings for preaching, and without the special excitement or influence of evangelists or noted preachers of any kind. Not that prayer meetings had been little used before, but they had not been the main dependence and chief means of influence. Daily prayer meetings first commenced in New York, became common in very many of the cities and villages of this state, as throughout the land. The Spirit of the Lord descended and largely blessed these seasons of spiritual communion, together with the means of personal conversation with the unconverted, and the ordinary preaching of the gospel on the Sabbath and occasionally on other days. It is thus demonstrated that these diversities of gifts and of operations, are of one Spirit that worketh withal, in his own way, so that God and His grace are alone to be honored and have all the praise.

The results of revivals in Connecticut it is easy to tell. Since the controversies of the great awakening and the disorders of Davenport and the Separates, the measures adopted having been for the most part wise and spiritual, the results have been most happy. Not a single church is known to have been excepted from the blessing of these divine effusions of grace. Sometimes ten or twenty, and sometimes 100, 150 and even 200 in a single congregation have been the reputed converts in these seasons of religious interest. Men, women and children have come to see themselves as sinners, in the light of the divine law, and been led by the spirit of God, through the truth and the motives of the gospel, to penitence for sin, and to lead a new life,—a life of penitence and prayer and godliness. Experimental religion has thus been proved before the eyes of the irreligious, the worldly, the universalist, the sceptic, and the infidel of every town and neighborhood in the state, to be a solemn and blessed reality. These classes have had the purity and consistency of the new life in men, once their companions and sympathizers to preach to them of the reality of true religion. Many have thus been convicted and ultimately converted to God. On the whole, these Connecticut revivals, in the main pure and genuine, have been the life of spirituality, and the sources of perpetuity to our churches. We have now no regular supply of church members by probation, or a half-way covenant, or confirmation at a certain age, to replenish our churches. The most of our flocks owe their perpetuity, increase and prosperity, some of them their very existence to revivals. None look at them in doubt or with discredit. Though a perpetual revival is a beautiful theory, ordinary revivals are a blessed reality. May they always, and with increasing frequency and power bless our land and our fallen world.

CONTRIBUTIONS FOR BENEVOLENT PURPOSES.

Among the inquiries of the circular to the churches, for facts and statistics, were the items and amount of charitable donations for a single year. Replies were received from 224 churches and the amount of their contributions $90,870, or an average of $406 each. Allowing but one-sixth of this average for the remaining 60 churches, the amount raised and paid for benevolent objects is $95,000 ; which will very soon reach $100,000, if it be not as much the current year. It requires only three-eighths of said average to make that amount. This is exclusive of the support of the Gospel, and many other expenses for the poor, sabbath schools, and a few *pastoral* libraries, and other items frequently referred to, but not named. The sum raised for all these objects in many of the churches equals the expense of public worship, including salaries ; and in a few of the more wealthy churches much exceeds that amount. From nothing, fifty years ago, the churches have gradually advanced to this standard, and yet it seldom has arisen to the point of real self-denial of luxuries, much less of any of the comforts of life, to save a perishing world. Though inquiries have been repeated on this subject, the failure of obtaining complete returns has been owing principally to the want of a record of contributions. Some few reports have made no allusion to this topic ; but in no instance has it been said that there are no benevolent contributions made. There is occasion for gratitude to God, that all our churches acknowledge the obligation of practical benevolence. Though in a considerable number of them, there is need of training in the habit of giving ; yet in the most of those reported, it was said that such offerings were made as often as from four to six times in a year, and in a few, for some object, nearly every month. It is noticeable that where contributions were small, the reason frequently assigned was, that the church had no stated minister through the year ; showing that the great causes of benevolence mainly depend for their prosperity upon the interest taken in them by pastors and upon the efficiency of the ministry.   It was intended to tabulate the donations, or at least to give the aggregate for the several objects ; but the amount of other materials for this volume, and the imperfection of returns in this first attempt in this direction, has precluded both.   The lessons learned however, from these data, are not without great value.   The influence of the ministry, and the ability of the church in the work of providing means for the salvation of the world, when a high standard of benevolence, and true self-denial shall be reached, by doubling the amount now given, or still further multiplying it, show our high responsibility to the great Head of the Church, and together with the calling forth of true faith in the prophecies and promises of God, hold out to the humble Christian the great hope of the perishing millions.

CONNECTION OF THE CONGREGATIONAL MINISTERS AND CHURCHES OF CONNECTICUT, WITH THE RISE AND PROGRESS OF THE TEMPERANCE REFORMATION.

BY REV. JOHN MARSH, D. D., NEW YORK.

As in the dawn of morning it is difficult to determine which ray of light is first in the work of illumination, so in a great social and moral reform, it is often impossible to decide who first aroused the community to a sense of the existing evil, or first prompted in turning back the tide of desolation. Both Massachusetts and Connecticut may well contend for precedence in the temperance movement; and among the good men of Connecticut who early bewailed the ravages of the destroyer, we may never know which first of all cried, "How long, O Lord, holy and true! Cannot the plague be stayed?" but certain it is that no impression had before been made upon the public mind like that produced by a sermon preached by Rev. Ebenezer Porter, of Washington, Litchfield county, in the winter of 1806, on the discovery of a man lying dead in the snow, with a bottle of spirits at his side. The discourse was entitled "Fatal Effects of Ardent Spirits." Text, Isaiah v. 11. "Woe to them that rise up early," &c. After describing the sin, intemperance, in all its bearings, showing that it destroyed industry and health; produced poverty; impaired reason; unfitted men for all the duties and comforts of life; led to gaming, swearing, talebearing, extinguishing the best sensibilities of the heart and producing a miserable death, the preacher made a solemn appeal to various classes, inquiring, What is to be done? He computed that one in every fifteen of all the deaths in the year was caused by the use of ardent spirits. No man in Connecticut had ever fallen in a duel, but thousands had fallen by strong drink.

The sermon was printed and widely circulated, and was afterwards adopted as one of the permanent tracts of the American Tract Society.

The condition of the country at that time was very alarming. In a note attached to Mr. Porter's sermon, it was stated officially, that 7,641,207 gallons of foreign spirits and 2,604,207 gallons of wine, paying duties of more than three millions of dollars, were introduced annually to the United States ; that the number of distilleries was 30,000, and that the spirits consumed would load 100,000 wagons, which in compact order, would extend 1000 miles ; and that the annual expense of it all, if paid in silver, would exceed 600 tons of dollars.

In Connecticut and throughout New England at that period, the most unbounded license was given to the use of strong drink. It was considered a luxury, a necessity, and universal panacea. It was in all families and on all tables, in all pleasures, recreations and labors; a regular ration in the hay and harvest field, in all manufactories and ship yards, in fishing, boating and coasting, in the cold of winter and the heats of summer. It was the universal proffer of hospitality, freely given and partaken of at weddings and funerals ; at ministerial calls, at ordinations and associations, without the least sense of impropriety, provided it was not used to excess. It was too the universal panacea, good in heat and cold, in weariness and painfulness, when sick and when exposed to sickness; the cure of children in all their complaints, the support of the mother nursing her offspring, and of the old man going down to the grave. It helped the lawyer plead, the minister preach, and the physician go his rounds of duty. None could tell its worth, but all were made to feel its curse. Not a family was there in which there was not, at some time or other, one dead. Sottishness and drunkenness marked every village. The high-minded lawyer, the able physician, the eloquent preacher, were found filling the drunkard's grave. The church was cursed with a blight, if not as bad as in the days of Jeremiah, yet one that filled good men with alarm as they looked into the future. Such was the state of things when Ebenezer Porter, then a young man, preached his sermon.

Litchfield County, trained under the ministry of Bellamy and

Backus, and Hooker and Mills, had a high tone of Christian morals and was ready for resistance to all evil. As early as 1789, twenty of the leading citizens of Litchfield, had combined in a resistance to the universal custom of furnishing laborers with strong drink, and yet none that we know of, commenced a work of reform in their own persons or households. Excommunications were frequent for drunkenness, and yet no church action was known to reach its cause. Roused by the sermon of Porter, the South Association of the county appointed a committee to inquire into the extent of the growing evil and report a remedy. In 1811, five years after the sermon was preached, that committee reported that the evil was wide spreading, but no remedy was feasible. Rev. Lyman Beecher, then recently installed as pastor of the Congregational Church at Litchfield, with characteristic energy moved that the committee be discharged, (of how long standing they had been, does not appear) and that a new committee be appointed. His motion was agreed to. The committee was appointed and he was made chairman. They immediately reported that there was "a remedy in the universal disuse of spirituous liquors by all good men and Christians;" but what was implied in this does not appear; such disuse does not seem then to have been adopted or recommended by them, or by any other body as a practical principle, or in the least binding the conscience. About the same time, and even before, President Dwight, in his discourses to students, had assumed the position, that the man who found in himself any peculiar relish for spirituous liquor was bound to abstain from it wholly, and that total abstinence was the only hope of the drunkard; but this too made no impression; all assented to it, ministers and people, and yet all kept on drinking as in no danger and doing no harm.

In 1812 the Fairfield Consociation entered zealously into the work of reform, and issued an address to the ministers and churches on the prevailing intemperance. It was the joint work of the Rev. Rowell R. Swan of Norwalk, and the Rev. Heman Humphrey of Fairfield, both Congregational ministers. Few temperance publications of equal power have, to this day, been sent from the press. The Consociation showed themselves to be in earnest, and on the 13th of October, they unanimously

Resolved, "That the customary use of ardent spirits shall be wholly discontinued from that hour."

This was, doubtless, the first decided movement of any ecclesiastical body in the country. In their address they said nothing about entire abstinence in the community at large ; but in recommending remedies for the evil they did say :

" 1. We suggest particularly to those whose apppetite for drink is strong and increasing, total abstinence from all intoxicating liquors.

" 2. Let those who are yet temperate, let him who thinketh he standeth, take heed lest he fall. In short, let him consider that he is a weak, depraved creature, and that total abstinence from strong drink is the only course in which he can be certain that he shall not be injured and even destroyed by it."

Out of this attempt at reform in that Consociation arose the Connecticut Society for the Reformation of Morals, which, for several years, was powerful in its attacks upon gambling, lottery dealing, Sabbath breaking and intemperance ; but made no special assault upon this last vice, and prescribed no special remedy. The masterly sermons, however, of Humphrey, Chapin and others at the annual meetings, did much to prepare the ministers and churches for some bold and decided action. The demoralizing influence of the war of 1812, created much alarm among the ministers and churches ; and on the return of peace, great anxiety was felt for a better state of religion and morals ; and the use of strong drink, which had increased on all occasions to the ruin of thousands, was greatly reprobated. In private circles and at ordination dinners and meetings of ministers, its use was soon materially lessened ; and through the wide circulation in the State of the " Well Conducted Farm," a tract written in 1822, by Rev. Justin Edwards, of Andover, Mass., ardent spirits began to be dispensed with in the hay and harvest field, in raising and removing buildings, though often occasioning much trouble among the employed. But nothing occurred to electrify and move the great body of ministers and churches until 1826, a memorable year for temperance.

In January of that year, the Rev. Calvin Chapin, D. D., of Rocky-hill, who, in a missionary tour through Ohio, had become deeply impressed with the whisky plague of that region, and the belief that nothing would save the nation but an entire abandonment of spirituous liquors by the ministers and churches, commenced in the Connecticut Observer at Hartford, a series of short but caustic pieces, entitled " Entire Abstinence the only Infallible Antidote," over the signature T. I. A. Some laughed ; some mocked ; some were indignant, and the editor was assured by ministers and church members that if the articles were continued, it would be the ruin of his paper. He nobly replied, " If the paper stands on spirit drinking, let it fall." They were continued weekly for a considerable period, carrying conviction to many inquiring what is duty, and what can and must be done ?

Another memorable event in that year was the delivery of six sermons at Litchfield by Rev. Lyman Beecher, D. D., on the nature, signs, evils and remedy of intemperance. Those were printed and scattered widely abroad, and were destined to have a mighty influence on the church and the world. A third important event the same year was the formation at Boston of the American Temperance Society, and the employment of the Rev. Nathaniel Hewit, the successor of Rev. Heman Humphrey in the pastoral office at Fairfield, in a temporary agency. This gentleman, who had already distinguished himself in such labor at home,* at once addressed several large bodies in Massachusetts, Rhode Island, and Connecticut. He appeared before the General Association of Connecticut, the next year, 1827, in their meeting at Stratford, and made such an impression, that they unanimously

Resolved, That this Association do cordially approve of the principles and objects of the American Society for the promotion of temperance, and that we will use our influence as pastors to prevent entirely the use and all abuses of strong drink.

---

*Dr. Hewitt, *before* 1826, had " distinguished himself" by maintaining not only "at home" but in his exchanges with other pastors, the duty of entire abstinence from the use of spirituous liquors except as a medicine, and as prescribed by a *temperate* physician. *Committee of Publication.*

In their annual report that year on the state of religion, they said : " The progress of intemperance, which once seemed beyond control, is beginning to receive a check. In many places the important discovery has been made by actual experiment, that union and decision among the virtuous part of the community in discountenancing the use of ardent spirits, is effectual to check its progress, to guard the rising generation against it, and to diminish very greatly its attendant evils."

At this period most of the Congregational ministers and members of churches had become abstainers from ardent spirits, but not from vinous and fermented drinks. It took ten years more of discipline and suffering to bring them to this.

The pastor of the Stratford church at that time, was the Rev. Joshua Leavitt, who, for his clear understanding of the subject and devotion to its interests, had just been appointed to an agency for the American Society. He visited thirteen towns in the state and several in Massachusetts, preaching and obtaining pledges and donations ; but being considered as peculiarly fitted for the office of secretary to the Seamen's Friend Society in the city of New York, he was, after four months' labor, removed to that station.

While in Stratford, he ably vindicated the principle of total abstinence in an article published at New Haven in the Christian Spectator. The Rev. Nathaniel Hewit had returned to his pastoral labors ; but, on the 14th of November, 1827, he was appointed to a three years mission in behalf of the American Society, and was accordingly dismissed from his charge by the Consociation, greatly to the regret of his people and the people of the county. The United States, aye, the world, was his field ; and the amount of labor which this son of Congregationalism performed in all the large cities and towns and in Great Britain, cannot be known until the judgment day. At Hartford, in the succeeding May, he addressed the governor, legislature and a great crowd of citizens in the Center Church, with all the boldness of John Knox. His subject was " The Tree Known by its Fruit." The fruits of intemperance were all spread out and laid at the door of all who by example or legislation were in any manner accessory to them ; and, as was afterwards said of an address by the same fearless preacher of temperance and judgment to come,

"It hailed for about the space of two hours, and every stone was of the weight of a talent."

The earliest and most efficient county society in the state was that of Middlesex, organized in the Congregational Church at Haddam, September 2, 1828. It enrolled 600 members pledged to total abstinence from ardent spirits, (the extent of the pledge in that day) before there was half that number in the rest of the state. Every Congregational minister in the lower part of the county, and in Lyme in the county of New London, became an active and efficient member. It met monthly in rotation in the parishes. In each town or parish were one or more auxiliaries. Three of the monthly addresses were printed and widely circulated. Soon the moral and religious community were embued with the proper spirit. At a meeting of the Middlesex Consociation at Haddam, October 26, 1829, it was unanimously

Resolved, That this Consociation do highly approve of the measures which have been recently adopted for the suppression of intemperance, and that the success of these measures calls loudly for the gratitude of the churches to God under whose blessing it has been attained.

Resolved, That the Consociation do recommend to the members of the churches in their connection, total abstinence from the common use of ardent spirits and a union with the temperance societies—these societies being the most powerful antidote to the alarming evil of intemperance, which the providence of God has pointed out to his people.

In the autumn of this year, the Congregational minister of Haddam, delivered an address, " Putnam and the Wolf, or the Monster Destroyed," at Pomfret, before the Windham County Temperance Society. Of this, more than 100,000 copies were printed and scattered abroad, giving a new impulse to the cause.

The Connecticut State Temperance Society was organized at Hartford, May 20, 1829. The Rev. Jeremiah Day, D. D., President of Yale College, was chosen president, Rev. Calvin Chapin, D. D., chairman of the executive committee, and Rev. John Marsh, corresponding secretary. Its first anniversary was held at New Haven, and was addressed by Hon. Timothy Pitkin of Farmington, long a member of congress, Daniel Frost,

Esq., of Canterbury, Hon. Roger M. Sherman of Fairfield, and Hon. Judge Daggett of New Haven.   Seldom has such an array of talent been brought to the · support of any cause.   The governor and legislature were present, with most of the clergy and leading citizens of New Haven.   The annual report, read by the corresponding secretary, presented the following and many other appalling facts.

In addition to large annual importations of rum from the West Indies, there were in the state two rum distilleries and ten gin and whisky distilleries, all doing a large business, and 300 smaller distilleries, chiefly cider.   There were 1026 licensed retailers and 400 licensed taverners.   A population of 275,248 consumed annually, (besides an untold amount of cider and wines) 1,238,616 gallons of spirituous liquors, which, at 62 1-2 cents a gallon, cost the people $782,884.95.   Every twenty-fifth family among the 45,000 of the state was engaged in supplying the rest with intoxicating drinks.   As the frightful result, there were in the state 6,881 common drunkards.   In nine parishes in Hartford county, there were found by actual visitation, 594 drunkards, giving 2000 to the county.   Not far from 500 drunkards died annually in the state, while, by a horrid machinery, continually kept in motion, their places were punctually filled.   Of 172 paupers in Middlesex county, 114 were reduced to beggary by intemperance ; and the keeper of the State Prison, at Wethersfield, Moses C. Pillsbury, Esq., declared that all of 167 prisoners were brought, he was satisfied, to the commission of crime by intemperance.   The great foe to the church and the Sabbath, to education, to sound morals and the peace and thrift of the community was strong drink with the licensed grog shops.   The report, with its accompanying cheering intelligence of reform, then commencing and spreading throughout the United States, and the speeches of those distinguished men, made a deep impression.

Hitherto, the cause in Connecticut had been sustained chiefly by the Congregational ministry and members of their congregations.   Other denominations, as a general thing, had stood aloof from it, and even seemed willing for a time to profit by dissensions in what had been called " The Standing Order."   But they could not appear in opposition, and, therefore, took some independent ground.   The Hartford Baptist Association, October 14, 1829, resolved, that, in the opinion of their body, the time had arrived when no preacher of the Gospel could either habitually, or even occasionally, except as a medicine, use ardent spirits without greatly abridging his usefulness ; but at the same time they resolved that " All the churches were temperance societies by profession." This was enough for them, and precluded them, almost universally, from uniting with these organizations. The Episcopal church took no action in the matter, nor did her ministers and churches manifest any special interest in it, sympathising much with Bishop Hopkins, of Vermont, in his published views of the whole as at variance with the Gospel. But one of her most distinguished ministers, Rev. J. S. Stone, D. D., of New Haven, delivered a thorough and searching temperance sermon before the Young Mens' Temperance Society of that city. The Methodist preachers, at a camp-meeting in Somers, in 1829, adopted resolutions commending it to all their brethren to unite in the temperance societies as "a combination of all religious parties, and no religious party in a good cause ;" and the Rev. Wilbur Fiske, D. D., head of the school at Wilbraham, Mass., and afterwards president of the Wesleyan University, at Middletown, was a giant in the cause. But, as a general rule in the towns, the Methodists opposed whatever the Congregationalists favored, and furnished homes of refuge for disaffected members. Seldom were they found in a temperance meeting; but if they suffered the rum party to cleave to them, it was not always to their honor and glory, or even their own satisfaction. In a Congregational church in Middlesex county, controversy ran high. The pastor said, " Sink or swim, rum must be driven out of this church." A large disaffected body took refuge with the Methodists and worshiped there. The Congregationalists, hearing of the decision and boldness of Dr. Fiske, invited him to give them an address. He consented to do so. Consternation seized the Methodists as they heard of his coming, and on the appointed day they sent a delegation to meet him, and, if possible, turn him back. Upon coming near they besought him not to go on, saying to him, " The Congregationalists are falling in pieces and we shall get some of their heaviest men. If you go on, confusion will cover us, and our church will

fall." " Get out of my way, brethren," said he, " if the Methodist church stands on a rum barrel, the sooner it falls the
better," and, putting spurs to his horse, on he went, much to
the confusion of the remonstrants. As he ascended, however,
his mantle fell upon his denomination, and the Methodist
churches and preachers have now long been foremost in the
cause.

Almost each successive General Association for years adopted
some resolution in favor of temperance ; and its condition
entered into the annual reports on the state of religion ; but
individual church action was slow. The elder members, who
had been accustomed to the use of ardent spirits in the house
and the field, in coasting and fishing, in ship-yards and quarries,
never considering it inconsistent with Christian character if
moderately indulged in, though frequently called to excom-
municate a brother for drunkenness, were slow to make entire
abstinence a term of communion even to those who should
come after them, as being a reflection upon themselves and
their fathers, and a yoke too heavy to be borne. But in the
numerous revivals which were then powerful, the entire abandonment of spirit-drinking, as at variance with the true self-denial of the Gospel, was demanded before any expression of
Christian hope would be received as satisfactory ; and, ere
long, one church after another was found adopting it as a
standing rule, that no person should be admitted to church
fellowship but upon the principle of total abstinence. This
important action was much hastened by the Rev. Asahel Net-
tieton, the great revival preacher of that period. He narrowly
watched the effect of spirit-drinking upon awakened sinners,
removing their anxiety and alarm and causing them to indulge,
through momentary exhilaration, a false hope ; and also upon
hopeful converts, destroying their serious deportment and leading them to vain associations. He would not converse with
a man who came to know what he should do to be saved, if
his breath betrayed the use of spirits ; nor would he give
encouragement to any one who professed conversion, while
daily using the alcoholic stimulant. In long cases of deep
distress and earnestly expressed desire to become a Christian
and have the joy of God's salvation, he would, with wonderful

skill, ferret out the secret indulgence as the only hindrance, and either break it up, or see the subject, as he often did, turn and go away in a rage. In 1829 he gave the public his views in a letter through the Spirit of the Pilgrims, published at Boston. Wherever it was read, it deeply impressed ministers and members of churches with their deep responsibility to practice total abstinence, both to save themselves and those around them.

In 1835 the Rev. Dr. Chapin published his prize essay on sacramental wines. He considered the use of any intoxicating drink at the Lord's table inconsistent with the nature of the ordinance, not demanded by the Master, and a decided hindrance to the temperance cause. He viewed water as the emblem of purity and the fit representative of the Gospel. But while he excited attention, to no great extent has fermented wine been abandoned. Several Congregational churches, however, have provided themselves with the unfermented juice of the grape, while anxiety has increased for those wines which are least imbued with the intoxicating principle.

Into the pledge of total abstinence from all intoxicating drinks, fermented as well as distilled, adopted by the National Convention at Saratoga Springs, in 1836, the Congregational ministers and churches of Connecticut at once fully entered, and without any special attention, cider went, among all Christian families, into general disuse. White tumblers graced the tables of the high and the low, the rich and the poor ; and the Washingtonian movement, in which hundreds and thousands of miserable drunkards were reclaimed, was universally acknowledged with thankfulness as the extraordinary and gracious providence of God.

The reformation found many members of churches in the business of importing, distilling and vending that which was so destructive to the community and to the great interests of Christ's Kingdom. Churches were built, ministers were supported, and missionaries were sent forth by men who said, "By this craft we have our wealth," and whose traffic had been owned as legitimate by the churches as well as the state. With such, the conflict on the part of ministers and Christian brethren was often very severe, for were they not frequently pious and praying men, good friends and even bene-

factors of the minister, and how could he rebuke them before
all ?   But the declaration of the National Convention at Philadelphia, in 1833, that the traffic was morally wrong, the awful
result of the traffic as seen in suffering families and ruined
men, in jails, in poor houses, and in murders ; and more than
all, perhaps, the taunts of the ungodly that such and such
pious men and church members sold rum, soon aided their
pulpit remonstrances, and in a short time almost the entire
business changed hands, and the principle was established that
the traffic as well as the use must be abandoned by all
who would be like Christ.   If, at any time, deacons or other
influential men took offence at the fidelity of the ministry and
would cause disturbance, they soon found themselves in an
unpleasant position.   A pastor of a church in which were two
of the largest liquor dealers of the state, in a sermon fearlessly
and boldly denounced the traffic as at variance with all Christian character.   The anger of these brethren was greatly
kindled, and as publicly they denounced him.   They would
not stand such preaching.   "That's right," said a cool by-
stander."   "Do you gather J. B. and T. S. and B. U.,
(notorious infidels and scoffers,) and all the drunkards in the
place together, and drive this fellow out of town."   Looking
at him for a moment and seeing the drift of his advice, they
said (for they were good men at heart, though engaged in a bad
business,) " We'll do no such thing ; we'll not be found in such
company if we never sell any more rum."   And so ended the
matter.   In a short time after, though it had been very lucra-
tive, they had changed their business.

    In this connection it may not seem perfectly in place to refer
to the legislation of Connecticut on the subject of temperance ;
still, the legal and moral action have been so closely connected
that it cannot well be passed without notice.   Neither the
Congregational ministers or churches, nor any other class have
ever asked for the aid of legislation to compel men to be temperate.   Severe as were the early laws of Connecticut upon
habits and morals, no restraints have been laid by law upon
drinking, but there have been upon selling.   From the earliest
period, the state adopted the English excise system, licensed
individuals to keep public houses and sell spirituous liquors to

lodgers and travelers. Revenue was thus raised to the state and public houses were regulated by law ; and as men of good morals were required to keep them, deacons and members of churches became, to a considerable extent, in Connecticut, the licensed keepers. Over all the rest of the community was a strong prohibitory law, guarded strictly by the selectmen and town constables. But here, under this solemn commission, the infernal traffic held its revelries for two centuries. Here were manufactured out of sound men and useful fathers and sons, all that long line of drunkards who went in terrible procession, year after year, to the grave, dragging down with them and after them many a promising and lovely household. The license system held its monopoly of Satan's business until Maine broke its power and cast it off in 1851. Connecticut followed in 1854. The law in this state took effect on the first of August, and never, perhaps, was there a greater revolution in public morals and domestic comfort than was experienced throughout the state. At a public meeting in the city of New York, in the winter of that year, Gov. Dutton, then governor of the state, testified that not a grog shop to his knowledge, had been found open in the state since the law came into force ; that no drunkard had been publicly seen in the streets ; that crime had been materially diminished ; that hundreds of families which had been great sufferers had been comfortably supplied ; that public security had greatly increased, and that opposition to the law was scarcely heard of. In these operations of the law, the ministry and the churches of all denominations greatly rejoiced ; the Sabbath was saved from deep desecration, Sabbath-schools were filled up with children from once drunken families, and the sanctuaries opened their portals to men who had long spent their Sabbaths in the dram-shop, or at home in stupid sensuality. The law still remains unrepealed and unimpaired ; and if "eternal vigilance is the price of liberty," so is it of the enforcement of the law. If good men grow weary of watching their sacred trust—if violations there are—(and what law of God or man is not daily broken) —if public officers, secretly unfriendly to the law and in secret alliance with offenders, have winked at the violation, and there have been few prosecutions—if politicians and office-seekers, desirous of revolution, have heard all the complaints of the disaffected and drawn them in their train, and threatened its overthrow ; and fears of political changes have kept even the best friends of the law from action—if the large towns and cities filling up with a foreign population and subject to constant and great excitements seem to be beyond control, yet the great principles of temperance are firmly fixed in the minds of the people : the law spreads over the state its broad, protecting shield—it gives license to none, for a price, to do evil—it stamps with its true mark, before all men, that traffic which is a traffic in the souls and bodies of men—it deters all good men, conscientious men, from engaging in it—it enables very many of the towns of the state and all who please to keep themselves perfectly free from it ; and if the moral and Christian community do their duty—if the church sets an example of entire disuse in all her habitations and labors—if the pulpit speaks out its thunders, and the Sabbath-schools, those blessed nurseries of good, train up the children and youth to a right observance of the moral and physical laws of the great Creator, the future of Connecticut, will, it is believed, be becoming the glorious inheritance which the fathers have given.

Do any flauntingly say, all has been humbug, delusion, imposition! Connecticut is as bad as ever ; there is more drinking than ever! More than ever? Is it so? Where are those large rum distilleries, and those mammoth Warehouse-point gin-distilleries, and those one thousand cider mills, and the three hundred cider-brandy distilleries of former days ? Where the mugs of cider which were on every dinner table, and the decanters of wine and brandy which were on every sideboard, at every ministerial meeting, at conventions and ordinations, at births and baptisms, weddings and funerals ? Where the friendly greetings of every visitant and traveler, and almost every man on business, with something to drink ? Where the bottles under every tree in the hay and harvest field, in the workshop and shipyard, at raisings and huskings ? and where the regular rum rations in every stone-quarry, and on board every coaster and merchant ship ? and where the 594 miserable, bloated, tottering drunkards in nine small parishes in one county? Gone ! nearly all gone ! The plague spots of the days of our fathers are wiped out, though enough remains to move our fears and call for repentance. What the cause has poured into the bosom of the churches, what of health and wealth, what of physical energy, what of moral power, what of ability to tread all enemies under their feet, and what higher enjoyments of the presence of their great Head and His Holy Spirit can never be known. A Congregational minister, or a member of a Congregational church, and the same may be said of some other denominations in Connecticut, now habitually using intoxicating liquors, or giving or selling them to others as a beverage, is a rare spectacle. Thanks be to God for the timely redemption.

TEMPERANCE PUBLICATIONS ISSUED IN CONNECTICUT BETWEEN 1806 AND 1840.*

Fatal Effects of Ardent Sprits, a sermon by Ebenezer Porter, of Washington, Litchfield county, ... 1806.
Address on Intemperance, by the Fairfield Consociation, . 1812.
Entire Abstinence the only Infallible Antidote, by Calvin Chapin, D. D., ... 1826.
Six Sermons on the Nature, Signs, Evils and Remedy of Intemperance, by Lyman Beecher, D. D., of Litchfield, . 1826.
Address before the Canterbury Temperance Society, by Daniel Frost, Esq., ... 1826.
———————— Norwich Falls Society, by W. Hines, . . 1827.
Article on total Abstinence in the Christian Spectator, by Rev. Joshua Leavitt, ... 1828.
Address at Haddam, by Linus Parmelee, Esq., . . 1828.
——Before the Middlesex Society, by Charles Griswold, Esq., 1828.
Total Abstinence from Ardent Spirits: an Address delivered by request of the Young Men's Temperance Society of New Haven. By Leonard Bacon, Pastor of the First Church in New Haven. 1829.
Letter of Asahel Nettleton on Temperance and Revivals, . 1829.
Temperance Destructive of National Welfare, by Rev. Joel Mann, Suffield, ... 1829.
Evil and Cure of Intemperance, a sermon, by the Rev. Erastus Ripley, ... 1829.
Putnam and the Wolf, or the Monster Destroyed, an address at Pomfret, by Rev. John Marsh, ... 1829.

*This Catalogue, though made with much care, is doubtless imperfect.—*Com. of Pub.*

Appeal to the Professors of Religion on the Use of Ardent
     Spirits, by Rev. John Marsh, ... 1829.
Address to the Middlesex Temperance Society, by E. Selden,
     Esq., ... 1829.
The Rum Drinking Christian, a short sermon, by Rev. John
     Marsh, ... 1830.
Only This Once, a short poem, by Mrs. L. H. Sigourney,   1830.
Address before the Wintonbury Temperance Society, by
     Francis Gillette, Esq., ... 1830.
Address at Norwich, by Rev. C. W. Denison,   .   . 1830.
Address to the Young Mens' Temperance Society, at New
     Haven, by Rev. J. S. Stone, D. D.,   .   . 1830.
Report of the Connecticut State Temperance Society,   . 1830.
Report of the Hartford County Society,   .   . 1831.
Appeal to Christians on Using and Vending Ardent Spirits,
     by Rev. Joseph Harvey, ... 1831.
Bible Doctrine of Temperance, by Rev. G. T. Davis, Hart-
     ford, ... 1831·
The Upas Tree. a hymn, by Mrs. Sigourney,   .   . 1831·
Address before the Hartford County Society, by S. Sargent,
     M. D., ... 1831.
The Only Safe Expedient, a sermon, by the Rev. Samuel
     Spring, of East Hartford, ... 1832.
The Christian Rumseller in his Closet, by Mrs Sigourney,   1832.
The Intemperate, a tale, by Mrs. Sigourney,   .   . 1833.
Offence of Strong Drink, a sermon, by Rev. Edwin Hall,
     D. D., Norwalk, ... 1834.
Second Declaration of Independence, by Rev. John Marsh,   1834.
Prize Essay on Sacramental Wines, by Rev. Calvin Chapin,
     D. D., of Rocky Hill, ... 1835.
Rev. Joseph Harvey's Remarks at a County Meeting,   . 1837.
Discourse on the Traffic in Spirituous Liquors, by Rev.
     Leonard Bacon, Pastor of the Frist Church in New
     Haven, ... 1837.
Is it Right to Use Intoxicating Liquors at the Present Day, a
     sermon, by Rev. Samuel Andrew, Woodbury,   .   . 1840.

PASTORS AND STATED SUPPLIES.

BY REV. GEO. P. PRUDDEN, WATERTOWN.

It has been a custom, nearly uniform from the beginning of the churches of this state, to have their ministers duly installed over them as Pastors.

To some extent, however, an opposite course obtains. In some quarters there is a disposition to supersede this ministry of pastors, by a ministry of stated supplies;—men employed to perform the duties of a pastor, but not inducted, in any appropriate way into the pastoral office.

That it is eminently fit and proper, that one who in any church exercises the functions of a Pastor, should be duly inducted by some appropriate form of installation into the pastoral office, the following considerations will perhaps evince.

I. *The office is one involving important responsibilities, which ought, by a process of installation, to be recognized and pointed out.* A pastor is one appointed to the spiritual oversight of a flock of Christ's ransomed sheep ; one whose duty is, " to feed a church of God, which He purchased with His own blood." To him is committed as a trust, that "ministry of reconciliation," through which in Christ Jesus sinners are being reconciled to God.

Such a position is one of very great responsibility. The issues involved look forward through an eternity for their full development.

And the trust is committed to the hands of one who is a mere man, subject to all human frailties and imperfections. That such a one is to receive such a trust, renders it eminently fit and proper that he should, on receiving it, be reminded in some public way of the responsibility, and of his duty. He should enter upon it through some appropriate process, in which he is required openly to accept the trust involved, and is openly charged, and openly covenants to be faithful to

its duties. The customary services of an installation constitute such a process ; and to dispense with them entirely, without providing any substitute, as is done by those whose ministers are mere stated supplies, must be beyond measure unwise
and inexpedient.

II. *The scriptural theory or the pastoral office seems to involve the neceesity, not only of election to it, but of introduction
into it.*

A pastor is an officer in a local church. Hence it is eminently fit and proper, that the church to whom he is to
minister, should by their vote designate to the office the man
of their choice.

But the doctrine of the gospel is, that such a pastor holds an
office, and a trust, committed to him not by the church, but by
God himself. The pastoral office is Christ's, and has to do
with the enlargement of Christ's kingdom on the earth. Paul's
charge to some who held the office, was, " take heed to your-
selves, and to the flock *over which the Holy Ghost has made
you overseers.*" This teaches us, that however he may be
voted, nominated or appointed to the office, the trust that the
true pastor receives, is one committed to his hands by the Holy Ghost. The vote appointing him comes from the church
and congregation to which he ministers, but the office committed to him is from above.

Those who compare the office of a pastor to that of a business agent of a mercantile house, regarding him as employed
by the congregation, for a definite salary, to do a certain work
for them, entirely mistake the nature of the office. The work
of a pastor is work for Christ. He cannot be a faithful pastor
except as he daily asks his Lord and Master in reference to the
work, "Lord what will thou have me to do." Whatever he
clearly discerns to be the will of Christ, in reference to that
work, he is to do, whether it be the wish of those who pay his
salary or not. The church elects and employs him, and supports
him for this express purpose, that he may do the work of Christ
among them.

Since such is the nature of the pastor's office, since it is an
office that comes from Christ—the oversight of a flock committed to him by the Holy Ghost, it is not only eminently fit

and proper, but exceedingly important, that when one assumes this office, there should be, in addition to this vote appointing him, some religious service that will fitly represent to him the office and trust which he receives from above.

That there should be such a service is a direct inference from the nature of the office. The scriptures have not distinctly taught us what this service shall be ; leaving that to human discretion ; but when the churches by a custom that has been observed with great uniformity for generations and centuries, have established such a service—a service precisely adapted and peculiarly appropriated to the end in view, this custom, among those with whom it is established, is to be regarded as a divine ordinance.

It is not divine in the sense that it may not be changed, but divine as human governments are a divine ordinance. The nature of the pastoral office proves it to be the divine will that there be some process of induction into it that shall represent the fact that the office is from God, and when such a process has been established by usage, it may be regarded as the divine will that it shall not be set aside, except as something else is substituted equally fitted to the same end.

If serious evils have blended with the ordinary process of installation, they should be changed ; if sinful usages have crept in, they should be reformed. But if not, if the customary services are eminently fitted to the end in view, so much so that human wisdom can devise nothing fitter, then to set them aside entirely, without any substitute, to remove from what is virtually the pastoral office whatever points to its relations to God, must be to treat with contempt these relations, and therefore must be plainly contrary to the will of God.

Serious evil has come, from mixing up this question with that of permanency of pastors. With many, the one great argument for pastoral installations is that thus the ministry will be rendered more permanent. With many, again, this very permanency which it promises to give, is the one great argument against such installations. All this, however, is a diversion from the real issue. The question of permanency is a distinct question, standing on its own merits. And however desirable it might be, were this possible, that every pastor

should remain for life in his first field ; yet long usage has settled it, as the decision both of ministers and churches, that it is
neither desirable nor expedient that a pastor shall remain in
any field beyond the time, when, from any cause whatever, his
usefulness has ceased.   This decision, however, does not in
any degree weaken the position that he who acts the part of a
pastor, should be properly inducted into the pastoral office.

III. *The opposite custom is liable to serious evils and dangers,* against which every church ought to be on its guard. At
these, our space will allow merely a glance.

1. This custom of receiving a ministry of mere stated supplies, will cause men to be employed in the pastoral office, who
have not in any public way been charged with its responsibilities, nor instructed into its duties, nor required to make promises
of fidelity.

2. It will tend to degrade the office of pastor by giving
prevalence to the idea that it is simply a business relation,
founded upon a mere business contract between the acting
minister and those who employ him.

3. It will tend to weaken and corrupt the church, by throw-
ing the choice of the officiating pastor into the hands of the
Society and perhaps of a mere society's committee, thus de-
priving the church of its just share in electing its pastor, and
exposing it to be under the ministrations of one not chosen
with any reference to its own edification.

4. It will tend to interrupt that beautiful fellowship of the
churches, which exhibits and expresses itself so fitly in the
various councils that have to do with the settlement and dismission of pastors.   One most pleasant result of the present
system of installations, is, that it tends to bring the neighboring
Pastors and churches into full acquaintance with a new pastor
at the beginning of his ministry.

5. It will expose the churches to be imposed upon by unworthy ministers.   An installing council requires a stranger,
coming into any neighborhood, at once to show his credentials.

6. It will expose the churches to the assault of unexpected
heresies.   A church and congregation who have simply heard
a minister preach a few Sabbaths, have no means whatever of
assuring themselves that he is not holding in reserve fatal er-

rors. In this matter they can by no means afford to dispense with the safeguard of an appropriate examination before an installing council.

For these reasons, among others, it is to be hoped that the churches will adhere to past usage in this matter, and earnestly seek for themselves pastors duly installed, rather than mere stated supplies.

HISTORY AND RESULTS OF THE DIFFERENT METHODS OF RAISING THE SALARIES OF MINISTERS IN CONNECTICUT.

BY REV. HIRAM P. ARMS, NORWICH TOWN.

In the first settlement of the state all the inhabitants were substantially of the same faith. They all had a common interest in maintaining the institutions of religion. All were therefore justly required to contribute according to their ability for the support of the church as well as the state. Both were constituent parts of the same commonwealth. Not only were the men of that day required to support the ministry of the established church, but they were bound, under a penalty of three pounds for every instance of voluntary neglect, to attend public worship on the Lord's day, and on days of fasting and of thanksgiving appointed by the civil authority.

At an early day, however, provision was made that all sober orthodox persons, dissenting from the Congregational churches, should be allowed peaceably to worship in their own way. Still they were required to contribute to the support of "the standing order."

As the number of dissenters increased, complaint was made of the injustice of taxing men to support a church on whose ministry they did not attend. The Separates made this a matter of conscience, and refused to pay the assessment. Some of them consented to be imprisoned rather than pay their ecclesiastical tax. Underlying the action of the Separates, with all their fanaticism, was the principle of true religious liberty. But the Christian world was not then prepared for its full development. The Congregational churches, however, were the first of all established churches, to respect the rights of the minority, and to release dissenters from contributing to the support of the state religion.

In 1727, Episcopalians were by law allowed to draw from the public treasury, for the support of their own ministry, a sum equal to that which they had paid. They were also permitted to impose a tax upon their members to meet the expenses of their separate organization.

Two years later, in 1729, Quakers and Baptists, on certain conditions, were exempted from the support of the Congregational churches. In 1784 this exemption extended to all dissenters of whatever denomination. Every man was required to contribute to the support of public worship, somewhere, according to his ability, but he might choose his own place of worship, and lend his support to the ministry which he preferred.

These laws continued in operation without material alteration till the session of 1821.

Meantime, as other denominations increased, much dissatisfaction was expressed at the prominence given to the Congregregational churches. They still constituted a church establishment, and as such were subject to not a little undeserved odium.

By the revision of 1821, all denominations of Christians are put upon the same footing. No man is now a member of any ecclesiastical society till he voluntarily connects himself with it. Formerly, one would withdraw from a society by lodging a certificate with the clerk that he belonged to another society, —but he could not " sign off " to nothing. At present a man may withhold his support from all religious institutions, and enjoy the collateral advantage of them, at the expense of his neighbors.

Societies still have authority to impose a tax upon the property of their members, and some continue to do so, though most depend on voluntary contributions in one form or another. Various methods are employed to meet the annual expenses of our societies. The most common mode is, by the rent of pews from year to year to the highest bidder. Sometimes a valuation is apprised on the pews, and the applicants bid for a choice. In a few of our churches where pews are owned by individuals as real estate, resort is had to subscription or taxation.

Formerly, and within the present century, the seats were assigned by a committee of the society to the different families according to some not very definite rule of dignity,—a process which was called "dignifying the seats." This was always a source of not a little dissatisfaction, which is avoided by our modern method.

It was feared by good men, that the repeal under our present constitution, of all laws which were designed to favor the Congregational churches, and which required all men to contribute to the support of public worship somewhere, would prove disastrous to the cause of religion. These fears have not been realized.

The voluntary system has been found by experience to work better in every respect than taxation. It has lopped off many of the dead branches which were unsightly in themselves and impeded the growth of our churches. It allows men who are not of us to go out from us, and exhibit themselves in their true characters. It has relieved the Congregational churches from the odium which attached to them as creatures and proteges of the state. In the mean time, it has infused into them new life, and very much increased their strength and efficiency.

AMOUNT OF SALARIES.

Our churches have been disposed, from the first, to give a comfortable support to their ministers—not to surround them with the luxuries of life, but to provide for their reasonable wants. At the union of the two colonies of New Haven and Connecticut in 1665, the united colony contained about 1700 families, eight or nine thousand inhabitants, who enjoyed the instruction of about twenty ministers, an average of one to every eighty-five families. Some of the stronger churches had two ministers, a pastor and a teacher, besides ruling elders. In some of the new plantations thirty or forty families sustained a minister.

The salaries of these ministers would range from fifty to one hundred pounds. In addition to their salaries they were accustomed to receive, at the time of their installation, "a settlement" of two hundred pounds or more, which, invested in a homestead, formed an important item in their means of support. They were also exempted from taxation. If any minister felt himself aggrieved by too scanty allowance, although it was matter of agreement, he might apply to the General Assembly, whose duty it was to order his society to furnish him suitable maintenance.

By the revised statutes of 1821, ministers were allowed to hold property to the amount of twenty-five hundred dollars exempt from taxation. This law has since been repealed, and no discrimination is now made in favor of ministers. Nor have they any reason to complain of this.

The salaries paid to ministers in former times were nominally less than they receive at the present day. But if we consider the cost of living in those times, with labor at fourteen cents a day, and corn at nine pence a bushel, we must conclude that the earlier ministers received a more liberal support than their successors. Many of them accumulated handsome estates, and few of them suffered any greater privations than their people.

Salaries will necessarily regulate themselves by the cost of living. They will rise or fall as the value of money is diminished or increased. Few ministers of the present day are accumulating property, and few, we cannot say *none*, are subject to the privations of actual poverty. They who gather much have nothing over, and they who gather little have no lack. They gather every man according to his eating.

PARSONAGES AND PERMANENT FUNDS.

At the organization of churches, and of parishes or ecclesiastical societies, in the settlement of towns, it was customary in order to secure a home for the minister, to set off to him a certain portion of land, and aid him in building a house. This was expected to be done as a matter of course, among their first acts with reference to the establishment of the ministry among them. The incorporation of any new town or ecclesiastical society was not only controlled by the Legislature; it was also made to depend very much on the ability and disposition of the inhabitants to support the gospel, without unduly weakening the towns or societies to which they had previously belonged, since the preaching of the gospel was ever considered essential to the prosperity of the civil state in every community. The grant of land by each town to its first minister, when land was of little comparative value, by vesting the title in him, (as was right, because its chief value arose from the improvements he made upon it,) left the people without a home for the next or any succeeding minister. As the great idea they had in mind was that of a permanent ministry, and of course they saw the propriety of making provision for it, the next movement for their second or any subsequent minister, was, after sufficient trial of his gifts and acceptableness, to offer him a certain sum for a "settlement," wherewith he might provide himself a home besides his regular salary. If this had continued to be the arrangement, as it has in some places, till within thirty or forty years past, it would have been an important check on the people, against moving for a dismission of their pastors.

After the practice of offering settlements was done away, ministers themselves made arrangements to provide a home from their own,—too often scanty resources, even by running into debt. But their own changing spirit and the instability of their people, have come to make this a useless, an embarrassing and a losing operation. Hiring such dwellings as could be obtained was the next resort. At length the plan was adopted of securing a parsonage by the society itself,—in some few cases, by individuals for the use of their successive ministers,—a measure quite consonant and almost indispensable with the too prevalent custom of frequent change and an unsettled ministry. With some pastors there is still a decided preference for the more ancient custom of a minister's having a house of his own; but if the people are restless, difficult to please, and changeable, as they frequently become even after a long pastorate, that arrangement accomplishes little to secure permanency. Until the evils of frequent change are thoroughly proved, in disaster and decline by many churches, and a reaction takes place, the only convenient course is to have a parsonage provided, to make dismission and re-settlement as easy as possible. In the present state of things, some are decidedly of the opinion, that parsonages are rather favorable to permanence than otherwise.

There are 115 ecclesiastical societies, that own 116 parsonage houses, the aggregate value of which is given in the footing, with the permanent funds.

Some ecclesiastical societies have possessed funds for the support of the ministry from the beginning. In some instances lands were reserved for that purpose at the first settlement of the towns. But more generally permanent funds have been established by voluntary subscription or by legacies. The support of the gospel, partly in this way, seems to be more general in Connecticut than in any other state. To favor this object, the Legislature has sometimes incorporated banks with a clause in their charter, allowing ecclesiastical societies a certain proportion of their stock if they desired, exclusive of all other applicants.

The amount of funds held for the support of the ministry in a few cases comes up to $10,000, in one the value is $50,000. More generally, they vary from a few hundred to five or six thousand. The number of ecclesiastical societies that hold such funds in the state is 197, and the whole amount of funds is $820,511,34.

This amount of property is owned and improved by all these different corporations, and not by any one ecclesiastical or consolidated establishment; it is owned and controlled by the people and not by any association, conference, convention, bishop or pope. It is safe in the keeping of the people, and nōt liable to be perverted or abused. There are special provisions and safeguards to prevent its misuse. In a few cases some of the funds raised have been lost, by unsafe deposits ; but as the general rule, they are well invested, and sacredly held by the appropriate officers, in trust for their high and noble purpose. A few of the most able churches were far better without these funds, except it be a parsonage ; but in a large majority of cases, they greatly subserve the interests of true religion, by rendering the burdens of annual expense lighter, and by increasing the annual salaries, asthe increased expenses of living and therefore the real wants of ministers require. If the more able churches could and would part with the most or all of their funds, and bestow them on the weaker, or make some provision for more generous salaries, and for proportionate contributions for benevolent objects, their funds would still do good and not evil.

PERMANENT FUNDS.

BY REV. G. A. CALHOUN, D. D., NORTH COVENTRY.

No doubt the system of Permanent Funds for supporting the gospel, in connection with the churches of our denomination, originated in a sincere desire to render enduring the institutions of religion, and to perpetuate the usefulness of benefactors beyond the short period of their generation. But in the inauguration of the system in Congregational churches, two mistakes were committed. First, the application of the funds to the specific objects designed was not sufficiently defined and guarded against perversion. They were often instituted without designating what system of doctrines they were given to support; leaving those who should have control of them, to apply them to the promulgation of truth or error according to their pleasure.

And in the next place, funds, especially parochial funds, were formed where they were not required. Large and wealthy ecclesiastical societies are better without permanent funds for the support of the gospel than with them. It is no favor to them to be entirely exempt from pecuniary expense in sustaining the institutions of religion for themselves, and the communities with which they are connected. As a general principle, that which costs nothing is lightly esteemed. It is believed that there are churches and societies in Connecticut which have been essentially injured by being freed from care and effort in supporting the ministrations of the gospel. They have not had imposed upon them the care and exertion needful to awaken interest and efficiency in ecclesiastical matters; and hence their inactivity and indifference have reared a barrier against benevolent exertions and spiritual progress. Historic facts in connection with our large churches and wealthy societies lead us to expect a clearer manifestation of the spirit of Christ where there are pecuniary sacrifices annually made, than where they are not demanded for sustaining religious institutions among themselves. They who have necessity laid upon them of looking to God for their daily bread, in consequence of this necessity may be brought nearer to God, have a deeper sense of dependence on Him, and of their obligations of gratitude, than if provision had been made for an abundant supply of all their wants. We would aid poor churches in sustaining religious institutions among them, and we would do it in the way which will best subserve their permanent interests ; while we would be sure to let the wealthy churches enjoy the favor of making annual provision for themselves, believing that permanent funds are rather an injury than a benefit to them. As the Congregational churches of this state have been kept thus long from a forfeiture of their evangelical character, so funds consecrated to the service of evangelical religion have been wonderfully preserved from a perverted application. As no original Congregational church in the state has fully changed its denominational character, we know of no funds which have been taken from our denomination and applied to the support of a church of another name, or to the promulgation of fatal error. But the history of Congregational churches and institutions out of Connecticut admonishes us of danger, and the need of much caution. And close corporations entrusted with treasures consecrated to the service of the Lord, are invested with a power to do great evil whenever they prove recreant to the trust reposed in them. The ecclesiastical history of New England, for the last half century, is proof of this, without going further back, or to a greater distance. But the churches cannot be supplied with well qualified pastors and missionaries without the endowment of literary and theological institutions.

Theological instruction must be gratuitous, and even beyond that ; students in theology must be aided in their self-denying, struggling efforts to enter the ministry. The question has long been settled, even from the first planting of Congregationalism in New England, that a system of permanent funds must be adopted for the education of Christian ministers. And this system has become imperative and more extended since the establishment of theological seminaries. We have no desire to see these seminaries so richly endowed as to present a strong temptation to worldings to become occupants of their professorships. A chair of gold, in process of time, would probably be in the possession of a thief. A Judas "had the bag and bare what was put therein." But professors in these institutions should be relieved from distressing anxiety in reference to their pecuniary support ; and they and their pupils should be supplied with accommodations and means requisite to the most efficient and successful prosecution of their appropriate work. This end cannot be attained without permanent funds. And if there are permanent funds for the support of professors, for the provision of needful buildings and large and well selected libraries, a field will then be left open for benevolent exertion in aiding indigent students in meeting their necessary expenses. The danger of a perversion of funds in connection with our theological institutions is probably greater than from any other quarter.

It is a singular fact, that most of the theological seminaries of New England, established by Congregationalists are, in their organic form, more thoroughly anti-congregational than those of other denominations. They have been committed to the management of self-perpetuating bodies, over whom neither the churches, nor their pastors have any control. In these seminaries, so long as they are held in reputation, centers a powerful influence for or against evangelical religion. And instructors in them are in circumstances most favorable for swaying public sentiment according to their pleasure. As it is expected that they will take the sons of the churches, impress on them their own views of the revealed will of God, and send them forth to be pastors and missionaries of the churches, a godly jealousy in reference to the kind of instruction given in these seats of learning, is not out of place. The influence of universities in Europe in opposition to evangelical religion, as also that of one planted by our Puritan Fathers, admonishes us of danger from these needful engines of great power.

The system of Permanent Funds in supporting the gospel should not be applied to our charitable institutions but to a limited extent, especially to voluntary associations. We do not ob-

ject to the Foreign Missionary Board possessing their mission
house, and funds to support their secretaries; but the spirit of missions would not be sustained, much less increased, were it not for
an annual application to the churches for means to continue the
work of faith and labor of love.   And to secure permanency
and efficiency to the other great charitable societies, they should
be intrusted with property sufficient to give them a local and
convenient position for transacting the business allotted them ;
but we would have them dependent on annual contributions
for means to sustain their operations.   We should deeply regret the loss of the fund created by the missionary societies of
Connecticut, or what is denominated the " Everest Fund."
There are metes and bounds set to the application of these
charities, and the General Association of this state is constituted
the almoner.   We do not discover ground to fear, that they
will not be hereafter, as they have thus long been, a means of
great good to the destitute.

But while we would be thus cautious in adopting the system of permanent funds for the support of the gospel ; we would
by no means discourage the benevolent, possessed of property,
from making friends of the mammon of unrighteousness, that
they may be doing good when they are dead and received into
everlasting habitations.   There are churches in the hill towns
of New England, sound in the faith once delivered to the
saints, long since planted, and often watered with the dews
and showers of grace, which are in pressing need of permanent funds to aid them in supporting the gospel.   Their necessitous condition has not resulted from any marked neglect of
theirs, but from the providence of God in taking from them
their members to form in part churches at the west, and in manufacturing villages, or to give additional strength and efficiency
to wealthy churches in our own state.   Most of the thirty-two
churches in Connecticut, assisted by the Home Missionary Society, were once, not only self-supporting, but were efficient
members of our ecclesiastical community.   They have made
great sacrifices to the spirit of emigration and to the extension
of the Kingdom of Christ.   Compared with wealthy churches,
theirs has been a double sacrifice—of helpers in the good cause
and of pecuniary ability.   Indeed to many of our wealthy

churches it might be said, that though they were rich, yet for your sakes they became poor, that ye through their poverty might be rich.

We understand it to be the purpose of our Home Missionary Society to prevent, if possible, any of these churches from becoming extinct, and eventually to repair all the waste places of Connecticut. Great good has been accomplished by the assistance granted ; but is an annual appropriation of a small sum to each of these churches to keep them from becoming at once defunct, the best method which can be adopted for effecting the purpose formed ? There are some evils attending these annual appropriations, and particularly to the old churches in our rural districts ; it is an annual proclamation of their pauperism, which is dispiriting to them, and gratifying to their enemies. A church receives from the Home Missionary Society an appropriation of $100, for which they are truly grateful. It may enable them to eke out the small salary of their pastor for the coming year ; but what will become of us, it is said, if this aid should hereafter be withheld, or if some of our members should be taken from us? And then, the unfavorable influence which this state of things must have on the pastor, can well be imagined. A bright boy in the poor house to-day, may be at a future period an honor to the pulpit, to the bar or to the congress of the nation ; but an old pauper, who will connect their interest with his ? An infant village church may be annually assisted by the missionary society, with the prospect, that when old enough it will take care of itself. And this assistance will not consign it, in public estimation, to hopeless pauperism. But facts disclose a reluctance in many men to becoming members of societies, connected with these old feeble churches, who would not hesitate to unite with them were their pecuniary condition fair and promising for the future. Were the system of permanent funds for the support of the gospel adopted so far as to give weak societies strength to sustain the institutions of religion without charitable assistance, and without a heavy burden to be borne by their members ; and also so far as to make the impression on friends and enemies, that these churches are to live while generations pass away ; their condition would be at once vastly improved.

The correctness of this position has been tested by experiment in the Consociation of Tolland County. When many of the churches of that Consociation began to decline in pecuniary strength, in consequence of emigration and the operation of other causes, six of them, aware of their tendency to weakness, secured each a permanent fund of some four or five thousand dollars. With the assistance thus derived, they have been self-supporting, and the prospect is, that they will continue to be thus independent : otherwise they would have ere this became beneficiaries of the Home Missionary Society. Neighboring churches, in like circumstances, not improving their opportunity, are now receiving charitable aid ; and we fear the amount now annually bestowed will not for many years continue unto them the stated ministrations of the gospel. They need each of them a fund of five thousand dollars, to awaken in them hope and expectation of good, to gather strength from the population around them, and with the blessing of God, to win souls to Christ. So do other churches in similar circumstances. And we know not where the system of permanent funds for the support of the gospel can be applied with less danger of perversion, or with a fairer prospect of lasting good. And we know not where emigrants from these churches, or other persons who have property to bestow in charity, can find objects more worthy of their generosity, than our feeble churches.

The friends of God in their operations to enlarge the Kingdom of Christ on earth, would be greatly embarrassed without the aid of permanent funds. These funds to be available of good should be put in the right place, and the application of them to the support of the faith and order of our churches be guarded by explicit legal instruments.

A PERMANENT MINISTRY.

BY REV. TIMOTHY TUTTLE, LEDYARD.

Time was, when the location of a minister in any particular place, as pastor of a church, was regarded as a permanent establishment. Until near the close of the last century, the dismission of a pastor was an event of uncommon occurrence; a thing which gave occasion for much remark, and the cause of dismission was the subject of earnest inquiry. Councils, when called to act on the question of dissolving the connection between a pastor and his church, long hesitated before coming to a decision. That churches and societies then considered the installment of a minister as a permanent thing is evident from the fact, that, in the call given to the candidate, they always offered what they called a *settlement*, that is, something beyond a yearly salary,—something to begin life with, or with which he might purchase a home. Now, that thing is entirely done away; and well it may be; for if it were continued, societies would often be subject to pecuniary loss.

The frequency of the dismission of ministers began about the commencement of the present century; and now it is an uncommon thing that a man continues the pastor of the same church during the whole period of his ministry, unless his ministerial life should end at a very early stage. In one District Association, (that of New London,) there have been, in less than half a century, nearly sixty removals of pastors by dismission alone, not including those who have been removed by death.

Now, if we inquire concerning the *causes*, or the circumstances, which have led to the frequency of dismissions, it may be observed, that the closing period of the last century, or more especially the beginning of the present, was an era, not only of the commencement of revivals of religion, but was also more distinguished than formerly for discriminating doctrinal preaching. The distinguishing doctrines of Calvinism were brought out more fully and pointedly than they had been, in some of the preceding years. They were dwelt upon by the younger class of ministers in almost every sermon. In many places, these doctrines were new to the people. By many, they were termed " New Divinity;" and much opposition to them was awakened. This opposition, becoming somewhat formidable, caused some instances of dismission. From that time onward, restless spirits in churches and societies—men of standing and influence, finding that they could worry out a minister whom they disliked, and whose preaching was too searching for them to bear submissively, began to make efforts to accomplish their object ; and now it is not uncommon that a very few, thus rising up, cause a minister's removal. Formerly, it seldom entered into the minds of the disaffected, that a minister could be dismissed ; or, if any had such an idea, and attempted to bring it about, they were put down by the general voice of the parish. But now, if the people composing our churches and congregations manifest more uneasiness under a permanent ministry than in former times ; if they are more given to change, more fastidious, or difficult to please, more fault-finding with their minister, and ready to turn him off, (especially if he has arrived at the age of fifty years or more, or if not thought to stand upon the very summit of modern excellence ;) the cause of this state of things, is the *ease*, with which it is now found that he can be removed.

At first, the reason assigned most commonly by ministers themselves, in asking for a dismission, was want of support ; though there might be, and often there were, other reasons underlying the request. If now the frequency of dismissions is a subject of lamentation, (and we know it has been by both ministers and churches,) the writer of this article must be allowed to express his opinion, that the action of ministers themselves, has, in many instances, tended to introduce this lamentable state of things ; and on them the blame must, in some measure rest. A minister is justified in asking for a dismission when his health fails ; and so he may be when there is an overbearing degree of disaffection in his parish ; but not because one or two individuals rise up against him. He may properly ask for a dismission, and he ought to do so, when it is clearly manifest that his usefulness among his people is at an end. But it must be admitted, that many have sought and obtained a dismission when there was no urgent occasion for it, and in cases, in which both the minister and the congregation have been sufferers in consequence.

In further proof that ministers should take a part of the blame to themselves in having prepared the way for the present state of things, when changes are so frequent, we would state the fact, that young men have sometimes consented to be settled in a parish, with the intention on their part of not continuing long in it. Perhaps it is some weak parish, or some obscure place. But they have concluded that it will do for the present, until they can make themselves better known, and rise to some eminence ; and then they "mean to go up higher."

Strong and wealthy parishes also do wrong in inviting a minister from one that is weaker. Sometimes they send spies to hear one preach, concerning whom a good report has reached them ; and if the spies, after hearing, recommend him, then a call is extended to him forthwith. This is not acting in accordance with the Savior's golden rule, not doing to others as they would that others should do to them. A small and weak parish needs an able minister, as well as a large one ; it needs such a minister to build it up, otherwise it is liable to remain always feeble. Ministers themselves ought to put down this kind of traffic, and to show that they are not to be taken by the highest bidder.

Now, as to the *permanence* of the pastoral office, we may say, that more importance should be attached to it than is usually done,—more than councils usually attach to it, when called to dismiss a minister ; more than churches and societies now attach to it. The reasons are,

1. The *migratory* condition of a minister often operates greatly to his disadvantage. It is possible that he may find a wider and a more inviting field of usefulness, and he may have a better support. But it is a common thing that he is no better situated—perhaps not so well ; especially, if he goes from a people strongly attached to him, and where his influence is powerfully felt. Sometimes, like Jonah, he goes away from

32

duty, and from the place where God sent him ; and though he may not be cast into the sea, and be swallowed by a whale, he becomes a wanderer on the land, having, it may be, no permanent location.   Thus, instead of being more useful, his usefulness may become in a measure abridged ; and if he has a family, his care and anxiety for them are greatly increased.   A minister may go from a place where he is pastor, and find another where he is only a stated supply ; and there, he knows not what shall be at the end of his term.   There, his days are as the days of a hireling.   Or, he may possibly find a place where all things look pleasantly.   But, has he, on the whole, gained anything by the change ?   It may be that he has gained by experience the knowledge of one thing, and that is, that it is not best to be unsettled again.   But, admitting that he has found another, and possibly a better place, still one thing may cause him some embarrassment ; he has the character of his people, as individuals, to learn ; and he may be left to find out things to his own disadvantage, and to learn that some, in whom he confided most, are the least friendly, or the least disposed to aid him in his work.

But these are not all the disadvantages of shifting from place to place.   In most cases, it is thought that migrating ministers do *not study* as much as those are under the necessity of doing, who are permanently located ; and consequently there is a lack of that mental improvement to which they might and ought to have attained.   Men are not apt to labor constantly and untiringly, unless they have something to impel them to action. They are liable to content themselves with the thought that old sermons will answer very well for a new place.   But if a minister continues long in the same location, he must do something to maintain his standing, as compared with others.   He must keep up with the advancement of society.   He must bring out of his treasure things new as well as old ; otherwise, as we sometimes say, " his pond will fail."

Further, as to the *influence* of a minister upon the minds of his people, we do not believe, in most instances, that it is diminished by a long continuance with them ; unless he should persist in laboring after his mental faculties have failed.   If he labors onward to advanced age in the same place, as ministers did formerly, he labors for those, the most of whom were born and educated under his ministry. The members of his church are the persons whom he has baptized. They regard him as their spiritual father ; and they scarcely know any other minister. He therefore exerts over their minds a powerful influence.

Such, to ministers themselves, are the advantages of a permanent ministry, as contrasted with frequent changes. Ministers cannot be absolutely sure of being more useful by a change of place ; and if they break away from a people who are strongly attached to them, God may frown upon their act, instead of adding his blessing.

2. The frequent dismission of ministers operates to the disadvantage of parishes.

Particularly, we may observe, that weak parishes, when called to part with their minister, especially if he be one to whom they are warmly attached, are very liable to be discouraged, and to be broken down. They are willing, we will suppose, to do all they can to retain him. But he has a call, it may be, from some other parish—from one greater in numbers and stronger in resources. Calls of this kind—the stronger from the weaker—if justified at all, must be so mainly on the principle, that power gives right. But suppose the minister, so called, consents to leave his people. He leaves the few sheep in the wilderness, it may be, to remain unfed, to be discouraged—perhaps to be scattered upon the mountains, and to become an easy prey to any devourer that may be lying in wait.

Another evil resulting to parishes is, that they are apt to content themselves with only a *stated supply*. We will suppose a parish, in which frequent dismissions have already occurred. It may not be one of the stronger parishes, but one able to support a pastor. Why then do they not settle one ? They may say, of what use will it be ? If we had one, we should probably soon have to dismiss him. His installation would be only a useless ceremony, and therefore we may as well content ourselves with hiring by the year, or by six months, as the case may be. Besides, he cannot feel at home among them as he otherwise would ; nor will he be apt to feel the responsibilities of a pastor ; nor can they speak of him as sustaining that endearing relation. A "stated supply" is comparatively a new order in our churches. Those of us, who are advanced in age, never heard of it in our boyhood, nor have we ever read of it among the different orders of officers in the church, as mentioned in the New Testament. If the practice of employing stated supplies continues to prevail, the time may soon come when there will be very few pastors in our churches.

A further evil, resulting from the frequent dismission of ministers, is the liability in parishes to become divided. If the dismission of a minister does not, of itself, cause division, the attempt to select another may have, and it often has had that effect. Many candidates, it may be, are tried; and some of the parish are for Paul, and some for Apollos, and some for Cephas; and it is found a difficult thing to agree upon any one. Thus divisions are caused, and, perhaps, animosities are enkindled, which may be lasting as a generation; and if another pastor should be settled, the disaffected ones may seek a home somewhere else. It may be a question whether the frequent dismission of ministers from our churches has not tended to strengthen other denominations.

Still another evil may be mentioned, and that is, that there is now less sacredness attached to the pastoral office, and that ordinations and installations are regarded with far less solemnity than they were in former times. Formerly, when such an occurrence was to take place, it was a thing of great notoriety, and there was a general gathering of the people, not only of the parish, but from neighboring towns. Now, because it is a thing of common occurrence, and there is so much uncertainty about the ministers continuing in the pastoral office, the importance of the transaction is not duly appreciated, and the solemnity of it is not felt. Formerly, the settlement of a pastor was considered in the light of a marriage—an agreement which was to be lasting as life. Now, there is almost a moral certainty, that, if the pastor should live a few years, a divorce will take place. Thus an installation is liable to be looked upon as a mere farce, and the office of the ministry is coming to be regarded too much as a secular concern.

Viewing the subject in the light which has now been presented, and in reference to the evils resulting from frequent dismissions, we may see what degree of importance ought to be attached to a permanent ministry.

Now, as to the *remedy* of the evils mentioned, it is difficult, under present circumstances, to prescribe any course of action which shall be effectual. Churches and societies, for their own interest, need enlightening on the subject, that they may learn how to appreciate the pastoral office. But much depends on the action of ministers themselves. They should learn wisdom from their own experience. Some ministers would, probably, do well to be less aspiring than they are, and endeavor to learn, as did the apostle, in whatever state they are, therewith to be content; especially to be content with the place where God, in his providence, has put them, so long as they can be sustained, and so long as they have the prospect of doing any good. Let them not seek to be dismissed, unless absolute necessity requires it ; and let all take a decided stand in favor of a permanent ministry. Truly the present may be termed a transition age, and it is considered to be an age of progress ; and though it may be thought that the world is becoming better, yet, in respect to the permanency of the ministry, happier would it be, if the present were like the age of our Puritan fathers. But it will never be such an age, unless ministers themselves do all they can to make it so. But how, it may be inquired, shall they attempt to make it so ? Let them not be too aspiring—not so much given to change—not so easily frightened by a few passing shadows; for shadows there will be in all their progress ; and let them labor on, contented with such things as God appoints to them. If they would have stable churches, they must themselves be stable.

[If ministers were not too modest, or too much affected by the fear of the charge of sinister motives, they might enlighten their people on the advantages of permanency, or at least preach for one another on this subject. But there are some things to be done also on the part of the people to favor a permanent ministry. Some things which they may and should do, we will briefly indicate, though they are often repeated at ordinations. Every church should devise generous things in their relations with their minister, and treat him liberally in in every respect; they should be cordial toward him and his family; show him due respect and reverence; make him feel at home, so that he can labor heartily for them as for his own people; seek to be united, frown on tattlers and mischief-makers, and use all practicable means to promote harmony; pray for their minister, for when they do not care to pray for him, he will soon, in their estimation, become unfit for their minister; in a word, the people should make provision for permanency in everything. A condition of "notice to quit" in the terms of settlement ought never to be allowed, for in nine cases out of ten, it will cause an unnecessary dismission; it shows a distrust of a minister's capacity or integrity, and is a libel on the Christian benevolence of both parties. Churches that are waning, in agricultural towns, should, of themselves, and with the aid of their sons who have gone abroad, seek to raise a moderate permanent fund, so as to be dependent on missionary aid as little as possible, which is needed in the new settlements of the West. Every church and society which desires a permanent ministry should with new effort, and self-denial if need be, give a more liberal salary, according to the changes of style and the habits of society, if they have not already done so. The cost of living has nearly or quite doubled within fifty years; but salaries have increased at a far less ratio. The people are also greatly increasing their gains, by extending their business and receiving higher prices for their products; but many churches are not in any like degree advancing in their liberality to their ministers. They charge double for what they furnish him by sale, but do not double his means of paying, or of educating his children, and meeting all other expenses at enhanced cost. Frequent and generous donations greatly strengthen the confidence, and encourage the hearts of a minister and his family; but unfortunately for them, every lamb and chicken, every peck of apples and potatoes, the people have to spare, now find so ready a market and at such advanced prices, that the gifts which were once so common, and which serve so well to inspire mutual interest and confidence, now seldom find their way to the minister's pantry or cellar. An inviting parsonage, with ample and efficient means for needed repairs, if not already provided, would secure and help to retain a desirable minister. Since few can furnish dwellings for themselves, this now seems almost indispensable under the new order of things—with "settlements" among the things which are now obsolete. And last, though not least, every church needs a pastoral library for the use of their successive ministers. Many of the best ministers, especially those with the smallest salaries, find it impossible to furnish themselves with the standard theological books—commentaries, and books of reference, which every minister needs for the most intelligent, satisfactory and useful discharge of his ministry. But a well selected library would be a great consideration with most ministers, in accepting a call to a church. It would be for the interest of any church to tax themselves 50 or $100 a year for a course of years for such a library; for they would be constantly receiving in return more that compound interest. A country or village church, paying from 600 to $1000 salary, could save one half of what they felt to be a necessary increase, by devoting a yearly sum to the purchase of books. A less salary would be accepted than otherwise, both for the sake of the attractiveness of the library itself, and because of the saving in that bill of personal expenses. When this measure shall be fully inaugurated, and a pastoral library become as common as a parsonage, a great stride will have been taken on the road to permanence in the ministry. Funds need to be established for this purpose, portions of overgrown funds, if possible, should be devoted to it, legacies given and annual contributions made by the people —funds and legacies conditioned, perhaps, on the raising of proportionate annual contributions.

With the use of these and kindred means, many an undesirable parish may gain and keep desirable ministers; and thus may permanency as of old, with all its blessings, return to our ministry.]—*Com. of Pub.*

COMMON SCHOOL AND ACADEMICAL EDUCATION AS INDEBTED TO CONGREGATIONALISTS.*

BY DAVID N. CAMP, ESQ., STATE SUPERINTENDENT OF SCHOOLS.

In speaking of the relations of any particular church or denomination to the school system of the state it is difficult to separate the distinctive denominational action from that of the whole community, for, in many instances, though action may have been by a particular body, the records of such action do not conclusively establish such fact. No one, however, who has been conversant either with the history of Congregationalism in Connecticut, or with the earlier history of common schools and academies, can have failed to see that elementary education has always found among Congregationalists warm advocates and firm supporters.

The early settlers of the towns which composed the two original colonies of Connecticut and New Haven were mostly Congregationalists. They came to these settlements with their families and all the family relations existing from the first. They came with all the elements of the state combined in vigorous action, and with a firm purpose to make the then wilderness their permanent home. They came with earnest religious convictions, made more earnest by the trials of persecution. United in a common faith, bound together by strong sympathies, and already organized in churches for religious improvement, it was in harmony with their circumstances that they should seek the intellectual and moral culture of their children. But there were other reasons why they should do this. They held the Bible as the only authoritative expression

---

* This article, prepared in ill health, and amid the pressure of official duties, is an inadequate exhibition of the subject. The hope has been indulged of making it more complete, but too much research and investigation seem to be required to render it practicable.

of the divine will, and that every man was able to judge for himself in its interpretation. Their civil government was organized, as they believed, on the principles of the Bible, and its teachings were their rule of faith and practice. It became, therefore, necessary that all should understand the Scriptures, and receive that intellectual culture which would enable them to read the Bible and judge of its meaning. Thus, among the earliest laws of the colonies, were statutes requiring parents and masters to teach their children, either themselves or by others, so as to enable them perfectly to read the English tongue, also to catechize them in the grounds and principles of religion.

The members of their churches had many of them received a good education in the best grammar schools of England. They knew the value of good schools, and felt the necessity of establishing them in the colonies, so that almost immediately on the formation of a settlement a school as well as a church was organized. And these pious men not only sought to provide for their own children, but also endeavored to make provision for the elementary education of all by establishing common schools, and, in some instances, making these schools free. The supervision of the schools, though provided for by the towns, was, generally, committed to the pastors of the churches. Thus, in the records of the New Haven colony, at a general court, held 25th of 12th month, 1641, it was ordered " That a free school be set up in this town, and our pastor, together with the magistrates, shall consider what yearly allowance is meet to be given to it out of the common stock of the town, and also what rule and orders are meet to be observed in and about the same." In the continued legislation, the pastor or minister is often referred to as superintending the schools. Not only were the individual pastors deeply interested in the common schools, but it appears that the governor, council and representatives in general court assembled, in May, 1714, recommended to the General Association of the churches, in this colony, to inquire into the state of religion in this government. In compliance wherewith, the Association reported to the Assembly several heads relating to religion and education. These were considered by the next General Assembly, and an

33

act was passed designed to secure the due execution of the law for the education of children. After the establishment of parishes or societies within the limits of incorporated towns, the common schools were under the supervision of officers appointed by school societies coterminous with the parishes. Among these officers was almost always found the "minister."

From that time to the present, the Congregational clergy have almost universally been actively engaged in promoting the cause of common schools.

The influence of the Congregational denomination on academies and high schools is seen chiefly in the results of individual or extraordinary action, while the benefits are undoubtedly much greater, from the constant influence of a deep and abiding feeling that pervaded the ministry, that it was important that the facilities for higher education should be abundantly provided.

Among the earliest and best established schools of higher order, were the Hopkins Grammar School of New Haven, and the Public Grammar School of Hartford. Both of these institutions received important bequests from Governor Edward Hopkins, who, at his death, left by will a sum for the education of hopeful youths, both at the Grammar School and College. Gov. Hopkins was, in early life, a convert to the religious doctrines and observances of the Puritans, and came to this state in 1637, where he resided for about fifteen years. His deep religious feeling, and his own high culture enabled him to see the need of such institutions as his wealth permitted him to foster and endow.

The Hopkins Grammar School at New Haven has been successfully maintained for nearly two centuries, and is still doing good service as a classical school of high character.

The Hartford Grammar School, after many vicissitudes, but with eminent success, has been united with the Public High School of that city, yet is still so far distinct as to answer the true "intent and purpose" of Mr. Hopkins, by being open to young men from abroad.

Dr. Dwight, afterwards president of Yale College, started an academy at Green's Farms, Fairfield, in 1783, and continued the same till his removal to New Haven, in 1796. This school obtained a high reputation, not only in Connecticut but in other states, and may be taken as the type of numerous similar institutions established by Congregational ministers and maintained by them at the same time that they were filling the office of pastors to large parishes.

The term "Academy," which in the mother country had been applied to seminaries of learning established by the non-conformists, to distinguish them from the schools and colleges of the Church of England, seems to have been applied, very naturally, by the sons of the Puritans to similar institutions in this country, and though not confined to schools founded by Congregationalists, was generally applied to such. Some of these institutions ceased to exist after a few years, while others were merged in the higher departments of common schools, but many of them were incorporated by the General Assembly, and became permanent educational institutions.

It is interesting to notice the date of incorporation of the principal of these schools, and the position which they occupied. Most of them were incorporated in the first thirty-five years of the present century, as follows:

In 1802	Berlin Academy	at Berlin.
" 1802	Woodstock "	" Woodstock.
" 1803	Bacon "	" Colchester.
" 1806	Stratford "	" Stratford.
" 1809	New Township Academy	" New Haven.
" 1814	Danbury "	" Danbury.
" 1821	Fairfield	" Fairfield.
" 1823	Goshen	" Goshen.
" 1825	Lee's	" Madison.
" 1829	Greenwich	" Greenwich.
" 1829	Tolland	" Tolland.
" 1830	Brooklyn "	" Brooklyn.
" 1833	Hill's	" Saybrook.
" 1834	Killingworth	" Killingworth.
" 1834	North Greenwich "	" N. Greenwich.
" 1334	Ellington "	" Ellington.

A few of the above had considerable endowments. Two or three others, as the Brainard Academy, Guilford Institute, and Norwich Free Academy, have been more recently endowed.

Besides these, there were two or three female academies, and a few others whose existence was brief. These mentioned were not usually denominational in character, but to a great extent had their origin in the efforts of Congregational pastors and laymen. Some of them were general in character, but the great object of their founders seems to have been to provide educational institutions, either academies or grammar schools, which would afford young men an opportunity to fit for college, and afford both young men and young women a place where they might obtain a better education than the common schools then offered.

The influence of these academies and high or grammar schools has been felt in the denomination and in the state at large.

The results of the action of Congregationalists cannot so easily be separated from the aggregate results of educational improvements and influences. It has generally been their aim not simply to provide means of instruction for their own children and those of their faith, but to extend the opportunities of a good education to all classes, and bring superior schools within the reach of all. Their efforts have been abundantly blessed to the Congregational church and to the state at large.

SEPARATE CHURCHES IN CONNECTICUT.

BY REV. ROBERT C. LEARNED, BERLIN.

It is commonly known that during the Great Awakening of the eighteenth century, there were in New England many divisions and contentions arising out of the fervent zeal of some members of the churches and the more conservative spirit of most of the pastors and brethren. As a consequence of these divisions there arose a class of churches, considerably numerous for a time, which though purely Congregational in their principles and practices were not in fellowship with the churches of "the standing order." They insisted strongly on the necessity of a clear evidence of regeneration and an open confession of faith with a public recital of religious experience ; they asserted the right of choosing and ordaining officers for themselves, and claimed the privilege for every member of the church to exercise the gifts which God had bestowed to the edification of their brethren. They were truly evangelical in their general doctrine, though somewhat enthusiastic in some of their views, and extravagant in their practices.

They seceded from churches on the Saybrook platform, and were therefore called Separatists. They *preferred* the name of Strict Congregationalists. These churches have, in some few cases, been received into fellowship with the other Congregational churches, the occasion of their separation having been obliterated in the lapse of time ; in others, their adherents have turned away to the Baptist connection. In many particular cases it is now diffcult to trace the history of these churches. In some, it is uncertain whether or not a church organization was ever effected. An attempt is here made to give an outline of the history of these churches in Connecticut.

The first Separate church was that in CANTERBURY. A division took place about the time of Dr. Coggswell's settlement in the old church in 1744. They had first as a pastor one of their own number. Solomon Payne,—ordained Sept. 10, 1746, died October 25, 1754. Mr. Payne was succeeded by Joseph Marshall,—ordained April 18, 1759, dismissed Aug. 20, 1768.

After this the church never settled a pastor. Efforts were repeatedly made to reunite this church to the church which stood on the old platform. However, in 1782 the Separate church was reorganized and was finally admitted into fellowship with the regular churches, being known as the church in the North Society, its house of worship having been removed to the north part of the town. There Rev. William Bradford, a native of Canterbury, ministered in his last years, and here other laborers were temporarily employed. At length, however, the old red meeting house fell into neglect and decay, and about the year 1853 was taken down.

In SCOTLAND, (then a part of Windham,) a Separate church of more than twenty members, cut off from Scotland church, was formed in 1746, known by the local name of "*Brunswick Church.*" It had only one pastor,—John Palmer,—who was ordained May 17, 1749, and continued in charge till his death, August 13, 1807, at the age of eighty-six. The church afterwards wasted away until, in 1813, it was dissolved by vote, most of the members going to the Presbyterian church, Canterbury, in which town part of them lived. The house of worship, south-east of Scotland Village, stood till about 1850.

In WINDHAM, (First Society,) there was a secession; but, if organized at all, it did not long continue its church-life. Backus says that Elihu Marsh was ordained pastor there Oct. 7, 1747, and afterwards became a Baptist.

In MANSFIELD, there was a Separate church formed Oct. 9, 1745, being the *first* after the division in Canterbury. They elected Dea. Thomas Marsh to be their Pastor, and appointed January 6, 1746, for his ordination; but the day before, he was seized and imprisoned for preaching the gospel without license. On the day appointed Mr. Elisha Paine preached to a great concourse of people. In February they chose John Hovey pastor, and ordained him, the first Separatist pastor. He continued in this office for many years, but died Oct. 28, 1775. Mr. Marsh having been released from prison was ordained colleague with Hovey in July, 1746. But this church had wasted so much, that in 1765, two men and two women, then "the remaining members," obtained "liberty of communion" with the church in South Killingly, "until God in his Providence should otherwise provide."

In KILLINGLY a Separate church was formed about 1746, located in the southern part of the town, over which were settled these pastors. Samuel Wadsworth, ordained Jan. 3, 1747, died 1762. Eliphalet Wright, ordained May 16, 1765, died Aug. 4, 1784. Israel Day, ordained June 1, 1785, dismissed May 23, 1826.

During Mr. Day's ministry, he was received by special vote into the County Association. After his death the church was supplied for a while by several ministers, and one was settled, the church being connected with the others of the county in full fellowship.

Since 1856, the meeting house has been loaned to the Free Will Baptists, and the church is nearly extinct.

There seems to have been a branch of this church in the eastern part of Killingly, which *perhaps* prepared the way for the Baptist church now established there.

In BROOKLYN, (then a society in Pomfret,) there was a separation, but whether a church was established is uncertain. The records of the Brooklyn Church show that in Dec., 1742, twenty-six persons signified by letter their "dissent and withdraws" from the pastor as from one that had the form but denied the power of godliness. Most of these persons after repeated admonitions were excluded from fellowship.

In PLAINFIELD a Separate church was formed about 1744, of which Thomas Stevens was ordained pastor on the 11th of September in that year. He was a man of some native talent, a worthy minister, and became one of the leaders of his party. He died in charge Nov. 15, 1755, and was succeeded by Alexander Miller about 1758, who ministered till his death. Their church being on the wane, and the old church being without a pastor and in a feeble state, a desire for re-union, felt in both churches, was realized in Feb. 1769 ; the house of worship was removed, and Mr. Fuller who had preached to other Separate churches was settled pastor of the united church.

In VOLUNTOWN there was a Separate church, over which Alexander Miller was ordained, April 15, 1851, and presided till his removal to Plainfield, when the two churches seemed to have united in one.

In PRESTON a Separate church was formed March 17, 1747, and Paul Park was ordained pastor July 15, 1747. He continued in office more than fifty years, and in 1797 preached a half century sermon. He had no regular successor in the pastorate, though the church held meetings for some time after his death, and their last records come down to 1817.

There was another Separate church in the "LONG SOCIETY" in Preston, over which Jonathan Story was ordained in 1742, but it seems to have been broken up in a few years.

In LISBON, (then a part of Norwich,) a Separate church was formed which had for its pastor Jeremiah Tracy, one of the seceders, but of its history no further particulars are known.

In BOZRAH (then called Norwich Plains,) there was likewise a Separate church, but no account can be given of it. Probably it was over this church that Bliss Willoughby was pastor in 1756.

In FRANKLIN (then Norwich Farms,) there was another Separate church, over which Thomas Denison was ordained pastor Oct. 29, 1746, and continued till about 1759. He appears at various places and times in the history of the churches of this order.

In NORWICH there was a Separate church, located at Bean Hill which began about 1745. Here Jedediah Hide was ordained Pastor Oct. 30, 1747, but was deposed Sept. 22, 1757. John Fuller was ordained Aug. 17, 1759, but removed and a Mr. Reynolds was ordained in his place, Dec. 22, 1762, who four years later became a Baptist, and the Separate church was scattered.

In MONTVILLE (then North Parish, New London,) there was a separation in 1747–8, and Joshua Morse was ordained pastor there May 17, 1750. They kept together about thirty years, but elder Morse removing in 1799 to Landisfield, Mass., the church became extinct.

In NEW LONDON there was a Separate church gathered, over which Rev. Timothy Allen presided for a time, who had been deposed at West Haven for his New Light views. This church, however, did not continue long.

In WATERFORD (then part of New London,) a Separate church was gathered about 1748 with Nathan Howard for its elder. This church early adopted Baptist principles.

In EAST LYME there was a Separate church, over which Ebenezer Mack was ordained June 12, 1749. They erected a meeting house in 1755, but most of them soon became Baptists.

In LYME there was another Separate church, of which John Fuller was ordained pastor Dec. 25, 1746. He removed to Norwich in 1759. Of the subsequent history of the church no account is at hand.

In NORTH STONINGTON a Separate church was formed Sept. 11, 1746, of which Matthew Smith was ordained pastor Dec. 10, 1746, but on the 3d of Aug., 1749, he was excommunicated by the church. Oliver Prentice succeeded him, ordained May 22, 1753, died in office Oct 18, 1755. Then succeeded Nathan Avery, ordained April 25, 1759 ; died in the 22d year of his ministry, Sept. 7, 1780. He was followed after an interval by Christopher Avery, ordained Nov. 29, 1786, who ministered till his death, July 5, 1819. This church finally coalesced with the church from which it had originally separated.

In LEDYARD, (then North Groton,) there was a small body of Separatists, of which Nathaniel Brown, Jr., was ordained pastor, Nov. 14, 1751, who fell under censure in 1755. It probably did not have a long life, but was supplied for a time by elder Park Allyn.

In ENFIELD there was a Separate church formed in 1770, which is supposed to have continued twelve or fifteen years, but no record of it now remains.

In SUFFIELD a Separate church was formed, of which Joseph Hastings was ordained pastor April 18, 1750. They built a house of worship in 1762, but soon became divided and broken up. Mr. Hastings became a Baptist, and, in 1769, the pastor of the Baptist church, into which a portion of his church had been organized. The Separatists then chose Israel Holley as their pastor, who was ordained June 29, 1763, but was afterwards dismissed, and preached in Granby and in Cornwall. This church was dissolved about 1784, the members mostly returning to the old church.

34

In MIDDLETOWN there was a Separate church which at first embraced members in Wethersfield, where Ebenezer Frothingham was ordained Pastor Oct. 28, 1747.   After a time the members in Wethersfield having removed to New York, Mr. Frothingham took up his residence in Middletown, and was installed there about 1754.   His people resided in the First and Fourth Societies, and in 1778 were divided into two parties, about which time Mr. F. was dismissed.   He died in Middletown Nov. 30, 1798, aged 81.   Stephen Parsons, his successor, was ordained Jan. 31, 1788 ; dis. Aug. 9, 1795. David Huntington, was ordained Nov. 8, 1797 ; dis. Oct. 1800.   Benjamin Graves was ordained Oct. 3, 1803 ; dis. 1812.   About the time of Mr. Graves' dismission, the church was dissolved, but was re-organized in 1816, and is now known as the South Church in Middletown.

In COLCHESTER there appears to have been a Separate church, of which Jabez Jones was ordained pastor in 1751.   Nothing more is at hand concerning it.

In SOMERS a Separate church was organized in 1769.   The First church had become very much distracted after the death of Mr. Leavitt in 1761, and was divided ; a part becoming Separates, built a meeting house, but returned in great harmony under Dr. Backus.   Mr. Ely who was the first pastor of the Separate church—from about 1769 to 1774—was afterwards prominent in Shay's rebellion in western Massachusetts, and ended his days in prison.

In HADDAM there were movements towards separation, and a society was formed in 1785, who in 1792 professed themselves Baptists.

In TOLLAND a number known as New Lights withdrew themselves from the communion of the church about 1740, but in 1760 only a few of them remained.   There is no evidence existing of their having formed a church.

In PROSPECT, formerly Columbia Society, there was a Separate church, probably formed between 1770 and '80, of which Benjamin Beach was several years pastor, till 1797, when the present church was formed in Prospect.   Being unable to support the gospel alone, the most of them united with that church.

In TORRINGTON a number of the members of the church united with a class denominated Separates and formed a society styled the Strict Congregational Society. The same year (1786,) they commenced a house of worship on the site of the present church. By a vote of this church, March, 1787, Rev. Lemuel Haynes, a colored preacher, became their pastor, an office which he held about two years, though not installed. In 1791, by the aid of a council, both churches adopted new articles of faith and a covenant and became re-united, and soon after made the new house their place of worship.

In BETHLEM Dr. Bellamy made record in 1740, "A number of the middle aged stand up for false religion and plead for the Separatists." But after a prevailing epidemic in 1750, he notes as one of the favorable results that "the separate spirit did not appear as before."

In COVENTRY and NEW MILFORD there are believed to have been movements towards separation, but no certain infor- mation has been obtained concerning them. The Second Church in Milford and the North Church in New Haven arose from the revival influences of the 18th century, but were not Separatists.

See Dr. Trumbull's History of Connecticut, Vol. 2, pp. 163—195; Tracy's Great Awakening, pp. 310—325; and Rev. Dr. McEwen's Historical Paper in this volume, p. 280.

ERRATA.

Page 254, line 1, put a comma after "number."

Page 254, line 13, put quotation marks around the words "the old red meeting house."

Page 254, line 22, for Presbyterian, read Congregational.

Page 255, line 7, for "Jan. 3," read "June 3."

Page 256, line 1, for "1851," read "1751."

Page 256, line 2, for "scemed," read "seem."

Page 256, line 11, for "1742," read "1752."

Page 256, line 35, for "Landisfield," read "Sandisfield."

ON THE RISE, GROWTH AND COMPARATIVE RELATIONS OF OTHER EVANGELICAL DENOMINATIONS IN CONNECTICUT TO CONGREGATIONALISM.*

BY REV. HENRY JONES, BRIDGEPORT.

PRESBYTERIANS.—In a survey of the minor evangelical denominations in Connecticut, the first place may be fairly assigned by us to the Presbyterians as next of kin.

In Voluntown a Presbyterian church was organized on the 15th October, 1723. Its first pastor, settled in 1723, was dismissed in 1770, and died in November, 1775. The church was reorganized as Congregational in June, 1779. The church in South Mansfield also is or has been nominally Presbyterian, but practically Congregational.

At the present time there are six Presbyterian churches in Connecticut, of which the Old School General Assembly claims five, and the New School one. Of these churches we present ths following tabular view :

Churches.	Date of organization.	Number of original members.	Number of members at the present time.
Thompsonville, O. S., ...	July 5, 1839.		162
Tariffville, O. S., ...	Oct. 24, 1844.		20
Hartford, O. S., ...	Oct. 4, 1851.	32	149
Stamford, N. S., ...	Feb. 25, 1853.	26	149
Bridgeport, O. S., ...	Oct. 31, 1853.	78	124
Deep River, O. S., ...	July 27, 1856.	19	18

The numbers in the last column are taken from the published minutes of the two General Assemblies for 1859.

The churches in Thompsonville, Tariffville, Hartford and

---

* The historical facts and statistics embraced in this paper are based mainly on the authorities given in the margin ; and from these, whatever seemed to the purpose, has been quoted without scruple.

Stamford were originally composed almost exclusively of those who had been previously members of Presbyterian churches elsewhere, and who imagined that their spiritual interests would be better secured under that organization.

The church in Bridgeport was the result of a secession from the Second Congregational church, on the dismission of Rev. Dr. Nathaniel Hewit, at his own instance, by the Consociation of Fairfield West.

The church at Deep River was also composed originally of members seceding from a Congregational church. The reasons distinctly assigned in this instance were, the refusal of that church to hear from its pulpit the doctrines of the Saybrook platform, and the dismission, without trial, by a unanimous vote of the council of consociation, of the pastor, whom the same council had, eighteen months before, with the same unanimity ordained.

But we must be allowed to doubt whether the council of consociation could have been led so summarily and unanimously to reverse its own recent action, had not the disaffection seemed to have been caused, not by the doctrines themselves of our platform, but by their nude and disproportionately frequent, and so far unscriptural exhibition. It may indeed be questioned which is the most lamentable in the Christian pastor, an affected championship of doctrines supposed to be specially offensive to the natural heart, or an over prudent silence in respect to them. And in the present case the Consociation might justly demand why has not this church been carefully and kindly trained to an intelligent acceptance of those doctrines, which by an over zealous assertion of them, have been rendered so distasteful. The seceding brethren, doubtless, felt themselves called upon thus to bear their testimony to the truth. But might they not have yielded a more quiet, indeed, but more effective testimony by remaining at their post? Two like secessions have taken place, (in Enfield and Fair Haven,) without a change of denomination, fully in the spirit of that at Deep River.

The church in Tariffville, in October, 1852, saw their pastor dismissed, and their church edifice soon after sold to Episcopalians. They have still an existence as a church, but have had no preaching except at long intervals for the last seven years.

It appears that within the last ten years, four Presbyterian churches have been organized in our state. If a necessity for these churches has in any instance arisen from a want of fidelity to the scriptural faith of our fathers, or from any failure in the duties of church fellowship, to which we are mutually pledged in our cherished system of consociation, let the churches receive the lessson in a spirit which may prevent such divisions in future years.

BAPTISTS.—In 1705, just seventy years from the settlement of the Connecticut River towns, a Baptist church was organized in Groton, by the Rev. Valentine Wightman, who removed to that town from North Kingston, Rhode Island. There had been previously a few scattered Quakers and Episcopalians within the limits of the colony, but this appears to have been the first attempt to establish a departure from the Congregational church order in Connecticut.

The Rev. Valentine Wightman remained pastor of the church in Groton forty-two years, till his death at the age of sixty-six. He was descended from the Rev. Edward Wightman, burnt at the stake in England in 1612, the last man who suffered death for conscience sake in the mother country by direct course of law. He was followed in the pastorate, after an interval of nine years, by his son, the Rev. Timothy Wightman, who retained the office forty years till his death in 1796, and was succeeded by his son John G. Wightman, who was pastor of the same church from 1800 to 1841, when he died. Thus the three Wightmans, father, son and grandson, sustained the pastoral office in this church one hundred and twenty-three years. Of the descendants of the Rev. Valentine Wightman, nineteen have sustained the pastoral office with usefulness and honor.

The church in Groton remained the only Baptist church in Connecticut for twenty years. In 1726 another was organized in New London, and in 1743 a third in North Stonington. ·

From these beginnings, small at first and slow in progress, have arisen, amid much opposition and many discouragements, we are told, the eight associations of Baptist churches in this state, embracing in 1850, 121 ministers, 113 churches, and 16,617 communicants.*

The Baptists have been supposed to have received considerable accessions from the Separatists of the last century. But it appears that out of twenty-five churches of the Separatists, not more than four or five joined the Baptist denomination. The rest resumed their communion with the Congregational churches.†

EPISCOPALIANS.—The origin of Episcopacy in Connecticut, as given by Trumbull, is substantially as follows :

The society for propagating the Gospel in foreign parts, in 1704, fixed the Rev. Mr. Muirson as a missionary at Rye. Some of the people at Stratford had been educated in the church of England, and others were not pleased with the rigid doctrines and discipline of the New England churches; and they made an earnest application to Mr. Muirson to visit Stratford and preach and baptize among them. About the year 1706, on their invitation, he came to Stratford. The novelty of the affair, and other circumstances, brought together a considerable assembly; and Mr. Muirson baptized twenty-five persons, principally adults. The churchmen in that town at first consisted of about fifteen families, among whom were a few landholders, but much the greatest number were tradespeople of English birth. In April, 1707, Mr. Muirson made another visit, and preached this time in Fairfield as well as Stratford, baptizing in both towns a number of children and adults. In 1722, the Rev. Mr. Pigot was established as a missionary at Stratford. He had twenty communicants and about a hundred and fifty hearers. In 1723 Christ Church was founded. ‡

Meantime a grand defection had occurred at the very center of things. In March, 1713, the trustees of Yale College, wishing to secure to the students the best advantages, had appointed Rev. Timothy Cutler of Stratford as resident rector. Mr. Cutler was acceptable to the legislature, and to the clergy, and the students were quiet under his instruction and govern-

---

* Hollister's Hist. of Conn., Vol. II., p. 560.
† New Englander, Vol. XI., p. 216.
‡ Trumbull's Hist. of Conn., Vol. I., p. 503.

ment. Says Dr. Stiles, "In the philosophy, metaphysics and
ethics of his day, he was great. He spoke Latin with fluency,
and with great propriety of pronunciation. He was a man of
extensive reading in the academic sciences, divinity and ecclesiastical history, and of a commanding presence and dignity in
government." The college, says Trumbull, appeared now to be
firmly established in a flourishing and happy state. But from
a quarter entirely unexpected, it suffered a sudden and great
change. At the commencement in 1722, it was discovered
that the rector and Mr. Brown, one of the tutors, had embraced
Episcopacy, and that they and two of the neighboring ministers, Rev. Samuel Johnson of West Haven, and Rev. James
Wetmore of North Haven, had agreed to renounce the communion of the churches in Connecticut, and to take a voyage to
England to receive Episcopal ordination.

Here was, indeed, a "*dignus vindice nodus.*" Gurdon Saltonstall had been for fourteen years the governor of the colony
by the annual vote of the people. In the first year of his
public service, through his personal influence, doubtless, to a
great extent, the Saybrook Platform had been carried, and our
admirable system of church consociation secured. Before his
election he had been ten years a Congregational pastor, was
well versed in the Episcopal controversy, and attached to the
prevailing order. Nor in the dignity of personal presence did
he yield anything to the learned Rector. So important did he
deem it that the public should be informed on this great
question of the liberty of the churches, that he came forward,
amid the universal surprise, and, as tradition relates, disputed
openly with Rector Cutler the claims of prelatical supremacy.
Moveover, he was judged to have been superior in the argument, and gave much satisfaction to the clergy and others who
were present.

The trustees at the commencement passed no resolve relative to the Rector, but gave themselves time to know the prevalent opinion of the people, and to consult the legislature on
the subject. But meeting in October, while the assembly
were in session at New Haven, they adopted the following
resolutions :

"*Voted,* That the trustees, in faithfulness to the trust reposed in them, do excuse the Rev. Mr. Cutler from all further services as rector of the college. That the trustees accept the resignation which Mr. Brown hath made as tutor.

" *Voted,* That all such persons as shall hereafter be elected to the office of rector or tutor in this college, shall, before they are accepted therein, before the trustees, declare their assent to the confession of faith, owned and assented to by the elders and messengers of the churches in this colony of Connecticut, assembled by delegation at Saybrook, September 9, 1708, and confirmed by the act of General Assembly, and shall particularly give satisfaction to them of the soundness of their faith in opposition to Arminian and prelatical corruptions, and of any dangerous consequence to the purity and peace of our churches. But if it cannot be before the trustees, it shall be in the power of any two trustees, with the rector, to examine a tutor with respect to the confession and soundness of his faith in opposition to such corruptions." *

It is impossible not to recognize an overruling providence in the fact that fourteen years before this time the churches of Connecticut had been led to provide themselves with a confession of faith, adopted as if with special reference to just such an emergency as had now so unexpectedly occurred. Who can fail to see that the Saybrook Platform was at that time, and has continued to be from that time, the sheet-anchor of the freedom and unity of our churches?—that it then held our beloved college, and has since held it firmly moored in its primitive and Puritan simplicity? Had Harvard College, founded in the united prayers and sacrifices of the sister colonies, been pledged to some such standard as our platform affords, could it have been so easily perverted from the holy purposes of its founders, and be lending, as at this day, its powerful influence to the propagation of fatal error.

Mr. Cutler and Mr. Brown, having been thus excused from their services at the college, and Mr. Johnson having been about the same time dismissed from his pastoral charge, as also Mr. Wetmore, they all soon after proceeded to England and received holy orders. Of these only one returned to the

---

* Trumbull's Hist. of Conn., Vol. II., p. 82.

colony. The Rev Samuel Johnson, about the year 1724, was stationed as missionary of the church at Stratford, in the place of Mr. Pigot. Mr. Johnson is described by Dr. Dwight as the father of Episcopacy in Connecticut, and, perhaps, the most distinguished clergyman of that order who had settled within its limits. In 1754, he was appointed president of King's College in New York. He received the degree of D. D. from the University of Oxford.

It was supposed that at this time several other gentlemen of considerable character among the clergy were in the scheme for declaring for Episcopacy, and of carrying over the people of Connecticut in general to that persuasion. But as they had not openly committed themselves, when they saw the consequences with respect to the rector and the other ministers, that the people would not hear them, but dismissed them from the service, they were glad to conceal their former purposes and continue in their respective places.* Three instances of defection, however, afterward occurred. The Rev. John Beach, who had been the approved pastor of the Congregational church in Newtown for seven years, seceded from the prevailing order, and sailed for England, where he was Episcopally ordained in September, 1732. He afterward preached as a missionary in Newtown and Reading. The Rev. Samuel Seabury, the father of the future bishop of the same name, likewise gave up his charge as stated supply at Groton, declared for Episcopacy, and sailed for England for holy orders.† And Rev. Ebenezer Punderson, ordained at North Groton (Ledyard) in 1728, after five years, relinquished his pastoral charge and sought Episcopal ordination in England. The two last named likewise returned to Connecticut and labored as missionaries in New London county.

In 1783, immediately after the close of the revolutionary war, the Episcopal clergy of Connecticut and those of New York held a private meeting and elected unanimously the Rev. Samuel Seabury as bishop of the diocese of Connecticut; and soon after the bishop elect proceeded to England for consecration. He had been ordained as presbyter by the bishop

---

* Trumbull's Hist. of Conn., vol. II., p. 33.
† Hollister's Hist. of Conn., vol. II., p. 544,

of London in 1753, and had sustained the pastoral office at New Brunswick, N. J., at Jamaica, L. I., and at Westchester, successively. It were long to tell the perplexity and delay which he encountered while urging in England his claim to the apostolic miter. Suffice it to say that on the 14th November, 1784, he received at Aberdeen in Scotland the consecration which England had refused, and returned speedily to take charge of the diocese of Connecticut and Rhode Island.*

With reference to the progress of Episcopacy in Connecticut, the following statistics are given on the best authority:

Ministers of the church of England in Conn. in 1740,   7
Fifteen years later, ... 11
Episcopal parishes in 1750, ... 25
Houses of worship,   "   24
Episcopal parishes in 1800, ... 62
Increase in the half century, ... 37

The increase was largest soon after Whitfield's first visits to New England, and just before the war of the revolution. During the struggle for independence, and the separation of the colonies from the mother country, there was a considerable loss, which was only beginning to be recovered at the opening of the present century.

The Episcopal clergy in 1800 numbered 17; the same as immediately before the revolution. The parishes had again multiplied, but so many families had been broken up by the war, or had withdrawn after the declaration of peace in 1783, that the communicants could not have numbered more than 1,500.

At the adoption of the present constitution in 1818, when the clergy began to report to the convention of the diocese in detail,

The communicants were   .   .   .   3,400
In 1825, 600 had been added, making   .   . 4,000
In 1850, the Journal of the Convention gives   9,360

METHODISTS.—The first seeds of Methodism were sown in Connecticut in 1789.† In June of that year, the Rev. Jesse

---

* Hollister's Hist. of Conn., vol. II., p. 548.

† This is the date given by Dr. Bangs, though it appears from the "Memorials of Methodism," by Rev. Abel Stevens, that Rev. Messrs. Cook and Black had preached in Connecticut a year or two previously.

Lee preached in Norwalk, Fairfield, New Haven, Reading, Hartford, Canaan, and other places, passing three months in the state.

The first Methodist society was formed at Stratford, 26th September, 1789, and consisted of three females. The next was at Reading, and embraced but two persons, one of whom, Mr. Aaron Sanford, became afterward a local preacher.

The first church edifice was built at Weston, and called Lee's Chapel, in honor of its founder.

In 1790, the circuits of New Haven, Hartford and Litchfield were established. There were at that time but four Methodist ministers in New England. Yet there were more ministers than classes, and scarcely more than two members to each preacher. Yet under the earnest and devoted labors of the pioneers of Methodism, the doctrine and discipline inculcated by Wesley gradually extended over the state.

At the close of the year 1802 the number of members was reported as 1,658. Efforts persistently made to obtain the number of members at later periods have been unavailing.

At the adoption of the present constitution in
    1818, the number of Methodist churches was, 53
In 1850, ... 185
Increase in thirty-two years, . . . 132
The increase of the number of Congregational
    churches in the same thirty-two years was, 42
Of the Episcopal, ... 29
Of the Baptist, ... 25
Of the three last named united, . . . 96

It thus appears that the excess of increase in the number of Methodist churches from 1818 to 1850, over that of the Congregational, the Episcopal, and the Baptist combined, was 36. The whole number of Congregational churches in 1850 was 252. Excess over the number of Methodist churches 67.

With the same rates of increase respectively, the Methodist churches would outnumber the Congregational in twenty-four years, that is to say, in fifteen years from the present time.*

* Since the above was written the Christian Advocate and Journal gives as the number of Methodist churches in Connecticut in April, 1859, 164; members and

To what causes is this large increase of the Methodist denomination to be ascribed?

Our Methodist brethren, if called on for their honest convictions, would probably assign, first and mainly, the formalism, the worldliness, and the want of vital piety in the prevailing order. And with too much reason, we must allow, especially if we look back to the close of the last century, when the mischief of the half-way covenant was at its hight, and when Methodism made its entrance among us. Let us hope that they could say it with less truth at the present time.

Another cause may, probably, be found in the fact that Methodism commends itself in various respects to the sympathy of the people. Its preachers are taken directly from the body of the people, and without any extended course of preparation, enter on their work with their previous habits of intellect and feeling still unchanged. Thus they are able to address the people more in accordance with their own modes of thought, and to carry their sympathies more entirely with them in their public devotions, than one can easily do, who has raised himself by years of study, and of communion with the choice minds of the world's history, to a higher sphere of thought and emotion. From the efforts, however, which are constantly made to elevate the tone of Methodist preaching, it would seem that either our Wesleyan brethren are not conscious of the advantage they have thus enjoyed, or are not careful to retain it. The people, again, are admitted to a large share of duty and responsibility in the common cause. Lay brethren are regularly employed as class leaders and exhorters, and amid volunteer prayers and exhortations, all raise, *ad libitum*, their fervent responses. In these respects Methodism may be characterized as the religion of the people.

Again, the Methodist organization should hold a place in our account of their success. No church calls its own minister, no preacher selects his own field. There is more than military

probationers, 18,500. The minutes of the General Association, just published, give as the number of members of the Congregational churches in Connecticut, Jan. 1st, 1859, 45,871. The numbers in the text were taken from the U. S. census for 1850, and ought to be reliable. If so, we have a loss of 21 Methodist churches in nine years. The respected historiographer of Methodism will, doubtless, be able to explain this.

subordination to the central power—a power which says to this man go, and he goeth ; and to another, come, and he cometh ; and to its servant, do this, and he doeth it.

Add to all this its intensely aggressive policy—aggressive not merely, it would seem, against the world lying in wickedness, but, to a good degree, against the churches and clergy of another name, who, perhaps, in its opinion, all need re-converting, with whom, on the other hand, there has been, proverbially, little or nothing of sectarian and proselyting zeal, and who, as their formularies show, have no other object in their organization than most effectively to fulfil the last command of our common Master.

GENERAL VIEW.—The change in the aspect of affairs since the opening of the last century is indeed marvellous. At that time not a single church existed in our Puritan Connecticut which was not of the Congregational order. In 1850 there were 734 churches, of which 252 only were Orthodox Congregational, 29 per cent., or less than one third of the whole number.

In view of this change, we rejoice to say that the legislation of Connecticut has never been opposed to the progress of the minor sects. In 1727, four years after the founding of Christ Church in Stratford, it was enacted that "If it so happen that there be a society of the church of England, where there is a person in orders according to the canons of the church of England, settled and abiding among them, and performing divine service, so near to any person that hath declared himself of the church of England, that he can conveniently and doth attend public worship there," whatever tax he shall pay for the support of religion shall be delivered " unto the minister of the church of England." Those who conform to the church of England were at the same time authorized to tax themselves for the support of their clergy, and were excused from paying any taxes for building meeting-houses. The Quakers and the Baptists received the same exemption and the same indulgence in 1729.

The reports of religious oppression under these provisions are, probably, to be traced to cases like the following. A meeting-house was to be built, or other unusual expense incurred by a Congregational society; and some who were opposed to the proceeding, would declare themselves Episcopalians or Baptists, and claim that they ought to be exempted from paying the new tax. But unless there was an established society and a resident minister of their professed faith, for whose support they were taxed, according to the letter of statute above quoted, the money was collected according to law, and this was called persecution.

The law of 1727 was modified by subsequent acts of the legislature, every change being intended to make a separation from the Congregational churches more easy to those who wished to leave them.*

By a statute passed October, 1708, the General Assembly did indeed approve the Saybrook Platform, and ordain that the churches within this government that were or should be thus united in doctrine, worship and discipline, be owned and acknowledged established by law, and from that time till the revision of the laws in 1784, the Congregational churches enjoyed the pre-eminence and patronage thus implied.

But in that revision of 1784, the legal establishment of the Saybrook Platform was repealed by being omitted, and liberty of conscience granted to Christians of every name. From that day no sect in Connecticut has been invested with privileges superior to another—no creed is established.

The state was divided into ecclesiastical societies, for the purpose of maintaining religious worship and instruction. Each society was at liberty to adopt such creed and form of worship as it might choose, and to change the same at the pleasure of the majority. To secure the consciences and property of minorities, it was provided that Christians, of whatever denomination, differing from the worship and ministry adopted by the majority in any "located society," might form themselves into distinct churches and congregations for public worship; that the churches or congregations thus organized should have all the corporate powers and privileges of the located societies; and that every person attending such churches or congregations, and lodging a certificate of the

---

* Kingsley's Hist. Discourse, pp. 94 and 96.

fact, signed by the minister or clerk of his own society, with the clerk of the located society, should be exempt from all taxation for religious purposes, except by the society of his choice.

Every person was bound, indeed, to belong ecclesiastically somewhere, and unless his certificate was given to the contrary, he was presumed to belong to the located society. The support of Christian worship and instruction was taken to be one of the great interests of the community ; and in theory no man was allowed to rid himself of his part of the burden.

In 1791 the system was completed by an act authorizing any man who might prefer some other place of worship to that of the located society, to give a certificate of the fact under his own hand, and by such a certificate to free himself from all further responsibility to that society.*

By the new constitution formed and adopted in 1818, the long cherished principle was given up that every citizen should bear his part in supporting public worship and Christian instruction, as a matter of public benefit. Thus was the last tie broken between church and state, and every man left to contribute or not to contribute as he might please to the support of religious institutions.

And all these acts, be it remembered, securing to the citizen of Connecticut the largest religious liberty, were passed, not by the minor sects, for in those times they together formed but a fraction of the people, but by the standing order.

It was certainly a picture fair to see, when the people of Connecticut, with their religious teachers, were united under one system of faith and worship. And if we might believe that under this appearance of external conformity, there were no jarring elements, that over all our hills and valleys heart beat to heart in Christian sympathy, it would be, indeed, a scene over which angels might love to linger.

But alas! the previous history of the Connecticut churches shows that the elements of discord were rife within them. The churches of Hartford, Windsor, Wethersfield and Stratford were rent with internal dissensions, which in the cases of

---

* Quarterly Christian Spectator, vol. VIII., p. 500.

Hartford and Stratford, were allayed only when one of the contending parties withdrew to seek a new home in the wilderness.*

And when we take into account the varying minds of men, their right to differ, and the fact that in a free country that right will be maintained, the only question seems to be, shall men differ under apparent and pretended unity, or in open and honorable dissent. Religious freedom was the boon which our fathers sought in coming to this land. In all consistency, then, let it prevail among us their descendants, and let us pretend to no unity which is not hearty and free.

---

* In 1659 Gov. John Webster, Elder William Goodwin, and about thirty others removed to Hadley; and the agreement by which they mutually bound themselves so to do, now stands on the records of that town.

36

CONGREGATIONALISTS IN THEIR RELATION TO OTHER RELIGIOUS SECTS, CHARACTERIZED BY ERROR, FANATICISM, OR DISORDER

BY REV. ABEL MC EWEN, D. D., NEW LONDON.

The Congregational ministry and churches of Connecticut have, from abroad, been reproached for not having any general confession of faith. The General Association has no confession of faith. Neither has any District Association, nor any Consociation of churches in the state, set forth any such formulary. Each particular church makes, or adopts, its own confession of faith. This has been deemed requisite to the religious freedom of individual Christians. Though the several churches have been indulged in this liberty, their confessions have, for substance, been so harmonious, that no embarrassment, during more than two centuries, has been experienced in transferring ordinary members, or pastors, from one church to another.

By ecclesiastical bodies which use general confessions of faith, Congregationalists have been admonished that they expose their churches, by the absence of a general creed, to apostacies from their faith and order into heretical sects.

, To this the pertinent reply is :

1. That no Congregational church in Connecticut has become UNITARIAN.

Our state borders upon a state, some of whose churches have made this departure from the religion of the Pilgrims. Strenuous efforts, have, in a few instances, been made to seduce churches in Connecticut from their Trinitarianism. But that class of the population, somewhat elevated by taste and education, which in Massachusetts became Unitarians, have, in our commonwealth, chosen to be Episcopalians, so that the material has here been wanting for proselytes to their faith.

Toward the close of the eighteenth century, the Rev. Stanley Griswold became the pastor of the church in New Milford.

Soon after his ordination he manifested religious sentiments diverse from those of his orthodox brethren. He labored to break the distinction between the church and the world, inviting all the congregation to the communion table. To this the church did not respond; nor is it known that any individual member became a Unitarian. Yet this church so far sympathized with its pastor, when he received the censure of the surrounding pastors and churches, that the Consociation of Litchfield South were constrained to exclude it from their fellowship. Soon, however, Mr. Griswold was dismissed, and immediately the church employed orthodox candidates, and, at length, settled Mr. Elliot, under whom and succeeding pastors of like soundness in the faith, this church returned to rejoice and to be welcomed in hearty fellowship with the other churches of the state.

Contemporary with Mr. Griswold, the Rev. Whitfield Cowles, pastor of a church in Granby, became a Unitarian, or something like one. He seems to have had no success in alienating his church and people from their established creed and practice; and his ministerial habits were such that he soon vanished from public observation.

A little subsequent to these events, the Rev. John Sherman was settled as an orthodox pastor of the South Church in Mansfield. He soon swerved from what the people of his charge and the surrounding clergy and churches took him to be. After a violent struggle, the church and society on one side and he on the other, called a mutual council, part orthodox and part Unitarian. After a session of heat and strife he was dismissed from his charge. The church having obtained relief has since progressed in its original integrity, accommodated with pastors faithful to their trust.

A sequel to the council at Mansfield is worthy of note. The Rev. Henry Channing, pastor of a church in New London, was the moderator of that council. He had been settled as an orthodox minister; but after two years, had become covertly a Unitarian, and remained such for seventeen years. Though in the chair, he so displayed himself as the advocate of Mr. Sherman, that the Association of New London County immediately passed and placed on record resolutions that they would not exchange pulpits with a man who denied the doctrine of the Trinity, of the divinity of Christ, or of the personality of the Holy Spirit. As a test to try his own church and people, Mr. Channing proposed to them to increase his salary, or to unite with him in calling a council for his dismission. They unanimously complied with the last item of his request, and he became a wandering apostle of the theology to which he gave himself a martyr.

While these events were passing, the Rev. Abiel Abbot was settled as pastor of the church in South Coventry. He was from Massachusetts. His ministry had not progressed far before he developed his Unitarian sentiments. For redress, or relief, the church called in the Consociation. He denied its jurisdiction ; nevertheless the Consociation dismissed him. He convoked an *ex-parte* council, which declared the result of the Consociation null, and that Mr. Abbot was still in his pastoral office. The decision of the Consociation, however, was respected, and Mr. Abbott withdrew.

In the old age of Dr. Whitney, of Brooklyn, Mr. Luther Wilson, a young clergyman, was brought in to aid the aged pastor in his services. Whatever might have been expected of Mr. Wilson, he was soon known as a preacher of Unitarian doctrines. The old tenant of the pulpit was aroused to a more distinctive exhibition of Calvinistic docrines than for years he had been accustomed to make. To him the church mainly adhered. The young man, however, attracted to himself a party who, acting as a majority, voted their aged pastor and his church out of the parochial house for worship, and subjected them to the expense of erecting a new building. This they manfully encountered, and, under a succession of able and faithful pastors, they have remained, and they still remain, the strong church of Brooklyn. Mr. Wilson, after a few years of isolated ministration and diminished influence, winning nothing from surrounding churches or societies, left for distant fields of enterprise. He left behind him a people obscurely known as prolonging an intermittent ministration of a changeful gospel.

Early in the present century a Mr. Leonard became the pastor of the church in Canterbury. He had studied theology with a clergyman of Connecticut, who taught the common faith of our churches. Mr. Leonard, however, so preached that he was soon regarded as a Unitarian, and he was, after a short time, dismissed from his charge. Trinitarian pastors have succeeded him, and no characteristic effects of his ministry in Canterbury have been reported.

These are the prominent instances—perhaps all the instances worthy of note—in which strenuous efforts have been made to seduce our churches from their faith in their Divine Saviour. They have all proved abortive, notwithstanding the churches have not been put under the shelter of a general confession of faith.

Besides these attempts to win some of our churches to Unitarianism, enterprises have been undertaken to establish a few original institutions of this exotic religion. In Hartford, Norwich, and in a few others of our populous towns, congregations have been gathered. The beginning of these ministrations have been proclaimed with the sound of a trumpet before them; yet, their progress has been feeble, their attainments have been unsuccessful, and their end has, in most instances, been witnessed.

The experiment, for more than half a century, shows that the population of our state, influenced directly or indirectly by our Congregational ministry and churches, is not a soil in which Unitarianism easily takes root.

2. Nor is it more congenial to the doctrine of Universal Salvation. People professing this are an omnipresent sect. Though they dwell in the presence of all their brethren, their institutions throughout Christendom are of a fluctuating character. In no part of the world have they been, it is conceived, more unstable than in Connecticut. The boon which their theory proposes may be had without institutions, without ministrations, and even without faith during the present life. Why should men tax themselves for what all may have, and all will have, whether they will or not, without money and without price? No one doctrine in the whole catalogue of errors has been more generally or constantly denounced, exposed and refuted by the Congregational ministers and churches of Connecticut than that of Universal Salvation. Still, so con-

venient and welcome a hiding place does it present from the
call to immediate repentance and faith, backed by the doctrine
of an endless reprobation, which may, any moment, become
irretrievable, that individuals will often be found loosely connected with orthodox congregations, or living in their neighborhood, who try to believe, or profess to believe, that none of
the human race will be subjected to endless punishment.
Such individuals, by experiment, find that it is no more practicable to shelter themselves from the appeals of the Gospel,
honestly expounded, under the doctrine of universal salvation,
than by an open profession of infidelity.

Occasionally, in the past, here and there in a parish, attempts,
with short lived success, have been made to gather a congregation of Universalists for public worship. A rich individual,
or a combination of a few such, has had the temerity to build
a church. The outlay, with rare exceptions, has proved an
entire failure. The stock in it has been found not to pay.
The zeal for an antagonistic Gospel has been quenched by the
subsequent and prospective experience of a prolonged ministration ; the house, with debt hanging over it, has gone into the
hands of some other denomination, or has been converted to
some secular use. To prevent such a catastrophe, resort has
sometimes been had to a metropolitan policy. A church has
been built in a populous town, and little streamlets of a liberal
Christianity, so called, have been caused to run into it from
many surrounding towns. By this device an institution, feebly
sustained by the population of the place where it is, has kept
itself in public observation and sustained public worship for
some length of time.

Murray, in his day, visited Connecticut not unfrequently, and
tarried and labored in much hope and with some effect. If he
gathered any church or congregation, it did not survive him in
any distinct and permanent existence. Winchester died at
Hartford. On his death bed he sought counsel from the distinguished pastor of the North Church in that city. Dr. Strong
testified that he manifested amiable affections, though lamentably deluded concerning one point of doctrine.

No Congregational church in the state has ever apostatized
to Universalism. Some few churches have at times suffered

from the infection of its doctrines, but no one has ever been extinguished. Very few of the pastors of our churches have been suspected of being even covertly tinctured with this heresy. Dr. Joseph Huntington, pastor of the church in South Coventry, who died more than half a century ago, preserved a reputation for orthodoxy until the close of his life. But he left a posthumous manuscript, in which he advocated the restoration of all men to holiness and salvation. His family divulged the fact, and submitted the disposal of the writing to the discretion of a company of ministers, by whose advice it was published, and soon received its quietus from a refutation by Dr. Strong, of Hartford, entitled " Benevolence and Misery."

` The theory of this sect, if theory it can be said to have, has undergone a very considerable change within twenty or thirty years past. During the early stages of the appearance of Universalists among us, they were ambitious to preach Calvinistic doctrines, until they came to the final point of the reprobation of a part of mankind. Orthodoxy was their grand proselyting argument. The reply of Congregationalists was, that the nearer a scheme of theology came to the truth, the more dangerous it was, if, in the end, it ignored or denied the great sanction of the divine law and Gospel. In late years Universalists seem to have relied very little on the atonement, or on the efficacy of any grace peculiar to the Gospel ; but, in common with infidels, they counsel men to confide in the uncovenanted gentleness and mercy of God. He is too good to inflict lasting evil upon his creatures.

Formerly, Universalists presented themselves in two divisions : Redemptionists, who ridiculed the fear of any punishment after death, and Restorationists, who inculcated the expectation of future punishment, which would be remedial, and would be successful in reclaiming all men to holiness and happiness. The great mass of the population of this state have, at all times, been preserved from confidence in either of these snares. Their distrust was well expressed by the celebrated Mr. Pierpont Edwards, who said to Mr. Dodd, of Hartford, that neither the doctrine of no punishment after death, nor that of a limited punishment was salutary for man while in this life ; " for," said he, " we are such rascals, that while the

Gospel, in its true import, is preached, we can hardly live to-gether ; but, were the doctrine of universal salvation generally credited, earth would be turned into a hell before the time."

3. About ninety years ago a secession from the Congrega-tional churches actually occurred of people who formed them-selves into churches of a distinct denomination called Sepa-rates.

After Whitfield had passed through the country, and great effects had been produced by divine grace attending his minis-trations, other ministers, especially one from Long Island, un-dertook to be his followers. They had his zeal, but not all of them his discretion. Some of the Congregational churches welcomed, and some of them discouraged and even withstood these itinerants. They were not sent, but they ran. They, perhaps without mistake, regarded some of the pastors who de-barred them from their pulpits as cold and unenterprising in the work of the ministry. Some of the members of our churches and congregations, disregarding the counsels of their ministers, were determined to hear and follow these new preachers. As a consequence, divisions occurred, separate con-gregations for worship were instituted ; some of these assumed permanence, and in some few of them churches were formally established. The churches, from which large secessions were made, were enfeebled ; some of them dwindled for a long time, but none of them became extinct ; all of them, by our domes-tic enterprise, have been restored to prosperity and strength.

The new churches, called Separates, or, as they preferred, Strict Congregationalists, were not a new sect in the main elements of evangelical doctrine. They were New Lights in common with many of the old churches and ministers. But they justified their separation from the churches from which they withdrew on other grounds. They objected to the ordination of ministers by councils, or, as the Gospel has it, " by the laying on of the hands of the Presbytery." Each of their churches ordained its own pastor. They objected to the support of the ministry by taxes authorized and regulated by civil law, and adopted what we have initiated, the voluntary policy, thus making an advance, which we concede to them, in religious liberty. They abhorred the civil enactments which authorized and regulated our associations and consociations, which enactments have, long since, become obsolete, and have left these institutions to rest, as they should, on the voluntary principle.

But two Congregational churches, as churches, in the state became Separates—that of Torrington and one in the south of Middletown. These reverted, one soon and the other after no long time, to their original connection with Congregationalists. The churches which were instituted as the result of separation, continued for one generation, some of them for two ; they then found it impossible to obtain ministers, their sentiment concerning ordination was corrected, the obnoxious civil enactments passed away, and they said that the reasons for their separation had ceased to exist, so they were merged again into Congregationalism, and, as a sect, are no longer known. They went out from us, but they were of us : their return was natural, pleasant to us, and honorable both to their candor and to our common religion.

4. Millerites, a sect of Second Adventists, have, within a few years, flashed upon Connecticut, as they have upon many parts of the country, and in many places have gained more adherents than they have in this state. They hold, in common with Christians at large, the doctrine of the second coming to this earth of the Lord Jesus Christ. The distinctive feature of the sect is, that they know and foretel the precise time of " the coming," fix the day, and when the event nullifies their prediction, they appoint the day again and again. They gain very few, if any, proselytes from our Congregational churches, and few from people instructed in our Sabbath schools or congregations. Individuals constitutionally fanatical, and without mental strength or culture to detect or resist imposition, have given in their zealous adhesion to the faith that the day of the Lord is at the door, and that it is as clearly revealed and precisely known as any day of any future month. To them it has availed nothing that Christ said, " But of that day and that hour knoweth no man ; no, not the angels which are in heaven ; neither the Son, but the Father." These people have had the calamity, and mortification of having their religious expectations again and again disappointed; and, as the

coming of the judgment was to bring with it the end of the world, the real believers, those who were actually deluded, parted with their property, and brought themselves and their families into want and distress. Less of this folly and suffering has been experienced in this state than in many other parts of the country. Hardly any, perhaps none, of the members of our Congregational churches have become spectacles of this kind, and very rarely have any people who have sat under the preaching of our ministry become the victims of this delusion.

5. Spiritualism has ventured within our borders, as it has into other parts of this country and other lands. It is a matter of jugglery, rather than a religion. Still, as it purports to bring intelligence from the world of the dead to people now on probation, it has the audacity to take precedence of the Bible as a basis of faith. The Bible commits the instruction of this world to the scriptures, and to living men, who expound and inculcate them, but ignores the teachings of dead men. Spiritualists fear not that their names will be taken from the Lamb's Book of Life, because they add to what is written in God's finished revelation.

Their assemblies are brought together more commonly for amusement, curiosity, and the detection of imposition, than to express veneration to God, or to engage in religious rites. Congregationalists find little occasion or motive to refute the pretence that intelligence is communicated by the dead to the living, for were the concesssion made to Spiritualists that through a medium they get communications from the unseen world, it is sufficient to ask what are these communications? No doctrines, no precepts of God, are brought to this world by what assumes to be a new revelation. Frivolous, and often absurd sayings of dead men, some of whom, while living, were respected, and some of whom were not respected for their veracity, are impudently reported. Were the sum total of all that has been paraded as communications from the dead written in a book, that book would not contain anything which would improve the morals of this world, or increase the knowledge or consolation of men now living, and soon to die. So confident are people instructed in our congregations and schools, that the apostles of spiritualism seek money, a sickly admiration, a renown tottering though it be on imminent exposure, and not the salvation of their disciples, that this new version of fanaticism is regarded as too impotent to make any inroad upon our religious denomination.

We have, in this country, the fulness of religious freedom. We have been abundantly warned that without a general confession of faith our churches will be swallowed up by wild doctrines and disorder ; but, counselled as we are by the experience of more than two centuries, we feel a strong assurance that these churches, organized as they are, connected and united as they are, will still rest upon Christ as their foundation, rejoicing in their integrity and peace.

ERRATUM.—Page 280, line 37, for "initiated" read "imitated."

[There have been also two small sects of religionists of the same class with the above who ought not to be passed by wholly unnoticed in this place,—especially as they belonged to Connecticut, and were mostly, if not wholly, confined to our borders. A few words are demanded concerning them from this circumstance, rather than because of their numbers or importance.

ROGERINES*.—This sect took their name from John Rogers, their chief leader. They first appeared in New London County about 1720. They took it upon themselves, as fanatics frequently do, to utter special denunciations and anathemas against the regular ministry, however useful and godly. Rogers, it is said, once met Dr. Lord of Norwich Town, at the door of his meeting-house, and accosted him after his usual manner of vulgar abuse with these words, as he took off his hat, displaying a majestic wig : "Benjamin, Benjamin, dost thou think that they wear white wigs in heaven?" Dr. Lord passed him and took no notice of the insult. The principal distinguishing tenet of this sect was, that worship performed on the first day of the week was a species of idolatry which they ought to oppose. They held it also to be their special

---

* Trumbull's Hist. of Conn., vol. II., pp. 38–40.

mission to destroy priestcraft. In carrying out their peculiar notions, they used a variety of measures to disturb those who were assembled for public worship on the Lord's day. They traveled about in small companies, and entered churches and other places of worship in a rude and boisterous manner, and sometimes engaged in different kinds of manual labor in order to break up and interrupt the religious services. Though claiming the right to dissent from the views of the ministry and churches among whom they had sprung up, they seemed to have no true idea of religious liberty and toleration, as was evident from their constant disturbance of the peaceful worship of others.

SANDEMANIANS.—This sect originated in Scotland. They received the name of Glasites after John Glas; but in England and in this country, they were called Sandemanians after Robert Sandeman. They held as one of their distinguishing tenets, in the language of Mr. Sandeman, that " the essence of justifying faith is nothing more nor less than the bare belief of the bare truth." By this they meant nothing more than mere speculative or intellectual belief; for, practically, they admitted all to their church privileges who avowed such faith, although in their lives they gave no evidence of vital piety. They also administered the Lord's Supper weekly; had love feasts, in which all were required to partake, dining together at each other's houses in the interval of divine service; they gave "the kiss of charity" in admitting new members and at other times; they had a weekly collection before the Lord's Supper for their necessary expenses and for the poor. They made much of mutual exhortations; abstinence from blood and things strangled; washing each others' feet; community of goods so far as the wants of the poor and of the church required; the unlawfulness of laying up treasures upon earth, or setting them apart for any future uncertain use,—all which things they understood to be taught in the scriptures. They held to the plurality of elders in each church, and the need of the presence of at least two elders in all cases of discipline and at the Lord's Supper; the want of learning or engagement in trade being no disqualification for the office. They were intolerant toward other Christians, and were not disposed to admit strangers to their worship. They declared that they took the Bible for their guide, discarding articles of faith and a paid ministry. They regarded the lot as sacred, and disapproved of all common forms of its use. In all their transactions, unanimity was regarded as essential. Their worship was orderly and to some extent, perhaps, profitable ; but some of their principles led them into error and disorderly practices.

Mr. Sandeman was invited to come to this country by some who had heard of his views; and, after forming a few societies, he died at Danbury in 1771. Three or four of the neighboring ministers were favorably impressed by his views and came under his influence. Much trouble was caused thereby in Danbury and Newtown. A majority of the church in Danbury became Sandemanian, and that in Newtown became so weakened as to be reorganized with nine members in 1799. In 1768, the Fairfield East Association, who had taken a decided stand against the innovation, stated publicly that as a body, they were tinctured with Sandemanianism. See the Historical Sketch of that body in this volume. The influence of the Sandemanian views has not spread, though they have not become extinct so rapidly as might have been expected. There is still a small community of them at Danbury. See Andrew Fuller's Works ; Historical Sketch Fairfield East Consoc., 1859 ; Sprague's Annals, 1. 297 ; Relig. Encyc.]—*Com. of Pub.*

SUMMARY OF DECISIONS OF THE COURTS OF CONNECTICUT IN ECCLESIASTICAL CASES.*

If a society vote to hold their annual meetings upon a certain day in each succeeding year, a meeting held on the day so fixed, without further notice, is not legal, even after a practice of holding them thus for fifty years.—4 *Day*, 62; *East Granby*, 1809.

The formation of a second ecclesiastical society within the limits of a town, vested all the rights which the town in its ecclesiastical capacity before had in the remaining inhabitants of the town as a first society; and a voluntary release from the first society to the second of a portion of the lands sequestered for the use of the ministry, and held by the town, vested a good title in the second society to the land released for such uses.—4 *Day*, 360; *Suffield*, 1810.

The pastoral office with which a minister, duly called by an ecclesiastical society, and set apart to the work of the gospel ministry, as pastor of such society and of the church therein, thus became vested, was an office not determinable at the will of either party, but for the life of the incumbent.

What acts or omissions of the incumbent create a forfeiture of the pastoral office, and thereby incapacitate him for the performance of pastoral duties, is a question not within the province of a court of law to determine—it being exclusively within the cognizance of an ecclesiastical tribunal.

The offering and attempt of a minister to preach, who was prevented by the society by a vote, and by a commitee shutting

---

* It was expected that a paper would have been prepared " on the rights and relations of pastors, churches and societies," to which this abstract of the " Decisions of the Courts" was to have been appended. The pressure of other duties has rendered it impossible for the gentleman who had it in charge to furnish the paper in season for the present volume. This is much to be regretted, since ignorance or misunderstanding on the subject is a source of much evil. The article may be given to our churches soon in another form.

him out of their meeting-house, was held equivalent to the actual performance of that pastoral duty.—*Whitney vs. Brooklyn, 5 Conn.,* 405, 1824.

An ecclesiastical society, established by local limits, before the adoption of the constitution of this state, is not by that constitution, and the subsequent laws relating to religious societies, divested of its local character.

The statute of 1702, exempting from taxation all such lands, tenements, hereditaments and *other estates* as had been or should be given, for the maintenance of the ministry of the gospel, extends to money at interest given for that object. The government has contracted that all such property shall be forever exempt from taxation, so long as it is applied to such uses; and has no constitutional right or power to rescind or impair such contract. It was held, therefore, that a tax laid by the town of Woodbridge on such funds in the society of Bethany, then in that town, was illegal.

It seems that the private property of the members of an ecclesiastical society, duly organized, may be taken on a legal warrant against the society.—*Atwater vs. Woodbridge, 6 Conn.* 223; 1826.

Where funds were subscribed to be appropriated to the support of a minister, *to be approved by the association,* within whose limits the subscribers lived—and he was ordained by the *consociation,* within the same limits (the ministers present and concurring being a majority of the members of the *association*)—and was ever afterward recognized by the association as a member, it was held, that this condition of the subscription was complied with.—*Somers vs. Miner, 9 Conn.,* 458; *Woodbury,* 1833.

The committee of an ecclesiastical society, appointed under the statute "for the year ensuing," continue to hold their offices after the expiration of the year, until suspended by the appointment of another committee.

To constitute a legal meeting of an ecclesiastical society, having a committee, it must be warned by that committee.

The power given by statute to an ecclesiastical society, to

prescribe the mode of warning its meetings, does not enable it to dispense with a warning by its committee.

Where the clerk of the society, there being a committee, affixed the names of the committee to a warning, and posted it upon the public sign post, without either the previous authority or subsequent ratification of the committee, it was held that such warning was ineffectual.—*Bethany Society vs. Sperry,* 10 *Conn.* 200 ; 1834.

The members of an ecclesiastical society, without local limits formed by voluntary association, pursuant to the 13th section of the statute, relating to religious societies, are not individually liable for the debts of such society.—*Jewett vs. Thames Bank,* 16 *Conn.* 511; *Norwich Falls Soc.,* 1844.

The name of a voluntary ecclesiastical corporation, formed under the laws of this state, without a special legislative act of incorporation, is arbitrary, and a change or alteration in its name does not affect its identity.—*Trinity Church, Portland, vs. Hall,* 22 *Conn.,* 125 ; 1852.

Since the adoption of our present state constitution, however it may have been before, it is not competent to the legislature to divide an ancient, local or territorial ecclesiastical society, into two or more such societies, or divide the fund owned by such ancient society, for the support of the ministry, and to assign a part of such fund to a new society, formed out of the ancient one.—23 *Connecticut,* 255 ; *Portland,* 1854.

The following list, collected from the church reports chiefly, compared with Dr. Sprague's Annals, and Dr. Allen's Biographical Dictionary, is intended to give the names of all ministers who were born in Connecticut, or here received their early education and license to preach the gospel, who attained to the ministerial age of fifty years. The list contains the names of two hundred and fifteen ministers, of whom twenty-two were supposed to be living July 1st, 1860, and only forty-one have not ministered to our churches. Of this latter class there are probably others who have been in the ministry fifty years, but the fact has not been ascertained. Of nine the age is put down as 49, but probably by reckoning from the date of their license, as Dr. Sprague does, the most of these attained the full period of 50 years. Many more were in the ministry nearly fifty years. The average of the whole is about fifty-five years. Five in italics, not counted above, did not continue in the Congregational ministry, though once pastors.

Abiel Abbott, D. D., . . . Coventry ; New Hampshire,	64
*Caleb Alexander, . . . Lic. New London, . . . Mass.; New York,	50
Timothy Allen, . . . West Haven ; Ashford ; Massachusetts,	68
Samuel Andrew, . . . Milford,	53
Samuel Allis, . . . Somers,	69
Thomas Andros, . . . n. Plainfield, . . . Lic. New London, . . . Berkley, Massachusetts,	58
Elisha Atkins, . . . East Putnam, (formerly North Killingly),	55
Jeremiah Atwater, D. D., . . . Pres. Middlebury Col., . . . Northford ; New Haven,	60
David Austin, . . . Bozrah,	51
†John Bacon, . . . n. Canterbury, . . . Boston ; Stockbridge,	50
Simon Backus, . . . Massachusetts ; North Madison,	66
‡Joseph Badger, . . . Lic. New Haven, . . . Plymouth ; Massachusetts ; Ohio,	60

---

*Sprague's An. 3, 405. Mendon Assoc. 128 †Spr. An. 1, 686, Allen. ‡ Spr. An. 3, 473.

Jonathan Bartlett, . . . Redding,	62
Nathaniel Bartlett, . . . Redding,	57
Shubael Bartlett, . . . East Windsor,	51
Archibald Bassett, . . . Winchester ; New York,	59
John Beach, . . . Newtown, . . . became an Episcopalian,	57
Lyman Beecher, D. D., . . . Litchfield ; Ohio, living,	60
George Beckwith, . . . Lyme ; Hamburgh,	55
Joshua Belden, . . . Newington,	66
Joseph Bellamy, D. D., . . . Bethlem,	50
Noah Benedict, . . . Woodbury,	53
Nathan Birdseye, . . . West Haven ; retired and lived in Stratford, 60 years,	76
John Bishop, . . . Stamford,	50
Joel Bordell, . . . Kent,	53
Joab Brace, D. D., . . . Newington ; Pittsfield, Mass., living,	54
Israel Brainerd, . . . Guilford ; Verona, New York,	54
Diodate Brockway, . . . Ellington,	50.
Gershom Bulkley, . . . New London ; Wethersfield,	52
Gershom Bulkley, . . . Cromwell,	54
*Samuel Buel, D. D., . . . n. Coventry, ... Lic. New Haven, . . . Long Island,	57
Platt Buffett, . . . Stanwich.	54
Eden Burroughs, D. D., . . . S. Ch. Killingly ; New Hampshire,	53
†Asa Burton, D. D., . . . n. Stonington ; . . . Vermont,	59
Thomas Canfield, . . . Roxbury,	51
Judah Champion, . . . Litchfield,	57
Calvin Chapin, D. D., . . . Rocky Hill,	60
‡Jedediah Chapman, . . . n. East Haddam, . . . Orange, New Jersey,	49
Amos Chase, . . . Morris, (formerly South Farms),	62
§Ebenezer Chaplin, . . . n. Chaplin , . . . Massachusetts.	58
Nathaniel Chauncey, . . . Durham,	50
Aaron Church, . . . Hartland,	50
Noah Coe, . . . New York ; Greenwich ; New Haven, living,	50
James Cogswell, D. D., . . . Canterbury ; Scotland,	63
Daniel Collins, . . . n. Guilford, . . . Lanesboro, Mass.,	58
Nathaniel Collins, . . . Enfield,	59
Timothy Collins, . . . Litchfield,	53
George Colton, . . . Bolton,	49
Andrew Croswell, . . . Ledyard ; Boston,	49
Jeremiah Curtiss, . . . Southington,	67

James Dana, . . . Wallingford ; New Haven,   54

*Henry Davis, D. D., . . . Lic. Tol. . . . President Middlebury
and Hamilton Coll., . . . Middletown,   54

Jeremiah Day, D. D., . . . Lic. 1800, . . . President Yale College, . . . New Haven, living,   60

†Jonathan Dickinson, D. D., . . . Lic. Fairfield, . . . President
Nassau Hall,   57

Moses Dickinson, . . . Norwalk,   59

Stephen Dodd, . . . Naugatuck ; East Haven,   50

Gordon Dorrance, . . . n. Sterling, . . . Mass. ; N. Y.,   50

Daniel Dow, D. D., . . . Thompson,   54

Timothy Edwards, . . . South Windsor,   62

Nathaniel Eells, . . . Stonington,   57

Jared Elliott, . . . Clinton,   54

John Ellis, . . . Franklin ; Rehoboth, Mass.,   52

Ezra Stiles Ely, D. D., . . . Westchester ; Philadelphia, living,   54

Richard Ely, . . . North Madison ; Centerbrook,   56

‡Nathanel Emmons, D.D., . . . n. East Haddam, . . . Lic. Hartford South, . . . Mass.,   71

Daniel Farrand, . . . Canaan,   51

David D. Field, D. D., . . . Haddam ; Stockbridge, living,   55

Joseph Fish, . . . North Stonington,   50

John Fisk, . . . East Putnam,   58

James Fitch, . . . Saybrook ; Norwich,   56

§Justus Forward, . . . n Suffield , . . . Belchertown, Mass.   59

Ebenezer Frothingham, . . . Middletown,   51

Ebenezer Gay, D. D., . . . Suffield,   53

Nathaniel Gaylord, . . . West Hartland,   59

Maltby Gelston, . . . Sherman,   59

Alexander Gillett, . . . Wolcott ; Torringford,   53

Timothy P. Gillett, . . . Branford, living,   52

Samuel Goodrich, . . . Ridgefield ; Berlin,   50

John Graham, . . . Stafford ; Southbridge,   51

John Graham, . . . West Suffield,   50

Sylvanus Haight, . . . Wilton ; South Norwalk, living,   50

||Enoch Hale, . . . n. Coventry, . . . Mass.,   58

Samuel Hall, . . . Cheshire,   52

**Walter Harris, D. D., . . . n. Columbia, . . . Dunbarton, N. H.,   54

††Roger Harrison, . . . n. Branford , . . . Mass.,   55

Rufus Hawley, . . , Avon,   57

---

*Spr. An. 4, 224. †Spr. An. 3, 14. ‡Spr. An. 1, 693. §Spr. An. 2, 297. ||Spr. An. 2, 572. **Spr. An. 2, 277. Mendon Assoc. 231. ††Spr. An. 2, 531.

Lemuel Haynes, . . . (col'd) . . . Torrington ; Vermont,	54
Jacob Hemmingway, . . . East Haven,	50
John Higginson, . . . Guilford ; Mass.,	72
*Abiel Holmes, D. D., . . . n. Woodstock ; . . . Mass.,	53
Samuel Hopkins, D. D., . . . North Stamford ; Rhode Island,	53
Frederic Wm. Hotchkiss, . . . Old Saybrook,	61
Heman Humphrey, D. D., . . . Fairfield, . . . Pres. Amh. Col., living,	53
†Daniel Humphreys, . . . Derby,	55
Aaron Hutchinson, . . . n. Hebron, . . . Ms. ; Vermont,	50
Elisha Hutchinson, . . . Westford ; Vermont,	55
Eli Hyde, . . . Salem ; New York ; Vermont,	50
‡William Jackson, D. D., . . . n. Cornwall ; . . . Vermont,	50
Evan Johns, . . . Berlin ; New York,	50
Samuel Johnson, . . . West Haven ; . . . became an Episcopalian,	52
Eliphalet Jones, . . . n. Fairfield, . . . Huntington ; Long Island,	55
Isaac Jones, . . . Bethany, . . . became an Episcopalian,	53
§Jonathan Judd, . . . n. Waterbury ; . . . Mass.,	60
Ebenezer Kellogg, . . . Vernon,	55
Aaron Kinne, . . . Groton ; Mass.	54
Daniel Kirkland, . . . Lisbon ; Groton,	50
Mark Leavenworth, . . . Waterbury,	57
‖Joseph Lathrop, D. D., . . . n. Norwich, . . . Mass.,	64
Andrew Lee, D. D., . . . Hanover, in Lisbon,	64
Chauncey Lee, D. D., . . . Colebrook ; Marlboro,	53
Amzi Lewis, . . . North Stamford ; New York,	49
Isaac Lewis, D. D., . . . Wilton ; Greenwich,	72
Isaac Lewis, . . . N. Y. ; Greenwich ; R. I.,	56
Ephraim Little, . . . Colchester,	55
Benjamin Lord, D. D., . . . Norwich Town,	67
Eliphalet Lyman, . . . Woodstock,	57
**Joseph Lyman, D. D., . . . n. Lebanon, . . . Massachusetts,	57
Abel McEwen, D. D., . . . New London, . . . living,	54
David McClure, D. D., . . . South Windsor,	50
Allen McLean, . . . Simsbury, living,	51
Frederick Marsh, . . . Winchester Center, living,	51
John Marsh, D. D., . . . Wethersfield,	56
Jonathan Marsh, . . . New Hartford,	55
Moses Mather, D. D., . . . Darien,	62

---

*Spr. An. 2, 240.   †Spr. 1, 452.   Mendon Assoc. 96.   ‡Spr. An. 2, 336.   §Spr. An. 1, 335.   ‖Spr. An. 1, 528.   Allen.   **Spr. An. 2, 10

Mark Mead, . . . Middlebury ; Greenwich, living,	51
Samuel Merwin, . . . New Haven,	51
Jonathan Miller, . . . Burlington,	49
Ebenezer Mills, . . . East Granby ; Massachusetts,	52
Jedediah Mills, . . . Huntington,	57
Samuel J. Mills, . . . Torringford,	65
Thomas Miner, . . . Westfield, (Middletown,)	53
Samuel Moseley, . . . Hampton,	57
Levi Nelson, . . . Lisbon,	51
Abel Newel, . . . Goshen,	58
*Asahel S. Norton, D. D., . . . n, Farmington ; . . . Clinton, New York,	61
Eliphalet Nott, D. D., . . . n. Saybrook, . . . (Lic. N. L.) . . . President Union College, living,	63
Samuel Nott, D. D., . . . Franklin,	70
James Noyes, . . . Stonington,	54
James Noyes, . . . Wallingford,	59
John Noyes, . . . Weston,	60
Matthew Noyes, . . . Northford,	50
Moses Noyes, . . . Old Lyme,	63
David Palmer, . . . n. Scotland, . . . Townsend ; Mass.,	50
John Palmer, (Sep.) . . . Brunswick, (Scotland,)	58
Paul Parks, (Sep.) . . . Preston,	50
Elijah Parsons, . . . East Haddam,	55
†William Patten, Jr., D. D., . . . n Hartford, . . . Rhode Island,	53
Nathan Perkins, D. D., . . . West Hartford,	66
‡John Pierson, . . . n. Clinton, . . . New Jersey,	57
Bealeel. Pinneo, . . . Milford,	53
Timothy Pitkin, . . . Farmington,	60
Benjamin Pomeroy, D. D. . . . Hebron,	50
§David Porter, D. D., . . . n. Hebron ; . . . Catskill, New York,	65
Noah Porter, D. D., . . . Farmington, living,	54
Thomas Potwine, . . . East Windsor,	49
Aaron Putnam, . . . Pomfret,	57
‖James Richards. D. D., . . . n. New Canaan, . . . (Lic. F. W.) New York, Prof. Aub. Theol. Sem.	50
John Richards, . . . North Guilford ; Vermont,	63
Hezekiah Ripley, D. D., . . . Green's Farms,	65
Ammi R. Robbins, . . . Norfolk,	52
Philemon Robbins, . . . Branford,	50

*Spr. An. 2, 332. †Spr. An. 1, 592. Allen. ‡Spr. An. 3, 16. §Spr. An. 3, 496.
‖Spr. An. 4, 99.

Thomas Robbins, D. D., . . . South Windsor ; Mass. ; Hartford,	49
*John Robinson, . . . n Lebanon, . . . Westboro, Massachusetts,	52
Ralph Robinson, . . . n. Scotland, . . . Pulaski ; New Haven ;	
New York, living,	51
William Robinson, . . . Southington,	49
John Rodgers, D. D., . . . Danbury ; Del. ; New York,	64
†William F. Rowland, . . . n. Plainfield, . . . Exeter, New	
Hampshire,	53
John Sawyer, D. D., . . . n. Hebron, . . . Maine,	72
Erastus Scranton, . . . Orange ; Burlington, living,	55
Samuel Shepard, . . . n. Portland ; . . . Massachusetts,	52
Ichabod L. Skinner, . . . North Coventry, became a lawyer,	58
John Smalley, D. D., . . . New Britain,	62
Cotton Mather Smith, . . . Sharon,	51
Daniel Smith, . . . Stamford,	53
David Smith, D. D., . . . Durham, living,	60
Zephaniah H. Smith, . . . Newtown, became a lawyer,	50
John Southmayd, . . . Waterbury,	55
James Sprout, D. D., . . . Guilford 4th ; Philadelphia,	50
Peter Starr, . . . Warren,	57
Stephen W. Stebbins, . . . Stratford ; West Haven,	57
‡John H. Stevens, . . . n. Canterbury, . . . Mass.,	60
Anthony Stoddard, . . . Woodbury,	58
Timothy Stone, . . . Cornwall,	50
Richard S. Storrs, D. D., . . . n. West Haven, . . . Massachu-	
setts, living,	50
Samuel Stow, . . . Middletown,	51
Nicholas Street, . . . Massachusetts ; North Haven,	51
Nicholas Street, . . . East Haven,	51
Joseph Strong, . . . Granby ; Massachusetts,	51
Joseph Strong, D. D., . . . Norwich Town,	56
Nathan Strong, . . . North Coventry,	50
Joseph Sumner, . . . n. Pomfret, . . . Shrewsbury, Mass.	62
Zephaniah Swift, . . . Roxbury ; Derby,	53
Nathaniel Taylor, . . . New Milford,	52
Jonathan Todd, . . . Madison,	58
Samuel Todd, . . . Plymouth ; Massachusetts,	50
Salmon Treat, . . . Preston,	64
Benjamin Trumbull, D. D., . . . North Haven,	60
Bennet Tyler, D. D., . . . South Britain ; Portland, Me.; Presi-	
dent East Windsor Seminary,	50

---

*Spr. An. 1, 697.   †Spr. An. 1, 722.   ‡Spr. An. 1. 598.

Alvan Underwood, . . . West Woodstock, 57
Joseph Vaill, . . . Hadlyme, 58
Daniel Waldo, . . . West Suffield; New York, living, 68
Simon Waterman, . . . Wallingford, 2d, 52
*Ezra Weld, . . . n. Pomfret; . . . Massachusetts, 50
Ludovicus Weld, . . . Hampton, 54
†Stephen West, D. D., . . . n. Tolland; . . . Stockbridge, Mass. 60
Nathaniel Whitaker, . . . Norwich, 2d, 60
Stephen White, . . . Windham, 53
Josiah Whitney, D. D.. . . . Brooklyn, 57
Jabez Wight, . . . Norwich, (Preston, Long Society,) 56
John Willard, D. D., . . . Stafford, 50
Eliphalet Williams, D. D., . . . East Hartford, 55
Joshua Williams, . . . Harwinton, 51
Nathan Williams, D. D., . . . Tolland, 69
Solomon Williams, . . . Lebanon, 54
Stephen Williams, . . . West Woodstock, 49
‡Thomas Williams, . . . n. Pomfret, . . . Lic. M., . . . Eastbury,
Rhode Island, living, 57
Noah Williston, . . . West Haven, 51
§Seth Williston, D. D., . . . n. Suffield, . . . Lic. T., . . . ord., H.
N.; . . . N. Y., 57
Samuel Wood, D. D., . . . n. Mansfield, . . . New Hampshire. 57
John Woodbridge, D. D., . . . Bridgeport; Hadley, Ms., living, 50

. *Spr. An. 1, 354. †Spr. An. 1, 548. Allen. ‡Mendon Assoc. 170. §Spr. An. 4, 140.
In this paper "n" signifies *native of*.

EARLY THEOLOGICAL EDUCATION.*

Before theological seminaries were established in this state, the professors of divinity in Yale College were in the habit of assisting in their studies such young men as were disposed to put themselves under their direction. But they were not the only instructors of candidates for the ministry. The custom was, to a great extent, for young men to fit for college with their pastors, and after graduation, to pursue their theological studies also under the same direction. In the case of those who were somewhat advanced in years, the pastors frequently gave instruction in academic studies, as a substitute for a public education, and our Associations granted licenses to the candidates who took this short course, when their hearts were set on the work of the ministry, and their other qualifications were peculiarly marked and complete.

There were several pastors, not only in this but also in other states, who became noted as theological teachers. Besides their natural qualifications for the work, the habit of instruction gave them facility and skill in their duties; and soon other pastors were, to a great extent, forsaken, and these came to have well known " schools of the prophets." These teachers were mostly of the New England or Edwardean stamp. They gave shape to the theology of the succeeding generations of ministers. There was an advantage in this method of instruction, that the teacher learned all the peculiarities of his pupils; and if any of them were warped in their views, a thorough sifting and drilling was sure to set them right, which is not always accomplished under the present method. The opportunities for becoming practically acquainted with pastoral duties was also peculiarly favorable under the eye of such teachers.

---

* In printing these " Historical Papers," of which this is the last, it has not been practicable to carry out any regular system of arrangement. This paper upon " Early Theological Education," should have had a place before that upon " The Theological Department of Yale College."—*Com. of Pub.*

The term of study was usually short; systematic theology, with some practice in sermonizing, being the principal subjects attended to. It is to be feared that, according to the present system, while great advantage is now gained in auxiliary branches, it is often with the sacrifice of these essential things.

Soon after the great awakening of 1740, Dr. Bellamy of Bethlem, whose pastorate was from 1737 to 1790, began to receive theological students, and was a pioneer in this department, and highly distinguished. Dr. Smalley, of New Britain, 1757 to 1820, Dr. Charles Backus, of Somers, 1773 to 1803, Dr. Levi Hart, of Griswold, 1761 to 1808, and Rev. Asahel Hooker in Goshen and Norwich, 1790 to 1813, were noted and much resorted to by theological students. Rev. Jedediah Mills of Huntington, 1724 to 1776, was the instructor of David Brainerd and some others; Dr. Wheelock of Columbia, 1735 to 1770, was an instructor of youth, a trainer of missionaries, and a teacher in theology; Rev. William Robinson of Southington, 1776 to 1825, received students; several others also, whom our imperfect knowledge does not enable us to enumerate. Dr. Stephen West of Stockbridge, Mass., 1756 to 1819, Dr. Samuel Hopkins, of Newport, R. I., 1742 to 1803, and Dr. Nathaniel Emmons of Franklin, Mass., 1769 to 1840, all natives of Connecticut, were also distingushed teachers of theological students, and did much to mold the theology of New England.

39

HISTORICAL SKETCHES

OF THE

DISTRICT ASSOCIATIONS.

FAIRFIELD EAST ASSOCIATION.

The Association of Fairfield County, in a meeting at Stamford, Aug. 27th, 1734, resolved itself into two Associations "by a line running on the east side of Fairfield and Greenfield, and on the west side of Redding and Danbury."

1735, Nov. 11th.—The associated elders resolved to move their several churches to form a Consociation. The Consociation of Fairfield county met at Fairfield June 8th, 1736 and resolved itself into two Consociations, and fixed upon the same dividing line.

1738, the Association voted that no person having a call to settle over any church in the Consociation should accept the same until he had been examined and approved by the Association.

1739–40, Jan. 22d.—Joseph Bellamy was recommended as a candidate for settlement at Bethlem.

1740.—It was decided that a man cannot scripturally marry his deceased wife's sister, and the reasons were put on record.

Circular fasts were agreed upon. These fasts were observed for twelve years in succession, though with some changes in the order of procedure. The usual course was to begin them in the fall, soon after the annual meeting of the Consociation, and hold them once a fortnight with each church until all the churches had been visited. They seem to have been greatly blessed at first, and in connection with the general awakening in and about 1740. They were afterwards appointed on account of the declension which followed that work of grace.

1740, October.—The Consociation resolved to endeavor to secure the labors of Rev. George Whitefield for this district.

1741, October.—The Consociation refer to the revival and to the circular fasts as productive of a glorious revival of religion.

1742, July 29th.—The Association licensed David Brainerd, and placed on record a vindication of themselves in so doing, while he was under the censure of Yale College.

At the same meeting they gave important advice in respect to lay meetings,—sanctioning them and showing how they should be conducted.

1763, May 29th.—The Association met at Bethel and heard complaints of false doctrine—Sandemanianism—aginst Rev. Noah Wetmore, of Bethel,

Rev. Ebenezer White, of Danbury; and Rev. James Taylor, of New Fairfield South—now New Fairfield. Mr. Wetmore was cleared, but Mr. White and Mr. Taylor were held to trial before the Consociation and silenced.

In 1768 the Association sent a delegate to a General Convention at Elizabethtown, which seems to have met yearly alternately in New Jersey, and in the western part of this State, as at Norwalk, Stamford and Greenfield, till broken up by the war.

In 1774 the Association memorialized the General Association with reference to devising some plan to provide the preached Gospel for the inhabitants who were scattered in the wilderness in various provinces.

In 1778 it was voted to continue public lectures and special services on account of the war. And because of the low state of schools, and the incompetency, immorality and Toryism of some of the teachers, the Association resolved to apply to the General Association for some action suited to revive learning and religion.

1783, Oct. 28th.—The members resolve to preach to the vacant churches and stir them up to the work of getting pastors.

1805, May 28th.—The Association of Fairfield West having inquired of this Association if it would not be best to admit lay delegates to the meetings of the District Associations as witnesses of their proceedings, and to show that they were not engaged in political intrigues, this Association replied in the negative, and gave their reasons.

1812, Oct. 7th.—The Association accepted and approved the recommendation of the General Association not to introduce ardent spirits at meetings of this Association.

1814, May 31st.—Measures were taken to form an Auxiliary Bible Society.

1821.—Sabbath schools reported as generally established.

1821.—A Foreign Mission Society was formed, auxiliary to the American Board.

The years of general revivals in these churches were 1740–41, 1821, 1831, 1843 and 1858. That of 1831 was probably the most fruitful one which these churches have ever experienced.

The spirit of this body commends it to all who go through with its well-kept records. It has been zealous for purity of doctrine and the wholesome administration of discipline. Its measures have, as a general thing, been marked by sound wisdom. It has had the confidence of the churches, has been largely consulted by them in cases of difficulty, and has sympathized with them and aided them in their trials. It has been in favor of revivals and of an active piety from its organization until now. The associated pastors, with the exception of the White controversy, [Sandemanianism] have dwelt together in harmony and good fellowship, assisting each other in sickness or distress, advising each other in perplexity, and strengthening each other for the responsibilities of the gospel ministry.

LICENCIATES.

NAMES.	WHEN LICENSED.	NAMES.	WHEN LICENSED.
Ebenezer Dibble,	Mar, 4, 1734	Ebenezer Mills,	May 2, 1739
Robert Silliman,	May 2, 1739	David Judson,	Oct. 7, 1740

Samuel Buel,	Oct. 7, 1741	George Gilmore,	May 27, 1765
John Graham, Jr.,	Nov. 12, 1741	Ichabod Lewis, Jr.,	Oct. 29, 1766
Jacob Johnson,	Apr. 29, 1742	Isaac Lewis,	Feb. 24, 1768
Samuel Hopkins,	Apr. 39, 1742	Blackleach Burritt,	Feb. 24, 1768
Jonathan Judd,	Apr. 29, 1742	Samuel Mills,	May 31, 1768
Reuben Judd,	July 29, 1742	Peter Starr,	June 6, 1769
David Brainerd,	July 29, 1742	William Plum,	May 27, 1772
Nathan Strong.	Nov. 10, 1742	Abraham Camp,	Feb. 15, 1775
David S. Rowland,	Aug. 12,1746	Joshua Perry,	Oct. 30, 1776
Nathaniel Taylor,	Oct. 7,1744	Ard Hoyt,	Oct. 8, 1805
Daniel Brinsmade,	Oct. 7,1747	Nathaniel Kenneday,	Oct. 14, 1807
Ephraim Judson,	Dec. 1, 1747	Hezekiah G. Ufford,	Oct. 15, 1807
Chauncey Graham,	Jan 14, 1747	John Clark,	May 29, 1810
Jonathan Elmer,	May 4, 1748	Thomas F. Davies,	May 29, 1816
Gideon Hawley,	May 23, 1750	Charles F. Butler,	May 28, 1817
Deliverance Smith,	May 29, 1751	Charles A. Boardman,	Oct. 8, 1817
Hezekiah Gold,	May 16, 1753	Peter Lockwood,	Oct. 7, 1819
William Ramsey,	Nov. 25,1755	Laurens P. Hickok,	May 28, 1822
Abraham Ketteltas,	Aug. 23,1756	Ebenezer Platt,	May 28, 1822
Joseph Peck,	May 29, 1758	Alanson Benedict,	Apr. 24, 1824
Elnathan Gregory,	May 29, 1758	John Smith,	Apr. 24, 1824
Noah Benedict,	Oct. 14, 1758	Orrin Hyde,	Apr. 24, 1824
Hugh Williamson,	Mar. 20, 1759	Thomas T. Waterman,	June 1, 1825
Eden Burroughs,	May 30 ,1759	Epenetus Platt Benedict,	June 1, 1825
Caleb Barnum,	May 30, 1759	George Carrington,	1825
Ebenezer Kellogg,	May 28, 1760	Ransom Hawley,	May 28, 1828
Benjamin Dunning,	May 28, 1760	Platt Tyler Holley,	June 1, 1831
John Chandler,	Apr. 16, 1761	William F. Dibble,	Oct. 13, 1841
Joseph Moss White,	Oct. 28, 1761	Nathaniel Augustus Hewit,	Oct. 12, 1842
Benjamin Wildman,	Oct. 28, 1761	Samuel T. Seelye,	Oct. 15, 1845
James Johnson,	May 26, 1762	Charles S. Shelton,	Mar. 28, 1848
Noadiah Warner,	Oct. 31, 1764		

The Saybrook platform was adopted by the ministers and churches of Fairfield County, March 17th, 1709, at which time the County Association was probably first organized.

Fairfield County Association was divided into two bodies in 1734.

The records of this Association were burned in the house of Rev. Andrew Eliot, of Fairfield, July 8th, 1779, when the British, commanded by Gen. Tryon, entered and destroyed that town. From that date to the present the records are complete.

1787, May 29th.— "A method for celebrating public worship " was recommended. This is substantially the same with that now used.

1788, May 27th.—Mr. Ripley and Dr. Dwight "present a plan for promoting a general union among the Presbyterians throughout the United States," which it was ordered should be presented to General Association at their next annual meeting.

1788, Oct. 14th.—Six Sabbaths of supply were voted to the destitute congregations in Vermont, as recommended by General Association.

1789, May 26th.—The Association instructed its delegates to General Association to "move that a minister be appointed by said Association yearly to preach in the first church in Hartford, on the afternoon of the general election day, a sermon in support of the divine authority of the holy scriptures ;" also, in 1791, that "a preacher be appointed in the same way for the same object at New Haven, the day before commencement."

1790, May 25th.—The delegates to General Association were directed to move that the plan of union between Presbyterians and Congregationalists in this country, proposed by this Association in 1788, be again considered·

1794, May 27th.—The Association voted in favor of the formation of a General Consociation.

1795, May 26th—It was voted to comply with the recommendation of General Association to report annually the state of religion within the limits of the Association.

The "concert in prayers, proposed by several ministers of different denominations in the United States," was highly approved. It was thought, however, to be inconvenient for the churches to meet oftener than once in each quarter of the year, and that then "it will be expedient for each minister to deliver at every such meeting a sermon respecting the future advancement of Christ's kingdom, and that it will also be proper and desirable to make the prosperity of the civil government in these states a stated object of public prayer in the proposed meetings."

1797, May 30th.—It was proposed to General Association that a society be formed in this state "for the purpose of enlarging the Redeemer's kingdom and propagating the gospel among the heathen."

1799.—The Association voted that, in their opinion, the imposition of hands in the ordination of deacons is expedient, but not indispensably necessary.

The churches are directed to "collect a stock by free contributions for benevolent purposes, and particularly for the assistance of their indigent members."

The means adopted by "the Missionary Society of Connnecticut" are heartily approved.

1804, May 29th.—The Association decided "that the ministers should take a tour of preaching within the bounds of the district," "and that they go forth two and two." Four days were to be spent in this tour, and two rotations of this service to be performed during the year.

1808.—The report of the state of religion is such that the Association think "the friends of Zion have reason to thank God and take courage."

1812.—It was "voted to recommend the formation of a Foreign Missionary Society in this district." A society was accordingly formed which is now auxiliary to "The American Board."

Voted, also, "wholly to discontinue the use of ardent spirits at all future meetings of this body, except in cases of real necessity." Messrs. Roswell R. Swan, of Norwalk, Heman Humphrey, of Fairfield, and Wm. Bonney, of Canaan, were appointed a committee to prepare and lay before the Consociation "an address respecting the use of ardent spirits." This was the first decided movement on the subject of temperance made by any ecclesiastical body, and the address prepared by Messrs. Swan and Humphrey was one of unusual power.

1813.—Voted, that once a quarter the ministers and churches of three or more neighboring societies meet in rotation at their respective places of worship to unite in the monthly concert.

1814.—It was recommended that the ministers and churches hold meetings for extraordinary prayer. This is supposed to refer to the state of the country, then engaged in war with Great Britain.

In compliance with the recommendation of General Association, it was voted to use all practicable means for the formation of female charitable societies for the education of indigent and pious youth for the gospel ministry.

1817.—In view of furnishing a supply of future laborers in the vineyard of Christ, the Association resolved to pay special attention to the subject of providing means for the education of pious youth.

1819.—The members of the Association were desired to read publicly in all their churches the tract entitled "The Claims of Six Hundred Millions, or the Conversion of the World," and to make a new effort to increase the charitable contributions for the support of foreign missions.

1820.—It was recommended that extraordinary exertions on the subject of foreign missions should be continued. Notice was taken of the "alarming degree" to which "the intemperate use of ardent spirits prevailed."

1822.—The Association cordially approved of the efforts then being made to extend the theological department of Yale College, inasmuch as it was an important part of the design of the founders of that institution that it should be a school for the church.

1827.—Sabbath schools were found to be very generally established, and many of them very flourishing.

1828, May 27th. A general interest in all the churches on the subject of religion prevailed. The delegates to General Association were directed to use their influence to have means taken to have the Missionary Society of Connecticut become auxiliary to "The American Home Missionary Society."

1829.—The Association noticed that the cause of temperance was gaining ground, and that the number of those who espoused the doctrine of entire abstinence had considerably increased. The efforts of "The Connecticut Sabbath School Union" were highly approved.

1830.—The cause of temperance is observed to be rapidly advancing. The monthly concert of prayer for the conversion of the world is generally observed, and Bible classes and Sabbath schools exist generally and are in a flourishing condition.

1831.—The Association took notice of "the signal outpouring of the Spirit" in many of the churches.

1832.—Revivals are reported as in nearly all the churches to an extent never before experienced.

1835.—Auxiliary Home Missionary Society formed.

1836.—Certain measures were recommended to Association to be used for the revival of religion within its bounds.

1839.—Certain doctrinal errors alleged by the Pastoral Union's Protest are not held in this body.

1849.—It is believed that doctrinal errors concerning the Trinity, the Incarnation and the Atonement are extensively propagated in the state, and its delegates are to request action of General Association in the matter.

LICENCIATES.

NAMES.	WHEN LICENSED.	NAMES.	WHEN LICENSED.
John Noyes,	Oct. 14, 1783	Dennis Platt,	Oct. 10, 1826
James Noyes,	Oct. 12, 1784	Henry Dean,	Oct. 10, 1826
William Brintnal Ripley,	May 26, 1789	Charles G. Selleck,	Mar. 2, 1830
Samuel Sturges,	May 26, 1789	Frederick H. Ayres,	Oct. 12, 1831
James Richards,	May 26, 1793	Wm. B. Sherwood,	June 24, 1834
Jonathan Law Pomeroy,	Oct. 8, 1793	Samuel B. S. Bissell,	Oct. 15, 1834
Jonathan Bartlett,	Oct. 8, 1793	Alexander H. Bishop,	May 26, 1835
David Hill,	Oct. 8, 1793	Gilbert L. Smith,	May 26, 1835
Zachary Lewis,	Oct. 12. 1796	Benjamin L. Swan,	Oct. 14, 1835
Isaac Lewis, Jr.,	Oct. 12, 1796	Hiram Doane,	Mar. 22, 1836
Andrew Eliot, Jr.,	Oct. 12, 1796	Aaron M. Colton,	May 30, 1838
Daniel C. Banks,	Oct. 8, 1805	Daniel March,	May 31, 1842
Daniel Banks,	Oct. 9, 1810	Abel B. Burke,	May 31, 1842
Isaac Reed,	May 28, 1816	Samuel G. Coe,	Sep. 20, 1842
Orrin Fowler.	Oct. 28, 1816	Bronson C. Beardsley,	Oct. 11, 1848
Nathan Burton,	Dec. 26, 1820	David M. Elwood,	May 29, 1849
Richard V. Dey,	Aug. 27, 1822	Talmon C. Perry,	Oct. 9. 1850
Benaiah Y. Morse,	May 25, 1824	Benjamin Parsons,	May 31, 1853
Henry Benedict.	May 31, 1825	Edwin Hall, Jr.,	May 31, 1853

HARTFORD CENTRAL ASSOCIATION.

BY REV. NOAH PORTER, D. D.

Hartford Central Association was constituted October 10, 1843. At that time the old Hartford North Association had become inconveniently large in the number of its members, as it had before been in territory, and a division was agreed on by a line across the county from east to west, making the two parts, as nearly as could be, equal. In A. D., 1852, Hartford Fourth Association was formed by members seceding from this Association, on account of a difference of sentiment, growing out of certain publications of Dr. Bushnell, and uniting themselves with others from Hartford North and Hartford South Associations. This has made it difficult to describe the present local boundaries of this Association.

Its annual meeting is on the first Tuesday in June, when its officers for the year are chosen, except the register, whose office is permanent. It also meets on the first Tuesdays of September, December, and March for critical reading of the Greek Scriptures, discussion of subjects, and reading of dissertations, sermons, and plans of sermons, previously assigned, and for prayer. The meetings are ordinarily opened at 10 o'clock, A. M., and closed before sun-set. They are uniformly fraternal and highly useful. The churches whose pastors originally constituted this Association, except Hartford Fourth and the churches of Collinsville and Unionville, had belonged to Hartford North Consociation. In September, 1854, they obtained leave of the Consociation to form themselves into a distinct body, by the name of Hartford Central Consociation. But at a convention of the pastors and delegates of these churches, called for the purpose of forming either a consociation or a conference, as might be agreed on, it appeared that a majority of the churches preferred the latter. A conference was accordingly formed, incuding all the churches within the bounds of Hartford Central Association, except one or two, which afterwards joined it. The Conference meets statedly twice a year, and at other times on invitation of the churches and at the call of the moderator. Its exercises are not ecclesiastical, but consist of prayer, preaching, and conference on subjects pertaining to the spiritual state, and improvement of the churches. They have been found highly useful.

The writer will take occasion to say that he has been a member of HARTFORD CONSOCIATION more than fifty years, and its doings, so far as he has observed, have been salutary only. It has deposed one bad minister, who disowned its jurisdiction and refused submission of his case, on complaint of a deacon of his church, to the judgment of Consociation. It has dismissed another minister from his pastoral relation to the church, although both he and a majority of the church refused to submit the case, either to the Consociation or a select council, on complaint of a minority of aggrieved members. In another case, on application of a minority in a church, it has formed them into a distinct church against the will and without the consent of the majority and the pastor. On application of two members of another church, it has thrown out a complaint on which they were convicted by the church and restored them to good standing without confession, the case having been mutually submitted. I have mentioned only some of the extreme cases which have come before us within these fifty years. In all these cases the judgment of Consociation has terminated the quarrels, and the result in all, except one, which is too recent for the full and final effect to be seen, has been *peace.* And I know not how the same happy effect could have been secured in any other way. Of course I believe that Consociation ought to have the power of judicial and final determination—although, where mutual submission can be gained, it should be advisory only. Nor does it seem to me contrary to the principles of Congregationalism, for a church, having in itself the power of self-government, to constitute the Consociation a standing council for ultimate decision in those extreme cases which require it. Churches are liable to be rent into parties—to be biased in their judgment—to pass censures wrongfully—and their is need of some standing body to which the injured may appeal, with consent of the churches where it can be had, and without it when it is refused. Ministers too, sad experience shows, may come under charge of heresy or scandal, on which their churches cannot arraign them for trial, and which they will not consent to refer to select councils. And what can be done in such a case without Consociation? An *ex parte* council, indeed, may be called, but how inadequate this is to meet the exigencies of the case, especially if it be a doubtful one, and strong parties are enlisted, is manifest. You see, then, that I am strongly in favor of Consociation, and I believe that the excellent Dr. Bacon himself, had he lived in Thomas Hooker's time, would have been so also.

LICENTIATES.

Henry M. Goodwin,	S. Dwight Pitkin,
George Bushnell,	Stephen H. Bumond,
Isaac M. Ely,	William U. Colt,
Josiah T. King,	Pearl S. Cossit,
Charles K. McHarg,	Joseph M. Smith.
George W. Colman,	

40

HARTFORD FOURTH ASSOCIATION.

This Association was formed October, 18, 1852. Until this time the principle of the formation of Associations in the state had been with local and territorial bounds.—New Haven Central also departing from that rule, in May, 1853, both were received to the General Association at their next annual meeting.

This Association meets on the third Tuesday in every month, at 10 o'clock, and adjourns about 4 P. M. The ordinary exercises are of a social, literary and religious nature, designed for the mutual improvement of all the members. These meetings have, from the first, proved exceedingly pleasant, harmonious and profitable. The compact of the Hartford South Association of 1811, of individual amenability to the body, is assented to by each member.

LICENTIATES.

Henry Pratt,
Edwin Goodell,
Henry M. Adams,
Edward W. Bentley,
Henry M. Parsons,
Henry Kies,
Edward H. Pratt,
Erskine J. Hawes,
Charles B. Ball,
George H. White,

Samuel B. Forbes,
Frederick Alvord,
Thomas S. Potwin,
Lemuel S. Potwin,
Elijah Robbins,
Ezra Haskell,
Edward M. Pease,
William A. Hallock,
George A. Miller.

The Hartford North Association was organized at Hartford, March 9th, 1709, according to an agreement entered into by the assembled ministers of the county, at the same place, February 2d, 1709. This agreement provided that all the ministers of the county should form two Associations, the first consisting of the ministers of Hartford, Windsor, Farmington and Simsbury, and the second, (Hartford South Association) consisting of the ministers of Wethersfield, Middletown, Haddam, Waterbury, Windham, Glastenbury and Colchester.

The original members of the Association were

Timothy Woodbridge, minister of the	First Church, Hartford,	
Thomas Buckingham, "	Second " "	[Windsor,)
Timothy Edwards, "	East Windsor, (now 1st Ch., South	
Dudley Woodbridge,	Symsbury,	
Samuel Whitman,	Farmington,	
Samuel Woodbridge, ..	East Hartford.	

Jonathan Marsh, pastor of the church in Windsor was settled probably subsequently to the organization of the Association, but was present at its next meeting, two months later. The seven churches here mentioned were all that then existed within the northern half of the county, including the greater part of the present counties of Tolland and Litchfield. Hartford South Association embraced the same number of churches at first, the whole number of churches in the state at that time being thirty-nine. Two other churches, Enfield First and Suffield First, now connected with this Association, were organized before this date, but were then included within the limits of Massachusetts colony.

The existing records of the Association cover the whole period since its formation, except a hiatus of eighteen years between 1765 and 1783, and several other periods in the first half century, viz.: 1710–13, 1715–16, 1718, 1729, 1733,1736, 1739 and 1752. In many cases however we have the record of only one or two of the three regular sessions of the body each year, and the records which remain of the earlier years contain frequently little more than the names of the members present, always arranged according to seniority, and the appointment of meetings and preachers for the ensuing year. The Association undoubtedly maintained three sessions each year regularly, February, June and October, until 1801, when the October session was omitted, and semi-annual sessions were held until 1850. Since the last mentioned date the Association has held quarterly sessions.

The records first notice the great revival of 1740 in June 1741, when the Association advised a large increase of ministerial labor, frequent lectures, &c., neighboring ministers assisting each other. It is evident that all the churches were deeply moved, and the many disorders incident brought many questions of interest into the Association. In 1845 the Association adopted a "testimony against Mr. Whitefield," which is referred to, but not recorded.

October 7, 1788, the Association adopted " a plan for sending a missionary into the new countries (probably Vermont) for ten weeks," and appointed Rev. Mr. Perkins of West Hartford to the work, who accepted. This is, probably, the beginning of the modern missionary work by the churches of this country. The work thus begun seems to have been continued, and in October, 1797, the Association "resolved themselves into a missionary society," which was merged in the general society, subsequently formed in October of the following year.

In October, 1794, the Association established or recommended a " concert of prayer for the revival of religion," to be observed by their churches once a fortnight, and issued a circular on the subject to the other associations of the state. The churches of this Association seem to have shared largely in the revivals which marked the closing years of the last century.

Like all the other original Associations, Hartford North has been reduced in numbers from time to time, by the formation of new Associations. Five of the fifteen Associations in the state have come out of the original Hartford North Association; and 88 of the 284 churches in the state have grown from the churches originally connected with it, if we include Enfield and Suffield among them.

The whole number of churches which have been in connection with the Association from the beginning is forty-nine.

The meetings of the Association are quarterly, on the first Monday and Tuesday of March, June, September and December. The proceedings embrace public worship, reading of essays or reviews, sermons and plans of sermons for criticism, critical reading of Greek Testament, discussion of doctrinal and practical questions, and miscellaneous business.

The moderator and scribe are chosen at each session.

The Hartford North Consociation had the same bounds as the Association till the division of the latter in 1844. Subsequently it embraced the churches of the two Associations, Hartford North and Hartford Central. It now embraces all the churches of Hartford North Association, except two, and a portion of those of the Central and Fourth Associations.

LICENTIATES.

NAME.	DATE.	NAME.	DATE.
Daniel Newell,	Aug. 19, 1719	Ashbel Pitkin,	Feb. 7, 1758
Daniel Edwards,	May 9, 1723	George Colton,	Oct. 3, 1758
Jonathan Arnold,	June 2, 1724	Levi Hart,	June 2, 1761
Nehemiah Bull,	June 1, 1725	Seth Lee,	Oct. 6, 1761
Timothy Woodbridge, Jr.,	June 3, 1735	Jedediah Strong,	Oct. 4, 1763
Isaac Baldwin,	Oct. 4, 1737	Jesse Goodell,	Oct. 4, 1763
Joshua Belden,	Oct. 1, 1745	Simeon Miller,	June 5, 1764
Elijah Mason,	Oct. 6, 1747	Ebenezer Kingsbury,	June 6, 1786
Aaron Brown,	June 5. 1750	Abiel Jones,	June 2, 1789
Benjamin Griswold, Jr.,	Oct. 2, 1750	Calvin Chapin,	Oct. 6, 1791
Abel Newell,	Feb. 5, 1754	Gordon Johnson,	Oct. 1, 1799
Nathaniel Hooker, Jr.,	Feb. 1, 1757	Jonathan Belden,	Oct. 1, 1799

NAME.	DATE.	NAME.	DATE.
Nathaniel Dwight,	Oct. 7, 1801	Mark Ives.	June 7, 1836
James Wheelock Woodward,	Oct. 7, 1801	George W. Bassett,	Dec. 14, 1836
Bancroft Fowler,	June 1, 1802	Rufus C. Clapp,	Dec. 14, 1836
Oliver Wetmore,	Feb. 15, 1803	Ansel Dewey,	Dec. 14, 1836
Elisha Yale,	Feb. 15, 1803	Cushing Eells,	Dec. 14, 1836
Jeremiah Osborn,	Feb. 15, 1803	John F. Norton,	Dec. 14, 1836
Thomas Adams,	Feb. 7. 1804	Royal Reed,	Dec. 14, 1836
Nathan Strong, Jr.,	Feb. 7, 1804	Ezra Adams, Jr.,	Dec. 19, 1837
Cornelius Adams,	June, 1804	David Bancroft, Jr.,	Dec. 19, 1837
Silas Higley,	Feb. 6, 1805	Lumas H. Pease,	Dec. 19, 1837
Nathan Johnson,	Feb. 6, 1805	Lemuel Pomeroy,	Dec. 19, 1837
Roswell Swan,	Feb. 6, 1805	James P. Terry,	Dec. 19, 1837
Henry Chapman,	June 3, 1806	Augustus C. Thompson,	Dec. 19, 1837
Elijah G. Welles,	June 3, 1806	George Butterfield,	Dec. 19, 1837
Reuben Chapin,	Feb. 4, 1807	James A. Hazen,	Dec. 19, 1837
Chester Colton,	June 8, 1808	Benjamin B. Parsons,	Dec. 19, 1837
Gilbert R. Livingston,	June 8, 1808	Amos G. Beman, (African)	June 5, 1838
Nathaniel G. Huntington,	June 6, 1809	James A. Hawley,	June 4, 1839
Nathan Perkins, Jr.	Feb. 7, 1810	Charles B. McLean,	June 4, 1840
John Bartlett, Jr.,	Feb. 7, 1810	Collins Stone,	June 4, 1840
Amasa Loomis, Jr.,	Feb. 6, 1811	David F. Robertson,	Nov. 5, 1840
Cornelius B. Everest,	Feb. 3, 1813	Nahum Gale,	June 1, 1841
Cyrus Yale,	Feb. 3, 1813	Thomes O. Rice,	July 11, 1843
Royal Robbins,	Feb. 2, 1814	Charles F. Gleason,	July 11, 1843
Joseph Mix,	Feb. 2, 1814	Melzar Montague,	July 11, 1843
George Allyn,	Feb. 4, 1818	Alexander Yerrington,	July 11, 1843
Austin Dickinson,	Feb. 4, 1819	Samuel H. Galpin,	June 3, 1845
Anson Hubbard,	Feb. 4, 1819	John C. Strong,	June 3, 1845
Wm. C. Woodbridge,	Feb. 4, 1819	W. A. Benton,	Feb. 3, 1846
Epaphras Goodman,	June 6, 1820	Hiram N. Gates,	June 5, 1849
Amzi Francis,	June 4, 1822	Andrew C. Denison,	June 5, 1849
Flavel S. Gaylord,	June 4, 1822	Isaac N. Lincoln,	June 5, 1849
Elnathan Gridley,	June 4, 1823	Charles H. Norton,	June 5, 1849
Chester Isham,	June 4, 1823	Ira Case,	June 4, 1850
Charles Wadsworth,	June 4. 1823	Frederick H. Brewster,	June 4, 1850
Alpheus Ferry,	Feb. 3, 1824	Francis F. Williams,	June 4, 1850
John Richards,	June 1, 1824	David Breed,	June 4, 1851
Horatio M. Brinsmade,	June 1, 1824	Charles Hartwell,	June 4, 1851
Joseph Foot,	June 1, 1824	Robert D. Miller,	June 4, 1851
Reuben Porter,	June 1, 1824	Wm. R. Palmer,	June 4, 1851
Walter Colton,	June 7, 1825	George J. Stearns,	June 4, 1851
Horatio N. Hubbell,	Feb. 7, 1826	Joseph D. Strong,	June 4, 1851
Bennett Roberts,	Feb. 7, 1826	John M. Francis,	Sept. 3, 1851
Justin Marsh,	Feb. 6, 1827	Oscar P. Bissell,	June 1, 1852
Algernon L. Kennedy,	June 3, 1828	George W. Connitt,	June 1, 1852
Joel Talcott,	June 3, 1828	Timothy A. Hazen,	June 1, 1852
Lemuel Foster,	June 1, 1830	William B. Lee,	June 1, 1852
Elijah P. Barrows,	June 7, 1831	Marcus M. Carlton,	June 7, 1853
John L. Bartlett,	June 7, 1831	J. W. Marcussohn (Jew),	March 7, 1854
Abel L. Barber,	June 4, 1833	O. W. Merrill,	June 6, 1855
Noah Porter, Jr.,	June 2, 1835	* J. K. Nutting,	June 6, 1855
Wm. E. Dixon, Jr.,	Sept. 17, 1835		

* License withdrawn from Mr. Nutting, September 2, 1856.

In 1811, the following "associational compact" was adopted and signed by the members, and is the compact of the Association at this time:

" We the subscribers, who constitute the South Association of Hartford county, do engage and covenant to watch over each other in things pertaining to our Christian and ministerial conduct, and to consider ourselves individually as amenable to the said Association, whenever it shall call us to an account."

" We further agree that a subscription to this covenant shall constitute membership of the Association."

At the time this " compact" was adopted it was signed by twenty-four ministers.

In October, 1823,

Resolved, That the members of this Association will abstain in their persons and families from the use of ardent spirits; and also that they will not give such spirits either to those who labor for them or to those who enjoy hospitality at their houses.

On the subject of Domestic Missions the following passed October 6, 1829:

Resolved, That the members of this Association do cordially approve the object of the Domestic Missionary Society, and that we will exert ourselves in aid of such Society.

1832, the Association declare, with regard to religious charities, that they consider the most important objects to be Home and Foreign Missions, the Bible Society and the American Education Society. They assume the whole responsibility of raising funds, considering each minister to be an agent in his own parish; but in any special emergency, and at least once in four years, the Association will appoint one of their number to act as agent for each of these objects.

1845. *Resolved*, That the Association be an Auxiliary Home Missionary Society.

1856, June 3d, A resolution was passed "That it is competent for an Association to ordain a candidate to the work of the gospel ministry."

The Association regards with disapprobation the too common asperity in the tone and language of religious newspapers, and desires the General Association to give the weight of its influence against it.

LICENTIATES.

NAME.	DATE.	NAME.	DATE.
Josiah Wolcott,	Oct., 1744	Sylvester Sage,	June, 1788
Samuel Fisk,	Feb., 1745	Gad Newell,	June, 1789
Aaron Hutchinson,	Oct., 1747	Joseph E. Camp,	Oct., 1789
Samuel Lockwood,	"	Asahel Hooker,	"
Joseph Clark,	Feb., 1748	Silas Churchill,	Feb., 1790
Samuel Lankton,	Oct., 1749	Isaac Porter,	June, 1790
Izrahiah Wetmore,	June, 1750	Whitefield Cowles,	Oct., 1790
Joseph Fowler,	June, 1751	James K. Garnsey,	"
Noadiah Russel,	Oct., 1753	Israel B. Woodward,	June, 1791
Jesse Root,	June, 1757	Stephen Fenn,	"
Oliver Noble,	Feb., 1758	Asahel S. Norton,	June, 1792
John Eells,	Oct., 1758	Bezaleel Pinneo,	Oct., 1793
Benj. Boardman,	Feb., 1760	Ebenezer Porter,	June, 1794
Caleb Fuller,	"	Samuel Shepard,	"
Jacob Sherwin,	June, 1761	Joseph Washburn,	"
Night Saxton, Jr.,	"	William Hart,	June, 1800
Thomas Niles,	Oct., 1761	Mark Mead,	June, 1804
Eliphalet Huntington,	"	Eli Hyde,	"
Robert Robbins,	June, 1763	Samuel Whittlesey,	"
Jedidiah Chapman,	June, 1764	Hosea Beckley,	June, 1805
Daniel Fuller,	"	Samuel Rich,	"
Elijah Mason,	"	Jonathan Bird,	June, 1807
Samuel Woodbridge,	Oct., 1765	John Chester, Jr.,	Oct., 1807
Salmon Hurlbutt,	June, 1766	John Marsh, Jr.,	June, 1809
Chauncey Whittlesey,	June 1767	Charles A. Goodrich,	June, 1815
Sterling Graves,	Oct., 1767	William Chester,	Oct., 1817
Samuel Eells,	Feb., 1768	William Williams,	June, 1820
James Eells,	Oct., 1768	Joseph Goodrich,	June, 1822
Oliver Deming,	Oct., 1769	Edward Robinson,	Oct., 1822
Nathaniel Emmons,	"	Samuel H Cowles,	Oct. 1824
Robert Hubbard, Jr.,	Oct., 1771	Timothy Stillman, 2d,	Oct. 1829
Joseph Kirby, Jr.	"	Harvey R. Hitchcock,	Oct. 1830
Gershom Bulkley,	June, 1772	Judah Ely, (revoked June 5,	
Selden Church,	Feb., 1774	1832),	June 1831
Wm. Lockwood,	June 1777	Zebulon Crocker,	Oct. 1831
Joshua Johnson,	"	Samuel Porter,	June 1835
Timothy Woodbridge,	Oct., 1778	Luzerne Ray,	Oct. 1835
John Lewis,	June, 1780	Josiah Abbott,	June 1838
William Plum,	June, 1781	Henry Clark,	Oct. 1838
Joseph Barker,	"	Amos S. Chesebrough,	June 1839
Fred. W. Hotchkiss,	Oct., 1782	James Averill,	Aug. 1839
Joshua Williams,	"	Thomas Bailey,	"
Thomas Low,	"	Phineas Blakeman,	"
David Selden,	June, 1783	Sidney Bryant,	
Zephaniah Hollister Smith,	"	Charles P. Bush,	
Wait Cornwell,	Feb., 1784	David B. Coe,	
John Willard, Jr.,	"	Horace Day,	
Jonathan Fuller,	June, 1784	Friend A. Deming,	
Ethan Osborn,	June, 1786	Charles Dickinson,	
David Higgins,	"	Edgar J. Doolittle,	
Samuel Kellogg,	Oct., 1787	Stedman W. Hanks,	
Elija Gridley,	June, 1788	Philo R. Hurd,	

NAME.	DATE.	NAME.	DATE.
David Judson,	Aug. 1838	Ralph Perry,	Oct., 1842
Benjamin N. Martin,	"	James Kilbourn,	"
James P. McCord,	"	Wm. S. Wright,	June, 1843
Colby C. Mitchel,	"	Wm. A. Thompson,	"
Oscar F. Parker,	"	John S. Whittlesey,	"
Charles Rich,	"	Nathaniel H. Eggleston,	
Thomas Tallman,	"	Lewis Edwards Sykes,	"
Horace A. Taylor,	"	Rollin D. H. Allen,	June, 1844
Samuel M. Wood,	"	S. R. Davis,	June, 1845
Elias Clark,	"	W. W. Belden,	Oct., 1845
Israel P. Warren,	June, 1841	Guy B. Day,	Oct., 1847
Isaac W. Plummer,	Oct., 1842	John H. Newton,	June, 1854

The Association of Litchfield County was formed July 7th, 1752, and then embraced the pastors of all the Congregational churches within the county. The churches were at the same time organized into a Consociation. In 1791, the Consociation was divided, and the Association was divided the next year; the limits of each corresponding with those of the Consociation. The Association, when it embraced all the Congregational pastors in the county, were remarkably harmonious in their views of truth and duty.

The following extract from their minutes, dated May, 1757, shows what were their views on theological subjects: "Whereas, the Rev. General Association in their meeting, June, 1756, recommended it to the particular Associations of this colony to manifest their concurrence with the Saybrook Confession of Faith; this Association having taken it into consideration, do hereby declare their unanimous assent and consent to the articles of the Christian religion contained in said public confession so far as they are contained in the Assembly of Divines' Shorter Catechism; and as to the platform of discipline, we think it not expedient that any alteration be made in the public impression; but that every Consociation be at liberty to vary in such things as to them appear exceptionable."

A practice of the Association, designed to prevent the introduction of unsound men into their body, was that of *examining* those who had received a call for settlement before an answer to such call might be given. The following is an example of their practice: "Mr. Samuel John Mills [having] offered himself to examination, in order to his being approved of for ordination in the work of the gospel ministry over the church and people of Torringford, was examined and approved, and recommended to them as a meet person, qualified to settle with them in that work." Sept. 20, 1768.

It was customary, also, for destitute churches of that day to request the Association to recommend to them suitable persons to be employed as candidates for settlement.

The period, from the formation of these ecclesiastical bodies in 1752 to the division of them in 1791, was for the greater part of it a time of great calamity and distress, by reason of war and the unsettled state of the colonies. Instead of directing their attention to Christianizing the heathen, they had, in common with others, to exert all their influence to prevent their coming under the dominion of a persecuting Roman Catholic government. While everything was thus unfriendly to the religious prosperity of the churches, the Association yet ever evinced a readiness to engage in any enterprise which promised good to the cause of Christ or the welfare of man. Witness their annual delegation to the convention of ministers of the synods of New York and Philadelphia, from 1766 to 1775, when those conventions were terminated by the Revolutionary war. See the measures they adopted in 1774 for promoting the education of pious negroes for missionaries to Af-

41

rica, and for the extension of the gospel in Virginia in 1779. To this may be added their ready response to a call for a mission to Vermont in 1788.

Those fathers and brethren lived in times which occasioned hardships and self-denials of which *we* have no experience. The newness of the settlements—the imperfect state of the roads—the distance they had to travel in attending ecclesiastical meetings—the straightened condition of their churches and societies during the French and Revolutionary wars, and other difficulties with which they had to struggle, laid on them burdens of no ordinary weight. The manner in which most of them bore those burdens, proved them to be good soldiers of Jesus Christ. Some of them were chaplains in the army, and suffered privations and toils peculiar to that service.

The harmony, zeal, and *success* with which many of those fathers labored in promoting revivals of religion near the close of the last century and the former part of the present, are too well known to require a particular description.

Of the forty-four ministers who belonged to the Association previous to this division, twelve passed the fiftieth year of their ministry with the same people.

1795. The Association, after discussion, resolved, that the duty of family prayer is so clearly enjoined by the general tenor of scripture, that the habitual neglect of it in a professor of Christianity, is censurable even to excommunication.

1796. Resolved, That it is inexpedient for ministers to travel on the Sabbath for the purpose of exchange, except in cases of *urgent* necessity.

1798. Association drafted and adopted a constitution for a missionary society.

1811. Resolved, That the use of wine and all other ardent spirits shall henceforth be excluded from our associational meetings. That the members of the Association will use their influence to discountenance the use of wine and all ardent spirits in their families and in their social visits among their people.

LICENTIATES.

NAME.	WHEN LICENSED.	NAME.	WHEN LICENSED.
Daniel Smith,	Oct. 2, 1792	John Woodbridge,	June, 1807
Thomas Robbins,	Sep. 25, 1798	Wm. Bonney,	June, 1807
Josiah B. Hawes,	Sep. 28, 1802	Caleb Pitkin,	June, 1807
James Beach,	June 11, 1805	Allen McLean,	Sep. 29, 1809
John Keep,	June 11, 1805	Francis King,	June 14, 1808
John Hyde,	June 11, 1805	Horatio Waldo,	June 14, 1808
Josiah W. Cannon,	June 11, 1805	Daniel Haskell,	Sep. 27, 1808
Moses Gillett,	June 11, 1805	Lucas Hart,	Sep. 25, 1810
Abel McEwen,	Sep. 24, 1805	Francis L. Robbins,	Sep. 30, 1813
Experience Porter,	Dec. 21, 1805	Solyman Brown,	Sep. 30, 1813
Thomas Punderson,	June 11, 1806	Luther Humphrey,	Sep. 27, 1814
Prince Hawes,	June 11, 1806	Ruggles Gould,	Sep. 29, 1815
Timothy P. Gillett,	Sep. 30, 1806	Walter Smith,	Sep. 30, 1818
Bennett Tyler,	Sep. 30, 1806	Chauncey Lee,	Sep. 26, 1820
Heman Humphrey,	Sep. 30, 1806	Abraham Baldwin,	June, 1822
Frederick Marsh,	Sep. 30, 1806	James Ely,	June, 1822

Jacob Catlin,	Sep. 30, 1823	Ephraim Lyman,	June, 1835
John H. Prentice,	Sep. 30, 1823	Willis Lord,	May, 1834
George Cowles,	June 8, 1824	Milo N. Niles,	May, 1834
Stephen Peet,	Sep. 27, 1824	David C. Perry,	Mar. 28, 1836
Harley Goodwin,	Sep. 1825	E. W. Andrews,	May 23, 1837
Jairus Burt,	June 13, 1826	Oliver St. John,	June 9, 1841
Peter A. Brinsmade,	June 10, 1828	Almond B. Pratt,	June 9, 1841
Henry Cowles,	June 10, 1828	Hiram Harris Ruyter,	Sep. 29, 1841
Josephus B. Loring,	June 9, 1829	Henry B. Blake,	June 13, 1843
John M. S. Perry,	June 8, 1830	Azariah Eldridge,	Sep. 24, 1844
Eleazer Holt,	June 14, 1831	E. B. Andrews,	June 4, 1845
John P. Pepper,	June 11, 1833	Samuel J. Andrews,	June 16, 1846
Charles T. Prentice,	Sep. 30, 1834	Elisha Whittlesey,	June 12, 1849

LITCHFIELD SOUTH ASSOCIATION.

The Association of Litchfield County, formed in 1752, was divided in 1792. At first there were fifteen churches, and before the division they had increased to twenty-eight. At the close of a century from the organization of the original Association and Consociation, in 1852, both bodies, sixty years after the division, met in convention at Litchfield for a century celebration. There were then forty-four churches; and two have been since formed. Discourses were delivered on that occasion; a historical address by Rev. D. L. Parmelee; an address on the religious society of the olden time, by Rev. E. W. Hooker, D. D.; biographical sketches of Litchfield county ministers were read by Rev. Abel McEwen, D. D., and Rev. Cyrus Yale; and a report respecting revivals, by Rev. Joseph Eldridge, D. D.

During the first forty years, the Association rarely failed of two sessions annually, with many occasional meetings. Its advice was constantly sought by vacant churches in obtaining candidates. Pastors only were members of it. No one was dismissed by vote; its entire action was by those who were pastors; and its watch and care were extended over those who had been dismissed and continued unsettled. In the important duty of licensing candidates, the Association was strict and faithful; probably the majority of them were students of Dr. Bellamy, who kept one of the early "schools of the prophets."

In regard to the sacredness of the pastoral relation, as held in early times, the case of Dr. Bellamy is worthy of note. The Presbyterian church in New York City had given him a call, and the Consociation of Litchfield county, after several adjournments, found the affair attended with such difficulties, as well as in its own nature of such importance, that they did not look upon it as safe for them finally to determine on the case, but asked the assistance of the neighboring Consociation, (Fairfield East.) After two months the two bodies met at Bethlem, but did not come to their result till the fourth day. Though they commiserated the destitute and melancholy circumstances of the Presbyterian congregation in New York, yet, with all the attending circumstances, in the best light afforded, they thought it not for the honor of our common Lord and the best interests of our holy religion for Dr. Bellamy to be dismissed. Had he gone there, his ministry would have been suspended during the most of the period of the Revolutionary war; also his school of the prophets; and possibly his labors as a theological writer had not blessed the church.

Some few of the churches were for a time affected by the Separatists; two or three pastors, in a measure, sympathized or favored them; but, as sober second thoughts prevailed, the evil gradually ceased, in a way, that while some suffered loss, yet all escaped safe to land and returned to the old paths.

With regard to Sabbath schools, as their origin has been a question of interest, it is proper to state that Dr. Bellamy, whose ministry commenced in Bethlem, in 1740, had a Sabbath school from the beginning. It was composed of two classes; the older class was instructed by the pastor himself in the scriptures, from which they learned portions and were questioned upon them; and the other class studied the Assembly's Catechism, under the instruction of a deacon or some prominent member of the church.

The half-way covenant caused much trouble where it was adopted. For the sake of peace, it was recommended to churches to dismiss those who could not acquiesce in their practice to a neighboring church where the usage was the reverse. The great majority of the early pastors were firm in the faith; the influence of Dr. Bellamy and of others was for good beyond what the records show.

The pastors of the county, with scarcely an exception were, in instruction, influence and practice, on the side of temperance; they were pioneers in the work; they performed their full portion of labor in annual missionary tours among the forming settlements in Vermont and central and western New York. While annual collections were taken under a "brief" from the Governor for the Connecticut Missionary Society, the contributions of the churches were among the most liberal; and still later the various benevolent objects have been well sustained. It is said during the early years of the American Board, as the annual remittance from this county was received in a pressing emergency, that Dr. Worcester, its first secretary, thanked God that he had made Litchfield county.

The Consociational system of Litchfield South has generally commended itself to the churches in its successful workings. The opposition to it has been chiefly because it was not an ecclesiastical court, to accommodate those of such hasty spirit that they are not willing to wait peaceably for the result of peaceable reference. But such opposition has been chiefly occasional, temporary and spasmodic. Only one church in more than two-thirds of a century has withdrawn, and that more than half a century ago, but has long since retuned. The Consociation has combined every advantage of a select council, while it has given stability and influence to its results, which occasional councils could not have done in the same degree. It has been a bond of union and love among the pastors and churches. It is so estimated by ecclesiastical societies, and several of them hold their funds on condition that their ministers are approved by the Consociation. Of the influence of Consociations, whether their acts have been advisory or judicial, their doings have, with rare exceptions, been approved; though for a time, some may have been disappointed in their results and grieved or offended. The fact that nearly every church voluntarily continues its connection, is the best testimony that Consociations are a bond of union and fellowship among the churches, and of assistance to them. Their perpetuity is proof of their usefulness. See Proceedings at the Litchfield County Centennial Anniversary, 1852.

LICENTIATES.

NAMES.	NAMES.
1754 Noah Wadhams.	1816 Elias Cornelius,
" Benajah Roots,	1822 Erastus Clapp,
" Benjamin Chapman,	" Herman L. Vaill,
1755 Josiah Sherman,	1823 Giles Doolittle,
" Seth Norton,	" Benj. B. Smith,
1756 Simeon Stoddard,	1824 Samuel G. Orton,
1757 John Smalley,	1826 Moses Raymond, Jr.,
1758 Benoni Bradner,	1828 Isaac Beach, ──
" Caleb Curtis,	1829 Theron Baldwin,
1760 William Hanna,	" Julian M. Sturtevant,
1762 Benjamin Prince,	" Asa Turner,
" Richard Crouch Graham,	" David A. Grosvencr,
1763 David Brownson,	" James T. Dickinson,
1764 Ephraim Judson,	" George J. Tillotson,
1766 Samuel J. Mills,	1830 Wyllys Warner,
" Samuel Camp,	1831 Sidney Mills,
" Henry Jackson,	1832 John P. Cowles,
" Moses Hartwell,	1833 Levi S. Beebe,
" Job Smith,	1834 Richard M. Chipman,
" Jonathan Edwards,	1835 Merit T. Platt,
1767 Jeremiah Day,	" Isaac W. Warner,
1768 Jehu Miner,	" George T. Todd,
1769 Joel Benedict,	" William Pitcher,
1770 Abner Benedict,	1836 George Tomlinson,
" Josiah Graves,	" Samuel W. Pond,
" Lemuel L. Bacon,	1838 Henry F. Wadsworth,
" Isaac Story,	" Austin Isham,
" Thomas Miner,	" Nathaniel Richardson,
1771 Nathan Hale,	" Merritt Richardson,
" Joshua Knapp,	" Reuben Gaylord,
1772 Josiah Colton,	1839 Samuel G. Whittlesey,
1775 William Bradford,	" William T. Balch,
1778 Noble Everett,	" Walter Clark,
1779 Justus Mitchel,	1840 Isaac Striker,
1780 John Stevens,	" Henry Clarke,
1781 Benjamin Bell,	" Anson Smyth,
1784 Isaac Osborn.	1841 John H. Pettingell,
1789 Chauncey Lee,	" Andrew L. Stone,
1791 Nathan Eliot,	1842 James H. Howe,
1796 John Clark,	" William R. Chapman,
1800 Benjamin Prime,	" George T. Dole,
1803 Charles Prentice,	" Isaac Jennings,
1805 Aaron Dutton,	" Isaac G. Sawyer,
1806 Mills Day,	" Ephraim W. Allen,
1809 Joseph Harvey,	" Ebenezer P. Rogers,
" Judson Hall,	1844 Darius M. Hoyt,
" Austin Hazen,	" Ira H. Smith,
1811 John Seward,	" Charles Fabrique,
" Mathew Rice Dutton,	" Elisha W. Cook,
" Asa Blair,	" William Baldwin,
" Joseph Treat,	" Albert K. Teele,
" Alfred Mitchell,	" David B. Davidson,
1812 Ammi Linsley,	1845 Chauncey H. Hubbard,
1815 Edwin W. Dwight,	" William Smeaton,

When the Saybrook Platform went into operation, the ministers then living within the present limits of Middlesex Association belonged to the Associations in the counties of New London and Hartford. They and their churches were also connected with the Consociation in those counties. The erection of Middlesex county in 1785, consisting of towns taken from the counties of New London and Hartford, opened the way for an ecclesiastical change. Accordingly, at a meeting of the members of the Western Association of New London, living within the limits of the new county, held October 2d, 1787, a resolution was passed, That, whereas the Honorable General Assembly of this state have formed a new county by the name of Middlesex, it becomes expedient, according to the Platform, that an Association and Consociation should be formed consisting of ministers and churches within the county. These bodies were accordingly formed by the ministers and churches of Saybrook and Killingworth, (six churches and six pastors,) giving full liberty to those of Hartford South within the limits of the new county to retain their former connection or join the new body, as they might judge expedient; and also agreeing to receive the pastor and churches of Lyme according to their desire.

Agreeably to these provisions, the ministers of Haddam, Middle Haddam, East Hampton, Westchester in Colchester, East Haddam and Lyme, and also the churches at Deep River and Essex, since formed, united with the Association. The churches and ministers of Middletown and Portland, as a matter of convenience, retain their connection with Hartford South. Durham, annexed to the county in 1799, for the same reason retains its connection with New Haven East.

The rules and usages of this body are much like those of the other Associations of the State.

LICENTIATES.

NAME.	WHEN LICENSED.	NAME.	WHEN LICENSED.
John Ely,	June 3, 1788	William Bushnell,	"
Matthew Noyes,	Sep. 3, 1788	Josiah S. Emery,	"
John Eliot,	July 7, 1790	Isaac Hill,	June 4, 1833
Diodate Brockway,	Oct. 3, 1798	Ellery Bascom.	"
William F. Vaill,	Sep. 15, 1807	Marvin Root,	"
Jonathan Cone,	Mar. 1810	Samuel R. Ely,	"
Samuel T. Mills,	Oct. 2, 1810	Elias P. Ely,	Oct. 2, 1833
Sylvester Selden,	"	Oliver B. Butterfield,	June 7, 1836
Joseph Vaill, 2d,	June 1, 1813	Wm. C. Foote,	"
William Ely,	June 3, 1817	Z. R. Ely,	"
Israel Shaler,	June 2, 1818	Henry M. Field,	Oct. 6, 1840
William Mitchel,	June 5, 1821	Edward W. Champlin,	Oct. 5, 1841
Jonathan Silliman,	"	Frederick A. Pratt,	June 7, 1842
Noah Smith,	"	Edgar Perkins,	June 6, 1843
George W. Boggs,	June 8, 1831	Wm. W. Atwater,	Aug. 7, 1849

Franklin Holmes,	Aug. 7, 1849	Allyn S. Kellogg,	Aug.	7, 1849
Andrew F. Dickson,	"	Henry D. Platt,	"	
Benj. B. Hopkinson,	"	Edwin Johnson,	"	
Chester N. Righter,	"	Edward D. Chapman,	June	3, 1851
James Weller,	"	Richard B. Bull,	Oct.	4, 1854
Sylvanus P. Marvin,	"	John C. Hutchinson,	Oct.	4, 1859
Swift Byington,				

---◄•◄••►---

NEW HAVEN CENTRAL ASSOCIATION.

This Association was formed May 3d, 1853, by members from the New Haven West and New Haven East Associations—chiefly from New Haven West. Its local limits are not exactly defined. Its present members are chiefly in New Haven city and town, and in towns in New Haven county, upon the New York and New Haven and the Naugatuck railroads. The object of the Association is that the members may promote each other's improvement in all the qualifications for the ministry of the gospel, and to aid each other in the duties of the pastoral office, and in advancing the interests of the churches. For this object they meet every month, and have an annual meeting for review of the year in June.

LICENTIATES.

1853.
William Elliott Bassett,
Greenleaf Cheney,
Stephen Fenn,
James A. Gallup,
Leonard W. Bacon.
1854.
Willis S. Colton,
J. L. Jenkins,
J. Y. Leonard,
Theodore T. Munger,
C. T. Seropyan,
J. L. Tomlinson,
Henry Case.
1855.
Charles H. Bassett,
Henry Losch,
Andrew J. Willard.
1856.
Kinsley Twining,
Charles M. Tyler,

1857.
J. H. Anketell,
Henry Loomis,
C. C. Tiffany.
1858.
Edward A. Walker,
Edward P. Wells.
1859.
George M. Smith,
Charles B. Dye,
Richard Crittenden,
Horace H. McFarland.
1860.
George B. Bacon,
Charles C. Carpenter,
E. N. Crossman,
Edgar L. Heermance,
P. H. Holister,
Daniel A. Miles,
John L. Mills,
Chauncey D. Murray,

There are no records of the meetings of the Association back of March 28th, 1734 ; though the record book is dated May 27th, 1731. Long previous to this, the Association not only existed, but probably, as afterwards, embraced all the ordained ministers of the county. Soon after the adoption of the Saybrook Platform in 1708, the Association took a compact form ; though the ministers had frequent meetings before that time, as is evident from the comment on the 12th article of discipline in the Platform, agreed upon at the meeting which formed the Consociation, April, 1709.

The minutes of that meeting are contained in the first book of records of the Association ;—present Rev. Messrs. Andrew of New Haven, Pierpont of Milford, Russell of Branford, Moss of Derby, and Hart of East Guilford, with their delegates, of whom there were two from each church except Derby and East Guilford. The object of this organization was stated to be that communion which is a principal means for the preservation of the peace, order, establishment and consolation of the churches. Votes were also passed on thirteen "articles of the method of managing discipline as it was agreed on by the council at Saybrook, September, 1708," at the request of "some members desiring the council's sense" of those articles. Since these comments show the understanding of the system by its friends, they are here inserted. By comparing them with the text of the Platform, which they are designed to illustrate, their full meaning will be gathered.

1. As to the first article, we conclude, if the majority of the brethren do not consent, the elders cannot proceed to act. If the elders cannot consent, the fraternity cannot proceed, in which case it is proper to seek counsel.

2. The second article we understand to be an explanation and revival of that duty engaged by our churches when they give the right hand of fellowship.

3. The third article ; by "all cases of scandal," we suppose such cases as need a council for their determination.

4. A major part of the elders we suppose necessary ; as in a particular church the brethren cannot act without the elders, so in a council the messengers may not make an act of council without the elders, or a major part of them.

5. "Shall see their determination," &c., i. e. shall by themselves or by some of their members deputed thereunto, observe whether their counsel sought of God in this way be complied with or refused.

6. Contempt of counsel, sought or offered in the way of God, must be scandalous as a just offence, and should be dealt with ; and the clause, viz : "The churches are to approve of such sentence," &c., we understand as the Platform expresseth it, viz : The churches being informed of the council's judgment, and the churches approving of said sentence, then non-com-

munion to be declared.   Without the approbation of the churches there cannot be a non-communion of said churches.

7. The seventh article only provides for joining two councils in weighty, difficult, and dangerous cases.

8. Churches may call a council before they proceed to censure, if they see cause.   But without their allowance, no particular person may have a council before excommunication.

9. That as no member of a council can remain such for longer than one year, so the churches may choose new messengers for every council if they' see cause.

10. The tenth article directs with regard to the calling a first council and adjourning the same not beyond a year, and how further councils may afterwards be called.

11. The eleventh article shows how persons concerned may be obliged to attend with their cases and evidence on a council.

12. The twelfth article is a revival of our former ministers' meetings (Associations) for the ends and good service formerly aimed at, wherein our people did rejoice for a season and as we hope yet will.

13. The thirteenth article shows how a minister offending may be proceeded against, till by the council of that Consociation he be reclaimed or removed from his office.

This Association is one of the oldest in the state, and has been the battle-field for the discussion of some of the most important questions relating to ecclesiastical order, theological doctrines, ministerial duty and covenant obligations that have ever agitated the churches in the state.   Witness the controversies in Branford, New Haven, Wallingford, Cheshire and Guilford.

During the Great Awakening, Rev. Philemon Robbins, of Branford, preached by particular request to a congregation of Baptists at Wallingford, which led to the offering of a complaint against him, embracing several charges of incorrect doctrine and disorderly practice, though he was not accused of the violation of any of the divine commands, or of doing anything contrary to the word of God.   The charges were sustained, and he was excluded from the Consociation ; but the majority of his church having full confidence in him as a sound, faithful, godly minister, he was not dismissed, and after a few years the controversy died away, and he was at length invited to sit with the Consociation at an ordination, without objection.   *Trumbull's Hist.* 2, 196—233.

Of the difficulty in New Haven with regard to the organization of the North Church, see Dr. Dutton's address in this volume, page 120.   Similar troubles were experienced in Milford, in the formation of the Second church, as is related concerning it, in its place in the list of churches, *infra*.   Large and respectable minorities were harassed and oppressed for many years by legal exactions, not being allowed liberty of conscience and worship, and being taxed for the support of the ministers of the First church in each of these places.   *Trumbull's Hist.* 2, 335—50.

In 1729, Rev. Thomas Ruggles, Jr., was ordained in Guilford against the wishes of a large minority, who separated from the church and society.   The

Legislature interposed to effect a reconciliation in vain. They refused to comply with resolutions of the Consociation, and hence forty-six members of the church were suspended. Repeated acts of the Assembly, of committees and of councils, all failed to reconcile them. At length, after a contention of four or five years, with great irritations and alienations between brethren and neighbors, and great expense of time and money before courts, general assemblies and councils, the wishes of the minority were granted, and they were allowed to have a church and minister of their own. *Trumbull's Hist.* 2, 114—134.

Rev. Mr. Humphreys, of Derby, was deprived of his seat in the Association in 1747, for preaching to a Baptist society. Mr. Timothy Allen was dismissed from West Haven for an unguarded expression and being active in the revival of 1740, though he offered a confession for his imprudencies. In dismissing him, his brethren uttered this ill-natured speech in triumph, that they had blown out one " new light," and that they would blow them all out. The Association also suspended Rev. Messrs. Humphreys of Derby, Leavenworth of Waterbury, and Todd of Plymouth, for assisting in the ordination of Rev. Jonathan Lee, in Salisbury, because he and the church had adopted the Cambridge Platform. *Trumbull's Hist.* 2, 195—6.

At the ordination of Rev. James Dana, in Wallingford, opposition arose against him on account of his religious sentiments. The Consociation and an ordaining council were assembled at the same time, and he was ordained against the remonstrance of the Consociation. With the advice of Hartford South, they declared Mr. Dana and his church guilty of scandalous contempt, and recognized the minority as the church. Rev. Simon Waterman was afterwards ordained their pastor. *Trumbull's Hist.* 2, 480—526.

Action preliminary to the division of the Association was taken at Waterbury, September, 1786, and the division effected at Wolcott (Farmingbury) May, 1787. It was then voted to call a meeting of the Consociation before their next meeting to effect a like division in that body. We have in this vote a recognition of the relation between the Association and the Consociation in the county in conformity with the articles agreed upon at Saybrook in 1708. The dividing line fixed upon was the Quinnipiack river.

There was a tradition that one reason why the division of the Association took place at that time was *doctrinal*, and that the movement for a division came from those who favored the *New Divinity*, of which Edwards the younger, then a pastor in New Haven, was the champion, who, with him, would fall into the Western District or Association. Some color of truth is given to this tradition by the circumstance that Dr. Trumbull, of North Haven, and one or two others joined each the other Association than that into which they would fall by the territorial division. The records of the Association and Consociation were to remain in the Eastern District.

LICENTIATES.

NAMES.	NAMES.
1734.	Benajah Case,
Samuel Eaton,	Noah Merrick,
Eleazar Wheelock,	Daniel Bliss.

NAMES.

1735.

William Leete, Jr.,
Mr. Eaton,
Solomon Palmer,
Andrew Bartholomew,
Daniel Huntington,
William Seward.

1737.

Joseph Bellamy,
Nathan Birdseye.

1738.

John Bunnell,
Mark Leavenworth,
Moses Barr.

1739.

John Trumbull,
Timothy Judd,
Gideon Mills,
Samuel Walker,
Jared Harrison,
Stephen White.

1740.

Chester Williams,
Chauncey Whittelsey,
Amos Munson.

1742.

Benjamin Woodbridge,
Thomas Canfield.

1743.

Thomas Darling.

1744.

Edward Dow,
Jonathan Lyman.

1745.

Thomas Arthur,
Stephen Johnson,
Israel Bunnell,
Elnathan Chauncey,
Aaron Richards.

1746.

John Hubbard,
Ichabod Camp.

1748.

John Richards.

1759.

Chandler Robbins,
Noah Williston.

1760.

Jesse Ives,
Roger Newton.

1761.

Ebenezer Grosvenor,
Stephen Hawley,
Ammi Ruhamah Robbins,
Mathew Merriam.

NAMES.

1762.

Pelatiah Tingley,
Albert Hall,
Abner Johnson,
Daniel Collins.

1763.

William Southmayd,
John Bliss,
Burrage Merriam.

1764.

Jonathan Lyman,
Elisha Rexford,
Whitman Walsh.

1765.

David Rose,
Timothy Stone.

1766

Thomas Yale, ⟶
John Foot,
Samuel Munson.

1769.

Isaiah Potter,
John Hubbard, renewed.

1770.

David Brooks,
Caleb Hotchkiss.

1771.

Punderson Austin,
Seth Sage.

1772.

Nathan Strong,
John Lewis.

1773.

David Perry,
Aaron Hale.

1775.

Achilles Mansfield,
Noah Merwin,
Abraham Baldwin.

1776.

William Robinson,
Nehemiah Prudden,
Nathan Fenn.

1777.

Noah Atwater,
Aaron Hall, renewed.

1778.

John Camp,
Rozell Cook,
John Avery.

1779.

Joseph Vail.

1780.

Joel Barlow,
Medad Rogers,

NAMES.

David Austin,
Zebulon Ely.
1781.
Levi Lankton,
Samuel Nott,
John Barnett.
1782.
Jason Atwater,
Henry Channing.
1783.
Jonathan Maltby,
Stephen William Stebbins,
John Robinson.
1784.
David Tomlinson,
Samuel Goodrich.
1785.
Lemuel Tyler,
Jedediah Morse.
1786.
Walter King,
Thomas Holt,
Joseph Badger.
1787.
William Stone,
David Hale,
Samuel Perkins,
Isaac Clinton,
Aaron Collins.
1788.
Caleb Johnson.
1789.
Oliver Dudley Cook,
Isaac Maltby.
1790.
· Hezekiah Goodrich.
1791.
Caleb Johnson.
1795.
Roger Harrison,
Timothy Mather Cooley.
1797.
Erastus Ripley.
1798.
Jeremiah Atwater,
Archibald Bassett.
1799.
Timothy Field.
1801.
Ebenezer Grant Marsh.

NAMES.

1803.
David D. Field.
1804.
Moses Stuart,
Samuel Merwin,
Erastus Scranton,
William L.Strong,
Andrew Rawson,
Horace Holley.
1807.
Henry Frost,
Nathaniel Freeman.
1810.
Noah Coe,
Comfort Williams,
Philander Parmelee.
1811.
G. Garnsey Brown.
1812.
Henry Sherman, renewed.
John D. Fowler.
1814.
Timothy Harrison.
1825.
Stephen D. Ward.
1826.
George Coan.
1827.
Milton Badger,
Sylvester Harvey,
Hiram P. Arms,
Jason Atwater,
Xenophon Betts,
Sanford Lawton,
Zachariah Mead,
Stephen Topliff,
Martyn Tupper,
Asher H. Winslow,
Stiles Hawley,
Chester Birge.
1828.
Dyer Ball,
George W. Perkins.
1830.
Dana Goodsell.
1831.
Romulus Barnes,
John F. Brooks,
Orin Cooley,
Albert Hale,

---

*Voted, 1773, that for the future the examination of candidates shall be before the Association, and not by committees. The names of some candidates examined by committees are probably not on record.

NAMES.

Lent S. Hough,
William Kirby,
John B. Lyman,
Darius Mead,
Seth Sackett,
Alanson Saunders,
Theophilus Smith,
Flavel Bascom,
Frederick W. Chapman,
Erastus Curtiss,
Samuel J. Curtiss,
John H. Eaton,
Solomon W. Edson,
Joseph Eldridge,
Edwin R. Gilbert,
Elisha Jenney,
Edwin Stevens,
Horace Woodruff,
Mason Grosvenor.

1838.

John T. Avery,
Jonathan Brace,
Thomas Bronson,
Amasa Dewey,
Henry Eddy,
Robert B. Hall,
Hiram Holcomb,
Elihu P. Ingersoll,
J. M. McDonald,
Dwight M. Seward,
Albert Smith,
Rollin S. Stone,
James L. Wright,
Dorson E. Sykes,
John O. Colton,
Harvey D. Sackett,
James H. Carruth,
John Mattocks,
Ashbel B. Haile.

1840.

Isaac P. Langworthy,
James Birney.

1843.

Theodore A. Leete,
Lewis Edwards Sykes.

1844.

Charles Jerome,
Samuel W. Eaton,
Joseph Chandler.

1848.

Nathaniel P. Bailey,
W. Edwin Catlin,

NAMES.

Theron G. Colton,
George A. Howard,
William Mellen,
Samuel G. Willard,
Edward W. Root.

1850.

Charles H. Bullard,
Henry Wickes,
William Aitchison,
A. Henry Barnes,
William W. Chapman,
John Edmands,
James B. Cleaveland,
Charles O. Reynolds,
William B. Greene,
Albert A. Sturges,
William C. Scofield.

1851.

Andrew T. Pratt.

1852.

Henry A. Russell,
John C. Buel,
William B. Clark,
Elias B. Hillard,
Cordial Storrs,
Franklin W. Fisk,
Henry Blodget,
William D. Sands,
Jonathan E. Barnes,
Benjamin Talbot,
Samuel Johnson,
James M. B. Dwight,
Charles J. Hutchins,
William C. Shipman.

1853.

Nathaniel J. Burton,

1855.

Timothy Dwight,
John Elderkin.

1857.

Charles C. Salter,
Charles Brooks,
Ira W. Smith,
James Cruikshanks.

1858.

James R. Bowman,
William A. Bushee,
John Edgar,
Jesse Winegar Hough,
Edward A. Smith,
Pliny Warner.

The first meeting of this Association was held at the house of Mr Gillet, of Farmingbury, May 31, 1787. Present, Messrs. Leavenworth, Williston, Foot, Edwards, Wales, Gillet, David Fuller, Fowler, Perry, and Martin Fuller. Mr. Leavenworth was moderator, and Dr. Jonathan Edwards was scribe.

1787, Mr. Williston, with the advice of the Association, went to Vermont to spend a number of weeks in preaching the Gospel, and in laboring to promote true religion, in such parts of that state as he might judge most to stand in need of his labors. The next year Mr. Fowler was sent on a similar mission; and the Association prepared and presented to the General Association an address "on the subject of sending missionaries to the new settlements in Vermont and other parts." In May, 1788, the following vote was passed:

" *Voted*, That the delegates from this Association be instructed to use their influence in the General Association, that a dutiful petition be presented to the General Assembly of this state, praying that more effectual means be adopted to prevent the multiplicity of divorces, to preserve the rights of marriage, and to punish the violation of the marriage vow. Also, that a petition against the African slave trade be preferred to the General Assembly."

1788, September, voted to recommend to the General Association the adoption of measures for the preaching of a sermon annually at Hartford, at the time of the general election.

1789, May, Mr. Gillet was appointed a missionary into the new settlements; Mr. Williston the next year; and in 1796, an address was presented to the General Association on the subject.

1799, "The question, whether deacons are to be ordained, was taken into consideration, and, after mature deliberation, voted unanimously in the negative."

Measures were adopted for forming a Consociation in this district. Voted, to invite Dr. Dwight to join the Association, and also, with the church in Yale College, to come into the proposed Consociation.

Voted, in accordance with the recommendation of the General Association, "to tax ourselves fifty cents for the support of delegates to the General Assembly of the Presbyterian church."

The request of the General Association, to the particular Associations, to make annual returns of the number of communicants in their respective churches, together with the annual additions to their communion was negatived.

Voted, That a communication respecting the state of religion in our churches and societies be a part of associational business.

1805. It was unanimously agreed in the Association that the confessions of church members for public offenses should be before the church and congregation.

Voted, That the discussion of theological questions may be in future a part of associational business.

1806. It was voted that the moderator, scribe, preacher, and all appointments in this Association be by rotation, extraordinaries excepted.

1807. It was voted "that the members of this Association solicit their respective churches, once at least in each month, to meet and unite with them in prayer to God for the effusion of his Holy Spirit, and the revival of religion among our and other churches and congregations."

1808. The Association requested their delegates " to recommend to the General Association the expediency that no foreigner be ordained over any of our churches, until he has preached one year at least in the place where he is to be ordained."

1812. The opinions of the Association were taken on this question, "Is a minister, dismissed without a recommendation, amenable to the church of his former pastoral care?" A majority favored the affirmative.

" *Voted,* That in all future meetings of this Association, ardent spirits form no part of the entertainment."

The records of this Association from 1814 to 1832 are lost. Consequently no report of its doings or of its licentiates during this period can be given.

1834. The license of John H. Noyes was recalled on account of his views on the subject of Christian perfection.

1836. A special meeting was held in the room of Dr. Taylor, in Yale College, to discuss the subjects of slavery and intemperance.

1840. The Association made and put upon their records a declaration of their doctrinal sentiments in reply to a protest of the Pastoral Union against certain doctrinal errors alleged to be prevalent among the Congregational ministers and churches of this state. The declaration was made after a long and careful consideration, and discussion of the various matters embraced in it, and was unanimous.

1842. " *Resolved,* That the duty of preaching the gospel to every creature ought to be urged by all the ministers of Christ on all the churches with more zeal and diligence, and with increased expectation of early and great success."

1853. The Association was amicably divided, and the New Haven Central Association was formed.

The meetings are on Tuesday before the first Wednesday of May, and on Tuesday after the annual thanksgiving, at the room of President Woolsey in Yale College.

LICENTIATES.

1787.
Levi Lankton,
Reuben Hitchcock.

1788.
Ebenezer Fitch,
Daniel Crocker,
Reuben Morse,
Payson Williston.

1790.
David H. Williston,
Aaron Woodward,
Dan Bradley.

1791.
Joel Bradley,
Giles Hooker Cowles,
William Brown.

1792.
Amos Bassett,
Edward D. Griffin,
Benjamin Wooster,
Platt Buffett,
Joseph Goffe.

1794.
Maltby Gelston.

1795.
Abraham Alling.

1796.
John Sherman, Jr.,
Isaac Jones, Jr.

1798.
Ira Hart,
Lyman Beecher,
John Niles.

1800.
Jeremiah Day, Jr.,
Timothy Stone.

1801.
Asa King.

1806.
Charles Atwater,
Thomas Ruggles.

1808.
Bela Kellogg.

1809.
James W. Tucker.

1810.
Nathaniel W. Taylor.

1811.
Asahel Nettleton.

1812.
David A. Sherman.

1813.
Nathan S. Read.

1832.
Simeon North.

1833.
Henry Durant,
John Gridley,
Leverett Griggs,
Robert McEwen,
William M. McLain,
Seagrove W. Magill,
Henry N. Day,
Alfred Newton,
Henry B. Camp,
Oliver Ellsworth Daggett,
William B. De Forest,
John N. Goodhue,
Charles T. Gilbert,
Henry A. Homes,
Marcus A. Jones,
Jeremiah Miller,
John H. Noyes,
Ezekiel Marsh,
Peter Parker,
Thomas N. Wells,
Benjamin Lockwood.

1834.
John D. Baldwin,
Lewis Foster,
Benjamin B. Newton,
William B. Lewis,
James R. Davenport,
David C. Comstock,
Lyman H. Atwater,
Edward O. Dunning.

1835.
Samuel Beman,
William W. Backus,
John B. Lyman,
Thomas Dutton,
Daniel H. Emerson,
Lorenzo L. Langstroth,
Philetus Montague,
Julius A. Reed,
H. A. Sackett,
Samuel Lamson.

1836.
Jeremiah R. Barnes,
Thomas J. Bradstreet,
James A. Clark,
Erastus Colton,
Henry B. Eldred,
Zerah K. Hawley,
Hezekiah W. Osborn,
Edwin J. Sherrill,

1836.
George Tomlinson,
S. B. Morley.
1837.
William H. Adams,
Oliver B. Bidwell,
William Ives Budington,
Edward A. Cumpston,
George E. Day,
Samuel W. S. Dutton,
Benjamin W. Dwight,
Alfred E. Ives,
John R. Keep,
James D. Moore,
George A. Oviatt,
Aaron Snow,
Thomas B. Sturges,
Samuel H. Whittelsey,
George F. Wood,
Thomas Wickes,
William Wright,
D. D. Chesnut,
Charles S. Sherman.
1838.
Aaron C. Beach,
John Churchill,
Eli B. Clark.
Dan C. Curtis,
Elbridge G. Cutler,
William D. Ely,
Jonathan B. Hubbard,
Harvey Hyde,
Samuel Moseley,
Charles E. Murdock,
George P. Prudden,
J. Addison Saxton,
William B. Weed,
Dillon Williams.
1840.
Orlo D. Hine,
L. Smith Hobart.
1841.
Mathew Hale Smith,
Benjamin Griswold,
William S. Curtis,
Samuel H. Elliot,
Chauncey Goodrich,
E. Edwin Hall,
Oliver W. Mather,
Amasa C. Frissell,
William Russell.
1842.
Joseph D. Hull.

1843
Loring B. Marsh,
Martin Dudley,
Lavalette Perrin,
George Thacher.
1844.
Samuel W. Barnum,
S. J. M. Merwin.
1845.
William H. Gilbert,
Joel Grant,
Porter Le Conte,
Alexander McWhorter,
George Richards,
T. N. Benedict,
Birdsey G. Northrop.
1846.
J. Augustus Benton,
Mills B. Gelston,
James H. Dill,
James B. Gibbs,
Burdett Hart,
Jared O. Knapp,
George C. Lucas,
William H. Moore,
John Wickes,
Lewis Grout.
1847.
F. D. Avery,
John Avery,
William Burroughs,
William H. Goodrich,
Gordon Hall,
William L. Kingsley,
William De Loss Love,
Samuel D. Marsh,
James R. Mershon,
John D. Sands,
George S. F. Savage,
Robert P. Stanton,
Edward Sweet,
Martin K. Whittlesey,
Glen Wood.
1848.
William S. Huggins,
William J. Jennings,
William T. Reynolds,
Daniel S. Rodman.
1849.
George E. Hill.
1850.
Thomas K. Beecher.

1851.
Joseph W. Backus,
Henry M. Colton,
Josiah W. North,
David Peck,
J. Leonard Corning,
William A. Macy,
Silas W. Robbins,
James L. Willard,
D. H. Thayer.
1852.
George Bent.

1857.
Oliver S. Taylor.
1858.
Carrol Cutler,
Horatio W. Brown,
John Monteith.
William Hutchison.
1859.
Solomon J. Douglass,
Wilder Smith,
Fisk P. Brewer,
James M. Whiton.

NEW LONDON ASSOCIATION.

BY REV ABEL MC EWEN, D. D., NEW LONDON.

The records of the Association of New London county extend back to the year 1750. An Association was then instituted, or one was remodeled from a previously existing Association. The new institution was called "The Eastern Association of New London County." According to the record, it was established in conformity to the Saybrook Platform and the act of Assembly. In the year 1789 the epithet "Eastern" was dropped, and a constitution and rules of order were formed and adopted for the Association of the County of New London.

Its territory is large, embracing most of the pastors and resident ministers in the county. Occasionally one living on the borders has, for convenience, attached himself to an adjacent Association; and one living out of the county has, for the same reason, belonged to this body. At present three pastors in Lyme and one in Westchester find it convenient to belong to Middlesex Association. A few years past the transfer of the town of Lebanon from Windham to New London county, brought the pastors in that town into the Association of their new county. The Association has, within half a century, increased in the number of its members threefold.

This Association is favored with a pleasant harmony in sentiment and action.

A church in Chesterfield, the one in Long Society, (Preston,) and the Third church in Norwich, have become extinct.

Some Separatist churches were formed in the county seventy or eighty years ago, which have now become extinct, or have been merged in Congregational churches.

The time of the stated meeting of the Association is the first Tuesday of June annually.

Every clerical Association in Connecticut, that of New London county excepted, had, since 1708, a CONSOCIATION of churches connected with it. With the exception of two or three churches on the western line of the county, which, many years ago, connected themselves with a Consociation west of them, and two churches in Lebanon, which, until a few years past, belonged to Windham county, the churches in this county were never consociated until 1814. The pastors often proposed such a connection, but one pastor who had, covertly, become a Unitarian, and one layman, invariably met the proposition with the monitory cry of "hierarchy;" not understanding, or not admitting, that the design and effect of Consociations are to raise up a barrier to protect the churches from any hurtful administration of the ministry over them, and from the incursion of heresy from abroad.

The two uncompromising conservators of independency passed off the stage, and, in 1814, a convention of pastors and lay delegates from the churches was called, which formed and adopted a constitution for a Consociation of the churches. All the churches, one excepted, then existing within the bounds of the Association, came cordially into the connection. Eleven churches, since that date, have been instituted in the county, six of which have consociated themselves with the body; five of the eleven have not connected themselves with the Consociation, though one of the five has declared its intention of doing it. One Separatist church of the straightest sect knocked at the door of the Consociation and was admitted, and afterwards merged itself in another Congregational church which was already consociated.

The territory of the Consociation is large, embracing the whole county, with the exception of three churches in Lyme and the West church in Colchester, which, for convenience, are attached to Middlesex Consociation. The pastors and churches are so attached to each other that hitherto they have been unwilling to divide.

This Consociation has a special constitution, embracing the substance of the provisions in the Saybrook Platform, with additional and somewhat different rules for the introduction of ecclesiastical business. The Consociation is a council for the ordination, installation, and dismission of pastors ; provision being made, if a smaller council be preferred, for calling only the moderator and six other pastors, with delegates from their churches, in cases involving no complaint of moral delinquency. Within the forty-five years of its existence, the Consociation has acted upon one complaint brought against a pastor, and but one against a church, which was preferred by a sister church. Four appeals have been tried from the action of churches in matters of discipline, in two of which the results of church action were confirmed, and in the other two annulled. Many years back, one church, then recently instituted, withdrew from the Consociation, and soon became extinct. Since then, three churches have withdrawn: one, because its action in the excommunicaton of two members was disapproved; one because the Consociation did not, on complaint of the church against a sister church, carry discipline to a satisfactory length; and one, because it was required to disavow its action as disorderly in the admission of an excommunicated person, and, perhaps, because a pastor elect preferred Independency to Consociation.

In the annual meetings of this body, reports on the benevolent enterprises of the country are made, and these topics are canvassed with deep interest and great advantage. Beside the closer union and fellowship of the churches, and the mutual aid which they render each other, which are benefits derived from this Consociation, it has conformed us to the commonwealth of the churches in the state. New London county now comes up and takes her rank among the tribes in the sisterhood of Connecticut.

The mass of the churches in this county prefer an ecclesiastical council made up of pastors and delegates from churches in the vicinity, to one composed of members from other places, and a council statedly chosen and organized to one gathered for every occasion ; and, as the resort must sometimes be, to an *ex parte* council. A mutual council for the occasion is liable, when difficulty and excitement exist, to be chosen and to act under the influence of a partizan spirit. A council from abroad comes to a result, the provisions of which very little affect them, or religion, in their distant homes, and for which they feel little responsibility. A stated council of the vicinity makes a result for themselves, under the provisions of which they and their neighbors must live, and for the good or evil consequences of this result the council is held to a rigid and telling accountability. Consociated churches have a council which they freely and actually choose, and which they can repudiate by withdrawing from the Consociation, and to which abused churches, pastors, and church members can resort for redress, as Independents must to occasional councils. Regulated liberty is preferred to liberty more capricious. Consociated churches confide in their own mutual protection from the sway of metropolitan churches, and from the domination of that one-man power which Independency gives to an aspiring minister.

LICENTIATES.

NAMES.		NAMES.	
Elisha Fish,	1750	Joseph Hurlburt,	1822
Isaac Foster,	1761	Joseph Ayer,	1823
Levi Hart,	1762	Joseph Whiting,	1826
Ephraim Woodbridge,	1768	Joseph Tyler,	"
Charles Backus,	"	David B. Austin,	1830
Andrew Law,	1766	Stephen Ellis, Jr.,	"
Micaiah Porter,	"	Asa J. Hinckley,	1832
Eleazar Fairbanks,	"	Elisha C. Jones,	1834
Caleb Alexander,	1778	Joshua L. Maynard,	1840
William Patten,	"	Cyrus Brewster,	1841
John Wilder,	1784	Chester S. Lyman,	"
Aaron Woolworth,	1785	Frederick T. Perkins,	"
Christopher Page,	"	L. Porter,	
Elijah Parish,	1786	Owen Street,	
Thomas Andros,	"	John C. Avery,	
Hezekiah Woodruff,	1789	William Barns,	
Asahel Huntington,	"	William P. Avery,	
John D. Perkins,	1793	Lansing Porter,	
Elijah Waterman,	"	Wilford L. Wilson,	
Daniel Hall,	1794	Edward Strong,	
Eliphalet Nott,	1795	Buel M. Pearson,	
Aaron Cleaveland,	1799	Giles M. Porter,	
Asa Meech,	"	Abijah P. Marvin,	
Hubbel Loomis,	1800	Lanson Cary,	
Joshua Huntington.	1806	Zalmon B. Burr,	"
Jason Allen,	1808	Gould C. Judson,	1842
Nathaniel Dwight,	1810	Eliphalet Parker,	"
Daniel Huntington,	1811	Enoch F. Burr,	"
Nathaniel Hewit,	"	Myron N. Morris,	1843
Dudley Rossiter,	1814	John C. Downer,	"
Samuel Phinney,	1815	Orrin F. Otis,	"
John Ross,	"	Daniel W. Havens,	1845
Lavias Hyde,	1816	Elijah B. Huntington,	"
William Nevins,	1819	James T. Hyde,	1850
Elijah Hartshorn,	1820	Jacob Eaton,	1856
Jedediah L. Stark.	"	William F. Arms,	1859
Beriah Green,	1821		

TOLLAND ASSOCIATION.

The ministers of the county met at Tolland, August 14, 1789, and unanimously "voted to form an Association on the same footing with sister Associations in the state of Connecticut, professing their adherence to the public formulæ and the general plan of ecclesiastical polity adopted in the Saybrook Platform." Their meetings for a time were on the first Tuesday of June and October, at 11 o'clock, A. M. ; and there was a public lecture in the afternoon. Subsequently the meeting in October was discontinued. The Association appointed a standing committee, to examine candidates for the ministry, and to advise " vacant churches" in relation to the choice of a suitable individual to become pastor. At the organization of the Association, no constitution was framed, and no by-laws were adopted ; the members feeling competent to determine whether they would adhere to this or that particular feature of the platform or not, as occasion required. The Association has twice ordained Evangelists. From its existence, it has kept the records of all select councils within its limits in the same books in which its own doings are contained. Previous to the forming of this Association the ministers who first constituted it belonged either to the Association of Hartford North, or Hartford South. Besides attending to necessary business and holding a public religious service, this Association shows, in its records, that the great objects of the ministry have held a large place in its consultations and plans of doing good. Its action in regard to missions " in the new settlements ;" its care for the instruction of youth in the Shorter Catechism of Dr. Watts ; its interest in having tracts published before the formation of any society for the purpose ; its early efforts for the education of pious young men for the ministry who needed aid ; its monthly meetings for prayer, whenever there was a decline of religious interest ; and the early organization (1812) of a County Missionary Society to aid the American Board of Commissioners for Foreign Missions ; all manifest that the members of this Association have not been unmindful of the great work entrusted to them by the Lord. The Association has sometimes exercised its right in determining the question, with whom it would hold fellowship ; but while it has done this, we can see that the respect it has shown for ministerial character and for a sincere faith in true religion, is every way becoming the ministers of Christ. In this particular their influence, we believe, has been of the right kind and conducive of good. " The Ministers' Meeting," which was established more than thirty years since, and, for the greater part of this period, held once in two months, has proved highly profitable, and was never more so than at present. The minutes of the Association do not show that the churches experienced previous to 1815, much religious prosperity. The decline of religion was very great in the latter part of the last century and the opening years of the present. The ministers were led more and more under this state of things to seek for a revival of religion, by means of

prayer, for the outpouring of the Holy Spirit. Hence, arose the monthly
meetings of the Association for prayer with a "lecture," which were continued for several years. The blessing sought was found. The Spirit descended—*the present era of revivals dawned* upon these churches, while yet
many of the fathers of the Association had not fallen asleep. This Association, as early as 1824, took action in favor of total abstinence from ardent
spirits. It has been very decided in its testimony against slavery, regarding it to be a violation of the most sacred rights of man, as determined by reason and Scripture. One of the early "Schools of the Proph·
ets" was within the limits of this Association—that of Dr. Backus, of Somers, who was a "bright and shining light" in the ministry. The pastors of
this Association are much united in their views of the doctrines of the
Gospel, and co-operate very heartily in the great responsibilities and duties
of their work. They have been wont to use special means for promoting the
great interests of religion, such as seasons of special prayer, and conferences
of from two to four churches, which have proved means of much good.

LICENTIATES.

NAME.	DATE.	NAME.	DATE.
Azel Backus,	June 1, 1790	John Lord,	Oct. 6, 1801
Freegrace Reynolds,	"	Ezekiel J. Chapman,	"
Alvan Hyde,	"	Isaac Knapp,	June 1, 1802
Salmon Cone,	Oct. 5, 1790	James Eells,	"
Jesse Townsend,	"	Elihu Smith,	June 1, 1802
Uri Tracy,	June 7, 1791	William Boies,	Oct. 5, 1802
Silas Long Bingham,	"	Henry Bigelow,	June 7, 1803
Titus Theodore Barton,	"	Ebenezer Kellogg,	June 6, 1815
Asa Lyon,	Oct. 4, 1792	Hart Talcott,	June 4, 1816
Joseph Field,	June 4, 1793	William B. Sprague,	Aug. 28, 1818
Marshfield Steele,	June 3, 1794	Ebenezer Churchill,	June 5, 1821
Seth Williston,	Oct. 7, 1794	Ambrose Edson,	Sep. 3 1823
Thomas Snell,	Oct. 3, 1797	John Goddard,	Dec. 28, 1835
Robert Porter,	"	M. S. Goodale,	"
Sylvester Dana.	June 5, 1798	John Haven,	"
Salmon King,	Apr. 10, 1798	John C. Paine,	
John H. Church,	"	Josiah W. Turner,	"
Henry Davis,	Aug. 7, 1798	Anson T. Tuttle,	Dec. 28, 1835
Josiah B. Andrews,	June 4, 1799	John E. Tyler,	"
Vincent Gould,	"	Hiram Bell,	Oct. 9, 1838
Amasa Jerome,	"	Benjamin Howe,	Nov. 10, 1840
Israel Braynard,	Oct. 1, 1799	John A. McKinstry,	"
Ephraim T. Woodruff,	June 3, 1800	Isaac H. Bassett,	"
Gideon Burt, Jr.,	"	David N. Coburn,	"
Humphrey Moore,	"	Charles Hammond,	June 4, 1844
Jabez Munsell,	June 2. 1801	Thomas C. P. Hyde,	June 1, 1852
David B. Ripley,	"	Samuel R. Dimock,	Nov. 7, 1854
William Patrick,	"	Joel T. Bingham,	June 12, 1855
Caleb Knight,	"	Louis E. Charpiot,	June 1, 1858
Claudius Herrick,			

At the time when Saybrook Platform was adopted, most of the present territory of Windham county was included in New London county. The settlements in this quarter of the state were comparatively new and feeble, having advanced very little before the close of the 17th century. Such progress did they make, however, that in 1723, the ministers in Franklin, Lisbon, Plainfield, and towns north, formed the North Association of New London county. But in 1725 the General Assembly erected the county of Windham, and in 1726 the name of this Association was changed to Windham Association.

MEMBERSHIP.—According to Saybrook Platform every pastor of a church within the limits of an Association was, *of course*, to be a member of it. All the pastors in this county (*and only they*) seem for a time to have been members of this Association. There appears to have been no vote of admission, with few exceptions in unusual cases, for seventy years, and in case of discharge from the pastoral office, no vote of dismission passed in this body.

DIVISION.—In October 1799, James Cogswell, Josiah Whitney, and Andrew Lee, had leave to form the " Eastern Association of Windham County," and it was voted that any other member might join them who should signify his purpose within one year. In accordance with this vote, Messrs. Staples Atkins, and Putnam joined the three above named, as also Messrs. George Leonard, Luther Wilson and Abiel Williams, (of Dudley, Mass.,) who were never members of the " Original Association," as it came to be called. There was a theological difference at the foundation of this division; the new Association inclining to Arminianism, while the leading minds in the " Original Association " were Hopkinsian in their bias. The Eastern Association was represented for some years in the meetings of the General Association, but withdrew on account of objections made by the Original Association against the reception of new members by it, an objection sustained by the General Association on the ground of the fundamental agreement. It finally became extinct by the removal of its younger members and the death of its fathers. The book containing its records is now in the hands of Windham County Association. Since then there have been other proposals for a division of the Association, one of which was voted, but finally abandoned.

MEETINGS.—There were originally three meetings in a year; of late years but two; on the first Tuesday of June and November. On these occasions there is usually public worship with a sermon, besides more private devotional and literary exercises. Questions for advice are propounded. The decisions on some of these questions in the early meetings are curious as illustrating the methods of discipline and guidance then in vogue. Churches apply for recommendation of candidates, pastors for solution of cases of conscience or counsel in trouble. In later times agents of benevolent societies appear, asking approval and commendation—resolutions and

44

plans of effort are adopted—the affairs of the nation and the condition of the world are considered and discussed. The examination of candidates for licensure, or *approbation*, (as it was more properly called at first,) was sometimes entrusted, with other business, to a committee *ad interim:* Indeed, for many years the Association divided its members into an eastern and a western committee. Rules as to such examination have been adopted at various times, the tendency being to greater stringency in the requisitions.

1729.—Voted, that a church member who turns Anabaptist is to be argued and labored with ; but if obstinate, " the minister is publicly to bear testimony against his error, and declare the church discharged from any particular relation to him."

1730.—Confessions of public scandal should be made before the congregation.

1730.—Candidates elect to pastoral offices are to be called by the moderator before the Association to give satisfaction of their abilities, &c.

1744.—Baptism by a Popish priest is not to be held valid.

1744.—Voted, that a woman divorced from her husband on account of his absence for three years unheard of, has a lawful right to marry.

1744.—A letter to the several societies in Windham county on the Separatist movement was prepared and signed by the members.

1746.—Committee "to draw a narrative of the affair of a number of men at Mansfield, pretending to form themselves into a church state and to ordain officers."

1747.—Resolved, that baptism by unauthorized persons, such as Sol. Paine, Thomas Marsh, &c., is not valid.

1748.—Committee to represent the case of Sampson Occum to the Commissioners of Indian Affairs at Boston,—he having been ill-treated and discouraged while teaching last winter at Mohegan.

1752.—Committee to prepare a history of the Episcopal separation, in reply to the Bishop of London.

1756.—Monthly hours of prayer agreed upon, on account of earthquakes and war.

1757.—Mr. Devotion to reply to the misrepresentations of Willoughby and Morse in England, about the support of the clergy here and their conduct towards the Separatists.

1757.—Consented that a messenger have equal voice with pastor in council.

1767.—In case of a young man baptized by Solomon Paine, recomended re-baptism.

1778.—Voted, that a minister dismissed from his charge is not a member without restriction.

1778.—Proposed to General Association to consider expediency of reprinting, by subscription, books of piety, and of forming societies for promoting knowledge and special reformation of manners.

1780.—Renewal of covenant recommended.

A day of fasting to be observed by the Association, and an address to the people to be distributed.

1789.—Messrs. Welch and Lyon missionaries to Vermont, for seven months.

1799.—Inexpedient, without urgent necessity, to travel on the Sabbath for exchange.

Deacons to be ordained by prayer and the laying on of hands.

Rev. Israel Day voted a regular minister and admitted to Association, he having been ordained a pastor among the Separatists.

1800.—A volume of sermons proposed.

1802 —Voted to print 1500 copies of the address of Westminster Association on family religion.

1804.—Association cannot hold fellowship with one who denies the Trinity. Approved a proposal for Association with delegates.

1814.—Resolved, that belief in the Divine Trinity is a fundamental point.

1827.—Acknowledged a donation of books from Mr. Phillips.

Resolved to abstain from ardent spirits at Association meetings.

LICENTIATES.

NAMES.		NAMES.	
Seth Paine,	Aug. 29, 1727	Amasa Learned,	Oct. 12, 1773
John Whiting,	Oct. 10, 1727	Enoch Hale,	Oct. 10, 1775
Eleazar Wales,	"	Joseph Strong,	May 21, 1776
James Caulkin,	Aug. 1730	Ebenezer Williams,	"
Jonathan Trumble,	Oct. 13, 1730	Abraham Fowler,	"
William Metcalfe,	"	Moses C. Welch,	Oct. 8, 1782
Joseph Lovett,	Nov. 16, 1731	Samuel Austin,	Oct. 12, 1784
Shubael Conant,	May 31, 1734	Richard S. Storrs,	"
Benjamin Throop,	Aug. 31, 1736	Stephen Williams,	May 6, 1786
Abel Stiles,	Oct. 12, 1736	John Taylor,	"
Hobart Estabrook,	May 16, 1738	Jonathan Ellis,	May 15, 1787
Jacob Baker,	May 15, 1739	Solomon Spalding,	Oct. 9, 1787
Seth Dean,	Aug. 28, 1739	Hendric Dow,	May 20, 1783
Peter Pratt,	"	Gordon Dorrance,	Oct. 14, 1788
Thomas Lewis,	Oct. 12, 1742	Daniel Waldo,	Oct. 13 1789
James Cogswell,	May 15, 1744	William Storrs,	"
William Throope,	"	Dyer Throop Hinckley,	May 18, 1790
Nathaniel Draper,	Oct. 14, 1746	Amos Woodworth,	"
Daniel Welch,	May 15, 1750	Timothy Williams,	May 15, 1792
Joseph Strong,	May 21, 1751	Lathrop Rockwell,	"
David Ripley,	May 19, 1752	Lynde Huntington,	May, 1793
Samuel Cary,	Oct. 9, 1759	Daniel Dow,	May, 1795
Caleb Turner,	May 21, 1760	Joseph Russell,	"
Benjamin Trumble,	"	Asa Lyman,	May, 1799
Ephraim Hide,	Oct. 13, 1761	Aaron Hovey, Jr.,	May 18, 1802
Andrew Storrs,	May 18, 1762	Abiel Russell,	Oct. 12, 1802
Joseph Dennison,	May 15, 1764	Thomas Williams,	May 17, 1803
Eleazar Storrs,	Oct. 9, 1764	John G. Dorrance,	June 20, 1803
Hezekiah Ripley,	"	Ezra Stiles Ely,	Dec. 12, 1804
Eleazar Wales,	May 21, 1765	John W. Judson,	May 21, 1805
Simon Lane,	"	John Hough,	Oct. 8, 1805
Josiah Dana,	"	Richard Williams,	"
Enoch White,	May 17, 1768	Hollis Sampson,	May 19, 1809
Joseph Howe,	May 17, 1769	Nathan Grosvenor,	Oct. 8, 1811
Joseph Lyman,	Oct. 10, 1769	Israel Ely,	Oct. 13, 1812
Joseph Pope,	May 19, 1772	George Payson,	May 17, 1815
Nehemiah Williams,	May 18, 1773	Jason Park,	"

NAMES.			NAMES.		
Stephen Crosby, Jr.,	Oct.	4, 1815	Charles P. Grosvenor,	May,	1831
Eliakim Phelps,	"		Orson Cowles,	Aug.	30, 1831
Ludovicus Robbins,	Sept.	3, 1816	Harvey Gleason,	"	
Ebenezer Halping,	Sept.	2, 1817	James M. Davis,	"	
William Potter,	Jan.	20, 1820	William A. Larned,	Aug.	28, 1833
Aaron Putnam,	May	16, 1820	Andrew Sharpe,	Aug.	28, 1839
Archibald Burgess,	May	16, 1821	David E. Goodwin,	"	
Charles Walker,	June	18, 1821	Asa F. Clark,	"	
Nathaniel Kingsbury,	May	22, 1822	Thomas G. Clark,		
Daniel G. Sprague,	"		James C. Houghton,	"	
Samuel Porter Storrs,	Oct.	7, 1823	Ezra Gordon Johnson,	June	2, 1841
Nehemiah Brown,	May	20, 1823	Hiram Day,	Sept.	1, 1841
David Metcalf, Jr.,	"		Melzar Parker,	"	
George Marsh,	Sept.	6, 1825	Luther H. Barber,	"	
John Storrs,	May	17, 1826	Francis L. Fuller,		
George Shepard,	May	16, 1827	Jonas B. Clark,	"	
Charles Fitch,	Oct.	5, 1827	Henry C. Morse,	Aug.	28, 1844
William Fuller,	"		Alden Southworth,	Mar.	4, 1846
Barnabas Phinney,	Oct.	6, 1829	George Soule,	June	4, 1850
Mason Grosvenor,	May	19, 1830	John R. Freeman,	Nov.	4, 1852
John J. Clute,	"		Charles L. Ayer,		1855

HISTORICAL SKETCHES

OF THE

CONGREGATIONAL CHURCHES

IN

CONNECTICUT.

In the preparation of these Historical Sketches of the Congregational Churches in Connecticut, it has been found necessary to abbreviate and condense the reports which have been provided for the use of the committee. It is believed, however, that every fact of importance has been retained. It will be seen that frequent references are made to Dr. Sprague's "Annals," and to Dr. Allen's "Biographical Dictionary," wherever those volumes furnish more elaborate notices of the lives of the ministers of Connecticut than it was possible to insert in this work. Dr. Emerson Davis's "Sketches of the Ministers of New England," which is soon to be published, will also undoubtedly give much valuable information. It may be well, perhaps, to mention for the benefit of those who are making inquiries on this subject, that much may be learned by consulting the American Quarterly Register of the Education Society, particularly the volume for the year 1832, pp. 307—322; also the lists of ministers in Trumbull's History of Connecticut, vol. I, pp. 492—494; and vol. II. pp. 527—533; and the Associational and Church Manuals.

It was intended that the accounts of the Revivals of Religion in the state should be more complete than has been practicable. For everything additional respecting them, reference must be made to the "Christian History," Boston, 1743—44. The Connecticut Evangelical Magazine, Hartford, 1800—1814; and the Religious Intelligencer, New Haven, 1817—1834.

In the following pages (h) designates a Home Missionary; (f) a Foreign Missionary; (c) denotes that a minister received a "call to settle," which he did not accept. The names of Stated Supplies are printed in italics. Extinct churches have been designated by printing their titles in "Antique letter."

THE CHURCH IN ABINGTON, (IN POMFRET,) ORGANIZED JAN. 31st, 1753.

MINISTERS.	SETTLED.	DISMISSED.	DIED.
David Ripley,*	Feb. 1753	1778	Sept. 1785
Walter Lyon,	Jan. 1783		Feb. 1826

MINISTERS.	SETTLED.	DISMISSED.	DIED.
David B. Ripley,	1827–28		
Charles Fitch,	April, 1828	May, 1832	1843
William H Whittemore,	1833–34		
Nathan S. Hunt,	Feb. 1834	April, 1845	
Edward Pratt,	1847–48		
Sylvester Hine,	1850–51		
H. B. Smith,	Jan. 1852		

At the organization of the Church in Abington, it numbered 63 members, who were dismissed from the Church in Pomfret. Mr. Lyon left several hundred dollars as a fund to the society. The Church has enjoyed many revivals of religion. As the fruits of one in 1858, thirty-one were added.

MINISTERS RAISED UP.—Joseph Dana, Eleazer Craft, Jesse Goodell, Asa Lyon, Calvin Ingalls, Erastus Spaulding, David B. Ripley, Thomas Williams, John Paine, Andrew Sharpe, William Grow.

* Sp. An. 1. 648. Allen.

THE CHURCH IN ANDOVER, ORG. FEB. 14, 1749.

Samuel Lockwood, D. D,*	Feb. 1749		June, 1791
Royal Tyler,†	July, 1792	May, 1817	
Augustus B. Collins,	Sept. 1818	Oct. 1827	
Alpha Miller,	June, 1829	June, 1851	
Levi Smith,	April, 1852	April, 1853	1853
Eliphalet Birchard, lic.,	1853	1854	1855
Samuel Griswold,	Sept. 1854	Sept. 1855	
John R Freeman,	June, 1856		

The Society was incorporated May, 1747. Dr. Lockwood " was a firm ad. vocate of the doctrines of grace, and of evangelical purity in religion. He fulfilled the work of the ministry with ability, zeal and faithfulness."

MINISTERS RAISED UP.—Jesse Townsend‡, Silas L. Bingham, William B Sprague, D. D., Milton Badger, D.D., Ebenezer Loomis, (Bap.,) Charles C. Townsend, (Ep.,) Joel F. Bingham.

* Sp. An.1, 465, Allen. † Mendon Assoc. 240. ‡ Sp. An. 4, 572.

THE CHURCH IN ANSONIA, (IN DERBY,) ORG. APRIL 17, 1850.

James R. Mershon,	April, 1850	April, 1851	
Owen Street,	Sept. 1852	April, 1857	
Alvah L. Frisbie,	Mar. 1860		

Permanent religious worship was commenced in the village in the winter of 1849—50, and the church was organized with 31 members. In 1859 the number had increased to 158. The Home Missionary Society granted aid one year, and after this the increase of members and means rendered the church self-sustaining. The winter of 1851 was marked by a very extensive revival, adding 44 to the church; another in 1858, adding about 20; and other refreshings have been enjoyed.

FIRST CHURCH IN ASHFORD, ORG. NOV. 26, 1718.

MINISTERS.	SETTLED.	DISMISSED.	DIED.
James Hale,*	Nov. 1718		1742
John Bass,	Sept. 1742	June, 1751	1751
Timothy Allen,†	Oct. 1757	Jan. 1764	1806
James Messenger,	Feb. 1769		Jan. 1782
Enoch Pond,‡	Sept. 1789		Aug. 1807
Philo Judson,	Sept. 1811	Mar. 1833	
Job Hall,	Jan. 1834	July, 1837	
Charles Hyde,	Feb. 1838	June, 1845	
Charles Peabody,	Jan. 1847	Sept. 1850	
George Soule,	Jan. 1851	Jan. 1852	
Charles Chamberlain,	June, 1854	Mar. 1858	
Thomas Dutton,	May, 1859		

According to the town records of Ashford, the church was formed about ten years after the first inhabitants came to the place. The society gave Mr. Hall as a salary at first £45, which they increased to £60. They voted also to give him one hundred acres of land, to build him a house, and to supply him with fire-wood during his ministry. The meeting-house, somewhat enlarged in after years, served the society from 1716 to 1830. During the pastorate of Mr. Bass, the church was disquieted on account of his first inclining to, and then adopting Arminian sentiments, which produced so great disaffection as to result in his dismission. Between several of the early pastorates, there were long intervals, during which, several candidates were invited to become pastors, but because the calls were not sufficiently unanimous, or for other reasons, they declined. The first "revival of religion" in Ashford, was in 1798-9; fifty-eight persons united with the church as the fruits of it. The labors of Mr. Judson and Mr. Hyde were especially blest with revivals; eighty-three being added in 1819, and ninety-one in 1838 and 1845. The society was never, perhaps, weaker than it is at present. For the last seven or eight years, it has received aid from the Home Missionary Society; whereas it had always before been self-sustaining. The reasons for this decline in strength are emigration, the coming in of but few religious families, and the territory being reduced to less than a fifth of its original extent.

MINISTERS RAISED UP.—Eliphalet Nott, D. D., Daniel Dow, D. D., John Newman Whipple, Sylvester Dana.

* Allen. † Allen. ‡Mendon Assoc. 229. Sp. An. 2. 370. Allen.

THE FIRST CHURCH IN AVON, (WEST,) ORG. NOV. 20, 1751.

MINISTERS.	SETTLED.	DISMISSED.	DIED.
Ebenezer Booge,	Nov. 1751		Feb. 1767
Rufus Hawley,*	1769		1826
Ludovicus Robbins,	April, 1820	1822	
Harvey Bushnell,	Jan. 1824	1834	
John Bartlett,	Oct. 1835	Oct. 1847	
Joel Grant,	June, 1848	Oct. 1852	
William S. Wright,	Feb. 1853		

In 1746, thirty-one individuals presented a petition to the General Assembly, praying that they would be pleased to grant them "winter privileges," i. e. the right to hire a minister to labor with them four months in a year, from December 1, to March 1, and exemption from taxes to the society of which they were members, during that period; the petition was granted. When three winters had passed, they judged themselves "ripe for being a society among themselves," which was formed in 1750. In 1754 their first meeting-house was built amid the native forests, on the east side of the Farmington river, and about two miles east of the one now standing.

Mr. Hawley, in preaching, spoke from short notes, and made use of a conversational style. Professor Silliman, in his volume of travels, speaks of him as a patriarchal teacher, not caring much for balanced nicety of phrase, but giving his flock wholesome food and sound doctrine in plain speech. His prayers had that detail of petition, that specific application both to public and private concerns, and that directness of allusion to the momentous political events of the day, and their apparent bearing upon his people, which was common among our ancestors, and especially among the first ministers who brought with them the fervor of the times, when they emigrated from England."

Until the year 1830, when Avon became a town, the parish, which was part of Farmington, was called Northington. In 1808 a difficulty arose in the society respecting the location of a new meeting house. It grew so serious at length, that in 1818, when a vote was taken to erect the house of worship on its present site, the minority separated themselves and formed a new society, East Avon. During the excitement on this question, December, 1817, the old house took fire and burned to the ground.

A signal religious awakening occurred in this parish in the year 1800; as a fruit of which fifty were added to the church. There were two revivals under the ministry of Mr. Bushnell.†

MINISTERS RAISED UP.—Aaron J. Booge, Publius V. Bogue, Oswald L. Woodford.

* Allen.   † Evangelical Mag. 1-102.

THE CHURCH IN BARKHAMSTED, ORG. APRIL 20, 1781.

Ozias Eells,	Jan. 1787		May, 1813
Elihu Mason,*	Mar. 1814	1817	

MINISTERS.	SETTLED.	DISMISSED.	DIED.
Saul Clark,	Jan. 1819	1829	
William R. Gould,	Sept. 1832	1838	
Reuben S. Hazen,	May, 1843	1849	
Aaron Gates,	Jan. 1850		April, 1850
Hugh Gibson,	1850	1852	
A. B. Collins,	1852	1853	
P. T. Hawley,	1853	1855	
F. Norwood,	Jan. 1855	Mar. 1857	
T. E. Roberts,	April, 1858	April, 1859	

Since Mr. Hazen's dismission, the church has been in a very divided and broken condition, not having all the time even a stated supply, or missionary aid. There was a revival in 1840, which added thirty to the church, and another in 1848. The church needs sympathy as well as aid in the support of the gospel.

*Sp. An. 2, 3.

The Second Church in Barkhamsted.

William Goodwin,	1849	1850

Twenty members of the First Church were dismissed and organized as the Second Church. The division grew out of difficulties in regard to the location of a new church edifice. They occupied a house, then vacant, of another denomination, and were occasionally supplied till Nov., 1853, since which, they have had no preaching, and no public worship. Though not formally disbanded, the church cannot be revived.

THE CHURCH IN BERLIN, (WORTHINGTON SOCIETY,) NOW SECOND CHURCH IN BERLIN, ORG. FEB. 9, 1775.

Nathan Fenn,	May, 1780		April, 1799
Evans Johns,*	June, 1802	Feb. 1811	May, 1849
Samuel Goodrich,†	May, 1811	Nov. 1834	April, 1835
Ambrose Edson,	June, 1831	Nov. 1834	Aug. 1836
James M. McDonald, '	April, 1835	Nov. 1837	
Joseph Whittlesey,	May, 1838	Aug. 1841	
William W. Woodworth,	July, 1842	April, 1852	
William De Loss Love,	Oct. 1853	Nov. 1857	
Robert C. Learned,	Dec. 1858		

Worthington Society was included in Kensington Society, Berlin, until 1772. Their first meeting-house, (now used as a Town Hall,) was opened for worship Oct., 1774; the present one, Feb., 1851. The church, when formed, was the *Third* Church in Berlin, but since the separation of New Britain from Berlin, the Second. Mr. Johns was a native of Wales, educa-

45

ted in England, where he was some time minister at Bury St. Edmonds, Suffolk; he came to America in 1801. After leaving Berlin, he was pastor in Canandaigua, N. Y., and died aged eighty-six. There have been repeated revivals in this church, at least in ten different years, with marked and special interest, since 1812.

MINISTERS RAISED UP.—Hosea Beckley,‡ George Dunham, Simeon North, Josiah W. North, Andrew Pratt, (f.)

* Sp. An. 4, 566. † Sp. An. 1, 512. Allen. ‡ An. 2, 326.

THE CHURCH IN BETHANY, ORG. OCT. 12, 1763.

MINISTERS.	SETTLED.	DISMISSED.	DIED.
Stephen Hawley,*	Oct. 1763		Aug. 1804
Isaac Jones,	June, 1804	Nov. 1806	May, 1850
Nathaniel G. Huntington,	Oct. 1809	Mar. 1823	Feb. 1848
Abraham Alling,	Mar. 1823	Mar. 1827	July 1837
Tillotson Babbitt,	Mar. 1826	Mar. 1827	
Ephraim G. Swift,†	Jan. 1828	Jan. 1830	Aug. 1858
B. C. Baldwin,	1830		
George Goodyear,	1830–31		
N. W. Taylor, D. D.,	1831–32		
Jairus Wilcox,	Nov. 1832	June, 1834	Sept. 1851
John B. Kendall,	Aug. 1834	June, 1836	
Erastus Colton,	1836		
William H. Adams,	1838		
Saul Clark,	Mar. 1840	Mar. 1842	Dec. 1849
Cyrus Brewster,	1842		
George Thatcher,	1842–43		
D. B. Butts,	May, 1843	Jan. 1848	
W. W. Belden, (c)	1848		
Augustus Smith,	1848		
Fosdick Harrison,	Mar. 1849	Dec. 1851	Feb. 1858
Alexander Leadbetter,	Dec. 1851	Sept. 1854	
E. W. Robinson,	May, 1855		

Bethany was the second church in Woodbridge until 1832. It was a long time after first petitioning, before they could be released to become an ecclesiastical society. Two very important suits, in which decisions were made by the courts with regard to the rights of societies, originated in Bethany, with regard to the exemption of church funds from taxation, in 1826; and respecting the proper manner of warning meetings, and the rights of annual committees, 1832. See synopsis court decisions, page 286. Mr. Jones was deposed and became an Episcopalian, carrying off a large part of the people; from that time the church has been small. Mr. Kendall was also deposed at South Wilbraham, Mass., shortly after his dismission, on complaint of New Haven West Association. There have been several seasons of special religious interest. This would have long been a missionary church, except for the donations and legacies of the fathers. The instability of frequent changes in the ministry and the employment of supplies have been unfavorable to its prosperity. A small house of worship, one mile south of the present church, was used till 1769; a very large house was then built half a mile south, which stood until 1831, when the third was built; the dedication sermon was by Dr. N. W. Taylor.

Λ. INISTERS RAISED UP.—Israel P. Warren.

* Allen's Biog. Dict.   † Allen.

THE CHURCH IN BETHEL, ORG. NOV. 25, 1760.

MINISTERS.	SETTLED.	DISMISSED.	DIED.
Noah Wetmore,	Nov. 1760	Nov. 1784	
John Ely,	Nov. 1791	June, 1804	
Samuel Sturges,	April, 1806	Dec. 1811	
John G. Lowe,	Jan. 1822	Jan. 1829	
Erastus Cole,	Sept. 1830	Sept. 1837	
John Greenwood,	April, 1838	April, 1842	
James Knox,	1842		
Lent S. Hough,	1846		
Sylvanus Haight,	Nov. 1846	Feb. 1848	
John S. Whittlesey,	Dec. 1849	Jan. 1852	
W. Nye Harvey,	May, 1853	June, 1858	
Newell A Prince,	April, 1859		

There are few records before the settlement of Mr. Cole. His labors, and those of Mr. Greenwood, were greatly blessed. Mr. Cole took special pains to preach the distinguishing Calvinistic doctrines, as many of the older members, well established in the faith, gratefully remember. About 1840, dissensions arose, which increased until a final separation into two feeble churches was contemplated ; but the Lord rebuked this spirit, by the burning of their church building, July 21, 1842. This brought them to reflection, humiliation. and the renewal of their covenant with deep penitence, and there soon followed what is known as the great revival, as the fruit of which one hundred and nineteen entered into covenant with the church on the day of the dedication of their new church edifice, June, 1843. Cost $3000 ; enlarged 1856, cost $3000 more. Added to the church in 1858, sixty. The society received aid from the Home Missionary Society, until the great revival ; since then it is self-sustaining, with a great increase of salary, and making liberal benevolent contributions.

MINISTERS RAISED UP.—Ebenezer Platt, Dennis Platt, Laurens P. Hickok, D. D., George Barnum, John S. Ambler, Samuel T. Seelye, Julius H. Seelye, Bennet F. Northrop, Theodore Benjamin, Laurens C. Seelye.

The Church in Bethlem, Org. March 27, 1739.

MINISTERS.	SETTLED.	DISMISSED.	DIED.
Joseph Bellamy, D. D.,*	1738		1789
Azel Backus, D. D.,†	1791	1813	1816
John Langdon,‡	1816	1825	1830
Benjamin F. Stanton,	1825	1829	1843
Paul Couch, .	1829	1834	
Fosdic Harrison,	1835	1850	1858
Aretas G. Loomis,	1850	1860	

Bethlem was the eastern part of the north purchase of Woodbury. Dr. Bellamy entered at large on the church records an account of the revivals during his ministry. In 1740–41, according to his account, "religion was revived greatly, and flourished wonderfully. In 1740 every man, woman and child, above five or six years old, were under religious concern more or less; quarrels were ended, frolics flung up, praying meetings began, and matters of religion were all the talk. This universal concern about religion lasted about a year. In its hight many were seemingly converted, but there were false comforts and experiences among the rest, which laid a foundation for false religion to rise and prevail; and when that was down, some fell into a melancholy sour frame of spirit, bordering on dispair; and others into carnal security, and the truly godly seemed to be very few. And now very trying times follow. 1. A number of them who are elderly people, being ambitious, and having a grudge at each other, are continually fermenting contention, strife and division about society affairs. 2. A number of the middle aged stand up for false religion, and plead for the Separatists. 3. A number of the younger sort, set themselves to set up frolicing, and serve the flesh; true piety and serious godliness are almost banished." This is a summary of things from 1740 to 1750; and much so has it been in other places. "In the spring of 1750 there was a prevailing, malignant nervous fever, of which thirty died. God sent his destroying angel and filled the place with the greatest distress, and in some things a reformation followed; contentions, Separatism, and rude frolicing did not appear, and the people became in a good measure peaceable and orderly." Dr. Backus was dismissed to become President of Hamilton College. See Dr. Bellamy's Life and Works.

Ministers Raised Up.—Robert Crane, David Brown, Moses Raymond, Charles Prentice, Benjamin C. Meigs, (f) Julius Steel, Homer Prentice, Frederick Munson.

*Spr. An. 1, 404, Allen. Litchfield Centen., 18, 82. †Sp. An. 2, 281. Allen. Litchfield Centen. 86. ‡ Sp. An. 1, 410, Allen. Litchfield Centen., 117.

The Church of Birmingham, (in Derby,) Org. Feb. 25, 1846.

Charles Dickinson,	Sept. 1846		April, 1854
Zachary Eddy,	Dec. 1855	Feb. 1858	
Charles Wiley, D.D ,	Nov. 1858	July, 1859	

Fifty-nine members from the church in Derby were the original members of this church, which increased during the first year to 73. The church edifice was enlarged in 1859 by the addition of sixteen feet to the length, with a recess of six feet for the pulpit. There were two or three seasons of refreshing during Mr. Dickinson's pastorate, which furnished many additions to the church ; two hundred and thirty-two having united with it since its organization.

THE CHURCH OF BLACK ROCK, IN FAIRFIELD, ORG. SEPT. 11, 1849.

MINISTERS.	SETTLED.	DISMISSED.	DIED.
William J. Jennings,	April, 1850	Oct. 1857	
Marinus Willett,	May, 1858		

The church was originally composed of twenty-four members from the first church in Fairfield, and the South church in Bridgeport ; increased in eight years to seventy-one.

THE CHURCH IN BLOOMFIELD, (WINTONBURY,) ORG. FEB. 14, 1738.

Hezekiah Bissell,	Feb. 1738		Jan. 1783
Solomon Walcott,	May, 1786	1790	
William F. Miller,	Nov. 1791		1811
John Bartlett,	Feb. 1815	1831	
Ansell Nash,*	Sept. 1831	1835	
Cornelius B. Everest,	June, 1836	1840	
William W. Backus,	Mar. 1841	1844	
John Gibbs,	Aug. 1844	Aug. 1845	
Alfred C. Raymond,	Dec. 1845	1848	
Francis Williams,	Dec. 1851	1858	

The Church erected a house of worship during the past year, costing ten thousand dollars. The last revival was in 1858, when twenty members were added. It is thought that the Society, much more than the Church, has been the cause of the frequent dismission of ministers.

* Allen.

THE CHURCH IN BOLTON, ORG. OCT. 27, 1725.

Jonathan Edwards, (c.)	1722		
Thomas White,*	Oct. 1725		Feb. 1763
George Colton,†	Nov. 1763		June, 1812
Philander Parmelee,‡	Nov. 1815		Dec. 1822
Lavius Hyde,	Dec. 1823	Apr. 1830	April, 1830
James Ely,	Sept. 1830	1846	
Lavius Hyde,	Dec. 1849	Jan. 1860	

This town began to be settled in 1717 or 1718. · Rev. Jonathan Edwards preached during some part of the year 1722, and received a call to settle.— The terms stated were £200 settlement, one fiftieth part of the real estate held by the proprietors of the town ; £80 annually after the second year, increasing by £5 till it reached £100, and that continued as the stated salary. Every male inhabitant over sixteen was to labor for him in clearing his land, fencing it, cultivating and securing the crops. December 10, 1722, he wrote : "I assure you, I have a great esteem of, and affection to the people of your town, so far as I am acquainted with them, and should count it a smile of Providence upon me, if ever I should be settled amongst such a people, as your Society seems at present, to me, to be." Nov. 11, 1723. The following record is entered in his hand writing upon the town records: "Upon the terms that are here recorded, I do consent to be the settled pastor of this town of Bolton.   JONATHAN EDWARDS.

On the following January, he was performing the duties of a Tutor in Yale College.

Mr. White's successor made the following record : "He was a sound orthodox preacher, though never favored with any special out-pouring of the Divine Spirit, save what took place soon after 1740. He was a friend of peace and order. He admitted 310 ; baptized 914.

*Sp. An. 1. 528, Allen.   †Sp. An. 1. 180, Allen.   ‡Sp. An. 2. 546. Allen. Relig. Intel. 7. 780.

THE CHURCH IN BRISTOL, ORG. AUGUST 12, 1747.

MINISTERS.	SETTLED.	DISMISSED.	DIED.
Samuel Newell,*	Aug. 1747		Feb. 1789
Giles H. Cowles,†	Oct. 1792	May, 1810	
Jonathan Cone,	May, 1811	Mar. 1828	
Abner J. Leavenworth,	Dec. 1829	Sept. 1831 .	
David L. Parmelee,	Feb. 1832	Feb. 1841	
Raymond H. Seeley,	July, 1843	Jan. 1849	
William H. Goodrich,	Mar. 1850	Oct. 1854	
Leverett Griggs,	Feb, 1856		

In October, 1742, liberty was granted by the General Assembly for the inhabitants residing on the lands now embraced within the limits of the town, to hire for six months, during the winter season, annually, an orthodox and well qualified person to preach among them. In May, 1774, the society was incorporated by the name of New Cambridge. The ministry of Mr. Newell covered the periods of the old French and Revolutionary wars—periods of much absorbing interest; yet his ministry seems to have been blessed with several seasons of spiritual refreshing. Mr. Cowles's ministry was a valuable one. The refreshing showers of the Holy Spirit were enjoyed several times. The year 1799 was a season of great religious interest, and a

large number was added to the church. The first ten or twelve years of Mr.
Cone's ministry were pleasant and profitable—many were added to the
church. The five or six last years of his ministry were unpleasant and con-
tentious, causing his dismission. In the year 1858 ninety-four were added
to the church by profession.

MINISTERS RAISED UP. Ira Hart, Samuel Rich, Asahel Hooker, Cyrus Byington, (f.) Swift Byington.

* Allen. † Sp. An. 2. 330.

THE CHURCH IN BROAD BROOK, ORG. MAY 4, 1851.

MINISTERS.	SETTLED.	DISMISSED.	DIED.
Charles N. Seymour,	May, 1851	May, 1853	
William M. Brichard,	Sept. 1854	Dec. 1858	

The church was formed with twenty members. It is in a manufacturing
village, with a floating population, which renders it difficult to support the
gospel. A house of public worship was opened Jan. 1, 1854. In 1858 there
was unusual interest in the subject of religion, and ten were added to the
church.

THE CHURCH IN BROOKFIELD, (NEWBURY,) ORG. SEPT. 28, 1757.

Thomas Brooks,	Sept. 1757		Sept. 1799
Erastus Ripley,*	Mar. 1800	Nov. 1801	Nov. 1843
Richard Williams,	June, 1807	April, 1811	
Bela Kellogg,	Jan. 1813	Oct. 1816	1831
A. B. Hull,	Oct, 1819	Oct. 1820	
Abner Brundage,	May, 1821	Oct. 1839	
Dan. C. Curtiss,	Oct. 1843	Oct. 1855	
Thomas N. Benedict,	April, 1859		

There have been several seasons of special religious interest since 1807,
adding a goodly number to the church. The present neat and commodious
house of worship was built in 1853.

MINISTERS RAISED UP.—O. S. St. John, Oliver S. Taylor.

* Allen.

THE CHURCH IN BROOKLYN, (POMFRET,) ORG. NOVEMBER 21, 1734.

Ephraim Avery,	Sept. 1735		Oct. 1754
Josiah Whitney, D. D.,*	Feb. 1756		Sept. 1824
Luther Wilson,	June, 1813	Feb. 1817 (Deposed.)	
Ambrose Edson,	April, 1824	Dec. 1830	Aug. 1836
George J. Tillotson,	May, 1831	Mar. 1858	

MINISTERS.	SETTLED.	DISMISSED.	DIED.
Edward C. Miles,	Oct. 1858	Oct. 1859	
C. N. Seymour,	Dec. 1859		

Unitarianism was introduced into Brooklyn, in consequence of the settlement of Mr. Luther Wilson, as colleague pastor with Rev. Dr. Whitney, in 1813. At the time of his ordination he was, by some of the council, regarded as of somewhat *doubtful* orthodoxy; and he soon revealed himself to be an Arian, and increasingly bold and decided in his errors. The better portion of the church and society, after making long continued efforts in vain to get rid of him, left the old house of worship and set up worship by themselves in 1817; thus cutting themselves off from further influence in the old society for the removing of the offending pastor. Had they still more patiently and perseveringly continued with their former associates in ecclesiastical affairs, it is most probable, that ere long, *orthodox preaching* might have been *reinstated,* and a *Unitarian* church *prevented.* Yet the orthodox church steadily grew and prospered; and has been signally blessed with revivals; six of which were enjoyed during the pastorate of Mr. Tillotson, which continued for twenty-seven years. The church has been unusually *liberal* in the way of *contributions to benevolent objects,* in proportion to its *ability.* With the exception of the first two years of Mr. Tillotson's ministry, the contributions to charitable objects amounted to just about as much as his aggregate salary, ranging annually from about $450 to $700.

MINISTERS RAISED UP.—John Brown, D. D.,† William R. Weeks, D. D.,‡ John Dorrance, George Clark, Harvey Hyde. (h.)

* Sp. An. 1. 529. Allen. † Sp. An. 2. 589. ‡ Sp. An. 4. 473.

THE CHURCH IN BURLINGTON, ORG. JULY 3, 1783.

Jonathan Miller,*	Nov. 1783		1831
Erastus Clapp, (Colleague,)	Jan. 1823	Dec. 1828	
Erastus Scranton, do.	Jan. 1830	May, 1840	
Lumas Pease,	1840	Nov. 1841	
James Noyes,	Aug. 1843	Nov. 1846	
William Goodwin,	Jan. 1847	1848	
James L. Wright,	Mar. 1849	Dec. 1854	
Asa M. Train,	Jan. 1855	1856	
Henry Clark,	Jan. 1857	Nov. 1859	
George A. Miller,	Nov. 1859		

The Church in this place has done much for the evangelization of the country. It has sent out many excellent men to colonize the Western country, and to settle in neighboring towns. Indeed this church has at times been almost depleted by emigration. The consequence has been that to sustain the preaching of the gospel here, aid has been afforded by the Connecticut Missionary Society.

MINISTERS RAISED UP.—Heman Humphrey, D. D., Luther Humphrey, Lucas Hart.

* Sp. An. 1, 690. Allen.

The Church in Bozrah, Org. Jan. 3, 1739.

MINISTERS.	SETTLED.	DISMISSED.	DIED.
Benjamin Throop,*	Jan. 1739		Sept. 1788
Jonathan Murdock,†	Oct. 1786		Jan. 1813
David Austin,‡	May, 1815		Feb. 1831
Jared Andrus,	April, 1831	April, 1832	Nov. 1832
John W. Salter,	Sept. 1832	Mar. 1835	
John Hyde,	April, 1835	April, 1837	1849
Thos. L. Shipman,	Oct. 1837	May, 1841	
John W. Salter,	May, 1841	April, 1842	
William M. Birchard,	April, 1842	Oct. 1848	
Edward Eells,	June, 1849	April, 1850	
William P. Avery,	April, 1850	May, 1855	
T. D. P. Stone,	April, 1856	April, 1857	
N. S. Hunt,	April, 1858		

Added to the Church during the pastorate of the first minister, 277; 2d, 46; 3d, 208; 4th, 44.

Two colonies went from this Church; to Bozrahville in 1828, and Fitchville in 1854.

Ministers Raised Up.—David Smith, D. D., Charles Gager, Simon Waterman, Elijah Huntington, John C. Downer, (h.) Elijah Waterman, Jedeniah L. Stark.

*Sp. An. 1. 669. Allen. †Sp. An. 2. 41. Allen. ‡Sp. An. 2. 195. Allen.

The Church in Bozrahville, Org. April 10, 1828.

David Sanford,	1825	
Erastus Ripley,	1828	
Nathaniel Minor,	1829	1831
Mr. Read,	1831	1832
Rodolphus Lamphear,	1832	1834
Oliver Brown,	1834	1840
George Perkins,	1840	1845
Stephen Hayes,	1845	1849
D. C. Sterry,	April, 1851	April, 1852
George Cryer,	April, 1852	" 1853
D. C. Sterry,	1853	" 1855
J. C. Nichols,	April, 1855	" 1856
Phineas Crandall,	April, 1856	Dec. 1856
George Cryer,	Jan. 1857	Jan. 1860

The village came into the possession of the Thames Manufacturing Company in 1825, by whose aid and influence the interests of the Church have been greatly promoted. Before the Church was formed, an extensive revival, under the ministry of Mr. Sanford, added seventy at one time to the

46

Bozrah Church ; and another under Mr. Minor, which commenced after the sudden death of a young woman who had agreed with another, at the close of a solemn meeting, that they should need true religion if they were aged, or about to die, but that they did not then. Before the week was out, she was giving a dying warning to her family, not to do as she had done, and she concluded by saying, "I am lost." Revivals since have been frequent, with considerable additions. The monthly concert has been generally held, and a Sabbath School sustained with prayer meetings, and liberal contributions made to benevolent objects, although the Church has never had a settled pastor.

The Church in Branford, Org. 1647.

MINISTERS,	SETTLED.	DISMISSED.	DIED.
John Sherman,	1644	1646	1685
Abraham Pierson,*	1647	1667	1678
John Bowers,	1671	1678	
Samuel Mather,	1680	1684	
Samuel Russell,†	1687	.	June, 1731
Philemon Robbins,‡	Feb. 1733		Aug. 1781
Jason Atwater,	Mar. 1784		June, 1794
Lynde Huntington,	Oct. 1795		Sept. 1804
Timothy Phelps Gillett,	June, 1808		
Jacob G. Miller,	Oct. 1859		

The tract of land constituting the town of Branford was purchased of the town of New Haven in 1644, by immigrants from Wethersfield. The settlers of New Haven had purchased it of the Indian Sachems in 1638. The Indian name was *Totoket.* The tract included North Branford, and most of Northford, and constituted but one Ecclesiastical Society. The original records of the church, if any existed. were carried away in 1667. It is, therefore, uncertain, when and where it was organized, but it was certainly as early as 1647—when Mr. Pierson, with part of his church, came from South Hampton, L. I. He removed with a majority of the church, and settled in Newark, N. J. A new church was organized in Branford ,March 7, 1688. A colony from this church in 1725, was regularly organized into a church in the North Farms, and named the church in North Branford. At an early period, though at different times, the Society purchased lands of the Indians, and appropriated the rent of them to the support of the ministry. The annual rent is at present about $500.

Since the organization of 1688, all the pastors previous to the present one have died in office. There have been no dismissals up to the date of January, 1859. *See Mr. Gillett's Half Century Sermon,* 1858, *and Mr. Wood's Historical Discourse, North Branford,* 1850.

MINISTERS RAISED UP.—Samuel Russell, Roger Harrison,§ Chandler Robbins,‖ Ammi Robbins, Levi Frisbie,¶ Joseph Barber, Joel T. Benedict, Solomon Palmer, Jared Harrison, John Foot.

* Sp. An. 1. 116. Allen. Math. Mag. 1. 357. † Sp. An. 1. 175, 261. Allen. ‡ Sp. An. 1. 367. Allen. § Sp. An. 2. 531. ‖ Sp. An. 1. 573. ¶ Sp. An. 1. 402.

The Church in Bridgewater, Org. 1809.

MINISTERS.	SETTLED.	DISMISSED.	DIED.
Reuben Taylor,	Jan. 1810	April, 1815	
F. Harrison,	1824	1829	
Maltby Gelston,	1831	1832	
Albert B. Camp,	Dec. 1834	May, 1843	
James Kilbourn,	Aug. 1843	July, 1850	
Dillon Williams,	Sept. 1850	Dec. 1853	
F. Harrison,	Nov. 1854	Feb. 1858	

The Society was formed from a part of New Milford in 1803. The church has been favored with several revivals, one in 1816, under the preaching of Rev. Dr. Nettleton. Church edifice built in 1807 ; re-built in 1842 ; again re-built in 1855. From 1824 to 1859, Mr Harrison supplied the pulpit one third of the time.

Ministers Raised Up.—Joseph Treat, Wm. A. Hawley, Levi Smith, Isaac C. Beach, Julius O. Beardsley, (f.), Philo R. Hurd.

The First Church in Bridgeport, (formerly called Stratfield,) Org. June 13, 1695.

Charles Chauncey,*	June, 1695		Dec. 1714
Samuel Cooke,	July, 1715		" 1747
Lyman Hall,	Sept. 1749	June, 1751	1791
Robert Ross,†	Nov. 1753		Aug. 1799
Samuel Blatchford, d. d.‡	Nov. 1797	Mar. 1804	
Elijah Waterman,	Jan. 1806		Oct. 1825
Franklin Y. Vail,	Oct. 1826	July, 1828	
John Blatchford,§	Mar. 1830	" 1836	April, 1855
John Woodbridge, d. d.,	June, 1837	Nov. 1838	
John H. Hunter,	Mar. 1839	" 1845	
Benjamin S. J. Page,	Feb. 1847	Aug. 1853	
Joseph H. Towne,	June, 1854	June, 1858	
Matson M. Smith,	Jan. 1859		

Mr. Chauncey made the following record : "In May, 1708, the Legislature of Connecticut, it will be remembered, passed an act requiring the ministers and churches to meet and form an ecclesiastical constitution. It was ordained and required, in the words of the act, 'that the ministers of the several counties in this government shall meet together at their respective county towns, with such messengers as the churches to which they belong shall see cause to send them, on the last Monday in June next ; then to consider and argue upon those methods and rules for the management of ecclesiastical discipline, which by them shall be judged agreeable and conformable to the word of God ; and shall at the same meeting appoint two of their number to be their delegates, who shall all meet together, at Saybrook, at the next commencement to be held there, when they shall compare the results of the ministers of the several counties, and out of, and from them draw a form of ecclesiastical discipline, which, by two or more persons delegated by them, shall be offered to this court at their session, at New Haven, in October next, to be considered and confirmed by them.'" The action of the church is thus recorded : " July 27, 1708. Voted, on the Sabbath, that Leverett Bennet or Ensign Sherman, or both, be the messengers of this church at the meeting of the elders, at Fairfield, on ye 28th of ye same month, by the appointment of the General Assembly, at Hartford, in May last, ye end of which meeting of ye elders and messengers, is to cons. the matter of church discipline, &c." The Act of Assembly adopting the Saybrook Platform, was passed in the Oct. following. Thereupon Mr. Chauncey records: " Feb. 16th, 1708-9, I published the Confession of Faith, ye Articles of Union between the United Presbyterians and Congregational men in England, and also read the regulations for church discipline agreed upon in this colony, and confirmed by authority ; none among the brethren objecting."

Copied in the firm, clear hand of Rev. Samuel Cooke, March 16, 1708-9, is a record of the formation of the old Consociation of Fairfield County, then including the whole territory allotted forty years afterward to the county of Litchfield.

Art. 2, says in part: " That ye pastors met in our Consociation have power, with ye consent of the Messengers of our churches chosen, and attending, authoritatively, juridically and decisively to determine ecclesiastical affairs, brought to their cognizance, according to the word of God."

There is a tradition that Rev. George Whitfield visited and preached in this parish, and that considerable religious interest followed.

Subsequent records give account of four revivals of religion which the church has enjoyed in 1815, 1821, 1827, and in 1844, in common with several other churches in the city ; and in the great revival of 1858, it largely shared.

Four houses for public worship have been built by this Society, in 1695, 1717, 1807, and 1850.

The Rev. Charles Chauncey was the eldest son of Rev. Israel Chauncey, of Stratford, and grandson of Rev. Charles Chauncey, second President of Harvard College. Messrs. Cooke and Ross were gentlemen of great dignity, of the old school, clad in the ancient garb of hat, wig, and small clothes, and had a commanding influence over the people. Dr. Blatchford was afterwards settled in Lansingburg, N. Y. The ministry of Mr. Waterman was attended with large ingatherings to the church. These four issued several publications.

MINISTERS RAISED Up.—Henry Blatchford, John Blatchford, Peter Lockwood, Nathaniel Bouton, Epinetus Platt Benedict, Ransom Hawley (h.), Alanson Benedict, Thomas Tileston Waterman, Nathaniel Wade, Willis Lord, George Alexander Oviatt, Thomas Benedict Sturges, William Walter Woodworth, Bronson B. Beardsley.

*Sp. Au. 1. 114. Allen. †Allen. ‡Sp. An. 4. 158. § Sp. An. 4. 163.

THE SECOND CHURCH IN BRIDGEPORT, ORG. JAN. 30, 1830.

MINISTERS.	SETTLED.	DISMISSED.	DIED.
Nathaniel Hewit, D. D.	Dec. 1830	Sept. 1853	
Asahel L. Brooks,	Jan. 1854	March, 1856	
Benjamin L. Swan,	May, 1856	Oct. 1858	
Alexander R. Thompson,	Mar. 1859	March, 1859	

Original members, 117, dismissed from the First Church. Religious services were held temporarily in the High School House, till November, 1830, when their house of worship was opened. The church became consociated Oct., 1830. In Oct., 1853, 78 members were dismissed by their own request, to form a Presbyterian Church, of which Dr. Hewit became pastor.

MINISTERS RAISED UP.—Philo Canfield, John R. Freeman, Charles T. Prentice, Willis Lord, D. D., George I. Wood, Talmon C. Perry, Samuel W. Phelps, Nathaniel Hewit (Rom. Cath.)

THE CHURCH IN CANAAN, ORG. MARCH. 1741.

Elisha Webster,	Oct. 1740	Oct. 1752	
Daniel Farrand,*	Aug. 1752		March, 1803
Charles Prentice,†	Sept. 1804		May, 1838
Edward B. Emerson,	April, 1841	May, 1843	
Harley Goodwin,	Nov. 1845	1854	Jan. 1855
Isaac De Voe,	1855	1856	
Henry Snyder,	May, 1858	April, 1860	

This Church and Society included North Canaan, till a division was effected in December, 1769. About that time the house of worship was moved nearly a mile from the old site. It was occupied till 1804, when the present house was built, which has been twice repaired; the last time in 1859. This church has enjoyed repeated revivals, adding, in six different years, from twenty-one to fifty-two members, and less numbers in several other years. In 1858, the Consociation formed a church at Falls Village of some of its members who had been refused a dismission, whereupon this church felt so aggrieved that it left the Consociation.

MINISTERS RAISED Up.—Charles T. Prentice, Cyrus Prindle, Cyrus G. Prindle, Robert Campbell, Lyman Prindle.

*Sp. An. 1. 490. Allen. Litchfield Centennial, 88. † Allen, Litchfield Centen. 121.

The First Church in Canterbury, Org. June 13, 1711.

MINISTERS.	SETTLED.	DISMISSED.	DIED.
Samuel Estabrook,	June, 1711	June, 1727	
John Wadsworth,	Sept. 1729	May, 1741	June, 1766
James Cogswell,*	Dec. 1744	Nov. 1771	Jan. 1807
Nathaniel Niles.			
Ephraim Judson.			
Samuel Hopkins,			
Job Swift,			
Solomon Morgan, †	Sept. 1783	Mar. 1797	Sept. 1804
Daniel C. Banks.			
Thaddeus Fairbanks.			
George Leonard,	Feb. 1808	Aug. 1809	June, 1834
Asa Meech,	Oct. 1812	May, 1822	Feb. 1849
Thomas J. Murdock,‡	Nov. 1812	Dec. 1826	
James R. Wheelock,	Dec. 1827	April, 1829	Nov. 1841
Dennis Platt,	May, 1830	Jan. 1833	
Otis C. Whiton,	June, 1833	" 1837	
Charles J. Warren,§	Sept. 1837	April, 1840	
Walter Clarke,	May, 1842	May, 1845	
Alanson Alvond,	May, 1845–6		
Robert C. Learned,	Dec 1847	Nov. 1858	
Charles P. Grosvenor,	Mar. 1859		

This church was constituted with seven male members, including the pastor, who had preached there some years previous. Mr. Estabrook had sons who were pastors in Mansfield and Willington. Mr. Wadsworth is said to have died in the pulpit. Dr. Cogswell was 32 years pastor in Scotland, Conn., after leaving Canterbury. Mr. Morgan, from Nazareth Church, Volentown, went to North Canaan. Mr. Meech, first a pastor in North Bridgewater, Mass., went to Hull, in Canada, and was in the ministry nearly fifty years. The more zealous of the church were not pleased with Dr. Cogswell, and the church was rent asunder at the time of his ordination, and a part, claiming to be the majority, continued from this time for many years a separate organization. *Cong. Quarterly*, *Oct.* 1859, 352–7.

MINISTERS RAISED UP.—Hobart Estabrook, Ebenezer Fitch, Samuel Phinney (Ep.), Moses Bradford, Ebenezer Bradford, Amzi Lewis, William Bradford, John Cleaveland, Ebenezer Cleaveland, Daniel Adams, Nathan Waldo, Jr.‖ Parker Adams (Ep.), John Bacon,¶ John H. Stevens,** E. R. Johnson, Luther Clark, Daniel C. Frost, Asa F. Clark, Cornelius Adams, John Hough, J. S. Pattengill, —— Pattengill.

*Sp An. 1, 445. Allen. †Sp. An. 2. 526. Allen, ‡ Sp. An. 2. 356. § Mendon Assoc. 182. ‖ Mendon. Assoc. 275. ¶ Sp. An. 1. 598. ** Sp. An, 1. 686. Allen.

The North Church in Canterbury, Separated Dec. 1744.*

MINISTERS.	SETTLED.	DISMISSED.	DIED.
Solomon Payne,	Sept 1746		Oct. 1754
Joseph Marshall,	April, 1759	Aug. 1768	Feb. 1813
William Bradford,			Mar. 1808

The opponents of Dr. Cogswell at his settlement over the first church, became the first Separate church in Connecticut. They claimed to be the majority, retained the records and communion service, and always professed themselves the original church. About 1782, this church was re-organized, and its house of worship, which stood a little west of " The Green," was removed and set up in the north part of the town, where it stood till about 1853. The church, under its latter organization, was known as the church in the North Society, and was received into the communion of the regular Congregational churches. It had some other preachers, whose names are not at hand ; but it became virtually extinct before 1831.

* See Canterbury Separate Church, p. 253.

THE CHURCH IN CANTON CENTER, ORG. MAY, 1750.

Evander Morrison,	May, 1750	April, 1751	
Gideon Mills,	1759		1772
Seth Sage,	1774	1778	
*Abraham Fowler,**	1780	1783	1815
Edmund Mills,†	1783	1784	
Jeremiah Hallock,‡	Oct. 1785		June, 1826
Jairus Burt,	Dec. 1826		Jan. 1857
Warren C. Fiske,	Feb. 1858		

The first meeting house, built in 1763, was occupied fifty-one years. A second was then erected, which has been remodeled, and is now in use. After the dismission of Rev. Mr. Sage, the church was in a broken state—the records of the church were lost—there was not even a list of the church members to be found. Soon after Mr. Mills commenced his labors, a revival of religion commenced, and progressed with great power, and many were converted. It continued for nearly two years. Before this revival, the church had tried to exist under what was called the "Half-way Covenant System." But after the revival commenced, they voted to abandon that, and adopted a covenant purely orthodox, and requiring credible evidence of personal piety as requisite for admission to church membership. In 1798, there was a powerful work of the Holy Spirit in this place, and many were added to the church ; also in 1821, 1827, 1831, and 1858.

MINISTERS RAISED UP.—Hector Humphrey, Chester Humphrey, Sidney Mills, Levinette Spencer, Luther H. Barber.

* Sp. An. 2. 230. † Sp. An. 1. 696. ‡ Sp. An. 2. 229. Allen. Memoir, by Rev. Cyrus Yale. Litchfield Centen, 114.

THE CHURCH IN CENTERBROOK, IN ESSEX (PANTAPANG), ORG. 1725.

MINISTERS.	SETTLED.	DISMISSED.	DIED.
Abraham Nott,*	Nov. 1725		Jan. 1756
Stephen Holmes,	Nov. 1757		Sept. 1773
Benjamin Dunning,	May 1775		May. 1785
Richard Ely,†	Jan. 1786		Aug. 1814
Aaron Hovey,	Sept. 1804		Sept. 1843
Joseph D. Hull,	Jan. 1844	Oct. 1848	
John H. Pettingill,	April, 1849	Oct. 1852	
Joseph W. Sessions,	Dec. 1852	April, 1854	
Elijah D. Murphy,	Oct. 1854	Dec. 1855	
Henry K. Hoisington,	April, 1857		May, 1858
John G. Baird,	June, 1859		

The Society was incorporated as the Second Ecclesiastical Society of Saybrook in 1722, and then included the present towns of Saybrook, Essex and Chester. The early records were lost about 1756, by the burning of the house where they were kept. Mr. Ely received to the church 104 ; Mr. Hovey 403. There were revivals in 1791-2, and in several different years since, adding 90, 71, 50, 38, 22, 20, in a year. In 1834, 42 were dismissed to form the church in Deep River. In 1852, 62 were dismissed to form a church in Essex. Besides these offshoots, five churches of other denominations have been formed within the original bounds of the Society. The present is the second house of worship, built in 1789, and remodeled in 1839.

MINISTERS RAISED UP.—Samuel Nott, D. D., Edward Bull, Horace S. Pratt, Nathaniel A. Pratt, Handel G. Nott, (Bap.,) Aaron Snow, Augustus Pratt, Richard B. Bull.

* Allen. † Allen.

THE CHURCH IN CENTRAL VILLAGE (PLAINFIELD,) ORG. APRIL 15, 1846.

Jared O. Knapp,	Sept. 1846	Nov. 1850
Nathaniel A. Hyde,	Nov. 1852	March, 1853
James Bates,	Jan. 1853	July, 1855
Wm. Elliott Bassett,	Oct. 1856	April, 1859
George Hall,	Nov. 1859	

This church was organized with forty-six members, in the North part of the township, as the old church in Plainfield was too remote for the people to attend worship in it. One hundred and nine members have since been added. The present number is one hundred and five. There have been two or three seasons of marked religious interest.

THE CHURCH IN CHAPLAIN, ORG. MAY 31, 1810.

David Avery,	June, 1810	1817	Sept. 1818

MINISTERS.	SETTLED.	DISMISSED.	DIED.
Jared Andrus,	Dec. 1820	May, 1830	Nov. 1832
Lent S. Hough,	Aug. 1831	Dec. 1836	
Erastus Dickinson,	Oct. 1837	Jan. 1849	
Merrick Knight,	May, 1850	Dec. 1852	
John R. Freeman,	April, 1853	May, 1855	
Joseph W. Backus,	Jan. 1856	Dec. 1857	
Francis Williams,	Feb. 1858		

Benjamin Chaplin, Esq, a member of the church in South Mansfield, offered a certain amount of property, as a ministerial fund, for a new church and society, to be composed of portions of Mansfield, Ashford, Hampton, and Windham, provided such a church should be formed, and the gospel be preached at or near a given spot, within a limited time. The conditions prescribed by Mr. Chaplin were complied with, and thus the church originated. After a time the town was named Chaplin in honor of their benefactor. The church has always been self-supporting, and has enjoyed a good degree of prosperity, having been blessed with repeated revivals.

* History Mendon Assoc., p. 124.

THE CHURCH IN CHESHIRE, ORG. DEC. 9TH, 1724.

Samuel Hall,*	Dec. 1724		Feb. 1776
John Foot,†	Mar. 1767		Aug. 1813
Humphrey H. Perrine,	June, 1813	April, 1816	
Jeremiah Atwater, D. D.,‡	April, 1816	July, 1817	July, 1858
M. Kellogg,	Nov. 1818	Nov. 1819	
Roger Hitchcock,	Sept. 1820		Jan. 1823
Luke Wood,	Dec. 1824	1826	
Joseph Whiting,	Oct. 1827	Dec. 1836	
Erastus Colton,	Jan. 1838	July, 1843	
Daniel March,	April, 1845	Nov. 1848	
Daniel S. Rodman,	Oct. 1849	Dec. 1854	
C. W. Clapp	May, 1855	May, 1857	
David Root,	Oct. 1857	April, 1859	
J. S. C. Abbott,	April, 1860		

Cheshire was originally a part of Wallingford. The first settlement took place in 1719. The first meeting house was built in 1724 ; the second in 1738, on the public Green ; the present one in 1826. Mr. Hall received to the church 670, baptized 2013, buried 626; Mr. Foot, received into the church 603, baptized 1767, buried 1109 ; Mr. Whiting received into the church 241, baptized 165 ; Mr. Colton received into the church 133, baptized 61. Mr. Hitchcock had been a deacon of the church, and stipulated that one-fifth of his salary of $500 should be reserved by the Society annually and put at interest for the future support of the ministry. He was taken sick one year after his settlement, and was never afterwards able to preach. Calls

47

were extended (not accepted) to Revs. John Marsh, in 1817, Cornelius Tut-hill, in 1818, Handel Nott, in 1826, Judson A. Root, in 1827, Dwight M. Seward, in 1842. There was a continuous revival under Mr. Whiting's ministry. Extensive revivals also in 1838 and 1858, which added 88 and 104 to the church.

MINISTERS RAISED UP.—Reuben Moss, Reuben Hitchcock, Roger Hitch-cock, Sherlock Bristol, Asahel A. Stevens, Abraham Beach, D. D. § (Ep.)

* Sp. An. 287. Allen.   † Allen.   ‡ Cong. Year Book, 1859, p. 118.   § Allen.

THE CHURCH IN CHESTER, ORG. SEPT. 1742.

MINISTERS.	SETTLED.	DISMISSED.	DIED.
Jared Harrison,	Sept. 1742		1751
Simeon Stoddard,	Oct. 1759		Oct. 1765
Elijah Mason,	May, 1767		Feb. 1770
Robert Silliman,	Jan. 1772		April, 1781
Samuel Mills,	Oct. 1786		Feb. 1814
Nehemiah B. Beardsley,	Jan. 1816	Feb. 1822	
William Case,	Sept. 1824	Mar. 1835	1857 .
Samuel T. Mills,	July, 1835	April, 1838	1853
Edward Peterson,	Sept. 1838	Oct. 1839	1856
Amos S. Chesebrough,	Dec. 1841	Jan. 1853	
Edgar J. Doolittle,	April, 1853	April, 1859	
William S. Wright,	June, 1859		

Chester Parish, formerly called Patequonck, was set off from Petapaug, a parish of Saybrook in 1740. The church, though small and weak in its be-ginning, has (Jan. 1859) a membership of one hundred and fifty, a good church edifice erected in 1846, and a parsonage built in 1854. Its ministry has generally been devoted, able and efficient; it has enjoyed occasional re-freshings from on high by which it has been enlarged both in number and in graces.—*Ev. Mag.* 5, 109.

MINISTERS RAISED UP.—Jonathan Silliman, Samuel T. Mills, William Ely, John Mitchell, William Mitchell, William Baldwin.

The Church in Chesterfield, (in Montville,) Org. May 27, 1824.

Nathaniel Miner,	Oct. 1826	July, 1829

The Society of Chesterfield lies in the towns of Lyme, Salem and Montville. "Soon after 1758, the Chesterfield people made an attempt to found a Con-gregational Church." It cannot now be determined when the society was constituted; it took the designation of "The Ecclesiastical Presbyterian Es-tablishment of Chesterfield Society." Land for the site of a meeting-house, and for a burial ground adjoining, was given to the society by Jonathan Lat-timer, in 1773, at which time it is probable the meeting-house was built and opened for service. Whether there was a church regularly constituted, and connected with this society at so early a date, is now a matter of great uncertainty. Rev. David Austin, Dr. Lyman, and the ministers of Montville occasionally preached here; but the pulpit was mostly occupied by Methodists and Baptists. The old meeting-house being in a shattered condition and hardly fit for public worship, in 1824 the people resolved to take it down, and erect a new one about the time of the organization of the church. Mr. Miner was dismissed solely because of the inability of the people to raise his salary. The church has never been formally disbanded, but is virtually extinct. It was aided part of the time, between 1816 and 1833, by the Home Missionary Society.—*Rel. Intel.* 16, 280.

THE CHURCH IN CLINTON, ORG. 1667.

MINISTERS.	SETTLED.	DISMISSED.	DIED.
John Woodbridge,*	1667	1679	1690
Abraham Pierson,†	1694		Mar. 1707
Jared Elliot,‡	Oct. 1709		April, 1763
Eliphalet Huntington,	Jan. 1764		Feb. 1777
Achilles Mansfield,‖	Jan. 1779		July, 1814
Hart Talcott,¶	June, 1817	Jan. 1824	Mar. 1836
Peter Crocker,	1826	1830	
Luke Wood,	Oct. 1831	Mar. 1834	Aug. 1851
Lewis Foster,	Dec. 1834		Oct. 1839
Orlo D. Hine,	April, 1841	Oct. 1842	
Enoch S. Huntington,	May, 1843	Mar. 1850	
James D. Moore,	July, 1850		

"Approbation and encouragement" to organize the church were given by the "General Assembly" in Hartford, in October, 1667, upon petition of Rev. John Woodbridge and others. The Rev. Abraham Pierson, second pastor of this church was the first Rector of Yale College, and for several years instructed the students in his house in Killingworth, now Clinton. The church in Killingworth that *now* is, branched from this church early in the last century.

* Allen. † Sp. An. 1, 174. Allen. ‡ Sp. An. 1, 176, 270. Allen. ‖ Sp. An. 2, 321. Allen. ¶ Litchfield Centen. 119.

THE CHURCH IN COLEBROOK, ORG. 1795.

	SETTLED.	DISMISSED.	DIED.
Jonathan Edwards, D. D.,*	Dec. 1795	1799	Aug. 1801
Chauncey Lee, D. D.,†	Feb. 1800	Jan. 1828	Nov. 1842
Azariah Clark,	Mar. 1830		Oct. 1832
Edward R. Tyler,‡	Mar. 1833	June, 1836	Sept. 1848
Alfred E. Ives,	Sept. 1838	May, 1848	
Archibald Geikie,	1854		

The date of the first settlement of Colebrook is 1762; the date of the incorporation of the town is 1779. The people constantly assembled on the sabbath, and as far as they had opportunity and means, had preaching, before the church was formed. In the summer of 1783, God was pleased to visit them with the special influences of the Holy Spirit; also in 1799 they shared in the blessing which came down so copiously upon all the churches in the state, and twenty-six souls were added to their number. The church enjoyed seasons of refreshing in 1806, in 1813, and most extensively in 1815, when more than one hundred were added to their fellowship; also in 1858. Many circumstances, however, had tended to weaken the church, especially in later years, when the irregularity of supply, and the absence of a settled pastor, loosened its hold upon the people, and engendered an indifference to gospel ordinances.

MINISTERS RAISED UP.—Chauncey G. Lee, Charles Rockwell, Henry Cowles, John P. Cowles, Joel Grant, William H. Gilbert, Rufus Babcock, D. D. (Bapt.)

* Sp. An. 1, 653 Allen. Litchfield Centen. 93. † Sp. An. 2. 288, Allen. ‡ New Englander, 6, 603.

THE CHURCH IN COLCHESTER, ORG. DECEMBER 20, 1703.

MINISTERS.	SETTLED.	DISMISSED.	DIED.
John Bulkley,*	Dec. 1703		June, 1731
Ephraim Little,†	Sept. 1732		June, 1787
Salmon Cone,‡	Feb. 1792	Aug. 1830	Mar. 1834
Lyman Strong,	Aug. 1830	June, 1835	
Joel R. Arnold,	June, 1836	July, 1849	
Erastus Dickinson,	Oct. 1851	Sept. 1855	
Lucius Curtis,	May, 1856		

In a paper submitted by the church to Mr. Cone for his assent, as a condition of his settlement, it is stated that the half-way covenant, (so called,) had been a standing regulation of the church from the time of its organization, but during his ministry, it went out of use, without, it would appear, any formal action of the church on the subject. The following anecdote is given on the authority of Mr. Cone: While the society was holding their meeting to vote on the question of his settlement, and the members of the church were assembled by themselves in *one of the pews,* to act on the same question, a member of the society, casting his eyes toward the little company, enquired whether the same number of persons could not be picked from among them, equal in all respects to those church members? A venerable member of the society by the name of Wright made the laconic reply, "You need not pick." To so low a state was the church reduced in point of numbers and standing. Between the time of Mr. Little's death, and Mr. Cone's ordination, the pulpit was supplied by no less than fifteen candidates. There were three revivals during Mr. Cone's ministry, the most considerable of which was in the winter of 1823-24. There were considerable additions to the church during the ministry of Mr. Strong, but the largest number received into the church in any one year, was in 1839, during the ministry of Mr. Arnold. There have been three meeting-houses built by this society, the second of which was finished in 1771, at which time it was one of the finest in the state. It stood just seventy years, and then gave place to the present structure, much to the displeasure of some of the old inhabitants.

MINISTERS RAISED UP.—Noah Welles, D. D., Jeremiah Day, Thomas Niles, James Treadway, Eliphalet Gillett, D. D., Jared Reid, Hubbel Loomis, Calvin Foote, William Henry Foote, D. D., Joel W. Newton, Alfred Newton, Israel T. Otis, Orrin Otis, Ezra Hall Gillett, Dillon Williams, David Trumbull, James T. Hyde, Hobart M. Bartlett, Guy B. Day, Eleazer Avery.

*Sp. An. 1, 53, 235. †Allen. ‡Sp. An. 2. 204.

THE CHURCH IN COLLINSVILLE, ORG. JUNE 25, 1832.

MINISTERS,	SETTLED.	DISMISSED.	DIED.
H. N. Brinsmade,	1832	1835	
Stephen Mason,	1835	1836	
C. C. Vanarsdalen,	1836	1838	
F. A. Barton,	Oct. 1838	May, 1843	
Charles B. McLean,	Feb. 1844		

This church has grown up in the midst of a thriving business community, distinguished for enterprize, prosperity, and the high regard paid to education, for which they are largely indebted to the proprietor of the manufacturing establishment, from whom the village is named.

THE CHURCH IN COLUMBIA, (FORMERLY LEBANON CRANK,) ORG. 1720.

Samuel Smith,	1720	Dec. 1724	1725
William Gager,*	May, 1725	Sept. 1734	May, 1739
Eleazer Wheelock, D. D,†	June, 1735	1770	April, 1779
Thomas Brockway,‡	June, 1772		July, 1807
Thomas Rich,	Mar. 1811	June, 1817	Sept. 1836
William Burton,	Feb. 1818	June, 1819	
David Dickinson,	Jan. 1820	July, 1837	Jan. 1857
Charles B. Kittredge,	Mar. 1839	Feb. 1841	
James W. Woodward,	Mar. 1842	Oct. 1848	
Frederick D. Avery,	June, 1850		

This church was the first of four successive offshoots from the first church in Lebanon. The Ecclesiastical society was constituted in 1716, and known as the second society in Lebanon, or Lebanon-Crank, until 1804, when Columbia became a distinct town. Dr. Wheelock began his ministry just at the commencement of the "Great Awakening," and he became an earnest and efficient co-laborer with President Edwards. His own people shared largely in the blessing which everywhere attended his labors. At one time, he said he "had charity to address the body of his own people as Christians."

The success of his labors outside of his own field is exemplified by the fact, that being called to organize a church remote from his place of residence, it was found, on personal examination, that *all* who then united in church covenant referred to his preaching and efforts as the means of their conversion. While he brought upon himself the severe censure of some good men because he felt at liberty to reach over his parish lines in his labors, he escaped not, on the other hand, the denunciations of the Separatists of that day. In 1755 Dr. Wheelock established " Moor's Indian Charity School," which, after a prosperous growth of fifteen years. was transferred, against the earnest remonstrances of his people, to Hanover, New Hampshire, and there it became the foundation of Dartmouth College, Dr. Wheelock being its first President. His immediate successor, Rev. Thomas Brockway, in the troublous times of war, showed himself not only the faithful, devoted pastor, but the patriotic citizen, offering to relinquish £15 a year of his salary, during the struggle, and £10 until the continental debt should be paid. But *this* sacrifice, in the *security* of his *home*, was not enough ; no sooner did the news of the burning of New London reach the place, than "he started off with his long gun, and deacons and parishioners, to assist in doing battle with the enemy."

During Mr. Brockway's ministry, the church and people were blessed with two revival seasons,—in 1781 and in 1801, as the fruits of which, sixty-five were added to the church. The subsequent periods of special religious interest have been, in 1816, when fifty were gathered into the church ; in 1821, 1823, 1825 and 1831, adding one hundred ; in 1841, seventeen ; in 1854 and 1858, forty-three. The first meeting-house was completed in 1727, the second in 1748, the third in 1832.—*Rel. Intel.* 16, 126. *Ev. Mag.* 3. 368.

MINISTERS RAISED UP.—John Smalley, D. D., John Wheelock, Samson Occum §, Daniel Crocker, Elijah Parish, D. D., Walter Harris, D. D.||, Ariel Parish, Ezra Woodworth, Joel West, Bezaleel Pinneo, Diodate Brockway, Alfred Wright, James D. Chapman, Daniel Hunt, Amasa Dewey, Charles Little.

* Sp. An. 1, 180. †Sp. An. 1, 397. Allen. ‡ Sp. An. 1, 605. Allen. § Sp. An. 3, 192.
Rel. Intel. 7, 380, 393. || Mendon As. 231.

THE CHURCH IN CORNWALL, ORG. 1740.

MINISTERS.	SETTLED.	DISMISSED.	DIED.
Solomon Palmer,	Aug. 1741	1754	
Hezekiah Gold, Jr.,	Aug. 1755		1790
Hercules Weston,	June, 1792	Nov. 1803	1811
Timothy Stone,*	Nov. 1803	May, 1827	April, 1852
William Andrews,†	July, 1827		Jan. 1838
Nathaniel M. Urmston,	June, 1838	May, 1840	
Hiram Day,	Feb. 1844	Sept. 1848	
Ralph Smith,	Sept. 1851	1855	
Ira Pettibone,	Sept. 1854	Sept. 1857	
Stephen Fenn,	May, 1859		

The organization of this church was at the same time and place of that of the town. Whole number of families at the time, twenty-five. The first vote, passed at this first town meeting, after the election of town officers, was "to provide for the preaching of the gospel among them." "Mr. Palmer continued with them in peace until March, 1754, when, on the sabbath, to the great surprise of the people, he declared himself an Episcopalian. He soon after went to England and obtained orders." There were three revivals somewhat extensive, during the ministry of Mr. Stone, by whom, over two hundred were received into the church by profession. During the ministry also of Mr. Andrews, through the blessing of God on his labors, there were sixty or more added to the church. There were some indications of the divine presence and blessing during the labors of most, if not all those worthy men who have fulfilled their work among this church and people.

During the ministry of Mr. Stone, the Foreign Mission School was established here, for the education of heathen youth, of different nations and tribes, to prepare them to be missionaries of the gospel to their countrymen. It commenced in 1818, and was closed in 1826. Henry Obookiah, from the Sandwich Islands, died and was buried here; seemingly at that time, a dark providence for the cause of missions. See article on Foreign Mission School, p. 160.

MINISTERS RAISED UP.—William Bonney, Cornelius B. Everest, Thomas R. Gold, T. D. P. Stone, Lucius C. Rouse, William Jackson, D. D.,‡ William W. Andrews, Samuel J. Andrews, Ebenezer B. Andrews, E. Warner Andrews.

* Sp. An. 1, 634, Allen. Litchf. Centen. 130. † Sp. An. 2, 237, Litchf. Centen. 120.
‡ Mendon Assoc. 250, Sp. An. 2, 336.

THE FIRST CHURCH IN COVENTRY, (SOUTH,) ORG. 1712.

MINISTERS.	SETTLED.	DISMISSED.	DIED.
Joseph Meacham,*	Oct. 1714		Dec. 1752
Oliver Noble,†	1759	June, 1761	Dec. 1792
Joseph Huntington,‡	June, 1763		Dec. 1794
Abiel Abbot,§	Oct. 1795	April, 1811	Jan. 1859
Chauncey Booth,	Sept. 1815	Mar. 1844	May, 1851
Henry B. Blake,	Jan. 1845	Sept. 1848	
Charles Hyde,	Oct. 1849	June, 1854	
J. R. Arnold,	Dec. 1854		

Of the early history of this church but little is known. The central period of its history furnishes proof that orthodoxy and vital godliness were safer in the keeping of the church, than in that of the ministry. See page 276. In the spring and summer of 1736, the Church was blessed with an interesting revival. But from the year 1736 to the year 1811, it is not known that there was a single revival of religion.

Under the ministry of Mr. Booth, there were added to the church two hundred and ninety-two, mostly the fruits of five revivals ; under Mr. Hyde, forty-nine were added. The ministry of Mr. Booth would seem to have constituted the David-and-Solomon period of the church, in which it saw the days of its greatest prosperity. It is now but a fragment of what it might have been, on account of the loss of a pastor in whom they were happily united ; and of near fifty members, who left to form the "village church" in consequence of a disagreement as to the site of the meeting-house.

MINISTERS RAISED UP.—Enoch Hale,‖ Samuel Buell, D. D.,¶ David Hale.

* Sp. An. 1. 217. Allen. † Sp. An. 1, 602. Allen. ‡ Sp. An. 1, 602. Allen. § Sp. An. 2, 346. ‖ Spr. An. 3, 102. ¶ Spr. An. 2, 572.

THE VILLAGE CHURCH IN (SOUTH) COVENTRY, ORG. JAN. 10, 1849.

MINISTERS.	SETTLED.	DISMISSED.	DIED.
Marvin Root,	1848		
Henry B. Blake,	May, 1850	March 1855	
Louis E. Charpiot, May, 1858	Ord. May, 1859.		

The Society was formed about a year before the Church, and had preaching in a private hall. This Church is a colony from the First Church in Coventry, organized (with fifty members,) to accommodate the inhabitants of that part of the town called "The Village." It has enjoyed several seasons of revival. During the three years after Mr. Blake's dismission, preaching was very irregular and mostly by the students from the Seminary at East Windsor.

THE CHURCH IN CROMWELL, ORG. JAN. 1705.

Joesph Smith,	Jan. 1705		Sept. 1736
Edward Eells,*	Sept. 1738		Oct. 1776
Gershom Bulkley,	June, 1778	July 1808	April, 1832
Joshua L. Williams,†	June, 1809		Dec. 1832
Zebulon Crocker,	May, 1833		Nov. 1847
George A. Bryan,	June 1849	Oct. 1857	
James A. Clark,	" 1858		

Cromwell was formerly the second or North Ecclesiastical Society in Middletown, called "Upper Houses" in Middletown. The Society was incorporated May, 1703. Mr. Smith was born in Concord, Mass., and graduated at Harvard University. Mr. Eells was a son of Rev. Nathaniel Eells of Scituate, Mass., and graduated at Harvard University, in 1733. He published a pamphlet on the "Wallingford Case ;" and had three sons who became clergymen in Eastbury, North Branford, and Barkhamsted.

Mr. Bulkley was born in Wethersfield, and graduated at Yale College in 1670. He died in his former parish, aged 84. Mr. Williams was born in Wethersfield, and graduated at Yale College in 1805.

MINISTERS RAISED UP.—Wm. W. Woodworth, Jairus Wilcox.

* Spr. An. 1, 383. Allen.

THE FIRST CHURCH IN DANBURY, ORG. 1696.

MINISTERS,	SETTLED.	DISMISSED.	DIED.
Seth Shove,*	1696		Oct. 1735
Ebenezer White,†	March 1736	March, 1764	1779
Noadiah Warner,	Feb. 1765	Feb. 1768	
Ebenezer Baldwin,‡	Sept. 1770		Oct. 1776
Ebenezer Bradford,	April, 1777	Nov. 1779	
John Rodgers, D. D.,§	" 1780	Jan. 1782	
Timothy Langdon,	Aug. 1786		Feb. 1801
Israel Ward,	May, 1803		Aug. 1810
William Andrews,‖	June, 1813	May, 1826	Jan. 1838
Anson Rood,	April, 1829	Dec. 1837	
Rollin S. Stone,	Jan. 1838	Feb. 1850	
Samuel G. Coe,	Dec. 1850		

The early records of the Church being lost, if any were ever kept, little is known of its origin.

Mr. White, after officiating acceptably for nearly thirty years, withdrew and formed a separate society under the name of "New Danbury," which finally coalesced with the sect of the Sandemanians, followers of one Robert Sandeman, a Scotchman. This breach is the only one in the history of the Church occasioned by theological controversy. The heretical offshoot has nearly run out, while the original stock is yet firm and vigorous.

The Church has enjoyed several seasons of religious awakening, and most of the additions within the last forty years have been the fruits of revivals. The years 1815, 1824, 1831, 1855, and 1858, were specially years of ingathering. Seventy-five years ago the number of communicants was 63; now it is 300. In 1851, eighteen persons went off harmoniously from the Church and formed a second Church. In the same year, the same number of persons took letters and formed themselves into a Church at Mill Plain.

The Church has worshiped in four successive Church edifices; the last one, a new and commodious structure, being occupied within the last year.

MINISTERS RAISED UP.—Caleb Barnum,¶ James Beebee, Nathaniel Taylor, Ebenezer White, Benjamin Wildman, Noah Benedict, John Langdon, Samuel Cooke, (Ep.) Henry Lobdell,** (f.)

---

* Sp. An. 1, 116. Allen. † Sp. An. 1, 315. ‡ Sp. An. 1, 635. Allen. § Sp. An. 3, 154. ‖ Sp. An. 2, 237. Litchfield Centen. 120. ¶ Mendon Assoc. p. 100. ** Mendon Assoc. p. 332.

THE SECOND CHURCH IN DANBURY, ORG. JULY, 1851.

MINISTERS.	SETTLED.	DISMISSED.	DIED.
William C. Scofield,	July, 1851	April, 1854	
E. S. Huntington,	Sept. 1854	Sept. 1856	
Richard Hooker,	Nov. 1856	April, 1857	
Samuel N. Howell,	Nov. 1857	April, 1820	
David Peck,	June, 1858		

Twenty-five or thirty years ago some members of the First Congregational Church had their attention called to the formation of a colony, for the purpose of extending the influence of religion. Other denominations however sprang up in the vicinity, and supplied for a period the spiritual wants of an increasing population.

About 1850 it was again thought that there was a demand for a Second Congregational Church. Accordingly in May, 1851, sixteen individuals received the consent of the First Church to hold separate religious services, on condition that *they* were to be held responsible "neither for the success nor support" of the enterprise.

The house belonging to the Universalist Society was rented, and divine services commenced June 1st. Such was the encouragement which a gracious Providence afforded, that the brethren resolved, June 17, to proceed to the formation of a Church.

During the subsequent Fall and Winter there was a revival of religion, as the result of which about 15 souls were added to the Church on confession of their faith. Within a year after the commencement of religious services, the Church erected a house of worship at an expense of $2500.

In the early part of 1858 this Church enjoyed another revival, as the fruit of which about 35 persons, most of whom were young men, were added to its membership. A revival also in 1859.

THE CHURCH IN DARIEN, (FORMERLY MIDDLESEX,) ORG. JUNE, 1744.

Moses Mather, D. D.	June, 1744		Sept. 1806
William Fisher,	July, 1807	March, 1819	
John Noyes,	1820?	1823?	
Ebenezer Platt,	Sept. 1825	Aug. 1833	
B. Y. Messenger,	1834	1835	
Ulrie Maynard,	June, 1835	April, 1838	
Ezra D. Kinney,	Aug. 1838	May, 1859	
Jonathan E. Barnes,	Aug. 1860		

The town of Darien formerly belonged to Stamford. This Society was incorporated under the name of Middlesex, which name it retained till Nov. 1858, when it was voted that it should be called *Darien.* There have been frequent revivals in this Church, which have kept it from becoming extinct.

One Sabbath, during the Revolution, the Church was suddenly surrounded by Tories and the British, and forty men, (nearly all who were in Church, including Dr. Mather,) and as many horses, were carried off to Long Island. Many of them never returned.

MINISTERS RAISED UP.—Charles G. Selleck, (h.) Charles Richards. (h.)

THE CHURCH IN DAYVILLE, (IN KILLINGLY,) ORG. MAY, 1849.

MINISTERS.	SETTLED.	DISMISSED.	DIED.
Roswell Whitmore, (c.)	April, 1849	Oct. 1857	
D. C. Frost,			
G. F. R. Bacheller, (c.)			
John D. Potter,			
William W. Belden,	1859		

There was a revival in 1858–9, under the preaching of Mr. Potter. This is one of the manufacturing villages that have sprung up in Connecticut within a few years, which have felt the need of a Church and the ministrations of the gospel for their own convenience.

THE CHURCH IN DEEP RIVER, (IN SAYBROOK,) ORG. APRIL, 1834.

Darius Mead,	May, 1835	Oct. 1837		
Zabdiel R. Ely,	Dec. 1837	May, 1839	Nov. 1839
Frederick W. Chapman,	May, 1839	Oct. 1850		
James A Clark,	Dec. 1850	Nov. 1853		
George W. Connitt,	Dec. 1854	July, 1856		
N. A. Hyde,	1857			
D. Mead,	1858			
Henry Wickes,	Dec. 1858			

The members of the Churches of Saybrook 2d, and Chester, residing in Deep River, feeling that the religious welfare of themselves and their children required the erection of a house of worship, and the organization of a Church and congregation within their limits, adopted measures to carry their desires into effect. The house of worship was completed in December, 1833, and a Congregational Society was formed the same month.

Members in 1834, 68; added by Mr. Mead, 90 ; by Mr. Chapman, 148. During the next two years after Mr. Connitt's dismission, the Church was in a distracted state, and was at length divided, and a Presbyterian Church formed, but the Church was blessed with a revival in which 36 were added.

MINISTER RAISED UP.—Jackson J. Bushnell.

THE CHURCH IN DERBY, ORG. 1677.

MINISTERS.	SETTLED.	DISMISSED.	DIED.
John Bowers,	1677		1688
Mr. Webb,	1638	1700	
John James,	1700		
Joseph Moss,	1706	1731	1732
Daniel Humphreys,*	1733		1787
Martin Tuller,	1783	1796	1813
Amasa Porter,	1797	1805	
Thomas Ruggles,	1809	1812	
Zephaniah Swift,	1813		1848
Lewis D. Howell,	1836	1838	
Hollis Read,	1838	1843	
George Thacher,	1844	1848	
Jesse Guernsey,	1849	1852	
R. P. Stanton,	1853	1856	
C. C. Tiffany,	1857		

The Church has had three houses of worship; the first was destroyed more than one hundred years since, the second gave place to the present, 45 years since, which was refitted very tastefully 15 years ago, and is beautifully situated in a grove.

There have been several revivals of religion, when quite a large number have been received into the church. The most extensive was in 1812, when there was no pastor; nearly 100 were then added; in 1852, 34; and in 1858, 49.

It was the custom, some years since, under the ministry of Mr. Swift, to hold protracted and three-days meetings, when several ministers would assemble and occupy the time in preaching and devotional exercises. These meetings were almost always the occasion of the awakening and conversion of many. The Churches in Birmingham and Ansonia were formed by members from this Church They are in a flourishing condition.

. MINISTERS RAISED UP.—Amos Bassett, D. D., Daniel Tomlinson, Charles Nichols, Isaac Jennings, Daniel S. Dickinson, Archibald Bassett, John L. Tomlinson, Truman Coe, Wales Coe, William E. Bassett.

* Sp. An. 1, 315. Allen.

THE FIRST CHURCH IN DURHAM, ORG. FEB. 11, 1711.

Nathaniel Chauncey,* Feb. 1706, ord. Feb. 1711			Feb. 1756
Elizur Goodrich, D. D.,†	Dec. 1756		Nov. 1797
David Smith, D. D.,	Aug. 1799	Jan. 1832	
Henry Gleason,	Aug. 1832		Sept. 1839
Charles L. Mills,	April, 1841	Sept. 1845	
Merrill Richardson,	Jan. 1847	Jan. 1849	

MINISTERS.	SETTLED.	DISMISSED.	DIED.
L. H. Pease,	Jan. 1849	Jan. 1851	
J B. Cleaveland,	Jan. 1852	1853	
B. S. J. Page,	Oct. 1853	Oct. 1856	
A. C. Baldwin,	Oct. 1857		

The first permanent white settler in Durham removed to that place in 1698. In 1708, the male adult population had increased to thirty-four. In that year they took measures to secure a permanent settled ministry. The town proposed to give Mr. Chauncey a salary of £60 "*in grain at country price,*" also a settlement of £55 "*in grain at country price,*" together with a house, and certain lands which had previously been set apart for the first minister, which he was to hold in his own right; *provided* he continued their pastor during his natural life. Mr. Chauncey accepted their invitation, but was not ordained until February, 1711, after preaching there five years. The ordaining council consisted of Revs. Timothy Woodbridge of Hartford, Noadiah Russell of Middletown, Thomas Ruggles of Guilford, and Samuel Russell of Branford. The following year, the town voted to build a meeting-house 40 feet square. In 1735 larger accommodations being necessary, a second house of worship was commenced and finished in 1737. This house continued just one century. In 1835, the third house was erected on the site of the first. This building was consumed by fire in 1844. The fourth church edifice was located half a mile north of the place where the others had stood, and was dedicated June, 1847. During this year a second church and society were organized, who erected a house of worship on the old site; the dedication sermon by Professor W. C. Fowler, contains much historical matter. Mr. Chauncey, born September 26, 1681, was grandson of Rev. Charles, second President of Harvard College, and son of Rev. Nathaniel, of Windsor, and Hatfield, Mass. He was a member of the first class that graduated at Yale College, 1702. Dr. Goodrich, born at Rocky Hill, October 26, 1734 was, in 1777, a candidate for the Presidency of Yale, in connection with Dr. Stiles. On counting the votes of the Corporation, they were found to be equally divided; whereupon Dr. Goodrich insisted upon his right to vote as a member, and gave the Presidency to Dr. Stiles.

MINISTERS RAISED UP.—William Seward, Elnathan Chauncey, Ichabod Camp, (Ep.) Roger Newton, D. D., Ebenezer Guernsey, Samuel Johnson, Noah Merwin, Lemuel Parsons, Samuel Goodrich, Joseph E. Camp, Noah Coe, Timothy Tuttle, David Marsh Smith, William C. Fowler, Elizur G. Smith, Talcott Bates, Henry B. Camp, Dwight M. Seward, Collins Stone.
* Allen. † Sp. An. 1, 506. Allen.

THE CHURCH IN DURHAM CENTER, ORG. MAY 4, 1847.

James R. Mershon,	April, 1848	April, 1850
George E Hill,	July, 1850	July, 1851
L. H. Pease,	July, 1851	July, 1852

MINISTERS.	SETTLED.	DISMISSED.	DIE D.
R. G. Williams,	Oct. 1853	April, 1855	
Richard Hooker,	Dec. 1857	Dec. 1858	
Irem W. Smith,	Aug. 1858		

On the 16th of November, 1844, the house of worship belonging to the Congregational Church in Durham, took fire and was burned to the ground. In making arrangements for the erection of a new building, the members of the church and society were unable to agree upon a location. After many months spent in unavailing efforts to attain unity of feeling and action, it seemed to the members of the church residing in the south part of the town that their duty clearly directed them to the formation of a new church and society ; accordingly a church was organized by a committee of the Consociation. In 1858, forty-four united with this church, as the result of a revival.—*Prof. Fowler's Dedication Sermon.*

THE CHURCH IN EAST AVON, ORG. MARCH 17, 1819.

Bela Kellogg,*	Nov. 1819	Sept. 1829	April, 1831
Francis H. Case,	Dec. 1830	April, 1840	
Stephen Hubbell,	Dec. 1840	May, 1853	
J. S. Whittlesey,	July, 1853	Oct. 1854	
H. M. Colton,	Feb. 1855	April, 1857	
E. D. Murphy,	April, 1858, inst. June, 1859.		

Some unhappy divisions having existed in the society of Northington, for a number of years, relative to the most convenient place for erecting a new meeting-house, the former one having been consumed by fire in 1817, and the society continuing unable to unite on any place for the erection of a house of worship, in 1818 they erected two, about two and a half miles from each other. The proprietors of this place petitioned the General Assembly in October, 1818, for an act of incorporation, which was granted. The old church declining to give letters of dismission for the organization of a new church, even after the incorporation of the society, the Consociation, being called, judged it best that there should be another formed, and so constituted the petitioners a church. This church, from its commencement, has had a steady and permanent growth; has ever contributed to the various benevolent societies, and has been blessed with several interesting revivals of religion. It has ever been prompt to the day in paying the minister's salary. It has not been destitute altogether of troubles and divisions, yet the blessing of the Lord has been upon it; and during the year 1858 it shared richly in the precious outpouring of the Spirit.

* Allen.

THE CHURCH IN EASTFORD, ORG. SEPT. 23, 1778.

MINISTERS.	SETTLED.	DISMISSED.	DIED.
Andrew Judson,*	Dec. 1778		June, 1808
John Judson,	1807?	1809?	
Hollis Sampson,	Dec. 1809	1815	
John Nichols,	1816	1818	
Reuben Torrey,	May, 1820	April, 1840	
Francis Williams,	Sept. 1841	Nov. 1851	
William M. Birchard,	1853	1854	
Henry Hanmer,	1854	1855	
Sumner Clark,	1856	1857	
Charles Chamberlin,	April, 1858		

Mr. Sampson came from the Methodists; had gifts, but little education. His ministerial character suffered from habits of drinking, till at length he was carried home intoxicated. He made confessions, but it was feared never wholly reformed. His truthfulness was often very seriously questioned. A member commenced discipline with him, whereupon he disciplined the member, and had him excommunicated. On an appeal, the Consociation, without deciding the case, advised both parties to make confession, with which Mr. Sampson complied. He was afterwards dismissed without complaint; but finally silenced by Consociation; after which, he went into Vermont, and preached Universalism many years. Mr. Nichols was unstable, anti-Calvinistic, and led many away from the truth. In the fall of 1818, Dr. Nettleton came and preached here and at Ashford alternately, through the winter, and a most glorious revival was experienced. Almost all the youth, all the choir but one, who were not previously professors, and many of our most substantial men and women were the subjects, and the church was greatly strengthened. There were several revivals during the ministry of Mr. Torrey and Mr. Williams.

MINISTERS RAISED UP.—John Judson, Chester Carpenter.

* Allen.

THE CHURCH IN EAST GLASTENBURY, (FORMERLY EASTBURY,) ORG. 1727.

Ebenezer Wright, (c.)			
Jonathan Hubbard, (c.)			
John Williams, (c.)			
Daniel Blish, (c.)			
William Gager, c.)			
Chiliab Brainard,	Jan. 1736		Jan. 1739
Nehemiah Brainard,	Jan. 1740		Nov. 1742
Isaac Chalker,	Oct. 1744		May, 1765
Samuel Woodbridge,	June, 1766	June, 1768?	1797
James Eells,	Aug. 1769		Jan, 1805
Joseph Strong, Jr.*	April, 1806	1817	1823

MINISTERS.	SETTLED.	DISMISSED.	DIED.
Jacob Allen,	July, 1822	1835	Mar. 1856
Thomas Williams,	1839	1840	
Aaron Snow,	April, 1841		

The society was formed 1731, and a meeting-house was soon built. Rev. N. Brainard was a brother of David Brainard. Mr. Woodbridge lost his reason about a year after his settlement, owing to unremitting study, as he allowed but four hours daily for sleep. After recovering his reason, he preached in Virginia and Georgia, and was a chaplain in the army; at length he located in W. Hartland. Mr. Eells found his salary too small. His property passed into the hands of trustees, of whom it was rented for the nominal sum of £5 per annum. During the last two years of his life, the society provided him with a home, board, clothing, and $50 a year. Some of the votes respecting the matter may interest the curious. Oct. 11, 1803, "Voted that Capt. —— take care of Mr. Eells the ensuing year. Voted that Capt. —— shall procure clothing for Mr. Eells, as shall be necessary, the ensuing year. Nov. 4, 1804, Voted that the committee dispose of Mr. Eells as they shall think best." After his death, March, 1805, "Voted that Deacon G— go among the neighboring priests to see if they will give us assistance. Voted S— C— take care of the priests, Sundays." Mr. Williams has preached in various places in Conn. for short periods; in all, five or six years, during fifty seven years ministry. There have been frequent revivals during the last two pastorates. The society received Home Missionary aid till 1858.

* Allen.

The Church in East Granby, (formerly Turkey Hills,) Org. 1737.

Ebenezer Mills,	1742	1755	1799
Nehemiah Strong,*	Jan. 1761	1767	Aug. 1807
Abel Forward,	Jan. 1773	Jan. 1774	
Aaron J. Booge,	Nov. 1776	Dec. 1785	
Whitfield Cowles,	May, 1794	Nov. 1808	Nov. 1840
John Taylor,	1810?	1815?	
Eber L. Clark,	July, 1816	July, 1820	1857
Erastus Ripley,	1820	1822	
Chester Chapin,	1822	1823	
Ebenezer Holping,	1824	1826	
Stephen Crosby,	Nov. 1826	Jan. 1832	
Daniel Hemenway,	July 1832	June, 1842	
J. Bowen Clarke,	Nov. 1842	Aug. 1845	
Pliny F. Sanborne,	April, 1846	Feb. 1853	
Sidney Bryant,	Oct. 1855	April, 1860	

Rev. Mr. Wolcott was the preacher here in 1737, and during that year the ecclesiastical society was formed, but there are no records of the church previous to 1776. The Rev. Whitfield Cowles became, during his ministry, an open believer in universal salvation, and was silenced Nov. 1808, but his influence for evil long continued.

MINISTERS RAISED UP.—Alexander Gillet, Newton Skinner.

*Sp. An. 1, 481.

THE FIRST CHURCH IN EAST HADDAM, ORG. MAY 3, 1704.

MINISTERS.	SETTLED.	DISMISSED.	DIED.
Stephen Hosmer,	May, 1704		June, 1749
Joseph Fowler,	May, 1751		June, 1771
Elijah Parsons,*	Oct. 1772		Jan. 1827
Isaac Parsons,	Oct. 1816	April, 1856	
Silas W. Robbins,	Oct. 1856		

The town of East Haddam was originally included in the town of Haddam, and the inhabitants on the east side of Connecticut river, previous to the year 1700, went over the river to attend public worship, and to transact town business. The Ecclesiastical Society, formed in 1700, at first embraced the entire town of East Haddam; the church was organized of members detached from the Church in Haddam. Their first house of worship was occupied twenty-three years; the second, sixty-six; their third, built in 1794, at an expense of $4000, having been remodeled and improved, in accordance with the taste of the age, is still a commodious, tasteful and desirable church edifice. Added to the church in the first pastorate, of forty-five years, two hundred and fifty-four; second pastorate, of twenty-one years, one hundred and thirty-two; third pastorate, of forty-four years, one hundred and sixty-two; fourth pastorate, of forty years, four hundred and fifty-two; fifth pastorate, to Jan. 1859, ninety-four. There were eight revivals of religion during the ministry of Mr. Isaac Parsons, and the additions to the church were for the most part, fruits of these revivals; though in every year, with only one or two exceptions, one or more were added by letter or profession.

MINISTERS RAISED UP.—Jedediah Chapman,† Elihu Spencer, D. D.,‡ George Hall, Epaphras Chapman,(f.) Robert D. Gardner, Henry M. Parsons, Stephen Fuller, (f.)

*Sp. An. 1. 607. Allen. †Sp. An. 3. 165. ‡Sp. An. 4. 95.

THE CHURCH IN EAST HAMPTON, IN CHATHAM, ORG. NOV. 30, 1748.

John Norton,*	Nov. 1748		Mar. 1778
Samuel Parsons,	Feb. 1779		Feb. 1791
Joel West,†	Oct. 1792		Oct. 1825
Timothy Stone,‡	June, 1828	Feb. 1832	1852
Samuel J. Curtis,	Nov. 1832	Nov. 1837	

*Allen. †Allen. ‡Sp. An. 1. 634, Allen.

MINISTERS.	SETTLED.	DISMISSED.	DIED.
Rufus Smith,	Sept. 1838	June, 1845	
William Russell,	Oct. 1846	Oct. 1855	
S. H. Pease,	1856	1858	
Henry H. Russell,	Dec. 1859		

The Society was incorporated May, 1746. Mr. Norton was settled in Bernardston, Mass., in 1741, but dismissed in 1748 by reason of disturbances in the French war. In the second French war he went as chaplain in the expedition to Crown Point, and his association, (Hartford South,) agreed to supply his pulpit in his absence, from October 12, 1755, to the next February. Mr. Stone first studied the art of painting under the celebrated John Trumbull ; and afterwards studied theology under Dr. Dwight.

The old house of worship was torn down in 1854, having stood nearly 100 years, and a new one was erected on the same site.

* Allen. † Allen. ‡ Sp. An. 1. 634. Allen.

The Church in East Hartford, Org. 1695.

Samuel Woodbridge,*	1705		1746
Eliphalet Williams, D. D.†	1748		June, 1803
Andrew Yates, D. D.	1801	1813	1844
Joy H. Fairchild,	1816	1827	Feb. 1859
Asa Mead,	1830		1831
Samuel Spring, D. D.,	1833		

This was known as the Third Church in Hartford, till the town of East Hartford was incorporated in 1784. Dr. Yates left to fill a professorship in Union College. Mr. Mead died after a ministry of 11 months.

Three houses of worship have been built by this congregation since the settlement of the town. The first was a small, low building, and stood about 45 years. The second was built in 1740, and taken down in 1835, having been occupied 95 years. The present house was dedicated January 20, 1836. There have been several marked seasons of revival since the formation of this church ; but as the present pastor's private papers, together with some of the most reliable and valuable records of the church, were destroyed by fire in 1858, no minute and correct account can be given of these. Six "times of refreshing" since 1833 are well remembered, during which nearly 300 have been added to the church.

Ministers Raised Up.—Allen Olcott, Eliphalet Williams, Jr. (Bap.) Chas. O. Reynolds, Frederick H. Pitkin (h.)

*Allen. † Sp. An. 1. 323. Allen.

The Church in East Haven, Org. Oct. 8, 1711.

Jacob Hemingway, 1704, ord. Oct. 1711			Oct. 174
Nicholas Street,*	Oct. 1755		Oct. 1860

MINISTERS.	SETTLED.	DISMISSED.	DIED.
Saul Clark,	Jan. 1808	May, 1817	Dec. 1846
Stephen Dodd,†	Dec. 1817	April, 1847	Feb. 1856
D. W. Havens,	June, 1847		

Mr. Hemingway preached about seven years before the church was formed, the original members having belonged to the church in New Haven. Mr. Street died on the 51st anniversary of his ordination. Added during his ministry, 230; in a revival in 1817, 118; under Mr. Dodd, 181; in 1852, 85, as the fruits of an extensive work of divine grace.

MINISTERS RAISED UP.—Jacob Hemingway, Dana Goodsell, Owen Street.
* Sp. An. 2. 202. Allen. † Allen. Cong. Y.B. 3, 95.

THE CHURCH IN EAST LYME, ORG. 1719.

Ebenezer Mack,			
George Griswold,	1724		1761
George Osborn,	1816	1817	
William Lockwood,	1817		
Beriah Green,	1821	1822	
John R. St. John,	1823	1827	1828
Herman L. Vaill,	1823	1836	
Frederick Gridley,	1836	1856	
Joseph Ayer,	1857		

Mr. Griswold was an active promoter of the great awakening. He labored not only at home, but also in other parishes. The work continued nearly two years, and one hundred white persons, and thirteen Indians became members of the church. *Tracy's Great Awakening*, pp. 150. 156. From 1761, the church was able to have but little preaching, until 1793, when it had become virtually extinct. In that year it was re-organized. Henceforth it maintained public worship constantly, by services of the brethren, in prayers and the reading of sermons, and by occasional preaching. In 1816, domestic missionaries began their labors in this place; under which the church and congregation increased, until the settlement of Mr. St. John, in 1823. Since that time it has been favored with constant preaching, and with occasional revivals of religion. It is still feeble; but with some aid from the Domestic Missionary Society, it continues, and has a prospect of being perpetuated.

MINISTERS RAISED UP.—George Griswold, Daniel Smith, Samuel Griswold, Seth Lee (Bap.), Jason Lee (Bap.)

THE CHURCH IN EASTON (FORMERLY NORTH FAIRFIELD,) ORG. DEC. 13, 1763.

James Johnson,*	Dec. 1763		Sept. 1810
Henry Sherman,	April, 1813	June, 1815	
Nathaniel Freeman,†	Feb. 1819	April, 1832	June, 1854

MINISTERS.	SETTLED.	DISMISSED.	DIED.
Geo. H. Hulin,	April, 1833	Oct. 1834	
Chas. T. Prentice,	June, 1836	April, 1851	
Martin Dudley,	Dec. 1851		

This church at its organization embraced nine male members, of whom its first pastor was one. After the Council had "owned them" as a consociated church, " the church proceeded to invite Mr. Johnson to take the pastoral care and charge of them." Mr. Johnson accepted the invitation. "The council then proceeded to the ordination." During a part—if not the whole of Mr. Johnson's ministry—the practice of " owning the covenant" prevailed ; 33 being received to full communion—and 87 " owning the covenant," had their children baptized—295 in all. From being a beneficiary of the A. H. M. S., the church has become self-supporting, having a fund of $3,200.

* Allen. † Allen.

THE CHURCH IN EAST PUTNAM, (FORMERLY NORTH KILLINGLY,) ORG. OCT. 1715.

John Fisk,*	Oct. 1715	Aug. 1741	May, 1773
Perley Howe,	1746		Mar. 1753
Aaron Brown,	Jan. 1754		Sept. 1775
Emerson Foster,	" 1788	1779	
Elisha Atkins,†	June, 1784		June, 1839
William Bushnell,	Aug. 1832	Mar. 1835	
Sidney Holman,	Mar. 1836	Apr. 1838	
Henry Robinson,	Nov. 1838	" 1845	
John D. Baldwin,	April, 1846	Sept. 1849	
Norris G. Lippitt, (Meth.)	1850	1851	
Benj. B. Hopkinson,	June, 1851	June, 1855	
Edward F. Brooks,	April, 1856	" 1858	
Hezekiah Ramsdell, (Meth.)	1858		

The church has enjoyed repeated seasons of revival, in which large numbers were received into it. The whole number of members from the beginning is about 750 ; the number of baptisms, about 1600.

MINISTERS RAISED UP.—Perley Howe, Joseph Howe, Manasseh Cutler, D. D., LL. D.,‡ Erastus Larned.

* Allen. † Allen. ‡ Sp. An. 2. 14.

THE FIRST CHURCH IN EAST WINDSOR, ORG. JUNE, 1752.

Thomas Potwine,*	May, 1754		Nov. 1802
Shubael Bartlett,†	Feb. 1804		June, 1854
Samuel J. Andrews,	Oct. 1848	May, 1855	
Frederick Munson,	Sept. 1856		

This church, at its foundation, was the sixth in the ancient town of Windsor. When East Windsor was incorporated as a town in 1768, this church was the third in that town ; when Ellington was set off in 1786, it became the second; and when Windsor became a distinct town, it became the first church in East Windsor. It has been blessed with stability in the pastorate.

In 1827, an addition to the society funds was made, which became available in 1849. They then amounted to $4,000, and were held on the following conditions : " That the Society shall maintain a decent meeting-house for public worship ; that the meeting-house shall be entirely the property of the Society ; that the Society shall not at any time be destitute of an ordained minister more than two years, which minister shall be a learned man of true orthodox principles, according to the sense in which our fathers maintained the same."

MINISTERS RAISED UP.—Henry Bissell, (h.) Sanford Bissell, (h.) Lemuel Bissell, (f.) Eldad Barber, I. N. Tarbox, Thomas S. Potwin, Lemuel S. Potwin.

* Sp. An. 2. 9. Allen. † Sp. An. 2: 192. Allen.

THE CHURCH IN THE THEOLOGICAL INSTITUTE, EAST WINDSOR HILL, ORG. NOV. 18, 1835.

MINISTERS.	SETTLED.	DISMISSED.	DIED.
Bennet Tyler, D. D.*	Nov. 1835		May, 1858

The church was organized for the accommodation of the professors of the Theological Institute, together with their families and the students—the nearest place of worship being about two miles distant. Their worship is conducted in the chapel of the Institute, and some of the families in the immediate neighborhood attend with them. Rev. Asahel Nettleton, D. D., resided near the Seminary, from 1834 to 1844, made donations to its funds, and gave the students familiar lectures on revivals and kindred topics. *See notice of him in Dr. Sprague's Annals, Vol. 2. 542 ; also, Memoir by Dr. Tyler, 1844.*

MINISTER RAISED UP.—Josiah Tyler (f.)

* New Englander, 1859, p. 746.

THE CHURCH IN EAST WOODSTOCK, ORG. 1759.

Abel Stiles,*	1759		July, 1738
Joshua Johnson,	Dec. 1780	Sept. 1790	
Wm. Graves,†	Aug. 1791		Aug. 1813
Samuel Backus,	Jan. 1815	June, 1830	
Ezekiel Rich,	1830	1831	

MINISTERS.	SETTLED.	DISMISSED.	DIED.
Wm. M. Cornell,	1831	1832	
Orson Cowles,	April, 1832	Sept. 1837	
Thos. Boutelle,	Dec. 1837	Mar. 1849	
Jas. A. Clark,	1850		
Michael Burdett,	April, 1852	Jan. 1854	
Jas. A. Roberts,	Mar. 1854	1855	
Edward H. Pratt,	Dec. 1855		

About the year 1759, a part of the First Congregational Church of Woodstock (South), removed from South Woodstock, to the then North Woodstock, comprising the present Societies of East and North Woodstock. It seems hardly probable that this church was ever regularly organized; but taking the original records, and the pastor of the old church, it proceeded without a new organization after the removal. It has been blessed with frequent revival seasons. Some of these occurred in the years 1815, '31, '32, '39, '42, '55, and '58. In 1831, a difficulty concerning the site of the meeting-house, led to the formation—by a part of the church—of a new church in North Woodstock; and this church, which, in some sense, appears to be the original church, removed again, taking once more a new name, and leaving the secession to form anew, at the location of the first removal.

MINISTERS RAISED UP.—Willard Child, D. D., Albert Paine, Charles Walker, D. D.

* Sp. An. 1. 470. Allen. † Sp. An. 2. 10. Allen.

THE CHURCH IN ELLINGTON, ORG. 1730.

John McKinstry,*	1730	1749	Jan. 1753
Nathaniel Huntington,	Oct. 1749		April, 1856
Seth Norton,	1756?		Jan. 1762
John Bliss,	Oct. 1764	Dec. 1780	Feb. 1790
Joshua Leonard,	Sept. 1791	Oct. 1798	
Diodate Brockway,†	Sept. 1799		Jan. 1849
Lavius Hyde,	Nov. 1830	Feb. 1834	
Ezekiel Marsh,	April, 1835	April. 1844	Aug. 1844
Nathaniel H. Eggleston,	Feb. 1845	Mar. 1850	
George I. Wood,	June, 1850	June, 1854	
Thomas K. Fessenden,	Jan. 1855		

The first settlement of Ellington was made in 1720; though the town was not incorporated till 1786. In 1730 there were eleven families in the place, at which time Mr. McKinstry, a native of Scotland, purchased land there; though he was not installed till three years after. Mr. Huntington, born in Windham, died at the age of 31, much beloved. Mr. Norton, born in Farmington, died at the early age of 30.

MINISTERS RAISED UP.—Wm. Andrews, Horace Belknap, Otis Saxton,

(Meth.), J. M. Willey, (Ep), Darius Morris, Roswell Shurtleff, John Ells-worth, Norman Nash, J. Addison Saxton, S. D. Pitkin.

* Sp. An. 1. 357. Allen. † Sp. An. 1. 605. Allen.

THE CHURCH IN ELLSWORTH, IN SHARON, ORG. MARCH, 15, 1802.

MINISTERS,	SETTLED.	DISMISSED.	DIED.
Daniel Parker,	May, 1802	Nov. 1812	1832
Orange Lyman,	Aug. 1813	Sept. 1816	July, 1851
Frederick Gridley,	June, 1820	Mar. 1836	
John W. Beecher,	Dec. 1841	Sept. 1847	Jan. 1858
William W. Baldwin,	1849	1851	
William J. Alger,	Feb. 1852	Dec. 1853	
Porter B. Parry,	1853	Aug. 1857	
Robert D. Gardner,	June, 1858		

A boarding school was established by the Rev. Daniel Parker, which attained to considerable celebrity, and was continued by him for some time after his dismission. Several men who have risen to eminence, are said to have been members of this school. A fund was raised by subscription about the time of the organization of the church, amounting to one thousand pounds (to which was added $2,500 in 1813,) the subscription payable in farmer's produce, or bar iron, at the market price, with provision that it should be loaned on mortgage for double the amount, and in case of any loss, it was to be made good by the society, under the penalty of the income's reverting to the subscribers, or to their heirs, until the conditions are complied with. A similar penalty is annexed to a failure to provide preaching for the term of a year, either by a pastor or candidates for settlement.

MINISTERS RAISED UP.—Gad Smith, (Meth.) Gad Smith, 2d, (Meth.) Edwin Baily, (Bap.) Seymour Landon, (Meth.) Walter Chamberlain, Alvin Somers, Charles Y. Chase, Thomas Beebe, (Bap.) Milo N. Miles, (h.) Elisha Frink, (Meth.)

THE FIRST CHURCH IN ENFIELD, ORG. 1683.

Mr. Welch,			
Nathaniel Collins,*	1699	1724	1856
Peter Raynolds,†	1725		1768
Elam Potter,	1769	1776	
Nehemiah Prudden,‡	1782		1815
Francis L. Robbins,§	1816		1850
Charles A. G. Brigham,	1851	1855	
Abraham L. Bloodgood,	1855		

When Mr. Prudden was settled, the church was in a very divided state. He was a peace-maker, a wise and judicious man, and Calvinistic in his views, and under his ministry the church was built up. Mr. Robbins was a Calvinist ; his preaching was more practical and experimental than his predecessor. Under his ministry there were several revivals ; in 1821 more than 100 were added to the church ; also in 1830 and 1841, large additions, and he died in the midst of a revival. When Mr. Brigham was settled, the church and society were harmonious ; but soon discord and contention sprang up, on account of the sentiments he advanced, which ended in his dismission, and the division of the church, and his settlement over the secession.

For an account of the revival in 1740, and President Edwards' noted Enfield sermon, see Tracy's Great Awak. 276, and Trumbull's Hist. 2. 145.

MINISTERS RAISED UP.—Origen Morrison, James P. Terry, Nehemiah P. Pierce, Joseph Meacham, William Dixon, Calvin Terry.

* Sp. An. 1. 183. Allen. † Sp. An. 1. 180, Allen. ‡ Sp. An. 1. 585. Allen. § Sp. An. 1. 370.

THE NORTH CHURCH IN ENFIELD, ORG. MARCH 7, 1855.

MINISTERS.	SETTLED.	DISMISSED.	DIED.
Charles A. G. Brigham,	Mar. 1855		

This church separated from the First Church in consequence of the dismissal of their pastor, Mr. Brigham, by the Consociation, in disregard of the protest of both the pastor and the church. They did this on grounds of expediency, in view of the divided state, and deep feeling of the church, on account of the extreme Calvinistic views of the pastor advanced in his preaching. A majority of the church took letters of dismission, and organized a new church, leaving a majority of the society, and the remainder of the church to retain their old organization, with all the ecclesiastical property. The house of worship of the new society was built the same year.

THE CHURCH IN ESSEX, ORG. SEPT. 1, 1852.

E. W. Tucker,	Aug. 1852	Aug. 1853	
James A. Gallup,	May, 1854		

The church in Essex is a branch from the church at Center Brook, formed with 52 members ; since added ninety-two. Efforts were immediately made to erect a house of worship, and the society have now, free from debt, a very tasteful and commodious house, built at a cost of $8,000 ; and also a very fine and capacious lecture room. The entire current expenses are raised promptly from the income of pew rents and subscriptions, and about $200 are contributed annually to benevolent objects abroad. Several seasons of spiritual refreshing have been enjoyed, but none of such power as during the winter and spring of 1858. The chief characteristics of the church and society have been from the beginning an entire unity of feeling and action—a self-denying liberality, and a deeply felt dependence on the divine presence and aid to give success to all plans and labors.

THE CHURCH IN EXETER, IN LEBANON, ORG. 1773.

MINISTERS.	SETTLED.	DISMISSED.	DIED.
John Gurley,*	May, 1775		Feb. 1812
John H. Fowler,	Oct. 1813	Mar. 1821	1829
Daniel Waldo,	Sept. 1823	Sept. 1834	
Lyman Strong,	1835	July, 1841	
Stephen Hayes,	July, 1841	April, 1846	
John Avery,	June, 1848		

The church in Exeter is a branch of the church in Goshen. The separation was occasioned principally by the fact that the people could not unite on a position for a church edifice. There have been several revivals since 1809; adding 67 in 1821; 26 in 1845; and 55 since 1848. The first church edifice was erected in 1773; the second in 1844. The church received aid from the Home Missionary Society in former years; but since 1852, it has been self-sustaining.

MINISTERS RAISED UP.—Shubael Bartlett, John Bartlett, Ralph R. Gurley, Flavel Bascom, Hobart Bartlett.

* Sp. An. 2. 192. Allen.

THE FIRST CHURCH IN FAIRFIELD, ORG. 1650.

John Jones,*	1639		1664
Samuel Wakeman,	Sept. 1665		Mar. 1692
Joseph Webb,	Aug. 1694		Sept. 1732
Noah Hobart,†	Feb. 1733		Dec. 1773
Andrew Eliot,‡	June, 1774		Sept. 1805
Heman Humphrey, D. D.,	April, 1807	May, 1817	
Nathaniel Hewit, D. D.,	Jan. 1818	Dec. 1827	
John Hunter,	Dec. 1828	1834	
Lyman Atwater, D. D.,	July, 1835	Sept. 1854	
Willis Lord,	Nov. 1854	1856	
Alexander McLean, Jr.,	Jan. 1857		

Mr Hobart, in consequence of the springing up of Episcopacy around him, undertook the vindication of ordination other than prelatical; whence arose a controversy which continued several years. The opponents of Mr. Hobart were Dr. Johnson, and Messrs. Beach, Wetmore, and Caner, who had swerved from Congregationalism. He had few equals in this country for acuteness and learning. He published two addresses to the members of the Episcopal separation in New England. Mr. Eliot was the son of Rev. Andrew Eliot, of the North Church, Boston, and his son, of the same name, was pastor at New Milford.　Mr Eliot is highly extolled by Dr. Dana in *Sprague's Annals.*　When Gen. Tryon burnt the town of Fairfield in 1779, his house, with a large and choice library, was burnt; the latter was restored by contributions of his friends in Boston.　Hon. Roger M. Sherman left to the society a parsonage valued at $10,000, and $2,500 as a fund to keep it perpetually in repair.　The ministerial fund of the society is also $5,700.

Ministers Raised Up.—Eliphalet Jones,§ Andrew Eliot, Jonathan Rowland, Oliver Dimon, Richard Woodhull, Ebenezer P. Rogers, Benjamin Parsons, Isaac M. Ely, E. P. Humphrey,D. D., John Humphrey,‖

* Allen. †Sp. An. 1. 375. Allen. ‡Sp. An. 1. 420. § Sp. An. 3. 31. ‖Sp. An. 4, 821.

First Church in Fair Haven, (in New Haven,) Org. June 23, 1830.

MINISTERS.	SETTLED.	DISMISSED.	DIED.
John Mitchell,	Dec.　1830	Nov.　1836	
B. L. Swan,	Nov.　1836	June, 1845	
Burdett Hart,	Sept. 1846	Aug.　1860	

On the same day that this church was organized, a commodious house of worship was dedicated.　The number of original members was fifty-three; thirty of whom were from the East Haven church, and twenty-three from the North Church in New Haven; eighteen more were soon after added from the North Church.　This church was founded with no sectarian or partisan intent, nor to carry any points of theological difference : but to meet the actual want of the community for the means and agencies of worship, and to secure here the great ends of religion, the observance of Christian ordinances, and the preaching of the free and blessed gospel of Christ.　Soon after it was formed it was favored with successive revivals.　The year 1848 was also peculiarly distinguished in its history as a season of refreshing from the Lord.　On the 20th day of April, 1854, the new edifice of the First Society was publicly set apart for the uses of divine worship.　It is a large, substantial and attractive church, seating fourteen hundred persons.　It belongs to the society, and its slips are annually rented to defray the current expenses.　Under the first pastorate there were added to the church one hundred and nineteen; under the second, seventy-three; under the third, thus far, three hundred and eighty.　A colony of one hundred and nineteen members from the First Church was organized as the "Second Congregational Church in Fair Haven," on the 31st day of March, 1852.—*Rel. Intel.* 17, 250.

Second Church in Fair Haven, (in East Haven,) Org. March 31, 1852.

Nathaniel J. Burton,	July, 1853	Sept. 1857	
Timothy Dwight,	Sept. 1853	Aug.　1859	

MINISTERS.	SETTLED.	DISMISSED.	DIED.
C. D. Murray, lic.	1860		
Edwin Dimock, lic.	1860		

To furnish needed church accommodations, a house of worship, costing, with organ, $16,000, was erected on the east side of the river, and completed March, 1852. The church was formed with ninety-three members from the First Church, and twenty-six more soon after. In March, 1853, forty-one members were dismissed, to form the Third Church. The revival of 1858 added sixteen.

THE CENTER CHURCH IN FAIR HAVEN, (IN NEW HAVEN,) ORG. MAY 3, 1853.

W. B Lee,	Aug, 1853	Mar. 1860

There were thirty-eight members in this church at the time of its organization, who had taken letters, in regular form, from the Second Congregational Church in Fair Haven. They met in Walworth Hall, on Grand street, until their church edifice was completed and dedicated, Sept. 6th, 1854.

THE CHURCH IN FALLS VILLAGE, (IN CANAAN,) ORG. OCT. 27, 1858.

H. A. Russell,	Oct. 1858	Oct. 1859
John Edgar,	Oct. 1859	

Formed by Consociation with twelve members. Twenty-seven persons were added in the year following. A house of worship has been erected thirty-four feet by forty-eight, at a total cost with the land on which it stands, of $2,400. Expenses and benevolent contributions for the year $902.

THE CHURCH IN FARMINGTON, ORG. OCT. 13, 1652.

Roger Newton,*	1652	1657	June, 1683
Samuel Hooker,†	1661		1697
Samuel Whitman,‡	1706		1751
Timothy Pitkin,§	1752	1785	1811
Allen Olcott,‖	1787	1791	1811
Edward D. Griffin, D. D.¶	June, 1793	1794	
Joseph Washburn,**	1795		1805
Noah Porter, D. D.	1806		

The church in Farmington was constituted with seven male members, including the pastor. The half-way covenant was adopted under Mr. Whitman's ministry, and discontinued after much debate and difficulty under his successor, Mr. Pitkin. The present meeting house was built in 1771, in the best manner, and of the choicest materials—an evidence of which is, that the outside covering, first put on, (including the shingles,) is yet sound and good. The steeple, above the belfry, was raised entire, where it has stood unimpaired, to the present day. The present town, till 1825, when a Methodist church was formed, was one Ecclesiastical Society or Parish, with no house of worship, church or religious teacher, besides the Congregational. Nov. 4, 1840, a historical discourse was delivered before the citizens of Farmington, in commemoration of the original settlement of the ancient town, in 1650, by Noah Porter, Jr., now Professor in Yale College. The discourse, together with valuable historical and biographical notes, was published. There have been revivals of religion in the Congregational church of this town from its first organization to this time ; and more frequently since 1793. *Memoir of Dr. Nettleton*, 140. *Ev. Mag.* 1. 378, 420.

MINISTERS RAISED UP.—Daniel Hooker, Elnathan Whitman, John Hart, Lathrop Thomson, Edward Porter, Giles H. Cowles, D. D., Isaac Porter, Robert Porter, Hezekiah N. Woodruff, Asahel Hooker, Ephraim T. Woodruff, Noah Porter, D. D , Elnathan Gridley (f.), John Richards, D. D.,[††] James Wilcox, Horace Woodruff, George J. Tillotson, William S. Porter, Noah Porter, Jr., D. D., Walter Clarke, D. D., Giles M. Porter, Chauncey D. Cowles, Lewis Bodwell, (h.)

* Sp. An. 1. 37. Allen. † Sp. An. 1. 37. Allen. ‡ Sp. An. 1. 315. Allen. § Sp· An. 1. 347. Allen. ‖ Allen. ¶ Sp. 4. 26. Allen. ** Allen. †† Cong. Quar. 1. vol. 1. Allen.

THE CHURCH IN FRANKLIN, ORG. JAN. 4, 1718.

Henry Willes,*	Oct. 1718		Sept. 1758
John Ellis,†	Sept. 1753	1779	Oct. 1805
Samuel Nott, D. D.‡	Mar. 1782		May, 1852
George Justus Harrison,	Mar. 1849	Oct. 1851	
Jared Reid Avery, Dec. 1851, installed Mar. 1854			

This church was organized with eight members, all males. The Ecclesiastical Society was in existence more than a year before this. Provision for religious worship was made during the winter of 1716-17, in private houses: and the following summer, the people worshiped in a barn. At this time, there was in the neighborhood an old meeting house, in ruins, whose "pulpit, and seats, and canopee" the society agreed to take *at five pounds, ten shillings, money, or as money.* By vote of society, Nov. 22, 1716, the new meeting house was located "at the place commonly known by the name of Arnold's barn, or about 12 rods southward therefrom:" house to be "forty foot long, thirty-five feet wide, and eighteen foot between joints." It was finally left with the carpenter to decide whether the house should "stand at the place where the timber lies, or down at the walnut bush where the path comes up the hill." The meeting-house was *seated* by a committee, according *to age and estate.*

Norwich, West Farms, was constituted the town of Franklin in 1786. A great revival added to the church 100 members in 1741-2 ; one in 1855 added 33. In 1753, there were more than 100 members of the society. The ministry of the first three pastors embraces a period of 136 years, or two years more than the whole period of the church's existence, prior to the death of Dr. Nott. The present house of worship was erected in 1836.

MINISTERS RAISED UP.—David Avery,§ Oliver Ayer, Eliphalet Nott, John Hyde, Eli Hyde, Samuel Nott, Charles Hyde, Lavius Hyde, Elijah Hartshorn, Beaufort Ladd, Stephen T. Nott, Robert P. Stanton, Joseph W. Backus, Alvan Hyde,‖ Asahel Huntington.**

* Sp. An. 1. 299. Allen. † Sp. An. 1. 604. ‡ Sp. An. 2. 190. Allen. § Mendon As. 124. ‖ Sp. An. 2. 300. Allen. ** Allen.

THE CHURCH IN FITCHVILLE, IN BOZRAH, ORG. DEC. 1, 1854.

William Aitchison,	April, 1852	April, 1855	Aug. 1859
W W. Belden,	" 1855	" 1857	
T. D. P. Stone,	" 1857	Jan. 1859	
Joseph A. Saxton,	Jan. 1859		

The house of worship was erected by Asa Fitch, Esq., the owner of the factory and village ; and the ministers have been supported mainly by him, on a liberal salary. After more than two years from the erection of the house, the church was formed.

THE CHURCH IN GILEAD (IN HEBRON,) ORG. (PROBABLY) 1748.

MINISTERS.	SETTLED.	DISMISSED.	DIED.
Samuel Langdon,	1750	1751	
Elijah Lothrop,*	April, 1752		Aug. 1797
Ammi Rogers,	1797 ?	1799 ?	
Nathan Gillet,	Nov 1799	Jan. 1824	July, 1845
Charles Nichols,	Sept. 1825	Oct. 1856	

The Ecclesiastical Society in Gilead was organized May, 1748. The first church edifice was erected in 1749. The occasions of special religious interest during the century were in the years 1824 and 1831. During the revival in 1831, there were 54 persons added to the church. During the early part of the year 1858, a work of grace resulted in upwards of twenty cases of hopeful conversion. A fund established in 1794, by Mr. John Gilbert, now amounts to $4,000.

MINISTERS RAISED UP.—Eleazar C. Hutchinson, D. D., Edwin R. Gilbert, Samuel Post.

* Allen.

THE FIRST CHURCH IN GLASTENBURY, ORG. JULY, 1692.

Timothy Stevens,*	Oct. 1693	April, 1726
Ashbel Woodbridge,†	" 1728	Aug. 1758

MINISTERS.	SETTLED.	DISMISSED.	DIED.
John Eells,	June, 1759		May, 1791
William Brown,‡	May, 1792	Jan. 1797	
William Lockwood,§	Aug. 1797	May, 1804	June, 1828
Prince Hawes,	June, 1807	1820	
Caleb Burge,	Aug. 1821	Nov. 1825	
Samuel A. Riddel,	June, 1827	Feb. 1837	
James Smith,	Dec. 1837	Jan. 1858	
Amos L. Chesebrough,	July, 1858		

Those members of the First Church in Wethersfield who resided on the east side of the Connecticut River, were duly organized into a distinct church July 28, 1692—denominated the *First Church in Glastenbury.* In May, 1731, a new Ecclesiastical Society was incorporated within the limits of Glastenbury, *by the name of Eastbury,* and a church immediately organized, consisting of those members of the First Church whose home was within the bounds of the new society. The First Church was again divided by the organization of the church in *South Glastenbury,* Dec. 22, 1836. *Rel. Intel.* 11. 460.

MINISTERS RAISED UP.—John Bulkley, Samuel Welles, Charles Treat, Jonathan Hubbard, Richard Treat, Samuel Woodbridge, Timothy Woodbridge, William Woodbridge, Anson Hubbard, Albert Hale, Isaac Plummer, James L. Wright, William S. Wright.

* Allen. † Allen. ‡ Sp. An. 1. 657. § Sp. An. 1. 413. Allen.

THE CHURCH IN GOSHEN, ORG. NOV. 1740.

Stephen Heaton,	Nov. 1740	May, 1753	Dec. 1788
Abel Newel,*	Aug. 1755	Jan. 1781	1813
Josiah Sherman,	June, 1783	Feb. 1789	
Asahel Hooker,†	Sept. 1791	June, 1810	April, 1813
Joseph Harvey,	Oct. 1810	Sept. 1825	
Francis H. Case,	Feb. 1826	" 1828	
Grant Powers,‡	Aug. 1829		April, 1841
Lavalette Perrin,	Dec. 1843	Sept. 1857	
Joel F. Bingham,	Jan. 1859	May, 1860	

The lands in Goshen were originally divided, in 1739, into 53 shares—one for the ministry, one for the first settled minister, one for schools, and the other fifty were sold at public vendue. At the first town meeting, in that year, it was voted " that the selectmen shall ascertain the places of holding the meetings for the public worship of God." Mr. Heaton's salary was £100 "settlement," to be paid in labor in two years, and £110 the first year, increasing £10 a year to £170. But he was found not to have much fixedness of opinion on theological subjects, sometimes preaching to please Arminians, and again to please the Orthodox, the consequence of which was, that he lost the confidence of all. Complaint was at length made to the Consociation, *by the town*, against him, of "immoral conduct;" "imprudent conduct unbecoming a minister;" "a great deficiency in ministerial qualifications." Six years were spent in the trial. His confession was ac-accepted as *Christian* satisfaction, and he was dismissed. He died at Goshen, leaving a large estate.

Mr. Sherman (brother of Hon. Roger Sherman, of New Haven,) wore a large white wig, and was very imposing and winning in appearance. He had popular talents, and at first was very acceptable. But alienation arose, in consequence of his avowing, in his preaching, Arminian sentiments. When the leading members of the church who felt aggrieved went to him to talk about it, he took offense, and they complained that he treated them in a very arbitrary way, "overrating human knowledge as essential to conversion." Three brethren, at this time, attended service one Sabbath at a neighboring church, for which they were disciplined; and things grew worse till Mr. Sherman agreed to a dismission,—the town paying him £50. Then the church were in a confused state, and called a council of ministers for advice; which was to annul all votes during Mr. Sherman's ministry.

Messrs. H Bingham and Thurston were ordained missionaries to the Sandwich Islands, at Goshen, Sept. 1819   There have been frequent revivals in the last sixty years,—in six cases adding from 30 to 72 members in a year *Ev. Mag.* 1. 341.   *Rel. Intel,* 7 232 ; 12. 731.

MINISTERS RAISED UP.—Noah Wadhams, Elisha Parmelee, Reuben Parmelee, Darius O. Griswold, Edward W. Hooker, D. D., William Thompson, D D., Orlo Bartholomew, A. T. Norton (h), Luther Hart., Ephraim Lyman, Mark Ives (f.), John F. Norton, Augustus Thompson, Luther H. Beecher, D. D.

* Allen. † Sp. An. 2. 317. Allen. Litchf. Centen. 92. ‡ Allen. Litchf. Centen. 123.

THE CHURCH IN GOSHEN (IN LEBANON,) ORG. NOV. 26, 1729.

MINISTERS.	SETTLED	DISMISSED.	DIED.
Jacob Eliot,*	Nov. 1729		April, 1766
Timothy Stone,†	Oct. 1766	Sept. 1767	May, 1797
Wm. B. Ripley,‡	Nov. 1798		July, 1822
Erastus Ripley,§	Sept. 1823	Feb. 1832	Nov. 1843
Salmon Cone,	1832		Mar. 1834
Israel T. Otis,	June, 1835	Mar. 1844	
Joshua R. Brown,‖	May, 1845	June, 1852	Sept. 1858
Elijah W. Tucker,	Sept. 1853	1858	
Aaron R. Livermore,	Feb. 1860		

This church was formed by a colony of twenty-nine males from the First Church in Lebanon. On the following year, (1730) 56 females were received. About the year 1770, a part of the church was dismissed, for the purpose of forming a church in Exeter Society.

Ministers Raised Up.—Abraham Fowler, Dyar T. Hinkley, Timothy Stone, Orrin Fowler, Salmon McCall.

*Sp. An. 1. 322. †Sp. An. 1. 631. Allen. ‡Allen. §Allen. ‖Cong. Y. B. 6. 119.

The Church in Granby, Org. 1739.

MINISTERS.	SETTLED.	DISMISSED.	DIED.
Eli Colton,	Dec. 1740	Nov. 1742	
David S. Rowland,	Feb. 1745	Aug. 1747	1794
—— *Burr,*	Aug. 1747	Dec. 1748	
Aaron Brown,	Oct. 1750	Dec. 1751	
Joseph Strong,*	Nov. 1752	Nov. 1779	Jan. 1803
Israel Holly,	Oct. 1784	1793	
Isaac Porter,†	June, 1794	Dec. 1832	1844
Charles Bentley,	Aug. 1833	Mar. 1839	
Chauncey D. Rice,	Oct. 1839	July, 1841	
Israel P. Warren,	April, 1842	May, 1845	
James C. Houghton,	June, 1845	April, 1847	
Alfred White,	July, 1847	July, 1848	
Samuel W. Barnum,	April, 1849	April, 1850	
C. F. Page,	Oct. 1850	Mar. 1854	
Wm. H. Gilbert,	July, 1856		

The earliest Ecclesiastical record extant pertaining to this church and society, is dated May, 1739. In the volume which contains it, a part of which is obliterated, the records of the church and society are blended. On the 27th page—the 21st now existing, we find the first distinct notice of the church, as follows :

" Att a meeting of ye Northwest Society of Simsbury on ye last Monday of January, 1746-7. Voted,

1. Yt we chuse yt ye church in this society shall be settled a Congregational church.

2. Voted yt ye Scriptures of ye Old and New Testaments, as they are ye only unering rule of faith and practis to Christians, so they are ye only unering rule of church government and discipline.

3. Yt as we know of no human composition yt comes nearer to ye Scriptures than Cambrig platform in ye substance of it, so we chuse yt ye church in this society, shall take it in ye substance of it under ye scriptures for their rule of church government and discipline.

4. Yt in ye administration of church membours, we judge it necessary yt ye porsons to be admitted, give to ye minister an account of their knoleg in ye fundamental docterings of ye gospel, their faith therein to his satisfaction and acceptance, and yt every such person being free from scandal, and of regular conversation, being propounded to ye church 3 Lords days before admition, may then be admited, by and with ye consent of ye church, provided no valid objection be laid against them.

5. Voted yt we naurtheless are not straited in our charity towards

our neighboring churches yt are settled under Saybrook platform, or those called Presbyterians, but are willing yt any of their members in good standing in their churches shall be admitted to communion in this church as opportunity may present—as also yt we are willing yt our ministers for ye time being shall exchang labours with any of ye ministers of any of s'd churches yt are in good standing, then alway provided yt it be with ye consent of ye church."

The whole number of additions to the church, exclusive of its original founders, is 604.

MINISTERS RAISED UP.—Joel Hayes, Silas Higby, Harvey Hayes, John C. Strong, Joseph D. Strong, Reuben Holcomb, Gordon Hayes, Amasa A. Hayes, James B. Cleaveland.

* Sp. An. 2. 229.   † Allen.

THE CHURCH IN GRASSY HILL, (IN LYME,) ORG. 1755.

MINISTERS.	SETTLED.	DISMISSED.	DIED.
Daniel Miner,	1757		April, 1799
Seth Lee,	Oct. 1817		Oct. 1826
Nathaniel Miner,	Mar. 1827	Mar. 1829	
A. Alden,	May, 1830	Sept. 1831	
Mark Mead,	July, 1833	July, 1836	
—— Warner,	1837	1838	
Oliver Brown,	May, 1839		Feb. 1853
Alpha Miller,	May, 1853		

The original members constituting the Strict Congregational, or Separate Church of Grassy Hill, mostly withdrew from the church of North Lyme, now Hamburg. This church united with the Middlesex Consociation Oct. 1834. Their records were destroyed by fire, with the house of the first minister. It is not known precisely when the church was gathered.

A very interesting revival of religion, which resulted in a very considerable addition to the numbers and strength of the church, commenced in the winter of 1842. There was also one in 1858. In 1847, their house of worship was remodeled. They have during a series of years received $100 from the Home Missionary Society. The whole number of families embraced in the Congregation does not exceed twenty.

MINISTERS RAISED UP.—Noah H. Gillett, Sylvester P. Marvin, Oliver Brown, Jr., George A. Miller.

THE CHURCH IN GREENFIELD, (IN FAIRFIELD,) ORG. MAY 18, 1726.

John Goodsel,	May, 1726	April, 1756	
Seth Pomeroy,*	Jan. 1758 ?		1769

MINISTERS.	SETTLED.	DISMISSED.	DIED.
William M. Tennent,†	June, 1772	Dec. 1781	1810
Timothy Dwight,D. D.,‡	Nov. 1783	1795	Jan. 1817
Samuel Blatchford, D. D.,§	1796	1797	Mar. 1828
David Austin,‖	1797	1798	Feb. 1831
Horace Holly, D. D.,	Sept. 1805	Sept. 1808	1827
William Belden,	Oct. 1812	1821	
Richard V. Dey,	Jan. 1823	1828	1836
Nathaniel Freeman,¶	April, 1833	1840	June, 1854
T. B. Sturges,	June, 1842		

This church has had five houses of worship. Dr. Dwight had a noted classical school at Greenfield. He left to accept the Presidency of Yale College. ✓

MINISTERS RAISED UP.—Aaron Burr, D. D.,** President of New Jersey College, Daniel Banks, —— Pomeroy.

* Allen. † Sp. An. 3, 26. ‡ Sp. An. 2. 152, Allen. § Sp. An. 4, 158. ‖ Sp. An. 2, 195. Allen. ¶ Allen. ** Allen.

THE CHURCH IN GREEN'S FARMS, (IN WESTPORT,) ORG. OCT. 26, 1715.

Daniel Chapman,	Oct. 1715		Nov. 1741
Daniel Buckingham,*	Mar. 1742		May, 1766
Hezekiah Ripley,D. D.,†	Feb. 1767	Aug. 1821	Nov. 1831
Edward W. Hooker,	Aug. 1821	Jan. 1829	
Thomas F. Davies,	Oct. 1829	Aug. 1839	
Dan C. Curtiss,	June, 1840	Jan. 1843	
Giles M. Porter,	Dec. 1844	Mar. 1850	
Charles Bentley,	May, 1850	May, 1858	
R. S. Egleston,	April, 1859		

From the state records, in Hartford, it appears that West Farms, Fairfield, was made a distinct society and parish in May, 1711, and that at their October session, 1714, the General Assembly did allow the inhabitants of West Farms, in Fairfield, to embody themselves into a Church Estate. The original covenant was subscribed by seven persons besides Mr. Chapman. *There was no Confession of Faith distinct from this Covenant*, which as it appears to have been retained, without alteration or addition for ninety-three years, is here given:

" We do, in the humble sense of our deep unworthiness of an acknowledgement in the covenant of divine grace and also of our inability unto the performance of the duties of the holy covenant, through the strength and grace of Christ alone, heartily and sincerely engage and promise, in the presence of God and his people, denying all ungodliness and worldly lusts, to live soberly, righteously and godly in this present world, solemnly devoting ourselves and our seed unto the Lord, to be his people ; avouching Almighty God for our God and portion ; avouching the Lord Jesus Christ for our only Prophet and Teacher, and for our only Priest and Propitiation, and for our only King and Lawgiver ; avouching the Holy Ghost for our Sanctifier ; professing our subjection to the gospel of Christ, and that we will walk together in a conscionable attendance upon all the ordinances of the gospel, and in a member-like communion, helpfulness, and watchfulness according unto Christ."

Members at the close of the first pastorate, eighty; of the second, seventy-five; of the third, one hundred and thirty; added during the fourth, nineteen ; the fifth, one hundred and ten ; the sixth, thirty-one ; the seventh, eighteen; the eighth, seventy-seven. Present number one hundred and thirty.

In 1831, about forty were dismissed to unite in the formation of a church in the village of Westport. The present meeting-house is the fourth which has been erected. . The second was destroyed by the British troops in 1779, when many dwellings, including that of the pastor, were consumed. The third house of worship was lost by accidental conflagration in April, 1852.

MINISTERS RAISED UP.—Samuel Sherwood, Samuel Sturges, William B. Ripley, Daniel C. Banks, Zalmon B. Burr, Enoch F. Burr, William J. Jennings, Edward Allen.

* Sp. An. 1, 648, †Sp. An. 1. 647. Allen.

THE FIRST CHURCH IN GREENWICH, ORG. 1670.

MINISTERS.	SETTLED.	DISMISSED.	DIED.
Jeremiah Peck,	1679	1689	
Abraham Pierson,	1691	1694	
Salmon Treat,	1695	1697	
Joseph Morgan,	1697	1700	
Nathaniel Bowers,	1700		
Ephraim Bostwick,	1730 ?	1746	
Ebenezer Davenport,	1767		1773
Robert Morris,	1785		1794
Platt Buffet,	1794	1796	
—— Simons,	1796		
Abner Benedict,		1800	
Samuel Sturges,	1800	1807	
John Noyes,	1810	1824	
Charles F. Butler,	1824	1835	
Thomas Payne,	May, 1837	Feb. 1842	
S. B. S. Bissell,	Sept. 1842	Sept. 1853	
William A. Hyde,	Sept. 1854		

This church has had four houses of worship. The first existed previous to 1694, as in that year a vote was passed to build a new meeting-house. Two others were successively occupied till 1838, when the present house was erected. For many years previous to 1835, this church was small and feeble, and in a very low state; since then it has been greatly blessed, and sustained. As the fruits of a revival in 1839, thirty-nine were added; in 1843, thirty-two ; in 1855, thirty.

THE SECOND CHURCH IN GREENWICH, ORG. 1705.

MINISTERS.	SETTLED.	DISMISSED.	DIED.
Joseph Morgan,	1705	Oct. 1708	
Richard Sackett,	1717	1727	
Stephen Monson,	May, 1728	1733	
Abraham Todd,	May, 1734	1773	
Jonathan Murdock,*	June, 1774	Mar. 1785	Jan. 1813
Isaac Lewis, D. D.,†	Oct. 1786	1818	Aug. 1840
Isaac Lewis, Jr.‡	Dec. 1818	1828	Sept, 1854
Noah C. Saxton,			
Albert Judson,			
Elam Clark,			
Joel Mann,	Sept. 1830	Aug. 1836	
Noah Coe,	May, 1837	May, 1845	
Frederic G. Clark,			
George Bushnell,			
Ebenezer Mead,			
Joel H. Linsley,	Dec. 1847		

This church is located in the west part of the town of Greenwich, and its separation from the first church appears to have arisen from the jealousy of the proprietors of the town, lest the holding of worship at Horseneck (as the west part was then called,) should injure their interests. The society was weak till after the close of the revolution, at which time tradition says that the society owed £30, and it was admitted that the money was not in the place. Since 1793 there has been a great increase of wealth in this community, so that there are now eleven houses of worship in the town, west of Mianus river, occupied by four denominations. A stone meeting-house, the contract for which was $32,500, was built in 1859. There are few records of the church for the first seventy years. In the revolutionary war, this society suffered severely, being between the British and American lines for about four years, in which there was no law, but robbery and plunder ran riot; the minister parolled by the British, and nearly all the stable inhabitants were compelled to flee; a few that were too poor to remove, remained to be made still poorer or join the enemy. A dread of revivals which grew out of the excesses in the great revival of 1740 has had an extended influence down to the present day; and yet God has favored this church above many in this respect, for since 1816, when the first revival after 1740 occurred, there have been revivals in 1822, in 1828, in 1831, in 1839, in 1843, in 1850, in 1854, in 1858, besides several others which did not bring so many into the church.—*Rel. Intel.*, 13, 188; 16, 620.

The settlement of Rev. Isaac Lewis, D. D., appears to have been one of the events that turned the tide in favor of this church. His long faithful ministry was the means of raising the church from forty-seven members to one hundred and eighty-five. One of his best measures was leading the church to abandon the "half-way covenant," and to admit only professors of piety to the communion, and only the children of such persons to baptism. In

March, 1831, the first "four days" or "protracted meeting" east of Byram river was held in this church, which was attended with a great blessing.

MINISTERS RAISED UP.—Mark Mead, Samuel Howe, Platt Tyler Holley, Ebenezer Mead, Zachariah Mead, (Epis.,) Whitman Peck, John Peck, Isaac Peck. (Epis.,) Enoch Mead.

* Allen. Sp. An. 2. 41. † Allen. Sp. An. 1. 662. ‡ Allen. Sp. An. 1. 667.

THE CHURCH IN GREENEVILLE, (IN NORWICH,) ORG. JAN. 1, 1833.

MINISTERS.	SETTLED.	DISMISSED.	DIED.
Dennis Platt,	Sept. 1832	1833	
John Storrs,	Mar. 1834	April, 1835	1854
Spencer F. Beard,	1835	1837	
Stephen Crosby, (c.)	1837	June, 1838	
Alphonso L. Whitman,	Dec. 1838	Mar. 1846	
Charles P. Bush,	Dec. 1846	Jan. 1856	
R. P. Stanton,	June, 1856		

Soon after the commencement of works for the manufacturing establishments in the village in 1829, a prayer meeting was commenced by brethren of the second church. In 1832, when the inhabitants were multiplied, the prayer meeting was changed to a regular sabbath service, and a Sabbath School was gathered in the autumn, and a minister employed. A meeting house, commenced in 1834, was completed in the spring of 1835. The Sabbath School has here, as elsewhere, proved a nursery of the church. One of its members, Rev. William Aichison who went as a missionary to China has fallen at his post. There have been frequent revivals, and in five several years there have been added from twenty-six to forty-three members.

MINISTER RAISED UP.—William Aichison, (f.)

THE FIRST CHURCH IN GRISWOLD, ORG. NOV. 20, 1720.

Hezekiah Lord,	Nov. 1720		June, 1761
Levi Hart, D. D.,*	Nov. 1762		1808
Horatio Waldo,†	Feb. 1810	Aug. 1828	
Spofford D. Jewett,	Feb. 1830	June, 1836	
William R. Jewett,	Dec. 1836	July, 1843	
Roswell Whitmore,	1844	1846	
Calvin Terry,	Nov. 1846	April, 1851	
Bennett F. Northrop,	July, 1853		

Dr. Hart was a man of eminence, and conducted the studies of some theological students. There were extensive revivals in 1820, and 1831, and more limited revivals in 1852 and 1858.—*Rel. Intel.* 5, 376; 13, 551.

MINISTERS RAISED UP.—Asa Burton, D. D.,‡ Daniel Haskell,§ Punderson

Tyler, Stephen Johnson, (f.) Robert Staunton, James Averill, William Clift, William P. Avery, (h.) Alexander Yerington, William R. Palmer.

* Sp. An. 1. 590. Allen. † Sp. An. 4. 630. ‡ Sp. An 2. 140. § Sp. An. 2. 526.

The Church in Groton, Org. 1705.

MINISTERS.	SETTLED.	DISMISSED.	DIED.
Ephraim Woodbridge,	Nov. 1704	1724	Dec. 1725
John Owen,*	Nov. 1727	1753	June, 1753
Daniel Kirkland,†	Dec. 1755	1758	May, 1773
Jonathan Barber,	Nov. 1758	1768	1783
Aaron Kinne,‡	Oct. 1769	Nov. 1798	1824
Timothy Tuttle,	Aug. 1811	Apr. 1834	
Jared R. Avery,	Oct. 1839	Apr. 1851	
George H. Woodward,	Oct. 1851	Jan. 1856	
Sylvester Hine,	1856		

The church was formed from the church in New London. The records were destroyed, or disappeared, amid the terrible scenes through which the people here were called to pass during the war of the revolution, and the inhuman massacre at the Fort in 1781; they are very meager till within the last fifty years. The first house of worship was located near the center of the town, as at present bounded. A house of worship was subsequently erected three-fourths of a mile east of the present village of Groton, and was occupied for a considerable time previous to the Revolution, and after, till the present house in Groton village was dedicated in 1834.

Ministers Raised Up.—Elisha Fish,§ Solomon Morgan, Colby C. Mitchell, (f.) Joseph Morgan,‖ Jared R. Avery, Frederick D. Avery.

* Sp. An. 1. 235. Allen. Tracy's Great Awak. 307-9. † Sp. An. 1. 623. Allen. ‡ Allen. § Mendon. Assoc. 89. ‖ Sp. An. 3. 19.

The First Church in Guilford, Org. June 19, 1643.

Henry Whitfield,*	1639	1650	1658
John Higginson,†	1643 ?	1659	1708
John Bowers,	1660 ?		
Joseph Eliot,‡	1664		May, 1694
Thomas Ruggles,§	Nov. 1695		June, 1728
Thomas Ruggles, Jr.,§	Mar. 1729		Nov. 1770
Amos Fowler,‖	June, 1758		Feb. 1800
Israel Brainerd,**	June, 1850	Jan. 1806	Oct. 1854
Aaron Dutton,††	Dec. 1806	June, 1842	June, 1849
E. Edwin Hall,	Oct. 1843	July, 1855	
Henry Wickes,	May, 1856	July, 1858	
Wm. S. Smith,	May, 1859		

Mr. Whitfield, with a large part of those who had been under his charge in England, began a settlement in Guilford in 1639. He returned to England, and died at Winchester. Mr. Higginson, his son-in-law, was " teacher" till his removal, and left himself to return to England, but was induced to settle at Salem, Mass. Mr. Brainerd's ministry of thirty years at Verona, N. Y., was attended with several extensive revivals. Mr. Dutton was an able and devoted minister, and his labors were eminently blessed with several revivals of great power. On taking leave of the old meeting-house, in 1830, he stated that about eight hundred had professed religion, and sixteen hundred had been baptized in it.

MINISTERS RAISED UP.—Jared Eliot, Daniel Collins, Timothy Collins, Edmund Ward, Bela Hubbard, D. D. (Ep.) Samuel Johnson, D. D. (Ep.) Thomas Ruggles, William Seward, Timothy Stone, Andrew Fowler, (Ep.) Thomas Ruggles, Jr., Joy H. Fairchild,§§ William Leete, Jr., Thomas Dutton, Edwin D. Seward, Theodore A. Leete, Beriah Hotchkin, John H. Fower, Henry Robinson, Sherman Griswold, (Bap.) S. W S. Dutton, D. D., Martin Dudley.

* Math. Mag. 1. 541. Sp. An. 1. 10. Allen. † Sp. An. 1. 91. Allen. ‡ Sp. An. 1. 22. Allen. § Sp. An. 1. 261. Allen. ‖ Sp. An. 1. 383. ** Cong. Y. B. 2. 89. †† Sp. An. 2. 489. Allen. ‡‡ Sp. An. 3. 497. §§ Sp. An. 3. 497. §§ Cong. Quar. 1. 314.

THE THIRD CHURCH IN GUILFORD, ORG. NOV. 23. 1843.

MINISTERS.	SETTLED.	DISMISSED.	DIED.
David Root,	Jan. 1845	April, 1851	
R. M. Chipman,	Jan. 1852	May, 1858	
Geo. I. Wood,	Nov. 1858		

This church was formed by a secession from the First Church. The church in Madison (East Guilford,) was formerly the Third Church ; that at North Guilford being the Second ; and a church formed in 1773, (now extinct, on account of the disagreement of a large majority of the First Church in the settlement of Mr. Ruggles, Jr.,) having been the Fourth in Guilford.

The Fourth Church in Guilford, Org. 1733.

Edmund Ward,	Sept. 1733	1735	
Joseph Lamb,			
James Sprout, D. D.,*	April, 1743	Oct. 1768	1793
John Hunt,	1769 ?	1771	
Daniel Brewer,	Sept. 1771	1778	
Beriah Hotchkin,	Aug. 1785	1790 ?	1829

This church was formed by reason of a controversy arising in 1729, with reference to the settlement of Mr. Ruggles, Jr. A meeting-house was erected in 1730. Dr. Sprout, after an able and prosperous ministry, was re-settled in Philadelphia. Mr. Hotchkin, after a few years, removed to Western New York, where he was eminently useful in preaching and planting new churches. The church became extinct soon after 1800. *See Trumbull's History, Vol. 2, Chap. 7, p. 114.*

* Sp. An. 3. 125.

The Church in Haddam, Org. 1700.

MINISTERS.	SETTLED.	DISMISSED.	DIED.
Jonathan Willowbe,			
*Nicholas Noyes,**	1668	1682	
John James,	1686		
Jeremiah Hobart,†	1690, inst. Nov. 1700		Nov. 1715
Phinehas Fiske,	Sept. 1714		Oct. 1738
Aaron Cleaveland,	July, 1739	1746	1757
Joshua Elderkin,	June, 1749	1753	
Eleazar May,‡	June, 1756		April, 1803
David D. Field, D. D.	April, 1804	April, 1818	
John Marsh,	Dec. 1818	April, 1834	
Tertius S. Clark,	April, 1834	Feb. 1837	
David D. Field, D. D.	April, 1837	April, 1844	
Elisha W. Cook,	Nov. 1846	April, 1852	
Erastus Colton,	Dec. 1852	May, 1854	
James L. Wright,	May, 1855		

As no church records exist in Haddam of an earlier date than 1756, it cannot be determined with certainty when the church was organized; it is supposed to have been at the time of the ordination of Mr. Hobart. Some circumstances, however, lead to a belief that it was done at a much earlier period. Public worship appears to have been observed from the first settlement. For a time the people met in a private house. The first meeting-house was built in 1673-4; the second in 1721; the third in 1770-1, (still standing;) the present house in 1847.

The first preacher here of whom mention is made in the records of the town, was Mr. Jonathan Willowbe. In 1668, Mr. Nicholas Noyes began to preach here, and continued thirteen or fourteen years; though it is said he was not ordained. Mr. John James preached here as early as 1686. How long he continued is unknown. Mr. Hobart came to Haddam in 1690 or 1691. "As he had been consecrated to the ministry before," the people seem to have recognized him as their minister without a formal installation. In 1695, they voted that they did not consider themselves under the charge of Mr. Hobart as pastor; and " that with the consent of the General Assembly, and the approbation of the neighboring churches, they would embody in church way, and order, according to the gospel." Mr. Hobart was, however, not installed till November, 1700.

MINISTERS RAISED UP.—David Brainerd,§ John Brainerd,‖ Hezekiah May, Elijah Brainerd, Jonathan Hubbard, Eleazar Brainerd, Charles Dickinson, Henry Field, Chiliab Brainerd, Nehemiah Brainerd, Israel Brainerd, Israel Brainerd, 2d, James Brainerd, Israel Shailer, Davis S. Brainerd, Dan. C. Tyler.

* Sp. An. 1. 91. Allen. † Sp. An. 1. 69. Allen. ‡ Sp. An. 1. 414. Allen. § Sp. An. 3. 113. Allen. ‖ Sp. An. 149.

THE CHURCH IN HADLYME, IN EAST HADDAM, ORG. JUNE 26, 1745.

MINISTERS.	SETTLED.	DISMISSED.	DIED.
Grindall Rawson,*	Sept. 1745		Mar. 1777
Joseph Vaill,†	Feb. 1780		Nov. 1838
Ralph S. Crampton,	May, 1832	Nov. 1834	
George Carrington,‡	Feb. 1835	Feb. 1843	1843?
Stephen A. Loper, Mar. 1842, inst. May, 1845, June, 1850			
Wm. Goodwin,			
James Noyes,			
Elias B. Hillard,	Mar. 1855	1860	

Hadlyme lies partly in East Haddam, and partly in Lyme; whence its name; the society was formed Nov. 1742. Mr. Rawson was a plain preacher, gifted in prayer, remarkably social, and had an uncommon talent in reconciling parties at variance. Mr. Vaill was a man eminent in goodness, of substantial character, a faithful preacher, a devoted pastor, and a *man of God.* He conducted a school in his house for many years, where were instructed many men who became eminent in church and state, among whom were his own sons, Joseph and Wm. F. Vaill, and Griffin, Harvey, Hungerford, and others. There is no record of a revival till 1808. In 1813 a revival began, which continued two years, adding 30; 56 in 1827; also revivals in 1846, '54, and '58. The half-way covenant was practiced till the time of Mr. Vaill. The first meeting-house was erected in 1843; the second in 1840. *Nettleton's Mem.* 67. *Rel. Intel.* 13, 61.

MINISTERS RAISED UP.—Joseph Harvey, D. D., Joseph Vaill, D. D., Wm. F. Vaill, (h.)

* Sp. An. 1. 168. Allen. † Sp. An. 4. 26. ‡ Litchf. Centen. 117.

THE CHURCH IN HAMBURG, IN LYME, ORG. (PROBABLY) IN 1727.

George Beckwith,	Jan. 1730		Dec. 1785
David Higgins,	Oct. 1787	1801	
David Huntington,	Dec. 1803		April, 1812
Asahel Nettleton,	April, 1813		May, 1844
Josiah Hawes,	Nov. 1814	Jan. 1833	
Harvey Bushnell,	Jan. 1835	April, 1838	
Philip Payson,	Oct. 1838	Oct. 1841	

MINISTERS.	SETTLED.	DISMISSED.	DIED.
Charles E. Murdock,	June, 1842		Jan. 1844
James A. Moore,	1844		
Daniel C. Tyler,	Oct. 1844	Oct. 1845	
Samuel Griswold,	Oct. 1845	Sept. 1848	
E. F. Burr,	Oct. 1850		

Before the division of the town, this was the third church in Lyme ; now the first. After Mr. Huntington's death, the pulpit was supplied one year by the Middlesex Association. There was a revival under Mr. Nettleton's labors, attended with great solemnity and deep conviction of sin, promoted by the preaching of the distinguishing doctrines of the gospel ; 31 added. *Memoir,* 67. Also in April, 1824, a work of divine grace commenced under the ministration of Rev. Noah C. Saxton, progressed rapidly, and forty-eight were added, four of whom entered the ministry. In April, 1831, Rev. Warren G. Jones commenced assisting Mr. Hawes, and a powerful revival followed, adding forty-five to the church. There was also a revival in the winter of 1836, and there have been two within the last ten years. *Rel. Intel.* 9. 175.

Ministers Raised Up.—David Ely, D. D., Zebulon Ely, John Ely, Elias P. Ely, Daniel M. Lord, L. F. T. Huntington, Richard Ely, Samuel Ely, Zabdiel R. Ely, Joseph T. Lord, Abijah P. Marvin, George W. Sill.

The Church in Hamden, East Plains, Org. Aug. 18, 1775.

Abraham Alling,	Oct. 1797	Oct. 1822	July, 1837
George E. Delavan,	May, 1833	Aug. 1834	
Austin Putnam,	Oct. 1838		

For many years, under the ministry of Mr. Alling, the church enjoyed a good degree of prosperity. At the time of his dismission, it was afflicted and weakened by divisions. During 16 years after his dismission, the church was served by more than two hundred different ministers. These were years of severe trial to this little flock of Christ. They were few, poor and feeble. They had no pastor, no place of worship that was convenient, no parsonage, no fund. They feared that they should be obliged to disband and go to other churches. They had many a communion season, which they thought might be their last. They could pay only two dollars a Sabbath for preaching. But a few, faithful brethren, held on. The church still lives, having a comfortable house of worship, and a parsonage, and has been self-supporting fifteen years, paying a good salary, and $150 to $200 to benevolent objects, although there has been but little increase of business or population.

THE CHURCH IN HAMPTON, ORG., JUNE 5, 1723.

MINISTERS.	SETTLED.	DISMISSED.	DIED.
William Billings,	June, 1723		May, 1733
Samuel Moseley,*	May, 1734		July, 1791
Ludovicus Weld,	Oct. 1792	March, 1824	Oct. 1844
Daniel G. Sprague,	May, 1824	April, 1839	
Daniel C. Frost,	Sept. 1840	Oct. 1841	
William Barnes,	Sept. 1842	Sept. 1847	
Richard Woodruff,	Feb. 1848	April, 1852	
George Soule, Sept. '53· ord.	Sept. 1855		

This Church was called the church in Windham Village, then the Second or Canada Society Church, until the town (Hampton,) was incorporated. It consisted of a colony of 29 persons from the church in Windham. It has recently refitted its house of worship and received to itself a large number of new members as the results of the great revival of 1858. *Rel. Intel.* 16, 476.

MINISTERS RAISED UP.—Ebenezer Moseley, Charles Fitch, A. C. Denison, Ludovicus Robbins, Joseph Stewart.

* Sp. An. 1, 446. Allen.

THE CHURCH IN HANOVER, IN LISBON, ORG. MAY 13, 1766.

Timothy Stone,*	Oct. 1765		1766	May, 1797
Andrew Lee, D. D.,†	Oct. 1768			Aug. 1832
Barnabas Phinney,	Feb. 1830	Nov. 1832		
Philo Judson,	June, 1833	July, 1834		
Daniel Waldo,				
Edward Cleaveland,				
Joseph Ayer,	Sept. 1837	June, 1848		
Ebenezer W. Robinson,	Mar. 1849	April, 1852		
James A. Hazen,	Dec. 1852			

The Hanover Ecclesiastical Society in Lisbon was incorporated in 1761, including small portions of Canterbury and Windham. A fund of £1400 was raised by subscription for the support of the gospel ministry before the incorporation of the Society. The church at its formation consisted of fourteen members. It has been greatly blessed by revivals.

MINISTERS RAISED UP.—Ezra Witter, Horace Bushnell, James Abel, Anson P. Brooks, Charles L. Ayer.

* Sp. An. 1, 631. Allen. † Sp. An. 1, 668. Allen.

THE CHURCH IN HANOVER, IN MERIDEN, ORG. FEB. 13, 1853.

James A. Clark,	Dec. 1853	April, 1855
Jacob Eaton,	May, 1857	

Early in the year 1852 members of different Congregational Churches residing in Hanover, and attending worship at the chapel opened for that purpose, began to contemplate the organization of a Church; it had at first 25 members. This church has been repeatedly blessed with the outpouring of God's Spirit.

In the Spring of 1857 a most powerful work of grace was enjoyed, and 32 persons united with the church.

The First Church in Hartford, Org. 1633.

MINISTERS.	SETTLED.	DISMISSED.	DIED.
Thomas Hooker,*	Oct. 1633		July, 1647
Samuel Stone,†	Oct. 1633		July, 1663
John Whiting,‡	1660		Nov. 1689
Joseph Haynes,§	1664		May, 1679
Isaac Foster,	1679		Jan. 1683
Timothy Woodbridge,‖	Nov. 1685		April, 1732
Daniel Wadsworth,¶	Sept. 1732		Nov. 1747
Edward Dorr,**	Apr. 1748		Oct. 1772
Nathan Strong, D. D.,††	Jan. 1774		Dec. 1816
Joel Hawes, D. D.,	Mar. 1818		

This Church was originally gathered in Newtown, (now Cambridge) Mass., and was duly organized by the installation of Thomas Hooker as pastor, and Samuel Stone as teacher, Oct. 11th, 1633. It is supposed that William Goodwin was ordained as ruling elder, and Andrew Warner as deacon at the same time.

In June, 1636, Messrs. Hooker and Stone, with about one hundred of their people, removed to this place. Here the Church was permanently planted, being the first Church established in Connecticut; and here the ordinances of the gospel have been regularly administered from that time to the present.

This Church embraced the territory now occupied by the Churches of the City, of East Hartford, and of West Hartford.

Mr. Woodbridge was a member of the Saybrook Synod, 1708.

We give a list of Churches formed from this Church wholly or in part; viz:

South Church, Feb. 1669, 31 members; East Hartford, May 1702; West Hartford, Feb. 1713; North Church, Sept. 1824, 97 members; Fourth Church, Jan. 1832, 18 members; Pearl Street Church, Oct. 1852, 47 members. See *Dr. Hawes's Centennial Discourse, 1836; "First Church in Connecticut," Dr. Hawes's Address at Norwich, page* 85 (*supra;*) *also History of the Church in Windsor, (infra,) which also claims to be the First Church in Connecticut. Ev. Mag.* 8, 263, 470.

Ministers Raised Up.—Thomas H. Gallaudet,‡‡ James Anderson, Algernon S. Kennedy, Anson Gleason, (f.) Reuben Tinker,§§ (f.) Alfred Wright, Benj. B. Wright, H. J. Van Lennep, (f.) Shearjashub Bourne, George Thacher, Jonathan Brace, D. D., Asa T. Hopkins, D. D.,‖‖ Douglas K. Turner, Josiah H.

Temple, Charles O. Reynolds, William Bird, (f.) Erskine J. Hawes, John
Willard, William U. Colt, Chester Isham,¶¶ Marshfield Steele,***

* Sp. An. 1, 34. Math. Mag. 1, 302. † Sp. An. 1, 37. Math. Mag 1, 392. ‡ Sp. An.
1, 182. Allen. § Dr. Bacon's Historical Discourse, supra, 24–25. ‖ Allen. ¶ Allen.
** Sp. An. 1, 387. Allen. †† Sp. An. 2, 34. Allen. Am. Qr. Reg. 13, 129. ‡‡ Sp.
An. 2, 609. Allen. §§ Sp. An. 4, 770. ‖‖ Sp. An. 4, 741. ¶¶ Sp. An. 2, 704. *** Sp.
An. 2, 347.

THE SOUTH CHURCH, HARTFORD, ORG. FEB. 12, 1669.

MINISTERS.	SETTLED.	DISMISSED.	DIED.
John Whiting,	Feb. 1669		1689
Thomas Buckingham,*	1690		1730
Elnathan Whitman,†	1733		March, 1777
William Patten,‡	July, 1767	1773	Jan. 1775
Benjamin Boardman,§	1784		Feb. 1802
Abel Flint, D. D.,‖	Apr. 1791	Jan. 1824	
Joel H. Linsley, D. D.	Feb. 1824	Aug. 1832	
C. C. Vanarsdalen,	Dec. 1832	March, 1836	
Oliver E. Daggett, D. D.	Apr. 1837	June, 1843	
Walter Clark, D. D.,	June, 1845	Jan. 1859	
Edwin P. Parker,	Jan. 1860		

During the ministry of Mr. Whiting and Mr. Haynes, joint pastors of the
First Church, some difference of opinion arose, which resulted in a regular
and amicable division of the Church. The senior pastor and 31 members
withdrew and formed this Church. Mr. Whitman recovering his health,
was sole pastor about 4 years. During the troubles of the Revolutionary
war from '77 to '84, there was no pastor.

MINISTERS RAISED UP.—William Patten, Jr. D. D., John A. Hempsted,
Andrew Benton, Albert Smith, Charles Rockwell, W. H. Corning, Charles
N. Seymour, Elijah P. Barrows, Charles E. Linsley.

* Sp. An. 1, 260. Allen. † Sp. An. 1.315. ‡ Sp. An. 1, 592. Allen. § Sp. An.
1, 513. ‖ Sp. An. 2, 273. Allen.

THE NORTH CHURCH, HARTFORD, ORG. SEPT. 23, 1824.

Carlos Wilcox,*	Dec. 1824	May,	1826	May,	1827
Samuel Spring, D. D.	Mar. 1827	Jan.	1833		
Horace Bushnell, D. D.,	May, 1833	Nov.	1859		
James T. Hyde,	July, 1855	April,	1857		
George N. Webber,	Nov. 1859				

Organized by a Colony from the Center Church of Hartford. It has had
a steady and vigorous growth; and especially under the ministry of Dr.
Bushnell, enjoyed great prosperity, both in the increase of the congregation
and of the Church.

Ministers Raised Up.—Erastus Colton, Henry N. Day, Tryon Edwards, D. D., John Erskine Edwards, James M. Smith, Aaron L. Chapin.

* Sp. An. 2, 653. Allen.

The Fourth Church in Hartford, Org. Jan. 10, 1832.

MINISTERS.	SETTLED.	DISMISSED.	DIED.
William C. Walton,	Jan. 1833		Feb. 1834
Charles Fitch,	June, 1834	May, 1836	
Isaac N. Sprague,	Oct. 1837	Oct. 1845	
William W. Patton,	Jan. 1846	Dec. 1856	
Nathaniel J. Burton,	Oct. 1857		

The original members of the Fourth Church numbered thirty-three. The organization grew out of efforts to bring the gospel to bear more effectively on the mass of the people. To encourage the attendance of the poor, the "free seat plan" was tried for several years, after which it was abandoned as not securing a self-supporting Church, and as therefore endangering the safety of the enterprise. The Church worshiped for about two years in the old Baptist Church in Market Street, now Washington Hall; in 1835, removed to a new house they had built, now the Melodeon; and in 1850 to their present edifice. The Church has been greatly blessed with revivals, and is now one of the largest in the State.

The "Colored" (Fifth or Talcott St.) Church, Hartford, Org. 1833.

John A. Hempsted,	June, 1837	Aug. 1838	
E. R. Tyler,	1839	1840	Sept. 1848
J. W. C. Pennington, D. D.	July, 1840	Nov. 1847	
J. A. Prime,	Nov. 1849	May, 1851	
C. W. Gardner,	May, 1851	Mar. 1853	
J. W. C. Pennington,	1855		
Samuel Griswold,	1855	1856	
E. J. Adams,	Aug. 1857	Aug. 1858	
Joseph D. Hull,	1859		

The name of this Church was changed by vote, August, 1837, from "African," to "Colored Congregational Church." It was consociated with Hartford South, August, 1837. It has had but one settled pastor.

The Church has a fund yielding about $100 annually, a legacy from Catharine Freebody, a worthy colored woman of Hartford.

Ministers Raised Up.—E. P. Rogers, Amos G. Beman.

THE PEARL STREET CHURCH IN HARTFORD, ORG. OCT. 15, 1852.

MINISTERS.	SETTLED.	DISMISSED.	DIED.
Elias R. Beadle,	Dec. 1852		

The Pearl Street Church was formed from members of the four Congregational Churches in Hartford, who, with some others, were duly constituted a Christian Church, with appropriate religious services, in the edifice recently erected by the Pearl Street Congregational Society, and for the purpose of completing its ecclesiastical organization. The whole number of members was ninety-one, viz: forty-six males, and forty-five females.

MINISTER RAISED UP.—Theodore J. Holmes.

The Market Street Church, Hartford, Org. Jan. 8, 1854.

Warren G. Jones,	April, 1853	April, 1858

Organized with twenty-four members, after sustaining public worship nine months. It adopted the free Church system, but proved fully in five years not to be self-sustaining, and though remarkably blessed in the outward reformation and hopeful conversion of many, (147 being added to their number in four years,) was disbanded.

THE GERMAN MISSION, HARTFORD.

—— *Renner,*	1848
J. Conrad Buenner,	1849
Christopher Popp,	1850
John Kilian,	1855
F. M. Serenbetz,	1856

Without a Church organization, the preaching of the gospel among residents of German origin aided by the Connecticut Missionary Society, has been productive of good. There is also a German congregation connected with another denomination. H. S. Ollendorf, a converted Jew, of German origin, a member of Dr. Hawes's Church, not a licensed minister, labored a few months in 1858–9, among the Germans in Broad Brook, Ellington and Rockville, with favorable prospects, but was cut off by an early death.

THE FIRST CHURCH IN HARTLAND, (EAST,) ORG. MAY 1, 1768.

Starling Graves,*	July, 1768		1773
Aaron Church,	Oct. 1773	1815	April, 1823
Ammi Linsley,	July, 1815	Dec. 1835	
Aaron Gates,	1836	1841	Mar. 1849
J. C. Houghton,	1843	1845	
Nelson Scott,	Sept. 1846	June, 1857	

MINISTERS.	SETTLED.	DISMISSED.	DIED.
Ogden Hall,	Oct. 1858	1859	
Alfred White,	1859	1860	

Hartland was incorporated in 1761. It then belonged to Litchfield County, but was afterwards annexed to Hartford County. It is centrally divided by a branch of the Farmington River, and two Congregational Churches were early formed in the east and west divisions of the town,—the one in West Hartland twelve years after this Church. Mr. Graves was ordained in the open air, on a knoll about a mile south of the present church. The first Church edifice was erected in 1770.

MINISTERS RAISED UP.—Salmon Giddings, (h.) Lewis Foster, Orson Cowles, Elisha C. Jones, Lemuel Foster, Anson McCloud, Chas. L. Loomis.
* Sp. An. 2. 229.

THE CHURCH IN HARWINTON, ORG. OCT. 4, 1738.

Timothy Woodbridge, Jr.	1735	1737	
Andrew Bartholomew,	Oct. 1738	Jan. 1774	March, 1776
David Perry,*	Feb. 1774	Dec. 1783	June, 1817
Joshua Williams,†	Mar. 1790	Jan. 1822	Feb. 1835
George Pierce,	July, 1822	June, 1834	
R. M. Chipman,	Mar. 1835	March, 1839	
Charles Bentley,	Sept. 1839	Jan. 1850	
Warren G. Jones,	Oct. 1850	June, 1853	
Jacob G. Miller,	July, 1854	May, 1857	
John A. McKinstry,	Oct. 1857		

The ministry of Mr. Bartholomew was, so far as appears, generally prosperous, though not accompanied with those manifestations of divine power that have been witnessed since. Under his ministry the Half-way Covenant was adopted. Mr. Perry opposed it; was truly an evangelical man, and his labors were blessed by the Divine Spirit.

Since 1774, in six revivals there were added from 20 to 85; in five others, from 96 to 150 each. *Ev. Mag.* 1,462.

Under the ministry of Mr. Williams commenced that series of revivals which crowned the closing years of the last and the commencement of the present century. Mr. Williams was ordained pastor of a Presbyterian Church, Southampton, L. I., Dec., 1784. Mr. Pierce was dismissed to become President of Western Reserve College. See Chipman's History of the town.

MINISTERS RAISED UP.—Norris Bull, D. D.,‡ Richard Chester, David Butler, D. D., Jacob Catlin,§ Russell Catlin, Simeon Catlin, Clement Merriam, David Perry, (h.) Rodney Rossiter, (Ep.) H. C. Abernethy, (h.) Abner Wilcox, (lay missionary.)

* Sp. An. 2, 303. † Litchfield Centen. 114. ‡ Sp. An. 4, 615. § Sp. An. 2, 260. Allen.

THE CHURCH IN HEBRON, ORG. 1717.

MINISTERS.	SETTLED.	DISMISSED.	DIED.
Samuel Terry,	1714		
John Bliss,	1715, ord. Nov. 1717	1734	
Benjamin Pomeroy,*	1734, ord. 1735		Dec. 1784
Samuel Kellogg,	June, 1788	July, 1793	
Amos Bassett, D. D.,†	Nov. 1794	Sept. 1824	1828
Lyman Strong,	Aug. 1825	Feb. 1830	
Hiram P. Arms,	June, 1830	Sept. 1832	
Moses T. Harris,	Jan. 1834	Jan. 1835	
Sylvester Selden,	Sept. 1835	May, 1841	Oct. 1841
Edgar J. Doolittle,	May, 1842	Dec. 1852	
William M. Birchard,	April, 1853	April, 1854	
Merrick Knight,	June, 1854	June, 1850	

The first settlement was in 1704. In 1712, the town appointed a committee to procure a minister. In 1714, the town passed votes making grants of land to the first minister, (170 acres,) and "ordered that three or four acres be broken up and sowed with wheat, for the encouragement of a minister settling among us, and appointed a committee to inspect the aforesaid affair."

Public worship, until the erection of a meeting house, was held in private houses and in a *new barn,* where fourteen children were baptized in one day. The people disagreeing about the site for the meeting house, it was fixed by a committee of the General Assembly; soon after the house was raised, but it was not completed for several years.

Mr. Pomeroy's salary was to be paid "in grain, or as grain goes in market," but in a few years the "Old Tenor" currency of the country became very much depreciated, so that in the year 1747, he received for his salary of £100 lawful money, £420 of depreciated money, payable in corn at 12 shillings per bushel, pork at 18 pence, and beef at 11 pence per pound, and in another year £685, and £85 to get his fire wood.

In 1733 we find records of a movement for a division of the town into two Ecclesiastical Societies, resulting in 1747, in setting off Andover and Gilead.

An incendiary, Moses Hutchinson, set fire to the meeting house and it was burnt in Oct., 1747. He was prosecuted and committed to jail, and afterwards sold into service to Samuel Gilbert, Esq., to pay damages and costs. The present edifice was erected in 1828.

It is recorded of Mr. Kellogg, that he was ordained by the Rev. President Stiles and others, by the style and title of Bishop. Dr. Bassett was dismissed to take charge of the Foreign Mission School at Cornwall. The practice of half way membership was continued until 1793, there being as many as 60 thus received.

The history of the Church does not appear to have been marked by any particular seasons of general religious interest until 1817, which with 1824 and 1831, are to be remembered for a general and powerful outpouring of the Spirit. *Rel. Intel.* 16, 156.

MINISTERS RAISED UP.—Ambrose Porter, David Porter, D. D.,‡ Aaron Hutchinson, Oliver Noble, Benjamin Trumbull, Jacob Sherwin, John Sawyer,§ Amasa Porter, Flavel Bliss, Ralph Perry, Alfred White, Moses Smith.

* Sp. An. 1, 394. Allen, † Sp. An. 2, 294. Allen. ‡ Sp. An. 3, 496. § Cong. Y. B. 6,131.

THE CHURCH IN HIGGANUM, IN HADDAM, ORG. MAY 1, 1844.

MINISTERS.	SETTLED.	DISMISSED.	DIED.
David D. Field, D. D.,	May, 1844	June, 1850	
Stephen A. Loper,	July, 1850	June, 1856	
Charles Nichols,	April, 1857		

The village of Higganum is in the town of Haddam. The members of the Church and Society formerly belonged to the First Church and Society in Haddam; a division of that being effected, it resulted in the formation of this.

THE CHURCH IN HITCHCOCKVILLE, IN BARKHAMSTED, ORG. APRIL 19, 1842.

Luther H. Barber,   Oct. 1843

The Church at its organization consisted of 53 members. There was a revival in 1857–8. The pas·or commenced his labors in June, 1842, there being then no house of worship; the use of the Episcopal House being allowed them every alternate Sabbath, about one year. The Church was dedicated at the time of the ordination.

THE CHURCH IN HUNTINGTON, (FORMERLY RIPTON,) ORG. FEB. 12, 1724.

Jedediah Mills,*	Feb. 1724		Jan. 1776
David Ely, D. D.,†	Oct. 1773		Feb. 1816
Thomas F. Davies,	Mar. 1817	July, 1818	
Thomas Punderson,	Nov. 1818	Jan. 1844	Aug. 1848
Charles N. Seymour,	June, 1844	July, 1847	
Eliakim Phelps, D. D.,	Nov. 1847	March, 1849	
William B. Curtiss,	Feb. 1850	June, 1857	
John Blood,	Sept. 1858		

The Church was organized with 92 members. During Dr. Ely's ministry there were additions by profession every year, except six; in all 158. Dr. Ely instructed and prepared many young men for college and also for the ministry. The Panoplist contains a sketch of his life and character.

The following is a copy of the *Half Way Covenant* which stands upon the records of the Church at the date of 1773, which was done away in 1817 :—

" You do now, before God and these witnesses, avouch the Lord Jehovah to be your covenant God and Father, viewing yourself under solemn bonds and obligations to be the Lord's by your baptismal vows. You do, so far as you know your own heart, make choice of Jesus Christ to be your only Saviour and Redeemer, and the Holy Ghost to be your Sanctifier, solemnly engaging to serve the Lord and him only, as he shall by his grace enable you; that you will deny all ungodliness and worldly lusts; that you will be careful to keep a conscience void of offense, so as to do honor to God and the religion you profess; that you will endeavor by strength from God to walk in all his commandments and ordinances blameless, desiring to put yourself under the watch and care of this Church, to be trained up in the school of Christ for his heavenly kingdom; promising also that you will give up your children to God in baptism, and to bring them up in the fear of the Lord ; and to attend upon all the ordinances of Christ as administered in this place; also that it is your full purpose to obey God in the ordinance of the Holy Supper as God shall give you light, and show you his will herein. And you covenant, and you promise, relying for help, strength and ability on the blood of the everlasting covenant, to perform all and every duty to the praise and glory of God. "

During Mr. Punderson's ministry of 26 years, 28 persons were admitted to the Church by letter, and 186 by profession ; 214 in all.

Rev. Jedediah Mills was a warm hearted divine, and entered fully into the spirit and preaching of Whitefield and Tennent. He cooperated with Bellamy and Edwards. In 1742 he was a member of a voluntary association which met at Wethersfield to promote the awakening and salvation of souls. A copy of the doings of that meeting is in the hands of the Clerk of the Church in Huntington.

MINISTERS RAISED UP.—Isaac Lewis, D. D., Joshua Perry, David Perry, William A. Hawley,‡ George Carrington, Henry S. Nichols.

* Sp. An. 1, 462 ; 2, 5. Allen. † Sp. An. 2, 4. Allen. ‡ Cong. Y. B. 2, 97.

THE CHURCH IN JEWETT CITY, IN GRISWOLD, ORG. APRIL 14, 1825.

MINISTERS.	SETTLED.	DISMISSED.	DIED.
Seth Bliss,	June, 1825	April, 1832	
George Perkins,	Aug. 1832	Sept. 1838	Sept. 1852
William Wright,	Nov. 1838	April, 1842	
Thomas L. Shipman,	Apr. 1843	Sept. 1854	
Henry T. Cheever,	May, 1856		

The Church is an offshoot from the old church in Griswold. The Society is the 2d Congregational Society of Griswold. For several years the Church received aid from the Domestic Missionary Society of Connecticut. In 1855 a fund of $8000 was raised, which placed the support of the gospel upon a permanent basis.

MINISTERS RAISED UP.—Stephen Johnson, (f.) William A. Hyde.

THE CHURCH IN KENSINGTON, IN BERLIN, ORG. DEC. 10, 1712.

MINISTERS.	SETTLED.	DISMISSED.	DIED.
William Burnham,	Dec. 1712		Sept. 1750
Ezra Stiles, D. D.			
Aaron Brown,			
Samuel Sherwood,			
Elizur Goodrich, D. D.			
Samuel Clark,	July, 1756		Nov. 1775
Timothy Dwight, D. D.	1777		
Benoni Upson, D. D.	April, 1779		Nov. 1826
Royal Robbins,	June, 1816	June, 1859	
Elias B. Hillard,	May, 1860		

This church was originally the second church in Farmington. The Ecclesiastical Society in Kensington was probably set off from Farmington about the year 1712, and included New Britain and Worthington. At that time there were but fourteen families in the place ; the church had at first but ten members. Mr. Burnham was considered a sound preacher, and was accustomed to refer much to the scriptures in support of his doctrines. He possessed a large estate. Under his ministry, a prayer and conference meeting existed, at which the brethren presided in rotation, and each one, before closing the meeting of his charge, named the next brother to preside, and the theme for consideration. Mr. Clark appeared well in the pulpit ; and the epitaph on his tombstone mentions among other estimable qualities of the man, that he was "in the gift of preaching, excellent, laborious and pathetic." Dr. Upson was a wise and benevolent man, a lover of peace, and a peace-maker, and distinguished with his family for hospitality. There have been several seasons of special attention to religion in this place during the present century.

MINISTERS RAISED UP.—Thomas Hooker, Elijah Gridley, Uriel Gridley, Horace Hooker, John Gridley, Samuel Lee.

THE CHURCH IN KENT, ORG. APRIL 29, 1741.

Cyrus Marsh,	May, 1741	Dec. 1755	
Joel Bordwell,*	Oct. 1758		Dec. 1811
Asa Blair,†	May, 1813		Jan. 1823
Laurens P. Hickok, D. D.,	Dec. 1823	April, 1829	

MINISTERS.	SETTLED.	DISMISSED.	DIED.
Wm. W. Andrews,	May, 1834	April, 1849	
Wm. W. Page,	Dec. 1753	May, 1854	
Elisha Whittlesey,	1856	1858	
Evarts Scudder,	June, 1859		

The settlement of this town began in 1737 ; incorporated in 1739. The church has been blessed with repeated revivals ; as the result of the most extensive, fifty-six were added in 1812, fifty in 1816, and forty-two in 1831. The church has a considerable fund for the support of the gospel, and a good parsonage.

MINISTERS RAISED UP.—Samuel J. Mills, Walter Smith, Seth Swift,‡ Edmund Mills,§ Birdsey G. Northrop.

* Sp. An. 1. 672.   † Litchf. Centen. 118.   ‡ Allen,   § Mendon. Assoc. 133.

The South Church in Killingly, Org. 1746.

Nehemiah Barker,	1746	1755	
Eden Borroughs, D. D ,*	Jan. 1760	1771	May, 1813

This church was formed by a division of the First Chnrch, now East Putnam, on account of a controversy about the location of a meeting-house. Dr. Burroughs was the last pastor, and the church became extinct before the close of the century.

* Sp. An. 2. 53, 90.   Allen.

THE CHURCH IN KILLINGWORTH, ORG. JAN. 18, 1738.

William Seward,*	Jan. 1738		1782
Henry Ely,	Sept. 1782	Feb. 1801	
Josiah B. Andrews,	April, 1802	April, 1811	
Asa King,†	Nov. 1811	Aug. 1832	Dec. 1849
Ephraim G. Swift,‡	Dec. 1833	Nov. 1850	Aug. 1858
Hiram Bell,	Nov. 1850		

The church in Killingworth was formed for the most part, of members from the First Church, now Clinton. It was called North Killingworth till the division of the town. Original members, 50 ; added by the first pastor, 160 ; second, 131 ; third, 143 : fifth, 262 ; sixth, nine years, 114 ; total, 1002. *Ev. Mag.* 4. 419 ; 5. 31. The first revival ever enjoyed by this church, was at the commencement of Mr. Andrews' ministry, an account of which was published in the Connecticut Evangelical Magazine ; since which time it has been refreshed by frequent revivals up to the present year ; the most powerful of which were in 1811, when 133 were added—in 1836, 61 ; in 1843, 72 ; in 1854, 50 ; in 1858, 46. *Memoir of Dr. Nettleton*, 133. The congregation occupies its third meeting-house, which was built about thirty years ago, and it embraces a large portion of the inhabitants of the town, who may be designated as a church-going people.

MINISTERS RAISED UP —William Seward, Asahel Nettleton, D. D. § Josiah
Pierson, George Coan, Martin Wilcox, Alvin Parmelee, Henry Lord, Philander Parmelee,‖ Titus Coan, (f.) John Wilcox, Ebenezer H. Wilcox.

* Allen.   † Allen.   ‡ Cong. Y. B. 6.135.   § Sp. An. 2. 542.   ‖ Sp. An. 2. 546.

THE FIRST CHURCH IN LEBANON, ORG. NOV. 27, 1700.

MINISTERS.	SETTLED.	DISMISSED.	DIED.
Joseph Parsons,	Nov. 1700	1708	
Samuel Wells,	Dec. 1711	Dec. 1722	
Solomon Williams, D. D.,*	Dec. 1722		Feb. 1776
Zebulon Ely,†	Nov. 1782		Nov. 1824
Edward Bull,	Sept. 1825	1837	
John C. Nichols,	Feb. 1840	Mar. 1854	
O. D. Hine,	May, 1856		

The year in which the organization of the town was perfected, the church
was gathered, and a pastor ordained. The growth of the church was
rapid. In little more than half a century it became one of the strongest
and most influential churches in the colony. Its most prosperous days were
during the long ministry of Dr. Williams, when such men as the elder
Governor Trumbull, and William Williams, signer of the Declaration of
Independence, were active members. The population of the town was larger
before the war of the Revolution than it has been since. A dispute as to
the position of the meeting house had prevailed at intervals from the organization of the society. In 1730, those living north of a certain line entered into an agreement with the society that they would not vote in matters pertaining to the meeting-house. After a generation, this agreement
was forgotten or disregarded; and in 1804, those living north of the line,
who, with others acting with them, constituted a majority of the society, voted to pull down the existing meeting-house, and build another a mile north;
and persons acting in their interest, proceeded amid strife, and with much
violence, to demolish the meeting-house then in use. The civil courts decided that those living north of *the line* had no right to act in the case ;—and
the General Assembly set off those living south of the line into a separate
society, upon evidence being exhibited that they were able to sustain the institutions of the Gospel. In order to furnish such evidence, a *fund* was created, now amounting to $7,000. Dr. Williams was prominent among the
ministers of his time. He sympathised with the great awakening. There
is extant a printed sermon which he preached in 1741, occasioned by the occurrence of swooning and pretended revelations in an adjoining parish of
the town, entitled " *The More Excellent Way* ;" in which, while he
put these singular manifestations in their true place, he speaks of the revival generally—"as the glorious work of God." It is singular that with
such a character, and such views, he took ground against Edwards in his

great controversy as to the terms of admission to the church, involving the half-way covenant.

Mr. Ely was a good preacher and pastor. He was characterized by soundness and strength of intellect rather than by imagination, and was reserved in his manners. During his ministry, revivals were frequently enjoyed, and his labors were adapted to promote an earnest piety. It is a little remarkable that he preached at the funerals of the first and second Governors Trumbull, and of William Williams, signer of the Declaration of Independence.

MINISTERS RAISED UP.—Peter Pratt, Eliphalet Williams, D. D., Eliphalet Huntington, Joseph Lyman, D. D.‡ William Robinson, David Huntington, John Griswold, Eliphalet Lyman, John Robinson,§ Elijah Parish, D. D.‖ Lynde Huntington, Ariel Parish,‖ William Lyman, D. D., Asa Lyman, Andrew Huntington, Richard Williams,¶ Ezra Stiles Ely, D. D., Nathaniel Freeman, Dan Huntington, Jonathan T. Ely, David DeF. Ely, David Metcalf, Warren B. Dutton, D. D., Samuel G. Buckingham, Elijah F. Rockwell, James A. Clark, William M. Birchard.

THE FOLLOWING LICENTIATES WERE NEVER ORDAINED —Jonathan Seymour, Jonathan Trumbull, Eliphalet Birchard, Henry Woodworth, William Metcalf.

* Sp. An. 1. 207, 321. Allen. † Sp. An. 2. 192. Allen. ‡ Am. Qu. Reg. 12. 329. § Mendon As. 134. ‖ Sp. An. 2. 268. Allen. ¶ Sp. An. 3. 497.

The North Church in Lebanon, Org. 1804.

In consequence of a disagreement about the location of the house of worship, a new congregation was gathered, nearly a mile north of the old one, which at first conformed to Congregational usages, but has since become a Baptist Church. A little yielding on the part of those living in the southern part of the town, a Christian regard to the convenience and interests of the whole society, would doubtless have saved the integrity of the congregation, and entailed countless benefits on succeeding generations.

THE CHURCH IN LEDYARD, ORG. OCT. 1729.

MINISTERS.	SETTLED.	DISMISSED.	DIED.
Ebenezer Punderson,*	Dec. 1723	Feb. 1734	1771
Andrew Croswell,†	Oct. 1736	Aug. 1746	Apr. 1785
Jacob Johnson,‡	June, 1749	1772	1794
Timothy Tuttle,	Aug. 1811		

The town of Ledyard was formerly the second society in Groton, incorporated in 1724. The church remained vacant from 1772 to 1811. Mr. Punderson became an Episcopalian, and preached some years at New Haven. * As the former church had become entirely extinct, a new church was organized Dec. 12, 1810, consisting at the time of five members. From the

time of Mr. Tuttle's ordination, to April, 1834, his labors were equally divided between the two parishes, Groton and Ledyard; and since that time,
devoted to Ledyard only. It may be seen from the foregoing statement
that the society of Ledyard lay as a waste place during thirty-nine years.
Sometimes it employed preachers of different kinds, and sometimes nor .
Added to the church since 1811, 204.

MINISTER RAISED UP.—James A. Gallup.

* Allen. † Sp. An. 1. 322. Allen. ‡ Allen.

THE FIRST CHURCH IN LISBON, NEWENT SOCIETY, ORG. DEC. 1723.

MINISTERS.	SETTLED.	DISMISSED.	DIED.
Daniel Kirkland,*	Dec. 1723	1752	
Peter Powers,†	Dec. 1756	1764	
Joel Benedict, D. D.,‡	1770	1781	
David Hale,§	June, 1790	April, 1803	
David B. Ripley,	1803	1804	
Levi Nelson,‖	Dec. 1804		Dec. 1855
David Breed,	Feb. 1857		

A separate church formed during Mr. Kirkland's ministry, was soon disbanded. Dr. Benedict was dismissed on account of the severity of the
times, and their straitened circumstances; and the church was vacant eight
years. The inscription on Mr. Nelson's monument testifies that he was, "An
able divine, an impressive preacher, a good man, faithful to his trust." The
present tasteful church edifice was built in 1858; the former one stood 87
years. Rev. Samuel Kirkland, born here, was a missionary to the Indians, in
Oneida County, N. Y., and the founder of Hamilton College. *Rel. Intel.*
45. 376.

MINISTERS RAISED UP.—Samuel Kirkland, (f.) Caleb Knight,¶ William
Potter, (f.) Wm. A. Hyde, Hiram Tracy, Wm. R. Palmer, Aaron Kinne.**

* Sp. An. 1. 623. Allen. † Sp. An. 2. 346. Allen. ‡ Sp. An. 1. 682. Allen.
§ Allen. ‖ Mendon As. 276. Cong. Y. B. 3. 108. ¶ Cong. Y. B. 2. 100. ** Allen.

THE FIRST CHURCH IN LITCHFIELD, ORG. 1722.

Timothy Collins,*	June, 1723	Nov. 1752	1776
Judah Champion,*	July, 1753		Oct. 1810
Dan Huntington,*	Oct. 1798	Jan. 1809	
Lyman Beecher, D. D.,	May, 1810	Feb. 1826	
Daniel L. Carrol, D. D.,	Oct. 1827	Mar., 1829	
Laurens P. Hickok, D. D.,	July, 1829	Nov. 1836	
Jonathan Brace, D. D.,	June, 1838	Feb. 1844	
Benjamin Lincoln Swan,	Oct. 1846	May, 1856	
Leonard Woolsey Bacon,	Oct. 1856	June, 1860	

No great revival occurred here until the year 1808. During the progress of the "great awakening," this church by special vote expressed their aversion to that work, and their unwillingness to receive visits from the Evangelists. An account of the first revival in Litchfield may be found in the Connecticut Evangelical Magazine for 1813, from the pen of Rev. Mr. Huntington, and of Hon. Tapping Reeve. Since that time, the history of this community has been signalized by many and great revivals, especially under the ministries of Drs. Beecher, Hickok and Brace. *Memoir of Dr. Nettleton*, 158. *Ev. Mag*, 8. 155, 313. *Rel. Intel.* 15. 777 ; 16, 286. Under the administration of Dr. Beecher, the *Temperance Reformation* was powerfully advanced, if, indeed, it was not originated by his well known "Six Sermons." Owing, doubtless, to his influence, also, the *Litchfield County Missionary Society* was formed—the earliest of the auxiliaries of the A. B. C. F. M.

MINISTERS RAISED UP.—Charles Wadsworth, D. D., Herman L. Vaill, David L. Parmelee, James Kilbourn, (h.) —— McNeil, (Meth.) Joseph Vaill, Ethan Osborn, Benjamin Osborn, Edward P. Abbe, Frederick R. Abbe, Oscar Bissell, Horace Bushnell, D. D., Henry Ward Beecher, Charles Beecher, Thomas K. Beecher, Edward Nolen, Charles L. Brace, Ambrose Collins, John Churchill, Stephen Mason, Hezekiah B. Pierpont, Almon B. Pratt, Holland Weeks, Jeremiah Woodruff, Lewis H. Woodruff.

* Litchf. Centen. 70-72.

THE CHURCH IN LONG RIDGE, IN STAMFORD, ORG. JULY 5, 1843.

MINISTERS.	SETTLED.	DISMISSED.	DIED.
Frederick H. Ayers,	1843	1854	
A. B. Collins,	1854	1856	
John Smith,	1856	1858	
Ezra D. Kinney,	May, 1859	1860	
C. H. Powell,	1860		

The church was organized with seventeen members from the church in Stanwich. The enterprise is considered an experiment. They have a comfortable meeting-house, which is paid for, but are too poor to raise more than half the ordinary salary paid to a minister.

THE FIRST CHURCH IN MADISON, ORG. NOV. 1707.

John Hart,*	1705, ord. 1707	Mar. 1731
Jonathan Todd,†	Oct. 1733	Feb. 1791
John Eliot,‡	Nov. 1791	Dec. 1824
Samuel N. Shepard,§	Nov. 1825	Sept. 1856
Samuel Fiske,	June, 1857	

Organized as the church in East Guilford, the society being then included within the limits of the town of Guilford.

54

MINISTERS RAISED UP.—Moses Bartlett, William Hart, William Stone, Timothy Field, (h.) David D. Field, D. D., Erastus Scranton, Harvey Bushnell, William C. Fowler, Ralph S Crampton, Stephen A. Loper, Andrew L. Stone, Seth B. Stone, (f.) James L. Willard, William B. Lee, Chauncey D. Murray.

* Sp. An. 1. 260. † Sp. An. 1. 383. ‡ Sp. An. 2. 321. Allen. § Sp. An. 2. 365. Allen.

THE FIRST CHURCH IN MANCHESTER (FORMERLY ORFORD) ORG. July, 1779.

MINISTERS.	SETTLED.	DISMISSED.	DIED.
Beriah Phelps,*	Mar. 1780	June, 1793	Feb. 1817
Salmon King,	Nov. 1800	Oct. 1808	
Elisha B. Cook,	Mar. 1814		July, 1823
Enoch Burt,	July, 1824	1828	Nov. 1856
Bennett F. Northrop,	Feb. 1829	Oct. 1850	
Frederick T. Perkins,	June, 1851	Oct. 1856	
Samuel B. Forbes,	Oct. 1857	April, 1859	
Lester M. Dorman,	June, 1860		

* Allen.

THE SECOND CHURCH IN MANCHESTER, ORG. JAN. 8, 1851.

Geo. E. Hill,	June, 1851	Feb. 1853
Francis F. Williams,	Dec. 1853	Jan, 1856
Hiram Day,	May, 1857	Mar. 1859
Warren G. Jones,	1859	

For many years previous to the organization of the church, a Sabbath School was sustained in Union Village by the united efforts of the Congregational and Methodist brethren; and a few years before the erection of the church, it became entirely a Congregational Sabbath School. The efforts made in sustaining this school fully developed the necessity of establishing there the stated preaching of the gospel; and sixty-seven members, regularly dismissed from the First Congregational Church in Manchester, were duly organized, and their house of worship dedicated on the same day.

THE FIRST CHURCH IN MANSFIELD, ORG. OCT. 1710.

Eleazar Williams,*	Oct. 1710		Sept. 1742
Richard Salter, D. D.,†	June, 1744		April, 1787
Elijah Gridley,	April, 1789	July, 1796	
John Sherman,	Nov. 1797	Oct. 1805	
Samuel P. Williams,	Jan. 1807	Sept. 1817	
Anson S. Atwood,	Sept. 1819		

This was a colony from the Church in Windham. The first pastor, a son of Rev. John Williams of Deerfield, escaped being captured with his father's family by the Indians in 1704, as he was absent from home pursuing his studies for the ministry. He was a godly man, and a faithful, successful minister, receiving to the Church 409, and enjoying revivals in 1731 and '34· The early part of Dr. Salter's ministry was embarrassed and tried by the conduct of some of the members of his church who were the radicals of the memorable revival of 1740. These denounced the Church and Pastor as dead, hypocrites, and devoid of all spiritual religion, and went out from them in a disorderly manner, and formed a separate church. The Church after bearing with them for a time were constrained to cut them off. Dr. S., lived in that age of our ecclesiastical history, when "ministers were law and gospel" to their people, and after his first troubles were over he had a prosperous ministry, 347 being added to the church. He was a sound and able theologian, highly respected and beloved. Mr. Sherman became a Unitarian, but such was his hold on the community and his popularity that he took with him almost the entire congregation, and a large minority of the Church. The wonder is that the Church was not a perfect wreck ; but under God, *Consociation* saved it ; independency could not have done it. The Church was mercifully and unexpectedly delivered, by the dismission of the pastor by a council, when neither he nor the Society expected it. Eight years elapsed before the difficulties of doctrinal views were reconciled, the last element of Unitarianism removed from the Church, and her unity and peace restored. Thus ended the first conflict with Unitarianism in this State. Mr. S. P. Williams's labors were blessed with a revival the year before his dismission, and during the next 40 years, the Lord often refreshed his weary heritage with the influences of the Spirit. Whole membership 1325.

MINISTERS RAISED UP.—John Storrs, Eleazer Storrs, Andrew Storrs, Oliver Arnold, Jonathan Hovey, Jonathan Hovey, 2d., Samuel Wood, Asa King, Richard Salter Storrs, *Allen* ; Porter Storrs, John Storrs, *Allen* ; David A. Grosvenor, Mason Grosvenor, John W. Salter, (Ep.) Thomas G. Salter, Elijah P. Barrows, D. D., John A. Albro, D. D.

* Sp. An. 1, 226. Allen. † Sp. An. 1, 241. Allen.

THE CHURCH IN MARLBOROUGH, ORG. MAY, 1749.

MINISTERS.	SETTLED.		DISMISSED.	DIED.	
Samuel Lockwood, (c.)		1748			
Elijah Mason,	May,	1749	1761		1770
Benjamin Dunning,	Dec.	1762	1773		1785
David Huntington,		1776	1797		1812
David B. Ripley,	Sept.	1804	1827		1840
Chauncey Lee, D. D.*		1828	1837	Dec.	1842
Hiram Bell,		1840	1850		
Warren Fiske,		1850	1858		
Alpheus J. Pike,	Mar.	1859			

According to tradition, the Indian name of Marlborough was Terramuggus. Previous to 1747, the few families occupying the three contiguous corners of Colchester, Glastenbury and Hebron, assembled themselves occasionally for public worship.

Tradition says that Mr. Mason was ordained on the timbers, which, in the course of a year, were erected into a meeting-house, which was occupied till 1841, and then gave room for the present house. Before the erection of the house, the people assembled at the tavern, the minister occupying the bar. He soon formed the habit of intemperance, for which he was deposed, but afterwards was restored, and installed at Chester. Mr. Huntington took his dsimission against the wishes of the people, and settled at North Lyme. Mr. Ripley was a worthy man, and after a successful ministry, removed to Virgil, N. Y., and Northern Illinois, preaching in various destitute places.

MINISTER RAISED UP.—Lewis Dunham, (Meth.)

* Allen.

THE FIRST CHURCH IN MERIDEN, ORG. OCT. 22, 1729.

MINISTERS.	SETTLED.	DISMISSED.	DIED.
Theophilus Hall,*	Oct. 1729		Mar. 1767
John Hubbard,†	June, 1769		Nov. 1786
John Willard,	June, 1786	1802	1826
Erastus Ripley,	Feb. 1803	Feb. 1822	Nov. 1841
Charles J. Hinsdale,	Jan. 1823	Dec. 1833	
Wm. McLain,	1834	1835	
Arthur Granger,	Mar. 1836	Oct. 1838	
Charles Rich,	1840	1841	
George W. Perkins,‡	May, 1841	July, 1854	Nov. 1856
George Thacher,	Nov. 1854		

The First Church in Meriden was organized with fifty-one members. The society was within the limits of Wallingford, until May, 1806. There have been frequent revivals, adding many members to the church. Under the first pastorate, 250; the fourth, 100 hopeful converts; fifth, 50; seventh, about 250; and during the last year, 80 were added. Under the "stated supplies" in 1834 and 1840, 170. *Rel. Intel.* 14, 668. Two colonies have gone from this church—one in 1848 of one hundred members, to constitute the "Center Church;" the other in 1853, of thirty persons, to form the "Third Church," located in that part of Meriden called Hanover.

MINISTERS RAISED UP.—Matthew Merriman, Avery Hall, Isaac Foster, Thomas Holt,‖ Samuel J. Curtis, (h.) Erastus Curtis, Charles E. Murdock, (h.) Dan C. Curtis, (h.) Ralph Tyler, Lyman C. Hough.

*Sp. An. 1. 668. Allen. †Sp. An. 415, 537. Allen. ‡. Cong. Y. B., 1857, 124. ‖ Allen.

The Center Church, Meriden, Org. March, 1848.

MINISTERS.	SETTLED.	DISMISSED.	DIED.
Asahel H. Stevens,	Mar. 1848	Sept. 1854	
A. S. Chesebrough,	1855	1857	
Lewis C. Lockwood,	June, 1857	Feb. 1858	
O. H. White, (c.)	June, 1858		

The first house of worship was erected in 1727, in the south-eastern part of the town; the second in 1755, at the center; the third in 1830, near the same spot. In this house, the church continued to worship till 1848, when a majority, with the pastor, removed to West Meriden; and the remainder, forming the second church, occupy the house where their fathers had worshiped. There have been interesting revivals in this place both before and since the division,—some of them in their details of great power and thrilling interest.

The Church in Middlebury, Org. Feb. 10, 1796.

Ira Hart,	Nov. 1798	April, 1809	Oct. 1829
Mark Mead,	Nov. 1809	Mar. 1830	
Jason Atwater,	Oct. 1830	Oct. 1845	April, 1860
George P. Prudden,	Dec. 1845	Mar. 1851	
Joel R. Arnold,	Sept. 1851	Dec. 1853	
Revilo J. Cone.	May, 1854	Dec. 1855	
Jonathan S. Judd,	June, 1856		

Several eminent men have been candidates in Middlebury, as Dr. E. D. Griffin, Dr. E. Porter, Mr. Sherman of Mansfield, and Mr. Gelston of Sherman. Some of them were invited to settle.

The dismission of Mr. Hart, was the result of a struggle that was very fierce and long continued. The people were very generally alienated from their pastor. In those times it was customary for damages to be paid to the dismissed pastor. It was left to the council to award the damages, and the amounts set down by the different members were from five dollars to $1500. The average of these was the amount fixed,—being somewhere from $400 to $500.

There have been several seasons of special ingathering. Especially was the Church thus favored during the ministry of Mr. Atwater. *Ev. Mag.* 3,64, 102. *Rel. Intel.* 6,153.

MINISTERS RAISED UP.—Bennet Tyler, d. d., John B. Richardson, Nathaniel S. Richardson, d. d., (Ep). Sylvester Hine, George F. Bronson, Henry A. Russel.

The Church in Middlefield, in Middletown, Org. 1745.

Ebenezer Gould,*	1747	1756
Joseph Denison,	1765	1770

MINISTERS.	SETTLED.	DISMISSED.	DIED.
Abner Benedict,†	1771	1785	1818
Stephen Hayes,	May, 1820	May, 1827	
James Noyes,	July, 1829	Jan. 1839	
Dwight M. Seward,			
James T. Dickinson,			
James D. Moore,	Dec. 1846	Dec. 1850	
Willard Jones,			
Francis Dyer,			
S. D. Jewett,	July, 1858		

After the dismission of Mr. Benedict, the Church was for 23 years destitute of a settled minister. Other denominations pressed sore upon it. The sanctuary was obtained for erroneous preaching; piety declined, and the Church became nearly or quite extinct. The Church was reorganized in 1808, but passed on in darkness till 1820. It has now a neat and tasteful sanctuary, a good lecture room and parsonage; is united and harmonious, with prospects highly favorable for the future.

* Allen.   † Sp. An. 1, 682.

THE CHURCH IN MIDDLE HADDAM, IN CHATHAM, ORG. SEPT. 24, 1740.

Benjamin Bowers,	Sept. 1740		1761
Benjamin Boardman,*	Jan. 1762	1783	1802
David Selden,	Oct. 1785		Jan. 1825
Charles Bentley,	Feb. 1826	May, 1833	
Stephen A. Loper,	Jan. 1834	Oct. 1841	
William Case,	1842	1844	
Philo Judson,	1846	1847	
James C. Houghton,	Sept. 1847	Feb. 1851	
William S Wright,	1851	1853	
James Kilbourn,	May, 1853	July, 1857	
Benjamin B. Hopkinson,	1858		

Added to the Church under the first pastorate, 199; second, 171; third 281; fourth, 90, of whom 51 at one time, July 1, 1827; baptized under the second pastorate 690; third, 539; Marriages, 319.

From the formation of the Church the pulpit has very seldom been vacant. The Church has been blessed with revivals. *Rel. Intel.* 11, 619.

MINISTERS RAISED UP.—Israel Brainerd, James Brainerd Taylor, Thomas Tallman, Jacob H. Strong, David Selden, Sylvester Selden, William Wright, David A. Strong.

*Sp. An. 1, 513.

THE SECOND CHURCH IN MIDDLE HADDAM, IN CHATHAM, ORG. MARCH, 1855.

J. H. Newton,	March, 1855

This Church was formed at Middle Haddam Landing, in consequence of the inconvenience to many members of the Congregational Church of going a long distance to public worship, and of the need of having a house of worship of the Congregational denomination at the Landing. The Church was formed with 23 members.

THE FIRST CHURCH IN MIDDLETOWN, ORG. NOV. 4, 1668.

MINISTERS.	SETTLED.	DISMISSED.	DIED.
Samuel Stow,	1651 ?	1667 ?	
Nathaniel Collins,*	Nov. 1668		Dec. 1684
Noadiah Russell,†	Oct. 1688		Dec. 1713
William Russell,‡	June, 1715		June, 1761
Enoch Huntington,§	June, 1762		June, 1809
Dan Huntington,	Aug. 1809	Feb. 1816	
Chauncey A. Goodrich,D.D.‖	July, 1816	Dec. 1817	Feb. 1860
John R. Crane, D. D.,¶	Nov. 1818		Aug. 1856
James C. Crane,	Jan. 1854	April, 1856	
Jeremiah Taylor,	Oct. 1856		

The congregation was gathered as early as 1651. "The great object of the Colonists, who settled in Middletown, was to enjoy unmolested, the right of worshiping God according to the dictates of their own consciences." Difficulties arose in the congregation respecting Mr. Stow, and the question in debate became so serious that the aid of the General Court was finally invoked to bring matters to a crisis. The decree of the Court was "that the town of Middletown is free from Mr. Stow as their engaged minister, and that the Court appoint a committee to further a settled ministry in that place."

In the ministry of Mr. Collins the Church had great prosperity. Cotton Mather says of him. "The Church of Middletown, upon Connecticut River, was the golden candlestick, from whence this excellent person illuminated more than that whole colony; and all the qualities of most exemplary piety, extraordinary integrity, obliging affability, joined with the accomplishments of an extraordinary preacher, did render him truly excellent." He was a member of the Saybrook Synod: p. 7, 10. The Russells, father and son, were eminent in their day; the father was one of the founders of Yale College; the son died on the 46th anniversary of his ordination. Whitfield, having been his guest for a night, said of him, " I think him an Israelite indeed, and one who has been long mourning over the deadness of professors. Oh! that all ministers were like minded."

Enoch Huntington the fourth pastor, was a ripe scholar, and in connection with his parochial labors, engaged in teaching young men.

A number of seasons of revival have been enjoyed; and the numbers added to the Church from time to time, when such special seasons have not been enjoyed evinces a healthy tone of piety at all times.

The Church and Society are now occupying their third house of worship.

MINISTERS RAISED UP.—Nathaniel Collins, Jeremiah Leaming, D. D., (Ep.) Robert Hubbard, Joseph Washburn, J. P. K. Henshaw, D. D., (Ep.) James B. Crane, Jonathan E. Barnes, Seth Wetmore, Israhiah Wetmore, Wait Cornwell, Seth B. Paddock, (Ep.) Simeon North, D. D., John H. Newton, Enoch Huntington.

* Sp. An. 1. 183. Allen. † Sp. An. 1, 261 ; 2, 237. ‡ Sp. An. 2. 237. Allen. § Sp. An. 1, 606. Allen. | New Englander for 1860, 328. ¶ Sp. An. 2, 562. Cong. Y. B. 2, 93.

THE SOUTH CHURCH IN MIDDLETOWN., ORG. OCT. 28, 1747.

MINISTERS.	SETTLED.	DISMISSED.	DIED.
Ebenezer Frothingham,	Oct. 1747	1788	1798
Stephen Parsons,	Jan. 1788	Aug. 1795	
David Huntington,	Nov. 1797	Oct. 1800	
Horatio T. McGregor,	Oct. 1801	Jan. 1802	
Benjamin Graves,	Oct. 1803	Jan. 1812	
Ahab Jincks,	Aug. 1816	May, 1820	
Thomas T. De Verell,	May, 1822	1823	
Horàce Hooker,	1826	Sept. 1827	
Edward R. Tyler,	Dec. 1827	Apr. 1832	Sept. 1848
Wm. H. Beecher,	Mar. 1833	Sept. 1833	
Robert McEwen,	May, 1835	Aug. 1838	
Arthur Granger,	April, 1839	May, 1844	
Andrew L. Stone,	Sept. 1844	Jan. 1849	
John L. Dudley,	Sept. 1849	Jan. 1854	
John L. Dudley,	Jan. 1854		

This church originated in the great revival of 1740. It was but one of the organized results of the stirring preaching of Edwards, and men who sympathized with him. It was no stranger to the salutary discipline attendant upon such as strove for the direct spirituality, pure doctrines, and simple polity of the pilgrim fathers. Notwithstanding early trials, the church advanced. Under its first ministry, its records show peculiar thrift and vigor. That of Mr. Huntington contributed to the spiritual well-being of the church. He labored with eminent success, and was a man of ardent piety. From 1812 to 1827, the church passed through a varied history, and some very dark and discouraging days. But under Mr. Tyler, it rallied. The present church edifice was built during his pastorate; the first was built in 1774. To him the church and society owe much of their present vigor.

THE FIRST CHURCH IN MILFORD, ORG. AUG. 22, 1639.

Peter Prudden,*	April, 1640	July, 1656
Roger Newton,†	Aug. 1660	June, 1683
Samuel Andrew,‡	Nov. 1685	Jan. 1738

MINISTERS.	SETTLED.	DISMISSED.	DIED.
Samuel Whittlesey,§	Dec. 1737		Oct. 1768
Samuel Wales, D. D.,‖	Dec. 1770	May, 1782	1794
William Lockwood,¶	Mar. 1784	Apr. 1796	June, 1828
Bezaleel Pinneo,**	Oct. 1796		Sept. 1849
David B. Coe, D. D.,	Oct. 1840	Aug. 1844	
Jonathan Brace, D. D.,	Sept. 1845		

The church was organized before the settlement of the town was commenced. The formation of the church is thus referred to in Mather's Magnalia: "There were then two famous churches gathered at New Haven; gathered in two days, one following upon the other, Mr. Davenport's and Mr. Prudden's, and with this one singular circumstance, that a mighty barn was the place wherein the duties of that solemnity were attended." There have been two colonies from the church; the first in 1741; the second in 1805. Both of these colonies were the germs of two now flourishing churches, viz: the second church in Milford, and the Church of Christ in Orange.

Mr. Andrew was one of the three prime movers in founding Yale College; also a member of the Saybrook Synod, in 1708, and Rector of the college; pp. 4, 8, supra. The church has been destitute of a settled pastor, since its formation, twelve years and eight months. None of the nine pastors were driven away; and the average term of official service of each pastor is about a quarter of a century.

MINISTERS RAISED UP.—Samuel Treat, Job Prudden, Nehemiah Prudden,†† Gibson Tomlinson, Abijah Carrington, Samuel Rogers Andrew, Samuel Merwin, Elijah Baldwin, Joseph Fowler, Benjamin Fenn, ——— Platt, Joseph Whiting, Phineas Stowe, Samuel J. M. Merwin, William G. French, David B. Davidson, Green Tibbals, Lewis French, Elijah C. Baldwin, John Gunn Beard, W. I. Budington, D. D., Calvin Lord, Alanson Clark.

* Math, Mag. 1. 357.   †Sp. An. 1. 37.   Allen.   ‡Sp. An. 1. 269.   Allen.   § Allen.
‖Sp.An. 1. 710.   ¶ Sp. An. 1. 413.   Allen.   ** Sp. An. 1. 605.   †† Allen.

THE PLYMOUTH CHURCH, IN MILFORD, ORG. 1741.

Job Prudden,*	May, 1747		June, 1774
Josiah Sherman,	Aug. 1775	June, 1781	Nov. 1789
David Tullar,	Nov. 1784	Dec. 1802	
Sherman Johnson,†	Feb. 1805		May, 1806
Caleb Pitkin,	Mar. 1808	Oct. 1816	
Jehu Clark,	Dec. 1817	1826	
Asa M. Train,	July, 1828	Jan. 1850	
J. M. Sherwood,	May, 1841	Oct. 1852	
S. G. Dodd,	Oct. 1852	July, 1854	
Wm. Scofield,	Nov. 1854	Apr. 1858	
W. Nye Harvey, (c.)	Oct. 1858		

A large and respectable minority of the first church objected to the settlement of Mr. Whittlesey, on suspicion of his being an Arminian. After
several months trial, they failed to gain satisfaction, and applied to the
church, then repeatedly to the Association, and next to the town, to relieve
their grievances. Failing in these, they petitioned the County Court for relief, and next, they were induced to dissent from the constitution of our
churches, and "declare for the excellent establishment of the church of
Scotland." After this, they repeatedly applied in vain to the court for relief.
Gov. George Law, of the First Society, sent Mr. Benajah Case to prison for
preaching to them ; issued warrants to arrest other ministers ; and sentenced
Rev. Samuel Finley, afterwards President of Princeton College, to be trans-
ported from the colony ; and Mr. Pomeroy, of Hebron, was called to answer
to the General Assembly for preaching to them. At length, after five years,
the County Court granted them liberty to erect a house of worship, though the
doors of their own house were closed against five evangelical preachers during the very year of its completion. In seven years more, the Legislature
released them from taxes to the First Society, but did not grant them ample
society privileges till ten years later. At length, in 1770, thirty-three years
after they began their dissent, they were allowed their proportion of the
funds for the support of the gospel. While other denominations were early
tolerated, thus intolerant were "the powers that be" to dissenters of their
own order,—a course of procedure well calculated to build up other sects.
See Trumbull, 2, 335–9, and *Church Manual.*

* Allen. † Mendon. As. 278.

THE CHURCH IN MILLINGTON, IN EAST HADDAM, ORG. DEC. 2, 1736.

MINISTERS.	SETTLED,	DISMISSED.	DIED.
Timothy Symmes,	Dec. 1736	1743	
Hobart Estabrook,	Nov. 1745		Jan. 1766
Diodate Johnson,	July, 1767		Jan. 1773
Eleazer Sweetland,	May, 1777		Mar. 1787
William Lyman, D. D.*	Dec. 1787	Aug. 1823	1833
Herman L. Vaill,	April, 1825	Apr. 1828	
Nathaniel Miner,	May, 1833	Oct. 1857	
A. C. Beach,	Feb. 1859		

The Ecclesiastical Society was formed Oct. 1733. Till some time in 1743,
when their meeting house—fifty feet by forty—was prepared for use, the
people worshiped in the dwelling house of Jonathan Chapman.

MINISTERS RAISED UP.—Nathaniel Emmons, D. D,† Edward Dorr Griffin,
D. D.,‡ Warren G. Jones, George A. Beckwith.

* Allen. † Mendon Assoc. 109. Sp. An. 1. 693. Memoir and Works. ‡ Sp. An.
4. 26.

The Church in Millplane, in Danbury, Org. Oct. 29, 1851.

MINISTERS.	SETTLED.	DISMISSED.	DIED.
Enoch S. Huntington,	Oct. 1851	1854	
Nathan Burton,	Oct. 1854	Oct. 1855	

This church began with eighteen members, under the leading of a man of energy and property—Mr. Birchard. But he soon died ; and after that event it drooped and flagged. It had a neat meeting house, but no funds. After being supplied by Methodist ministers about four years, it disbanded April 28, 1860.

THE CHURCH IN MILTON, IN LITCHFIELD, ORG. AUG. 19, 1798.

Benjamin Judd,	May, 1802	June, 1804	
Abraham Fowler,*	Sept. 1807	1813	1815
Asahel Nettleton, D. D.	1813		
Levi Smith,	1825		
Ralph Smith,	Oct. 1841	1844	
John F. Norton,	Oct. 1844	Apr. 1849	
Herman L. Vaill,	June, 1849	Dec. 1851	
Francis F. Williams,	Dec. 1851	Apr. 1853	
James Noyes,	July, 1853	July, 1854	
George J. Harrison,	Sept. 1854		

This is the parish described in the Life of Nettleton (p. 67) as "a waste place"—"the people not only without a pastor, but so weakened by divisions, and by the loss of their parish fund, that they almost despaired of ever enjoying again the privilege of a preached gospel." The history of this feeble missionary church is a deeply interesting and eventful one ; filled with sadness—and yet with many signal interpositions of God in its behalf. For long periods of time, the regular services of the sanctuary have been suspended, and the scattered members of the church left to wander as sheep without a shepherd. But when the church seemed ready to perish, Nettleton, in 1813, and Levi Smith, in 1825, under the providence of God, were sent to revive his work, gather in a new band of converts, and so strengthen the things which remained. It appears to have been an error of great magnitude, that after the successful labors of Nettleton and Smith, the regular ministry of the word was not secured and sustained. God's providence was strikingly seen in causing the church to resume their efforts, and secure regular preaching in 1841. Had the effort been deferred for a single month, there is reason to believe that the church would have been now extinct.

MINISTERS RAISED UP.—Noah Bishop, James Kilbourn.

* Sp. An. 2. 229.

THE CHURCH IN MOHEGAN, IN MONTVILLE, ORG. JULY 9, 1832.

Anson Gleason,	April, 1835	Sept. 1848

MINISTERS.	SETTLED.	DISMISSED.	DIED.
D. W. C. Sterry,	June, 1848	Apr. 1851	
William Palmer, (Bapt.)	May, 1851	Dec. 1855	
Oliver Brown, Jr.	Oct. 1856	May, 1857	
H. C. Hayden,	June, 1857	June, 1858	
J. W. Salter,	Aug. 1858		

The meeting-house was erected by donations of their friends, in 1831. The people number about two hundred persons—one third Indians, and two-thirds whites, settled on the tribe land. The origin of the church was in this wise: "Miss Sarah L. Huntington, of Norwich, and Miss Elizabeth Raymond, of Montville, commenced a day school at the house of Deacon William Dolbeare, in December, 1829. Their compassion was moved, in view of the moral desolations, and in 1830, they commenced a Sabbath School, assisted by other sisters and brethren, of kindred spirit, from Norwich and New London. Miss Huntington furnished her own supplies; and often walked six miles to her charge. These labors of love she continued until her marriage with Rev. Eli Smith, and her entrance on a foreign mission. *See Memoir of Mrs. Smith, Sept.* 1831. Since the organization of the church in 1832, which was composed of five whites and one aged female Mohegan, there have been numerical and moral improvements in the church, schools and society. The funds for the support of the ministry and educational purposes, are obtained from the United States, and from friends in Norwich, New London and vicinity. Since 1848, Gen. William Williams, of Norwich, assisted by other brethren in Norwich and New London, has had a careful supervision of their religious affairs. For several years, Gen. Williams has left the ministrations of his own pastor, attended service here, superintended the Sabbath School, distributed thousands of tracts, and mostly supported the minister. Their schools, congregation, society, decorum and progress, would not suffer in comparison with those in any of our rural districts.

THE CHURCH IN MONROE, (FORMERLY NEW STRATFORD,) ORG. DEC. 14, 1764

Elisha Rexford,	Jan. 1765		Apr. 1808
John Noyes,	1813	1814	
Asahel Nettleton, D. D.	1814	1815	
Chauncey G. Lee,	Oct. 1821	Apr. 1826	
Amos Bassett, D. D.,*	1826		1828
Daniel Jones,	Sept. 1828	July. 1835	
James Kent,†	1837	1840	
Robert D. Gardner,	Mar. 1841	Sept. 1851	
Lewis M. Shepard,	Aug. 1853	June, 1857	
Edward B. Emerson,	April, 1858		

As the first volume of the Church records is lost, many important facts are buried in oblivion. Several revivals been enjoyed here; two while Mr. Nettleton was here; one in 1814, and one in 1815,—when about thirty were

added to the church. *Memoir of Nettleton,* 66. Also under, the ministry of Mr. Lee, Mr Jones and Mr. Kent. The last, and most powerful one, was in 1851, under Mr. Morgan's labors, when between thirty and forty were received to the church. The house of worship is new, handsome, and paid for.
MINISTER RAISED UP.—Tillotson Babbitt.

* Sp. An. 2. 294. Allen. Rel. Intel. 12. 735. † Allen.

THE CHURCH IN MONTVILLE, (FORMERLY NEW LONDON NORTH,) ORG. 1721.

MINISTERS.	SETTLED.	DISMISSED.	DIED.
James Hillhouse,	Oct. 1722		1740
David Jewett,*	Oct. 1739		June, 1783
Roswell Cook,	June, 1784		Apr. 1798
Amos G. Thompson,	Sept. 1799		Oct. 1801
Abisha Alden,	Aug. 1803	Apr. 1826	1836
Rodolphus Landfear,	Aug. 1829	May, 1832	
Erastus Ripley,	Jan. 1835	Nov. 1837	
Spencer F. Beard,	July, 1838	June, 1846	
John W. Salter,	Aug. 1847	Apr. 1858	
Thomas L. Shipman,	April, 1858	1859	
H. C. Hayden,	Sept. 1859		

Mr. Hillhouse received his call at Boston, Feb. 5, 1721. His family remain to this day. The distinguished Senator, James Hillhouse, of New Haven, was his son. The church has been blessed with revivals at several different times. For an account of a revival in 1741, see Tracy's Great Awakening, pp. 156–8. The house of worship is new and commodious.

* Sp. An 3. 192. Allen.

THE CHURCH IN MORRIS, (FORMERLY LITCHFIELD SOUTH FARMS,) ORG. 1768.

George Beckwith,*	1772	1781	
Amos Chase,†	1787	1814	Dec. 1849
William R. Weeks, D. D.,‡	Jan. 1815	Oct. 1815	June, 1848
Amos Pettengill,§	April, 1816	1822	Aug. 1830
Henry Robinson,	1823	1829	
Veron D. Taylor,	1831	1833	
James F. Warner,	1833	1834	
Ralph S. Crampton,	1834	1836	
Stephen Hubbell,	June, 1836?	1837?	
B. Y. Messenger,	1837?	1838?	
Richard Woodruff, (c.)	Oct. 1838?	Jan. 1841	
David L. Parmelee,	Aug. 1841		
H. H. McFarland,	Nov. 1859		

The grant for "winter privileges" dates back to 1747; the incorporation

of the Society, 1767. There have been several revivals, with considerable ingatherings at frequent intervals, from 1799 ; in six different years, from 23
to 73 were added.   In 1814, was the most extensive work, under the labors
of Dr. Nettleton ; an account of it was written by James Morris, and carefully
preserved in manuscript. It gives the names and age of 80 individuals, the
time of each one's hopeful conversion, and some account of the religious exercises of almost all of them.   *See extracts in Memoir of Dr. Nettleton,* pp.
70–77.

South Farms Society became the town of Morris in 1859.

MINISTERS RAISED UP.—Samuel Whittlesey, Simeon Woodruff, Samuel G.
Orton, John Pierpont, (Unita.) John W. Peck, D. D. (Bapt.)

* Litchf. Centen. 72. † Sp. An. 1, 592. Litchf. Centen. 72. ‡ Sp. An. 4, 473. § Sp.
An. 2, 524. Allen. Litchf. Centen. 127. Memoir by Rev. L. Hart, 1834.

THE CHURCH IN MT. CARMEL, IN HAMDEN, ORG. JAN. 26, 1764.

MINISTERS.	SETTLED.	DISMISSED.	DIED.
Nathaniel Sherman,*	May, 1769	Aug. 1772.	1797
Joshua Perry,†	Oct. 1783	1790	1812
Dan Bradley,‡	1792	1800 ?	1838
Asa Lyman,§	Sept. 1800	April, 1803	1836
John Hyde,‖	May, 1806	Jan. 1811	1849
Eliphalet B. Coleman,	Feb. 1812	Nov. 1825	1857 ?
Stephen Hubbell,	May, 1830	May, 1836	
James Birney,	June, 1842	March, 1846	
Israel P. Warren,	July, 1846	Sept. 1851	
D. H. Thayer,	Jan. 1853		

This Church has had a frequent change of ministers, and none have ever
died among them in office.   Revivals have been usual, as in other Churches
in the vicinity.   The Church and Society have for several years been growing in numbers and strength, with some increase of population and the introduction of manufactures.   *Rel. Intel.* 13, 218.

MINISTER RAISED UP.—George A. Dickerman.

*Sp. An. 1. 480. Allen. †Allen. ‡ Sp. An. 1. 656. § Allen. ‖ Sp. An. 2. 192.

THE CHURCH IN MYSTIC BRIDGE, IN STONINGTON, ORG. JAN. 20, 1852.

Walter R. Long,   Sept. 1853

The Church was organized with a membership of 37, mostly from the
First Church in Stonington.   There have been four seasons of revival
during its brief existence, one immediately after its organization, also in
'53, '55 and '58.

The Nazareth Church, in Sterling, (formerly Voluntown,) Org. Feb. 13, 1772.

MINISTERS.	SETTLED.	DISMISSED.	DIED.
Solomon Morgan,*	April, 1772	Feb. 1782	Sept. 1804
Allen Campbell,	1794		

This Church has had but one pastor, who afterwards was settled in Canterbury and North Canaan. They encouraged Mr. Campbell, one of their own members to preach for them, in which they had the approbation of the Association. The Church though not formerly dissolved, is virtually extinct.

* Allen. Sp. An. 2, 526.

The Church in Naugatuck, (formerly Salem Society,) Org. Feb. 22, 1781.

Medad Rogers,	1781	1784 ?	
Abraham Fowler,*	Jan. 1785	Mar. 1799	Nov. 1815
Noah J. Simons,	Oct. 1799	1800	
Jabez Chadwick,	Dec. 1800	Mar. 1803	
Matthias Cazier,	May, 1804		
Stephen Dodd,†	1811	April, 1817	Feb. 1856
Amos Pettengill,‡	Jan. 1823		Aug. 1830
J. B. Richardson,	1832	1834	
Seth Sackett,	Oct. 1834	Jan. 1838	
Chauncey G. Lee,	Jan. 1838	Nov. 1840	
H. A. Taylor,	1840	1841 ?	
Marshall Eames,	1842	April, 1843	
C. S. Sherman,	July, 1843	April, 1844	
Albert K. Teele,	June, 1845	Oct. 1849	
Charles S. Sherman,	Nov. 1849		

This Church was originally formed of 16 members, mostly from the First Church in Waterbury. The town was then a parish of Waterbury, and known by the name of Salem.

In January, 1781, it was "voted to make a petition to the General Assembly, to lay a land tax of one shilling upon the acre, upon all the land in the Society of Salem, for the purpose of building a meeting house." This meeting house was completed in 1782. Another was built occupying a new and more central site in 1831. In 1853 this was sold and removed, and the present house of worship dedicated in Sept. 1855.

The Church has experienced a varied and often a trying history; at one time the Presbyterian and Congregational elements in it refused to coalesce; at another, intemperance affected the standing and divided the ranks of its members; and still later, there was a division of feeling on the question of Old and New School Theology.

In addition to these troubles, the Society has had to struggle with limited means and a change of ministry, the latter growing in part out of the former.

With the growth, however, of the manufacturing interests of the town, the Society has increased in ability and has erected its present beautiful edifice at a cost of $16,000, expecting at the time to cancel every pecuniary obligation in a period of five years. This would probably have been done but for the commercial distress which intervened. It is gratifying, however, to add that the Church has for a long time been in a very harmonious state, has gradually increased in membership, and been repeatedly favored with the gentle and refreshing dews of the Holy Spirit. The whole number of persons who have been admitted to the Church is 645.

MINISTERS RAISED UP.—John H. Pettengill, John G. Hull, (Ep.) Thomas Lewis.

* Sp. An. 2. 230.   † Allen.   ‡ Sp. An. 2. 524.   Allen.   Litchf. Centen. 127. Memoir by Rev. L. Hart, 1834.

THE FIRST CHURCH IN NEW BRITAIN, ORG. APRIL 19, 1758.

MINISTERS.	SETTLED.	DISMISSED.	DIED.
John Smalley, D. D.,*	April, 1758		June, 1820
Newton Skinner,†	Feb. 1810		March, 1825
Henry Jones,	Oct. 1825	Dec. 1827	
Jason Atwater,	1827	Nov. 1828	
Jonathan Cogswell, D. D.,	April, 1829	April, 1834	
Dwight M. Seward,	Feb. 1836	June, 1842	
Chester S. Lyman,	Feb. 1843	April, 1845	
C. S. Sherman,	May, 1845	1849	
E. B. Andrews,	June, 1850	Nov. 1851	
Horace Winslow,	Dec. 1852	Dec. 1857	
Lavalette Perrin,	Feb. 1858		

This Church has been greatly blessed of God, having enjoyed frequent revivals, and some of great power. The frequent changes in the ministry during the last twenty years have been occasioned chiefly by failure of health in the pastors.

The most signal work of the Spirit under Dr. Smalley's ministry was in 1784–5, adding 38; 253 in all, during his ministry; 28 admitted to certain Church privileges, previous to 1767, without professing vital piety. There was a signal revival under the second pastor in 1821, 119 making profession of faith, 248 in all. Mr. Skinner was a man of great physical as well as mental strength. Under every pastor there have been consideraable accessions, and also in 1828–9, when without one. The progressive and conservative elements, which agitated churches largely through New England, led to a division of the church in 1842.

The first meeting house, a plain building, has long since disappeared; the second, a house much admired in its time, built in 1822, is now used for secular purposes; the third, built in 1855, is regarded as a model of church architecture. Its centennial anniversary was observed April 19, 1858.

MINISTERS RAISED UP. —William Whittlesey, Eliphalet Whittlesey, Levi W. Hart, Henry Eddy, John S. Whittlesey, Jonathan Bird, Burdett Hart.

* Sp. An. 1 559. Allen. ¶ Sp. An. 1. 563.

THE SOUTH CHURCH IN NEW BRITAIN, ORG. JULY 5, 1842.

MINISTERS·	SETTLED.	DISMISSED.	DIED.
Samuel Rockwell,	Jan. 1843	June, 1858	
C. L. Goodell,	Feb. 1859		

The growth of the village prepared the way for a second church, besides those of other denominations. Its house of worship was erected immediately. Original number of members, 120, who were dismissed from the Central Church. Added during fifteen years, 270; baptisms, 144. Contributions for benevolent objects in fifteen years, $13,418.91 ; in 1854, $1,983.49. Aggregate with home expenses, $26,000, exclusive of cost of house of worship.

MINISTERS RAISED UP.—Levi W. Hart, E. Maynard, (f.)

THE CHURCH IN NEW CANAAN, ORG. JUNE 20, 1733.

John Eells,	June, 1733	June, 1741	
Robert Silliman, *	Feb. 1742	Aug. 1771	April, 1781
William Drummond,	July, 1772	May, 1777	
Justus Mitchell,†	Jan. 1783		Feb. 1806
William Bonney,	Feb. 1808	Aug. 1831	
Theophilus Smith,‡	Aug. 1831		Aug. 1853
Frederick W. Williams,	Feb. 1854	Dec. 1859	
Ralph Smith,	May, 1860		

The Canaan Society, lying in Norwalk and Stamford, and occupying the same territory with the present town of New Canaan, was incorporated in 1731 ; the town in 1801. The church was formed with twenty-four members, thirteen from the Norwalk church, and eleven from Stamford ; in one hundred and twenty-six years, nine hundred and twenty-six persons have been received into the church. Mr. Silliman settled in Chester in 1772.

MINISTERS RAISED UP.—James Richards, D. D.,§ Amzi Benedict, William Carter, William B. Weed, James S. Hoyt, Daniel Smith, Edwin Stevens, (f.) Darius Hoyt, (h.) David C. Comstock.

* Allen. †Sp. An. 1. 666. Allen. † Cong. Y. Book, 2. 104. §Sp. An. 4. 99. Allen.

THE CHURCH IN NEW FAIRFIELD, ORG. NOV. 9, 1742.

Benajah Case,	Nov. 1742	Jan. 1753
James Taylor,	Mar. 1758	June, 1764

MINISTERS.	SETTLED.	DISMISSED.	DIED.
—— *Davenport*,	1769		
Joseph Peck,	June, 1769	1775	
—— *Mills*,	1780		
—— Kittleton,	1782		
Medad Rogers,*	1786	Oct. 1822	Aug. 1824
Abraham O. Stansbury,	Oct. 1824	Jan. 1827	
Daniel Crocker,	Oct. 1827		Mar. 1831
George Coan,	June, 1833	May, 1835	
Benajah Y. Morse,	Apr. 1835	Mar. 1838	
David C. Perry,	Dec. 1838	Nov. 1844	
Henry H. Morgan,	Dec. 1845	May, 1849	
Lewis Pennell,	Oct. 1849	Oct. 1853	
Aaron B. Peffers,	May, 1855	May, 1858	
Frederick J. Jackson,	June, 1858	1859	
Ezra D. Kinney,	1859		

There was a noted revival of religion in 1818, by which the whole community was moved, and there was an ingathering of one hundred or more to the kingdom of Christ. There was a meeting house in 1755, and the society built another in 1786. In 1836, the society removed the site of the house, by which some became disaffected and withdrew.

* Allen.

The First Church in New Hartford, Org. 1738.

Jonathan Marsh,	Oct. 1739	July, 1794	
Edward D. Griffin, D. D.*	June, 1795	Aug. 1801	Nov. 1837
Amasa Jerome,†	Aug. 1802	Dec. 1813	
Cyrus Yale,‡	Oct. 1814	Dec. 1834	
Cyrus Yale,‡	1837		May, 1854

This church was greatly reduced in numbers by the formation of the South Church in 1848. Public worship was suspended after Mr. Yale's death, and it disbanded Oct. 1859. The location of the house, on a high bleak hill, also conspired to effect this result. There were extensive revivals, particularly under Dr. Griffin and Mr. Yale. In three different years, one hundred to one hundred and ten were added, and in four other years, 48 to 78. *Ev. Mag.* 1. 217, 265. *Rel. Intel.* 16. 702.

* Sp. An. 4. 26. Allen. Litchf. Centen. 109. Am. Qu. Reg. 13, 365. † Allen. Litchf. Centen. 118. ‡ Sp. An. 2. 615.

The North Church in New Hartford, Org. Sept. 25, 1828.

Burr Baldwin,	Jan. 1830	Feb. 1833	
Willis Lord,	Oct. 1834	Dec. 1838	
John Woodbridge, D. D.,	April, 1839	Jan. 1842	

MINISTERS.	SETTLED.	DISMISSED.	DIED.
Hiram Day,	1842	1844	
Alexander Leadbetter,	May, 1844	May, 1849	
Joseph A. Saxton,	Jan. 1851	Oct. 1852	
Franklin A. Spencer,	Sept. 1853		

This Church was originally a colony from the First Church of the town, and consisted of 62 members. Out of the thirty years since it was organized, it has had only 23 years of pastoral labor. The remaining portion of time has been supplied temporarily by different persons.

There were limited revivals under the ministry of the first and fifth pastors. Mr. Day's ministry was attended with many conversions. There have been three refreshings from the presence of the Lord since the settlement of the present pastor.

In 1850 the church edifice underwent a very extensive and thorough repair, and is now one of the best in the County. It is lighted with gas.

MINISTER RAISED UP.—William Goodwin, (Bap.)

THE SOUTH CHURCH IN NEW HARTFORD, ORG. AUG. 8, 1848.

James C. Houghton.	Dec 1851	Feb. 1854
Edwin Hall, Jr.	Dec. 1854	

The South Church was formed from the First Church of New Hartford, whose house of worship is located on what is called Town Hill, nearly two miles north of the house of worship occupied by the South Society. The principal reason for the separation was the inconveniently long distance the people in the south part of the town were compelled to travel in order to attend public worship.

The Church has never been a very strong one, and has enjoyed few extensive revivals of religion, though it has not been without some seasons of refreshing from on high.

THE FIRST CHURCH IN NEW HAVEN, ORG. AUG. 22, 1639.

Public worship had been maintained, and the word of God preached, under a provisional arrangement or "plantation covenant," from the landing of the first settlers, April 18, 1638. Rev. John Davenport, B. D. and Rev. Samuel Eaton, being the ministers.

John Davenport,* Pastor.	Aug. 1639	1667	Mar.	1670
William Hooke,† Teacher,	1644	1656	Mar.	1678
Nicholas Street,† Teacher,	Nov. 1659		April,	1674
John Harriman,‡	1674	1682		
Joseph Taylor,‡	1674		April,	1682
James Pierpont,§ Pastor,	July, 1684		Nov.	1714
Joseph Noyes,‖	July, 1716		June,	1761
Chauncey Whittelsey,**	Mar. 1758		July,	1787

MINISTERS.	SETTLED.	DISMISSED.	DIED.
James Dana,††	April, 1789	Nov. 1805	Aug. 1802
Moses Stuart,‡‡	Mar. 1806	Jan. · 1810	Jan. 1852
Nathaniel W. Taylor, D. D.,§§	April, 1812	Dec. 1822	Mar. 1858
Leonard Bacon, D. D.,	Mar. 1825		
Nathaniel H. Eggleston,‖	Sept. 1850	1851	

*Sp. An. 1, 93, 96 ; Allen; Math. Mag. 1, 292. †Sp. An. 1, 104; Allen. ‡ Neither were settled nor dismissed, but labored in the ministry of the word from 1674 to 1682. §Sp An. 1, 205 ; Allen. ‖ Sp. An. 1, 362 ; Allen. ** Sp. An. 1, 414; Allen. †† Sp. An. 1, 565 ; Allen. ‡‡ Sp. An. 2, 475. §§ Memorial Discourses; Cong. Qr. 2, 245. ‖ Mr. Eggleston had charge of the pulpit during Dr. Bacon's absence in Europe.

The first pastor and leading members of the Church came from the parish of St. Stephens, Coleman Street, London, to Boston, in 1637, arriving June 26. In April, 1638, they came to New Haven. The Church is the oldest institution in the New Haven colony. Its first connection in the support of public worship was with the town. East Haven, North Haven, and West Haven, having been successively established as parishes, the separate records of the First Ecclesiastical Society in New Haven begin on the first of July, 1715.

The Society has a permanent "ministerial fund" of about $15,000, partly the result of ancient donations and endowments, and partly the proceeds of a subscription made under the pastorate of Dr. Dana.

This Church has shared in the revivals which in successive ages have been granted to New England. In the pastorate of John Davenport, there appears to have been a special efficacy in the means of grace, as is evidenced by the number of the sons of this Church that entered the work of the ministry at that period. An allusion to the multiplied conversions at that time is made in the Election Sermon of James Fitch, who could speak from his own recollection. In 1735, while Joseph Noyes was pastor, there was some special revival, forerunning "the great awakening" that came a few years later. In the conflict incidental to "the great awakening" of 1740, and subsequent to it, the Church was divided. The next marked revival was in the pastorate of Moses Stuart, in the year 1808. The years 1815, and 1820–21, in the pastorate of the late Dr. Taylor, were memorable as years of gracious visitation. Under the ministry of the present pastor, the years 1828, 1831, 1832, 1837, 1841 and 1858, have been the years most marked with blessing. *Mem. of Nettleton,* 81, 125—33, 159. *Rel. Intel.* 5, 668, 762 ; 6, 26.

Mr. Pierpont was one of three prime movers in founding Yale College, and a member of Saybrook Synod, 1708, pp. 7, 8.

In connection with this church there is a City-mission Chapel, built by subscription in 1858, and know as the Davenport Chapel. Public worship is regularly maintained there nnder the patronage of the First Church, the Rev. Edward E. Atwater being the minister in charge.

MINISTERS RAISED UP.—Michael Wigglesworth,* Samuel Cheever,† Samuel Street,‡ John Harriman, Thomas Cheever,§ Noadiah Russell, John Davenport, (Stamford,) Stephen Mix, Joseph Moss, Amos Munson, Samuel

Pierpont, John Hubbard, Samuel Munson, Stephen White, Benjamin Tal-madge,‖ John Noyes,¶ Jason Atwater, Achilles Mansfield, Sereno Edwards Dwight, D. D., Gardiner Spring, D. D., George Chandler, (h.) David L. Ogden, Charles C. Darling, Daniel D. Tappan, Seth Bliss, William Bush-nell, Jonathan Rowland, Abraham C. Baldwin, Joseph B. Stevens, John Mitchell, Oliver B. Bidwell, Jeremiah R. Barnes, (h.) Lyman H. Atwater, D. D., John C. Backus, Phineas Blakeman, (h.) Joseph D. Hull, Aldace Walker, William T. Bacon, John H. Pettingill, Alfred E. Ives, Alfred C. Raymond, John E. Chandler, (f.) James C. Moffatt, Charles A. Raymond, (Bapt.) Matthew Hale Smith, George B. Hubbard, (h.) Elisha W. Cook, Chauncey Goodrich, William H. Goodrich, William L. Kingsley, William A. Macy, James R. Mershon, (h.) Charles Henry Emerson, (h.) Kinsley Twining, Leonard W. Bacon, Edward Chester, (f.) Jonathan L. Jenkins, John H. Anketell, (Ep.) Edward Walker, George M. Smith, George B. Bacon.

* Sp. An. 1, 143.   † Sp. An. 1, 253.   ‡ Sp. An. 1, 104.   Allen.   § Sp. An. 1, 244.
‖ Sp. An. 3, 35.   ¶ Sp. An. 1, 363.   Allen.

THE NORTH CHURCH, OR THE CHURCH IN THE UNITED SOCIETY, NEW HAVEN,
ORG. MAY 7, 1742.

This Church, under the name of the Church of Christ in White Haven Society, was organized May 7, 1742.

MINISTERS.	SETTLED.	DISMISSED.	DIED.
Samuel Bird,	Oct. 1751	Jan. 1768	May, 1784
Jonathan Edwards, D. D.,*	Jan. 1769	May, 1795	Aug. 1801

A Church was formed by secession from this, called The Church of Christ in the Fair Haven Society, June 20, 1771.

Allyn Mather,†	Feb. 1773		Nov. 1784
Samuel Austin, D. D.,‡	Nov. 1786	June, 1790	Dec. 1830

These Churches were united under the name of The Church of Christ in the United Societies of White Haven and Fair Haven, Nov. 27, 1796.

John Gammil, D. D.,§	Nov. 1798	Nov. 1801	
Samuel Merwin,‖	Feb. 1805	Dec. 1831	Sept. 1856
Leicester A. Sawyer,	June, 1835	Nov. 1837	
Samuel W. S. Dutton, D. D.,	June, 1838		

This Church was formed during "The Great Awakening," at the time of Whitfield's second visit to this country. The pastor of the first and only Church in New Haven, and a majority of the Church and Society, were op-posed to the revival and to Whitfield's preaching. Those who favored the revival, called "New Lights," seceded, and were formed into a Church, by some of the leading ministers of the "New Lights," convened in Council, viz: Rev. Messrs. Samuel Cook, John Graham, Elisha Kent, and Joseph Bellamy. Under the partial union of Church and State which then existed, oppressive laws were passed to embarrass and suppress them, and those like them; the "Old Lights," being a majority, both in the State and in the Associations and Consociations. This Church could legally have no one to preach to them, except by consent of the pastor and a majority of the parish of the First Church, which of course they could not obtain. Under this restriction, eminent and excellent men, like Rev. Dr. Finley, afterwards President of Princeton College, were arrested and punished for preaching to this Church. Its members and adherents were taxed for the support of the First Church, besides sustaining the expense of their own religious services. This oppressive treatment continued for 15 years, until the New Lights became a majority in the town, and in the Ecclesiastical Society, from which they had never been released, and proceeded to vote the salary to the minister of the New Church : whereupon, on the petition of the " Old Lights," the Legislature interposed, and divided the Society into two, according to elective affinity ; there being of the "Old Lights" 111, and of the "New Lights " 212. The new Society was called "The White Haven Society." One of the professed reasons for the original secession in 1742, was the adherence of the First Church and pastor to the Saybrook platform, which the New Lights insisted had never been adopted by the Church.

After about fifty years the two Churches became, and have ever since been, harmonious.

MINISTERS RAISED UP.—They cannot now be mentioned except for the last half century, and those but partially. Frederick W. Hotchkiss, Joseph Mix, Thomas Punderson, Samuel Austin, D. D.,¶ David A. Sherman, Prof. Eleazar T. Fitch, D. D., Prof. Chauncey A. Goodrich, D. D.,** Henry Herrick, (h.) O. E. Daggett, D. D., Edward O. Dunning, A. Hamilton Bishop, John D. Smith, William W. Woodworth, Samuel J. M. Merwin, Joseph Brewster, (Ep.) Andrew T. Pratt, William B. Clarke.

*Sp. An. 1, 653. Allen. Am. Qr. Reg. 8, 290. † Allen. ‡ Mendon As. 156. Sp. An. 2. 21. Allen. § Allen. ‖ Cong. Y. Book, 1857, 118. ¶ Am. Qr. Reg. 9, 201. Sp. An. 2, 221. ** New Englander, 18, 328.

THE CHURCH IN YALE COLLEGE, NEW HAVEN, ORG. JUNE 30, 1757.

MINISTERS.	SETTLED.	DISMISSED.	DIED.
Naphtali Daggett, D. D.,*	1755		1780
Samuel Wales, D. D.,†	1782		1794
Timothy Dwight, D. D.‡	1805		1817
Eleazar Thompson Fitch, D. D.,	1817	1852	
George Park Fisher,	1854		

The existence of the College Church is due in part to the commotions which followed the great awakening of 1740; in particular, to a dissatisfaction on the part of the College government with the doctrinal views and the preaching of Rev. Mr. Noyes, the pastor of the First Church, where the students attended worship from the time of the removal of the College to New Haven. It was also believed by President Clapp, who had a leading part in the establishment of the Church, that the members of College would be more profited by preaching and pastoral service, which should be provided for them exclusively, and adapted to their peculiar character.

In 1746, the corporation voted to choose a Professor of Divinity, as soon as they could procure the means of support for him. This they were enabled to do by a gift from Hon. Philip Livingston, and by other donations.

Pres. Stiles,§ acted as College pastor for a time after the death of Prof. Daggett. The College Church has enjoyed great prosperity. Numerous revivals of religion have occurred, at short intervals since its formation, which have given to the Church a large number of devoted and able minis- ters, and to the State a large body of public men of enlightened Christian principle. The most remarkable of these revivals were those of 1802, 1831 and 1858. The number of members belonging to the College Church is larger at present than at any former time. *See Prof. Fisher's Century Sermon*, 1857.

* Sp. An. 1. 479. Allen. † Sp. An. 1. 710. ‡ Sp. An. 2. 152. Allen. § Sp. An. 1. 470. Allen. Sparks' Amer. Biog., Second Series, vol. 6.

THE THIRD CHURCH IN NEW HAVEN, ORG. SEPT. 6, 1826.

MINISTERS.	SETTLED.	DISMISSED.	DIED.
Nathaniel W. Taylor, D. D.,*	1826	1830	March, 1858
Charles A. Boardman,	March, 1830	Sept. 1832	
Elisha Lord Cleaveland,D. D.,	July, 1833		

The Church has occupied three houses of worship; the first on the cor- ner of Chapel and Union streets, from 1830 to 1838; the second in Court street, between State and Orange, from 1841 to 1856; and the third in Church street, fronting the public square.

Since Jan. 1st, 1856, the congregation has doubled its numbers; one hun- dred and ninety-eight have been added to the Church, of whom ninety-seven were by profession. Seventy of these made profession since the great revi- val of 1858. The Church has enjoyed many seasons of refreshing from the Lord, but none so remarkable as that of the last year. Within the above named period of three years, the annual contribution to the cause of foreign missions has increased from $300 to about $1000.

MINISTERS RAISED UP.—Andrew Benton, (h.) Edward E. Atwater, Da- vid Breed, Charles H. Bullard, Joseph Rowell, (h.) Everet W. Bedinger, John C. Shackleford, (h.) Henry Powers.

* Cong. Y. Book, 6, 136.

THE TEMPLE ST. CHURCH, NEW HAVEN, (COLORED,) ORG. SEPT. 1829.

Simeon S. Jocelyn,	1829	1834
David Dobie,	1835	1837
Amos G. Beman,	Sept. 1841	Jan. 1853
Hiram Bingham,	Mar. 1859	Jan. 1860
William T. Catto,	Jan. 1860	

THE COLLEGE STREET CHURCH, ORG. AUG. 31, 1831.

Henry G. Ludlow,	May 1837	Mar. 1842
Edward Strong,	Dec. 1842	

For two years the Church worshiped in the Orange Street Chapel; three years in a large hall in the Exchange building; and from September, 1836, in a house of worship erected for it in Church street. Here it remained struggling along with various success, sustained chiefly by the self-denying and extraordinary sacrifices of a few leading men. Its house of worship being found less convenient and pleasant than had been anticipated, it was sold in 1848, and its present commodious and beautiful sanctuary erected in College st. From the period of this last removal, the growth and general prosperity of the church have been uniform and comparatively rapid. For the first six years of its existence, it had no pastor, but had the ministrations, for periods of from three to six months, of Revs. Waters Warren, Samuel Griswold, James Boyle, Dexter Clary, Austin Putnam, John Ingersoll, and the late N. W. Taylor, D. D.

MINISTERS RAISED UP.—Enoch Hewitt, (h.) William W. Atwater, (h.) Wm. A. Thompson, Joseph Chandler, Joseph A. Prime, (h.) Henry Losch (h.) Darius Hoyt, (h.) Samuel W. Strong, H. M. Colton, (h.) A. B. Hitchcock, (h.) Irem W. Smith Glen Wood, (h.) James A. Brainerd.

THE HOWE STREET CHURCH IN NEW HAVEN, ORG. MARCH 14, 1838.

MINISTERS.	SETTLED.	DISMISSED.	DIED.
Leicester A. Sawyer,	July, 1838	Oct. 1840	
Abraham C. Baldwin,	Jan. 1842	June, 1845	
William D. L. Love,	Apr. 1848	Mar. 1852	
S. Hale Higgins,	Mar. 1852	May, 1855	
David H. Hamilton,	Mar. 1855	Jan. 1858	
C. D. Murray, (lic.)	May, 1859		
Edwin Dimock,	Jan. 1860		

This church originated with the efforts of the City Missionary Society in parts of the city remote from other places of worship. Public worship was held for a few weeks in the Broadway School-house,—then for about four years in a carriage shop, fitted up for the purpose in Park street,—till a church edifice was opened in Howe street, in Jan. 1842. The church, though laboring under embarassments and discouragements, has ever been harmonious and united. It has been much blessed with revivals,—there having been years at a time, when additions were made by profession at every communion season.

THE CHAPEL STREET CHURCH IN NEW HANEN, ORG. NOV. 4, 1838.

N. W. Taylor, D. D.,	Nov. 1838	1839	Mar. 1858
John O. Colton,*	Nov. 1839		Apr. 1840
Joseph P. Thompson, D. D.,	Oct. 1840	Mar. 1845	
Leverett Griggs,	Aug. 1845	Sept. 1847	
William T. Eustis,	Mar. 1848		

There were sixty-one members at the organization. The death of the first pastor, following so soon after his ordination, was a severe trial. Although the house of worship is somewhat removed from the dwellings of the citizens, yet the church and congregation have steadily grown, and have been compelled to enlarge their accommodations; having outlived the days of feeble infancy, and attained a position of strength and stability which may well compare with any of the city congregations.

The church has shared largely in the outpouring of the Holy Spirit. The years 1840, (while the Church had no pastor,) 1841, '42, '43, '49, '51, '55, and '58, have been specially marked for the manifestations of the Divine Power in conversions; and during the existence of the church, three hundred and sixty-four have been added to its membership on profession of their faith in Jesus Christ.

THE SOUTH CHURCH IN NEW HAVEN, ORG. NOV. 8, 1852.

MINISTERS.	SETTLED.	DISMISSED.	DIED.
Joseph C. Stiles, D. D.,	Nov. 1852	Nov. 1857	
Gurdon W. Noyes,	Apr. 1854	May, 1858	
Gurdon W. Noyes,	May, 1858		

In 1850, Gerard Hallock, Esq., residing in the south-eastern part of the city, felt that accommodations for religious worship were needed in that vicinity —a Sabbath School being already in successful operation there. He, accordingly, in connection with one or two land-holders in the neighborhood, erected a large and convenient church and chapel, which were opened for use in the summer of 1852. There was no ecclesiastical society till the beginning of the year 1858; and then, Mr. Hallock, being the chief and almost entire owner of the church buildings, gave them up for the free use of the church, besides meeting most of the expenses, as he had done from the beginning. From this time the other members of the church have felt a deeper interest than before, and raised more to sustain it, though never more than $700 annually. The members of the congregation are generally from the middling classes in society, and have but small worldly means at their command; many of them being mechanics and operatives without families. The house of worship is three-quarters of a mile from any other of the Congregational denomination, and was much needed. There are now over two hundred members of the church, and there is a growing congregation, which may become, in time, pecuniarily strong.

The Wooster Place Church in New Haven, Org. Dec. 18, 1855.

Samuel H. Cox, D. D.	1855	
J. G. Hamner, D. D.	Nov. 1855	Oct. 1856

Owing to the pecuniary embarrassments of Mr. Jerome, at whose cost the church edifice was erected, it became necessary that the building should be

57

sold; and the society finding themselves unable to command the funds requisite to purchase it—a contingency not thought of in the commencement of the enterprise—voted, Oct. 28, 1856, that it was expedient to discontinue public worship as a separate congregation, and the church was dissolved Oct. 1857, having had ninety-five members.

THE GERMAN MISSION, NEW HAVEN.

MINISTERS.	SETTLED.	DISMISSED.	DIED.
Christian Popp,	1851		
J. E. Rau,	1855		
C. F. Sleidel,	1855		
C. G. Bentel,	1860		

This mission, with an organized Moravian church, has been under the patronage of the Connecticut Missionary Society. The congregation appears to promise well.

THE CHURCH IN NEWINGTON, IN WETHERSFIELD, ORG. OCT. 3, 1822.

Elisha Williams,*	Oct. 1722	1726	July, 1755
Simon Backus,†	Jan. 1725		1745
Joshua Belden,	Nov. 1747		July, 1813
Joab Brace, D. D.,	Jan. 1805		
Samuel J. Andrews,	Mar. 1856	Jan. 1857	
William P. Aikin,	Jan. 1857		

Newington was a branch of the Wethersfield Church. Mr. Williams resigned, to accept the Presidency of Yale College. Mr. Backus went as chaplain in the army to Cape Breton, where he died,—no doubt expecting to return, as no record is made of his dismission. Dr. Brace resigned the active duties of the ministry at the close of his fiftieth year. It is worthy of note that the active pastorates of Mr. Belden and Dr. Brace covered a period of nearly 108 years. Among the revivals, one in 1820 was conducted by Dr. Nettleton, with marked and blessed results. *Memoir,* 137. *Rel. Intel.* 6. 793, 16. 445.

MINISTERS RAISED UP.—Simon Backus, Zadock Hunt, Silas Churchill, Martin K. Whittlesey, (h.) Edward Joab Brace, Seth C. Brace.

*Sp. An. 1. 281. Allen. †Sp. An. 1. 231. Allen.

THE FIRST CHURCH IN NEW LONDON, ORG. 1650.

Richard Blinman,	1650	1659	
Gershom Bulkley,*	1661	1666	Dec. 1713
Simon Bradstreet,	1670		1683
Gurdon Saltonstall,	Nov. 1691	Aug. 1707	

MINISTERS.	SETTLED.	DISMISSED.	DIED.
Eliphalet Adams,†	July, 1708		Oct. 1753
Mather Byles,‡	Nov. 1757	Apr. 1768	
Ephraim Woodbridge,§	Oct. 1769		Sept. 1776
Henry Channing,	May, 1787	May, 1806	
Abel McEwen, D. D.	Oct. 1806		Sept. 1860
Thomas P. Field,	June, 1856		

The records commence in 1670 ; members admitted under the several pas‑ torates since—58, 128, 410, 59, 23, 191 and 723, the last including four years of Mr Field as colleague ; in all, 1592. Mr. Saltonstall left the ministry for civil life, and was for several years Governor of the State.

Repeated revivals of religion have occurred ; in 1807, over one hundred were added ; in other years, 60, 50 and 40 in a year. *Ev. Mag.* 9. 339. In 1835, the congregation having become inconveniently large, a colony was set off, now the large Second Church. Prior to 1806, this church was under the ministry of a Unitarian pastor for seventeen years. But this ministry produced no Unitarianism in the church or congregation, which survived his dismission. Nothing but the remarkable interposition of Divine Providence prevented the most disastrous results. For some time under that ministry, religious meetings, except those on the Sabbath, and the preparatory lec‑ ture, were very unpopular. Evening services, especially, encountered much prejudice. Now, and for many years past, churches and people of all de‑ nominations here, hold many such meetings. The Sabbath is much better observed in this place now than it was fifty years ago, and family prayer and family religion, generally, are more prevalent now than in the prior period.

MINISTERS RAISED UP.—William Adams,‖ John Avery, Joshua Hunting‑ ton,¶ Joseph Hurlbut, Nathaniel Hewit, D. D., Daniel Huntington, John Ross, Nathan Douglass, Thomas Huntington, Thomas W. Coit, D. D., (Ep.) Gurdon S. Coit, (Ep.) William Harris, Robert McEwen, D. D., Robert C. Learned, George Richards, John Eliot.

* Sprague's Annals, 1. 53. † Sp. An. 1. 182, 233. ‡ Sp. An. 1. 879. Allen. § Al‑ len. ‖ Sp. An. 1. 235. ¶ Allen.

THE SECOND CHURCH IN NEW LONDON, ORG. APRIL, 28 1835.

Joseph Hurlbut,	April, 1835	Mar. 1837	
James Macdonald, D. D.,	Dec. 1837	Jan. 1840	
Artemas Boies,*	Mar. 1841		Sept. 1844
Tryon Edwards, D. D.,	Mar. 1845	Aug. 1857	
G. B. Wilcox,	1859		

This church originally consisted of nineteen members of the First Church in New London who, " believing that the increase of the city required, and its resources would justify an extension of religious accommodations, and that the cause of truth and piety would be promoted by the organization of another church, of their own faith and order," were most amicably dismissed to unite in forming it.

MINISTERS RAISED UP.—Joseph Hurlbut, Jr., Joshua Coit.

Sp. An. 2. 664.

THE CHURCH IN NEW MILFORD, ORG. NOV. 2, 1716.

MINISTERS.	SETTLED.	DISMISSED.	DIED.
Daniel Boardman,*	1716		1744
Nathaniel Taylor,†	1748		1800
Stanley Griswold,‡	1790	1802	
Andrew Eliot,§	1808		1829
Heman Rood,	1830	1835	
Noah Porter, Jr.,	1836	1842	
John Greenwood,	1844	1849	
David Murdoch, Jr.,	1850		

By means of the "settlement" anciently given to ministers at their ordination, "the two fathers of New Milford, were able to give their families foothold in their native town ; hence to the honor and gratification of the parish, they have remained there, distinguished parts of the aristocracy of that aristocratic town." Mr. Boardman lived strong in the confidence and affection of his parishioners, and had not a little to do with and for the aborigines of the country, a conspicuous tribe of whom were located in his neighborhood. Mr. Taylor was something of a farmer, and had also a controlling influence, through his long ministry, in his large church and congregation. Mr. Griswold gradually developed himself as a Unitarian, and sought to break down the distinction of the church from the world. He was dismissed, but brought disaster upon the church, and so far misled them, as to procure their exclusion from the Consociation,—a severe, but ultimately a beneficial measure. It was several years, under the next pastorate, before prosperity, order and orthodoxy were restored. *Rel. Intel.* 16. 285.

MINISTERS RAISED UP.—David Sanford,‖ John Stephens, Benjamin Wildman, Gideon Bostwick, David Bronson, Whitman Welch, Joseph Treat, David Baldwin, Daniel Marsh,¶ Nathaniel W. Taylor, D. D., Charles A. Boardman, Orlando Hine, David Bostwick.**

* Sp. An. 1. 468. Litchf. Centen. 66.   † Sp. An. 1. 467. Allen. Litchf. Centen. 66.
‡ Sp. An. 1. 468. Litchf. Centen. 66.   § Sp. An. 2. 421.   ‖ Mendon As. p. 105. Sp. An. 2. 42. Allen.   ¶ Sp, An. 2. 116.   ** Sp. An. 3. 131.

THE FIRST CHURCH IN NEW PRESTON, IN WASHINGTON, ORG. 1757.

Noah Wadhams,	1757	1768	
Jeremiah Day,*	Jan. 1770		Sept. 1806

MINISTERS.	SETTLED.	DISMISSED.	DIED.
Samuel Whittlesey,†	Dec. 1807	Apr. 1817	
Charles A. Boardman,	June, 1818	Mar. 1830	
Robert B. Campfield,	Nov. 1831	1834	
Columbus Shumway,	1834	1835	
Merit S. Platt,	1836	1837	
Benjamin B. Parsons,	Apr. 1839	Sept. 1842	
Hollis Read,	1845	1851	
Samuel F. Bacon,	1851	1853	
Charles S. Smith,	Sept. 1853	Mar. 1855	
Jacob H. Strong,	Dec. 1857		

In October, 1748, twenty persons obtained leave of the General Assembly to hire a minister for six months in the year, on the ground of their living from seven to ten miles from their places of worship in Kent and New Milford. In May, 1752, forty-one individuals petitioned the General Assembly for a new Ecclesiastical Society. The societies of East Greenwich, (now Warren,) Kent and New Milford, opposed the application, and it failed, but was granted in October. In December, 1753, it was voted to lay a tax of 12 pence on the pound to hire a minister for a season; and to build two school-houses, by subscription, for the use of the society. Nov. 1754, it was voted to build a meeting-house, 36 by 26 feet, with five windows, of 12 lights each, 100 rods west of the present stone meeting-house. Dec. 1766, it was voted to build another meeting-house 50 by 40 feet. This house was enclosed three years later, but was not entirely finished until 1798. In 1806, a permanent fund of $5,000 was raised. In 1824, a third meeting-house was built of stone, 54 by 44 feet. In 1853, a majority of the church, with a minority of the society, upon their own responsibility, built a fourth meeting-house in the village of Waramaug, 60 by 39 feet, at an expense of about $6,000, and the church, by a majority vote, on the 27th of Jan. 1854, voted to remove their place of worship to this house. The minority of the church, with a majority of the society, maintain worship at the stone house.

· There were added to the church by the first minister, 54; second, 123, and 300 baptized; third, 142, 167 baptized; fourth 134, 200 baptized; fifth, 88, 79 baptized. The most extensive revival was in 1816, when eighty were added to the church.

MINISTERS RAISED UP.—Jeremiah Day, D. D., Benjamin B. Smith, Levi Smith, Joseph Whittlesey, Henry N. Day, Horace Bushnell, D. D., George Tomlinson, Charles W. Camp, William Baldwin, Johnson L. Tomlinson, George Bushnell.

‡ Sp. An. 1. 688. Allen.   † Sp. An. 2. 326. Litchf. Centen. 118.

THE CHURCH IN NEW PRESTON HILL, (IN WASHINGTON.)

A minority of the old church was left Jan. 27th, 1854, at the old house of worship, but there was no new organization.

Levi S. Beebe,	Feb. 1854	Feb. 1855
John A. Hempstead,	1855	1856

MINISTERS.	SETTLED.	DISMISSED.	DIED.
Noah Coe,	Feb. 1856	Jan. 1857	
Williams H. Whittemore,	1859	1860	
George Tomlinson,	Mar. 1860		

An unhappy division arose in New Preston in 1853–4, on account of a disagreement about the place of worship. The majority of the society and the minority of the church claim the original organization, though the Consoci·ation decided that the majority of the Church, who removed, are to be considered the original church; while the minority retain the records and communion service, and the society, with them, have the funds for the support of the gospel. The old house has since been extensively repaired.

MINISTER RAISED UP.—Philander Hollister.

THE CHURCH IN NEWTOWN, ORG. OCT. 19, 1715.

	SETTLED	DISMISSED	DIED
Thomas Tousey,	Oct. 1715	1724	Mar. 1761
John Beach,*	1724	Feb. 1732	Mar. 1782
Elisha Kent,	Sept 1732	Feb. 1743	July, 1776
David Judson,†	Sept. 1743		Sept. 1776
Zephaniah H. Smith,	Mar. 1786	Feb. 1790	Feb. 1836
Jehu Clarke,	Oct. 1799	Aug. 1816	May, 1838
William Mitchell,	June, 1825	May, 1831	
Nathaniel M. Urmston,	Dec. 1832	Apr. 1838	
Alexander Leadbetter,	1839	1842	
John N. Ambler,	1843	1845	May, 1859
Jason Atwater,	1846	1856	Apr. 1860
William H. Moore,	Nov. 1856		

The tract embraced by this town was called Pohtatuck, by the Indians, and was deeded by them to certain men from Stratford, in 1705. The town was incorporated by an act of the General Court, Oct. 11, 1711. Before this date, the people had tried to secure a minister, but without success. The town voted Oct. 1, 1712, to invite the neighboring ministers to come and spend a day with them in advice, humiliation and prayer, that they might be directed and encouraged in trying to maintain the worship of God among them.

Mr. Tousey began to preach here in May, 1713. In May, 1715, the town got permission of the General Court to have a church gathered, in order that Mr. Tousey might be regularly settled among them. After his dismission, he gave his attention to secular affairs, and was a prominent and influential man in the town. Mr. Beach became an Episcopalian, went to England for ordination, and ministered to Episcopal churches in Redding and Newtown forty years, and in Newtown alone till his death.

Mr. Judson's salary varied from £50 to £75 a year, and in 1758, the lowest sum was paid, in part at the following prices: wheat 3s. 6d., rye 2s. 4d. and corn 1s. 9d. per bushel, flax 5d. a pound, and work 1s. and 9d. per day.

During his ministry there were 226 marriages, (from 1756 to 1776,) 378 deaths, 887 baptisms, a yearly average of 27 ; half-way covenant dismissions, 90 ; about 300 added to the church.

Mr. Smith adopted some of the errors of Sandemanianism, and by his indiscretion and discipline, involved the church in trouble, from the disastrous effects of which, it became so reduced, as to be organized anew in 1799, having but nine male members.

Under Mr. Atwater, 69 were added, the meeting-house repaired, a conference room provided, and the society brought into a more hopeful condition than for seventy-five years before. Without aid from the Home Missionary Society, from 1825, it would have become extinct.

MINISTER RAISED UP.—Isaac Beach.

* Allen.   † Allen.

THE CHURCH IN NORFOLK, ORG. DEC. 24, 1760.

MINISTERS.	SETTLED.	DISMISSED.	DIED.
Ammi Ruhamah Robbins,*	Oct. 1761		Oct. 1813
Ralph Emerson, D. D.,	June, 1815	Nov. 1829	
Joseph Eldridge, D. D.,	Apr. 1832		

Mr. Emerson was dismissed to accept the professorship of Ecclesiastical History in Andover Seminary. The town was incorporated in 1758. The church has never had a " stated supply," except a few weeks at a time. The church and people have never had any serious trouble among them, or with their ministers. A serious quarrel in the choir has never occurred ; it has generally been harmonious in every sense. Interesting and refreshing revivals of religion have been granted to the church, at intervals, through the whole century of its existence. *Ev. Mag.* 1, 211, 338. For a long time, it has been subject to a heavy drain from emigration, particularly to the West. During the ministry of the present pastor, all the other churches of the Consociation have had at least two pastors, and most of them three and four, or more.

MINISTERS RAISED UP.—Thomas Robbins, D. D.,† Asahel Gaylord, Nathan Turner, Francis L. Robbins,† Isaac Knapp,‡ Eleazar Holt, Joseph L. Mills, Sheridan Guiteau, James W. Robbins, Reuben Gaylord.

* Sp. An. 1. 869.   Allen.   Litchf. Centen. 90.   † Allen.   ‡ Allen.

THE CHURCH IN NORTH BRANFORD, ORG. MAY 18, 1724.

Jonathan Merrick,*	1726		June, 1772
Samuel Eells,†	1769		Apr. 1808
Charles Atwater,	1809		Feb. 1825
Judson A. Root,	1828	1834	1855
Henry B. Camp,	1835	1836	
John D. Baldwin,	1838	1844	

MINISTERS.	SETTLED.	DISMISSED.	DIED.
George I. Wood,	Dec. 1844	June, 1850	
Whitman Peck,	Mar. 1851	July, 1855	
George I. Wood,	Oct. 1855	Nov. 1858	
William B. Curtis,	Dec. 1859		

This church was a colony from the church in Branford. Its first house of worship was erected in 1724, at the expense of the town of Branford. At the institution of the church, the funds owned by the society in Branford, were equitably divided between the two societies. The settlement of this part of Branford commenced about 1680; and in 1701, they were numerous enough to have occasional preaching among themselves. The town at first voted to support both ministers; but six months after revoked this action, and the North Branford society was then organized. Mr. Merrick was a man of decision and energy, beloved and respected among his people. Mr. Eells had £200 settlement, besides materials for building a house and barn. He was a man of great versatility and sympathy, and practiced to some extent as a physician. He also became the captain of a company of 60 men from his parish, in the Revolutionary war, though fortunately there was no occasion for their services. The half-way covenant prevailed here, a source of trouble in the church. *See Mr. Wood's Historical Discourse,* 1850.

MINISTERS RAISED UP.—David Rose, Roger Harrison, Fosdick Harrison, Levi Rose, Alonzo Loper.

　　　　* Sp. An. 1. 631. Allen. † Allen.

THE CHURCH IN NORTH CANAAN, ORG. DEC. 5, 1769.

Asahel Hart,	Mar. 1770		Mar. 1775
Amos Thompson,	June, 1782	1788	
Joshua Knapp,	1791	1795	
Solomon Morgan,*	April, 1798		Sept. 1804
Pitkin Cowles,†	Aug. 1805	Jan. 1833	Feb. 1833
Henry H. Woodbridge,	Oct. 1833	Oct. 1842	
Daniel D. Francis,	May, 1844	Mar. 1850	
Elisha Whittlesey,	June, 1851	Sept. 1853	
Hiram Eddy, 1854, inst. June, 1856		1860	

This church was originally formed upon the application of eleven members of the First Church, who were dismissed and recommended to organize themselves into a church in the second Ecclesiastical Society in Canaan. It is now, since the division of the town, the Congregational Church of North Canaan.

Mr. Knapp had been seventeen years pastor in Winsted. Mr. Cowles studied with Dr. Charles Backus, of Somers. He was a warm friend of evangelical truth and practical religion, an affectionate pastor, an instructive and impressive preacher. His ministry was blessed with several revivals; in one of them 100 were added to the church. *See Litchf. Centen.* 1852.

MINISTERS RAISED UP —Grove L. Brownell, Zalmon Tobey, Linus Fellows, Timothy Benedict, Aaron Peale, Calvin Peale.

　　　　*Allen, Sp. An. 2. 526. † Litchf. Centen. 116.

THE CHURCH IN NORTH CORNWALL, ORG. 1782.

MINISTERS.	SETTLED	DISMISSED.	DIFD.
John Cornwall,			
Israel Holley,	1795	1801	
Josiah Hawes,	March, 1805	July, 1813	
Grove L. Brownell,	1817	1818	
Walter Smith,	June, 1819	April, 1838	
S. J. Tracy,	1838	1839	
Joshua L. Maynard,	Jan. 1841	May, 1852	
W. B. Clarke,	May, 1855	May, 1859	
Charles Wetherby,	Sept. 1859		

Formed from the First Church (South Cornwall,) by secession. Has been very greatly blessed with revivals from its beginning until the present time, and is now in a prosperous condition. This Church was for several years, in the early part of its existence, under the care of the Morristown Presbytery, in New Jersey; but was received into the Litchfield North Consociation in 1809.

MINISTERS RAISED UP.—John C. Hart, Henry Wadsworth, Almon B. Pratt, Henry G. Pendleton, Abram Baldwin.

THE CHURCH IN NORTH COVENTRY, ORG. OCT. 8, 1745.

Nathan Strong,*	Oct. 1745			Nov.	1795
Ichabod Lord Skinner,†	Oct. 1794	Oct.	1798		1852
Ephraim T. Woodruff,	Apr. 1801	Oct.	1817		
George A. Calhoun, D. D.,	Mar. 1819				

Previous to 1736 the inhabitants of North Coventry were embraced in the Congregational Church and Society of South Coventry. During three winters after that date, the town assisted the inhabitants of this section of it in supporting public worship at the house of Mr. Noah Russ; and the Society was incorporated in 1740. In May, 1742, the Legislature of this State enacted a law prohibiting ministers from preaching and exhorting out of their respective parishes, unless they were invited by the minister, if there was no minister, by the Church, and if there was no Church, by the Society.

This Society voted, June 21, 1742, that any of 24 ministers named, might preach or exhort at any time in this Society upon invitation. "Then voted, that any Church member, or any head of a family may invite any of the above ministers to preach in said Society."

The building of the first meeting house occasioned much trouble. In regard to it the Legislature was repeatedly memorialized. The parish was once and again surveyed to find the center; and finally a Legislative committee was employed to determine the site. After years of agitation, the second house was built in 1792, the third in 1847.

The Society agreed to give Mr. Strong for his support £600 old tenor bills as a settlement, and £200 (increasing to £270,) old tenor bills as an

58

annual salary, to vary nominally according to the change in the value of produce. This arrangement for the support of the minister occasioned trouble in after years.

For a number of years previous to 1828 the ability of this Society to support the gospel, gradually decreased, by emigration; when a parochial fund of $5,000 was raised to supply the deficiency.

This place has been repeatedly blessed with special effusions of the Holy Spirit. There was a revival of religion in 1742, while there were two societies in the town, also in 1765, 1781, 1800 and in the years of general revival in the present century. Added in 1819, 65; 1822-3, 70. *Ev. Mag.* 9, 379. *Rel. Intel.* 5, 173.

During the last 50 years the Church has received 501 members, and has dismissed on recommendation to other Churches 147 more than it has received from them.

MINISTERS RAISED UP.—Nathan Strong, D. D., Joseph Strong, D. D., Thomas Page, (h.) Ebenezer Kingsbury, (h.) Gershom E. Lyman, Horatio Waldo, Jacob Allen, Clement Parker, Hervey Talcott, Eber Carpenter, Addison Kingsbury, D. D., Marvin Root, Nathan S. Hunt, Milton Badger, D. D., R. R. Gurley, D. D., John A. Woodruff, Diodatius Babcock.

* Sp. An. 1, 28. 2, 34. Allen. † Sp. An. 2, 37.

THE CHURCH IN NORTHFORD, IN NORTH BRANFORD, ORG. JUNE 13, 1750.

MINISTERS.	SETTLED.	DISMISSED.	DIED.
Warham Williams,*	June, 1750		April, 1788
Matthew Noyes,†	Aug. 1790		Sept. 1839
William J. Boardman,	Dec. 1835		Oct. 1849
Henry S. Clark, D. D.,	April, 1847	June, 1849	
E. W. Root,	July, 1849	July, 1850	
Charles H. Bullard,	Oct. 1850	Oct. 1851	
Asa C. Pierce,	June, 1853		

Meetings for public worship were held as early as 1746, when measures were adopted for building a meeting house; and soon after a committee was appointed "to apply to the Rev. Association's Committee for advice in respect to a candidate for a preacher."

Mr. Williams was descended from Revs. Robert Williams of Roxbury, Mass., who came from England, John Williams of Deerfield, and Stephen Williams, D. D., of Long Meadow, where he was born. He admitted to the Church 256. Mr. Noyes, born in Lyme, also of Puritan ancestry, was a descendant of James Noyes, who came from Wiltshire, England. He studied Theology with Dr. Whitney, of Brooklyn; admitted to the Church 201. He was "distinguished as the richest minister in Conn.". Mr. Boardman, from North Haven, born in Dalton, Mass., resigned his charge some years before his death, through ill health, but not dismissed. The Church was in a divided and troubled state for years after. Revivals in 1856 and 1858.

MINISTERS RAISED UP.—Oliver D. Cook, Medad Rogers, Lemuel Tyler, Jonathan Maltby, Isaac Maltby, L. Ives Hoadley, John Maltby, Erastus Maltby, Samuel Whitney, (f.) Eli Smith, D. D.,‡ (f.) Benjamin S. J. Page.

* Sp. An. 1. 287. Allen. † Sp. An. 1, 513. Allen. ‡ Cong. Y. Book, 5, 116.

THE CHURCH IN NORTHFIELD, IN LITCHFIELD, ORG. JAN. 1, 1795.

MINISTERS.	SETTLED.	DISMISSED.	DIED.
Joseph E. Camp,*	Feb. 1795	1837	May, 1838
J. S. Dickinson,	Feb. 1844	June, 1851	
Lewis Jessup,	Nov. 1851	Nov. 1854	
Noah Coe,	Nov. 1854	Feb. 1856	
Stephen Rogers,	Nov. 1856	Feb. 1859	
James Richards, D. D',	Feb. 1859	Aug. 1860	

The Church and Society had a fund which a few years since was invested in a parsonage, all but $500. Have since received $10,000, a legacy from Asa Hopkins.

Mr. Richards is not in good standing, having been deposed from the ministry, several years since, by the Presbytery of New Orleans. The Church since engaging his services, with the disapprobation of the Consociation, have voted to dissolve their connection with that body.

MINISTERS RAISED UP.—Wyllys Warner, Isaac Warner, William H. Guernsey, Albert B. Camp, Lewis Smith, (Meth.)

* Sp. An. 2. 592.

The "Enrolled Church," in Northford, Org. 1801.

——— *Huntington*,
Claudius Herrick,
Eliphalet B. Coleman,
Jeremiah Atwater, D. D.

A house of worship was erected in 1805. This Church was a secession from Mr. Noyes's Church, on account of an unhappy division of feeling which prevailed at that time. Its existence continued till 1833, when by advice and assistance of the Association, a reunion was effected.

The names of Revs. Messrs. Huntington, Claudius Herrick, Eliphalet B. Coleman, and Jeremiah Atwater, D. D., are given as having supplied their pulpit, but no dates have been furnished; the first is said to have aided in the formation of the Church, and the second in erecting its house of worship.

The Church in North Goshen, Org. 1828.

George Carrington,*	Aug. 1829	Sept. 1833
Guy C. Sampson,	Jan. 1836	May, 1837

MINISTERS.	SETTLED.	DISMISSED.	DIED.
C. J. Tracy,	1837 ?	1839 ?	
Chester Colton,	1839 ?	1845 ?	
Frederick Marsh,	May, 1846	Nov. 1847	

During Mr. Tracy's labors, there was some revival and several additions to the Church. The death of the leading man in the Society, and the removal of the only deacon depended on for conducting religious meetings, to Michigan, so weakened the Society as to prevent further attempts to sustain preaching. By vote of the Church, the communion service was given to the Congregational Church in Chelsea, Mich.

* Litchf. Centen. 117

The Church in North Greenwich, Org. Dec. 25, 1827.

Chauncey Wilcox,	June,	1828	May,	1846	Jan. 1852
Frederick Munson,	Sept.	1847	April,	1856	
John Blood,	Nov.	1856	Oct.	1858	
William H. Knouse,	May,	1859			

A considerable part of the region from which this Church is now gathered, was formerly included in the parish of the Second Congregational Church in Greenwich. Another portion was united with the Society of Stanwich ; and a district in which several families now connected with the Church and congregation reside, belonged as at present to the State of New York. Some of those who desired to enjoy the privileges of the sanctuary, regularly traveled the distance of eight miles for this purpose. A Church edifice was erected in the summer of 1827, and dedicated the same day that the Church was organized.

The Church in North Guilford, Org. June 16, 1725.

Samuel Russell,*	June,	1725			Jan.	1746
John Richards,†	Nov.	1748	1765			
Thomas W. Bray,‡	Dec.	1766			April,	1808
William F. Vaill,	Dec.	1808	April,	1820		
Zolva Whitmore,§	Sept.	1821	Aug.	1846		
John L. Ambler,	Jan.	1848	Jan.	1849		
Henry Eddy,	Jan.	1849	March,	1851		
Fosdick Harrison,	Nov.	1851	Nov.	1854		
Abraham C. Baldwin,	Nov.	1854	Oct.	1855		
Thomas Dutton,	Dec.	1855	May,	1859		
Richard Crittenden,	Aug.	1860				

North Guilford was made a distinct parish, May, 1720. The first inhabitants were people of property, and of strong religious principles and purposes. It indicates the elevation of their views and aims respecting education, that there were graduated at Yale College, from this small community, with in fifty years after its separation from Guilford, five, who became eminently useful members of the learned professions, viz: Revs. Nathaniel Bartlett of Redding, Amos Fowler of Guilford, and Daniel Collins of Lanesboro, Mass., (all these, after long pastorates, died in old age among the people of their charge,) Thomas Russell, a physician, in Sheffield, Mass., and Piermont, N. H., and Abraham Baldwin, member of the Continental Congress from Georgia, one of the framers of the Constitution of the United States, and Senator in Congress from 1799 to 1807.

After the death of the first minister in 1746, a division arose on the question of settling Mr. Chauncey, a son of Rev. Mr. Chauncey of Durham. A majority feared that he was not sound in the faith; and therefore voted against him, whereupon, a minority, who were strongly in favor of him, seceded and formed an Episcopal Church, with which about one-third of the 102 families of the parish are connected. Since that time, there have been two occasions, when three or four families at once, have left the Congregational for the Episcopal Society. One was when Mr. Bray refused to baptize on the "half way covenant" plan; the other when Mr. Vail preached zealously on the doctrines of Divine Sovereignty and Election.

An increase from 20 to 70 in 33 years, and in so small a community, shows a good measure of religious prosperity. This number was increased during the 42 years of the third pastorate, by the addition of 152. There were almost every year additions to the Church from 1 to 6 or 7. There were at almost all times, individuals in the congregation, who were under solemn religious impressions.

About the time of Mr. Bray's death, began the first revivals of religion. Even in the days of Whitefield, Edwards, and Bellamy, there was no unusual religious interest here. This work continued with increased power after the settlement of Mr. Vaill. Then began, also, the era of social prayer meetings, and benevolent contributions. And thenceforward the Church has been blest with pentacostal visits of the Divine Spirit; almost all who have been added to it since Mr. Bray's day, having been converted in seasons of revival.

MINISTERS RAISED UP.—Nathaniel Bartlett, Amos Fowler, Daniel Collins, Aaron C. Collins, Lyman Beecher, D. D., Augustus B. Collins, Jared Tyler, Abraham C. Baldwin, John E. Bray, Stephen A. Loper.

* Sp. An. 1, 261. Allen.   † Allen.   ‡ See account of Thomas B. Wells in Allen. § Mendon As. 300.

THE CHURCH IN NORTH HAVEN, ORG. 1718.

MINISTERS.	SETTLED.		DISMISSED.		DIED.	
James Wetmore,	Sept.	1718	Sept.	1722		1760
Isaac Stiles,*	Nov.	1724			May,	1760
Benjamin Trumbull, D. D ,†	Dec.	1760			Feb.	1820
William J. Boardman,	Sept.	1820	Oct.	1833	Oct.	1849

MINISTERS.	SETTLED.	DISMISSED.	DIED.
Leverett Griggs,	Oct. 1833	July, 1845	
Ira H. Smith,	Feb. 1846	March, 1848	
Theron G. Colton,	Sept. 1849	Aug. 1851	
Silas W. Robbins,	June, 1853	Oct. 1856	
Benjamin S. J. Page,	Oct. 1856		

Mr. Wetmore, says Dr. Trumbull, "was one of the first ministers who declared for Episcopacy in the colony of Connecticut." At that time, there was but one Episcopal Church in the whole colony, and but few of that persuasion. Mr. Cutler, the Rector of the College in New Haven, and Mr. Johnson, of West Haven, declared for Episcopacy at the same time, and may be considered the fathers of the Episcopalians in Connecticut. Dr. Trumbull was the author of a celebrated "History of Connecticut," and of other valuable religious works.

MINISTERS RAISED UP.—Samuel Todd, Ezra Stiles, D. D.‡

* Sp. An. 1, 470. Allen.   † Sp. An. 1, 584. Allen.   ‡ Am. Qu. Reg. 8,193.

THE CHURCH IN NORTH MADISON, (FORMERLY NORTH BRISTOL,) ORG. 1757.

John Rundle,	1753	Dec. 1754		
Richard Ely,*	June, 1757	1785	Aug. 1814	
Simon Backus,	Oct. 1790	April, 1801	1823	
John Ely,	Oct. 1812		Nov. 1827	
David Metcalf,	May, 1829	Sept. 1831		
Jared Andrus,	June, 1832		Nov. 1832	
Stephen Hayes,	June, 1833	June, 1838		
Amos LeFavor,	Dec. 1838	Dec. 1840		
Judson A. Root,	April, 1841	April, 1842	Sept. 1855	
Lent S. Hough,	April, 1842	April, 1845		
Martin Dudley,	April, 1845	April, 1846		
William Case,	April, 1846	April, 1847	1857	
James T. Terry,	April, 1847	April, 1848		
Reuben Torrey,	April, 1848	Oct. 1852		
Phineas Blakeman,	Jan. 1853	April, 1858		
Samuel Howe,	Aug. 1858			

A committee from the Church in North Bristol met Consociation at Guilford, when convened for the ordination of Rev. Amos Fowler, and presented the act of Assembly, making them a legal ecclesiastical society, and a certificate of the regular formation of the Church, requesting them to ordain their pastor. Rev. R. Ely was accordingly ordained at Guilford. The name of the Church and Society was changed from North Bristol to North Madison about 1830, soon after Madison became a town. Mr. Le Favor, the last pastor, was found guilty of scandalous and immoral conduct at New Berlin, N. Y., and upon the representations of the Chenango Presbytery, was deposed by the Consociation, July 28, 1842. The Church has experienced several revivals; is poor in the things of this world, and has recently been weakened by the spirit of proselytism. *Dr. Nettleton's Memoir*, 135.

*Allen.

THE CHURCH IN NORTH MANSFIELD, ORG. OCT. 11, 1744.

MINISTERS.	SETTLED.	DISMISSED.	DIED.
William Throop,	Oct. 1744	Jan. 1746	
Daniel Welch,*	Jan. 1752		April, 1782
Moses C. Welch, D. D.,†	June, 1784		April, 1824
William Ely,‡	Aug. 1825	May, 1841	Nov. 1850
Reuben Torrey,	June, 1841	April, 1843	
A. R. Livermore,	Aug. 1843	Nov. 1858	
Edward F. Brooks,	Feb. 1860		

The Society was incorporated in 1737. The second house of worship was built in 1793, would seat 700, and was generally filled. The third, built in 1848. The Church has been weakened by division, (as is true of many churches,) by the coming in of other denominations, by the great political excitement at the beginning of the present century, and by other causes since; and so must they continue till such time as they again go up each Sabbath to one house of worship, one people. The first pastor was resettled in Southold, L. I., where he was highly successful. The second was taken ill in the pulpit and died the same night; a good man, a good preacher, respected, beloved and lamented. The third, son of the second, "was an able defender of the faith; in prayer devout; in preaching plain and pungent." The fourth "was a sound, faithful, discreet pastor, and appeared to have a hand, a head and a heart ready to every good work." There was a great awakening in 1822-3. Other seasons of special interest in 1798, 1810, '32, '41, '49, and '58. The humbling doctrines of the cross have been plainly preached with happy effect.

MINISTERS RAISED UP.—Abner Goodell, S. W. Hanks, Marcus Cross, Samuel R. Dimock, Edwin Dimock.

* Sp. An. 2, 234. † Sp. An. 2. 234. Allen. ‡ Allen.

THE CHURCH IN NORTH STAMFORD, ORG. JUNE 4, 1782.

Samuel Hopkins, D. D.,*	1782	1784	Dec. 1803
Solomon Wolcot,	March, 1784	June, 1785	
John Shepherd,	June, 1787	June, 1794	
Amzi Lewis,†	June, 1795		April, 1819
Henry Fuller,	June, 1812	Jan. 1844	
Nathaniel Pierson,	April, 1844	Jan. 1846	
William H. Magie,	Jan. 1846	Jan. 1849	

MINISTERS.	SETTLED.	DISMISSED.	DIED.
William E. Catlin,	March, 1849	March, 1850	
F. E. M. Bacheler,	July, 1851?	Jan. 1852 ?	
Livingston Willard,	March, 1852	June, 1856	
John White,	May, 1857	Oct. 1858	
W. Simpson Clarke,	April, 1859		

This Church has been blessed with many precious revivals; but has suf-fered much for want of a more permanent ministry. *Rel. Intel.* 16, 76, 156.

*Sp. An. 1, 428. †Sp. An. 4. 155.

The Church in North Stonington, Org. Feb. 22, 1727.

William Worthington,		1720 ?	1722	
Thomas Craghead,		1722 ?	1724	
Jabez Wight,		1724 ?	1726	
Ebenezer Russell,	Feb. 1727			May, 1731
Joseph Fish,*	Dec. 1732 .			May, 1781
Barnabas Lathrop,	May, 1783	Feb. 1785		
Joseph Ayer,	June, 1825	March, 1837		
Peter H. Shaw,	May, 1837	Feb. 1839		
Philo Judson,	April, 1841	April, 1845		
Myron N. Morris,	April, 1846	June, 1852		
Stephen Hubbell,	Aug. 1853			

The North Society in Stonington was incorporated in 1720, seven years before the organization of the Church, and 81 before the act incorporating the present town of North Stonington.

The earlier years of the ministry of Mr. Fish were marked by great suc-cess, but soon after that great religious movement in connection with the labors of Davenport, alienations and strifes began to spring up in the Church. About two-thirds of the members seceded, some to unite with the Baptists, and some to organize themselves into a new body under the name of "Sep-arates," or "Strict Congregationalists."

At the death of Mr. Fish, a long period commenced, during which the Church was without a settled minister and was at times nearly extinct. In August, 1791, the Church was reorganized with eighteen members, and a fresh effort made to secure a pastor. The attempt however failed, and a succession of persons, none of them remaining more than four months, sup-plied all the pulpit instruction which was given for the next thirty years.

The Separates kept up their organization about 70 years. At the expira-tion of that time, the old Society and the Separates so far united as to build a house of worship, to be occupied alternately, with certain limitations.

In 1824, the Rev. Joseph Ayer was employed by both Churches to supply their alternate worship, and at last the two Churches were formally and happily reunited on the 15th of March, 1827.

A fund, early commenced, helped to prolong the existence of the Church during its trials. *See Mr. Morris's Historical Discourse,* 1848.

MINISTERS RAISED UP.—Joseph Ayer, Isaac P. Langworthy.

* Sp. An. 1. 359. Allen.

The North Windsor Church, Org. Sept. 2, 1761.

MINISTERS.	SETTLED.	DISMISSED.	DIED.
Theodore Hinsdale,	April, 1766	1795	

In 1757 a contention arose about the location of a new meeting house. It was built on the South side of the (Farmington) river. This change led to the organization of the North Windsor Church, by Consociation. In 1795 it was disbanded, and the members returned to the first Church.

MINISTER RAISED UP.—Nathaniel Gaylord.

THE CHURCH IN NORTH WOODSTOCK, ORG. 1756.

Foster Thayer,	July, 1831	Oct. 1836	
Lent S. Hough,	Jan. 1837	May, 1841	
Willard Child, D. D.,	1841	1842	
D. C. Frost,	1843	1844	
William H. Marsh,	Nov. 1844	Apr. 1851	
O. D. Hine,	Jan. 1852	Oct. 1855	
D. M. Elwood,	Apr. 1857	May, 1859	
John White,	1859		

This church claims to be the original North Woodstock church, organized in what is now East Woodstock, in 1756. A division having arisen as to the site of a new meeting-house, a church edifice was erected at " Village Corners," in 1830, and on " Feb. 25, 1831, votes were passed by a majority of said church removing their place of worship from the old meeting-house to the new," "and providing for the administration of the ordinances at the latter place." The church, or that portion of it remaining at East Woodstock, also built a new meeting-house, and continued without a new church organization. The church at North Woodstock carried with it (after litigation) the funds of the original church, amounting to some three or four thousand dollars. These funds it still retains—a portion having been expended in the purchase of a parsonage. *Rel. Intel.* 16. 415.

MINISTERS RAISED UP.—Joseph Chandler, (h) John E. Chandler, (f.) Augustus Chandler.

THE CHURCH IN NORWALK, ORG. 1652.

Thomas Hanford,*	1652, ord. 1654		1693
Stephen Buckingham,†	Nov. 1697	Feb. 1726	Feb. 1745

MINISTERS.	SETTLED.		DISMISSED.		DIED.	
Moses Dickinson,‡		1727			May,	1778
William Tennent,‡		1765		1772		
Matthias Burnet, D. D.,§	Nov.	1785			June,	1806
Roswell R. Swan,‖	Jan.	1807			Mar.	1819
Sylvester Eaton,¶	Oct.	1820	Feb.	1827		
Henry Benedict,	Aug.	1828	Feb.	1832		
Edwin Hall. D. D.,	June,	1832		1855		
William B. Weed,	June,	1855				

A settlement was commenced in the town of Norwalk in 1650, and public worship was undoubtedly established at that time. Without certain information, it is believed that the first Congregational church was organized in 1652—the year in which the Rev. Thomas Hanford, the first minister, commenced his labors. Until the year 1726, the parish and the town were identical. In that year, in pursuance of an act of the General Assembly, the Congregational society was organized. The churches of Wilton, Ridge field, New Canaan, Norfield, Weston, Darien, Westport and South Norwalk, are in whole, or in part, colonies from this church.

This church has enjoyed the labors of ten pastors, men devoted to their work, sound in the faith, and some of them distinguished in their profession. Many "times of refreshing from the presence of the Lord" have blessed this church, and crowned the labors of her faithful ministers.

MINISTERS RAISED UP.—Samuel Lockwood, D. D., William Hanford, Stephen Saunders, James Lockwood, Nathaniel Bouton, D. D., Henry Benedict, Ebenezer Kellogg, Charles G. Selleck, S. B. S. Bissell, Melancthon Hoyt, Benjamin Lockwood, Charles A. Downs, Augustus F. Beard, Edwin Hall, Jr.

* Allen. † Sp. An. 1. 261. ‡ Sp. An. 1. 311. 3. 242. Allen. § Sp. An. 2. 92. ‖ Sp. An. 2. 485. Allen. ¶ Sp. An. 4. 405.

THE FIRST CHURCH IN NORWICH, (IN "NORWICH TOWN,") ORG. 1660.

James Fitch,*		1660			Nov.	1702
Jabez Fitch, (c.)		1694		1695		
Henry Flint (c.)						
Joseph Coit, (c.)						
John Woodward,*	Dec.	1699	Sept.	1716		1746
Benjamin Lord,*	Nov.	1717			Mar.	1784
Joseph Strong, D. D.,†	Mar.	1778			Dec.	1834
Cornelius B. Everest,	Nov.	1829	Apr.	1836		
Hiram P. Arms,	Aug.	1836				

The church, with their pastor, removed from Saybrook. Mr. Fitch was a native of Bocking, in Essex, England. In 1646, he was ordained and installed pastor of the church in Old Saybrook. Rev. Mr. Stone, of Hartford, and other ministers assisted in the ordination services ; but so jealous was the church of any ecclesiastical power out of themselves, that the imposition of hands was by a "presbytery" chosen from the church for this purpose.

Mr. Fitch being disabled by palsy, retired to Lebanon in 1694, where he spent the evening of his life with his children. He was distinguished for the penetration of his mind, the energy of his preaching, and the sanctity of his life. Soon after coming to Norwich, he received a call to settle in Hartford. His laconic reply was : "With whom shall I leave these few sheep in the wilderness ?" He preached to the Mohegans in their native tongue, and gave them of his own lands to induce them to adopt the habits of civilized life. Mr. Woodward (Assistant Scribe of Saybrook Synod, 1708, *see p.* 3,) was in favor of consociation. The church insisted on their independence, in accordance with the Cambridge Platform, and this caused controversies and dissensions, during his ministry, respecting "the order and exercise of church discipline." At the time of Dr. Lord's ordination, the church, by a formal vote, renounced the Saybrook Platform, and adopted the Cambridge Platform, and has ever since maintained its independence. Dr. Lord was an earnest friend of revivals of religion, and had the satisfaction of witnessing several in connection with his labors. He lived to see eight religious societies grow out of the one of which he had charge. During Dr. Strong's ministry, two seceding congregations became extinct, and a considerable portion of their members returned to his church.

MINISTERS RAISED UP.—Jabez Fitch,‡ Isaac Backus, (Bap.)§ Charles Backus, D. D., Azel Backus, D. D., Aaron Cleaveland, Ebenezer Fitch, D. D.‖ Charles Cleaveland, (h.) Richard F. Cleaveland, (h.) Simon Huntington, Daniel W. Lathrop, (h.) Miron Winslow, (f.) William Nevins, D. D.,¶ Thomas L. Shipman, (h.) Simeon Hyde, David R. Austin, Charles Hyde, James T. Hyde, Erastus Wentworth, D. D., (f. Meth.) Gilbert Beebe, Zedediah H Mansfield, (Ep.) Henry Case, (h.) George Strong, (Ep.) Charles Porter, William F. Arms, (f.) D. W. Havens, Lynde Huntington, Fred. Charlton, (Bap.) David Wright, Thomas Baldwin,** D. D., (Bap.) John Huntington, Stephen Tracy, Joseph Lathrop, D. D.†† John Lathrop, D. D.‡‡ Nathan Perkins, D. D.

* Sp. An. 1. 297. Allen. † Sp. An. 2. 41. Allen. ‡ Sp. An. 1. 180. § Memoir by Prof. Hovey, 1859. ‖ Sp. An. 3. 511. ¶ Sp. An. 4. 629. ** Allen. †† Sp. An. 1. 528. Allen. ‡‡ Allen.

THE SECOND CHURCH IN NORWICH, ORG. 1760

MINISTERS.	SETTLED.	DISMISSED.	DIED.
Nathaniel Whitaker, D. D.,*	Feb. 1761	Mar. 1769	Mar. 1795
Ephraim Judson,†	Oct. 1771	Dec. 1778	Feb. 1813
Walter King,‡	May, 1778	July, 1811	Jan. 1812
Asahel Hooker,§	Jan. 1812		Apr. 1813
Alfred Mitchel,‖	Oct. 1814		Dec. 1831
James T. Dickinson,	April, 1832	Aug. 1834	
Alvan Bond, D. D.,	May, 1835		

It was one hundred years subsequent to the settlement of the town, before a church was organized in what was called "Norwich Landing," now the city of Norwich. As this part of the town gradually increased in population, in consequence of facilities for commercial pursuits, the few resident members of churches became organized into a Congregational church, and immediately provided for the support of the ministry. For want of ac commodations for the increased number of attendants, a colony from the church formed a new ecclesiastical organization in the year 1842. In 1844, the house was so much damaged by fire, that it was taken down. The present building, which is of stone, was dedicated Jan. 1, 1846, and has seats for about eight hundred persons. *Rel. Intel.* 18. 731, 747.

Ministers Raised Up.—Silas H. Hazzard, Albert T. Chester, d. d., Charles H. Chester, William Tracy, (f.) Elijah B. Huntington, Henry L. Carey, Giles B. Wilcox, Henry D. Woodworth.

* Sp. An. 1. 299. Allen. † Sp. An. 2. 20. ‡ Sp. An. 2. 319. Allen. § Sp. An. 2. 317. Allen. ‖ Sp. An. 2. 601. Allen.

The Church at Norwich Falls, Norwich, Org. Aug. 29, 1827.

MINISTERS.	SETTLED.	DISMISSED.	DIED.
Benson C. Baldwin,	Jan. 1828	Aug. 1829	
Charles Hyde,	June, 1830	Oct. 1834	
Joel W. Newton,	Oct. 1834	Jan. 1837	
Thomas K. Fessenden,	Oct. 1839	Feb. 1841	

The pastors were all respected and beloved by the people. This church had a brief, but blessed history. A Sabbath school was formed in the year 1816. At the organization of the church in 1827, there were only ten members, two of whom presented letters from the Second Congregational Church in Norwich, seven came from churches in other towns, and one was received on profession. The church was much united ; was blessed with seasons of revival ; did not forsake the assembling of themselves together, when without a minister, and reached the number of 167 in all. Disbanded May 23, 1842.

The Broadway (formerly Main St.) Church in Norwich, Org. June, 1842.

Willard Child, d. d.,	Aug. 1842	Aug 1845
John P. Gulliver,	Oct. 1846	

This church was originally organized with 112 members, under the name of the Fifth Congregational Church in Norwich. On the completion of its first house of worship on Main street, one of the Congregational churches of the town having meanwhile become extinct, the name was changed to Main St. Church. Their house of worship was completed and dedicated Oct. 1, 1845. It was destroyed by fire Sept. 1854. The site having been found too contracted for the erection of a house of sufficient size, a removal to the corner of Broadway and Bath streets was determined upon. This removal rendered necessary another change of name, and the present title was accordingly given.

THE CHURCH IN OLD LYME, (FORMERLY LYME,) ORG. 1693.

MINISTERS.	SETTLED.	DISMISSED.	DIED.
Moses Noyes,*	1666, inst. 1693		Nov. 1729
Samuel Pierpont,*	Dec. 1722		March, 1723
Jonathan Parsons,†	1730	1745	
Stephen Johnson,*	Dec. 1746		Nov. 1786
Edward Porter,	Feb. 1790	Sept. 1792	
Lathrop Rockwell,‡	Jan. 1794		March, 1828
Chester Colton,	Feb. 1829	1840	
Davis S. Brainerd,	June, 1841		

Mr. Noyes, for some unexplained cause, was minister at Lyme 27 years before the formation of the Church, though he was a man of mark and without reproach. He was also a member of the Saybrook Synod, 1708. *See Dr. Bacon's Discourse*, p. 4.

Mr. Parsons was one of the most efficient promoters of the revival of 1740. His account of the revival in Lyme and his labors in the vicinity, dated April, 1744, is one of the most valuable documents of the time, especially when read with his sermon of the same date entitled " A needful caution in a critical day." *See Tracy's Great Awakening*, pp. 133—150, and *Christian Hist.*, 2, 118. About 180 were reckoned as hopeful converts, and 150 were added to the Church in nine months. The purity of the revival was very much owing to the above named sermon, of which see an outline in *Tracy*, pp. 146—150. Parsons' account of his itinerating, pp. 152-5.

Revivals of religion have occurred in this Church and community at different intervals, from the days of Mr. Parsons, who was contemporary with the elder Edwards down to the last year ; in which, perhaps, the revival then enjoyed more resembled the revival under the ministry of Mr. Parsons than any previous one.

MINISTERS RAISED UP.—Moses Mather, D. D., Edward Dow.

* Allen. † Sp. An. 3, 47. Am. Qr. Reg. 14, 109. ‡ Sp. An. 1. 634. Allen.

THE CHURCH IN OLD SAYBROOK, (FORMERLY SAYBROOK,) ORG. 1646.

*John Higginson,**	1636	1640	
Thomas Peters,†	1643	1646	
James Fitch,†	1646	1660	Nov. 1702
Jeremiah Peck,	1660 ?	1670 ?	
Thomas Buckingham,‡	1670		April, 1709
Azariah Mather,†	1710	1732	
William Hart,§	Nov. 1736		July, 1784
Frederick Wm. Hotchkiss,‖	Sept. 1783		March, 1844
Ethan B. Crane,	June, 1838	Sept. 1851	
James Beattie,	Feb. 1851	Nov. 1852	
Salmon McCall,	Dec. 1853		

There are no records till 1736, and nothing of importance till 1783.   Yale College was first located here, and the noted Saybrook Platform was formed here in 1708.   Mr. Buckingham being assistant Moderator, (p.3.)   The ministry of Mr. Hotchkiss was eminently successful, the increase being from 69 to 330, and more than 600 being added in all.   Additions in the next pastorate 130; in the present 56.   *See Dr. Field's History of Middlesex Co., and Hotchkiss's Half Century Sermon.*

MINISTERS RAISED UP.—Benjamin Lord, D D., Daniel Chapman, Hezekiah Chapman, Ezekiel J. Chapman, (h.) Chas. Chapman, Jedediah Bushnell, (h)¶ Harvey Bushnell, Jackson J. Bushnell, Joseph A. Canfield, William Champlin, Elias Dudley.**

* Sp. An. 1, 91.   † Allen.   ‡ Sp. An. 1, 260.   § Sp. An. 2, 62.   Allen. ‖ Sp. An. 1, 262.   Allen.   ¶ Sp. An. 2, 422.   ** Mendon Assoc. 236.

THE CHURCH IN ORANGE, ORG. MARCH 13, 1805.

MINISTERS.	SETTLED.		DISMISSED.		DIED.
Erastus Scranton,	July,	1805	Jan.	1827	
Horatio A. Parsons,	Dec.	1829	April,	1832	
Horace Woodruff,	Aug.	1832	June,	1836	
B. Y. Messenger,	May,	1837	May,	1838	
John Starkweather,	April,	1839	April,	1840	
Anson Smyth,	Nov.	1840	Dec.	1842	
Cyrus Brewster,	Aug.	1843	Aug.	1848	
William W. Belden,	Aug.	1848	May,	1852	
Dillon Williams,	Jan.	1853	April,	1855	
Alfred C. Raymond,	June,	1855			

The inhabitants of North Milford, (now called Orange,) attended meeting in Milford until 1805.   They were incorporated as a Society in Oct., 1804, by request of 50 petitioners.   The Church was begun with five members. The inhabitants of this parish, fourteen years before this, erected a meeting house, where they had preaching in the winter season, by the alternate labors of the ministers in Milford.   While Mr. Scranton continued at North Milford, the Society greatly prospered.

MINISTERS RAISED UP.—Benjamin Fenn, George P. Prudden, Elias Clarke, (h.)

THE CHURCH IN OXFORD, ORG. JAN. 9, 1745.

	SETTLED.		DISMISSED.		DIED.	
Jonathan Lyman,	Jan.	1745			Oct.	1763
David Brownson,*	April,	1764			Nov.	1806
Nathaniel Freeman,	May,	1811	July,	1814		
Saul Clark,		1816?		1817	Dec.	1849
Ephraim G. Swift,	Dec.	1818	June,	1822	Aug.	1858

MINISTERS.	SETTLED.	DISMISSED.	DIED.
Sayres Gazley,	July, 1827	Jan. 1829	
Abraham Brown,	June, 1830	Aug. 1838	
Stephen Topliff,	Sept. 1841	July, 1860	

The early records are lost, and some of the later are defective; other "supplies" unrecorded. The Church has been limited in numbers and strength, (there having been for many years, four other places of worship in town,) and was for a time aided by the Missionary Society. It has been repeatedly blessed with revivals. In 1842, 30, and in 1851, 33 were added to the Church, and a less number in several other years of revival.

* Sp. An. 1, 468.

THE CHURCH IN PLAINFIELD, ORG. JAN. 3, 1705.

Joseph Coit,*	1699? ord. Jan. 1705	March, 1748	July,	1750
David S. Rowland,	March, 1748	April, 1761	Jan.	1794
John Fuller,	Feb. 1769		Oct.	1777
Joel Benedict, D. D.†,	Dec. 1784		Feb.	1816
Orin Fowler,‡	March, 1820	Jan. 1831	Sept.	1852
Samuel Rockwell,	April, 1832	April, 1841		
Andrew Dunning,	May, 1842	Jan. 1847		
Henry Robinson,	April, 1847	April, 1856		
William A. Benedict,	Oct. 1857?			

Mr. Coit declined a call to Norwich before 1799, then went to Plainfield. He ranked high among the ministers of his time. Mr. Rowland's ministry was in troublous times, on account of the Separatist movement, and after passing through many discouragements he took a dismission. He was afterwards settled in Providence and Windsor, and sustained the character of a faithful minister of Christ. Mr. Fuller had previously preached to the Separate Churches at Lyme and Bean Hill, and had the reputation of a godly and excellent minister. The Separate Church formed soon after Mr. Rowland's settlement having declined, and the old Church being also in a feeble state after his dismission, a desire for reunion was felt in both Churches, which was effected at Mr. Fuller's settlement. After Mr. Fuller's death, the people were again as sheep without a shepherd, being supplied only a part of the time. Dr. Benedict was a fine scholar, an able divine, a devoted pastor, and will be long held in cherished remembrance by the people of Plainfield. During the vacancy after his death, the Church was in very unfavorable circumstances, and had but four male members. Their house of worship, which had stood about 30 years, was entirely prostrated by the gale of Sept. 23, 1815. The present stone house was begun soon after, but not finished till the spring of 1819; the place of worship in the mean time being ill suited to the purpose. There was unusual religious interest in 1810–11, adding 30 to the Church; a powerful revival in 1821, adding 71, and also in 1831, adding 28; in 1838, adding 28, and in 1843, adding 30. In 1846, 50, or half the resident members, were dismissed to form the Church at Central Village.

MINISTERS RAISED UP.—Thomas Stevens, Josiah Whitney, D. D., Josiah Spalding,§ Elijah Parish, D. D.,‖ Alfred Johnson, Jonathan Kinne, Thomas Andros,* William F. Rowland,¶ Ariel Parish,** John D. Perkins, George Perkins, Richard H. Benedict, Evan M. Johnson, George Shepard, D. D., Edward J. Fuller, Elderkin R. Johnson, Cyrus Marsh.

* Allen. † Sp. An. 1. 682. Allen. ‡ Sp. An. 2. 648. Allen. § Mendon. As. 119. ‖Sp. An.2. 268. ¶Sp. An. 2, 722. Allen. ** Sp. An. 2. 269.

THE CHURCH IN PLAINVILLE, IN FARMINGTON, ORG. MARCH 16, 1840.

MINISTERS.	SETTLED.	DISMISSED.	DIED.
Chauncey D. Cowles,	June, 1841	April, 1843	
William Wright,	Nov. 1843	Sept. 1851	
Joel L. Dickinson,	June, 1852	1858	
Edward L. Wells,	Aug. 1858	Aug. 1859	
Moses Smith,	Sept. 1859		

March 5th, 1840, eighteen individuals petitioned to be set off as a distinct church from the first Congregational Church in Farmington, and were, in accordance with that petition, formed into a Church by an Ecclesiastical Council.

Since then the Church has steadily increased and God has wonderfully blessed it in numerous revivals.

THE CHURCH IN PLYMOUTH, (FORMERLY NORTHBURY,) ORG. MAY, 1740.

Samuel Todd,*	May, 1740	Aug. 1764	June, 1789
Andrew Storrs,†	Nov. 1765		March, 1785
Joseph Badger,‡	1786	1787	1846
Simon Waterman,	Aug. 1787	Nov. 1809	Nov. 1813
Luther Hart,§	Sept. 1810		April, 1834
Ephraim Lyman,	Oct. 1835	June, 1851	
Israel P. Warren,	Oct. 1851	Feb. 1856	
Erskine J. Hawes,	Jan. 1858		July, 1860

The Ecclesiastical Society of Northbury, the third in Waterbury, (Westbury, now Watertown, being the second,) was formed Nov. 1739. It has had four houses of worship. The first stood in Plymouth Hollow village. The other two occupied nearly the same ground on the Hill as that occupied by the present edifice, which was erected about the time the Churches in the Hollow and Terryville were formed. The Church has enjoyed several seasons of religious awakening, eight of which were during Mr. Hart's ministry, and at his death; adding from 19 to 92 members each, 344 in all; and a good number at eight or ten other seasons. *Ev. Mag.* 2. 60.

In 1837, 49 persons were dismissed to constitute the Church in Terryville, and at the same time, 51 to form the Church in Plymouth Hollow.

*Sp. An. 2, 288.   †Sp. An. 1, 406.   ‡Sp. An. 9. 473.   ♀Sp. An. 2, 523.   Allen. Litchf. Centen. 124.

The Church in Plymouth Hollow, Org. Dec. 7, 1837.

MINISTERS.	SETTLED.	DISMISSED.	DIED
Harvey D. Kitchell, D D.,	July, 1839	Sept. 1848	
Joseph D. Hull,	May, 1849	June, 1851	
James Averill,	Oct. 1852		

This was a colony of 51 members from the first Church. The occasion of its organization was the springing up of the villages in the west part of the town, and especially that in Plymouth Hollow. This Church has enjoy-ed revivals in 1838-9, 1846-7, and 1858-9.

The First Church in Pomfret, Org. Oct. 26, 1715.

Ebenezer Williams,*	1713	Oct. 1715	March, 1753
Aaron Putnam,†	March, 1756	May, 1802	
Asa King,‡	May, 1802	June, 1811	Dec. 1849
James Porter,§	Sept. 1814	April, 1830	
Amzi Benedict,	Oct. 1831	July, 1834	
Daniel Hunt,	April, 1835		

Mr. Williams was a native of Roxbury, Mass , and a nephew of Rev. John Williams of Deerfield. Mr. King, afterwards of Killingworth and West-minster.

This Church has had periods of trial in its history. Sometimes the time between pastorates has been longer than was desirable on account of the difficulty of uniting upon a candidate. But the people have never had a stated supply, and have never been without the preaching of the gospel for any great length of time. They have always been self-supporting, and have done something to help the weak.

The first meeting house in Pomfret was built in the summer of 1734. The Churches in Brooklyn and Abington were subsequently formed from this.

MINISTERS RAISED UP.—Chester Williams, Ezra Weld, Joshua Paine,‖ Ebenezer Grosvenor, Ephraim Hyde, Holland Weeks, Joseph Pope, Joseph Sumner, D. D.,¶ Joseph Dana, D. D , Eleazer Crofut, Abraham Salim, John Salim, Thomas Williams, Daniel Grosvenor, Aaron Putnam, William Morse. Henry Gleason, Nathan Grosvenor, George Payson, Joshua P. Payson, Mason Grosvenor, Charles P. Grosvenor, Job Hall, Elijah Wheeler, Nehemiah Williams, George N. Webber.

* Sp. An. 1,323. Allen. †Sp. An 1,358. Allen. ‡Allen. §Cong. Y. B. 1857, 128. ‖Allen. ¶Sp. An. 4, 680.

The Church in Poquonnock, Org. about 1720.

MINISTERS.	SETTLED.	DISMISSED.	DIED.
John Woodbridge,	1731 ?	1736	
Samuel Tudor,	1737 ?	1758 ?	
Dan Foster,	1774	1784	

This church had no minister for many years after the dismission of Mr. Tudor, and was in a very sad condition. Mr. Foster became a Universalist, and left the people in a worse condition than he found them. There was no minister after him. The church perished by the decrease of its members, and their house of worship passed into the hands of the Universalists. The present church at Poquonnock is a new organization, formed in 1841.

THE CHURCH IN POQUONNOCK, IN WINDSOR, ORG. JUNE 2, 1841.

Cornelius B. Everest,	1843	1852
Thomas H. Rouse, 1852, ord. July, 1854	Oct. 1856	
Henry J. Lamb,	May, 1857	1859
Ogden Hall, (c.)	May, 1859 ?	

The church worshiped in a hall till 1854, when they completed their house of worship.

THE FIRST CHURCH IN PORTLAND, ORG. OCT. 25, 1721.

Daniel Newell,	Oct. 1721	Sept. 1731
Moses Bartlett,	June, 1733	Dec. 1766
Cyprian Strong, D. D.,*	Aug. 1767	Nov. 1811
Eber L. Clark,	Sept. 1812	Aug. 1815
Hervey Talcott,	Oct. 1816	

The first settlers of the place were from Middletown. The society was organized in 1714, and the first meeting-house was built in 1716, the second in 1750, and the third in 1850. In 1851, 38 members of the church were dismissed, and formed into what is called the Central Church. The greatest religious revivals were in 1823 and 1831. In several other years there have been smaller revivals. The church at first had 29 members. The several pastors have admitted to the church 50, 114, 193, 24 and 228,—total, 638.

MINISTER RAISED UP.—Samuel Shepard, D. D.†

* Sp. An. 1. 651. Allen. † Sp. An. 2. 364.

THE CENTRAL CHURCH, PORTLAND, ORG. JAN. 27, 1851.

Samuel G. W. Rankin, (c.) Jan. 1851 ?

A colony from the First Church, occasioned by the removal of the old meeting-house. There is room enough for two churches, but many do not avail themselves of the benefit of either. This Church has a very comfortable house of worship, which cost $4,500; it has enjoyed two revivals with good results.

THE CHURCH IN PRESTON, ORG. NOV. 16, 1698.

MINISTERS.	SETTLED.	DISMISSED.	DIED.
Salmon Treat,*	Nov. 1698	1744	1762
Asher Rosseter,†	1744		1781
Jonathan Fuller,	1784		1786
Lemuel Tyler,	1789		1808
John Hyde,	1812	1827	Aug. 1848
Augustus B. Collins,	1828	1847	
Nathan S. Hunt,	1847	1858	
Elijah W. Tucker,	1858		

The church was very small for forty or fifty years, having become reduced during the ministry of Mr. Rosseter to 17, and numbering only 28 at the death of Mr. Tyler. In the next fifty years it increased to more than 100, being nearly as large as at any time in its history. A large fund renders the support of the gospel very easy. The house of worship was repaired and remodeled in 1849.

MINISTER RAISED UP.—Alexander Yerrington.

* Allen. † Allen.

The Church in Long Society, in Preston, (Norwich 5th,) Org. about 1726.

Jabez Wight,*	1726		1782
Roswell Whitmore,	1848 ?	1849 ?	
Jacob Allen,	1850	1851	

Dr. Benjamin Lord, of Norwich Town, preached Mr. Wight's ordination sermon, in 1726, which was published. The records speak in 1758 of a meeting-house, and a minister, then settled in the "East Society of Norwich." None has been settled since his death. After that the meeting-house was open to all denominations who chose to occupy it. The second house was built in 1817, and several years since was sold to the town for a town-house. At one time it was voted that any one in the society might invite a minister of any denomination to preach, and a collection would be taken up to pay him. The records often speak of unsuccessful efforts to raise money to support preaching for six months at a time. An attempt was made to resuscitate this waning church in Oct. 1837, but paucity of members and inefficiency finally prevailed, and it was disbanded in 1857.

* Sp. An. 1. 299. Allen.

THE CHURCH IN PROSPECT, (FORMERLY COLUMBIA,) ORG. MAY 14, 1798.

MINISTERS.	SETTLED.	DISMISSED.	DIED.
Reuben Hitchcock,	1790	1794	
Oliver Hitchcock,	Sept. 1798	Jan. 1812	
David Bacon,	April, 1813	1814	
Abraham Fowler,	Jan. 1815	Jan. 1816	
Gideon Burt,	Jan. 1816	Jan. 1817	
John Marsh,	1817	1818	
Samuel Rich,	May, 1818	May, 1824	
John E. Bray, July, 1825, ord.	May, 1827	Sept. 1832	
James D. Chapman,	Sept. 1832	Sept. 1833	
Sylvester Selden,	1834	1836	
Zephaniah Smith,	1836	1837	1848
Ammi Linsley,	May, 1837	1839	
Edward Bull,	May, 1840	May, 1843	
Reuben Torrey,	June, 1843	April, 1848	
John L. Ambler,	Jan. 1849	Feb. 1851	
James Kilbourn,	Oct. 1851	Mar. 1854	
Asa M. Train,	Mar. 1855	Mar. 1856	
Joseph H. Payne,	April, 1856	Jan. 1858	
Asa M. Train,	Feb. 1858	1860	
William W. Atwater,	1860		

The Columbia Society was formed from portions of the towns of Water-bury and Cheshire, giving 17 members of those societies liberty of retaining their former connection. The society, with original bounds, became the town of Prospect, in 1827. An old Separate meeting-house was at first occupied, being repaired in 1801. The present house was built, with some aid out of town, in 1841. Sermons were delivered at the dedication, and installation of Mr. Torrey by Mr. Bull. The church has long been dependent on home missionary aid. There have been interesting revivals of religion.

———

THE CHURCH IN PUTNAM VILLAGE, ORG. JULY 9, 1848.

E. B. Huntington,	Nov. 1848	Feb. 1851	
J. Leonard Corning,	June, 1852	Jan. 1853	
Sidney L. Dean, (Meth.)	April, 1853	Nov. 1854	
J. R. Johnson,	Mar. 1855	April, 1856	
Eliakim Phelps, D. D.,	May, 1856	Jan. 1858	
George J. Tillotson, (c.)	Mar. 1858		

This church has grown up in the large and thriving village which has arisen around the Putnam depot of the Norwich and Worcester Railroad. The attention of the association of Windham County was turned to the desirableness of establishing a church here in 1846, by whose direction and aid the present minister left his charge several weeks to labor here. Preaching continued from that time. Though the church has had some trials, yet it has been generally making progress. Within the last two or three years especially, it has greatly advanced in numbers and efficiency, and now has the prospect of becoming a strong and useful member of our fraternity of Puritanical churches.

The Church in Redding, Org. 1733.

MINISTERS.	SETTLED.	DISMISSED.	DIED.
Nathaniel Hunn,*	1733		1749
Nathaniel Bartlett,†	May, 1775		1810
Jonathan Bartlett,	Feb. 1796	June, 1809	Mar. 1858
Daniel Crocker,	Oct. 1809	Oct. 1824	1831
William C. Kniffin,	June, 1825	Dec. 1828	1858
William L. Strong,	June, 1830	Feb. 1835	
Jeremiah Miller,	July, 1837	July, 1839	
David C. Comstock,	Mar 1840	April, 1845	
Daniel D. Frost,	Dec. 1846	Oct. 1856	
Enoch S. Huntington,	1858	1859	
William D. Herrick,	Jan. 1860		

Jonathan Bartlett, son of Rev. Nathaniel Bartlett, was a pupil of President Dwight, and was converted under his ministry. He was ordained as a colleague with his father, and was dismissed on account of ill health. In the latter part of his pastorate, there was a powerful revival of religion among the people of his charge. After his health was restored, he used to preach to destitute congregations in the vicinity, as well as to his own people when they were without a pastor. He was a good preacher, and mighty in the scriptures; being so familiar with them, that he could recite several entire epistles from memory : and it is supposed that he could repeat more of the New Testament in Greek, than any other minister in the land. He always loved the flock over whom he had been settled, and gave them at various times more money than they paid him during his pastorate. He left them, in addition, a legacy of $3,000 at his death. At the time of his decease, he was the oldest Congregational minister in Connecticut, being in the 62d year of his ministry, and in the 94th year of his age. He lived and died in the house where he was born, and his end was peace.

Ministers Raised Up.—Jonathan Bartlett, Thomas F. Davies.

* Allen. † Sp. An. 1. 638.

The Church in Ridgebury, in Ridgefield, Org. Jan. 18, 1769.

Samuel Camp,*	Jan. 1769	Nov. 1804	Oct. 1813
Nathan Burton,	Nov. 1821	June, 1841	Aug. 1859
Zalmon B. Burr,	June, 1843	May, 1850	
Philo Canfield,	Sept. 1852	April, 1856	

MINISTERS.	SETTLED.	DISMISSED.	DIED.
William W. Page,	Aug. 1856	Aug. 1859	
Enoch S. Huntington,	Oct. 1859		

This church ever has been, and must of necessity be, small in numbers, being located on a narrow ridge of land, and having to suffer embarrassment from a Baptist church located in their midst, and more particularly from being so near to Danbury. Ridgebury being a farming community exclusively, and Danbury a large manufacturing town, the tendency is to make farming unpopular, particularly with the young men, so that as soon as they get to years of majority, they move away, greatly to the embarrassment of the church.

MINISTERS RAISED UP.—Nathan Burton, Oliver St. John, Jacob St. John.

* Sp. An. 1. 664.

THE CHURCH IN RIDGEFIELD, ORG. 1712.

Thomas Hawley,*	1712		Nov. 1738
Jonathan Ingersol,†	July, 1740		Oct. 1778
Justus Mitchell,	1779 ?	1782 ?	
Samuel Goodrich,‡	July, 1786	Jan. 1811	April, 1835
Jonathan Bartlett,	1811	1814 ?	Mar. 1858
John Noyes,	1814	1817	May, 1846
Samuel M. Phelps,	June, 1817	Dec. 1829	Dec. 1841
Charles G. Selleck,	May, 1831	Sept. 1837	
Joseph Fuller,	Feb. 1838	May, 1842	
James A. Hawley,	Oct. 1843	Nov. 1849	
Clinton Clark,	June, 1850		

The township of Ridgefield was purchased of the Indians by a company of twenty-nine individuals from Norwalk and Milford. The deed bears date 1707-8. In Oct. 1712, the General Assembly, upon the petition of the inhabitants of Ridgefield, passed an order "that all the lands lying in the town of Ridgefield, be taxed in proportion for four years, towards the settling and maintaining of the ministry in the said town of Ridgefield." *Rel Intel.* 16. 540.

* Sp. An. 1. 438. Allen. † Allen. ‡ Sp. An. 1. 512. Allen.

THE FIRST CHURCH IN ROCKVILLE, IN VERNON, ORG. OCT. 26, 1837.

Ansel Nash,	Jan. 1839	July, 1841
Augustus Pomroy,	Sept. 1841	Sept. 1844
Horace Winslow,	Oct. 1845	Nov. 1852
John W. Ray,	Dec. 1853	Feb. 1854
Thomas O. Rice,	April, 1856	April, 1857
Smith B. Goodenow,	Nov. 1858	May, 1860

Rockville is a manufacturing village in the northern part of Vernon, on the Hockanum River. The first factory was erected in 1821, at which time there were thirteen families within the present limits of Rockville. Since that time the population has been regularly increasing, and is now (1859) about 2500. The people here attended church at Vernon Center till 1836, at which time the population was 444. The time had now arrived when it seemed necessary that the ministrations of the gospel should be enjoyed by the people, without being obliged to travel the distance of three miles. Accordingly, a petition was drafted and signed by fourteen petitioners, which was presented to the Congregational church in Vernon, asking permission to hold meetings in a room already provided, and to make an effort to sustain the gospel ministrations in this place, with a view, if they were prosperous, of eventually asking that their special relations with the church in Vernon might be dissolved, and *they* be organized into a church of the same order. The petition was readily granted. The first preaching on the Sabbath in this place, was Dec. 18, 1836, by Rev. Bennet Tyler, d. d., of East Windsor.

THE SECOND CHURCH OF ROCKVILLE, IN VERNON, ORG. FEB. 22, 1849.

MINISTERS.	SETTLED.	DISMISSED.	DIED.
Andrew Sharp,	Sept. 1849	Dec. 1851	
C. H. Bullard,	Nov. 1853	Jan. 1857	
C. W. Clapp,	May, 1857		

In eleven years after the formation of the First Church, it had increased to such an extent, as to vote that "the time had come for the formation of a second church." The society was formed in February, 1848. The church adopted a rule for a "triennial deaconship." The prevailing Christian influence in the village, from the first, has been Congregational. The church has enjoyed frequent tokens of Divine favor in outpourings of the Spirit, especially in 1850, '52, '54 and '58. The Sabbath school contains children of many foreign families, who can scarely be reached in any other way. The church is steadfast in devotion to the principles of liberty, temperance and Christian enterprise at home and abroad.

MINISTER RAISED UP.—E. C. Bissell.

THE CHURCH IN ROCKY HILL, (FORMERLY STEPNEY,) ORG. JUNE 7, 1727.

Daniel Russell,*	Jan. 1727		Sept. 1764
Burrage Merriam,	Feb. 1765		Nov. 1776
John Lewis,†	Jan. 1781		April, 1792
Calvin Chapin, d. d.,‡	April, 1794		Mar. 1851
L. B. Rockwood,	July, 1850	Jan. 1859	
George M. Smith,	Oct. 1859		

This church has had but six pastors since its organization. The first four died as pastors, and were buried in Rocky Hill. The church has had a good degree of prosperity from its first formation. The year 1858 was one of unusual religious interest. Dr. Nettleton labored here in 1818, with happy results. *Memoir*, 97.

MINISTER RAISED UP.—Nathaniel G. Huntington.

    * Allen. † Sp. An. 2. 324. Allen. ‡ Sp An. 2. 323. Allen.

THE CHURCH IN ROXBURY, ORG. JUNE 1744.

MINISTERS.	SETTLED.	DISMISSED.	DIED.
Thomas Canfield,	1744		1795
Zephaniah Swift,	1795	1812	1848
Fosdic Harrison,	1813	1835	Feb. 1858
Austin Isham,	1839		

The Church in Roxbury, like many other churches, began with few in number and at times seemed struggling between life and death. But the Great Head of the Church has in a wonderful manner fulfilled to His people here His gracious promises, so that they may truly say "hitherto hath the Lord helped us."

Our fathers, who now "rest from their labors," established a permanent fund, now amounting to between five and six thousand dollars, the interest of which goes to sustain a preached gospel. From time to time, the Holy Spirit has been signally manifested, greatly refreshing the hearts of believers and bringing numbers, especially of baptized children and youth, into the fold of the blessed Redeemer.

THE CHURCH IN SALEM, (FORMERLY COLCHESTER, 2d,) ORG. 1719.—RE-ORGANIZED, 1793.

Joseph Lovett,	1719	1745	
David Huntington,	1775	1796	April, 1812
Amasa Loomis, Jr.,	May, 1813	Jan. 1817	
Royal Tyler,*	Jan. 1818	Dec. 1821	April, 1826
Eli Hyde,†	Nov. 1822	April, 1831	Oct. 1856
Charles Thompson,†	Oct. 1833		March, 1855
B. B. Hopkinson,	May, 1855	May, 1857	
Nathaniel Miner,	May, 1857		

There are traditions extant concerning Mr. Lovett, and some living who recollect Mr. Huntington, who went to Hamburg in Lyme. Almost nothing is known of the Church before its re-organization. After that, they had preaching but seldom, and being reduced in numbers by death and removals, they ceased to meet as a Church until May 5th, 1813, when the prospect of enjoying the ministry regularly settled among them, and the application of several persons for admission into covenant with them, induced them to meet.

    * Mendon As. 240. † Cong. Y. B. 3. 120.

The Church in Salisbury, Org. Nov. 22, 1744.

MINISTERS.	SETTLED.	DISMISSED.	DIED.
Jonathan Lee,* Nov. 1743, ord. Nov. '44			Oct. 1788
William F. Miller, (c.)	1790		
John Eliot, (c.)	1791		
James Glassbrook,	1792	1793	Oct. 1793
Ebenezer Porter, D. D., (c.)	1795		April, 1834
T. M. Cooley, D. D., (c.)	1795		Dec. 1859
Joseph W. Crossman, June, 1796, ord. June, 1797			Dec. 1812
John B. Whittlesey, (c.)	Dec. 1812	Aug. 1813	
William R. Weeks, D. D., (c.)	1814	1815	1848
Chauncey A. Goodrich, D. D., (c.)	1815		Feb. 1860
Asahel Nettleton, D. D.,	1815	1816	May, 1844
Federal Burt, (c.)	1816		
Lavius Hyde, Mar. 1817, ord. Mar. 1818		Aug. 1822	
William C. Fowler, (c.)	1823		
Amzi Benedict,	1823		
L. E. Lathrop, D. D., Jan. '24, inst. Feb. 1825		Oct. 1836	1857
Adam Reid, Nov. 1836, ord. Sept. 1837			

The town transacted ecclesiastical business till the Society was organized in 1804. Public worship was attended for several months in three dwelling houses, and then in a log house built for the purpose, and for the use of the minister's family, till 1749, when a meeting house was built; the second house in 1800. The Church and first pastor favored the Great Awakening. The Association of New Haven County reprimanded the Church for adopting the Cambridge Platform, and suspended Rev. Messrs. Humphreys of Derby, Leavenworth of Waterbury, and Todd of Northbury, for ordaining Mr. Lee. He was a man fitted for the exigencies of the times, and to his influence is to be attributed much of the manly, independent spirit, intelligence, sagacity, breadth and weight of character by which the town has ever been characterized. He received to the Church 252. There was a very extensive revival under Dr. Nettleton's labors ; (*Memoir,* 81,) and another under Dr. Lathrop. *See Centennial Address of Judge Church ; and Historical Address of Mr. Reid,* 1844. *Rel. Intel.* 12, 795.

MINISTERS RAISED UP.—James Hutchinson, Samuel Camp, Chauncey Lee, D. D., Henry P. Strong, Horace Holley, D. D., William L. Strong, Isaac Bird, (f.) Jonathan Lee, George A Calhoun, D. D., Edward Hollister, (h.) Edwin Holmes, Edmund Janes, Edwin Janes, Joseph Pettee, Josiah Turner, Eliphalet Whittlesey, (f.) Elisha Whittlesey, Henry Pratt.

*Sp. An. 2, 288. Allen. Litchf. Centen. 115.

The Church in Scotland, Org. Oct. 22, 1735.

Ebenezer Devetion,*	Oct. 1735		July, 1771
James Cogswell, D. D.,†	Feb. 1772	Dec. 1804	Jan. 1807

MINISTERS.	SETTLED.	DISMISSED.	DIED.
Cornelius Adams,	Dec. 1805		Nov. 1806
Elijah G. Welles,	Jan. 1808	May, 1810	1855
Jesse Fisher,‡	Mar. 1811		Sept. 1836
Otis C. Whiton,	June, 1837	April, 1841	Oct. 1845
Thomas Tallman,	Mar. 1844		

The third Society in Windham, (now Scotland,) was incorporated May 11, 1732; the town, July 4, 1857. Eighty-nine were dismissed from the First Church in Windham, to constitute the Church.

The whole number who have joined the Church in Scotland is 746. The Church has not been visited by very frequent revivals. The most powerful was in 1832, when 54 were added. The Church has been destitute of a pastor only about seven years in all.

The Society is now occupying its third meeting house. *See Brunswick Separate Church.*

MINISTERS RAISED UP.—Joseph Huntington, D. D., Enoch Huntington, David Ripley, Hezekiah Ripley, D D., John Palmer, David Palmer, Daniel Waldo, Ralph Robinson, Lucien Farnham, (h.) Ebenezer Jennings, Asa A. Robinson, (Bapt.)

* Allen.   †Sp. An. 1, 445.   Allen.   ‡Sp. An. 1. 538.

THE CHURCH IN SEYMOUR, (FORMERLY HUMPHREYSVILLE,) ORG. MAR. 12, 1817.

Ephraim G. Swift,	1825	1827	Aug. 1858
Chas. Thompson, June,'28, ord. Apr. 1830		June, 1833	March, 1855
John E. Bray,	Sept. 1834	April, 1842	
William B. Curtis,	Aug. 1843	Oct. 1849	
E. B. Chamberlain,	April, 1850	April, 1852	
James L. Willard, (lic.)	Sept. 1852	April, 1855	
H. D. Northrop, (lic.)	Aug. 1857	March, 1859	
E. C. Baldwin, (lic.)	May, 1859	May, 1860	

The first house of worship was built about the time of the organization of the Church; the second in 1846. There were revivals under the ministry of Mr. Bray and Mr. Northrop. The failure of an extensive branch of manufacture, in 1855, removing about 30 families from the congregation, greatly reduced the resources of the society, and made the Church, after several years of self-support, again dependent on home missionary aid.

MINISTERS RAISED UP.—Ira Smith, (h.) H. A. DeForest, (f.)

THE CHURCH IN SHARON, ORG. 1740.

Peter Pratt,*	April, 1740	Oct. 1747	1780
John Searl,*	Aug. 1749	June, 1754	1787

MINISTERS.	SETTLED.	DISMISSED.	DIED.
Cotton Mather Smith,†	Aug. 1755		1806
David L. Perry,	June, 1804		1835
Mason Grosvenor,	Sept. 1836	June, 1839	
Grove L. Brownell,	May, 1840	Aug. 1848	
Charles Rockwell,	April, 1850	June, 1851	
Thomas G. Carver,	Oct. 1851	1853	
L. E Lathrop, D. D.‡	July, 1854		Aug. 1857
D. D. McLaughlin,	Jan. 1859		

The town was incorporated Oct. 1739, and as appears from the records, the Church was organized about the time of Mr. Pratt's settlement. In 1822 a general revival of religion was experienced throughout the Society and large accessions made to the Church, also general revivals in 1806 and 1839, and less extensive at several other times. In 1824, the present church edifice was built with great unanimity. Within a few years past their numbers have been diminishing by deaths and removals.

MINISTERS RAISED UP.—Jeremiah Day, Daniel Smith, Vinson Gould, David R. Gould, Charles Y. Chase, Alvin Somers, William Jewell, Hiram White, (Meth.) John M. S. Perry,* (f.) David C. Perry, Gilbert L. Smith, Charles H. Read, James Cleaveland, George I. Kaercher, Jesse W. Guernsey.

* Allen. † Sp. An. 1. 500. Litchf. Centen. 96. ‡ Cong. Y. Book, 5. 108.

THE CHURCH IN SHERMAN, (FORMERLY NORTH NEW FAIRFIELD,) ORG. 1751.

Thomas Lewis,	Mar. 1744	· Oct. 1746	
Elijah Sill,	Oct. 1751	Oct. 1779	
Oliver D. Cook,	May, 1792	Nov. 1793	
Maltby Gelston,	April, 1797		Dec. 1856
N. M. Urmston,	May, 1841	May, 1843	
Elijah Whitney,	Nov. 1843	Nov. 1844	
Judson B. Stoddard,	Oct. 1845	Oct. 1854	
Revillo J. Cone,	Jan. 1856	July, 1858	
William Russell,	1859		

This Church and Society have always been small, being originally called North New Fairfield, and set off from New Fairfield, as the town of Sherman, in 1803. The only deacon died in 1810, and Mr. Gelston officiated both as pastor and deacon till 1813; and for several years, there were but three male members. The first house of worship was small, much like a common school house; the second was built in 1785–9; the third in 1836.
See Mr. Gelston's Funeral Sermon, 1857. *Cong. Y. B.* 1857, 108.

MINISTERS RAISED UP.—Maltby Gelston, Jr., Mills B. Gelston.

The Church in Simsbury, Org. 1682.

MINISTERS.	SETTLED.	DISMISSED.	DIED.
Samuel Stone,	1682 ?	1687 ?	
Edward Thompson,	1687	1691	
*Seth Shove,**	1691	1695 ?	Oct. 1735
Dudley Woodbridge,	Nov. 1697		Aug. 1710
Timothy Woodbridge, Jr.	Nov. 1712		Aug. 1742
Gideon Mills,†	Sept. 1744	Sept. 1754	1772
Benajah Roots,	Aug. 1757	1772	
Samuel Stebbins,	Dec. 1777	Nov. 1806	Jan. 1820
Allen McLean,	Aug. 1809		
Samuel T. Richards,	May, 1850	July, 1858	
O. S. Taylor,	Sept. 1859		

The settlement of Simsbury commenced about 1661. A number of enterprising farmers, from Windsor, were attracted there by the broad and fertile meadows on the river, and by the beautiful and rich forests on the plain. The first settlers took early measures to establish the ministry, and erect a house for public worship. The half-way covenant was in use till after Mr. McLean's settlement. In 1813–14 the Spirit of God descended with great power, and wrought a wonderful work of grace, in which the whole population were more or less affected. Since that time there has been a season of refreshing once in about seven years. For its very existence and prosperity the Church has been dependent on revivals of religion ; a remarkable one occurred in 1858, 100 making a profession. Various forms of error, attempted to be introduced, have all failed. No individual for 50 years has been publicly arraigned for trial before the Church, but private admonition has uniformly reclaimed the wandering. Mr. McLean had been for eleven years before his 50th anniversary totally blind, after two years of impaired vision. *See his Half Century Discourse,* 1859.

Ministers Raised Up.—Charles B. McLean, Amos A. Phelps,‡ John W. Adams, D. D.§

* Sp. An. 1. 116. Allen.   † Sp. An. 2. 229. Allen.   ‡ Mendon As. 184. Allen.
§ Sp. An. 4, 688.

The Church in Somers, (formerly East Enfield,) Org. March 15, 1727.

Samuel Allis,	Mar. 1727	1747	Dec. 1796
Freegrace Leavitt,	July, 1748		1761
Charles Backus, D. D.*	Aug. 1774		Dec. 1803
William L. Strong,	April, 1805	July, 1829	
Rodney G. Dennis,	June, 1830	June, 1839	
James P. Terry,	Dec. 1839	Aug. 1845	
Joseph Vaill, D. D.,	Aug. 1845	Dec. 1854	
George A. Oviatt,	Dec. 1855		

This church has been blessed with many interesting revivals of religion— three during the ministry of Mr. Allis ; and adding under the ministry of

Dr. Backus and his successors, severally, 280, 296, 143, 52, and 106. *Memoir of Dr. Nettleton,* 159 ; *Ev. Mag.* 1. 19 *; Rel. Intel.* 7. 170 ; *S.* 60. The Society was at first called East Enfield. Its remoteness from the First Church (eight miles) led to the formation of the church, which was with nine members, all males,—the inhabitants being then less than 200. Mr. Allis, born at Hatfield, Mass., studied divinity with Mr. Stoddard of Northampton ; he published an account of the revival of 1740–41, in Gillie's Hist. Coll. Mr. Leavitt, born in Suffield, was a superior scholar, and a strong, earnest, and faithful preacher, and died greatly lamented. Dr. Backus kept "a school of the prophets." After the death of Mr. Leavitt, the church was without a pastor thirteen years, and became divided by the Separates, four or five years before the settlement of Dr. Backus, under whom both branches united in great harmony. The first meeting-house was built in 1739 ; the second in 1787 ; the third in 1842.

MINISTERS RAISED UP.—Alonzo B. Chapin, D. D., (Ep.) Reuben Chapin, Levi Collins, William H. Thompson, Seth Chapin, (Ep.) Giles Pease, Freegrace Reynolds,† Anson Sheldon, Epaphras Kibbe, (Meth.) Silas Billings, Luke Wood, Abiel Jones, Gideon Clark, Rollin Porter.

*Sp. An. 2. 61. Allen. † Cong. Y. Book, 2. 100.

THE CHURCH IN SOUTH BRITAIN, IN SOUTHBURY, ORG. 1769.

MINISTERS.	SETTLED.	DISMISSED.	DIED.
Ichabod Lewis,	Nov. 1767		
Samuel Camp,	Dec. 1766		
Jehu Minor,	April, 1768	1790	
Benjamin Wooster,	May, 1794		
Ebenezer Porter, D. D.,	Aug. 1795		April, 1834
Lathrop Thompson,	May, 1796	1798	
Matthias Cazier,	Aug. 1799	Jan. 1804	
Thaddeus Osgood,	1807	1808	
Bennet Tyler, D. D.,	June, 1808	Mar. 1822	May, 1858
Noah Smith,*	Oct. 1822		Oct. 1830
Seth Sackett,	May, 1831	1832	
Darius Mead,	Feb. 1832	July, 1834	
Seth Sackett,	Aug. 1834	1835	
Benoni Y. Messenger,	Sept. 1835	June, 1837	
Oliver B. Butterfield,*	June, 1837		Nov. 1849
William T. Bacon,	Jan. 1850	1851 ?	
Amos E. Lawrence,	Dec. 1851	July, 1860	

The church in South Britain came off from the church in Southbury, about the year 1769, and were allowed what was called winter privileges. A committee was appointed to confer with the General Association's Committee in regard to the matter, and a rate bill allowed for the payment of the minister, and other expenses. In 1807, a fund of $7,000 was raised by subscription for a permanent fund ; but they realized the truth, that riches take to themselves wings and fly away,—and the wisdom of having every generation support the institutions of the gospel for itself; for they lost $4,500 of the fund by the failure of the Eagle Bank of New Haven. The sale of the slips, and the balance of the fund, support them now. Dr. Nettleton labored here in a revival in 1812. *See his Memoir, p.* 63.

MINISTERS RAISED UP.—George E. Pierce, Asa Bennet, Cyrus Downs.

* Litchf. Centen. 117.

THE CHURCH IN SOUTHBURY, ORG. 1732.

MINISTERS.	SETTLED.	DISMISSED.	DIED.
John Graham,*	1732		Dec. 1774
Benjamin Wildman,†	1766		1812
Elijah Wood,	1813	1815	
Daniel A. Clark,‡	1816	1819	Mar. 1840
Thomas L. Shipman,	1826	1836	
William H. Whittemore,	1836	1850	
George P. Prudden,	1852	1856	
Jason Atwater,	1856	July, 1859	April, 1860
A. B. Smith,	Jan. 1860		

The first house of worship was erected in 1732; the second in 1772; the third and present house in 1844. The years of the largest accessions to this church were 1813, 1821, 1831, and 1842.

MINISTER RAISED UP.—John W. Beecher.

*Sp. An. 1. 314. Allen. Litchf. Centen. 75--7. †Litchf. Centen. 75-7 ‡Sp. An. 4. 460. Litchf. Centen. 119.

THE CHURCH IN SOUTH GLASTENBURY, ORG. DEC. 22, 1836.

Warren G. Jones,	July, 1837	Aug. 1850
Frederick W. Chapman,	Oct. 1850	Oct. 1854
Lewis Jesup,	Dec. 1854	April, 1856
John A. Seymour,	Oct. 1857	

This church and that in the north part of the town were originally one. The house of worship stood midway between the two villages. In the course of time, this arrangement was found inconvenient. Each part of the town needed a church of its own. The division was effected in a happy way. Harmony was undisturbed, and brotherly love was quickened. This part of the town derived much of its importance from manufacturing interests. Fire consumed the property, and scattered a large portion of the inhabitants. The church and society were much affected.

THE CHURCH IN SOUTHINGTON, ORG. NOV. 19, 1728.

Jeremiah Curtiss,	Nov. 1728	1755	Mar. 1795

MINISTERS.	SETTLED.	DISMISSED.	DIED.
Benjamin Chapman,	Mar. 1756	Sept. 1774	June, 1786
William Robinson,*	Jan. 1780	April, 1821	May, 1825
David S. Ogden,	Oct. 1821	Sept. 1836	
Elisha C. Jones,	June, 1837		

Prior to 1721, the present town of Southington was included within the limits of the town and parish of Farmington; and there its few families attended upon religious worship, and paid their taxes for its support. They were called "The Farmers, South of the Town," and sometimes "The Southern Farmers." In 1721, on account of the great inconvenience of going so far on the Sabbath, especially in cold weather, they were allowed the privilege of setting up a meeting among themselves a part of the year; and their ecclesiastical tax, payable at Farmington, was abated to them, at first one-third, and afterwards one-half, on condition that they should hire a minister to preach among them three months in the winter season; and in 1723, their petition was granted to become a ministerial society by themselves, on condition that at their first meeting they should fix upon a place for a meeting-house, and should lay a tax sufficient to raise the sum of one hundred and fifty pounds, current money, which should be carefully expended in building it. The society was incorporated in 1724. The first meeting-house was built about the year 1726; the second in 1757; and the third in 1830. The whole number connected with the church (there being no record from 1756 to 1780,) is 1535. The church has been blessed from time to time with revivals of religion. The years most distinguished for these seasons were 1831, when 68 were added to the church; in 1834, 136; in 1838, 128; and 1858, 80. *Rel. Intel.* 18. 713. The church and society have generally been very harmonious and united, no difficulty having ever arisen that called for the interposition of a Council or Consociation. The Confession of Faith, and the Church Covenant, now used by the church, are essentially the same that were adopted in 1779, about the commencement of Mr. Robinson's ministry, and, in sentiment, are highly Calvinistic.

MINISTERS RAISED UP.—Jeremiah Curtiss, Samuel Newell, Levi Lankton, Levi Hart, D. D., Whitfield Cowles, Gad Newell,† Josiah B. Andrews, Pitkin Cowles, Elisha D. Andrews, Fosdick Harrison, Edward Robinson, D. D., Jeremiah R. Barnes, Henry Clark.

* Sp. An. 2. 131. Allen. Memoir by his son, Prof. Edward Robinson, D. D.
† Cong. Qu. 1. 314.

THE CHURCH IN SOUTH KILLINGLY, ORG. 1746

Samuel Wadsworth,	June, 1747				1762
Eliphalet Wright,	May 1765				784
Israel Day,	June, 1785	May,	1826	Dec.	1831
John N. Whipple,	1831		1834		
George Langdon,	1842		1844		

MINISTERS.	SETTLED.	DISMISSED.	DIED.
Israel C. Day,	1846	1848	
Joseph Ayer, Mar. 1849, inst. Jan. 1851		Mar. 1856	

This was originally a Separate church, and after a few years, returned to the faith and practice of the churches from which it separated. The church has been blessed with revivals. In 1776–7, there was one which brought about 50 into the church; in 1788, about 49; in 1800, 64; and in 1832, 40. *Ev. Mag.* 3. 225. It has long been feeble, depending on Home Missionary aid, and is now virtually extinct.

MINISTERS RAISED UP.—Joshua Spalding, Daniel G. Sprague.

THE CHURCH IN SOUTH NORWALK, ORG. JAN. 3, 1836.

James Knox,	1836	April, 1839	
John B. Shaw,	1839	1841	
Francis C. Woodworth,	Feb. 1842	Feb. 1844	1859
Z. K. Hawley,	April, 1844	May, 1848	
Sylvanus Haight,	July, 1848	Sept. 1851	
D. R. Austin, Oct. 1851, inst. May, 1853			

The church originally consisted of sixty-four members, dismissed from the First Church, and was called the Second Church in Norwalk, till 1852. Public worship and a Sabbath school were commenced Feb. 14th, and the house of worship opened on the last Sabbath of March, 1836.

THE CHURCH IN SOUTHPORT, IN FAIRFIELD, ORG. MARCH 7, 1843.

S. J. M. Merwin,	Dec. 1844	May, 1859
Charles E. Linsley,	Feb. 1860	

THE CHURCH IN SOUTH WINDSOR, ORG. 1690.

Timothy Edwards,*	March, 1695		Jan.	1758
Joseph Perry,*	April, 1755		April,	1783
David McClure, D. D.,†	June, 1786		June,	1820
Thomas Robbins, D. D.,‡	1808	1827		1857
Samuel Whelply,	April, 1828		Dec.	1830
Chauncey G. Lee,	Aug. 1832	1836		
Levi Smith,	May, 1840	1849		1852
Edward W. Hooker, D. D.,	1849	1856		
J. B. Stoddard,	1856			

South Windsor is a part of the former town of East Windsor.

The first settlers of East Windsor came from Windsor, and for many years attended public worship on the West side of the river, and belonged to the Church and congregation there. But finding it inconvenient to cross the river, and being grown sufficiently numerous and able to support public worship among themselves, they proceeded to build a meeting-house, which stood near the north burying yard, and invited Mr. Timothy Edwards, son of Richard Edwards, Esq., of Hartford, to preach to them, who was ordained in March, 1695. He studied under the Rev. Mr. Glover, of Springfield; and received the degrees of Bachelor and Master of Arts in one day at the College in Cambridge, Massachusetts, which was an uncommon mark of respect paid to his extraordinary proficiency in learning. He married the daughter of the Rev. Solomon Stoddard, of Northampton, Mass., who was a divine of eminence in his day. By her he had ten daughters and one son—the Rev. Jonathan Edwards, President of New Jersey College, whose writings rank him high among the first geniuses and divines of that or any other age.

The second meeting house was built in 1709, near the north burying yard. The third meeting house was built in 1761; and in 1804, ground was purchased near it for a burying place. This building was taken down in 1845, and a new one erected on nearly the same ground.

This Church early adopted the Cambridge Platform of Church government and worship, and the Westminster Confession of Faith; as the Church in West Windsor, from which they originated, had also done; but has ever united in associations and ecclesiastical councils, with the neighboring churches, who are generally settled on what is called the Saybrook Platform.

South Windsor partook, with the neighboring towns and churches, in the great and general revival of religion through New England and America, in the years 1741-2.

The practice of admitting persons into the Church on what was called the half-way-covenant plan, continued here until March 27, 1808, when it was quietly abolished. A relation of Christian experience was required of all candidates for full communion, from an early period.

MINISTERS RAISED UP.—Jonathan Edwards, Pres. of New Jersey College, Julius Read, Amasa Loomis, Samuel Wolcott.

* Sp. An. 1, 230. Allen. † Sp. An. 2, 7. Allen. ‡ Allen.

THE SECOND CHURCH IN SOUTH WINDSOR, ORG. FEB. 2, 1830.

MINISTERS.	SETTLED.		DISMISSED.		DIED.
Henry Morris,	July,	1826	July,	1829	
David L. Hunn,	July,	1832	May,	1835	
Marvin Root,	July,	1835	April,	1840	
Augustus Pomeroy,		1840		1841	
O. F. Parker, Jan. '43, ord. Jan.		1844	Oct.	1848	
William Wright,	Aug.	1854			

The inhabitants within the limits of this Society formerly worshiped with the First Church of South Windsor, originally East Windsor. This portion of the town was settled about the year 1700. In 1826, the people concluded that it was best to secure religious privileges among themselves, when Rev. Mr. Brinsmade of the "Asylum," Hartford, labored here six months, and several others for short periods after, till 1829. By Mr. Brinsmade's labors about 20 indulged hope ; 28 at first composed the Church ; in August, 1831, a protracted meeting resulted in about 50 hopeful converts ; and good numbers were added at other times. Pres. Tyler and others from the Seminary supplied for some years before the settlement of Mr. Wright. The members of the Church and Society gave him $1000, on condition that he would not seek and obtain a dismission in ten years. The congregation is more than a quarter larger than formerly ; all pertaining to it is seemingly prosperous by the Divine blessing ; and the effect of the permanency given to the ministry by the terms of settlement is eminently desirable.

THE FIRST CHURCH IN STAFFORD, (EAST,) ORG. MAY 22, 1723.

MINISTERS.	SETTLED.	DISMISSED.	DIED.
John Graham, [*]	May, 1723	1731	Dec. 1774
Seth Payne,	June, 1734	July, 1740	
Eli Colton,	Sept. 1744		June, 1756
John Willard, D. D.,[†]	March, 1757		Feb. 1807
Cyrus W. Gray,	July, 1817		Aug. 1821
Hervey Smith,	Oct. 1822	1830	
Moses B. Church,	Aug. 1831	Feb. 1837	
George H. Woodward,	Jan. 1840	April, 1850	
Allen Clark,	March, 1851	March, 1852	
Merrick Knight,	1853	1854	
Mr. Gardner,	1854	1855	
Joseph Knight,	May, 1855		

This Church has passed through seasons of prosperity and adversity. Universalism has done much mischief. The apostasy of their pastor Moses B. Church, was a source of much affliction. The Church is but a feeble band, two churches, at Stafford Springs and Staffordville, having colonized from it, but the aid of funds renders it independent of foreign aid in the support of the gospel.

MINISTERS RAISED UP.—John Graham, Jr., Joseph Blodgett, Elisha Alden.

* Sp. An. 1. 314. Allen. † Sp. An. 2, 30. Allen.

THE CHURCH IN STAFFORD SPRINGS, ORG. DEC. 10, 1850.

George H. Woodward,	1850	1851
Hiram Day,	April, 1851	May, 1856
Alexis W. Ide,	July, 1859	

The Society was formed in March, 1850, and Mr. Woodward, who helped to commence the enterprise was obliged to abandon it in a few months through ill health. The old Society, two miles distant, contemplated moving their place of worship, to accommodate the growing population at the "Springs," but a Council thought it more advisable to form a new church. It was thought wise to build a house of worship large enough for prospective growth in the village; but this led to the contracting of a debt of $4000, more than half the cost; and death, losses and other circumstances taking away some who were willing to help, the burdens came on a few. But the debt was cancelled in 1858, and every encouragement for future prosperity now appears, in enlarged Congregations, Sabbath School, and donations for benevolence.

THE CHURCH IN STAFFORDVILLE, ORG. DEC. 1853.

MINISTERS.	SETTLED.	DISMISSED.	DIED.
Allen Clark,	April, 1852	Oct. 1852	Dec. 1852
John M. Francis,	Oct. 1852	April, 1853	
George W. Connitt,	. 1853	1854	
Charles Hyde,	Jan. 1855	April, 185 6	
Hiram Day,	1859		

House of worship, 40 by 54, erected in 1859, cost $4000. The church has been supplied when destitute of a resident minister, from East Windsor Seminary.

THE FIRST CHURCH IN STAMFORD, ORG. MAY, 1641.

	SETTLED	DISMISSED	DIED
Richard Denton,*	May, 1641 ?	1643 ?	1663 ?
John Bishop,	1644		1694
Mr. Jones,	1672		1676
John Davenport,	1694		Feb. 1731
Ebenezer Wright,	May, 1732		May, 1746
Noah Welles, D. D.,†	Dec. 1746		Dec. 1776
John S. Avery,	Jan. 1779		Sept. 1791
Daniel Smith,‡	June, 1793		June, 1846
John W. Alvord,	March, 1842	Oct. 1846	
Isaac Jennings,	Sept. 1847	April, 1853	
James Hoyt,	June, 1853	Jan. 1855	
Henry B. Elliot,	Dec. 1855	July, 1858	
Joseph Anderson,	March, 1860		

The Church in Wethersfield fell into unhappy contentions and animosities, and the minority, 30 or 40 families, removed to Stamford in 1641, with their minister, of whom Cotton Mather speaks in high terms. Mr. Denton from Wethersfield, went to Hempstead, L. I. Two brethren took a journey on foot, nearly to Boston, through the wilderness, to find Mr. Bishop, of whom they had heard, and were well repaid for their trouble, for he was long their faithful pastor. Mr. Davenport was the only son of the only son of Rev. John Davenport of New Haven. The records are fruitful of votes to prepare a parsonage as a gift to him, and making grants of land, firewood, &c., during his ministry. He was a member of the Synod of Saybrook in 1708, (p. 11;) and was held in high estimation for his piety and learning, and exercised a wide influence among the Churches. Mr. Wright is said to have been a powerful preacher. Dr. Welles was considered one of the most eminent scholars of his day, and was untiring in his zeal as a pastor. For years after his death, the country was in such an unsettled state that it was impossible to procure a pastor, and they had only temporary supplies.

The first meeting house, built in 1642, soon proved unfit for use, but not till 1672, after about 30 years discussion, did it yield to the second, the form of which was decided by lot, and stood till 1790. The present house was built in 1858.

The external history of the Church is a record of long continued peace and prosperity. It has at six different times parted with members who have withdrawn to form new Churches, some of which have become large and flourishing. It has at various times been greatly revived and blessed by large accessions of converts. Some of the most noted revivalists, George Whitfield among them, have labored among the people with great success.

* Mather's Magnalia, 1, 860. † Sp. An. 1, 461. Allen. ‡ Allen.

The Church of Stanwich, in Greenwich, Org. June 17, 1735.

MINISTERS.	SETTLED.	DISMISSED.	DIED.
Benjamin Strong,	June, 1735	March, 1763	
William Seward,	Feb. 1774	Feb. 1794	
Jonathan Edwards, D. D.,	1795		
Platt Buffett,	May, 1796	June, 1835	May, 1850
Daniel B. Butts,	Oct. 1839	Dec. 1842	1851
Alonzo B. Rich,	April, 1848	Nov. 1852	
Henry G. Jessup,	April, 1854		

Records burnt with the house of Mr. Buffett in 1821. Like many of the pastors of his day, Mr. Buffett was for many years an instructor of the young, and among his pupils were not a few who became ministers of the gospel, missionaries, or filled offices of trust and profit.

During the last 30 years, the Church in Stanwich has been favored with several powerful revivals of religion. Those of 1831, '39, '45, and '54 added very much to its members, life and strength. The last three occurred when there was no settled pastor.

In matters of reform this Church has always been active, oftentimes taking the lead among her sister churches, and in no case falling behind them. In short, despite the constant influence of emigration, the gathering of other churches in the neighborhood, and the comparatively stationary character of all agricultural communities, it continues steadily to maintain its position as to numbers and influence among the older churches of the Commonwealth.

MINISTERS RAISED UP.—W. L. Buffett, F. H. Ayres, M. Palmer, M. D. (f.)

THE FIRST CHURCH IN STONINGTON, ORG. JUNE 3, 1674.

MINISTERS.	DISMISSED.	SETTLED.	DIED.
Mr. Thompson,	1658		
Mr. Chauncey,	1659		
Zechariah Bridgden,	1660	1663	
Mr. Fletcher,	1663	1664	
James Noyes,* 1665, ord.	Sept. 1674		Dec. 1719
Ebenezer Rossiter,†	Dec. 1722		Oct. 1762
Nathaniel Eells,‡	1762		June, 1786
Hezekiah N. Woodruff,§	July, 1789	1803	1833
Ira Hart,‖	Dec. 1809		Oct. 1829
Joseph Whittlesey,	May, 1830	Dec. 1832	
Peter H. Shaw,	Jan. 1835	May, 1837	
Nehemiah B. Cook,	Mar. 1838	May, 1859	
Pliny F. Warner,	Jan. 1860		

Mr. Blinman, minister at New London, preached here a part of the time between 1648 and 1658, and received from this people a part of his support. Mr. Noyes was the moderator of the Synod that formed the Saybrook Platform in 1708, p. 7. The East Society was formed from this in 1733. Within the last twenty-five years, three Congregational churches have been organized in this town, two of which were composed, at their organization, almost entirely of members belonging to the First Church ; and it furnished at its commencement, a substantial part of the strength of the other. Admissions to the church from the beginning, to Aug. 1858, 1037.

MINISTERS RAISED UP.—Asa Burton, D. D.,¶ Joseph Noyes, Jonathan Copp, B. F. Stanton,** Roswell Swan, Dudley Rossiter, Zabdiel Rogers, Clark Brown, Hezekiah Woodruff, Nathaniel Miner, Amos S. Chesebrough, Joshua B. Brown, Gurdon W. Noyes.

* Sp. An. 1. 234. Allen. † Allen. † Sp. An. 1. 362. Allen. § Sp. An. 2. 485. Allen. ‖ Rel. Intel. 14. 460. Allen. ¶ Am. Qu. Reg. 10. 321. Sp. An. 2. 140. ** Sp. An. 4. 524.

The Church in the East Society, in Stonington, Org. 1733.

Nathaniel Eells,	1733	1762

During Mr. Rossiter's pastorate in the First Church, a part of the people left, formed the East Society, erected a house of worship, and settled Mr. Eells as their pastor. At the death of Mr. Rossiter in 1762, Mr. Eells succeeded him, and his society gave up their separate worship and united with the First Society.

THE SECOND CHURCH IN STONINGTON, ORG. NOV. 14, 1833.

John C. Nichols,	May, 1834	April, 1839
J. Erskine Edwards,	April, 1840	April, 1843
William Clift,	Dec. 1844	

This church enterprise was projected by members of the First Church residing at Stonington Borough, where meetings had been held for half of the time for many years. It was the result of the increasing population and wealth of the place. Eighteen hundred dollars of the fund of the first parish were given to the new society, and their present house of worship was immediately erected. The parish expenses are paid by the annual sale of slips. A noticeable feature in these expenses is one hundred dollars, annually, devoted to a pastor's library. The church has been blest with frequent revivals of religion, and more than one-third of the population are now members.

THE CHURCH IN STRATFORD, ORG. 1640.

MINISTERS.	SETTLED.	DISMISSED.	DIED.
Adam Blackman,*	1640		1665
Israel Chauncey,†	1665?		Mar. 1703
Zechariah Walker,‡	1667?	1674	Jan. 1700
Timothy Cutler, D. D.,§	1709	1719	Aug. 1765
Hezekiah Gold,‖	1720	July, 1752	May, 1790
Izrahiah Wetmore,¶	May, 1753	1780	1798
Stephen W. Stebbins,**	1784	Aug. 1813	1843
Matthew R. Dutton,††	Sept. 1814	Oct. 1822	July, 1825
Joshua Leavitt, D. D.,	Feb. 1825	1828	
Thomas Robbins, D. D.,‡‡	Feb. 1830	Sept. 1831	1857
Frederick W. Chapman,	Sept. 1832	April, 1839	
William B. Weed,	Dec. 1839	May, 1855	
Joseph R. Page,	Feb. 1857	Sept. 1858	
Benjamin L. Swan,	Oct. 1858		

Mr. Chauncey was the youngest son of President Chauncey, of Harvard, born in Scituate, Mass., in 1644, and graduated at Harvard in 1661. With his profession as a clergyman, he united the practice of medicine, and had a high reputation for medical skill, as well as pastoral fidelity. Mr. Cutler was the second President of Yale College ; he became an Episcopalian, and was dismissed from his office. *Trumbull,* 2. 32–4.

MINISTERS RAISED UP.—Benjamin Blackman,‡‡ Hezekiah Gold, Jr., Chas. Chauncey,§§ Nathan Birdseye, Isaac Chauncey,‖‖

* Allen. † Sp. An. 1. 114. Allen. ‡ Allen. § Allen. ‖ Allen. ¶ Allen. ** Sp. An. 1. 439. Allen. †† Sp. An. 2. 592. Allen. ‡‡ Allen. §§ Sp. An. 1. 114. ‖‖ Sp. An. 1. 114.

THE CHURCH IN SUFFIELD, ORG. APRIL 26, 1698.

John Younglove,	1680		June, 1690
George Philips,	1690	1692	
Nathaniel Clapp,	1693	1695	

MINISTERS.	SETTLED.	DISMISSED.	DIED.
Benjamin Ruggles, July, 1695, inst April, 1698			Sept. 1708
Ebenezer Devotion,*	June, 1710		April, 1741
Ebenezer Gay, D. D.,†	Jan. 1742		Mar. 1796
Ebenezer Gay, Jr.†*	Mar. 1793		Jan. 1837
Joel Mann,	Dec. 1826	Dec. 1829	
Henry Robinson,	June, 1831	April, 1837	
Asahel C. Washburn,	Jan. 1838	July, 1851	
John R. Miller,	Dec. 1853		

The grant for the settlement of this town from the General Court of the Massachusetts Colony, in 1670, required the maintainance of a gospel ministry here; and early measures were taken for that purpose. Owing to the disturbance occasioned by the Indian war of 1675, known by the name of Philip's War, the proprietors were unable to carry this provision into effect until 1680, when Mr. John Younglove came among them in the ministry, and continued till his decease. None of Mr. Ruggles' predecessors were ordained here. The doings of the Court of Quarter Sessions of Hampshire County, Massachusetts, and the records of this town, show that a council of ministers was called April 26, 1698, (May 7, N. S.,) to consider upon and advise with respect to the settlement of Mr. Ruggles in the ministry here; and other circumstances, notices and facts point to that as the period when the First Church in Suffield was organized, and Rev. Benjamin Ruggles ordained its pastor. Mr. Devotion was pastor nearly thirty-one years, and received into the church 334 members. Of him it is inscribed,— "He was a man of sound judgment, great stability of mind, and singular modesty and humanity, a true friend and faithful minister, steady in his attendance upon the altar, close and pungent in his preaching, and very exemplary in his life, a pattern of industry and resignation, and of all Christian graces." During the nine months after his decease, 176 individuals were admitted to the communion of the church—97 by Rev. Jonathan Edwards, of Northampton, and 79 by Rev. Peter Reynolds, of Enfield. Within a year of his decease, 207 were received. In 1747, a number withdrew from the church, and formed a Separate church, a part of whom were ultimately formed into the Baptist Church. The third pastor received into the church 167 members; the 4th, 138; 5th, 25; 6th, 25; 7th, 211; and the 8th, in five years, 109, 65 of them in 1858.

MINISTERS RAISED UP.—John Trumbull, Benjamin Pomeroy, Jonathan Leavitt,‡ John Devotion, Cotton Mather Smith, Aratus Kent, Francis E. Butler, Seth Williston, D. D.§ Ebenezer Devotion, Elisha Kent, Ebenezer Gay, Jr., Arthur Granger.

* Allen. † Sp. An. 1. 537. Allen ‡ Mendon. As. 197. § Sp. An. 4. 140.

The Church in Tariffville, Org. Oct. 29, 1832.

William Parsons,	1841	1842
Calvin Terry,	1842	1843

It is thought that this Church never had a pastor. It is set down as "vacant" in the minutes, except as above. It received aid from the Home Missionary Society the most of the time from 1833 to 1845. It was composed to a considerable extent of members trained in Scotch Presbyterianism, and their influence availed to change its order. The last of its records is dated May, 1845, a Presbyterian Church having been organized in October previous, which in its turn, after seven years pastorate, (though yet nominally alive,) gave place to an Episcopal Church.

The Church in Terryville, in Plymouth, Org. Jan. 1838.

MINISTERS.	SETTLED.	DISMISSED.	DIED.
Nathaniel Richardson,	Aug. 1838	July, 1840	
Merrill Richardson,	Oct. 1841	July, 1846	
Judson A. Root,	Oct. 1846	April, 1847	
Merrill Richardson,	May, 1849	Jan. 1858	
John Monteith, Jr,	Oct. 1858	1860	

Its original members numbered forty-nine persons, dismissed by letter from the Congregational church in Plymouth. The congregation is for the most part composed of manufacturers and mechanics. It meets in a neat and comfortable edifice, which seats about 500 persons. Sixty-four members were added by profession in the spring of 1858.

MINISTER RAISED UP.—Edwin Johnson.

The Church in Thompson, (formerly Killingly 2d,) Org. Jan. 38, 1730.

Marston Cabot,	Feb. 1730	Apr, 1756
Noadiah Russell,*	Nov. 1757	Oct. 1795
Daniel Dow,† D. D.,	April, 1796	July, 1849
Andrew Dunning,	May, 1850	

This church is a colony of what was "the First Church in Killingly,"— now "the First Church in Putnam." Its history has not been marked by any striking changes, whether adverse or prosperous. In common with most churches at that early day, it had to struggle through an infancy of weakness and poverty. But its early members trusted in God, and so were helped. Under his care and conduct, its progress has been steadily onward. The church was organized with twenty-seven members. The whole number received to its communion is 1230, or nearly ten per year. It has never dismissed a pastor. This church has enjoyed several seasons of revival,— times of refreshing from the presence of the Lord. In 1858, it received a precious portion of the pentecostal blessings which so richly descended upon our American Zion. A new house of worship, one of the finest in the State, was erected in 1856.

Ministers Raised Up.—Joseph Russell, Stephen Crosby, Henry Gleason, William A. Larned, Joseph T. Holmes, David N. Coburn, John Bowers, Herbert A. Read, Charles Thayer, Joseph P. Bixby.

* Sp. An. 2. 237.   † Sp. An. 2. 365.

THE CHURCH IN TOLLAND, ORG. 1717.

MINISTERS.	SETTLED.	DISMISSED.	DIED.
Stephen Steel,*	Feb. 1722		1758
Nathan Williams, D. D.,	April, 1760		Apr. 1829
Ansel Nash,	Jan. 1813	May, 1831	
Abram Marsh,	Nov. 1831		

Rev. Stephen Steel labored earnestly to promote the great revival of 1740, and also to save its character from the excesses that damaged it in other places. He was an able and faithful minister. Dr. Williams was a good minister, and a very pleasing man in his manners and conversation. There were revivals in 1790 and 1800. Mr. Nash was active, ready of speech, and one who used well his gifts and knowledge. There were two important revivals under his ministry,—in 1814 and 1822. In the latter, Dr. Nettleton aided him. Additions in all by the third pastor, 265 ; by the fourth, 212. Directly after Mr. Nash was dismissed, a revival commenced; and at Mr. Marsh's installation, about 90 were indulging hope. A general revival in 1857 and 1858, added 34. From 1831 to 1857, three-fifths of all the male members of the church removed to churches in other towns ; and owing to changes in business, the population of the town decreased 300. Still the heart of the church in regard to the support of the gospel beats better than in 1831. Many a church is receiving missionary aid that could not be induced to tax itself as this church does for the support of the ministry.

The first house of worship was small, and was never finished; the second was built in 1784 ; the third in 1838—a neat and tasteful structure. The church has been blessed in having only four pastors. It lives because it has a living Redeemer.

Ministers Raised Up.—Stephen West, D. D.,† Gordon Hall, (f.)

* Allen.   † Sp. An. 1. 237.   Allen.   ‡ Sp. An. 1. 548.   Allen.

THE CHURCH IN TORRINGFORD, IN TORRINGTON, ORG. ABOUT 1759.

Mr. Heaton,	1761		
Mr. Davenport, (c.)	1764 ?	1767 ?	
Samuel J. Mills,*	June, 1769		◄ May, 1833
Epaphras Goodman,	Mar. 1822	Jan. 1836	
Herman L. Vaill,	July, 1837	Sept. 1839	
Brown Emerson,	July, 1841	Sept. 1844	
William H. Moore,	Sept. 1846	Aug. 1854	

MINISTERS.	SETTLED.	DISMISSED.	DIED.
Stephen Fenn,	Nov. 1854	Sept. 1857	
Charles Newman,	May, 1858		

In 1755, the town voted that their minister should preach on the east side of the town in proportion to the support that the people there afforded. In 1759, four and a half tiers of land were set off for an ecclesiastical society, and from that time public worship was generally maintained. Mr. Mills was a godly man, and as a preacher, plain, simple, and highly interesting. During his last years, he was left quite dependent; yet he never complained. Every mercy he recognized as "wonderful, *wonderful* goodness." Mr. Goodman removed to Dracut, Massachusetts, and since has preached in several places at the West.

Torringford has shared largely in those divine blessings—revivals. In 1773, 1793, and 1799 mercy drops and the copious shower were granted; in 1816, 60 were added, and in 1821, 60 more. During Mr. Goodwin's ministry, about 100 were received, and different numbers at various seasons of interest since. By these divine visitations, the Lord has granted prosperity. *See Mr. McKinistry's History of Torrington. Ev. Mag.* 1. 27.

MINISTERS RAISED UP.—Jonathan Miller, Harvey Loomis, Stanley Griswold, E. D. Moore, Samuel J. Mills, Jr., (f.)† Lucius Curtis, Orange Lyman.

* Sp. An 1. 672.   Litchf. Centen. 99.   † Sp. An. 2. 566.   Allen.

THE CHURCH IN TORRINGTON, ORG. OCT. 21, 1741.

Nathaniel Roberts,*		1741	Mar. 1776
Noah Merwin,†	Oct. 1776	Nov. 1783	1795
Lemuel Haynes,‡	1787	1789	Sept. 1834
Alexander Gillett,§	May, 1792		Jan. 1826
William R. Gould,	Feb. 1827	Feb. 1832	
Milton Huxley,	1832	1842	
John A. McKinstry,	Oct. 1842	Sept. 1857	
Charles B. Dye,	Oct. 1859		

At the laying out of the town in 1737, 100 acres of land were reserved for a minister's lot. In 1737, the Torringford Society laid a claim to a portion of this land, and ultimately a little more than one-third of it was granted them. Mr. Roberts was one of the fourteen ministers present at the institution of the original Consociation of Litchfield County, in 1752. He was an eccentric man, characterized by honesty, sincerity, and a humor peculiarly his own. Mr. Haynes was a colored man, of great shrewdness and wit, and was a useful minister of white congregations about fifty years; he died in Granville, N. Y. Torrington has been the theater of frequent and precious revivals, 70 being added as the fruits in each of the years, 1799 and 1816, with goodly numbers at other times. *Dr. Nettleton's Memoir*, 89. *Ev. Mag.* 1. 131.

MINISTERS RAISED UP. Timothy P. Gillett, James Beach, Luther Hart, Abel K. Hinsdale,‖ (f.)

*Sp. An. 1. 410. Allen. Litchf. Centen. 79, 82. * Sp. An. 2. 351. Allen. ‡Sp. An. 2. 176. Allen ‡Sp. An. 2, 68. Allen. Litchf. Centen. 79, 80. ‖ Allen.

THE CHURCH IN TRUMBULL, (FORMERLY UNITY, IN NORTH STRATFORD,) ORG. NOV. 18, 1730.

MINISTERS.	SETTLED.	DISMISSED.	DIED.
Richardson Miner,	1730	Mar. 1744	
James Beebe,	May, 1747		Sept. 1785
Izrahiah Wetmore,*	1785		Aug. 1798
John Giles,†	May, 1802	Sept. 1802	
Daniel C. Banks,	Aug. 1807	Feb. 1813	
Reuben Taylor,	Sept. 1817	Feb. 1824	
James Kent.*	Nov. 1825	Nov. 1835	
Wlliam T. Bacon,	Dec. 1842	May, 1844	
John L. Whittlesey,	Oct. 1844	Nov. 1849	
David M. Elwood,	Feb. 1850	June, 1853	
William T. Bacon,	Sept. 1853	Sept. 1854	
Ralph Smith,	Dec. 1854	Dec. 1855	
Stephen A. Loper,	June, 1856	June, 1858	
Benjamin Swallow,	Jan. 1859		

MINISTER RAISED UP.—Daniel Brinsmade.

* Allen. † Sp. An. 3. 437.

THE CHURCH IN UNION, ORG. DEC. 13, 1738.

Ebenezer Wyman,	Dec. 1738		Jan. 1745
Caleb Hitchcock,	Jan. 1749	1759	
Ezra Horton,	June, 1759	June, 1783	
David Avery,	April, 1797	Aug. 1799	1817
M. Chapin, (Meth.)	1803	1809	
Nehemiah B. Beardsley,	April, 1824	April, 1831	
Elliot Palmer,	Jan. 1832	June, 1833	
Alvan Underwood,	June, 1833	June, 1834	April, 1858
Samuel J. Curtiss, Mar. '40, inst. Apr. '42			

Mr. Hitchcock was deposed for intemperance. The Church has been 43 years out of 121, destitute of a pastor or stated supply. During this time, the ministration of the word was only occasional and generally there was no preaching during the winter, no minister spending a whole year with the people. The Church has long been dependent on home missionary aid.

THE CHURCH IN UNIONVILLE, IN FARMINGTON, ORG. MARCH 30, 1841.

MINISTERS.	SETTLED.	DISMISSED.	DIED.
John R. Keep,	1840	1841	
Richard Woodruff,	June, 1842	May, 1846	
James O. Searl, Apr. '47, inst. Sept. 1848		April, 1851	
Giles M. Porter,	Oct. 1852	Oct. 1856	
Hiram Slauson,	Dec. 1857	Dec. 1858	
James A. Smith,	1859		

Previous to the organization of the Church, public worship had been maintained in a school house, with a good degree of regularity, for more than ten years; preaching by ministers of different denominations. Society organized in 1839, from which time the ministers were Congregational, and missionary aid was granted till 1852. Revivals in 1846 and 1858. House of worship built in 1842, enlarged and remodeled in 1852.

THE CHURCH IN VERNON, (FORMERLY NORTH BOLTON,) ORG. OCT. 1762.

Ebenezer Kellogg,*	Nov. 1762		Sept. 1817
William Ely,*	March, 1818	Feb. 1822	Nov. 1850
Amzi Benedict,†	June, 1824	Feb. 1830	Nov. 1856
David L. Hunn,	Nov. 1830	March, 1832	
Chester Humphrey,	Oct. 1832		April, 1843
Albert Smith,	May, 1845	Oct. 1854	
Mark Tucker, D. D.,	April, 1857		

The Society was organized Nov. 1760, and called North Bolton, containing, probably, a little more than 400 inhabitants.

The Church formed with 35 members from Bolton; the number doubled in seven years, and in 89 years since 1769, but two years have passed without additions being made to the Church; in all 971. It is probable that more than two-thirds of those here first professing their faith in Christ, were the children of professed believers.

The early history of the Church was not marked by frequent revivals. The first pastor, in his half-century discourse, preached in 1812, notices four "seasons of uncommon awakening; in and about the years 1772, 1782, 1800, and 1809." He was blessed with a still greater "awakening," in 1814–15, when 40 united with the Church; about 80 in 1830–31. Other principal revivals in 1819, '30, '35, '41, '51, and '58. *Rel. Intel.* 16, 637.

Before 1807, 136 were received on the "half-way covenant," 19 of them afterwards received to full communion. The first meeting house was erected in 1762, (Sabbath worship having been maintained at a dwelling house a year or two,) though without pews till 1770, and unplastered till 1774. This was used until the present house of worship was completed in 1827.

Until 1852, the expenses of the Society were provided for by taxation. There are small funds for sacred music, and the Sabbath school library.

MINISTERS RAISED UP.—Salmon King, Francis King, Allen McLean, Ebenezer Kellogg, Joel Talcott, Eliot Palmer, Jr., Cyril Pearl, Lavalette Perrin, Martin Kellogg, Allyn S. Kellogg.

* Allen. † Cong. Y. B. 1857.

THE CHURCH IN VOLUNTOWN AND STERLING, ORG. OCT. 15, 1723.

MINISTERS.	SETTLED.	DISMISSED.	DIED.
Samuel Dorrance,	Dec. 1723	1770	Nov. 1775
Micaiah Porter,	Nov. 1781	Aug. 1800	
Elijah G. Welles,	June, 1811	June, 1812	
Otis Lane,*	Oct. 1828	Sept. 1834	May, 1842
Jacob Allen,†	Oct. 1837	Nov. 1849	
Jacob Allen,	April, 1851		March, 1856
Charles L. Ayer,	Jan. 1859		

For revivals and Dr. Wheelock's preaching at Voluntown, see Tracy's *Great Awakening* 201. The Church was originally Presbyterian: was reorganized as Congregational, June 30, 1779. In the year 1794 the town of Voluntown was divided and the north part called Sterling. Since then the Church has been called the Congregational Church in the First Ecclesiastical Society in Voluntown and Sterling, and the meeting house is on the line between the towns. In 1858, the Society erected a neat and convenient meeting house at an expense of $2,500, with a good bell and other conveniences for public worship, and in 1859, a parsonage. With the settlement of a pastor also, a new day of hope seems to have dawned on this old desolation.

MINISTER RAISED UP.—Gordon Dorrance.‡

* Sp. An. 2, 243   † Cong. Y. Book, 1857, 1858.   ‡ Sp. An. 1, 549.   Allen.

THE CHURCH IN WALLINGFORD, ORG. IN 1675.

Samuel Street,*	1675		Jan. 1717
Samuel Whittlesey,†	Apr. 1709, ord. May, '10		April, 1752
James Dana, D. D.,‡	Oct. 1758	Feb. 1789	Aug. 1812
James Noyes,§	May, 1785	June, 1832	Feb. 1844
Edwin R. Gilbert,	Oct. 1832		

The first settlers of Wallingford were from New Haven. The town was incorporated in 1670, and embraced what are now the towns of Wallingford, Meriden, Cheshire, and Prospect. The Church was organized in 1675. The first pastor was one of "the undertakers and committee," for the settlement of the town. "He was esteemed an heavenly man." It is said of Mr. Whittlesey that "he was one of the most eminent preachers in the colony in his day, a laborious, faithful minister of Christ, applying his whole time to his work, and that he shone with distinction in intellectual and moral attainments."

After the death of Mr. Whittlesey, the Church was without a pastor for about six years, and became somewhat divided into parties in consequence of hearing various candidates. They "called" at length Rev. James Dana, D. D., of Cambridge. In connection with his settlement arose what is historically known as "the Wallingford controversy," an account of which may be found in Trumbull's History of Connecticut, Bacon's Historical Discourses, and in a volume of pamphlets in the Library of the Connecticut Historical Society.

Dr. Dana, on the restoration of his health, was dismissed, and became pastor of the First Church in New Haven, April 29, 1789. He was noted for his discretion and dignified propriety of conduct, and the venerable beauty of all his public performances, particularly his prayers; and his reputation for learning and wisdom was unquestionable.

Mr. Noyes belonged to a line of ministers, which at the time of his death had existed during two hundred years in uninterrupted succession. He was a lover of peace and harmony. In his public discourses he was always discreet, amiable and conciliating; and his prayers, especially on peculiar occasions, such as domestic affliction, were remarkable for their elevation, spirituality and adaptation to the circumstances of every case. His pastorate continued 47 years.

The Church has existed 183 years, and has had but five pastors. Such an instance of pastoral permanence and longevity may not be unworthy of record in grateful remembrance of the mercy of God.

MINISTERS RAISED UP.—Samuel Whittlesey, Chauncey Whittlesey, James Noyes, Lent S. Hough, Edgar J. Doolittle, Ogden Hall, Andrew Bartholomew, Joseph Bellamy, Matthew Merriam,‖ Thomas Yale, Comfort Williams, David Brooks.

* Sp. An. 1, 104. Allen. † Sp. An. 1, 268. Allen ‡ Sp. An. 1, 565. Allen. § Sp. An. 1, 362. Allen. ‖ Sp. An. 2, 689.

The Second Church in Wallingford, Org. April 3, 1759.

MINISTERS.	SETTLED.	DISMISSED.	DIED.
Simon Waterman,	Oct. 1761	June, 1787	Nov. 1813

This Church originated in what is known as the Wallingford controversy. A minority of the First Church who were opposed to the settlement of Dr. Dana, were owned and acknowledged to be the first consociated church in Wallingford, by the united council of the Consociations of New Haven County and Hartford South. They were incorporated, with others associated with them, into the "Wells Ecclesiastical Society" in 1763, having opened their meeting house Dec. 8, 1762. The Church and Society each by separate vote, declared themselves unable longer to support Mr. Waterman, May 3, 1787. Nov. 1788, they voted unanimously that they were "desirous of holding Christian fellowship and communion with the church under the care of Rev. James Noyes, notwithstanding the sentence of non-communion passed some years since by a consociated council against said Church." Some of them returned to the old church, and others went to other ecclesiastical organizations; and their church edifice passed into the hands of the Episcopalians about 1831.

THE CHURCH IN WARREN, (FORMERLY EAST GREENWICH,) ORG. SEPT. 1756.

MINISTERS.	SETTLED.	DISMISSED.	DIED.
Silvanus Osborn,*	June, 1757		May, 1771
Peter Starr,†	Mar. 1772		July, 1829
Hart Talcott,‡	May, 1825		March, 1836
Harley Goodwin,	June, 1838	Dec. 1843	Jan. 1855
John R. Keep,	May, 1844	Nov. 1852	
M. M. Wakeman,	Sept. 1853	June, 1856	
Francis Lobdell,	Nov. 1859		

Universal harmony has prevailed from the formation of the Church to the present time. During the ministry of Mr. Osborn there was no general revival of religion, but a constant attention to the things of another world, which resulted in numbers being added to the Church every year. Since which God has been pleased to pour out His Spirit from time to time during each successive ministry. The most powerful work was in 1799 and 1800, when it seems almost the whole town was brought under the influence of the Gospel. *Ev. Mag.* 1, 100.

MINISTERS RAISED UP.—Reuben Taylor, Urban Palmer, Alanson Sanders, Josiah Hawes, Charles G. Finney, Seth Sackett, Prince Hawes, Charles Everitt, John Smith Griffin, Nathaniel Swift, Jr., Lucius C. Rouse, Tertius Reynolds, John L. Taylor, Julian M. Sturtevant, Myron N. Morris.

*Sp. An. 1. 690. Allen. †Sp. An. 1. 692. Allen. Litchf. Centen. 78. †Litchf. Centen. 119. Allen.

THE CHURCH IN WASHINGTON, (FORMERLY JUDEA SOCIETY,) ORG. SEPT. 1, 1742.

Reuben Judd,	Sept. 1742	May, 1747	
Daniel Brinsmade,*	Mar. 1749		April, 1793
Noah Merwin,†	Mar. 1785		April, 1795
Ebenezer Porter, D. D.,‡	Sept. 1796	Dec. 1811	April, 1834
Cyrus W. Gray,	April, 1813	Aug. 1815	
Stephen Mason,	Feb. 1818	Dec. 1828	
Gordon Hayes,	Oct. 1829	Dec. 1851	
Ephraim Lyman,	June, 1852		

There have been several revivals, in which large additions have been made to the church. Besides seasons of less importance, three or four have been specially remarkable in extent, viz : in 1804, in which 54 were added,

58 in 1824, 131 in 1831, and 43 in 1843. *Ev. Mag.* 7. 143. · *Rel. Intel.* 16.
331.   Dr. Porter was eminent both as a minister and an instructor in Andover Theological Seminary, whither he removed.   He labored for many
years under the embarrassment and trial of ill health, but accomplished
much, notwithstanding.

MINISTERS RAISED UP.—John Clark, John Clark, ——— Davies, Thomas
Knapp, Daniel Parker, George A. Calhoun, Elisha Mitchell, Henry Calhoun,
Bennitt B. Burgess, William Sidney Smith, Samuel Pond, (f.) Gideon H.
Pond, (f.) Lewis Gunn.

*Sp. An. 1. 631. Allen.   †Sp. An. 2. 351. Allen.   ‡Sp. An. 2. 351. Allen.
Litchf. Centen. 106. Am. Qu. Reg. 9. 9.

THE FIRST CHURCH IN A TERBURY, ORG. AUG. 26, 1683.

MINISTERS.	SETTLED.	DISMISSED.	DIED.
Jeremiah Peck,*	Aug. 1689		June, 1709
John Southmayd,† 1700, ord.	June, 1715	1739	Nov. 1755
Mark Leavenworth,‡	Mar. 1740		Aug. 1797
Edward Porter,	Nov. 1795	Jan. 1798	1828
Holland Weeks,	Nov. 1799	Dec. 1806	Aug. 1842
Luke Wood,	Nov. 1808	Nov. 1817	Aug. 1851
Asahel Nettleton, D. D.,	1815	1816	
Daniel Crane,	July, 1821	April, 1825	
Henry Benedict,	1826	1827	
Jason Atwater,	Mar. 1829	June, 1830	April, 1860
Joel R. Arnold,	Jan. 1831	June, 1836	
Henry N. Day,	Nov. 1836	Oct. 1840	
David Root,	July, 1841	1844	
Henry B. Elliott,	Dec. 1845	April, 1851	
William W. Woodworth,	Sept. 1852	May, 1858	
George Bushnell,	Sept. 1858		

This church was formed eleven years after the first settlement was made
in the town by a small colony from Farmington.   Like many of the churches
which were formed during the early period of its history, this church consisted at first of seven male members, who were the " seven pillars of the
church."   For a long time the church was small; for in 1705 there were
only twelve male members.   The territory occupied by the early members
of this church was large.   The church in Westbury (now Watertown,) was
formed mostly by members from this church, in 1738 ; the church in Northbury (now Plymouth,) in 1740; the church in Middlebury about 1790 ; the
church in Salem (now Naugatuck,) in 1781 ; the church in Wolcott in 1773 ;
the Second Church in Waterbury in 1852 ; and the original members of the
church in Prospect were also partly from this church.

Mr. Southmayd, a native of Middletown, commenced preaching here soon
after the death of Mr. Peck, but owing to the poverty and distress of the
town, occasioned by its exposure to attacks from the Indians, and by de-

structive floods, was not ordained till June 20, 1715. He was dismissed, at his own request, in 1739, and continued to reside in the place till his death, at the age of 79. The weakness of the church 50 years ago, is also shown in the fact that Mr. Weeks was dismissed for want of support. The old, uninteresting village, with one feeble church, has become the thriving city with half a dozen strong and vigorous churches.

The church has shared frequently in revivals. Mr. Leavenworth was an active promoter of the Great Awakening. Dr. Nettleton labored here with great success. *Memoir* 90.

MINISTERS RAISED UP.—Samuel Hopkins, Samuel Hopkins, D. D., Daniel Hopkins, D. D., Jonathan Judd, Benoni Upson, D. D., Benjamin Wooster, Ebenezer Cook, Thomas Bronson, Abner J. Leavenworth, Eli B. Clark, Ira H. Smith, George A. Bryan.

*Allen. † Allen. ‡ Sp. An. 2. 288. Allen.

THE SECOND CHURCH IN WATERBURY, ORG. APRIL 4, 1852.

MINISTERS.	SETTLED.	DISMISSED.	DIED.
S. W. Magill,	May, 1852		

This church was formed to meet the necessities of a rapidly growing population, and is steadily working its way to an independent and easily sustained position.

THE CHURCH IN WATERTOWN, (FORMERLY WESTBURY,) ORG. 1738.

John Trumbull,*	1739		Dec. 1787
Uriel Gridley,*	1784		Dec. 1820
Horace Hooker,	April, 1822	Oct. 1824	
Darius O. Griswold,†	Jan. 1825	Jan. 1835	Dec. 1841
William B. DeForest,	Jan. 1835	June, 1837	
Philo R. Hurd,	July, 1840	Jan. 1849	
Chauncey Goodrich,	Aug. 1849	Nov. 1856	
George P. Prudden,	Nov. 1856		

Watertown was originally a part of Waterbury. In 1732, the inhabitants of this part of the town requested of the town what were called winter privileges. Their request being denied, in October of the same year they petitioned the General Assembly on the same subject. Their petition was granted, and the privilege allowed for four years.

In May, 1734, they petitioned to be made a separate society, but their petition was successfully resisted by the town. In Oct. 1736, they petitioned again, and were again refused. Their winter privileges, however, were continued, and extended to five months instead of four. In May, 1737, the attempt was renewed, but unsuccessfully. In October, however, of this year, a committee was appointed to visit them and investigate the circumstances·

64

This committee reported in May, 1738, in favor of the petitioners, and recommended a division line. The town remonstrated, and so earnestly, that another committee was appointed, who reported in October, recommending the same line. Their report was adopted, and the society incorporated by the name of Westbury. *See Bronson's History of Waterbury.*

The first house of worship was erected in 1741; the second in 1772; and the third in 1839.

MINISTERS RAISED UP.—Stephen Fenn, Israel Beard Woodward, Aaron Dutton, Matthew Rice Dutton, Frederick Gridley, Anson S. Atwood, Jesse Guernsey, John L. Seymour.

     * Litchf. Centen. 77, 78. † Sp. An. 2. 524. Allen. Litchf. Centen. 118.

THE CHURCH IN WAUREGAN, IN PLAINFIELD, ORG. JUNE 17, 1856.

MINISTERS.	SETTLED.	DISMISSED.	DIED.
Charles L. Ayer,	Dec. 1855	April, 1858	
E. F. Brooks,	May, 1858	April, 1859	
S. H. Fellows,	1859		

This enterprise was originated to give the means of grace to the population collected by a new manfacturing establishment erected on the Quinebaug River, and that the people might not be left in a state of destitution, or to the inroads of other sentiments and influences. The church is largely dependent on Home Missionary aid.

THE CHURCH IN WESTBROOK, ORG. JUNE 29, 1726.

William Worthington,*	June, 1726		Nov. 1756
John Devotion,†	Oct. 1757		Sept. 1802
Thomas Rich,	June, 1804	Sept. 1810	Sept. 1836
Sylvester Selden,	June, 1812	Mar. 1834	Oct. 1841
Jeremiah Miller,	Feb. 1835	Mar. 1837	
William A. Hyde,	June, 1838	July, 1854	
Henry T. Cheever,	May, 1855	May, 1856	
Stephen A. Loper,	Sept. 1858		

The settlement of this place commenced as early as 1664. The inhabitants attended public worship at Saybrook sixty years, until they became sufficiently numerous to form a separate society. Five of the six pastors began their ministry here. The early history of the church, extending through more than half a century, shows that there were additions to it almost every year, varying in number from 2 or 3, up to 15 and 16. In 1809 and 1810, a revival extended through the society, and, as the fruits of it, more than sixty were added to the church. Since that time, there have been nine or ten other revivals, which have resulted in the addition of about five hundred.

The first house of worship was built in 1726; the second in 1828; re-built and re-modcled in 1859. The church has a small fund to assist its needy members; another for the support of the communion table; and another for the support of the ministry, besides a valuable parsonage. There is here a "Ministerial and Parish Library," the foundation of which was laid a few years since by the Rev. James Murdock, D. D., who gave for this purpose 78 volumes of valuable books; and $200, to which Mrs. Nancy Lay, a member of the church, added $200, the interest of which is to be expended for new books.

MINISTERS RAISED UP.—Jonathan Murdock, James Murdock, James Murdock, D. D.,‡ Jedediah Bushnell, Calvin Bushnell, John Whittlesey, Nathan F. Chapman, William Bushnell, Charles Murdock, William H. Moore.

* Sp. An. 1. 501. Allen. † Sp. An. 1. 262. Allen. ‡ Allen. Cong. Y. B. 1857, 119.

THE CHURCH IN WESTCHESTER, IN COLCHESTER, ORG. DEC. 1729.

MINISTERS.	SETTLED.	DISMISSED.	DIED.
Judah Lewis,	Dec. 1729		Apr. 1739
Thomas Skinner,	April, 1740		Oct. 1762
Robert Robbins,	Oct. 1764		Jan. 1804
Ezra S. Ely, D. D.	Oct. 1806	April, 1800	
Nathaniel Dwight,*	Jan. 1812	Aug. 1820	1831
Jacob Scales,	Dec. 1820	May, 1826	
Joseph Harvey,	Jan. 1827	Dec. 1835	
Daniel G. Sprague,	July, 1839	Jan. 1844	
Spofford D. Jewett,	May, 1844	May, 1858	
A. C. Denison,	1858		

The Westchester Society was set off from Colchester in the year 1729. Original members, 16; added by Mr. Lewis, 182; by Mr. Skinner, 60, dismissed, 80, baptized, 400; by Mr. Robbins, 87, dismissed 29, baptized, 207.

At Mr. Ely's settlement, the church was reduced to 10 males and 20 females. It has a fund of about $8000, pays a liberal salary, and its ministry has generally been able, faithful and devoted. It has enjoyed occasional seasons of the outpouring of the Spirit, and has thus been enlarged; 32 were added in 1857.

MINISTERS RAISED UP.—Judah Lewis, John Niles, Chauncey Robbins, Jonathan Cone, George Champion, (f.) William Olmsted, Jeremiah Day.

* Allen.

THE CHURCH IN WESTFIELD, IN MIDDLETOWN, ORG. DEC. 28, 1773.

Thomas Miner,	Dec. 1773		Apr. 1826
Stephen Hayes,	May, 1820	June, 1827	
Stephen Topliff,	May, 1829	Sept. 1838	
James H. Francis,	Dec. 1840	June, 1845	
Lent S. Hough,	Feb. 1847		

The Fourth Church in Middletown is in Westfield Society, which was incorporated in 1766, about 46 years from the time of the first settlement.

Mr. Hayes, from Newark, N. J., was pastor of the churches in Westfield and Middlefield, giving two-thirds of his time to Westfield. During Mr. Hough's ministry, thus far, a new school-house, with modern improvements, has been built in each of the four school districts, a new church edifice has been erected, and a building has been purchased and fitted up very conveniently for a lecture room. To the praise of the people, it may be said, "They have had a mind to work."

The society raised, in 1818, a fund, so guarded that it cannot be destroyed by a majority vote of the society, and that none but a Congregational minister can have the avails of it, in which they were encouraged by Prof. C. A. Goodrich, D. D., by a handsome donation from the first money of his own earning. Added to the church in the several pastorates, 88, 21, 62, 31, and 130.

MINISTER RAISED UP.—Samuel Lee.

The Church in Westford, in Ashford, Org. Feb. 11, 1768.

MINISTERS.	SETTLED.	DISMISSED.	DIED.
Ebenezer Martin,	June, 1768	1777	Sept. 1795
Elisha Hutchinson,	Mar. 1778	Sept. 1783	Apr. 1833
William Storrs,	Nov. 1790		Nov· 1824
Luke Wood,*	Dec. 1826	Sept. 1831	Aug. 1851
Alvan Underwood,	April, 1858		

Charles S. Adams, Sept. 1844, inst. Jan. 1846. April, 1858

Mr. Hutchinson became a Baptist after leaving Westford. See *Am. Bap. Mag.*, Dec. 1833. During Mr. Storrs' ministry there were several revivals, especially in 1799, 1809, and 1819, the last being a powerful work, adding more than 50 to the church. Mr. Wood was eminently successful as a pastor, and did much to heal the wounds in Christ's church, and build up her waste places. See a notice of him in *Cong. Journal*, Feb. 4, 1852; also notice of Westford pastors in *Cong. Quarterly*, July, 1859, p. 268.

* Allen,

The Church in West Hartford, Org. Feb. 24, 1713.

Benjamin Colton,	Feb. 1713		Mar. 1759
Nathaniel Hooker,*	Dec. 1757		June, 1770
Nathan Perkins, D. D.*	Oct. 1772		Jan. 1838
Caleb S. Henry,	June, 1833	Mar. 1835	
Edward W. Andrews,	Nov. 1837	Dec. 1840	
George I. Wood,	Nov. 1841	June, 1844	
Dwight M. Seward,	Jan. 1845	Dec. 1850	
Myron N. Morris,	July, 1852		

The following may serve to illustrate the fact that divisions among a peo_ple do not *necessarily* involve the dissolution of the church and society, nor preclude the possibility of their enjoying a permanent and highly useful ministry. It also suggests how a certain kind of divisions may be avoided ; and on what ground—when they exist—harmony may be restored.

Dr. Perkins, in his Half-Century Sermon, preached Oct. 13, 1822, refer_ring to the condition of the people at the time he came—a youth and stran_ger—among them, remarked: "The church and parish were vacant two and a half a years before my ordination to the pastoral office, in which time you had sixteen candidates on trial for settlement, each of whom, as was to be expected, would have some fast friends. In consequence of a measure of this nature, the church and society were miserably rent and divided. They were greatly distracted,—so much so, that neighboring ministers, whom they consulted, advised them to dismiss all thoughts of settling any of the nu_merous candidates whom they had already employed, and apply to one whom they had never seen nor heard, as the most likely means to accom_plish a union, if possibly a union might be accomplished." Mr. Perkins was sent for; he came, and was settled, and thus commenced a pasto_rate which continued to the day of his death, a period of more than *sixty_five* years. "But," he remarks, "it was several years before individuals could *wholly* forget their past bitter contentions and divisions."

Ministers Raised Up.—Eli Colton, George Colton, Eliphalet Steele, Marsh_field Steele, (h.) Nathan Perkins, George Colton, (h.) Chester Colton, (h.) Harry Croswell, D. D., (Ep.) Joab Brace, D. D., Epaphras Goodman, Evelyn Sedgwick, Seymour M. Spencer, (f.) Richard Woodruff, (h.) Amzi Francis, Chester Isham, Austin Isham, Hiram Elmer.

*Sp. An. 2. 1. Allen.

THE CHURCH IN WEST HARTLAND, ORG. MAY 4, 1780.

MINISTERS.	SETTLED.	DISMISSED.	DIED.
Nathaniel Gaylord,*	Jan. 1782		Apr. 1841
William Ely,	1823	1824	1850
Adolphus Terry,	Nov. 1824		Apr. 1832
John A. Hempsted,	Oct. 1833	Sept. 1835	185–
Luke Wood,	Oct. 1838	May, 1842	Aug. 1851
Aaron Gates,	May, 1843	Apr. 1846	Apr. 1850
Pearl S. Cossitt,	June, 1847	Nov. 1848	
Charles G. Goddard,	June, 1850	Feb. 1854	
Henry A. Austin,	May, 1854	1855	
Charles G. Goddard,	June, 1856		

Rev. Nathaniel Gaylord, the first pastor, died in the 90th year of his age, and the 59th year of his ministry.

Ministers Raised Up.—Flavel S. Gaylord, —— Taylor.
* Allen.

The Church in West Haven, in Orange, Org. 1719.

MINISTERS.	SETTLED.	DISMISSED.	DIED.
Samuel Johnson,	1720	1722	1772
Jonathan Arnold,	1725	1734	
Timothy Allen;*	1738	1742	1806
Nathan Birdseye,†	1742	1758	Jan. 1818
Noah Williston,‡	1760		Nov. 1811
Stephen W. Stebbens,§	1815		Aug. 1843
Edward Wright,	1843		Oct. 1852
Hubbard Beebe,	1854	1856	
Erastus Colton,	June, 1856	Jan. 1858	
George Andrew Bryan,	Sept. 1858		

Mr. Johnson, with Rector Cutler, and Mr. Wetmore of North Haven, declared for Episcopacy, and opened the advance movement in dissent, when the churches of the State had almost with one consent belonged to the "standing order" for nearly one hundred years. Mr. Arnold also followed in the steps of his predecessor. Mr. Allen was summarily dismissed as a New Light, but long labored as a faithful minister. It is remarkable that except Mr. Arnold, the first five pastors were in the ministry, respectively, 52, 68, 72, 51 and 57 years,—300 in all, or an average of 60 years. West Haven was taken from New Haven in 1822, and united with the society of North Milford to form the town of Orange. This society had its neat and valuable house of worship burnt in 1859, and with great effort opened a new house—larger and much better, with a Conference room attached, in July, 1860.

Ministers Raised Up.—Payson Williston,‖ Seth Williston, D.D.,¶ Richard S. Storrs, D.D., William T. Reynolds, John Bunnel.

* Tracy's Great Awak. 314, 368.   † Sp. An. 1. 436. Allen.   ‡ Sp. An. 1. 586. Allen.   § Sp. An. 1. 439. Allen.   ‖ Cong. Y.Book, 3. 125.   ¶ Sp. An. 4. 140.

The Church in West Killingly, Danielsonville, (formerly Westfield,) Org. Aug. 1801.

Gordon Johnson,	Dec. 1804	Jan. 1809	
Roswell Whitmore,	Jan. 1813	May, 1843	
Thomas O. Rice,	Jan. 1845	March, 1856	
Thomas T. Waterman,	Jan. 1858		

The Church has been repeatedly and richly blessed with the outpourings of the Holy Spirit, some 800 persons having been connected with it by letter and profession. Some 570 of these were added during the long and effective ministry of Rev. Mr. Whitmore.

The Church and Society have one of the largest and most beautiful church edifices in Connecticut, built in 1853, on a new site, which was required by the change of population in the growth of the village.

Ministers Raised Up.—Zolva Whitmore, N. E. Johnson, Herbert A. Reid, (h.) Ezra G. Johnson, (h.) George I. Stearns, (h.) Henry Kies, (h.) Isaac N. Cundall, (h.)

THE CHURCH IN WESTMINSTER, IN CANTERBURY, ORG. DEC. 20, 1770.

MINISTERS.	SETTLED.	DISMISSED.	DIED.
John Staples,	April, 1772		Feb. 1804
Erastus Learned,*	Feb. 1805		June, 1824
Israel G. Rose,	Mar. 1825	Oct. 1831	
Asa King,*	Jan. 1833		Dec. 1849
Reuben S. Hazen,	Sept. 1849		

The Church in Westminster was originally formed of members belonging for the most part to the Church in Canterbury; embracing most or all those residing in the western part of the town, now called Westminster. The Church and Society in Westminster have almost constantly enjoyed the stated means of grace, and have been generally united and prosperous from the first. Seasons of revival have been enjoyed from time to time, the last of which was during the year 1858, as the fruits of which about 30 have been added to the Church.

MINISTERS RAISED UP.—William Bradford, James Bradford, Josiah Bradford, Archibald Burgess, Zedekiah Barstow, D. D., Samuel Backus, Jason Park, Hiram Dyer, Seth Waldo.

* Allen.

THE CHURCH IN WESTON, (FORMERLY NORFIELD,) ORG. AUG. 17, 1757.

Samuel Sherwood,	Aug. 1757		May, 1783
John Noyes,*	May, 1786	May, 1807	
John Noyes,	April, 1823	1836	May, 1846
George Hall,	Jan. 1837	March, 1841	
Mark Mead,	July, 1841	Jan. 1844	
Lewis Pennell,	Aug. 1844	Oct. 1849	
Z. B. Burr,	June, 1850		

The Rev. J. Noyes, who resided in Weston after his dismissal, supplied the pulpit a portion of the time from 1808 till 1823, (being the regular supply in Greenwich First 1810 to '24,) during which period there was no settled minister or stated supply. *See Rev. J. Noyes's Half Century Sermon,* 1836.

MINISTER RAISED UP.—Daniel Banks.

* Sp. An. 1. 362. Allen.

THE CHURCH IN WESTPORT, ORG. JULY 5, 1832.

Charles Boardman,	Feb. 1833	Dec. 1836	
Henry Benedict,	Jan. 1840	March, 1852	
Joseph D. Strong,	April, 1853	Feb. 1855	
Timothy Atkinson,	Jan. 1856		

In 1831, measures were adopted for the building of a meeting house, which was opened on the 5th of July, 1832. The Church in the village of Saugatuck was constituted with 36 members dismissed from Green's Farms, and in 1835, the village with adjoining territory was incorporated as the town of Westport.

Mr. Boardman was dismissed to become Secretary and General Agent of the Western Reserve Branch of the Presbyterian Education Society.

Mr. Strong was dismissed to take the pastoral charge of the Second Foreign Church in the Sandwich Islands. The meeting house was enlarged and repaired in 1857.

THE CHURCH IN WEST STAFFORD, ORG. OCT. 31, 1764.

MINISTERS.	SETTLED.		DISMISSED.		DIED.	
Isaac Foster,*	Oct.	1764	Deposed, 1781			
Calvin Ingals,	Dec.	1796	March,	1803	Sept.	1830
Joseph Knight,	Nov.	1816	Dec.	1829		
Stephen Ellis, (c.)	Sept.	1831 ?	Dec.	1833 ?		
Elliot Palmer,	May,	1834	April,	1847		
Augustus B. Collins,	May,	1848	April,	1852		
Charles Galpin,		1852		1853		
Alvah Page,	Jan.	1854 ?	April,	1856 ?		
Frederick W. Chapman,	Oct.	1856 ?				

For a number of years Mr. Foster and his people were on good terms, being mutually agreed and happy. But at length difficulties arose on account of certain doctrines advanced by Mr. Foster, whereby several of the members of the Church were aggrieved; and having labored with Mr. Foster to no purpose, they complained of him to the North Association of the county of Hartford. The Association convened, and becoming satisfied of Mr. Foster's departure from some of the fundamental doctrines of the Gospel, deposed him from the ministry. A large minority, however, still adhered to him. The majority therefore called a council of the Association for advice, and were declared by said council to be the Church of Christ in West Stafford, on their subscription to certain articles of Faith, similar to those of sister Congregational Churches. Said articles were subscribed to by 25 members, April 17, 1781. The seeds of Universalism and Infidelity, sown by Mr. Foster, produced an abundant harvest. As the result, the Church has had difficulties to contend with, and has been too feeble most of the time to sustain the preaching of the gospel without foreign aid.

The Church was destitute of a pastor for 15 years before, and 13 years after Mr. Ingals's pastorate, having only occasional preaching. Mr. Ingals, after being absent from Stafford for a few years, returned again, and administered the ordinances of the Church occasionally until the settlement of Mr. Knight. He was chosen a deacon of the Church, March 3, 1820, in which capacity he served until his death.

* Sp. An. 2. 142.

THE CHURCH IN WEST SUFFIELD, ORG. 1744.

MINISTERS.	SETTLED.	DISMISSED.	DIED.
John Graham,*	Oct. 1746		April, 1796
Daniel Waldo,	May, 1792	Dec. 1809	
Joseph Mix,	Dec. 1814	Nov. 1829	
Erastus Clapp,	*five years,*		
Benjamin J. Lane,	*two years,*		
Joseph W. Sessions,	Jan. 1843	Nov. 1852	
Henry J. Lamb,	June, 1853	March, 1857	
Henry Cooley, June, 1857, inst. Mar. 1860			

Apparently this Church has not been in a more favorable and promising condition than at present, for half a century.

MINISTER RAISED UP.—Sylvester Graham.†

* Sp. An. 1, 315.   † Mendon As. 309.

THE CHURCH IN WESTVILLE, IN NEW HAVEN, ORG. DEC. 25, 1832.

John E. Bray,	Sept. 1832	Sept. 1834
Judson A. Root,	April, 1842	Sept. 1846
Samuel H. Elliot,	Dec, 1849	May, 1855
J. L. Willard,	Oct. 1855	

The rising of the thrifty and growing village where this Church is located demanded its existence, though the number of Congregationalists here was for several years insufficient for self-support. Aid was afforded by the Home Missionary Society, till 1855, which has proved a very wise and profitable expenditure. Preaching was supplied for several years from the Theological Seminary, New Haven.

From a small beginning, this Church and Society are now in a flourishing condition. The house of worship was enlarged to meet the demands of a growing congregation, in 1859.

THE CHURCH IN WEST WINSTED, IN WINCHESTER, ORG. JAN. 18, 1854.

C. H. A. Buckley,	Dec. 1854	May, 1859
Arthur T. Pierson,	1859	

A Church having existed in the thriving village of Winsted nearly 65 years, a division was amicably effected, local circumstances and the increase of population seeming to demand it, and both Churches are vigorously sustained. The benevolent contributions, for the year ending May, 1860, amounted to $700, besides paying a liberal salary.

65

The Church in West Woodstock, Org. 1747.

MINISTERS.	SETTLED.	DISMISSED.	DIED.
Stephen Williams,*	June, 1747		April, 1795
Alvan Underwood,†	May, 1801	March, 1833	April, 1858
John D. Baldwin,	Sept. 1834	July, 1837	
Benjamin Ober,	Dec. 1839	March, 1846	
Edward F. Brooks,	April, 1846	April, 1850	
William Allen,	April, 1850 ?	Nov. 1852	
Alvan Underwood,	Nov. 1852	April, 1854	
Joseph W. Sessions,	June, 1854		

This Church was formed chiefly of members, who were dismissed for the purpose, from the Church in South Woodstock, then under the care of Rev. Abel Stiles. This Church and Society have never been large, though once much larger than at present. Within the bounds of the parish there are now three other religious societies,—one Baptist, one Methodist, and one Universalist, all having places of worship and regular services on the Sabbath. This Church and Society have always lived in peace among themselves, and with others around them.

Ministers Raised Up.—Stephen Williams, Jr., Alvan Underwood.

* Sp. An. 1, 287. † Cong. Y. Book, 6, 146.

The Church in Wethersfield, Org. 1641.

	SETTLED	DISMISSED	DIED
Henry Smith,	1636	1639	1648
*Richard Denton,**	1636	1639	1663
Peter Prudden,†	1639	April, 1640	July, 1656
Henry Smith,	1641		1648
John Russell,†	1650	1659	
John Cotton, Jr.,	1659 ?		
Joseph Haynes,			
Thomas Buckingham,			
Jonathan Willoughby, Jr.,		1667 ?	
Gershom Bulkley,‡	1667	1677	Dec. 1713
Samuel Stone,	1667	June, 1669	
Joseph Rowlandson,†	1677		1678
John Woodbridge,†	1679		1691
Stephen Mix,§	1694		Aug. 1738
James Lockwood,‖	Feb. 1739		July, 1772
John Marsh, d. d.,¶	Jan. 1774		Sept. 1821
Caleb J. Tenney, d. d.,**	Mar. 1816	Jan. 1841	Sept. 1847
Charles J. Warren,††	July, 1835	Feb. 1837	
Robert Southgate,	Feb. 1838	Nov. 1843	
Mark Tucker, d. d.,	Oct. 1845	April, 1856	
Willis S. Colton,	Sept. 1856		

Wethersfield was one of the three first settled towns of Connecticut. Sir

Richard Saltonstall with his company settled at Watertown, Mass, but on account of the great number of immigrants from England, some of the people at Watertown left and settled Wethersfield; likewise from Dorchester and Newtown or Cambridge, settlers came to Windsor and Hartford. Those who first came to submit again to the hardships of a new settlement, were men of character and high standing both in Church and State. Wethersfield was more unfortunate than the other two churches, in not having at first a permanent, unchanging ministry. *Trumbull's Hist.* 1, 22, 23, 59 and 63. Account of revivals in *Memoir of Dr. Nettleton,* 135. *Rel. Intel.* 6, 730 ; 11, 123, 140.

Mr. Mix was one of the Scribes of Saybrook Synod, 1708.

The Church is now in a flourishing condition as to wealth, numbers and general unanimity among the members in feeling and action. More than 70 were added by profession in 1857–8.

MINISTERS RAISED UP.—Gershom Bulkley, Joshua L. Williams, John Marsh, Jr., D. D., Jonathan Russell,† Daniel Boardman, Samuel P. Williams,‡‡ John Chester, D. D.,§§ William Williams.

* Mather's Mag. 1, 360. † Allen. ‡ Am. Qr. Reg. 9, 366. § Sp. An. 1. 281. ‖ Sp. An. 1. 413. Allen. ¶ Sp. An. 1. 619. Allen. ** Sp. An. 2. 472. †† Mendon As. 182. ‡‡ Sp. An. 4. 370. §§ Sp. An. 4, 401.

THE CHURCH IN WILLINGTON, ORG. SEPT. 11, 1726.

MINISTERS.	SETTLED.		DISMISSED.		DIED.	
—— Fuller,	Sept.	1728			Dec.	1758
Gideon Noble,*		1759		1790		
Abishai Alden,		1791		1802		
Hubbell Loomis,	Aug.	1804	Sept.	1828		
Francis Wood,	Dec.	1829	July,	1838		
David Bancroft,	Oct.	1839	Jan.	1858		
Charles Bentley,	Oct.	1858				

By the town records we learn that Mr. Fuller was ordained at the house of Mr. John Merick. No records of any house of worship being erected till 1798. The one then built is now occupied by the Church, although extensive alterations were made in it in 1840.

In the early part of this century, the Church and Congregation, by subscription, raised a fund, the amount of which is now $5000, (a part of it having been lost by failure of a Bank.)

There were revivals in the Church during the ministry of Messrs. Loomis, Wood and Bancroft, and also, soon after the dismission of Mr. Bancroft, as fruits of which 30 were added to the church. Mr. Noble was dismissed for intemperance. Mr. Loomis, during his pastorate, became a Baptist, and as a consequence, a large portion of the church seceded when he was dismissed, and formed the present Baptist Church, which weakened and discouraged this Church. *Rel. Intel.* 14, 550 ; 18, 715.

MINISTERS RAISED UP.—Zebulon Crocker, Stephen Topliff, Benjamin Sharp.

* Allen.

The Church in Willimantic, in Windham, Org. Jan. 22, 1828.

MINISTERS.	SETTLED.	DISMISSED.	DIED.
Dennis Platt,	Aug. 1827	Oct. 1829	
Ralph S. Crampton,	April, 1830?	April, 1832	
Philo Judson,	Dec. 1834	March, 1839	
Andrew Sharpe,	Sept. 1840	June, 1849	
Samuel G. Willard,	Nov. 1849		

Previous to 1821, what is now Willimantic contained only about 20 families. Soon after, several factories were erected, and the population in 1827 was perhaps 1000. Up to 1827 there was no church or stated preaching— except in a school house—nearer than Windham Center, three miles distant. In August, 1827, on application of a few persons in Willimantic, made with the hearty approbation of Rev. C. B. Everest of Windham, the Directors of the Domestic Missionary Society sent Mr. Dennis Platt to labor for twelve weeks in the new Village. Mr. Platt states that they designed this as an experiment "to test the question whether an Evangelical Church could be established in a manufacturing village."

Up to this time there was not even a Sabbath School. With the aid of a Society of Ladies in Tolland County, he labored about six months without expense to the people, except for board. Before the six months elapsed a Church of 16 members was organized.

The Church was much blessed by the Holy Spirit, and four years from its organization it contained about 100 members. During the first ten years of its existence, the Church was aided by the Domestic Missionary Society of Connecticut. The whole sum thus received was $1213, a large sum compared with the annual contributions of many churches to Home Missionary purposes, but less than it often costs to educate one man for the ministry.

The Church and Society for 15 or 20 years had pecuniary as well as moral difficulties to contend with. Their house of worship was dedicated in the autumn of 1828, and was paid for with much difficulty. Several years after it was enlarged. Up to the time of its enlargement it was difficult to meet the annual expenses. The Church has never had either numbers or wealth to aid it in commanding the respect of the community.

The Church in Wilton, Org. June 20, 1726.

Robert Sturgeon,	July, 1726	1732	
William Gaylord,*	Feb. 1733		Jan. 1766
—— Mills,	1765	1767	
Isaac Lewis, D. D.,†	Oct. 1768	June, 1786	Aug. 1840
Aaron Woodward,‡	Jan. 1794	1800	
John I. Carle,	June, 1801	1804	
Samuel Fisher,	Dec. 1805	July, 1809	
Sylvanus Haight,	Oct. 1810	Aug. 1831	
Samuel Merwin,	Feb. 1832	Sept. 1838	Sept. 1858

MINISTERS.	SETTLED.	DISMISSED.	DIED.
John Smith,	Feb. 1839	June, 1848	
Gordon Hall,	Oct. 1848	May, 1852	
Thomas S. Bradley,	July, 1853	Oct. 1857	
Charles B. Ball,§	June, 1858		Jan. 1859
Samuel R. Dimock,	Dec. 1859		

Wilton was originally a part of Norwalk. The half-way covenant occasioned much difficulty in the Church during the ministry of Dr. Lewis. By his influence the Church passed a vote, Oct. 1783, to abolish it, and the Society also voted a year after to "sustain the Church and pastor in their principles." But after a stormy debate, two months after the dismission of their pastor, the half-way covenant was restored, and was not finally abolished until the present confession of faith was adopted in its stead, soon after the settlement of Mr. Fisher. There were three extensive and powerful revivals under the labors of Mr. Haight and Mr. Smith, and large additions by other pastors. In the second house of worship, Whitfield preached in 1740, from Job 40, 4, "Behold I am vile." The first house was built at the time of organization, but being too small, another was begun in 1738, but was not finished, for lack of funds, till 1747; the present house in 1790, dedication sermon by Dr. Timothy Dwight, from Gen. 28, 17. *Rel Intel.* 6, 762.

MINISTERS RAISED UP.—Moses Stuart, Samuel G. Willard.

* Allen. † Sp. An. 1, 662. Allen. ‡ Sp. An. 1, 585. § Cong. Qu. 1859, 225.

THE FIRST CHURCH IN WINCHESTER, (CENTER,) ORG. OCT. 30, 1771.

Joshua Knapp,*	Nov. 1772	Oct. 1789	March, 1816
Publius V. Bogue,	Jan. 1791	March, 1800	Aug. 1836
Archibald Bassett,	May, 1801	Aug. 1806	July, 1860
Frederick Marsh,	Feb. 1809	Oct. 1851	
James H. Dill,	Aug. 1846	Oct. 1851	
J. W. Cunningham, (c.)	1852 ?	1854?	
Ira Pettibone,	Oct. 1857		

The Consociation declined to install Mr. Cunningham, on account of opposition and remonstrance. Since 1783, there have been repeated revivals, adding in seven different years from 21 to 70 members each. *Rel. Intel.* 16, 413.

MINISTERS RAISED UP.—Noble Everitt, Abel McEwen, D. D., James Beach, Eliphaz Platt, Daniel E. Goodwin, Henry B. Blake.

* Sp. An. 1. 870. Allen.

THE CHURCH IN WINDHAM, ORG. DEC. 10, 1700.

Samuel Whiting,* 1692 inst. Dec. 1700			Sept. 1725
Thomas Clap,†	Aug. 1726	1739	Jan. 1767

MINISTERS.	SETTLED.		DISMISSED.		DIED.	
Stephen White,‡	Dec.	1740			Jan.	1793
Elijah Waterman,§	Oct.	1794	Feb.	1805	Oct.	1825
William Andrews,‖	Aug.	1808	April,	1813		
Cornelius B. Everest,	Nov.	1815	Nov.	1827		
Richard F. Cleaveland,	Oct.	1829	Oct.	1832		1855
John Ellery Tyler,	Oct.	1837	Dec.	1851		
Geo. Ingersol Stearns,	Dec.	1852				

This town voted June 11, 1692, to employ Mr. Whiting as their minister. This church during a part of its history enjoyed a good degree of prosperity. One pastor, (Mr. Clap,) was called directly from this Church to the Presidency of Yale College. Dr. Eleazar Wheelock was the son of one of the deacons. This Church has sent off four colonies from the limits of the original parish, viz: the Churches in Mansfield, (South,) Scotland, Hampton, and Willimantic.

Ever since the Revolutionary war, there has been much irreligion here. The Separatist movement did some mischief. An Episcopal Church and Society started in 1832, which withdrew from us a large share of the wealth of the place; and, added to all this, was a removal of the County Courts, and a large part of the profitable business once flourishing here. The result is that this is a comparatively feeble church.

MINISTERS RAISED UP.—Elijah Fitch, ¶ Augustine Hibbard, Eleazar Wheelock, D. D.,** Allen Clark.

* Sp. An. 1, 182. Allen. † Sp. An. 1, 234, 343. Allen. ‡ Sp. An. 2, 235. Allen. § Sp. An. 2. 342. Allen. ‖ Sp. An. 2. 237. Litchf. Centen. 120. ¶ Mendon Assoc. 117. ** Am. Qr. Reg. 10, 9.

THE FIRST CHURCH IN WINDSOR, ORG. MARCH, 1630, IN PLYMOUTH, ENGLAND.

John Warham,*		1630		April,	1670
John Maverick,*		1630		Feb.	1636
Ephraim Hewit,*		1639		Sept.	1644
Nathaniel Chauncey,†		1667	1680	Nov.	1685
Samuel Mather,‡		1682			1727
Jonathan Marsh,‡		1709		Sept.	1747
William Russell,‡	July,	1751			1775
David S. Rowland,‡		1776			1794
Henry A. Rowland,‡	May,	1790	July, 1835		1835
Charles Walker,	March,	1836	1837		
Royal Reed,	Oct.	1837	Oct. 1838		
Spofford D. Jewett,	June,	1839	Oct. 1843		
Theodore A. Leete,	Sept.	1845	Sept. 1859		
Benjamin Parsons,	July,	1860			

The people who originally composed the First Church of Windsor were from the Counties of Devon, Dorset, and Somerset, England. They had met by previous appointment at Plymouth, their port of embarkation, and on a day set apart for fasting and prayer they were organized into a church, and Rev. John Warham and Rev. John Maverick were chosen and installed Pastor and Teacher. They set sail, (probably but a few days after,) on the 20th of March, 1630. They arrived in New England, May 30, and settled in Dorchester, Mass. In the summer of 1635, and the spring of 1636, most of them came to Windsor, accompanied by their pastor, bringing their Church organization with them.§ Mr. Maverick, the teacher, died in Dorchester.

Mr. Warham was one of the four ministers appointed by the General Court of Connecticut, in 1657, to meet in Boston, such Divines from the other colonies as should be sent to discuss certain Ecclesiastical questions, among others that of Baptism. The next Jan. (1657–8) he commenced the practice of baptizing under the half-way covenant, which it has been supposed was first practiced in Connecticut, in Hartford, in 1666. The practice was still continued in this Church in 1822, but probably only in families where the older children had been baptized under that system.

In 1664, the record was made: "the General Court doth approve of the pious and prudent care of Windsor in seeking out for a supply and help in the ministry, Mr. Warham growing ancient."

Cotton Mather says of him, "I suppose the first preacher that ever preached with notes in our New England, was the Rev. Warham; who though he were sometimes faulted for it by some judicious men who had never heard him, yet when once they came to hear him, they could not but admire the notable energy of his ministry. He was a more vigorous preacher than the most of them who have been applauded for never looking into a book in their lives. His latter days were spent in the pastoral care and charge of the Church in Windsor, where the whole colony of Connecticut considered him as a principal pillar and father of the colony." *Sprague's Annals,* 1, 11.

In 1667, the General Court authorized "all the freemen and householders of Windsor and Massano, (Simsbury,) to meet on Monday next, at the meeting-house, by sun an hour high in the morning, to bring their votes to Mr. Henry Wolcott. Those that would have Mr. Chauncey to be settled minister in Windsor, are to bring in a paper to Mr. Wolcott with some writing on it. Those that are against his continuance are to bring a white paper to Mr. Wolcott. And this court doth hereby require and command that during this meeting they forbear all discourse and agitation of any matter as may provoke and disturb the spirits of each other, and at the issue of the work that they repayre to their severall vocations as they will answer to the contrary." The result was 86 votes for Mr. Chauncey's continuance, and 52 against it. Jan. 12, 1667–8, Mr. Chauncey made public declaration of his faith in Christian principles, and the manner of God's working on his soul.

§ There is a mistake in the note on page 86, owing to not allowing for the difference of reckoning in Old Style. The Church in Windsor was formed "in the beginning of the year," that is in March, at Plymouth, England, just before their embarkation; and the Church in Wethersfield not till the February after, 1630–31.

The minority were dissatisfied, and the court authorized such as could not close with Mr. Chauncey, to procure an orthodox minister, such as the court will approve, and the Church to settle Mr. Chauncey.

Mr Chauncey and Mr. Woodbridge, continued to minister to their separate Churches until 1680, when the court directed that both be dismissed, and the second Church disband and unite with the first. The difficulty was kept up two or three years longer, the First Church urging that those who had made a profession in the Second Church should undergo an examination by the first Church before being received. This point was finally yielded to the First Church, and the Rev. Samuel Mather settled over the united Church.

In 1685 there was a powerful revival and about 30 added to the Church.

And now as to the evidence that the Church in Hartford was on the ground before the Church in Windsor. This, to say the least, is not positive. The early records of the Windsor Church are not as entire as those of the Hartford Church. Here lies, as we think, the main difficulty. The evidence is decisive that the Church in Dorchester started for its destination in Windsor, several months prior to the removal of the Newtown Church to Hartford. (*See Stiles's History of Windsor, p.* 28.) The presumption therefore is, that they were first on the ground. And Dr. Hawes does not furnish any historic proof that such was not the fact. He does indeed assert, on the authority of Trumbull, that Mr. Warham did not come to Windsor till September, 1636. But this statement of Trumbull is more than balanced by counter statements, which affirm that Mr. Warham, with his Church, had removed to Windsor prior to April, 1636. (*Life of Richard Mather.*) As early as April of this same year, an attempt was made to form a new Church in Dorchester, because, as Mather says, the Church which was first planted in that place had removed with the Rev. Mr. Warham, to Connecticut. Here then is presumptive evidence that they were first on the ground. They had left Massachusetts ; where were they if not in Connecticut?

Besides, it is in evidence that Matthew Grant, a prominent member of the Church at Windsor, was there in 1635, and it may be inferred from the record (*See note p.* 635, *Stiles's History of Windsor,*) that he was permanently settled there, and that he was not alone. Some think that Mr. Warham was there at that time. *See note p.* 25 *as above.*

Unless, therefore, proof positive can be produced, showing that the Windsor Church did not reach its destination prior to June, 1636, we must consider the claims of the Windsor Church as valid against all others. *Compare with Dr. Hawes's address, page* 85.

MINISTERS RAISED UP.—Jonathan Marsh, Abel Stiles, Daniel Marshall, (Bap.) Abraham Marshall,(Bap.) Eliakim Marshall, Joseph Marshall, Jedediah Mills, Hezekiah Bissell, Solomon Wolcott, Samuel Chauncey, Allyn Mather, Henry A. Rowland, James Rowland, Oliver W. Mather.

*Sp. An. 1. 11. Allen. Math. Mag. 399. †Sp. An. 1. 114. 263. ‡ Allen.

The Second Church in Windsor, Org. 1669.

MINISTERS.	SETTLED.	DISMISSED.	DIED.
Benjamin Woodbridge,	1668	1680	

A division arose in the First Church with reference to the settlement of Mr. Chauncey; the minority seceding and calling Mr. Woodbridge, applied May 18, 1668, to the General Court for their approbation, which then took cognizance of all such matters. " The Court declare that they shall not disapprove of Mr. Woodbridge's continuance as a lecturer there, and recommend that the Church of Mr. Warham permit him to preach once a fortnight on the Sabbath." May 19th, "Mr. Warham inquires whether members of the Church are included in the order that granted liberty for choosing Mr. Woodbridge," and received an affirmative answer. In 1669, " The Court see not cause to deny liberty to those dissenters to embody themselves in a church state." Mr. Woodbridge was dismissed in 1680 by order of Court, and this church disbanded to unite with the First Church.

THE CHURCH IN WINDSOR LOCKS, ORG. FEB. 28, 1844.

Samuel H. Allen,	April, 1846	

This church was organized with fifteen members, mostly from the First Church in Windsor. It has enjoyed but one season of revival, in 1857 and 1858; the fruits 43 members. Its place of worship was at first a small chapel, built in 1834, in which public worship and a Sabbath school were regularly sustained from that time. The church edifice, now occupied, was built in 1846, and dedicated March 17, 1847.

THE FIRST CHURCH IN WINSTED, IN WINCHESTER, ORG. 1790.

Ezra Woodworth,	Jan. 1792	1799	
James Beach,*	Jan. 1806	1842	June, 1850
T. M. Dwight,	1842	1844	
Ira Pettibone,	Jan. 1846	1854	
Henry A. Russell,	April, 1854	1858	

Situated in a prosperous and enterprising manufacturing village, at the terminus of the Naugatuck Railroad, this church had so increased as to afford materials for a colony in 1854, and thus was formed the church in West Winsted, which is also well sustained. There have been several revivals, the most extensive in 1816, adding 112, and in 1843, adding 52 members.

MINISTERS RAISED UP.—Samuel Rockwell, Lumas H. Pease, John W. Alvord, Willard Burr, Jonathan Coe. (Ep.)

* Sp. An. 2. 319. Litchf. Centen. 123.

THE CHURCH IN WOLCOTT, (FORMERLY FARMINGBURY,) ORG. Nov. 15, 1773.

Alexander Gillett,*	Dec. 1773	Nov. 1791	Jan. 1826
Israel B. Woodward,	June, 1792		1810

66

MINISTERS.	SETTLED.		DISMISSED.	DIED.
Thomas Rich,		1811	1812	
Lucas Hart,		1812		1813
John Keyes,	Sept.	1814	1824	
Erastus Scranton,		1827	1830	
James D. Chapman,		1833	1840	
Aaron C. Beach,		1842	1857	
Stephen Rogers,	May,	1859		

Wolcott was originally the Society of Farmingbury, situated between Farmington and Waterbury, and taking its name by a combination usual in the early formation of Connecticut societies. In the vacancy of 1824 to 1833, there were supplies by Rev. Messrs. Vaill, Gaylord, Shaw, Sackett and others, but the dates are not preserved. Being a rural and hill town, with but indifferent encouragement to agriculture, the young men of energy and enterprise, leave to build up the cities and villages; reducing the church to a state of dependence in the support of the gospel. The revival of 1858, however, brought a considerable accession, mostly of the young, to the church, and rendered its spiritual state very desirable. *Rel. Intel.* 13. 398.

* Sp. An. 2. 68. Allen. Litchf. Centen. 80 ; Memoir by Rev. Luther Hart, 1826.

THE CHURCH IN WOLCOTTVILLE, IN TORRINGTON, ORG. JULY, 1832.

	SETTLED	DISMISSED
H. P. Arms,	Feb. 1833	July, 1836
Stephen Hubbell,	Feb. 1837	Sept. 1839
Samuel Day,	Sept. 1840	June, 1845
S. T. Seelye,	Jan. 1846	Mar. 1855
Ralph Smith,	April, 1856	Sept. 1857
E. L. Clark,	1857 ?	1859
R. M. Chipman,	July, 1859	

This church at first comprised 29 members; 58 others were afterwards received by the first pastor; 19 by the second; 61 by the third; and 90 by the fourth. This church has suffered the fluctuations usual to churches in manufacturing villages.

THE CHURCH IN WOODBRIDGE, (FORMERLY AMITY,) ORG. NOV. 2, 1742.

	SETTLED	DISMISSED	DIED
Benjamin Woodbridge,*	Nov. 1742		Dec. 1785
Eliphalet Ball,	Dec. 1783	1790	1797
David L. Beebee,	Feb. 1791	Mar. 1800	
Claudius Herrick,†	Mar. 1802	Sept. 1806	1831
Jason Allen,	April, 1810	April, 1826	
Prince Hawes,	Dec. 1828	April, 1834	
Walter R. Long,	Oct. 1837	Sept. 1841	
Samuel H. Elliot, Sept. 1842, ord. Nov. 1843		Dec. 1849	
Owen Street,	Dec. 1850	May, 1852	

MINISTERS.	SETTLED.	DISMISSED.	DIED.
Alfred C. Raymond,	Oct. 1852	Dec. 1855	
Jesse Guernsey,	May, 1856	Oct. 1857	
Alexander D. Stowell,	Nov. 1858	April, 1860	

The ecclesiastical society in Amity, (including Bethany, till 1762,) was formed, in 1737, (after petitioning twenty years,) from the north-west part of the town of New Haven, with the addition of "one mile and six score rods in width" from the north-east part of Milford; and in length, from an east and west line about four miles north of the State House, to Waterbury line. The town was formed with the same bounds in 1784, and named in honor of its first minister; and Bethany Society became a town in 1832. In Jan. 1782, this church voted that its government should be agreeable to the Congregational plan; and in Jan. 1801, it united with the New Haven West Consociation. A separate religious society was formed by Methodists about 1833, which continued but a few years. Besides this, there has been no other religious organization within the present bounds of the society and town. The church has for long periods, in the intervals of pastorates, been supplied from Yale Theological Seminary. There have been several revivals; the one in 1858, when the Church was without a pastor, adding 60 to its membership. *Rel. Intel.* 5. 521.

The house of worship was built in 1832, and repaired in 1860.

Ministers Raised Up.—L. S. Parsons, Artemas Hull.

* Allen. † Rel. Intel. 16. 15.

THE FIRST CHURCH IN WOODBURY, ORG. MAY 5, 1670.

Zechariah Walker,*	1668 ord. 1670		Jan. 1700
Anthony Stoddard,†	1702		1760
Noah Benedict,‡	1760		1813
Worthington Wright,	1811	1813	
Henry P. Strong,	1814	1816	
Samuel R. Andrew,§	1817	1846	1853
Lucius Curtis,	1846	1854	
Robert G. Williams,	1855	July, 1859	

This church was organized as the Second Church in Stratford. It had separated from the original church, some years before, on the "Half-Way Covenant" question. A new location was sought, and in May, 1672, a grant for a township of land was obtained for this church at Pomperaug, the Indian name of the river. Early the next year, a majority of the members removed to this place, and became the First Church in Woodbury.

Mr. Walker ministered to both portions of his church till June 27, 1678, when he took up his abode permanently in Woodbury. The church maintained the half-way covenant system till the ordination of Mr. Benedict.

The limits of the original and first church embraced the present towns of Bethlem, Washington, Roxbury, Southbury, and a portion of Middlebury, and the churches in those towns were formed from this. The ministry of the first three pastors, with little interval, covered a period of 143 years. By its eight pastors, 1410 persons have been gathered into its fold. It has had three different houses of worship, and, in 1857, remodeled its present house at an expense of $4,200. *See History of Woodbury ; also Bi-centennary*, 1859.

There is within its history abundant evidence of the covenant keeping mercy of God. Some of its original office bearers have had one or more of their descendants to represent them in the office, without a break in the succession to the present time. The present condition of many families is a living testimony to the covenant faithfulness of God—to those who observe the rite of infant baptism.

MINISTERS RAISED UP.—Ephraim Judson, Adoniram Judson, Philo Judson, Samuel Judson,‖ Everton Judson, Justus Mitchell, Thomas Miner, Anson S. Atwood.

* Allen. Litchf. Centen. 73-75.   † Sp. An. 1, 173.   Allen.   Litchf. Centen. 73, 75. ‡ Sp. An. 1, 407.   Allen.   Litchf.   Centen. 73, 75.   § Cong. Y. Book, 6, 118. ‖ Mendon Assoc. 138.

THE FIRST CHURCH IN WOODSTOCK, ORG. 1686.

MINISTERS.	SETTLED.	DISMISSED.	DIED.
Josiah Dwight,	1686	1726	
Amos Throop,	1727		1736
Abel Stiles,*	1737	1759	1783
Abiel Leonard,	1763	1777	1780
Eliphalet Lyman,†	1779	1824	1836
R. S. Crampton,	1827	1830	
W. M. Cornell,	1831	1834	
Otis Rockwood,	1834	1843	
Jonathan Curtis,	1846	1852	
Henry M. Colton,	1853	1855	
Lemuel Grosvenor,	1855	1860	

This church originated with a company of settlers from Roxbury, Mass. parishioners of Rev. John Eliot. The church enjoyed numerous revivals of religion during the pastorates of Mr. Lyman, Mr. Rockwood and Mr. Curtis, and in 1858, shared in the general shower of divine grace.

Three houses of worship have been built since the organization of this church. The present one was built in 1821, at a cost of $4,000, and was repaired and remodeled inside in 1858. This church was governed under the Cambridge Platform till 1815, when they joined the Consociation of Windham County.

MINISTERS RAISED UP.—Ezra Ripley, D. D.,‡ Thomas R Chandler, D. D., Jedediah Morse, D. D.,‖ James Davis, Abiel Holmes, D. D.¶ Lucien Burleigh, Newton Barrett, Charles Burleigh, Anthony Palmer, George Webber, Samuel Palmer, George Bugbee, John Bowers, Ralph Lyon.

* Sp. An. 1.470. Allen.   † Allen. ‡ Allen. § Allen. ‖ Sp. An. 2. 247. ¶ Sp. An. 2. 240.

APPENDIX.

CHURCHES WITH DIFFERENT SOCIETY NAMES AND POST OFFICE
ADDRESSES FROM THOSE OF THE TOWNS IN WHICH THEY
ARE LOCATED.

Ashford, Westford.
Avon, (West Avon P. O.)
    East Avon, (Avon P. O.)
Barkhamsted, Hitchcockville.
Berlin, Kensington.
Bozrah, Bozrahville, Fitchville.
    (B. P. O.)
Canaan, (So. Canaan P. O.)
    Falls Village.
Canterbury, Westminster.
Canton, (C. Center P. O.,) Collinsville.
Chatham, East Hampton.
    Middle Haddam.
Colchester, Westchester.
Colebrook, (C. Center P. O.)
Cornwall, North Cornwall.
Coventry, South, (C. P. O.)
    North Coventry.
Darien, (D. Depot, P. O.)
Derby, Birmingham, Ansonia.
Durham Center, (P. O.)
East Haddam, Millington, Hadlyme.
East Haven, Fair Haven, (2d.)
East Lyme, (Niantic P. O.)
East Windsor, Broad Brook.
Essex, Centerbrook.
Fairfield, Greenfield, (G. Hill P. O.)
    Southport, Black Rock.
Farmington, Plainville, Unionville.
Glastenbury, East Glastenbury, (G.
    P. O.) South Glastenbury.
Greenwich 1st. (Mianus P. O.,) Stan-
    wich, North Greenwich.
Griswold, (J. C. P. O) Jewett City.
Guilford, North Guilford.
Haddam, Higganum.
Hamden, Mt. Carmel.
    East Plain, (Whitneyville P. O.)
Hartland, West Hartland.
Hebron, Gilead.
Killingly, West Killingly, South Kil-
    lingly, Dayville.

Lebanon, Goshen, (L. P. O.) Exeter,
    (L. P. O.)
Lisbon, (Jewett City P. O.)
    Hanover, (Lord's Bridge P. O.)
Litchfield, Northfield, Milton.
Lyme, Hamburg, Grassy Hill.
Madison, North Madison.
Manchester, M. 2d, (M. Station P. O.)
Mansfield, (M. Center P O.)
    North Mansfield, (M. P. O.)
Meriden 1st, (West Meriden P. O.)
    Hanover, (W. Meriden P. O.)
Middletown, Westfield, (M. P. O.)
    Middlefield.
Montville, Mohegan, (Norwich P. O.)
New Hartford North, (N. H. P. O.)
New Hartford South, (N. H. Center
    P. O.)
New Haven, Fair Haven (1st,) Fair
    Haven (Center,) Westville.
North Branford, Northford.
North Canaan, (East C. P. O.)
Norwich 1st, (Norwich Town P. O.)
    Greeneville.
Old Lyme, (Lyme P. O.)
Old Saybrook, (Saybrook P. O.)
Orange, West Haven.
Plainfield, Central Village, Waure-
    gan, (C. V. P. O.)
Plymouth, Plymouth Hollow, Terry-
    ville.
Pomfret, Abington.
Putnam, East Putnam, (P. P. O.)
Ridgefield, Ridgebury, (Ridgefield P.
    O.)
Sharon, Ellsworth.
Southbury, South Britain.
South Windsor, S. W. 2d, (Buckland
    P. O.) Church of Theological In-
    stitute, (East Windsor Hill P. O.)
Stafford, West Stafford, Stafford
    Springs, Staffordville.

Stamford, North Stamford, Long Ridge.
Stonington, 2d ; (S. 1st, M. B. P. O.,) Mystic Bridge.
Suffield, West Suffield,
Torrington, Torringford, Wolcottville.
Vernon, Rockville 1st and 2d.
Voluntown and Sterling, (Collamer P. O.)
Washington, New Preston.
 New Preston Hill, (N. P. P. O.)
Westport, Green's Farms,(W. P. O.)

Wethersfield, Newington.
Willington, (West Willington P. O.)
Winchester Center, (P. O.) Winsted, West Winsted.
Windham, Willimantic.
Windsor, Poquonnoc.
Woodbridge, (Westville P. O.)
Woodbury, North Woodbury, (W. P. O.)
Woodstock (So.) East Woodstock. West Woodstock, North Woodstock.

EARLY THEOLOGICAL EDUCATION, CONTINUED FROM PAGE 296.

In the first generation of New England history, several ministers, who afterwards became in various degrees distinguished, appear to have been trained, in part, under the teaching of Thomas Hooker and Samuel Stone, at Hartford. Whether any other pastors in the Connecticut and New Haven colonies at that period, gave special instruction to candidates for the ministry, is less clearly indicated.

The names of some of the pastors who, since the "Great Awakening" of 1740, have served as theological instructors, are given in the brief paper on Early Theological Education, pp 296, 297; to those names the following may be added.

Rev. Joel Benedict, D. D., Plainfield.
Calvin Chapin, D. D , Rocky Hill.
Rev. Timothy Dwight, D. D., Greenfield ; New Haven.
Rev. David Ely, D. D., Huntington.
Rev. Elizur Goodrich, D. D., Durham.
Rev. Nathan Perkins, D. D., West Hartford.
Rev. Bezaleel Pinneo, Milford.
Rev. Cyprian Strong, D. D., Portland.
Rev. Nathan Strong, D. D., Hartford.
Rev. Josiah Whitney, D. D., Brooklyn.

THE NAMES OF THE FOLLOWING "HALF CENTURY MINISTERS." SHOULD BE ADDED TO THE LIST ON PAGES 289–295.

Asa Burton, D. D., . . . n. Stonington, . . . Thetford, Vt.   59
Jedediah Bushnell, . . . n. Saybrook, . . . Cornwall, Vt.   53
Joseph Coit, . . . Plainfield,   52

Timothy M. Cooley, D. D., . . . Lic. N. II. E., . . . Granville,
Mass., ... 65
Manasseh Cutler, D. D., . . . n. East Putnam, . . . Hamilton, Mass., 52
Timothy Cutler, D. D., . . . Stratford, . . . Pres. Y. C.; became
Ep. 56
Gordon Dorrance, . . . Voluntown, 52
Joseph Fish, . . . North Stonington, 49
Jabez Fitch, . . . n. Norwich, . . . Portsmouth, N. H., 52
Eliphalet Gillett, D. D., . . . n. Colchester, . . . Hallowell, Me., 54
John Griswold, . . . n. Lebanon, . . . Pawlet, Vermont, 60
John Keep, . . . Lic. Litchfield N., . . . Ohio ? living, 55
Caleb Knight, . . . n. Lisbon, . . . Berkshire Co., Mass., 52
Joseph Lathrop, D. D., . . . n. Norwich , . . . West Springfield,
Massachusetts, 66
John Marsh, Jr., D. D., . . . Haddam, . . . New York; living 51
Joseph Marshall, . . . (Sep.) . . . Canterbury, 54
Asa Meech, . . . Canterbury, . . . Canada, 50
James Murdock, D. D., . . . n. Westbrook, . . . Andover, Mas-
sachusetts; New Haven, 55
Roger Newton, D. D., . . . n. Durham, . . . Greenfield, Mass., 55
Isaac Porter, . . . Granby, 50
John Prudden, . . . n. Milford, . . . Long Island, (see Allen.) 55
Ezra Ripley, . . . n. Woodstock. 63
David S. Rowland, ... Granby ; Plainfield ; Windsor, 50
Samuel Shepard, D. D., . . . n. Portland, . . . Lenox, Mass. 52
Thomas Snell, D. D., . . . Lic., Tolland, ... North Brookfield,
Massachusetts, living, 63
Joseph Sumner, D. D., . . . n. Pomfret, . . . Shrewsbury, Mass., 62
Ezra Weld, . . . n. Pomfret, . . . Lic. W. . . . Braintree, Mass. 54
Elisha S. Williams, . . . (Bap.) . . . n. East Hartford, . . . Bev-
erly, Mass., 65
Solomon Williams, Jr., . . . n. East Hartford, . . . Northampton,
Mass., 56
Payson Williston, . . . n. West Haven, . . . Easthampton, Mass., 67

ERRATA.

The Committee exceedingly regret that many errors have crept into a work that they had hoped to make entirely accurate. Their excuse must be the impracticability of their giving that personal superintendence to the press which would have been desirable.

Page 17, line 28, read 1656.
Page 32, line 5, read Scriptures.
"   34,   "   17, read 1680.
"   47,   "   22, read Arminianism.
"   73,   "   19,   "   Mr. Warham.
"   83,   "   2,   "   Rev. Theodore D. Woolsey, D. D.
Page 146, line 45, read Thos. K. Fessenden.
"   146,   "   49,   "   1859, Norwich, S. W. S. Dutton, D. D., A. S. Chesebrough, Jeremiah Taylor, Enoch F. Burr.
Page 148, line 34, read solicit.
"   154,   "   10,   "   William F. Arms.
"   "   "   37,   "   State.
"   "   "   39,   "   States, et passim.
"   155,   "   4,   "   Mr. Hanover Bradley.
"   "   "   7,   "   David Brainerd.
Page 155, line 28, read E. C., E. Haddam, Osages.
"   "   "   44, read Mr. Stephen Fuller, E. H., Osages.
Page 156, line 48, read Whitneyville.
"   157,   "   10,   "   Mrs. Dwight W. Marsh.
"   "   "   28, read Mrs. Munger.
"   "   "   31,   "   Rev. Samson Occum.
"   158,   "   21,   "   Rockville.
"   169,   "   16,   "   H. C., New York.
"   176,   "   36,   "   western boundary.
"   178,   "   37,   "   Norfield in Weston.
"   184,   "   6,   "   1846.
"   190,   "   33,   "   to be aided.
"   199,   "   12,   "   1763.
"   204,   "   6,   "   have precluded.
"   207,   "   34,   "   Fairfield West.
"   "   "   37,   "   Roswell R. Swan.
"   219,   "   18,   "   Fairfield West.
"   220,   "   37,   "   Samuel R. Andrew.
"   231,   "   18,   "   218—own 119.
"   "   "   37,   " $826, 980, 34.
"   238,   "   11,   "   become.
"   246,   "   2,   "   erase in
"   247,   "   17,   "   than, for that.
"   254,   "   23,   "   Congregational, for Presbyterian.
Page 256, line, 2,   "   1751.
"   "   "   36,   "   Sandisfield.
"   263,   "   39,   "   N. E. Vol. xi. p. 195.
"   283,   "   1,   "   Rogerenes; do line 25.
"   285,   "   19,   "   were not tinctured.
"   290,   "   14,   "   Joel Bordwell.
"   "   "   43,   "   * Sp. An., 3, 102.
"   291,   "   18,   "   Nathanael Emmons.
"   "   "   30,   "   Torrington.
"   "   "   33,   "   Southbury.

Page 292, line 10, change † to next line.
"   "   "   18, read Huntington, L. Isl.
Page 293, line, 13, " n. Ashford.
"   "   "   28,   "   Bezaleel Pinneo.
"   "   "   36,   "   N. Jersey for N. York
"   294,   "   45,   "   New Haven, N. York.
"   "   "   29,   "   New Haven.
"   295,   "   19, " Lic. Windham.
"   296,   "   30,   "   were, for was.
"   297,   "   24, " distinguished.
"   300,   "   11, " N. T., 1747 ; line 18, read H. Gold, Jr. ; line 21, 22, read March 29, 1758 ; line 30, read N. A. Hewit became a Roman Catholic.
Page 303, line 30, read William Brentnal Ripley ; line 32, erase May 26 ; line 38, read Andrew Elliot, Jr., May, 1803 ; line 42, read Orrin Fowler, Oct. 1817 ; also Bronson B. Beardsley.
Page 304, line 36, read HARTFORD NORTH.
"   395,   "   22, " there is need, for their.
"   308,   "   2, " 1745.
"   309,   "   14, " Roswell R. Swan ; line 23, George I. Stearns.
Page 311, line 55, read Elijah Gridley.
Page 314, line 7, read straitened ; line 18, read its, for this.
Page 316, line 39, read sympathized with.
"   317,   "   31, Northfield has since withdrawn.
Page 317, line 33, read, since returned.
"   320   "   26, " Edward L. Wells.
"   "   "   34, " Carlos C. Carpenter.
"   321,   "   24, read article.
"   324,   "   37, read Aaron Hall ; line 50 read, Bezel Cook.
Page 325, line 20, read Guernsey Brown.
"   326,   "   13, read Samuel I. Curtiss.
"   326,   "   23, read John J. Avery.
"   326,   "   44, read Irem W. Smith ; line 53, read Pliny F. Warner.
Page 331, line 5, read Carroll Cutler.
"   334, line 31, read H. Porter ; line 23, read David R. Austin ; line 34, read William Barnes ; line 51, read Lavius Hyde.
Page 335, line 15, read During, for From.
"   336,   "   41, read Israel Brainerd ; line 47, read Joel F. Bingham.
Page 337, line 1, WINDHAM ASSOCIATION.
Page 343, line 8, read J. H., died Nov. 1742 ; " 9, read J. B., settled Sept. 1743 ; " 22, read Hale, at first £40.
Page 344, " 10, W. S. W., dismissed 1858 ? " 14, read to April 1.

Page 345, line 17, read *William Goodwin.*
line 27, read Evan Johns.
Page 346, line 8, read Andrew T. Pratt;
line 33, E. W. R., dismissed Aug.
1860.
Page 347, line 15, read S. S., settled April,
1805.
Page 349, line 16, read FORMERLY WINTON-
BURY; line 24, read Daniel Gibbs; line
37, erase died April, 1830.
Page 351, line 13, read William M. Birch-
ard; line 18, read FORMERLY NEWBURY;
line 33, read FORMERLY POMFRET, 2D.
Page 350—352, Bristol, Broad Brook,
Brookfield, Brooklyn, and Burlington,
should follow Bridgeport 2d, p. 357.
Page 353, line 2, read BOZRAH, NEW CON-
CORD SOCIETY; line 23, read Jedediah
L. Stark; line 38, read Nathaniel Mi-
ner, also 354, line 1; line 30, read Ro-
dolphus Landfear.
Page 355, line 9, Fosdick Harrison, also
line 14; line 33, read J. H. H., settled
Feb. 1839.
Page 357, line 2, read Raised Up.—Gideon Hawley; line 13, erase dis. March,
1859; line 22, read Nathaniel A. Hewit.
Page 358, line 4, read S. E., died June,
1727; line 16, read T. J. M., settled
1821, died Dec. 1826; line 19, read O.
C. W., died Oct. 1845; line 22, *Alanson Alvord*; 27; read, a son, pastor in
Millington; line 30, read Voluntown.
Page 360, line 2, read PAUTAPAUG; line 13,
read Henry R. Hoisington; line 32,
read J. B., settled June, 1853; line 34,
read G. H., dismissed June, 1860; line
40, read CHAPLIN.
Page 365, line 32, read Charles Kittredge.
" 368, " 24, read ORG. JAN. 1715;
line 25, read Joseph Smith, Jan. 1715.
Page 369, line 39, read Ebenezer R. White.
" 370, " 7, read S. N. H. dismissed
April, 1858.
Page 377, line 33, read S. F., Lay Missionary.
Page 378, line 5, read *L. H. Pease,*; line
6, read Henry A. Russell; line 42,
read 1806; line 41, read J. H., died
1754.
Page 379, line 14, E. Mack, see p. 257;
Page 380, line 21, read E. F., settled Jan.,
1778; line 35, read Erastus Learned.
" 381, " 5, read South Windsor;
line 36, read Died July, 1783.
Page 382, line 27, read Died April, 1756.
" 383, line 33, read Died 1756.
" 384, " 3, read than that of.
" 385, " 30, Lyman H. Atwater, D. D.
" 386, " 40, read *Timothy Dwight*, lic.
Sept. 1858.
" 387, line 4, erase " lic ;." line 19,
read *John Edgar*, lic.
Page 388, line 9, read in 1640.
" 390, " 8, read Samuel H. Riddel;
line 9, read James A. Smith; line 10,
read Amos S. Chesebrough.
Page 391, line 4, read six days; line 31,
read Oct. 1766, ord. Sept. 1767.
" 397, line 24, read Aitchison; also
line 17.

Page 398, line 5, ORG. NOV. 8, 1704; line
37, read I. B. settled June, 1800.
Page 399, line 29, read 1733.
" 400, " 7, read supposed to be organized 1675.
Page 401, line 4, read Henry M. Field;
line 13, read G. C., dismissed Feb.'
1842; line 19, read Nov. 1743; line 29,
read erected in 1743; line 41, read
Philips Payson.
Page 402, line 4, read *James D. Moore.*
" 403, " 11, read G. S., ord. Oct. 1855,
line 22, read *Timothy Stone.*
Page 404, line 13, read J. W., dis. 1669.
" 405, " 12, read T. B., died 1731.
" 407, " 22, read *Christian Popp.*
" 408, " 20, read George E. Pierce.
" 411, " 39, read T. L. S., May, 1842,
inst. April, 1843.
Page 413, line 3, read W. W. A. dis. May,
1849; line 4, read W. W. P., settled
Dec. 1853, dis. 1854; line 17, read
Eden Burroughs.
Page 415, line 31, read NORTH GROTON.
" 416, line 18, read Separate; line 36,
read Daniel L. Carroll, D. D.
Page 418, line 11, read Qu. Reg. has Benajah Phelps.
Page 419, line 37, erase (Ep.); put it after
T. G. S.
Page 420, line 38, read Matthew Merriam;
line 39, read Samuel I. Curtis.
Page 422, line 41, read Org. Feb. 1, 1855.
" 423, " 17, read James B. Crane.
" 424, " 17, read Ahab Jinks.
" 425, " 41, read J. M. S. settled
1851; line 43 read Wm. C. Scofield.
Page 426, line 10, read Gov. Jonathan Law.
" 427, " 2, read **Mill Plain.**
" 428, " 39, read James Kant; also
page 429, line 3.
Page 431, line 10, read formally dissolved.
" 432, " 43, read secular purposes.
" 434, " 3, read Davenport, 1765;
line 6, read probably Abraham Kettel-
tas; line 13, read H. H. M., settled
May, 1845.
Page 439, line 36, read A. G. B., dis. Jan.
1858.
Page 441, line 40, read *J. G. Hanmer*, D. D.
" 443, " 29, read T. H. (Bapt.) Nathan B. Derrow, Charles Thompson.
Page 446, line 4, read *William H. Whitte-
more*; line 16, read J. B. settled 1725;
line 24, read *John L. Ambler.*
Page 447, line 3, read admissions; line 6,
read in discipline; line 12, read from
1817.
Page 451, line 9, read Joel L. Dickinson.
Page 453, line 32, read pentecostal.
" 456, " 7, read *W. Simpson Clarke.*
" 458, " 36, read Benjamin Lord, D.D.
" 459, " 26, read Zebediah H. Mansfield.
Page 463, line 23, read before 1699.
" 465, " 14, read E. W., 1731, ord.
Oct. 1715; line 37, read Abraham Sabin, John Sabin.
Page 466, lines 21, 22, 23, transfer " dismissed " dates, to " died."

Page 469, line 9, read N. B. died Jan. 1810.
" 470, " 39, read J. W. R., dismissed Feb. 1856.
Page 472, line 7, read ORG. AUG. 22, 1744; line 25, read RE-ORGANIZED MAY 15, 1793.
Page 474, line 4, read E. G. W., died May, 1855; line 5, read J. F., settled May, 1811.
Page 475, line 24, read ORG. MARCH 28, 1744.
Page 477, lines 23, 24, transpose I. Lewis and S. Camp; line 38, read *William T. Bacon.*
Page 479, line 5, read David L. Ogden; line 42, read E. W. died 1784.
Page 480, line 31, read Samuel W. Whelpley.
Page 481, line 35, read M. R. July 1835, inst. June, 1836.
Page 482, line 21, read G. H. W., 1837, inst. Jan. 1840.
Page 483, line 27, read John L. Avery.
Page 484, line 29, read Henry G. Jesup.
" 485, " 3, transpose DISMISSED and SETTLED; line 29, read Joshua R. Brown.
" 486, " 16, read Z. W., was pastor of the Second Church, that removed to Woodbury, *which see.* Line 18, read H. G., settled June, 1722.
Page 489, line 16, read in 1816; line 30, erase Gordon Hall, (f.) also add Leverett Griggs, William A. Benton.
Page 490, line 16, read Mr. Goodman's; line 19, read *Mr. McKinstry's;* line 33, read in 1773.
Page 491, line 6, read OR NORTH STRATFORD, line 27, read C. H., June, 1749, line 34 read Samuel I. Curtiss.
Page 493, line 27, read C. Y. B., 1857, p. 87.
Page 494, line 29, Sp. An. 1. 689; line 32, reference from S. W. is *Allen.
Page 495, line 28, ‡ Litchfield Centen. 119.
Page 496, line 7, read Jehu Clark; line 13, read WATERBURY—ORG. 1689.
Page 499, line 12, read Charles E. Murdock; line 19, read E. S. E., dism., April, 1810.
Page 500, line 24, read A. U., died April, 1858.
Page 501, line 33, read Adolphus Ferry.
" 502, line 9, read Stephen W. Stebbins; line 26, add David H. Williston; line 43, add Joseph R. Johnson.
Page 503, line 2, read Nov. 20, 1770; line 18, read Zedekiah S. Barstow, D.D.; line 21, erase FORMERLY NORFIELD; line 36, read Charles A. Boardman.
Page 504, line 13, read I. F. Died 1807.
" 509, line 6, read C. B. B., settled Jan. 1858; line 36, read Noble Everett.
" 510, line 9, read G. Ingersoll S., Sept. 1852.

TOPICAL INDEX.

INDEX OF NAMES.

The committee have met with a difficulty in the preparation of this index, to which they call attention. In the reports which they have received, there is a want of uniformity in the spelling of names. As a result of this, it may sometimes be found that there are two references to the same person, according to each of the methods of spelling. So in the case of persons who have "middle" names, the reference may be, in a few cases, both to the Christian name alone, and to the name in full. Whenever an error of importance in the spelling of any name has been discovered in the volume, the name, as incorrectly spelled, has been entered in the Index, inclosed in brackets.

Attention is also called to the fact that not unfrequently in the "History of the Churches" the same person is claimed to have been "raised up" for the ministry within the bounds of two or more societies.

On the other hand, it should be noticed that from several of the churches no list of ministers "raised up" has been furnished; and the names of "Licentiates" of the District Associations for the first hundred years are almost entirely wanting.

Barnes, William, 403, 334.
Barnet, John, 325.
Barnum, Caleb, 300, 360.
　George, 347.
　Samuel W., 330, 392.
Barr, Moses, 324.
　Thomas, 170.
Barrow, ———, 136.
Barrows, E. P. 103, 309, 405, 419.
Barstow, Zedekiah S., 503.
Bartholomew, Andrew, 322, 408, 494.
　Orlo, 391.
Bartle, W. T. 175.
Bartlett, E. N., 175.
　Hobart, 385.
　Hobart M. 365.
　John, Jr., 309, 344, 349, 385.
　John L., 309.
　Jonathan, 290, 303, 469-70.
　Moses, 418, 466,
　Nathaniel, 144, 290, 453, 469.
　Shubael, 290, 380, 385.
　William, 151, 152.
Barton, F. A., 365.
　Titus F., 336.
Bascom, Flavel, 326, 385.
　John, 171.
　Ellery, 319.
Bass, John, 343.
Bassett, Amos, 161, 165, 169, 176, 329, 372, 409. 428.
　Archibald, 170, 290, 325, 372, 509.
　Charles, 320.
　Isaac H., 336.
　George W., 309.
　William Elliott, 320, 360, 372.
Bates, James, 360.
　Talcott, 373.
Beach, Aaron C., 330, 426, 514.
　Abraham, 362.
　Benjamin, 258.
　James, 145, 146, 314, 491, 509, 513.
　John, 266, 290, 446.
　Isaac, 318, 447.
　Isaac C., 355.
Beadle, E. R., 407.
　Mrs. E. R., 154.
Beard, Augustus F., 458.
　Spencer F., 397, 429.
Beardsley, Bronson B., 303, 357.
　Julius O., 355.
　Nehemiah B., 362, 491.
Beattie, James, 461.
Beckley, Hosea, 311.
Beckwith, George, 143, 144, 290, 401, 429.
　George A. 426.
Bedinger, Everett, W. 439.
Beebe, David H., 514.
　Levi S., 318, 445.
　Gilbert, 459.
　Hubbard, 502.

Beebe, James, 369, 491.
　Thomas, 383.
Beecher, Charles, 417,
　Henry Ward, 417.
　John W., 174, 383, 478.
　Luther H., 391.
　Lyman, 145, 176, 207, 209, 219, 290, 329, 416, 453.
　Thomas K., 417, 330.
　William H. 424.
Beers, Joshua, 170.
Belden, Joshua, 290, 308, 442.
　William, 391.
　Jonathan, 308.
　Wm. W. 312, 346, 371, 389, 462.
Belknap, Horace, 382.
Bell, Benjamin, 318.
　Hiram, 336, 413, 418.
Bellamy, Joseph, 52, 144, 191, 199, 259, 290, 297, 298, 324, 348, 494.
Beman, Amos G. 309, 406, 439.
　Samuel, 309.
Benedict Abner, 318.
　Abner, Jr., 171, 395, 422.
　Alanson, 300, 357.
　Amzi, 433, 465, 473, 492.
　Epenetus P. 320, 357.
　Joel, 165, 318, 416, 463, 518.
　Joel F., 471.
　Joel T., 355.
　Noah, 144, 145, 290, 300, 369, 515,
　Henry, 303, 458, 496, 503.
　Richard H., 464.
　Timothy, 448.
　T. N., 330, 351.
Benjamin, Theodore, 347.
Bennet, Asa, 468.
Bent, George, 331.
Bentel, C. G., 442.
Bethune, ———, 191.
Bentley, Charles, 392, 394, 408, 422, 507
　Edward W., 306.
Benton, Wm. A, 154, 180, 309.
　Andrew, 405, 439.
　J. Augustus, 330.
Betts, Alfred H., 171.
　Edward C., 174.
　Xenophon, 175, 325.
Bidwell, Oliver B., 330, 437.
Bigelow, Henry, 336.
Billings, Silas, 477.
　William, 403.
Bingham, Joel F., 336, 342, 390.
　Hiram, 439.
　Hiram, Jr., 181.
　Luther G., 173.
　Silas L., 170, 336, 342.
Birchard, Eliphalet, 342, 415.
　Wm. M. 351, 353, 375, 409, 415.
Bird, Isaac, 154, 180, 473.
　Jonathan, 311, 433.
　Samuel, 437.

Dodd, Stephen, 291, 379, 431
  S. G., 425.
Dole, George T., 318.
Doolittle, Edgar J., 311, 362, 409, 494.
  Giles, 318.
Dorman, Lester M., 418.
Dorr, Edward, 404.
Dorrance, Gordon, 291, 339, 493, 519.
  John, 352.
  John G., 339.
  Samuel, 493.
Douglas, Nathan, 443.
  Solomon J., 331.
Dow, Daniel, 145, 291, 339, 343, 488.
  Edward, 324, 461.
  Hendric, 339.
Downer, John C., 334, 353.
  Miss Lucinda, 155.
Downs, Charles A., 458.
  Cyrus, 478.
Draper, Nathaniel, 339.
Drummond, William, 433.
Dudley, Elias, 462.
  J. L., 146, 426.
  Martin, 330, 380, 399, 454.
Dulles, John W., 180.
Dunham, George, 346.
  Lewis, 420.
Dunning, Andrew, 463, 488.
  Benjamin, 300, 360, 419.
  Edward O., 329, 438.
Durant, Henry, 329.
Dutton, Aaron, 145, 318, 398, 498.
  Henry, 217.
  Matthew R., 318, 486, 498.
  S. W. S., 118, 146, 330, 399, 437.
  Thomas, 329, 343, 399, 452.
  Warren B., 415.
Dwight, Benjamin W., 330.
  Edwin W., 160, 318.
  James M. B., 326.
  Josiah, 516.
  Nathaniel, 309, 334, 499.
  Sereno E., 437.
  Timothy, 151, 164, 166, 182, 183, 184, 207, 250, 302, 394, 412, 438, 518.
  Timothy, Jr., 182, 183.
  Timothy, 183, 184, 326, 386.
  T. M., 513.
Dye, Charles B., 320, 490.
Dyer, Francis, 422.
  Hiram, 503.
Eames, Marshall, 431.
Eaton, ——, 324.
  Jacob, 334, 403.
  John H., 326.
  Samuel, 435.
  Samuel, 323.
  Samuel W., 326.
  Sylvester, 458.
Eddy, Henry, 326, 433, 452.
  Hiram, 448.

Eddy, Zachary, 348.
Edgar, John, 326, 387.
Edmands, John, 326.
Edson, Ambrose, 336, 345, 351.
  Solomon W., 326.
Edwards, Daniel, 308.
  J. Erskine, 406, 485.
  Jonathan, 181, 197, 198, 318, 349, 350, 481.
  Jonathan, 144, 164, 166, 363, 437, 484.
  Justin, 208.
  Pierpont, 279.
  Timothy, 5, 48, 143, 291.
  Tryon, 146, 406, 443.
Eells, Cushing, 309.
  Edward, 143, 368.
  Edward, 353.
  James, 311, 336, 375.
  John, 311, 390, 433.
  Nathaniel, 291, 485.
  Ozias, 344.
  Samuel, 165, 311, 447.
Eggleston, Nathaniel H., 312, 382, 436.
  R. S., 394.
Elderkin, Joshua, 400.
  John, 326.
Eldred, Henry B., 329.
Eldridge, Azariah, 315
  Joseph, 125, 146, 316, 326, 447.
Elmer, Hiram, 501.
  Jonathan, 300,
Elwood, David M., 303, 457, 491.
Elliot, Andrew, 144, 385.
  Andrew, Jr., 303, 386, 444.
  Henry B., 483, 496.
  Jacob, 143, 391.
  Jared, 143, 291, 363, 399.
  John, 144, 145, 319, 417, 443, 473.
  Joseph, 27, 29, 399.
  Moses, 171,
  Nathan, 318.
  Samuel H., 330, 505, 515.
Ellis, John, 291, 388.
  Jonathan, 339,
  Stephen, Jr., 334, 504.
  Mrs. Sylvester, 155.
Ellsworth, J. C., 155.
  William W., 168.
  John, 383.
Ely, ——, (Sep.) 258.
  David, 144, 145, 402, 410, 518.
  David D. F., 415.
  Elias P., 319, 402.
  Ezra S., 291, 339, 415, 499.
  Henry, 413.
  Isaac M., 305, 386.
  Israel, 339.
  James, 155, 314, 349.
  Mrs. James, 155.
  Jonathan T., 415.
  John, 319, 347, 402, 454.

Griffin, John S., 495.
Griggs, Leverett, 146, 329, 350, 440, 454.
Griswold, Benjamin, Jr., 308.
  Benjamin, 330.
  Charles, 219.
  Darius O., 391, 497.
  George, 199, 379.
  John, 415, 519.
  Samuel, 342, 379, 402, 406, 440.
  Sherman, 399.
  Stanley, 274, 444, 490.
Grosvenor, Charles P., 340, 358, 465.
  Daniel, 465.
  David A., 318, 419.
  Ebenezer, 324, 465.
  Lemuel, 516.
  Mason, 326, 340, 419, 465, 475.
  Nathan, 339, 465.
Grout, Lewis, 180, 330.
Grow, William, 342.
Guernsey, Ebenezer, 373.
  Jesse, 372, 498, 515.
  Jesse W., 475.
  William H., 451.
Guiteau, Sheridan, 447.
Gulick, Mrs. Peter J., 156.
Gulliver, John P., 460.
Gunn, Lewis, 496.
Gurley, John, 166, 385.
  Ralph R., 385, 440.
Haile, Ashbel B., 326.
Haight, Sylvanus, 291, 347, 480, 508.
Hale, Aaron, 324.
  Albert, 325, 390.
  David, 325, 368, 416.
  Enoch, 291, 339, 368.
  Nathan, 318.
Hall, Albert, 324.
  Avery, 420.
  Mrs. C., 156.
  Daniel, 334.
  Edwin, 146, 220, 458.
  Edwin, Jr., 303, 435, 458.
  E. Edwin, 330, 398.
  George, 360, 377, 503.
  Gordon, 330, 509.
  Judson, 318.
  Lyman, 355.
  Ogden, 408, 466, 491.
  Robert B., 326.
  Samuel, 143, 291, 361.
  Theophilus, 420.
  Mrs. William, 156.
Hallock, Gerard, 441.
  Jeremiah, 169, 200, 359.
  William A., 306.
Halping, Ebenezer, 340, 376.
Halsey, Herman, 173.
Hamilton, David H., 440.
Hammond, Charles, 336.
Hanford, William, 458.

Hanks, S. W., 455.
Hanna, William, 318.
Harding, Charles, 181.
  Mrs. Charles, 156,
Harris, Moses T., 409.
  Timothy, 170.
  Walter, 291, 366.
  William, 443.
Harrison, Fosdick, 346, 348, 355, 448, 452, 472, 479.
  George J., 388, 427,
  Jared, 324, 355, 362.
  Roger, 291, 325, 354, 448.
  Timothy, 325.
Harrower, David, 170.
Hart, Asahel, 448.
  Burdett, 146, 175, 330, 386, 433.
  Edson, 173.
  Ira, 145, 170, 176, 329, 351, 424, 485.
  John, 388, 417.
  John C., 449.
  Levi, 58, 144, 165, 166, 297, 308, 334, 397, 479.
  Levi W., 433.
  Lucas, 171, 314, 352, 514.
  Luther, 145, 391, 464, 491.
  William, 311, 418, 461.
Hartshorn, Elijah, 334, 389.
Hartwell, Charles, 309.
  Moses, 318.
Harvey, Joseph, 145, 160, 220, 318, 390, 401, 499.
  Sylvester, 325.
  W. Nye, 347, 425.
Hanford, Thomas, 457.
  William, 172.
Hanks, Steadman W., 311.
Hanmer, J. G., 441.
  Henry, 375.
Harriman, John, 435-6.
Haskell, Daniel, 314, 397.
  Ezra, 306.
  Mrs. Sarah, 156.
Hastings, Joseph, 257.
Haven, John, 336.
Havens, Daniel William, 334, 379, 459.
Hawes, Erskine J., 306, 405, 464.
  Joel, 85, 190, 404.
  Josiah, 401, 449.
  Josiah B., 314, 495.
  Prince, 173, 314, 390, 495, 515.
Hawley, Gideon, 300.
  James A., 309, 470.
  P. T., 345.
  Ransom, 300, 357.
  Rufus, 291, 344.
  Stephen, 324, 346.
  Stiles, 325.
  Thomas, 470.
  William A., 355, 411.
  Zerah K., 174, 329, 480.
Hayden, H. C., 428-9.

70

ADDENDA.

BOOKS ON CONNECTICUT HISTORY.

BY DANIEL C. GILMAN, YALE COLLEGE LIBRARY.

The following list is intended to include the titles of some important books which have a bearing upon the ecclesiastical and religious history of Connecticut. Some well known works, of a popular character, are not mentioned, partly for want of room, and partly that the student may not be misled in hunting up books which have been superseded by works of a more recent publication or of more complete character. It is probable that many anniversary discourses, and church manuals, quite as important as those which are mentioned, are omited from the list. All who are interested in these inquiries are requested to point out to the publisher any important omissions which they may notice, that the deficiencies may be supplied in future editions of this list. It is obvious that most of the books illustrative of the general history of the United States or of New England, such as Bancroft, Hildreth, the Historical Publications of the various Societies, Biographical Dictionaries, Family Genealogies and the like cannot be here enumerated. It is, perhaps, worth while to add that most of the books and pamphlets which are named below may be found in the Library of Yale College, New Haven, or of the Connecticut Historical Society, Hartford, and it is quite important that all who print discourses, church manuals, histories, or other books and pamphlets illustrating the present or the past condition of the State, should bear in mind the importance of preserving copies of their work in both the libraries we have named.

GENERAL HISTORY; *including Colonial Records.*

TRUMBULL, (BENJ.) HIST. OF CONNECTICUT, 1630,—1764, (2 vols. 8vo, 1818.)

This volume remains to the present day the most complete work in existence on the early history of Connecticut. A considerable portion of the manuscripts of the author, including letters addressed to him by persons in different towns on local matters, are preserved in the Library of Yale College.—President Stiles's manuscript diary, full of notes on ecclesiastical affairs, belongs to the same library.—Hollister's History of Connecticut, (2 vols. 8vo. 1855,) is brought down to the time of publication.— Peters's History, sometimes quoted by ignorant persons, is never to be trusted.—Dwight's History, (18mo. 1841,) was meant for schools.—Dr. Palfrey's History of New England, two volumes of which are now finished, (Boston, 1859–60, 8vo.) discusses with liberality and fulness, the early history of Connecticut.

TRUMBULL (J. HAMMOND,) *Colonial Records of Connecticut.*
Three vols. 8vo.—Vol. 1, 1636—1665, (1850.)—Vol. 2, 1665—1677, (1852.)—Vol. 3, 1678—1689, (1859.)

HOADLY (CHARLES J.) *Colonial Records of New Haven.*
Two Vols. 8vo.—Vol. 1, 1638—1649, (1857.)—Vol. 2, 1653—1665, (1858.)

CONNECTICUT HISTORICAL SOCIETY COLLECTIONS.
Vol. 1, (1860, 8vo.)

BARBER (JOHN W.) CONNECTICUT HISTORICAL COLLECTIONS.
Second Edition Revised, (pp. 594. 8vo. 1856.)

BUSHNELL (HORACE) SPEECH FOR CONNECTICUT. (pp. 32. 8vo.)

LOCAL HISTORIES.

1. TOWNS AND COUNTIES.

Canton see Simsbury.
Chatham, see Middletown.
Cromwell, see Middletown.
East Haven,
Dodd's Register, 1824.
Farmington,
Porter's Historical Discourse, 1840.
Glastenbury,
A. B. Chapin's History, 1853.
Granby see Simsbury.
Greenwich,
Mead's Hist., pp. 318. 12mo. 1857.
Hartford,
Hawes's Hist. Discourse, 1836.
Stuart's Olden Time, 1853.
Harwinton,
Chipman's History.
Litchfield,
County Jubilee,
Biography by Kilbourne, 1851.
Meriden,
Perkins's History, 12mo. 1849.
Middlesex County,
Field's Account of
Middle Haddam, see Middletown,
Middletown,
Field's History, including Cromwell, Chatham, Middle Haddam and Portland, 1853.

New Haven,
Kingsley's Hist. Discourse, 1838.
Bacon's Historical Discourse, 1839.
New London,
Caulkins's History, 1852.
Norwich,
Caulkins's Hist. 1845.
2d, Centennial "Jubilee," 1859.
Gilman's Hist. Discourse, 1859, 2d. edition.
Norwalk,
Hall's History.
Pomfret,
Hall's Discourse, 1840.
Portland see Middletown,
Sharon,
Sedgwick's History, 1858.
Simsbury, Granby and Canton.
Phelps's Hist., 1845.
Waterbury,
Bronson's Hist., 1858.
Windham County Ministers,
Learned's Biography of, in Cong. Qu. Vol. 1.
Windsor,
Stiles's History, 1860.
Woodbury,
Cothren's Hist., 1854.
2d Centennial Jubilee.

2. CHURCHES.

New Haven,
Benjamin Trumbull's North Haven.
Bacon's Hist. Discourses, . 1839
Dutton's North Church, 1842
Fisher's Yale College Church, 1858
Cleaveland's Third Church, 1859
Eustis's Chapel Street Church, 1859
Norwich,
Strong's First Church, . 1823
Arms's First Church, . 1859
Bond's Second Church, . 1860
North Haven,
B. Trumbull, . . . 1801
Durham,
Dedication—W. C. Fowler, 1847

Abington,
H. B. Smith, . . . 1753
Branford,
T. P. Gillett, . . .
Franklin,
S. Nott, ... 1832
Newington,
J. Brace, . . . 1855
New London,
A. McEwen, . . . 1858
Wallingford,
J. Dana, ... 1770
Weston,
J. Noyes, . . . 1839
Windham,
First Church, E. Waterman, 1801

3. INSTITUTIONS.

Yale College,
Clap's History,
Baldwin's Annals,
Kingsley's Sketch, . . 1835
Woolsey's Discourse, . . 1850
Fisher's Yale College Church, 1858
Kent's Φ. B. K. Address.

Silliman's Alumni Address, 1842
Sprague's Alumni Address, 1860
Indian Charity School, Lebanon,
Wheelock's Account of, 1771–3.
Cornwall Mission School,
Missionary Herald, 1816–'27.

PERIODICALS ;

Published in the State, or Containing Important Articles Relating to the State.

American Quarterly Register, Boston, 1827—1843.
Christian History, Prince's, Boston, 1743–4.
Christian Sentinel, East Windsor, 1838–41.
Christian Spectator, New Haven, 1819—1838.
Congregational Quarterly, 1859, continued.
Congregational Evangelical Magazine, Hartford, 1800—1814.

Congregational Observer, (Weekly,) Hartford.
Missionary Herald, Boston, 1817–26, on Foreign Mission School.
New Englander, New Haven, 1843, continued.
New Haven Record, (Weekly.)
Panoplist, Boston, 1802—1813.
Religious Intelligencer, (Weekly,) New Haven, 1817—1834.
Spirit of the Pilgrims.

Articles of Special Value.

Review of the early History of Cong. Churches in New England; *Christian Spectator*, June, 1830.
Review of Hawes's Tribute to the Pilgrims, by Rev. Joshua Leavitt, D. D. ; *Christian Spectator*, Sept., 1831.
Review of Palfrey's History of New England, by Rev. L. Bacon; *New Englander*, Nov. 1860.

Religious Declension of 1750–1800, by Rev. Luther Hart; *Christian Spectator*, June, 1833.
Separatists of Eastern Connecticut, by Rev. R. C. Learned ; *New Englander*, May, 1853.
Baptists in Connecticut, by Rev. R. C. Learned; *New Englander*, May, '60·
Windham Co., Ministers, by R. C. Learned; *Cong. Quart.* 1859.

Note.—There are many things among the papers with which the committee of publication have been furnished, which might to advantage have been added to these Contributions to the Ecclesiastical History of the State ; but the size of the volume has already become much greater than was anticipated, and they have been reluctantly omitted. It is believed, however, that all important facts respecting the History of the Congregational churches in the State, which are not to be found here, may easily be learned by consultation of the authorities to which reference is made.

It is hoped that what is here published may lead others to collect a more full and particular account of the churches and ministers of the State ; this part of the work having been in a measure sacrificed to the press of other matters. It is particularly desirable that all the historical materials that can be collected in the several churches should be put on record and preserved. It would be well, too, if some one interested in historical research, in each Association, would follow the example of what has been done in Windham, and persuade each minister to prepare a full account of his church, and of its several ministers, with statements concerning their families, and see that it is copied into a book provided by the Association for the purpose. Future additions could then be made to the record.

It is requested also that those who discover errors in this work, not mentioned in the ERRATA, should give information of them to Mr. William L. Kingsley, of New Haven ; and if it seems desirable, they will, either under the direction of the General Association or otherwise, hereafter be given to the public, together with other historical facts and statistics.—*Com. of Pub.*

[The article on page 560 was attributed by a mistake to Mr. Gilman.]

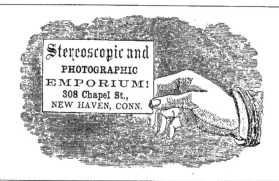

THE NEW ENGLANDER.

The present is a favorable time to procure COMPLETE SETS OF THE NEW ENGLANDER, from the commencement. These are now becoming very rare. For a short time the few which are on hand will be furnished at rates which can never, probably, be offered again.

COMPLETE SETS OF THE EIGHTEEN VOLUMES, already published, (from 1843 to 1860,) will be sold for $24. (Express charge, except to some address in New York City or Boston, to be at the expense of the purchaser. Sets of the first FIFTEEN VOLUMES, *with the exception of five numbers*, will be sold for $13. (Express-charge, except to some address in New York City or Boston, to be at the expense of the purchaser.)

Persons who now have incomplete sets, are invited to correspond with the subscriber, who will inform them of the price of the numbers and volumes they need.

The SEVENTEENTH VOLUME, (for 1859,) 1104 pages, and the EIGHTEENTH VOLUME, (for 1860,) 1150 pages, are offered at $2 each, (postage prepaid,) a price which is below cash cost. In these volumes will be found a fuller account of the new publications of these two years than in any other magazine in the country.

A complete INDEX of the NEW ENGLANDER will soon be published, (probably during the year 1861,) of the writers of Articles, of the subjects discussed, and of the titles of books noticed and reviewed, which will make the 20th volume of the series. Further notice will be given respecting it.

Address all communications and all inquiries to

WILLIAM L. KINGSLEY, Editor and Proprietor,
NEW HAVEN, CONN.